The

RIVERSIDE
READER

The
RIVERSIDE
READER

FIFTH EDITION

Joseph F. Trimmer
Ball State University

Maxine Hairston
University of Texas at Austin

Houghton Mifflin Company   Boston   Toronto
Geneva, Illinois   Palo Alto   Princeton, New Jersey

Senior Sponsoring Editor: Dean Johnson
Associate Project Editor: Elena Di Cesare
Senior Design/Production Coordinator: Sarah Ambrose
Senior Manufacturing Coordinator: Marie Barnes
Marketing Manager: Charles Cavaliere

Cover design: Harold Burch, Harold Burch Design, New York City
Cover image: Claude Monet "The Seine at Giverny," courtesy of the National
          Gallery of Art

Acknowledgments appear on pages 655–658, which constitute a continuation
of the copyright page.

Printed in the U.S.A.

Library of Congress Catalog Card Number: 95-76991

ISBN: Student text 0-395-72972-6
      Examination text 0-395-72973-4

123456789-QM-99 98 97 96 95

CONTENTS

CAUSE AND EFFECT   371

THEMATIC TABLE OF CONTENTS

The Other

Women

The Family

Heroes

Teaching and Learning

Leisure and the Arts

Science and Technology

Business and Ethics

- **Study questions and writing assignments** throughout the book have been extensively revised.

- A thematically organized final section, **Resources for Writing,** focuses on the subject of health and includes seven essays (each exemplifying one rhetorical mode), one short story, and a student essay that contains several strategies. The writing assignments following each reading encourage students to use what they already know to *respond, analyze,* and *argue* about the essays.

- A **student essay,** Ann Juralbal's "How to Avoid Second-Semester Burnout," draws on the subjects and strategies of the pieces in Resources for Writing to demonstrate how students can combine writing strategies effectively to attract their audience and advance their purpose.

THE RIVERSIDE TRADITION

The first seven sections in this reader are arranged in a sequence that is familiar to most writing teachers. Beginning with narration and description, moving through the five expository patterns, and ending with persuasion and argument, these sections group readings according to traditional writing strategies.

Each section begins with a simple, direct introduction previewing that writing strategy and helping the student become an active reader of that type of writing. Each section introduction ends with a professional and a student paragraph illustrating the strategy in action and with a convenient Points to Remember summary of the strategy's essential tasks and techniques. The headnote for each selection contains basic biographical information about the writer. This introductory material focuses on four questions about the writing situation: *Who* is writing? What is the writer's *purpose? Whom* is the writer addressing? *How* does the writer accomplish his or her purpose?

The readings within each section have been chosen to illustrate what the section introductions say they illustrate:

there are no strange hybrids or confusing models. Within each section, the selections are arranged in ascending order of length and complexity. The readings at the beginning are generally shorter and simpler than those near the end. The ultimate purpose of *The Riverside Reader* is to produce writing. For that reason, the writing assignments in this book are presented as the culminating activity of each section. Six assignments at the end of each section ask students to write essays that cover a range of writing tasks from personal response to analysis and argument.

Instructor's Guide

The new Instructor's Resource Manual by Rai Peterson of Ball State University is available to any instructor using *The Riverside Reader*. The Manual includes extensive rhetorical analysis of each essay and story, reading quizzes and vocabulary lists, and additional student essays and writing assignments. The Manual also includes advice on teaching the reading and writing strategies.

ACKNOWLEDGMENTS

We are grateful to the following writing instructors who have provided extensive advice and commentary on *The Riverside Reader* for this revision:

  Martha Bergland, Milwaukee Area Technical
    College—South, WI
  Beverly K. Burch, Vincennes University, IN
  Jeffery E. Cupp, University of Charleston, WV
  Dean Dillard, Neosho County Community
    College, KS
  Will Hochman, University of Southern Colorado, CO
  Robert Hokon, San Juan College, NM
  Sally C. Hoople, Maine Maritime Academy, ME
  Fred Kille, Western Nevada Community College, NV

Karen Lee, Northeast Iowa Community College, IA
Lynne Lerych, Grays Harbor College, WA
David Shevin, Tiffin University, OH

We are also thankful to our students for allowing us to reprint their work in this edition: Lauren Briner, Sara Temple, Nathan Harms, Gareth Tucker, Jason Utesch, Emily Linderman, Jim Saloman, and Ann Juralbal. A special thanks goes to Karen Taylor for her help in manuscript preparation. And, of course, our debt to all our students is ongoing.

INTRODUCTION

As a college student, you are necessarily a reader and a writer. Not that either role is new to you—certainly you were a reader and a writer before you started college, and you read and write outside of college. In college, however, you're in a different kind of reading and writing environment: the stakes are higher and you often have to work under pressure. You have to read a broad variety of material, some of it difficult and unfamiliar, and write more demanding kinds of assignments, many of them about or in response to your reading. Your success in college depends, in part, on how well you can read and write and how well you can connect these two processes. Why is the connection important? Because the processes interact closely: as you become a more skillful and knowledgeable reader, you will also become a better writer. In turn, as you become a more competent writer, you will become a more skilled reader.

BECOMING A READER WHO WRITES

The first time you read one of the essays or short stories in this book, move along steadily and enjoy it just because it's entertaining or because you are learning something. Unless you get lost or have to go back to pick up meaning, don't stop to analyze what you're reading. Instead, try to absorb the main ideas and come out with a dominant impression of the theme and of the essay's impact on you. Don't stop to annotate or underline.

When you've finished your first reading, take a look at the questions or comment that follows each selection. They are designed to start you thinking about your reactions to the reading and to get you ready for the second reading that is almost always necessary for mastering serious nonfiction writing.

The Second Reading

When you read the piece for the second time, you need to read more actively. Do more than notice your reactions. Think about why you have those reactions and how the author provoked them. Start moving back and forth between the roles of reader and writer, interacting with the piece of writing—looking for key points or weak spots and making associations and asking questions. Get ready to start making notes in the margins.

Begin an imaginary conversation with the author. Ask, "*Why* are you writing this? *For whom* are you writing? *What strategies* are you using?" If you keep these questions in mind during your second reading, you'll begin to get a picture of the writer behind the page, someone who has something to say and is working at getting it across to his or her readers.

React to what you're reading. Don't accept the author's

claims passively. Instead, ask questions, argue, comment, and test what the writer is saying against your own knowledge and experience. Say, "Yes, I agree," or ask, "What's your evidence?" or "Why do you say that?" Such comments and questions help you to decide what an essay or story means *for you*.

The phrase *for you* is important because a piece of writing never means exactly the same thing for every reader. Nor should it. You are a special reader who brings unique experiences and attitudes with you, and you create your own meaning when you combine what you know and feel with what the writer tells you.

For example, as you read you may be comparing the author's account of something that happened to her—perhaps an encounter with stereotyping or sex discrimination—with a similar experience of yours and thinking about how differently you reacted. Or in reading another essay, you may disagree with the author's analysis of an American political problem and decide you'd like to refute him in your next paper. As you respond, write your reactions down. If you don't, you may forget them.

Notes and Questions in the Margins

On your second reading, interact with what you read by underlining and writing in the margins as you read—just highlighting usually isn't enough. Jot notes and questions in the margins (or on a separate piece of paper if you have to), and summarize key points. Also note any ideas the essay may trigger for your own writing.

This kind of reading is such an essential part of understanding serious material that most experienced readers underline and write in margins almost routinely when they are reading to absorb content. If they don't own the book they have to master, they buy it or photocopy parts of it so they can read with a pencil in hand. At the end of this introduction, we include a short annotated essay that shows how one reader used this method to interact with a piece of writing.

We believe that trying this method and using the guideline questions on pages 9–11 will help you to become a good reader who enjoys serious reading and knows how to use it for your own writing.

BECOMING A WRITER WHO READS

When you *write* college essays, you need to move back and forth between the roles of reader and writer. As you move through the writing process, you need to be aware that you are interacting with different readers.

The Self as Reader

Your first reader is yourself. You write, read what you've written, and in response to that reading write more. You're creating as you go. When you get to the revision stage, you rewrite because you realize, as a reader, that your essay didn't come out quite as you wanted it to. When you're satisfied with content but go back to tinker and polish, you're doing so in response to your own reading. And when you get to the final editing stage, you edit and proofread because you are acting as the most critical of all readers: an editor.

Other Readers

As you write, you need to think about the other people who will read what you write. To help you do so, look at the suggestions in Parts IV and VI of Guidelines for Writing an Essay (see pages 17–20). Ask yourself, "For whom am I writing, and what do my readers expect? How can I get my ideas across to them?" When you have finished your first draft, it's particularly important for you to stand back from it, put yourself in the place of your readers, and ask yourself what questions they might have for you.

READING TO BECOME MORE AWARE OF THE WRITING PROCESS

As you read and react to a piece of writing, you can sharpen your own writing skills by thinking about the writing process in the essay you're reading. Try to see what's going on beneath the surface of the words; try to get into the writer's mind and watch her or him at work. By asking certain questions, you can do a kind of simulation exercise that can help you understand the writer's thinking process.

Ask About Purpose

We know that most writers have goals when they write, certain things they want to accomplish. So ask yourself,

- Why is the author writing? What motivated him or her?
- Does the author tell me the purpose directly? How can I determine it?

Ask About Audience

We know that most writers—especially professionals—write for a definite audience and tailor their writing to meet that audience's needs and expectations. So ask yourself,

- For whom is the writer writing? Why did he or she choose that audience?
- What does the writer know about that audience? How does that knowledge affect his or her writing?

Ask About Strategies

You can learn from other writers by noticing how they work and what kinds of appeals they use. So ask yourself,

- How does the writer go about putting the essay together? How is it organized?
- What kind of strategies does the writer use? Is he or she

telling stories, giving evidence, using examples, employing metaphor and images? How well do those strategies work and why?

Reading a well-crafted essay critically is like watching a well-made movie on two levels: on one level you can enjoy the drama itself, and on another level you appreciate the talent and skill of the artists at work.

Do we guarantee that close analysis of a professional writer's work will make you a better writer? No, of course we don't. But we do believe that learning to read responsively, critically, and analytically will give you insights into the craft of writing and make it a less intimidating and more manageable process.

READING TO LEARN ABOUT WRITING STRATEGIES

In *The Riverside Reader* you will find essays and short stories that comment on events and concerns that affect all our lives—social programs such as welfare, the experiences of different ethnic groups, women's roles, and politics, to name just a few. The essays connect to other strands in your college education and are as pertinent in sociology, history, or environmental courses as they are in your college writing course. The short stories expand your understanding of the essay by showing how nonfiction connects with the worlds of fiction. All these readings touch on matters that affect your personal life or your job. The last section of the book, Resources for Writing, is devoted to issues about health and health care.

Common Writing Strategies

The essays in *The Riverside Reader* are arranged according to common patterns of organization that have been serving writers well for centuries: *narration and description, process analysis, comparison and contrast, division and classification, definition, cause and effect,* and *persuasion and argument.*

These patterns can serve as *strategies* for the development of ideas in writing. Study how professional writers use these traditional strategies in their writing. If you know from your reading how these strategies are used, you will be able to choose one that fits your writing situation. For example, if you notice how Maya Angelou uses narrative to dramatize racial stereotyping, you may see how you can relate an incident from your life to illustrate a point. If you are convinced by Cathy Young's claim that radical feminists are harming the cause of women's liberation by portraying women as victims, you may want to use the same kind of cause-and-effect argument in a paper for sociology or ethnic studies.

Not that you have to limit yourself to a single strategy for the entire paper—certainly professional writers don't. Often, however, they do structure a piece of writing around one central pattern, and for *The Riverside Reader* we have chosen essays with one dominant strategy so that you can see particularly strong examples of each strategy in action.

Strategies for Your Writing

You can also use the traditional strategies to generate resources and then transform them into writing. Suppose you are trying to get started writing an essay on the early impressionist painters for a humanities course. One way to start thinking would be to *define* the impressionist school of painting. Another would be to explore what *caused* the rise of impressionism in the nineteenth century—what were the artists in the movement reacting to? Another potentially rich approach would be to *compare* these painters to other painters of the time. You could also *describe* an important early impressionist painting or relate a *narrative* about one of the early painters. Each of the strategies provides a kind of special lens for viewing your topic, a different way of looking at it so that you can see its possibilities.

When you become aware of how these lenses work—how each one helps you see and shape your subject—you can select one strategy or combine two or three to draft and revise your essay. That is the procedure you can follow in Resources for Writing. Each selection in that section uses one of the common writing strategies to explore a different aspect of health and health care. As you read these selections, recalling what you know about those topics, you can expand and shift your perspective on the subject, uncovering all sorts of resources to develop in your writing.

USING *THE RIVERSIDE READER*

The Riverside Reader will help you become an active, critical reader and an effective writer. At the start of every section, you will find an introduction that previews the strategy, gives you clues about what to look for as you read, and concludes with the key "Points to Remember." Examples from both a professional and a student paragraph show how the strategy works. Before each essay and short story, you will find a headnote that tells you about the author's background and credentials and about how and where the selection originated. After each essay and short story, you will find study questions or commentary to help you connect your reading to the author's writing process. At the end of each section, you will find writing assignments that give you opportunities to respond to your reading using your own experiences and knowledge.

On the next few pages, you will find a set of questions titled Guidelines for Reading an Essay. The guidelines will help you to preview an essay, to read and respond to it critically, and to see it from a writer's point of view. After these guidelines, you will find a sample analysis of Anna Quindlen's essay "Enough Bookshelves"; it shows how one reader read, responded to, and annotated the essay. Also included are three writing topics that grew out of the reader's responses to Quindlen's piece. This Introduction to *The Riverside Reader* then closes with Guidelines for Writing an Essay, a brief review of the writing process that should help you to get started with your own writing.

Guidelines for Reading an Essay

Most of us don't sit down to read essays or anything else with a set of guidelines in our hand. Sometimes we read so casually that if someone were to ask about the article later, we'd have a hard time giving an accurate summary. That's fine—no one wants to be taking tests on his or her leisure reading.

However, when we read to grasp ideas and to appreciate the style and language of an essay, reading becomes serious work, something that we need to do intelligently and systematically. We have no magic formula for that kind of reading, but we think the following guidelines can be helpful.

I. READ THE ESSAY THROUGH COMPLETELY

a. Notice the title, and consider what it may mean. Note the author's name and whether it's familiar to you. Read any introduction and any summary sentence such as the one on the second page of each essay in this volume.
b. Read slowly, looking up important words if necessary, but don't stop to reread unless you think you've missed some major point.
c. When you finish, think about the dominant impression the essay made on you. Was it powerful? Persuasive? Comic? Moving? Baffling?
d. If there are questions at the end of the essay, read them through to determine their focus. Prepare to read the selection again, this time with a pencil in hand.

II. ANALYZE YOUR RESPONSE

a. Think about any personal experience that the essay brings to mind. How does that experience affect your response?
b. Jot down any questions the essay raised for you. Put a check in the margin where you want to say "Yes!" Put a cross where you want to say "No way!"

c. Consider what you'd say to the author if you wanted to talk back to him or her.
d. Reflect on the emotional or intellectual impact the essay had on you.

III. ANALYZE THE AUTHOR'S PURPOSE

a. Decide what the author is trying to accomplish with the essay. That goal can range from trying to amuse to inspiring outrage and action.
b. Ask yourself what in the writer's experience or background motivated him or her to write the essay. How does it seem to grow out of that experience?
c. Mark sentences or sections in the essay that show the writer's purpose.
d. When you finish, consider how well the writer achieved his or her purpose with you. What are some of the reasons he or she succeeded or failed with you?

IV. ANALYZE THE WRITER'S AUDIENCE

a. Identify the audience you think the writer is appealing to. If the essay was first published in a magazine, try to analyze the type of magazine and what characteristics its audience would have.
b. Identify the beliefs or values the author assumes the readers share with him or her. To what extent do you think that assumption is justified?
c. Authors also assume their readers have a certain amount of background knowledge. What knowledge does this author take for granted? How do you know?
d. Consider how well you fit the profile the author probably constructed of his or her readers. How does that fit, or lack of it, affect your response to the essay?

V. ANALYZE AND EVALUATE THE WRITER'S STRATEGIES

a. The most effective writers catch their readers at the very beginning of an essay. Read a few paragraphs, and decide how well they work and why.

b. Look for the dominant patterns—definition, narration, cause and effect, and so on—in the essay. How do they serve the writer's purpose?

c. Look for metaphor, vivid description, personal experience, the use of authority and statistics, or other strategies. What do they accomplish?

d. What strategies of the writer worked best with you? Why do you think so?

VI. IDENTIFY ISSUES RAISED BY THE ESSAY

a. What larger social issues do you think the essay raises? How does it contribute to the ongoing conversation about those issues?

b. What, if anything, has happened in the field the author is writing about since the time the essay was written? How is the essay still relevant, or is it?

c. What impact do you think the essay may have had on its original readers?

Sample Analysis of an Essay

ANNA QUINDLEN

Anna Quindlen was born in Philadelphia, Pennsylvania, in 1952 and was educated at Barnard College. After working on the *New York Post,* she became a reporter for the *New York Times,* then a columnist writing the feature "About New York," which covered City Hall and some of the "worst back alleys in New York." Her next column, "Life in the Thirties," featured personal reflections and reminiscences, later collected in her book *Living Out Loud.* She went on to write a column for the *Times* called "Public and Private"; in 1992 she won the Pulitzer Prize for that series. She published her first novel, *Object Lessons,* to wide acclaim in 1991 and followed it with *One True Thing* in 1994. At the end of 1994 she resigned from the *New York Times* to pursue a full-time career as a writer of fiction. In "Enough Bookshelves," reprinted from *Living Out Loud,* she reveals herself as a lifelong book addict, delighted that she has passed her habit along to her eldest child.

In the essay Quindlen demonstrates her special ability to use the small domestic details of her life to connect with her readers and put fresh life into commonplace observations. Her point here is that reading is an adventure of the mind. She starts with an intimate anecdote that almost every parent or child can identify with: reprimanding a child who has gotten back up after he's been put to bed. Her annoyance quickly fades when she realizes her son wants to share his excitement over a book. As one who has had a lifelong love affair with books, she's thrilled to see her son following her lead because it establishes a special bond between them.

Her son's delight with reading makes her reflect on what reading has meant to her: "a way of understanding the world" and a way of connecting with others who have a passion for books. She also feels that by transmitting her love of reading to her children, she is giving them a gift: "an infinite number of worlds in which to wander, and an entry to the real world, too." Her wish that they'll be the kind of people whose idea of decorating will be to build enough bookshelves puts her hope of their being lifelong readers into a visual image.

At the end, seeking once more to convince her readers of the joys of reading, she tells of taking her son upstairs with a new adventure book that starts him "moving through the high seas with the help of my compass," and she sees again "the making of my self and the making of his" from the same material: books.

Comments in the left margin summarize Quindlen's main points and note her strategies. In the right margin, the reader notes her responses to Quindlen and jots down ideas and questions the essay raises. This process of annotating and responding has generated several ideas that one might write about. Some of those are given after the essay.

Enough Bookshelves

Domestic scene taking readers into her home — The voice I assume for children's bad behavior is like a winter coat, dark and heavy. I put it on the — Nice image

other night when my eldest child appeared in the kitchen doorway, an hour after he had gone to bed. "What are you doing down here?" I began to say, when he interrupted: "I finished it!" — I used to read under the covers with a flashlight.

The dominatrix tone went out the window and we settled down for an old-fashioned dish about the fine points of *The Phantom Tollbooth*.

It is the wonderful tale of a bored and discontented boy named Milo and the journey he makes one day in his toy car with the Humbug and the Spelling Bee and a slew of other fantastical characters who change his life. I read it first when I was ten. I still have the book report I wrote, which began "This is the best book ever." That was long before I read *The Sound and the Fury* or *Little Dorrit*, the Lord Peter Wimsey mysteries or Elmore Leonard. I was still pretty close to the mark.

Identifies herself as a lifelong reader

All of us have similar hopes for our children: good health, happiness, interesting and fulfilling work, financial stability. But like a model home that's different depending on who picks out the cabinets and the shutters, the fine points often vary. Some people go nuts when their children learn to walk, to throw a baseball, to pick out the "Moonlight Sonata" on the piano. The day I realized my eldest child could read was one of the happiest days of my life.

Our routine concerns our children

Shows importance of reading in their home

"One loses the capacity to grieve as a child grieves, or to rage as a child rages: hotly, despairingly, with tears of passion," the English novelist Anita Brookner writes in *Brief Lives*, her newest book. "One grows up, one becomes civilized, one learns one's manners, and consequently can no longer manage these two functions—sorrow and anger—adequately. Attempts to recapture that primal spontaneity are doomed, for the original reactions have been overlaid, forgotten."

Hmm— seems to me I know lots of adults in a rage.

And yet we constantly reclaim some part of that primal spontaneity through the youngest among us, not only through their sorrow and anger but simply through everyday discoveries, life unwrapped. To see a child touch the piano keys for the first time, to watch a small body slice through the surface of the water in a clean dive, is to experience the shock, not of the new, but of

Pleasure of reliving discoveries through her son

the familiar revisited as though it were strange and wonderful.

Reading a way of learning about world and the self

Reading has always been life unwrapped to me, a way of understanding the world and understanding myself through both the unknown and the everyday. If being a parent consists often of passing along chunks of ourselves to unwitting—often unwilling—recipients, then books are, for me, one of the simplest and most surefire ways of doing that. I would be most content if my children grew up to be the kind of people who think decorating consists mostly of building enough bookshelves. That would give them an infinite number of worlds in which to wander, and an entry to the real world, too; in the same way two strangers can settle down for a companionable gab over baseball seasons past and present, so it is often possible to connect with someone over a passion for books.

Yes—for me too!

"Enough book-shelves" shorthand for a life-time of reading

Has the media room taken the place of book-shelves in new homes?

Books connect us to others.

(Or the opposite, of course: I once met a man who said he thought *War and Peace* was a big boring book, when the truth was that it was only he who was big and boring.)

Notice we make judgments about people by their reading.

Always a book pusher

I remember making summer reading lists for my sister, of her coming home one day from work with my limp and yellowed paperback copy of *Pride and Prejudice* in her bag and saying irritably, "Look, tell me if she marries Mr. Darcy, because if she doesn't I'm not going to finish the book." And the feeling of giddiness I felt as I piously said that I would never reveal an ending, while somewhere inside I was shouting, yes, yes, she will marry Mr. Darcy, over and over again, as often as you'd like.

Rejoice in others' reading

You had only to see this boy's face when he said "I finished it!" to know that something had made an indelible mark upon him. I walked him back upstairs with a fresh book, my copy of *A Wrinkle in Time*, Madeleine L'Engle's unforgettable story of children who travel through time and space to save their father from the forces of evil. Now when I leave the room, he is reading by the pinpoint of his little reading light, <u>the ship of his mind moving through high seas with the help of my compass.</u> Just before I close the door, <u>I catch a glimpse of the making of my self and the making of his, sharing some of the same timber.</u> And I am a happy woman.

Final metaphor of book as an adventure

Are computers a new way of doing this?

She's good with visual images.

Possible Writing Topics

1. What were your experiences with books and reading as a child, both in and out of school, and how did those experiences affect the kind of reader you are now? Writing for parents or English teachers, write a short essay in which you use that experience to give your recommendations for helping children to become readers.

2. Although for many youngsters computer programs and video games seem to be taking the place of reading books, those who make predictions about future trends say that people who hope to flourish on the information superhighway are going to need excellent literacy skills. Interesting contradiction, isn't it? For an audience of the school board of the town where you went to high school, write a persuasive essay describing a course of study that you think would best prepare students to do well in the technological world that you expect to be a part of. Give specifics such as what the schools should emphasize and how courses should be balanced between history, literature, and languages on the one hand and mathematics, science, and computer skills on the other. Finally, speculate about how students can be motivated to prepare themselves for the future.

3. In "Enough Bookshelves" Quindlen writes about the joys of reading fiction and says it "unwraps" the world. Yet other readers feel fiction is a waste of time because "you aren't learning anything" and read almost entirely nonfiction. For the book page of your local paper, write a short essay in which you argue for one of these views—or perhaps you might want to argue for some combination of the two views.

Guidelines for Writing an Essay

Because writing is a complex, often messy process that varies greatly from one writer to another and from one task to another, we're not going to offer you a formula that says "Here's how you write." It's never that simple. Nevertheless, it's possible to rough out guidelines that can be useful for getting started on a writing assignment. Here is what we suggest.

I. ANALYZE YOUR WRITING SITUATION

Every time you write, you write in a specific set of circumstances that has four elements to it: topic, purpose, audience, strategy. If one of these elements changes, so do the others. The successful writer always keeps that in mind. So start your writing process each time by analyzing the overall writing situation:

a. What do you want to say?
b. Why do you want to say it?
c. To whom do you want to say it?
d. How can you say it effectively?

Write out your analysis, and use it as a chart to keep you on course as you develop your paper. For instance, perhaps you are taking a children's literature course or have been reading to your own children and have noticed how few women heroes there are in traditional children's literature. Using that experience as a writing prompt, you could set up this writing situation:

> *I want to persuade librarians to look for more children's books that have women heroes because girls today need role models for bravery and leadership. I'll use my own experience in the argument.*

Now you have your writing situation in a nutshell. It will help get you started.

II. SELECT AND NARROW YOUR TOPIC

a. Select a topic you are genuinely interested in and about which you already have some information. The children's books topic meets both criteria.
b. Brainstorm, free-write, and talk to people to generate information on your topic. Narrow your topic to one main idea; for example, traditional children's books lack the strong women role models that today's youngsters need.
c. For a topic that requires factual information, research your topic to find out what material is available. For the topic given above, you could talk to librarians, elementary teachers, and the owners of children's book stores.
d. Write a tentative thesis sentence to anchor your writing. For example, "Today's children, especially girls, need books showing women as heroines and leaders; traditional children's books have few powerful role models for girls."

III. DECIDE ON YOUR PURPOSE IN WRITING

a. Decide what you want to achieve by writing. Is your purpose to inform, entertain, persuade, bring about change? You will probably have more than one.
b. When you know what you want to do, decide what readers you need to reach. In an essay about children's books, the audience could be librarians and educators.
c. Consider how you want your readers to respond, what action you hope for. For the topic given above, you want librarians and educators to find books with strong role models for girls.

IV. ANALYZE YOUR AUDIENCE

a. Identify your target audience, and decide what is important to those readers. What kinds of appeals would they respond to? For example, librarians and educators want books that will appeal to young readers, and they want their readers to learn and benefit from the books they read.

b. Consider how much your audience already knows about the topic. What new information do they need? What examples would persuade them?

c. Anticipate what questions your argument will raise in readers' minds and plan to respond to those questions.

d. Identify a place where an essay like yours might be published. For the model topic, you could consider journals for librarians, *Scholastic* magazine, or an editorial on the school page of the local newspaper. Look over those publications.

V. DECIDE ON YOUR STRATEGIES

a. Make a plan of organization and rough out a working outline; jot down ideas for supporting evidence.

b. Decide what kind of arguments you can use. For instance, you could use *narration* to give your own experience, *definition* to show what kind of books girls need, and *comparison and contrast* to compare the number of men and women heroes in children's books.

c. Review the discussions of the strategies you're going to use to find what techniques you can use to develop the ones you've chosen.

d. Consider what kind of opening will catch and hold your readers' interest.

e. Find evidence to support your argument. For instance, examples of favorite children's books that focus on males could include *The Jungle Book, King Arthur and His Knights, Huckleberry Finn,* and the tales about Greek heroes.

f. Refine your thesis sentence to help you focus your topic. For example, "Because strong role models are so important for a child's development, librarians and educators need to make special efforts to locate books with women heroes and leaders in order to compensate for the lack of such figures in most traditional children's literature."

VI. WRITE A DRAFT, REVISE, AND EDIT

a. Write your first draft, let it sit for several hours or overnight, and then reread it. Ask yourself: Does it have a clear, specific focus? Is your purpose clear? Do you keep your audience in mind? Have you supported your claims with evidence? Is it clearly organized? Do you need more examples?

b. Mark changes, deletions, and additions on your first draft and reorganize where you need to do so. Write a second draft.

c. Revise the second draft, pruning excess words and sentences, improving word choice, smoothing out transitions, and polishing the opening and closing paragraphs.

d. Edit for spelling, grammar, and typographical errors. Proofread once again, and print out or type a final clean copy.

NARRATION
AND
DESCRIPTION

The writer who *narrates* tells a story to make a point. The writer who *describes* evokes the senses to create a picture. Although you can use either strategy by itself, you will probably discover that they work best in combination if you want to write a detailed account of some memorable experience— your first trip alone, a last-minute political victory, a picnic in some special place. When you want to explain what happened, you will need to tell the story in some kind of chronological order, putting the most important events—I took the wrong turn, she made the right speech, we picked the perfect spot—in the most prominent position. When you want to give the texture of the experience, you will need to select words and images that help your readers see, hear, and feel what happened—the road snaked to a dead end, the crowd thundered into applause, the sunshine softened our scowls. When you show and tell in this way, you can help your readers see the meaning of the experience you want to convey.

PURPOSE

You can use narration and description for three purposes. Most simply, you can use them to introduce or illustrate a complicated subject. You might begin an analysis of the energy crisis, for example, by telling a personal anecdote that dramatizes wastefulness. Or you might conclude an argument for gun control by giving a graphic description of a shooting incident. In each case, you are using a few sentences or a detailed description to support some other strategy such as causal analysis or argument.

Writers use narration and description most often not as isolated examples but as their primary method when they are analyzing an issue or theme. For example, you might spend a whole essay telling how you came to a new awareness of patriotism because of your experience in a foreign country. Even though your personal experience would be the center of the essay, your narrative purpose (what happened) and your descriptive purpose (what it felt like) might be linked to other purposes. You might want to *explain* what caused your new awareness (why it happened) or to *argue* that everyone needs such awareness (why everyone should reach the same conclusion you did).

The writers who use narration and description most often are those who write autobiography, history, and fiction. If you choose to write in any of these forms, your purpose will be not so much to introduce an example or tell about an experience as to throw light on your subject. You may explain why events happened as they did or argue that such events should never happen again, but you may choose to suggest your ideas subtly through telling a story or giving a description rather than stating them as direct assertions. Your primary purpose is to report the actions and describe the feelings of people entangled in the complex web of circumstance.

AUDIENCE

As you think about writing an essay using narration and description, consider how much you will need to tell your readers and how much you will need to show them. If you are writing from personal experience, few readers will know the story before you tell it. They may know similar stories or have had similar experiences, but they do not know your story. Because you can tell your story in so many different ways—adding or deleting material to fit the occasion—you need to decide how much information your readers will need. Do they need to know every detail of your story, only brief summaries of certain parts, or some mixture of detail and summary?

In order to decide what details you should provide, you need to think about how much your readers know and what they are going to expect. If your subject is unusual (a trip to see an erupting volcano), your readers will need a lot of information, much of it technical, to understand the novel experience you are going to tell. They will expect an efficient, matter-of-fact description of volcanoes but also want you to give them some sense of how it feels to see one erupting. If your subject is familiar to most people (your experience with lawn sprinklers), your readers will need few technical details to understand your subject. But they will expect you to give them new images and insights that create a fresh vision of your subject—for example, portraying lawn sprinklers as the languid pulse of summer.

STRATEGIES

The writers in this section demonstrate that you need to use certain strategies to write a successful narrative and descriptive essay. For openers, you must recognize that an experience and an essay about that experience are not the same thing.

When you have any experience, no matter how long it lasts, your memory of that experience is going to be disorganized and poorly defined, but the essay you write about that experience must have a purpose and be sharply focused. When you want to transform your experience into an essay, start by locating the central **conflict.** It may be (1) between the writer and himself, or herself, as when George Orwell finds himself in a quandary about whether to shoot the elephant; (2) between the writer and others, as when Maya Angelou responds to Mrs. Cullinan and her friends; or (3) between the writer and the environment, as when Wakako Yamauchi tries to understand the changing landscapes of the Japanese-American migrant community.

Once you have identified the conflict, arrange the action so that your readers know how the conflict started, how it developed, and how it was resolved. This coherent sequence of events is called a **plot.** Sometimes you may want to create a plot that sticks to a simple chronological pattern. In "Basketball Season," Donna Tartt simply begins at the beginning and describes events as they occur. At other times you may want to start your essay in the middle or even near the end of the events you are describing. In "The Village Watchman," Terry Tempest Williams begins at the end, after her Uncle Alan's death, and works back to the beginning as she searches for "proper instruction." Each author chooses a pattern according to her purpose: Tartt wants to describe the evolution of a "social" season; Williams wants to describe the impact of a social stigma.

When you figure out what the beginning, middle, and end of your plot should be, you can establish how each event in those sections should be paced. **Pace** is the speed at which the writer recounts events. Sometimes you can narrate events quickly by omitting details, compressing time, and summarizing experience. For example, Yamauchi summarizes several episodes in her family's fractured history. At other times you may want to pace events more slowly and carefully because they are vital to your purpose. You will need to include every detail, expand on time, and present the situation as a fully realized scene rather than in summary form. Williams creates such a scene when she describes her Uncle Alan's baptism.

You can make your scenes and summaries effective by your careful **selection of details.** Just adding more details doesn't satisfy this requirement. You must select those special details that satisfy the needs of your readers and further your purpose in the essay. For example, sometimes you will need to give *objective* or *technical* details to help your readers understand your subject. Yamauchi provides this kind of detail when she describes her mother's boarding house. At other times you will want to give *subjective* or *impressionistic* details to appeal to your readers' senses. Orwell provides much of this sort of detail as he tries to recreate his physical and psychological response to shooting the elephant. Finally, you may want to present your details so they form a *figurative image* or create a *dominant impression.* Williams uses both of these strategies: the first when she describes the "Wolf Pole," for example, and the second when she describes the pattern of her uncle's seizures.

In order to identify the conflict, organize the plot, vary the pace, and select details for your essay, you need to determine your **point of view:** the person and position of the narrator (*point*) and the attitude toward the experience being presented (*view*). You choose your *person* by deciding whether you want to tell your story as "I" saw it (as Maya Angelou does in her story about her confrontation with Mrs. Cullinan), or as "he" saw it (as Williams does in her account of her uncle's last days).

You choose your *position* by deciding how close you want to be to the action in time and space. You may be involved in the action or view it from the position of an observer, or you may tell about the events as they are happening or many years after they have taken place. For example, George Orwell, the young police officer, is the chief actor in his narrative, but George Orwell, the author, still wonders, years after the event, why he shot the elephant. You create your attitude—how you view the events you intend to present and interpret—by the person and position you choose for writing your essay. The attitudes of the narrators in the following essays might be characterized as angry (Angelou), bemused (Tartt), reverent (Williams), perplexed (Yamauchi), and ambivalent (Orwell).

USING NARRATION AND DESCRIPTION IN PARAGRAPHS

Here are two narration and description paragraphs. The first is written by a professional writer and is followed by an analysis. The second is written by a student writer and is followed by questions.

MAXINE HONG KINGSTON
from "A Song for a Barbarian Reed Pipe"

Sets up conflict

Not all of the children who were silent at American school found a voice at Chinese school. One new teacher said each of us had to get up and recite in front of the class, who was to listen. My sister and I had memorized the lesson perfectly. We said it to each other at home, one chanting, one listening. The teacher called on my sister to recite first. It was the first time a teacher had called on the second-born to go first. My sister was scared. She glanced at me and looked away; I looked down at my desk. I hoped that she could do it because if she could, then I would have to. She opened her mouth and a voice came out that wasn't a whisper, but it wasn't a proper voice either. I hoped that she would not cry, fear breaking up her voice like twigs underfoot. She sounded as if she were trying to sing though weeping and strangling. She did not pause or stop to end the embarrassment. She kept going until she said the last word, and then she sat

Conflict
Slows pace; heightens suspense

Appeals to sense

down. When it was my turn, the same voice came
out, a <u>crippled animal running on broken legs.</u>   Creates new
You could hear splinters in my voice, bones rub-   image
bing jagged against one another. I was loud,
though. I was glad I didn't whisper.

Confirms point of view (margin note)

Comment This paragraph, taken from the final section of *The
Woman Warrior*, recounts an embarrassing scene involving
two Chinese sisters. Kingston describes how she and her sister
prepare for the expected recitation. The conflict occurs when
the teacher calls on the second-born sister first—a breach of
Chinese etiquette. By describing how she looks down at her
desk, Kingston slows the pace and heightens the anxiety of
the situation. She then selects details and images to evoke the
sound of her sister's and then her own voice as they complete
the lesson.

LAUREN BRINER
Deloris

"All right, how do you say 'dollars' in Spanish?"
Mrs. Tyrrel was setting the rules for Spanish II,
but we wanted the old rules. Last year Mr.
Kreuger, who taught Spanish I, loved to throw
parties. I guess he thought fiestas would make us
want to learn Spanish. What we really wanted was
more fiestas. But now, according to Mrs. Tyrrel,
the party was over. She peered at us over the top
of her glasses looking for a snitch. We avoided
her eyes by thumbing the sides of our new books.
"Lauren? How about you?" I looked for help.
No luck! My party friends were faking it, staring
at the unintelligible sentences in *Spanish II*. I was
on my own. I looked up at Mrs. Tyrrel.
"Lauren?" I was desperate, caught in her gaze. I
panicked. In a really hokey accent, I suggested a
possible answer, "Dellores?" "Deloris? Who's
Deloris? Is she a friend of yours?" Mrs. Tyrrel

was laughing. The whole class began laughing,
"Deloris! Deloris! Deloris!" The blood rushed to
my face and tears welled in my eyes. So much for
old rules and old friends.

1. How does Briner's description of the two teachers establish the
   conflict in this episode?
2. How do the responses of the teacher and the class to Lauren's
   answer reveal the writer's point of view?

NARRATION AND DESCRIPTION

Points to Remember

1. Focus your narrative on the "story" in your story—
   that is, focus on the conflict that defines the plot.
2. Vary the pace of your narrative so that you can summarize some events quickly and render others as fully
   realized scenes.
3. Supply evocative details to help your readers experience the dramatic development of your narrative.
4. Establish a consistent point of view so that your readers know how you have positioned yourself in your
   story.
5. Represent the events in your narrative so that your
   story makes its point.

Maya Angelou (given name, Marguerita Johnson) was born in St. Louis, Missouri, in 1928 and spent her early years in California and Arkansas. A woman of varied accomplishments, she is a novelist, poet, playwright, stage and screen performer, composer, and singer. She is perhaps best known for her autobiographical novels: *I Know Why the Caged Bird Sings* (1970), *Gather Together in My Name* (1974), *Singin' and Swingin' and Gettin' Merry Like Christmas* (1976), *Heart of a Woman* (1981), *All God's Children Need Traveling Shoes* (1986), and *Wouldn't Take Nothing for My Journey Now* (1993). Angelou's poetry is equally well respected and is published in her *Complete Collected Poems* (1994). In the following selection from *I Know Why the Caged Bird Sings,* Angelou recounts how she maintained her identity in a world of prejudice.

My Name Is Margaret

RECENTLY A WHITE woman from Texas, who would quickly describe herself as a liberal, asked me about my hometown. When I told her that in Stamps my grandmother had owned the only Negro general merchandise store since the turn of the century, she exclaimed, "Why, you were a debutante." Ridiculous and even ludicrous. But Negro girls in small Southern towns, whether poverty-stricken or just munching along on a few of life's necessities, were given as extensive and irrelevant preparations for adulthood as rich white girls shown in magazines. Admittedly the training was not the same. While white girls learned to waltz and sit gracefully with a tea cup balanced on their knees, we were lagging behind, learning the mid-Victorian values with very little money to indulge them. (Come and see Edna Lomax spending the money she made picking cotton on five balls of ecru tatting thread. Her fingers are bound to snag the work and she'll have to repeat the stitches time and time again. But she knows that when she buys the thread.)

We were required to embroider and I had trunkfuls of colorful dishtowels, pillowcases, runners and handkerchiefs to my credit. I mastered the art of crocheting and tatting, and there was a lifetime's supply of dainty doilies that would never be used in sacheted dresser drawers. It went without saying that all girls could iron and wash, but the finer touches around the home, like setting a table with real silver, baking roasts and cooking vegetables without meat, had to be learned elsewhere. Usually at the source of those habits. During my tenth year, a white woman's kitchen became my finishing school.

Mrs. Viola Cullinan was a plump woman who lived in a three-bedroom house somewhere behind the post office. She was singularly unattractive until she smiled, and then the lines around her eyes and mouth which made her look perpetually dirty disappeared, and her face looked like the mask of an impish elf. She usually rested her smile until late afternoon

---

During my tenth year, a white woman's kitchen became my finishing school.

---

when her women friends dropped in and Miss Glory, the cook, served them cold drinks on the closed-in porch.

The exactness of her house was inhuman. This glass went here and only here. That cup had its place and it was an act of impudent rebellion to place it anywhere else. At twelve o'clock the table was set. At 12:15 Mrs. Cullinan sat down

to dinner (whether her husband had arrived or not). At 12:16
Miss Glory brought out the food.

It took me a week to learn the difference between a salad 5
plate, a bread plate and a dessert plate.

Mrs. Cullinan kept up the tradition of her wealthy parents. 6
She was from Virginia. Miss Glory, who was a descendant of
slaves that had worked for the Cullinans, told me her history.
She had married beneath her (according to Miss Glory). Her
husband's family hadn't had their money very long and what
they had "didn't 'mount to much."

As ugly as she was, I thought privately, she was lucky to 7
get a husband above or beneath her station. But Miss Glory
wouldn't let me say a thing against her mistress. She was very
patient with me, however, over the housework. She explained
the dishware, silverware and servants' bells. The large round
bowl in which soup was served wasn't a soup bowl, it was a
tureen. There were goblets, sherbet glasses, ice-cream glasses,
wine glasses, green glass coffee cups with matching saucers,
and water glasses. I had a glass to drink from, and it sat with
Miss Glory's on a separate shelf from the others. Soup
spoons, gravy boat, butter knives, salad forks and carving
platter were additions to my vocabulary and in fact almost
represented a new language. I was fascinated with the novelty,
with the fluttering Mrs. Cullinan and her Alice-in-Wonder-
land house.

Her husband remains, in my memory, undefined. I 8
lumped him with all the other white men that I had ever seen
and tried not to see.

On our way home one evening, Miss Glory told me that 9
Mrs. Cullinan couldn't have children. She said that she was
too delicate-boned. It was hard to imagine bones at all under
those layers of fat. Miss Glory went on to say that the doctor
had taken out all her lady organs. I reasoned that a pig's
organs included the lungs, heart and liver, so if Mrs. Cullinan
was walking around without those essentials, it explained why
she drank alcohol out of unmarked bottles. She was keeping
herself embalmed.

When I spoke to Bailey about it, he agreed that I was right, 10 but he also informed me that Mr. Cullinan had two daughters by a colored lady and that I knew them very well. He added that the girls were the spitting image of their father. I was unable to remember what he looked like, although I had just left him a few hours before, but I thought of the Coleman girls. They were very light-skinned and certainly didn't look very much like their mother (no one ever mentioned Mr. Coleman).

My pity for Mrs. Cullinan preceded me the next morning   11
like the Cheshire cat's smile. Those girls, who could have been her daughters, were beautiful. They didn't have to straighten their hair. Even when they were caught in the rain, their braids still hung down straight like tamed snakes. Their mouths were pouty little cupid's bows. Mrs. Cullinan didn't know what she missed. Or maybe she did. Poor Mrs. Culli-nan.

For weeks after, I arrived early, left late and tried very hard   12
to make up for her barrenness. If she had had her own children, she wouldn't have had to ask me to run a thousand errands from her back door to the back door of her friends. Poor old Mrs. Cullinan.

Then one evening Miss Glory told me to serve the ladies   13
on the porch. After I set the tray down and turned toward the kitchen, one of the women asked, "What's your name, girl?" It was the speckled-faced one. Mrs. Cullinan said, "She doesn't talk much. Her name's Margaret."

"Is she dumb?"   14

"No. As I understand it, she can talk when she wants to   15
but she's usually quiet as a little mouse. Aren't you, Margaret?"

I smiled at her. Poor thing. No organs and couldn't even   16
pronounce my name correctly.

"She's a sweet little thing, though."   17

"Well, that may be, but the name's too long. I'd never   18
bother myself. I'd call her Mary if I was you."

I fumed into the kitchen. That horrible woman would   19
never have the chance to call me Mary because if I was starving I'd never work for her. I decided I wouldn't pee on

her if her heart was on fire. Giggles drifted in off the porch
and into Miss Glory's pots. I wondered what they could be
laughing about.

Whitefolks were so strange. Could they be talking about   20
me? Everybody knew that they stuck together better than the
Negroes did. It was possible that Mrs. Cullinan had friends
in St. Louis who heard about a girl from Stamps being in
court and wrote to tell her. Maybe she knew about Mr.
Freeman.

My lunch was in my mouth a second time and I went   21
outside and relieved myself on the bed of four-o'clocks. Miss
Glory thought I might be coming down with something and
told me to go on home, that Momma would give me some
herb tea, and she'd explain to her mistress.

I realized how foolish I was being before I reached the   22
pond. Of course Mrs. Cullinan didn't know. Otherwise she
wouldn't have given me two nice dresses that Momma cut
down, and she certainly wouldn't have called me a "sweet
little thing." My stomach felt fine, and I didn't mention
anything to Momma.

That evening I decided to write a poem on being white,   23
fat, old and without children. It was going to be a tragic
ballad. I would have to watch her carefully to capture the
essence of her loneliness and pain.

The very next day, she called me by the wrong name. Miss   24
Glory and I were washing up the lunch dishes when Mrs.
Cullinan came to the doorway. "Mary?"

Miss Glory asked, "Who?"   25

Mrs. Cullinan, sagging a little, knew and I knew. "I want   26
Mary to go down to Mrs. Randall's and take her some soup.
She's not been feeling well for a few days."

Miss Glory's face was a wonder to see. "You mean Mar-   27
garet, ma'am. Her name's Margaret."

"That's too long. She's Mary from now on. Heat that soup   28
from last night and put it in the china tureen and, Mary, I
want you to carry it carefully."

Every person I knew had a hellish horror of being "called   29
out of his name." It was a dangerous practice to call a Negro

anything that could be loosely construed as insulting because of the centuries of their having been called niggers, jigs, dinges, blackbirds, crows, boots and spooks.

Miss Glory had a fleeting second of feeling sorry for me.   30
Then as she handed me the hot tureen she said, "Don't mind, don't pay that no mind. Sticks and stones may break your bones, but words . . . You know, I been working for her for twenty years."

She held the back door open for me. "Twenty years. I   31
wasn't much older than you. My name used to be Hallelujah. That's what Ma named me, but my mistress give me 'Glory,' and it stuck. I likes it better too."

I was in the little path that ran behind the houses when   32
Miss Glory shouted, "It's shorter too."

For a few seconds it was a tossup over whether I would   33
laugh (imagine being named Hallelujah) or cry (imagine letting some white woman rename you for her convenience). My anger saved me from either outburst. I had to quit the job, but the problem was going to be how to do it. Momma wouldn't allow me to quit for just any reason.

"She's a peach. That woman is a real peach." Mrs. Ran-   34
dall's maid was talking as she took the soup from me, and I wondered what her name used to be and what she answered to now.

For a week I looked into Mrs. Cullinan's face as she called   35
me Mary. She ignored my coming late and leaving early. Miss Glory was a little annoyed because I had begun to leave egg yolk on the dishes and wasn't putting much heart in polishing the silver. I hoped that she would complain to our boss, but she didn't.

Then Bailey solved my dilemma. He had me describe the   36
contents of the cupboard and the particular plates she liked best. Her favorite piece was a casserole shaped like a fish and the green glass coffee cups. I kept his instructions in mind, so on the next day when Miss Glory was hanging out clothes and I had again been told to serve the old biddies on the porch, I dropped the empty serving tray. When I heard Mrs. Cullinan scream, "Mary!" I picked up the casserole and two

of the green glass cups in readiness. As she rounded the kitchen door I let them fall on the tiled floor.

I could never absolutely describe to Bailey what happened 37
next, because each time I got to the part where she fell on the floor and screwed up her ugly face to cry, we burst out laughing. She actually wobbled around on the floor and picked up shards of the cups and cried, "Oh, Momma. Oh, dear Gawd. It's Momma's china from Virginia. Oh, Momma, I sorry."

Miss Glory came running in from the yard and the women 38
from the porch crowded around. Miss Glory was almost as broken up as her mistress. "You mean to say she broke our Virginia dishes? What we gone do?"

Miss Cullinan cried louder, "That clumsy nigger. Clumsy 39
little black nigger."

Old speckled-face leaned down and asked, "Who did it, 40
Viola? Was it Mary? Who did it?"

Everything was happening so fast I can't remember 41
whether her action preceded her words, but I know that Mrs. Cullinan said, "Her name's Margaret, goddamn it, her name's Margaret." And she threw a wedge of the broken plate at me. It could have been the hysteria which put her aim off, but the flying crockery caught Miss Glory right over the ear and she started screaming.

I left the front door wide open so all the neighbors could 42
hear.

Mrs. Cullinan was right about one thing. My name wasn't 43
Mary.

For Study and Discussion

QUESTIONS FOR RESPONSE

1. In what ways do you identify with your name? How do you feel when someone mispronounces, changes, or forgets it?
2. What questions do you have about some of the unresolved issues

in the narration? For example, what do you think will happen when Margaret loses her job?

QUESTIONS ABOUT PURPOSE

1. In what sense does Mrs. Cullinan's kitchen serve as Angelou's "finishing school"? What is she supposed to learn there? What does she learn?
2. How does Angelou's description of Mrs. Cullinan's house as *exact* and *inhuman* support her purpose in recounting the events that take place there?

QUESTIONS ABOUT AUDIENCE

1. How does Angelou's comment about the liberal woman from Texas identify the immediate audience for her essay?
2. What assumptions does Angelou make about her other readers when she comments on the laughter of the white women on the porch?

QUESTIONS ABOUT STRATEGIES

1. How does Angelou use the three discussions of her name to organize her narrative? How does she pace the third discussion to provide an effective resolution for her essay?
2. How does Angelou's intention to write a poem about Mrs. Cullinan establish her initial attitude toward her employer? What changes her attitude toward Mrs. Cullinan's "loneliness and pain"?

QUESTIONS FOR DISCUSSION

1. How did you feel about Glory's and Bailey's reactions to the destruction of the fish-shaped casserole? Explain their strengths and weaknesses as a teacher or adviser.
2. Angelou admits that poor black girls in small southern towns and rich white girls in magazines do not receive the same training. What evidence in the essay suggests that both girls were given "extensive and irrelevant preparations for adulthood"?

Donna Tartt was born in 1964 in Greenwood,
Mississippi, and was educated at the University of
Mississippi and Bennington College. The setting
of her first novel, *The Secret History* (1992), bears
a strong resemblance to Bennington College and
concerns a group of college students who reject
the limits of morality to explore the banality of
evil. In "Basketball Season," reprinted from *The
Oxford American,* Tartt describes a world in which
girls are judged by how enthusiastically they can
cheer for boys.

Basketball Season

THE YEAR I was a freshman cheerleader, I was reading
1984. I was fourteen years old then and failing algebra
and the fact that I was failing it worried me as I would worry
now if the Mafia was after me, or if I had shot somebody and
the police were coming to get me. But I did not have an awful
lot of time to brood about this. It was basketball season then,
and there was a game nearly every night. In Mississippi the
schools are far apart, and sometimes we would have to drive
two hundred miles to get to Panola Academy, Sharkey-
Issaquena, funny how those old names come back to me;
we'd leave sometimes before school was out, not get home
till twelve or one in the morning. I was not an energetic
teenager and this was hard on me. Too much exposure to the
high-decibel world of teen sports—shrieking buzzers; roaring
stomping mobs; thunderous feet of players charging up the
court—kept me in a kind of perpetual stunned condition; the
tin roof echo of rural gymnasiums rang through all my silences, and frequently at night I woke in a panic, because I
thought a player was crashing through my bedroom window

or a basketball was flying at me and about to knock my teeth out.

I read *1984* in the back seats of Cadillacs, Buicks, Lincoln   2
Town Cars, riding through the flat wintry Delta with my
saddle oxfords off and my schoolbooks piled beneath my feet.
Our fathers—professional men, mostly, lawyers and optome-
trists, prosperous local plumbers—took turns driving us back
and forth from the games; the other cheerleaders griped
about this but though I griped along with them, I was secretly appalled at the rowdy team bus, full of boys who
shouted things when you walked by their table in the cafeteria

---

*I yelled as loud as anybody even though I
was suffused by an airy, perilous sense of
unreality, a conviction that none of it
meant anything at all.*

---

and always wanted to copy your homework. The cars, on the
other hand, were wide, spacious, quiet. Somebody's mother
would usually have made cookies; there were always potato
chips and old issues of *Seventeen*. The girls punched listlessly
at the radio; applied Bonne Bell lip gloss; did their homework
or their hair. Sometimes a paperback book would make the
rounds. I remember reading one book about a girl whose
orphaned cousin came to live with her, gradually usurping
the girl's own position in the household and becoming
homecoming queen and family favorite. ("'Why can't *you* be
more like Stephanie!' yelled Mom, exasperated.") It turned
out that Stephanie was not the girl's real cousin at all, but a
witch: a total surprise to the nincompoop parents, who had
not noticed such key signs as Stephanie failing to show up in
photographs, or the family dog ("Lady") and the girl's horse
("Wildfire") going crazy every time Stephanie came within
fifty feet.

Now that I think about it, I believe I read *Animal Farm*   3
before *1984.* I read it in the car, too, riding through monotonous cottonfields in the weak winter afternoon, on the way
to a tournament at Yalobusha Academy. It upset me a little,
especially the end, but the statement "All Animals are Equal,
but Some Animals are more Equal than Others" echoed
sentiments which I recognized as prevalent in the upper
echelons of the cheerleading squad. Our captain was a mean
senior girl named Cindy Clark. She talked a lot about spirit
and pep, and how important it was we work as a team, but
she and her cronies ostracized the younger girls and were
horrible to us off the court. Cindy was approximately my
height and was forced to be my partner in some of the cheers,
a circumstance which displeased her as much as it did myself.
I remember a song that was popular around that time—it had
lyrics that went:

> *We are family*
> *I've got all my sisters with me*

This had for some reason been incorporated into one of   4
the chants and Cindy and I were frequently forced to sing it
together: arms around each other, leaning on each other like
drunks, beaming with joy and behaving in every way like the
sisters which we, in fact, were most certainly not.

Though there was a sharp distinction between the older   5
girls and the younger ones, we were also divided, throughout
our ranks and regardless of age, into two distinct categories:
those of snob and slut. The snobs had flat chests, pretty
clothes, and were skittish and shrill. Though they were always
sugar-sweet to one's face, in reality they were a nasty, back-
biting lot, always doing things like stealing each other's boyfriends and trying to rig the elections for the Beauty Revue.
The sluts were from poorer families, and much better liked
in general. They drank beer, made out with boys in the
hallways, and had horrible black hickeys all over their necks.
Our squad was divided pretty much half and half. Physically
and economically, I fell into the category of snob, but I did

poorly in school and was not gung-ho or clubbish enough to fit in very well with the rest of them. (To be a proper snob, one had always to be making floats for some damn parade or other, or organizing pot-luck dinners for the Booster Club.) The sluts, I thought, took a more sensible view of such foolishness; they smoked and drank; I found them, as a rule, much nicer. Being big girls generally, they were the back-bones of the stances, the foundations from which the pyramids rose and, occasionally, fell; I, being the smallest on the squad, had to work with them rather closely, in special sessions after the regular cheerleading practices, since they were the ones who lifted me into the air, who spotted me in gymnastics, upon whose shoulders I had to stand to form the obligatory pyramid. They all had pet names for me, and—though vigorously heterosexual—babied me in what I am sure none of them realized was a faintly lecherous way: tickles and pinches, slaps on the rump, pulling me into their laps in crowded cars and crooning stupid songs from the radio into my ear. Most of this went on in the after-school practices. At the games they completely ignored me, as every fiber of their attention was devoted to flirting with—and contriving to make out with—various boys. As I was both too young to be much interested in boys, and lacking in the fullness of bosom and broadness of beam which would have made them much interested in me, I was excluded from this activity. But still they felt sorry for me, and gave me tips on how to make myself attractive (pierced ears, longer hair, tissue paper in the bra)—and, when we were loitering around after practices, often regaled me with worldly tales of various sexual, obstetric, and gynecological horrors, some of which still make my eyes pop to think about.

The gymnasiums were high-ceilinged, barnlike, drafty, 6 usually in the middle of some desolate field. We were always freezing in our skimpy plaid skirts, our legs all goose pimples as we clapped and stamped on the yellowed wooden floor. (Our legs, being so much exposed, were frequently chapped from cold, yet we were forbidden to put lotion on them,

Cindy and the older girls having derived a pathological horror
of "grease" from—as best as I could figure—the Clearasil ads
in *Tiger Beat* and *Seventeen*—this despite the fact that grease
was the primary element of all our diets.) Referee's whistle,
sneakers squealing on the varnish. "Knees together," Cindy
would hiss down the line, or "Spit out that gum," before she
hollered "Ready!" and we clapped our hands down to our
sides in unison and yelled the response: "O-Kay!" At halftime
there were the detested stances, out in the middle of the
court, which involved perilous leaps, and complex timing,
and—more likely than not—tears and remonstrations in the
changing rooms. These were a source of unremitting dread,
and as soon as they were over and the buzzer went off for
third quarter the younger girls rushed in a greedy flock to
the snack bar for Cokes and French fries, Hershey bars,
scattering to devour them in privacy while Cindy and her
crew slunk out to the parking lot to rendezvous with their
boyfriends. We were all of us, all the time, constantly sick—
coughing, blowing our noses, faces flushed with fever—a
combination of cold, bad food, cramped conditions, and
yelling ourselves hoarse every night. Hoarseness was, in fact,
a matter of pride: we were accused of shirking if our voices
weren't cracked by the end of the evening, the state to which
we aspired being a rasping, laryngitic croak. I remember the
only time the basketball coach—a gigantic, stone-faced, terrifying man who was also the principal of the school and who,
to my way of thinking, held powers virtually of life or death
(there were stories of his punching kids out, beating them till
they had bruises, stories which perhaps were not apocryphal
in a private school like my own, which prided itself on what
it called "old-fashioned discipline" and where corporal punishment was a matter of routine); the only time this coach
ever spoke to me was to compliment me on my burnt-out
voice, which he overheard in the hall the morning after a
game. "Good job," he said. My companions and I were
struck speechless with terror. After he was gone they stared
at me with awestruck apprehension and then, one by one,

drifted gently away, not wishing to be seen in the company
of anyone who had attracted the attention—even momentarily—of this dangerous lunatic.

There were pep squads, of a sort, in George Orwell's   7
Oceania. I read about them with interest. Banners, procession, slogans, games, were as popular there as they were at
Kirk Academy. Realizing that there were certain correspon-
dences between this totalitarian nightmare and my own high
school gave me at first a feeling of smug superiority, but after
a time I began to have an acute sense of the meaninglessness
of my words and gestures. Did I really care if we won or lost?
No matter how enthusiastically I jumped and shouted, the
answer to this was unquestionably No. This epiphany both
confused and depressed me. And yet I continued—outwardly
at least—to display as much pep as ever. "I always look
cheerful and I never shirk anything," says Winston Smith's
girlfriend, Julia. "Always yell with the crowd, that's what I
say. It's the only way to be safe." Our rival team was called
the Patriots. I remember one rally, the night before a big
game, when a dummy Patriot was hanged from the gymnasium rafters, then taken outside and burned amid the frenzied
screams and stomps of the mob. I yelled as loud as anybody
even though I was suffused by an airy, perilous sense of
unreality, a conviction that—despite the apparently desperate
nature of this occasion—that none of it meant anything at
all. In my diary that night—a document which was as secretive and, to my mind at least, as subversive as Winston's
own—I noted tersely: "Hell's own Pep Rally. Freshmen won
the spirit stick. Rah, rah."

It was on the rides home—especially on the nights we'd   8
won—that the inequity of not being allowed on the team bus
was most keenly felt by the cheerleaders. Moodily, they stared
out the windows, dreaming of back seats, and letter jackets,
and smooching with their repulsive boyfriends. The cars
smelled like talcum powder and Tickle deodorant and—if we
were with one of the nicer dads, who had allowed us to stop
at a drive-in—cheeseburgers and French fries. It was too dark
to read. Everyone was tired, but for some reason we were all

too paranoid to go to sleep in front of each other; afraid we might drool, perhaps, or inadvertently scratch an armpit.

Whispers, giggles, sighs. We rode four to a car and all four 9 of us would be crammed in the back seat; bare arms touching, goosebumped knees pressed together, our silences punctuated by long ardent slurps of Tab. The console lights of the Cadillac dashboards were phosphorescent, eerie. The radio was mostly static that time of night but sometimes you could get a late-night station coming out of Greenwood or Memphis; slow songs, that's what everyone wanted, sloppy stuff by Olivia Newton-John or Dan Fogelberg. (The cheerleaders had a virtual cult of Olivia Newton-John; they tried to do their hair like her, emulate her in every possible way, and were fond of speculating what Olivia would or would not do in certain situations. She was like the ninth, ghost member of the squad. I was secretly gratified when she plummeted—with alarming swiftness—from favor because someone heard a rumor that she was gay.)

Olivia or not, the favorite song that winter hands down 10 was "You Light Up My Life" by Debby Boone. It must have been number one for months; at least, it seemed to come on the radio just about every other song, which was fine with everybody. When it came on the girls would all start singing it quietly to themselves, staring out the window, each in their own little world; touching the fogged window-glass gently with their fingertips and each thinking no one could hear them, but all their voices combined in a kind of low, humming harmony that blended with the radio:

> *So many nights*
> *I sit by my window*
> *Waiting for someone*
> *To sing me his song . . .*

Full moon; hard frost on the stubbled cottonfields. They 11 opened up on either side of the car in long, gray spokes, like a fan.

For Study and Discussion

QUESTIONS FOR RESPONSE

1. To what extent did your high school social schedule revolve around sports? Describe some of that schedule.
2. What were the cliques in your school? How did you relate to these groups?

QUESTIONS ABOUT PURPOSE

1. How do Tartt's reading (homework) and writing (diary) establish her attitude toward "basketball season"?
2. How do her references to George Orwell's *Animal Farm* and *1984* clarify the purpose of her personal narrative?

QUESTIONS ABOUT AUDIENCE

1. How do Tartt's references to her size and maturity evoke the sympathy of her readers?
2. How do her responses to the head cheerleader and the coach help readers identify with her point of view?

QUESTIONS ABOUT STRATEGIES

1. How does Tartt use the car rides to and from the basketball games to frame the plot of her narrative?
2. How does she use popular songs ("We Are Family" and "You Light Up My Life") to establish the conflicts in her story?

QUESTIONS FOR DISCUSSION

1. How do peer groups (such as the *snobs* and the *sluts*) determine the social codes in high school?
2. In what ways has the development of women's sports changed the status of cheerleaders?

Terry Tempest Williams was born in 1955 in the Salt Valley of Utah and educated at the University of Utah. She has taught on a Navajo reservation and in the women's studies program at the University of Utah. She currently serves as the curator of education and naturalist-in-residence at the Utah Museum of Natural History in Salt Lake City. Williams has written children's books with nature themes, including *The Secret Language of Snow* (1984); a collection of short stories set in Utah, *Coyote's Canyon* (1989); and three works of nonfiction that blend natural history and personal experience: *Pieces of White Shell: A Journey to Navajo-Land* (1984), *Refuge: An Unnatural History of Family and Place* (1991), and *An Unspoken Hunger: Stories from the Field* (1994). In "The Village Watchman," reprinted from *An Unspoken Hunger,* Williams describes the remarkable lessons she learned from her Uncle Alan.

The Village Watchman

S TORIES CARVED IN cedar rise from the deep woods of Sitka. These totem poles are foreign to me, this vertical lineage of clans; Eagle, Raven, Wolf, and Salmon. The Tlingit craftsmen create a genealogy of the earth, a reminder of mentors, that we come into this world in need of proper instruction. I sit on the soft floor of this Alaskan forest and feel the presence of Other.

The totem before me is called "Wolf Pole" by locals. The Village Watchman sits on top of Wolf's head with his knees drawn to his chest, his hands holding them tight against his body. He wears a red-and-black-striped hat. His eyes are direct, deep-set, painted blue. The expression on his face reminds me of a man I loved, a man who was born into this world feet first.

"Breech—" my mother told me of her brother's birth.   3
"Alan was born feet first. As a result, his brain was denied oxygen. He is special."

As a child, this information impressed me. I remember   4
thinking fish live underwater. Maybe Alan had gills, maybe he didn't need a face-first gulp of air like the rest of us. His sweet breath of initiation came in time, slowly moving up through the soles of his tiny webbed feet. The amniotic sea

---

Alan was wild, like a mustang in the desert and, like most wild horses, he was eventually rounded up.

---

he had floated in for nine months delivered him with a fluid memory. He knew something. Other.

Wolf, who resides in the center of this totem, holds the tail   5
of Salmon with his feet. The tongue of Wolf hangs down, blood-red, as do his front paws, black. Salmon, a sockeye, is poised downriver—a swish of a tail and he could be gone, but the clasp of Wolf is strong.

There is a story of a boy who was kidnapped from his   6
village by the Salmon People. He was taken from his family to learn the ways of water. When he returned many years later to his home, he was recognized by his own as a Holy Man privy to the mysteries of the unseen world. Twenty years after my uncle's death, I wonder if Alan could have been that boy.

But our culture tells a different story, more alien than those   7
of Tlingit or Haida. My culture calls people of sole-births retarded, handicapped, mentally disabled or challenged. We see them for who they are not, rather than for who they are.

My grandmother, Lettie Romney Dixon, wrote in her   8

journal, "It wasn't until Alan was sixteen months old that a busy doctor cruelly broke the news to us. Others may have suspected our son's limitations but to those of us who loved him so unquestionably, lightning struck without warning. I hugged my sorrow to myself. I felt abandoned and lost. I wouldn't accept the verdict. Then we started the trips to a multitude of doctors. Most of them were kind and explained that our child was like a car without brakes, like an electric wire without insulation. They gave us no hope for a normal life."

Normal. Latin: *normalis; norma,* a rule; conforming with 9 or constituting an accepted standard, model, or pattern, especially corresponding to the median or average of a large group in type, appearance, achievement, function, or development.

Alan was not normal. He was unique; one and only; single; 10 sole; unusual; extraordinary; rare. His emotions were not measured, his curiosity not bridled. In a sense, he was wild like a mustang in the desert and, like most wild horses, he was eventually rounded up.

He was unpredictable. He created his own rules and they 11 changed from moment to moment. Alan was twelve years old, hyperactive, mischievous, easily frustrated, and unable to learn in traditional ways. The situation was intensified by his seizures. Suddenly, without warning, he would stiffen like a rake, fall forward and crash to the ground, hitting his head. My grandparents could not keep him home any longer. They needed professional guidance and help. In 1957 they reluctantly placed their youngest child in an institution for handicapped children called the American Fork Training School. My grandmother's heart broke for the second time.

Once again, from her journal: "Many a night my pillow is 12 wet from tears of sorrow and senseless dreamings of 'if things had only been different,' or wondering if he is tucked in snug and warm, if he is well and happy, if the wind still bothers him. . . ."

The wind may have continued to bother Alan, certainly 13 the conditions he was living under were less than ideal, but

as a family there was much about his private life we never
knew. What we did know was that Alan had an enormous
capacity for adaptation. We had no choice but to follow him.

I followed him for years.   14

Alan was ten years my senior. In my mind, growing up, he   15
was mythic. Everything I was taught not to do, Alan did. We
were taught to be polite, to not express displeasure or anger
in public. Alan was sheer, physical expression. Whatever was
on his mind was vocalized and usually punctuated with colorful speech. We would go bowling as a family on Sundays.
Each of us would take our turn, hold the black ball to our
chest, take a few steps, swing our arm back, forward, glide,
and release—the ball would roll down the alley, hit a few pins,
we would wait for the ball to return, and then take our second
run. Little emotion was shown. When it was Alan's turn, it
was an event. Nothing subtle. His style was Herculean. Big
man. Big ball. Big roll. Big bang. Whether it was a strike or
a gutter, he clapped his hands, spun around in the floor,
slapped his thighs and cried, "God-damn! Did you see that
one? Send me another ball, sweet Jesus!" And the ball was
always returned.

I could always count on my uncle for a straight answer.   16
He was my mentor in understanding that one of the remarkable aspects of being human was to hold opposing views in
our mind at once.

"How are you doing?" I would ask.   17

"Ask me how I am feeling?" he answered.   18

"Okay, how are you feeling?"   19

"Today? Right now?"   20

"Yes."   21

"I am very happy and very sad."   22

"How can you be both at the same time?" I asked in all   23
seriousness, a girl of nine or ten.

"Because both require each other's company. They live in   24
the same house. Didn't you know?"

We would laugh and then go on to another topic. Talking   25
to my uncle was always like entering a maze of riddles. Ask a
question. Answer with a question and see where it leads you.

My younger brother Steve and I spent a lot of time with   26

Alan. He offered us shelter from the conventionality of a Mormon family. At our home during Christmas, he would direct us in his own nativity plays. "More—" he would say to us, making wide gestures with his hands. "Give me more of yourself." He was not like anyone we knew. In a culture where we were taught socially to be seen not heard, Alan was our mirror. We could be different too. His unquestioning belief in us as children, as human beings, was in startling contrast to the way we saw the public react to him. It hurt us. What we could never tell was if it hurt him.

Each week, Steve and I would accompany our grandparents south to visit Alan. It was an hour's drive to the training school from Salt Lake City, mostly through farmlands.

We would enter the grounds, pull into the parking lot of the institution where a playground filled with huge papier-mâché storybook figures stood (a twenty-foot pied piper, a pumpkin carriage with Cinderella inside, the old woman who lived in a shoe), and nine out of ten times, Alan would be standing outside his dormitory waiting for us. We would get out of the car and he would run toward us, throwing his powerful arms around us. His hugs cracked my back and at times I had to fight for my breath. My grandfather would calm him down by simply saying, "We're here, son. You can relax now."

Alan was a formidable man, now in his early twenties, stocky and strong. His head was large with a protruding forehead that bore many scars, a line-by-line history of seizures. He always had on someone else's clothes—a tweed jacket too small, brown pants too big, a striped golf shirt that didn't match. He showed us appearances didn't matter, personality did. If you didn't know him, he could look frightening. It was an unspoken rule in our family that the character of others was gauged in how they treated him. The only thing consistent about his attire was that he always wore a silver football helmet from Olympus High School where my grandfather was coach. It was a loving, practical solution to protect Alan when he fell. Quite simply, the helmet cradled his head and absorbed the shock of the seizures.

"Part of the team," my grandfather Sanky would say as he

slapped him affectionately on the back. "You're a Titan, son, and I love you—you're a real player on our team."

The windows to the dormitory were dark, reflecting Mount Timpanogos to the east. It was hard to see inside, but I knew what the interior held. It looked like an abandoned gymnasium without bleachers, filled with hospital beds. The stained white walls and yellow-waxed floors offered no warmth to its residents. The stench was nauseating, sweat and urine trapped in the oppression of stale air. I recall the dirty sheets, the lack of privacy, and the almond-eyed children who never rose from their beds. And then I would turn around and face Alan's cheerfulness, the open and loving manner in which he would introduce me to his friends, the pride he exhibited as he showed me around his home. I kept thinking, Doesn't he see how bad this is, how poorly they are being treated? His words would return to me, "I am very happy and I am very sad." 31

For my brother and me, Alan was our guide, our elder. He was fearless. But neither one of us will ever be able to escape the image of Alan kissing his parents good-bye after an afternoon with family and slowly walking back to his dormitory. Before we drove away, he would turn toward us, take off his silver helmet, and wave. The look on his face haunts me still. Alan walked point for all of us. 32

Alan liked to talk about God. Perhaps it was in these private conversations that our real friendship was forged. 33

"I know Him," he would say when all the adults were gone. 34

"You do?" I asked. 35

"I talk to Him every day." 36

"How so?" 37

"I talk to Him in my prayers. I listen and then I hear His voice." 38

"What does He tell you?" 39

"He tells me to be patient. He tells me to be kind. He tells me that He loves me." 40

In Mormon culture, children are baptized a member of 41

the Church of Jesus Christ of Latter-Day Saints when they turn eight years old. Alan had never been baptized because my grandparents believed it should be his choice, not something simply taken for granted. When he turned twenty-two, he expressed a sincere desire to join the Church. A date was set immediately.

The entire Dixon clan convened in the Lehi Chapel, a few   42
miles north of the group home where Alan was now living. We were there to support and witness his conversion. As we walked toward the meetinghouse where this sacred rite was to be performed, Alan had a violent seizure. My grandfather and Uncle Don, Alan's elder brother, dropped down with him, holding his head and body as every muscle thrashed on the pavement like a school of netted fish brought on deck. I didn't want to look, but to walk away would have been worse. We stayed with him, all of us.

"Talk to God," I heard myself saying under my breath. "I   43
love you, Alan."

"Can you hear me, darling?" It was my grandmother's   44
voice, her hand holding her son's hand.

By now, many of us were gathered on our knees around   45
him, our trembling hands on his rigid body.

> *And we, who have always thought*
> *Of happiness as rising, would feel*
> *The emotion that almost overwhelms us*
> *Whenever a happy thing falls.*
> *—Rainer Maria Rilke*

Alan opened his eyes. "I want to be baptized," he said.   46
The men helped him to his feet. The gash on his left temple was deep. Blood dripped down the side of his face. He would forgo stitches once again. My mother had her arm around my grandmother's waist. Shaken, we all followed him inside.

Alan's father and brother ministered to him, stopped the   47
bleeding and bandaged the pressure wound, then helped him change into the designated white garments for baptism. He

entered the room with great dignity and sat on the front pew with a dozen or more eight-year-old children seated on either side. Row after row of family sat behind him.

"Alan Romney Dixon." His name was called by the pre- 48
siding bishop. Alan rose from the pew and met his brother Don, also dressed in white, who took his hand and led him down the blue-tiled stairs into the baptismal font filled with water. They faced the congregation. Don raised his right arm to the square in the gesture of a holy oath as Alan placed his hands on his brother's left forearm. The sacred prayer was offered in the name of the Father, the Son, and the Holy Ghost, after which my uncle put his right hand behind Alan's shoulder and gently lowered him into the water for a complete baptism by immersion.

Alan emerged from the holy waters like an angel. 49

> *The breaking away of childhood*
> *Left you intact. In a moment,*
> *You stood there, as if completed*
> *In a miracle, all at once.*
> *—Rainer Maria Rilke*

Six years later, I found myself sitting in a chair across from 50
my uncle at the University Hospital, where he was being treated for a severe ear infection. I was eighteen. He was twenty-eight.

"Alan," I asked. "What is it really like to be inside your 51
body?"

He crossed his legs and placed both hands on the arms of 52
the chair. His brown eyes were piercing.

"I can't tell you what it's like except to say I feel pain for 53
not being seen as the person I am."

A few days later, Alan died alone; unique; one and only; 54
single; in American Fork, Utah.

The Village Watchman sits on top of his totem with Wolf and 55
Salmon—it is beginning to rain in the forest. I find it curious that this spot in southeast Alaska has brought me back into

relation with my uncle, this man of sole-birth who came into the world feet first. He reminds me of what it means to live and love with a broken heart; how nothing is sacred, how everything is sacred. He was a weather vane—a storm and a clearing at once.

Shortly after his death, Alan appeared to me in a dream. 56 We were standing in my grandmother's kitchen. He was leaning against the white stove with his arms folded.

"Look at me, now, Terry," he said smiling. "I'm normal— 57 perfectly normal." And then he laughed. We both laughed.

He handed me his silver football helmet that was resting 58 on the counter, kissed me, and opened the back door.

"Do you recognize who I am?" 59

On this day in Sitka, I remember. 60

For Study and Discussion

QUESTIONS FOR RESPONSE

1. In what ways does our culture (television, movies) portray "special" people?
2. In what ways does Williams's essay correct or enrich your understanding of "special" people?

QUESTIONS ABOUT PURPOSE

1. How does Williams's title suggest the purpose of her description of her Uncle Alan's life?
2. How does Williams's description of the Wolf Pole present the purpose of her narrative?

QUESTIONS ABOUT AUDIENCE

1. How does Williams's use of the pronoun *our* in the following phrase identify her audience: "our culture tells a different story, more alien"?
2. How does the following sentence separate Williams's family from her audience: "His unquestioning belief in us . . . was in startling contrast to the way we saw the public react to him"?

QUESTIONS ABOUT STRATEGIES

1. How does Williams use the quotations from Rilke's poetry to interpret Alan's baptism?
2. How does she use the visits at the school, and particularly her last visit at the hospital, to slow the pace of her narrative?

QUESTIONS FOR DISCUSSION

1. What do the words *normal* and *special* mean in our culture?
2. How is it possible to hold opposing views in the mind at once? How does Alan do it?

Wakako Yamauchi was born in 1924 in Westmorland, California. In 1942, she was a high school senior in Oceanside, California, when she and her family, along with 120,000 other Japanese Americans, were sent to a relocation "camp." After the war, she worked briefly as a columnist and a graphic artist for the *Los Angeles Tribune*. She did not begin her own writing career until 1974, when she published a short story, "And the Soul Shall Dance," in an anthology of Asian-American authors, *Aiiieeeee!* In 1975, she adapted the story for the stage and began a career as a playwright, authoring a half-dozen plays such as *The Music Lessons* (1980) and *The Memento* (1987). Yamauchi has continued to contribute her stories and memoirs to *Amerasia Journal* and *Greenfield Review*. In 1994, she published a collection of her stories, plays, and memoirs in *Songs My Mother Taught Me*. In "Otoko," first published in the *Southwest Review*, Yamauchi describes her family's turmoil in the years just before and during World War II.

Otoko

T HIS IS THE summer solstice, the longest day of the year. Tomorrow will be shorter, each day thereafter slipping away, taking along a measure of light. In December the cycle starts again; light grows stronger, longer, bringing spring back to us. But today is the turning point, and though the long hazy summer stretches before us, we know this is the beginning of the waning.

On this day, my brother Kiyo drops by. He brings three

small boxes of berries from his in-laws' farm. They work a few acres of raspberries in West Covina, maybe twenty miles east of Los Angeles and seventeen more from Gardena, where I live. He shows me an album he found in a Japanese tape and record store there. He sets the berries in the sink and dusts the record with his sleeve. It's a reissue of vintage Japanese songs. My mother sang them often. In those Depression years the old Victrola was her trip home.

"Listen to this," he says.   3

> *Watashya ukiyo no watari dori* (I'm a bird of passage in a floating world) . . .

I hear her now. I see her dancing. She is younger than I   4
am today.

"We've outlived them both, Kiyo," I say.   5

"Remember that old abandoned house in Westmorland?"   6
he asks.

It was a time like now. The bottom fell out of the stock   7
market, they said. We didn't have stocks or money to lose, but my father did lose his job with the American Fruit Growers, a job that included housing with salary. Until then life

---

Otoko *was the word that said it all: man, virility, courage, endurance.*

---

was all right; there was good food, store-bought clothes, a house with running water and a telephone on the wall. These are what I remember of life before our fall. Then the Great Depression descended. For us, it happened in 1932.

There were lots of homeless people—even in Westmor-   8
land, a desert township near the Mexican border, where a shelter could be built with chaparral.

But a house of straw? The Japanese are proud. My father 9
took his family of four (Sachi was not yet born), borrowed
an old frame house from a friend of a friend, leased thirty
acres, moved the house onto it and went into farming independently—if you can call borrowing money from a produce
company and committing the entire harvest to them independent.

It was a struggle—too much rain, too little rain, frost. It 10
was the old "company store" syndrome: the loan, the high
interest, the fixed prices. But the worst was yet to come.

The friend's friend reclaimed the house he'd loaned us. 11
My mother said no friend would do such a thing; my father
said it was a friend's friend. We had to find a place to stay
until he decided what to do. He chose to remain in farming,
and he moved us into this deserted house that stood by the
dirt road we took to town.

We had passed it often. Kiyo and I used to throw stones 12
at the windows, called it the haunted house. We covered the
broken windows with cardboard, washed off the ancient feces
left by wandering (and prideless, my mother said) unfortu-
nates and moved in as squatters. It was summer; school was
out and there was no need to explain the embarrassing situation to anyone. We hardly saw a person, much less a friend
or a schoolmate. My mother said it wouldn't be for long.

My brother spent that summer working at a packing shed 13
making boxes, hammering nails into wooden slats all day, his
small fingers growing raw with tiny splinters. He was eleven
or twelve. He gave all his pay to my father. He tells me now
he's glad of that, because it turned out that was all he'd ever
do for him.

Kiyo's eyes swell with moisture. I see my brother with his hair 14
turning white and thinning, almost crying over something
that cannot be redone or even revised, and I too, almost cry.

    Otoko wa iji, onna wa nasake (man is will, woman
    is mercy) . . . The moisture dries before it falls.

Kiyo says he once drove with my father to Niland in the low   15
desert, a place drier, sandier, more barren and wind-swept
than our Westmorland. This was before car radios and air
conditioning. It was a hot and boring journey at thirty miles
an hour, my father's usual highway speed. The friend my
father went to see made a little money with early tomatoes
that year. Our tomatoes were too late (as usual, my mother
said) to cash in on the good price. Kiyo says now he believes
my father went to borrow money that day.

"They were rich. Radio—battery, of course. Console," he   16
says. "Sofa in the parlor . . . the works." He laughs and pats
my couch. "I guess they turned him down, because we left
early and Pop didn't say anything all the way home. Twenty
miles. Nothing. I remember that."

How do you ask for a loan? Do you wait 'til tea is served?   17
Do you touch the sleek new console and say, "You did good
this year, huh?" Most likely the friend suspected the nature
of the mission and immediately started talking poverty and
my father left as soon as it was convenient. I can't picture
him, cap in hand, rubbing the back of his neck: "My kids are
hungry; we have no place to live."

"Maybe he didn't ask," I say.   18

"I don't know. The kids were showing me the new radio   19
so I don't know. He was proud, all right," Kiyo says. "I
wonder what he was thinking on that ride back. Well, we
made it without their help." He takes a deep breath. "I guess
he felt bad. Pop was proud."

"He." We talk about him as we would a stranger. "Pop."   20
Calling him "Pop" after he's gone is a safe intimacy. He was
a stranger. I suppose his life was a string of enduring humili-
ations, rotating his failures and hanging in there—drawing
strength from beneath the silence, from his hope of one day
returning to Japan. I heard it in the songs he sang when he
drank.

I was a headstrong, impetuous, and demanding child—the   21
second of three: Kiyo, myself, and thirteen years below me,
a sweet cross-eyed sister, Sachi. I was the only one of the
bunch who was familiar with the knuckles of my father's

hand. "*Onna no kuse,*" he said. That's an admonition to know my place as a woman.

I looked just like him: the long face, angular frame, the   22
epicanthic fold. My mother was a beautiful woman, and mercifully the others inherited her looks and my father's suppressed temperament. I was given the other combination: his looks and her tenacious nature.

The spring of the great Imperial Valley earthquake was the   23
peak of my father's farming career—his grandest failure. One hundred and forty acres of lettuce nobody wanted.

I was fifteen. I was tired of hand-me-downs and recycled   24
clothes and I went to Los Angeles to earn a few dollars to buy a coat of my own and some finery that might help me with the fellows. At that time the only jobs available to Japanese were in fruit stands, garages, and, for women, domestic work. It was the summer of '39. In Europe World War II was already in progress.

I found a job in South Pasadena as a "school girl," a   25
euphemism for inexperienced servant. I worked three months at twenty-five dollars a month plus room and board, washing, ironing, polishing furniture, vacuuming, and caring for two small girls. Not a lot of money even for those days. Of the seventy-five dollars I earned, I spent twenty-five mostly for movies and restaurants on my days off. I bought a coral necklace and a pair of Gallen Kamp shoes with open toes. It was too warm to think about coats.

At the end of my stint, I was eager to come home. I missed   26
my family while I was away living with white folks. I had acquired a new appreciation for them along with the experience of being on the outside looking in. The grand piano with the velvet fringed scarf, mirrored bathrooms, red-meat dinners with cloth napkins and sterling flatwear brought me closer to my family—my carping mother, silent father, quarrelsome brother and my sweet Sachi.

In the meantime my family had gone to Oceanside to work   27
in the berry farms of Kumamoto-mura (Kumamoto Village), so named because most of the residents had immigrated from Kumamoto, Japan. It's now Camp Pendleton, a Marine base.

No doubt wild strawberries still stain the boots of bivouack-
ing soldiers—a stubborn memory of the Japanese community
that lived and farmed there.

In Oceanside, I was appalled to find my family in a make-   28
shift tent, using water from a communal faucet, washing,
shaving, brushing teeth publicly. Other families from Imperial
Valley were also there. It had been a disastrous year for a lot
of us. In the three months I'd been away, my little sister's
front teeth had rotted. She'd turned two and did not remember me.

Kiyo would not take the situation seriously: a few months   29
camping in Oceanside, cool weather, a beach nearby, a few
bucks, a kind of vacation. He laughed. My mother's lips
grinned but her eyes did not smile.

I gave my remaining fifty dollars to her. "We'll buy a   30
sweater for Father," she said, "and we'll give money to Kiyo
to go to Los Angeles. There's no future for him here."

Kiyo left for L.A. He wrote later that he'd found a day job   31
in a fruit stand and went to vocational school nights.

And we didn't stay in the tent. A kindly bachelor who   32
farmed a piece of land with a frame house on it offered us a
room. "It's not right for a young girl to sleep on the ground,"
he said.

My mother said, "Michiko, remember this kindness."   33

"It's only for a short while," I said. "We have to get back   34
home. School will start in two weeks."

"We have nothing to go back to," she said.   35

The following week my mother was offered a job in town   36
as cook in a boarding house for Japanese migrant workers.
The man who came was short and wiry. He wore boots laced
to his calves. He said she would cook for thirty, forty men
during peak seasons, and off-season there would be only a
few, say four or five, who chose not to move on.

"There are always some of them," Mr. Tano said. "They   37
get tired of moving, and if they don't have money to pay,
well, I got to carry them. What can I do? They're Japanese
too, eh? I'll give you a room for your family. Your husband
can work out of the hotel like the rest of them. When farmers

need help they come to me. I'll see that your husband always
has work," Mr. Tano said.

My father went to bed that day. He had a stomach condi- 38
tion that plagued him off and on for years. He took a chalky
white liquid for it.

My mother asked him, "What should I do? Should I take 39
the job?"

His face was ashy. His lips were dry and cracked. On this 40
hot day he pulled the blanket to his neck and turned away
from us.

My mother persisted. "What should I do?" 41

He answered without turning: "Do what you want." 42

We moved to the city and lived in a room with a double 43
bed and two cots and just enough space to move around
them. With the money Mr. Tano gave her, my mother bought
the supplies: rice, *shoyu, miso,* heart, liver, tripe—nether cuts.
My father rode to work in a truck with the rest of the men
and swallowed great quantities of chalky medicine. My
mother bought me a herringbone tweed jacket with shoulder
pads that made me look like a grown woman. I started my
junior year at Oceanside Carlsbad Union High School. When
the kids at school asked me where I lived, I said, "Out that
way," and waved vaguely westward, too ashamed to say I lived
in a hotel for transient men, afraid the down-cheeked youngsters would shrink from me, their mouths pursed.

> *Nokoru yume wo nanto shyo* (what shall we do with
> the dreams that remain) . . . Kiyo flips the record.

Most of the men in the boarding house were over fifty. There 44
were a few in their thirties—*Kibei,* men who were born in
America, sent back to Japan for an education, and, still seeking something they'd not found in Japan, they had returned
to join a legion of men who moved with harvests not their
own. In this land of plenty, they bought the clothes in fashion, which they kept in cleaners' bags, went to movies together, wrote long letters to Japan, and visited neighboring
farmers who had daughters. Sometimes in the evening some-

one would play a wistful Japanese melody on a harmonica or a wooden flute.

The older men were scruffy and bowed from years of scraping along on their knees picking strawberries (for tables not their own) and from bending over low grape vines. Their pants were caked with mud. They shook them out at night over the balcony. Conversations were colored with sexual reference, and they responded with high-pitched laughter. They spent their free time playing *hana* (cards), or drinking *sake,* which my mother warmed and sold to them for ten cents a cup. 45

Once a man staggered off to the courtyard and passed out on the dirt, the ocean breeze cooling him, the sun warming him like the fruit he'd spent his youth harvesting. In the late afternoon he woke and walked away brushing himself off, without shame, as though it were his natural right as a man. Fruit of the land. 46

Within months the hotel was condemned by the Oceanside Department of Health. Not enough bathrooms; too many men in one room. The men scattered—tangling with the law was bad business. Some were illegal aliens. Mr. Tano also left. We stayed in the back house where Mr. Tano had lived, and waited for something to turn up. Squatters again. 47

The landlord came to check on his property and found us there. He saw my little sister with the rotten teeth and the lazy eye and me, haughty and cold. Sachi sang, "Cielito Lindo" for him—a song she learned from the Mexican family next door. The landlord asked me to tell my mother that he was willing to remodel to meet health standards if she would run the hotel. He said he was through dealing with Tano. 48

My mother said to me, "You see? Someone is watching." 49

My father wasn't home that day; just my mother, Sachi— smiling, showing her nubs of teeth, confident the world was safe and loving—and me, unrelenting. 50

By the time the hotel was habitable, it was winter, and most of the rooms were empty. I asked my mother if I could have one room for myself; I would give it up during the season, I promised. She said no. I begged and pleaded, 51 sulked, slammed doors and cupboards, and banged dishes until she screamed, "All right! You can have a room!" She said I was a graceless brat, determined and self-centered. She said if I didn't change my ways I was in for a whole lot of trouble. "You'll find out!" she said.

> *Kiete kureruna, itsumade mo* (don't fade, remain forever) . . .

It was the first time I had a room to myself, excluding the one in South Pasadena. It was on the second floor overlooking the courtyard. I dragged in a table and our two best chairs, in case I had company. I sewed dimity curtains for the window and pushed my cot against it so I could see the stars at night. I bought a vase in a secondhand store for a nickel. 52

The old men thought I was an upstart. Some devised ways of getting back at me: one used to wait until my mother left the room and then would rub his leg against mine and laugh at my indignation. One passed me on my way to the bathroom and cackled, "Three. Count them and see. Three holes. Count them." Sexuality was a man's birthright and nothing, no circumstance, no employer or landlord or upstart kid would deny them that. From cradle to grave, theirs. *Otoko* was the word that said it all: man, virility, courage, endurance. 53

> *Tsuki ga noboreba rantan keshite* (as the moon rises, lanterns flicker out) . . .

My father went to work less and less. He found little jobs to do at home, sweeping the sidewalk, emptying ashtrays, turning the *tsukemono* (pickles). In the evenings he joined the gambling and drinking; during the day he ministered to his anxieties and griefs silently, orally with chalk. My mother sucked in her breath and said, "He drinks *sake* and takes medicine. *Sake* by night and medicine by day. What good does it do? *Sake* and medicine . . ." 54

I went to sleep to the sound of the cursing and laughing and reviling of the men gambling down the hall. My father 55 was always there, taking the house cut and plowing it back into the games (my mother said)—grimly smiling, squandering the money that meant so much to her, defending his last battle line: his manhood, his courage, his endurance.

Noda-san was among the group that drifted in from   56
Fresno after leaving the grape harvest early that year. He was about thirty, boyish and quiet. He didn't join the card games nor did he drink much. Sometimes if I was behind the counter, he'd ask for a cup of *sake,* counting the change in his palm slowly, flashing a shy smile with his white teeth.

One late night I was awakened by a gentle knock.   57
"Who is it?" I asked.   58
"*Boku yo. Noda. Chotto akete. Hanashi ga aruno.*" (It's me,   59
Noda. Let me in. I must talk to you.)

I opened the door and he quickly slipped in. We faced each   60
other in the dark.

"What do you want?"   61
"You," he said.   62
"Well, you can't have me," I said, and switched on the   63
light and made for the door. He turned off the light and barred the door with his arm.

"You ought not to be here," I said, but his smile was so   64
sad, so much in need, it was hard for me to hurt him. "You can't come in here like this," I said.

"But you let me in." He touched my face.   65
"You asked to come in." I pushed his hand away. "You   66
ought to get out of here. You ought not to be here."

"But you let me in."   67
This went on for a while until he got impatient and   68
reached for me. He tried to kiss me. He stroked my struggling body. He maneuvered me to the cot, squirming and sliding in his arms.

We could hear the gamblers down the hall. "Let me go or   69
I'll scream," I whispered.

"You won't do that."   70
"You can walk out of here. I won't tell anyone. Just let me   71
go." I think I heard that in the movies.

His hands worked to calm me, to arouse me. "Shhh . . ."   72
"One more chance," I warned. Still he didn't stop.   73

I yelled, "Father!" He released me instantly. We heard   74
footsteps thudding down the hall. He jumped away from me
and we stood facing each other in the dark just the way he
came in. The door opened. My father and two other men
peered into the room.

"Oh," one of them said. No other word was spoken. The   75
two men left, my father waited for Noda-san and followed
him out, closing the door quietly behind him.

In the morning my father put a hook and eye on my door.   76
And Noda-san smiled his sad boyish smile whenever he
passed me at the counter.

> *Shina no yoru. Shina no yoru yo* (China nights. O,
> China nights) . . . My brother says, "This was
> popular before the war. Remember Oceanside?"

> *Minato no akari, murasaki no yo ni* (lights of the
> harbor against the purple sky) . . .

Hostilities, always present between America and Japan, wors-   77
ened. The threat of war was constant. After a while we got
used to it.

My brother returned to Oceanside. "You never know," he   78
said. "We got to be together when whatever happens happens." He found work as a truck driver in Vista, a few miles
east of Oceanside. "Work days and study nights and still
driving a truck," he complained.

I had gone to see *Sergeant York* that Sunday. When I came   79
home my mother met me at the door. "America is at war with
Japan," she said. Her face was white.

Within months, plans to incarcerate us—alien and citi-   80
zen, rich and poor, sick and well—were implemented. They
herded us into ten isolated camps, 120,000 of us, and locked
the gates. They said it was for national security, even though
there was no incidence of sabotage, they said it was for our
own safety, even though the guns on the guard towers were
pointed at us. And one family, after all those years of struggle,
lost the boarding house that was their ticket to the promised
land.

Noboru janku no yume no fune (sailing upstream, the junk is a boat of dreams) . . .

"I wonder what happened to all those men at the boarding 81 house," I say.

"Why, they went to concentration camps like the rest of 82 us," Kiyo says.

"I mean now, Kiyo. What are they doing now?" 83

"Why, they were old. They died, of course. Heh. Like our 84 father and mother." He looks at his hands. "They never did get to Japan, did they?"

They never did. 85

My father died in camp after the war ended, just before 86 the camp closed. The government had been slowly dispersing the inmates over the past year; I was in Chicago and Kiyo was in Tule Lake expecting deportation. His citizenship was revoked when he answered "no" to the questionnaire asking him if he would go into combat for the country that gave him the opportunity to wash fruit, study nights, and still drive trucks; that took away every inch-by-inch gain in one swift stroke through incarceration without due process; that gave him the choice to bear arms against the country of his ancestry or be deported.

My father had said to him, "*Kimi wa otoko da*" (you are a 87 man), and had let his only son make his choice. I went to Chicago to work in a candy factory.

And so only my mother and Sachi, who was eight, were 88 with my father when he died.

Hiroshima ended the war. My mother said my father grew 89 despondent after the bombing. By this time, the government had set a November deadline for closing the camps. She said she'd asked my father, "Where shall we go? What shall we do?" and he'd not answered. He began to vomit black beads of blood and at the end of October died without making that decision. She said, "I joined the last group of people going out. What could I do?" My mother and Sachi left their home of four years with my father's ashes. They had been there longer than they were in Oceanside.

The war ended, and Kiyo, still in camp at Tule Lake, was 90
not deported. I left Chicago, and Kiyo and I joined my
mother and Sachi in San Diego. But my father died believing
the nucleus of his small family was shattered.

> *Yume mo nuremasho; shiwo kaze, yo kaze* (dreams
> may dampen; salt winds, night winds) . . .

Kiyo says, "These songs really get to me." He thumps his 91
chest. "It's like going back to the past—to Japan. You ever
want to go back, Michi?" he asks.

"Go back? Kiyo, we've never been there." 92

"Yeah. I guess we think of ourselves as them." 93

"Kiyo? What if there's no such place? What if it only existed 94
in their minds? And we believed them?"

"There is no such place. It's Fantasy Island, Michi," he 95
says.

The record spins silently before Kiyo turns it off. He tucks 96
it in its jacket. "I better get going." He looks at his watch.
"Mary's probably wondering what happened to me." He
looks out my window. "Hey, I thought you planted agapan-
thus last year."

"I did. They didn't take," I say. 97

"Did you water them? They're supposed to be the hardiest 98
plants around." He tucks the record under his arm. "Well,
maybe next year, huh?" He laughs.

And on the longest day of the year, he leaves me and 99
hurries home.

For Study and Discussion

QUESTIONS FOR RESPONSE

1. What have you been taught about the motives and actions of the
   Japanese and the Americans in World War II?
2. How do you respond to Yamauchi's description of the incarceration of Japanese Americans?

QUESTIONS ABOUT PURPOSE

1. How does Yamauchi's definition of the word used for the title of her essay—*otoko* (paragraph 53)—clarify the essay's purpose?
2. How does her characterization of the *Kibei* (paragraph 44) contribute to her purpose?

QUESTIONS ABOUT AUDIENCE

1. What assumptions does Yamauchi make about the American readers of her memoir?
2. How does Yamauchi's mother's portrayal of her older daughter as a "graceless brat" affect readers' view of Yamauchi's behavior?

QUESTIONS ABOUT STRATEGIES

1. How does Yamauchi use the lyrics from old Japanese records to comment on the events in her memoir?
2. What techniques does she use to compare herself and her mother, and her brother and her father?

QUESTIONS FOR DISCUSSION

1. How does Yamauchi characterize the *place* of men and women in the Japanese-American community?
2. Why does Kiyo describe Japan as "Fantasy Island"?

George Orwell, the pen name of Eric Blair (1903–1950), was born in Motihari, Bengal, where his father was employed with the Bengal civil service. He was brought to England at an early age for schooling (Eton), but rather than completing his education at the university, he served with the Indian imperial police in Burma (1922–1927). He wrote about these experiences in his first novel, *Burmese Days*. Later he returned to Europe and worked at various jobs (described in *Down and Out in Paris and London*, 1933) before fighting on the Republican side in the Spanish civil war (see *Homage to Catalonia*, 1938). Orwell's attitudes toward war and government are reflected in his most famous books: *Animal Farm* (1945), *1984* (1949), and *Shooting an Elephant and Other Essays* (1950). In the title essay from the last volume, Orwell reports a "tiny incident" that gave him deeper insight into his own fears and "the real motives for which despotic governments act."

Shooting an Elephant

I N MOULMEIN, IN lower Burma, I was hated by large num-   1 bers of people—the only time in my life that I have been important enough for this to happen to me. I was subdivisional police officer of the town, and in an aimless, petty kind of way anti-European feeling was very bitter. No one had the guts to raise a riot, but if a European woman went through the bazaars alone somebody would probably spit betel juice over her dress. As a police officer I was an obvious target and was baited whenever it seemed safe to do so. When a nimble Burman tripped me up on the football field and the

referee (another Burman) looked the other way, the crowd
yelled with hideous laughter. This happened more than once.
In the end the sneering yellow faces of young men that met
me everywhere, the insults hooted after me when I was at a
safe distance, got badly on my nerves. The young Buddhist
priests were the worst of all. There were several thousands of
them in the town and none of them seemed to have anything
to do except stand on street corners and jeer at Europeans.

All this was perplexing and upsetting. For at that time I   2
had already made up my mind that imperialism was an evil
thing and the sooner I chucked up my job and got out of it

As soon as I saw the elephant I knew
with perfect certainty that I ought not to
shoot him.

---

the better. Theoretically—and secretly, of course—I was all
for the Burmese and all against their oppressors, the British.
As for the job I was doing, I hated it more bitterly than I can
perhaps make clear. In a job like that you see the dirty work
of Empire at close quarters. The wretched prisoners huddling
in the stinking cages of the lock-ups, the gray, cowed faces of
the long-term convicts, the scarred buttocks of the men who
had been flogged with bamboos—all these oppressed me
with an intolerable sense of guilt. But I could get nothing
into perspective. I was young and ill educated and I had had
to think out my problems in the utter silence that is imposed
on every Englishman in the East. I did not even know that
the British Empire is dying, still less did I know that it is a
great deal better than the younger empires that are going to
supplant it. All I knew was that I was stuck between my hatred
of the empire I served and my rage against the evil-spirited
little beasts who tried to make my job impossible. With one
part of my mind I thought of the British Raj as an unbreak-

able tyranny, as something clamped down, in *saecula saecu-lorum,* upon the will of prostrate peoples; with another part I thought that the greatest joy in the world would be to drive a bayonet into a Buddhist priest's guts. Feelings like these are the normal by-products of imperialism; ask any Anglo-Indian official, if you can catch him off duty.

One day something happened which in a roundabout way 3
was enlightening. It was a tiny incident in itself; but it gave me a better glimpse than I had had before of the real nature of imperialism—the real motives for which despotic govern-ments act. Early one morning the sub-inspector at a police station the other end of town rang me up on the 'phone and said that an elephant was ravaging the bazaar. Would I please come and do something about it? I did not know what I could do, but I wanted to see what was happening and I got on to a pony and started out. I took my rifle, an old .44 Winchester and much too small to kill an elephant, but I thought the noise might be useful *in terrorem.* Various Bur-mans stopped me on the way and told me about the ele-phant's doings. It was not, of course, a wild elephant, but a tame one which had gone "must." It had been chained up, as tame elephants always are when their attack of "must" is due, but on the previous night it had broken its chain and escaped. Its mahout, the only person who could manage it when it was in that state, had set out in pursuit, but had taken the wrong direction and was now twelve hours' journey away, and in the morning the elephant had suddenly reappeared in the town. The Burmese population had no weapons and were quite helpless against it. It had already destroyed somebody's bamboo hut, killed a cow and raided some fruit-stalls and devoured the stock; also it had met the municipal rubbish van and, when the driver jumped out and took to his heels, had turned the van over and inflicted violences upon it.

The Burmese sub-inspector and some Indian constables 4
were waiting for me in the quarter where the elephant had been seen. It was a very poor quarter, a labyrinth of squalid bamboo huts, thatched with palm-leaf, winding all over a steep hillside. I remember that it was a cloudy, stuffy morning

at the beginning of the rains. We began questioning the people as to where the elephant had gone and, as usual, failed to get any definite information. That is invariably the case in the East; a story always sounds clear enough at a distance, but the nearer you get to the scene of events the vaguer it becomes. Some of the people said that the elephant had gone in one direction, some said that he had gone in another, some professed not even to have heard of any elephant. I had almost made up my mind that the whole story was a pack of lies, when we heard yells a little distance away. There was a loud, scandalized cry of "Go away, child! Go away this instant!" and an old woman with a switch in her hand came round the corner of a hut, violently shooing away a crowd of naked children. Some more women followed, clicking their tongues and exclaiming; evidently there was something that the children ought not to have seen. I rounded the hut and saw a man's dead body sprawling in the mud. He was an Indian, a black Dravidian coolie, almost naked, and he could not have been dead many minutes. The people said that the elephant had come suddenly upon him round the corner of the hut, caught him with its trunk, put its foot on his back and ground him into the earth. This was the rainy season and the ground was soft, and his face had scored a trench a foot deep and a couple of yards long. He was lying on his belly with arms crucified and head sharply twisted to one side. His face was coated with mud, the eyes wide open, the teeth bared and grinning with an expression of unendurable agony. (Never tell me, by the way, that the dead look peaceful. Most of the corpses I have seen looked devilish.) The friction of the great beast's foot had stripped the skin from his back as neatly as one skins a rabbit. As soon as I saw the dead man I sent an orderly to a friend's house nearby to borrow an elephant rifle. I had already sent back the pony, not wanting it to go mad with fright and throw me if it smelt the elephant.

The orderly came back in a few minutes with a rifle and   5
five cartridges, and meanwhile some Burmans had arrived and told us that the elephant was in the paddy fields below, only a few hundred yards away. As I started forward practically the

whole population of the quarter flocked out of the houses and followed me. They had seen the rifle and were all shouting excitedly that I was going to shoot the elephant. They had not shown much interest in the elephant when he was merely ravaging their homes, but it was different now that he was going to be shot. It was a bit of fun to them, and it would be to an English crowd; besides they wanted the meat. It made me vaguely uneasy. I had no intention of shooting the elephant—I had merely sent for the rifle to defend myself if necessary—and it is always unnerving to have a crowd following you. I marched down the hill, looking and feeling a fool, with the rifle over my shoulder and an ever-growing army of people jostling at my heels. At the bottom, when you got away from the huts, there was a metalled road and beyond that a miry waste of paddy fields a thousand yards across, not yet ploughed but soggy from the first rains and dotted with coarse grass. The elephant was standing eight yards from the road, his left side toward us. He took not the slightest notice of the crowd's approach. He was tearing up bunches of grass, beating them against his knees to clean them, and stuffing them into his mouth.

I had halted on the road. As soon as I saw the elephant I 6 knew with perfect certainty that I ought not to shoot him. It is a serious matter to shoot a working elephant—it is comparable to destroying a huge and costly piece of machinery—and obviously one ought not to do it if it can possibly be avoided. And at that distance, peacefully eating, the elephant looked no more dangerous than a cow. I thought then and I think now that his attack of "must" was already passing off; in which case he would merely wander harmlessly about until the mahout came back and caught him. Moreover, I did not in the least want to shoot him. I decided that I would watch him for a little while to make sure that he did not turn savage again, and then go home.

But at that moment I glanced round at the crowd that had 7 followed me. It was an immense crowd, two thousand at the least and growing every minute. It blocked the road for a long distance on either side. I looked at the sea of yellow faces above the garish clothes—faces all happy and excited over this bit of fun, all certain that the elephant was going to be shot. They were watching me as they would watch a conjurer about to perform a trick. They did not like me, but with the magical rifle in my hands I was momentarily worth watching. And suddenly I realized that I should have to shoot the elephant after all. The people expected it of me and I had got to do it; I could feel their two thousand wills pressing me forward, irresistibly. And it was at this moment, as I stood there with the rifle in my hands, that I first grasped the hollowness, the futility of the white man's dominion in the East. Here was I, the white man with his gun, standing in front of the unarmed native crowd—seemingly the leading actor of the piece; but in reality I was only an absurd puppet pushed to and fro by the will of those yellow faces behind. I perceived in this moment that when the white man turns tyrant it is his own freedom that he destroys. He becomes a sort of hollow, posing dummy, the conventionalized figure of a sahib. For it is the condition of his rule that he shall spend his life in trying to impress the "natives," and so in every crisis he has got to do what the "natives" expect of him. He wears a mask, and his face grows to fit it. I had got to shoot the elephant. I had committed myself to doing it when I sent for the rifle. A sahib has got to act like a sahib; he has got to appear resolute, to know his own mind and do definite things. To come all that way, rifle in hand, with two thousand people marching at my heels, and then to trail feebly away, having done nothing— no, that was impossible. The crowd would laugh at me. And my whole life, every white man's life in the East, was one long struggle not to be laughed at.

But I did not want to shoot the elephant. I watched him   8
beating his bunch of grass against his knees with that preoccupied grandmotherly air that elephants have. It seemed to
me that it would be murder to shoot him. At that age I was
not squeamish about killing animals, but I had never shot an
elephant and never wanted to. (Somehow it always seems
worse to kill a *large* animal.) Besides, there was the beast's
owner to be considered. Alive, the elephant was worth at least
a hundred pounds; dead, he would only be worth the value

of his tusks, five pounds, possibly. But I had got to act quickly. I turned to some experienced-looking Burmans who had been there when we arrived, and asked them how the elephant had been behaving. They all said the same thing: he took no notice of you if you left him alone, but he might charge if you went too close to him.

It was perfectly clear to me what I ought to do. I ought 9 to walk up to within, say, twenty-five yards of the elephant and test his behavior. If he charged, I could shoot; if he took no notice of me, it would be safe to leave him until the mahout came back. But also I knew that I was going to do no such thing. I was a poor shot with a rifle and the ground was soft mud into which one would sink at every step. If the elephant charged and I missed him, I should have about as much chance as a toad under a steam-roller. But even then I was not thinking particularly of my own skin, only of the watchful yellow faces behind. For at that moment, with the crowd watching me, I was not afraid in the ordinary sense, as I would have been if I had been alone. A white man mustn't be frightened in front of "natives"; and so, in general, he isn't frightened. The sole thought in my mind was that if anything went wrong those two thousand Burmans would see me pursued, caught, trampled on, and reduced to a grinning corpse like that Indian up the hill. And if that happened it was quite probable that some of them would laugh. That would never do. There was only one alternative. I shoved the cartridges into the magazine and lay down on the road to get a better aim.

The crowd grew very still, and a deep, low, happy sigh, as 10 of people who see the theater curtain go up at last, breathed from innumerable throats. They were going to have their bit of fun after all. The rifle was a beautiful German thing with cross-hair sights. I did not then know that in shooting an elephant one would shoot to cut an imaginary bar running from ear-hole to ear-hole. I ought, therefore, as the elephant was sideways on, to have aimed straight at his ear-hole; actually I aimed several inches in front of this, thinking the brain would be further forward.

When I pulled the trigger I did not hear the bang or feel 11 the kick—one never does when a shot goes home—but I heard the devilish roar of glee that went up from the crowd. In that instant, in too short a time, one would have thought, even for the bullet to get there, a mysterious, terrible change had come over the elephant. He neither stirred, nor fell, but every line of his body had altered. He looked suddenly stricken, shrunken, immensely old, as though the frightful impact of the bullet had paralyzed him without knocking him down. At last, after what seemed a long time—it might have been five seconds, I dare say—he sagged flabbily to his knees. His mouth slobbered. An enormous senility seemed to have settled upon him. One could have imagined him thousands of years old. I fired again into the same spot. At the second shot he did not collapse but climbed with desperate slowness to his feet and stood weakly upright, with legs sagging and head drooping. I fired a third time. That was the shot that did for him. You could see the agony of it jolt his whole body and knock the last remnant of strength from his legs. But in falling he seemed for a moment to rise, for as his hind legs collapsed beneath him he seemed to tower upward like a huge rock toppling, his trunk reaching skyward like a tree. He trumpeted, for the first and only time. And then down he came, his belly toward me, with a crash that seemed to shake the ground even where I lay.

I got up. The Burmans were already racing past me across 12 the mud. It was obvious that the elephant would never rise again, but he was not dead. He was breathing very rhythmically with long rattling gasps, his great mound of a side painfully rising and falling. His mouth was wide open—I could see far down into caverns of pale pink throat. I waited a long time for him to die, but his breathing did not weaken. Finally I fired my two remaining shots into the spot where I thought his heart must be. The thick blood welled out of him like red velvet, but still he did not die. His body did not even jerk when the shots hit him, the tortured breathing continued without a pause. He was dying, very slowly and in great agony, but in some world remote from me where not even a bullet could damage him further. I felt that I had got to put an end to that dreadful noise. It seemed dreadful to see the great beast lying there, powerless to move and yet powerless to die, and not even to be able to finish him. I sent back for my small rifle and poured shot after shot into his heart and down his throat. They seemed to make no impression. The tortured gasps continued as steadily as the ticking of a clock.

In the end I could not stand it any longer and went away.   13
I heard later that it took him half an hour to die. Burmans were bringing dahs and baskets even before I left, and I was told they had stripped his body almost to the bones by the afternoon.

Afterward, of course, there were endless discussions about   14
the shooting of the elephant. The owner was furious, but he was only an Indian and could do nothing. Besides, legally I had done the right thing, for a mad elephant has to be killed, like a mad dog, if its owner fails to control it. Among the Europeans opinion was divided. The older men said I was right, the younger men said it was a damn shame to shoot an elephant for killing a coolie, because an elephant was worth more than any damn Coringhee coolie. And afterward I was very glad that the coolie had been killed; it put me legally in the right and it gave me a sufficient pretext for shooting the elephant. I often wondered whether any of the others grasped that I had done it solely to avoid looking a fool.

For Study and Discussion

QUESTIONS FOR RESPONSE

1. How do you feel when you are laughed at? What do you do in order to avoid looking like a fool?
2. How did you react to Orwell's long introduction (paragraphs 1 and 2) to the incident? Were you attentive, bored, or confused? Now that you have finished the essay, reread these two paragraphs. How does your second reading compare with your first?

QUESTIONS ABOUT PURPOSE

1. What thesis about "the real nature of imperialism" does Orwell prove by narrating this "tiny incident"?
2. List the reasons Orwell considers when he tries to decide what to do. According to his conclusion, what was his main purpose in shooting the elephant?

QUESTIONS ABOUT AUDIENCE

1. How does Orwell wish to present himself to his readers in paragraphs 6 through 9? Do you follow the logic of his argument?
2. Which of the three positions stated in the final paragraph does Orwell expect his readers to agree with? Why is he "glad that the coolie had been killed"?

QUESTIONS ABOUT STRATEGIES

1. Although Orwell begins narrating the incident in paragraph 3, we do not see the elephant until the end of paragraph 5. What details do we see? How do they intensify the dramatic conflict?
2. How does Orwell pace the shooting of the elephant in paragraphs 11 and 12? How does the elephant's slow death affect Orwell's point of view toward what he has done?

QUESTIONS FOR DISCUSSION

1. Orwell was young, frightened, and tormented by strangers in a strange land. What parallels do you see between Orwell's plight and the plight of young American soldiers in Vietnam?
2. Much of Orwell's essay assumes a knowledge of the words *imperialism* and *despotism*. What do these words mean? How do they apply to the essay? What current events can you identify in which these words might also apply?

Alice Adams was born in 1926 in Fredericksburg, Virginia, and educated at Radcliffe College. After twelve years of marriage, she began working at various office jobs, including secretary, clerk, and bookkeeper, while she mastered the skills of a writer. Adams published her first book of fiction, *Careless Love* (1966), at the age of forty. Since that time she has published four widely acclaimed novels, *Families and Survivors* (1975), *Listening to Billie* (1978)—the title refers to the legendary blues singer Billie Holiday—*Rich Rewards* (1980), and *Superior Women* (1984), as well as three collections of short stories, *Beautiful Girl* (1979), *To See You Again* (1982), and *Return Trips* (1985). She has also contributed numerous short stories to magazines such as *The New Yorker, The Atlantic,* and *Paris Review.* The narrator of "Truth or Consequences," reprinted from *To See You Again,* tries to understand the "consequences" that resulted from her truthful answer in a childhood game.

Truth or Consequences

T HIS MORNING, WHEN I read in a gossip column that a man named Carstairs Jones had married a famous former movie star, I was startled, thunderstruck, for I knew that he must certainly be the person whom I knew as a child, one extraordinary spring, as "Car Jones." He was a dangerous and disreputable boy, one of what were then called the "truck children," with whom I had a most curious, brief and frightening connection. Still, I noted that in a way I was pleased at such good fortune; I was "happy for him," so to speak, perhaps as a result of sheer distance, so many years. And before I could imagine Car as he might be now, Carstairs Jones, in Hollywood clothes, I suddenly saw, with the most terrific accuracy and bright sharpness of detail, the schoolyard of all those years ago, hard and bare, neglected. And I relived the fatal day, on the middle level of that schoolyard, when we were playing truth or consequences, and I said that I would rather kiss Car Jones than be eaten alive by ants.

Our school building then was three stories high, a formi- 2 dable brick square. In front a lawn had been attempted, some years back; graveled walks led up to the broad, forbidding entranceway, and behind the school were the playing fields, the playground. This area was on three levels: on the upper level, nearest the school, were the huge polished steel frames for the creaking swings, the big green splintery wooden see-saws, the rickety slides—all for the youngest children. On the middle level older girls played hopscotch, various games, or jumped rope—or just talked and giggled. And out on the lowest level, the field, the boys practiced football, or baseball, in the spring.

To one side of the school was a parking space, usually filled 3 with the bulging yellow trucks that brought children from out in the country in to town: truck children, country chil-dren. Sometimes they would go back to the trucks at lunchtime to eat their sandwiches, whatever; almost always there were several overgrown children, spilling out from the trucks. Or Car Jones, expelled from some class, for some new acts of rebelliousness. That area was always littered with trash, wrappings from sandwiches, orange peel, Coke bottles.

Beyond the parking space was an empty lot, overgrown 4 with weeds, in the midst of which stood an abandoned trellis, perhaps once the support of wisteria; now wild honeysuckle almost covered it over.

The town was called Hilton, the seat of a distinguished 5 university, in the middle South. My widowed mother, Char-lotte Ames, had moved there the previous fall (with me,

Emily, her only child). I am still not sure why she chose Hilton; she never much liked it there, nor did she really like the brother-in-law, a professor, into whose proximity the move had placed us.

An interesting thing about Hilton, at that time, was that   6 there were three, and only three, distinct social classes. (Negroes could possibly make four, but they were so separate, even from the poorest whites, as not to seem part of the social system at all; they were in effect invisible.) At the scale's top were professors and their families. Next were the townspeople, storekeepers, bankers, doctors and dentists, none of whom had the prestige nor the money they were later to acquire. Country people were the bottom group, families living out on the farms that surrounded the town, people who sent their children in to school on the yellow trucks.

The professors' children of course had a terrific advantage,   7 academically, coming from houses full of books, from parental respect for learning; many of those kids read precociously and had large vocabularies. It was not so hard on most of the town children; many of their families shared qualities with the faculty people; they too had a lot of books around. But the truck children had a hard and very unfair time of it. Not only were many of their parents near-illiterates, but often the children were kept at home to help with chores, and sometimes, particularly during the coldest, wettest months of winter, weather prevented the trucks' passage over the slithery red clay roads of that countryside, that era. A child could miss out on a whole new skill, like long division, and fail tests, and be kept back. Consequently many of the truck children were overage, oversized for the grades they were in.

In the seventh grade, when I was eleven, a year ahead of   8 myself, having been tested for and skipped the sixth (attesting to the superiority of Northern schools, my mother thought, and probably she was right), dangerous Car Jones, in the same class, was fourteen, and taller than anyone.

There was some overlapping, or crossing, among those   9 three social groups; there were hybrids, as it were. In fact, I was such a crossbreed myself: literally my mother and I were town people—my dead father had been a banker, but since his brother was a professor we too were considered faculty people. Also my mother had a lot of money, making us further élite. To me, being known as rich was just embarrassing, more freakish than advantageous, and I made my mother stop ordering my clothes from Best's; I wanted dresses from the local stores, like everyone else's.

Car Jones too was a hybrid child, although his case was   10
less visible than mine: his country family were distant cousins of the prominent and prosperous dean of the medical school, Dean Willoughby Jones. (They seem to have gone in for fancy names, in all the branches of that family.) I don't think his cousins spoke to him.

In any case, being richer and younger than the others in   11
my class made me socially very insecure, and I always approached the playground with a sort of excited dread: would I be asked to join in a game, and if it were dodge ball (the game I most hated) would I be the first person hit with the ball, and thus eliminated? Or, if the girls were just standing around and talking, would I get all the jokes, and know which boys they were talking about?

Then, one pale-blue balmy April day, some of the older   12
girls asked me if I wanted to play truth or consequences with them. I wasn't sure how the game went, but anything was better than dodge ball, and, as always, I was pleased at being asked.

"It's easy," said Jean, a popular leader, with curly red hair;   13
her father was a dean of the law school. "You just answer the questions we ask you, or you take the consequences."

I wasn't at all sure what consequences were, but I didn't   14
like to ask.

They began with simple questions. How old are you?   15
What's your middle name?

This led to more complicated (and crueler) ones.   16

"How much money does your mother have?"   17

"I don't know." I didn't, of course, and I doubt that she   18 did either, that poor vague lady, too young to be a widow, too old for motherhood. "I think maybe a thousand dollars," I hazarded.

At this they all frowned, that group of older, wiser girls, whether in disbelief or disappointment, I couldn't tell. They moved a little away from me and whispered together.

It was close to the end of recess. Down on the playing field below us one of the boys threw the baseball and someone batted it out in a long arc, out to the farthest grassy edges of the field, and several other boys ran to retrieve it. On the level above us, a rutted terrace up, the little children stood in line for turns on the slide, or pumped with furious small legs on the giant swings.

The girls came back to me. "Okay, Emily," said Jean. "Just tell the truth. Would you rather be covered with honey and eaten alive by ants, in the hot Sahara Desert—or kiss Car Jones?"

Then, as now, I had a somewhat literal mind: I thought of honey, and ants, and hot sand, and quite simply I said I'd rather kiss Car Jones.

Well. Pandemonium: Did you hear what she said? Emily would kiss Car Jones! *Car Jones.* The truth—Emily would like to kiss Car Jones! Oh, Emily if your mother only knew! Emily and Car! Emily is going to kiss Car Jones! Emily said she would! Oh, Emily!

The boys, just then coming up from the baseball field, cast bored and pitying looks at the sources of so much noise; they had always known girls were silly. But Harry McGinnis, a glowing, golden boy, looked over at us and laughed aloud. I had been watching Harry timidly for months; that day I thought his laugh was friendly.

Recess being over, we all went back into the schoolroom, and continued with the civics lesson. I caught a few ambiguous smiles in my direction, which left me both embarrassed and confused.

That afternoon, as I walked home from school, two of the girls who passed me on their bikes called back to me, "Car

Jones!" and in an automatic but for me new way I squealed out, "Oh no!" They laughed, and repeated, from their distance, "Car Jones!"

The next day I continued to be teased. Somehow the boys had got wind of what I had said, and they joined in with remarks about Yankee girls being fast, how you couldn't tell about quiet girls, that sort of wit. Some of the teasing sounded mean; I felt that Jean, for example, was really out to discomfit me, but most of it was high-spirited friendliness. I was suddenly discovered, as though hitherto I had been invisible. And I continued to respond with that exaggerated, phony squeal of embarrassment that seemed to go over so well. Harry McGinnis addressed me as Emily Jones, and the others took that up. (I wonder if Harry had ever seen me before.) **27**

Curiously, in all this new excitement, the person I thought of least was the source of it all: Car Jones. Or, rather, when I saw the actual Car, hulking over the water fountain or lounging near the steps of a truck, I did not consciously connect him with what felt like social success, new popularity. (I didn't know about consequences.) **28**

Therefore, when the first note from Car appeared on my desk, it felt like blackmail, although the message was innocent, was even kind. "You mustn't mind that they tease you. You are the prettiest one of the girls. C. Jones." I easily recognized his handwriting, those recklessly forward-slanting strokes, from the day when he had had to write on the blackboard, "I will not disturb the other children during Music." Twenty-five times. The note was real, all right. **29**

Helplessly I turned around to stare at the back of the room, where the tallest boys sprawled in their too small desks. Truck children, all of them, bored and uncomfortable. There was Car, the tallest of all, the most bored, the least contained. Our eyes met, and even at that distance I saw that his were not black, as I had thought, but a dark slate blue; stormy eyes, even when, as he rarely did, Car smiled. I turned away quickly, and I managed to forget him for a while. **30**

Having never witnessed a Southern spring before, I was   31
astounded by its bursting opulence, that soft fullness of petal
and bloom, everywhere the profusion of flowering shrubs
and trees, the riotous flower beds. Walking home from
school, I was enchanted with the yards of the stately houses
(homes of professors) that I passed, the lush lawns, the rows
of brilliant iris, the flowering quince and dogwood trees,
crepe myrtle, wisteria vines. I would squint my eyes to see
the tiniest pale-green leaves against the sky.

My mother didn't like the spring. It gave her hay fever,   32
and she spent most of her time languidly indoors, behind
heavily lined, drawn draperies. "I'm simply too old for such
exuberance," she said.

"Happy" is perhaps not the word to describe my own state   33
of mind, but I was tremendously excited, continuously. The
season seemed to me so extraordinary in itself, the colors, the
enchanting smells, and it coincided with my own altered
awareness of myself: I could command attention, I was pretty
(Car Jones was the first person ever to say that I was, after
my mother's long-ago murmurings to a late-arriving baby).

Now everyone knew my name, and called it out as I walked   34
onto the playground. Last fall, as an envious, unknown new
girl, I had heard other names, other greetings and teasing-
insulting nicknames, "Hey, Red," Harry McGinnis used to
shout, in the direction of popular Jean.

The new note from Car Jones said, "I'll bet you hate it   35
down here. This is a cruddy town, but don't let it bother
you. Your hair is beautiful. I hope you never cut it. C. Jones."

This scared me a little: the night before I had been arguing   36
with my mother on just that point, my hair, which was long
and straight. Why couldn't I cut it and curl it, like the other
girls? How Had Car Jones known what I wanted to do? I
forced myself not to look at him; I pretended that there was
no Car Jones; it was just a name that certain people had made
up.

I felt—I was sure—that Car Jones was an "abnormal"   37
person. (I'm afraid "different" would have been the word I

used, back then.) He represented forces that were dark and strange, whereas I myself had just come out into the light. I had joined the world of the normal. (My "normality" later included three marriages to increasingly "rich and prominent" men; my current husband is a surgeon. Three children, and as many abortions. I hate the symmetry, but there you are. I haven't counted lovers. It comes to a normal life, for a woman of my age.) For years, at the time of our coming to Hilton, I had felt a little strange, isolated by my father's death, my older-than-most-parents mother, by money. By being younger than other children, and new in town. I could clearly afford nothing to do with Car, and at the same time my literal mind acknowledged a certain obligation.

Therefore, when a note came from Car telling me to meet   38
him on a Saturday morning in the vacant lot next to the school, it didn't occur to me that I didn't have to go. I made excuses to my mother, and to some of the girls who were getting together for Cokes at someone's house. I'd be a little late, I told the girls. I had to do an errand for my mother.

It was one of the palest, softest, loveliest days of that   39
spring. In the vacant lot weeds bloomed like the rarest of flowers; as I walked toward the abandoned trellis I felt myself to be a sort of princess, on her way to grant an audience to a courtier.

Car, lounging just inside the trellis, immediately brought   40
me up short. "You're several minutes late," he said, and I noticed that his teeth were stained (from tobacco?) and his hands were dirty: couldn't he have washed his hands, to come and meet me? He asked, "Just who do you think you are, the Queen of Sheba?"

I am not sure what I had imagined would happen between   41
us, but this was wrong; I was not prepared for surliness, this scolding. Weakly I said that I was sorry I was late.

Car did not acknowledge my apology; he just stared at me,   42
stormily, with what looked like infinite scorn.

Why had he insisted that I come to meet him? And now   43
that I was here, was I less than pretty, seen close up?

A difficult minute passed, and then I moved a little away. 44
I managed to say that I had to go; I had to meet some girls,
I said.

At that Car reached and grasped my arm. "No, first we 45
have to do it."

Do it? I was scared. 46

"You know what you said, as good as I do. You said kiss 47
Car Jones, now didn't you?"

I began to cry. 48

Car reached for my hair and pulled me toward him; he 49
bent down to my face and for an instant our mouths were
mashed together. (Christ, my first kiss!) Then, so suddenly
that I almost fell backward, Car let go of me. With a last look
of pure rage he was out of the trellis and striding across the
field, toward town, away from the school.

For a few minutes I stayed there in the trellis; I was no 50
longer crying (that had been for Car's benefit, I now think)
but melodramatically I wondered if Car might come back and
do something else to me—beat me up, maybe. Then a
stronger fear took over: someone might find out, might have
seen us, even. At that I got out of the trellis fast, out of the
vacant lot. (I was learning conformity fast, practicing up for
the rest of my life.)

I think, really, that my most serious problem was my utter 51
puzzlement: what did it mean, that kiss? Car was mad, no
doubt about that, but did he really hate me? In that case, why
a kiss? (Much later in life I once was raped, by someone to
whom I was married, but I still think that counts; in any case,
I didn't know what he meant either.)

Not sure what else to do, and still in the grip of a monu- 52
mental confusion, I went over to the school building, which
was open on Saturdays for something called Story Hours, for
little children. I went into the front entrance and up to the
library where, to the surprise of the librarian, who may have
thought me retarded, I listened for several hours of tales of
the Dutch Twins, and Peter and Polly in Scotland. Actually
it was very soothing, that long pasteurized drone, hard even
to think about Car while listening to pap like that.

When I got home I found my mother for some reason in   53
a livelier, more talkative mood than usual. She told me that
a boy had called while I was out, three times. Even before
my heart had time to drop—to think that it might be Car,
she babbled on, "Terribly polite. Really, these *bien élevé*
Southern boys." (No, not Car.) "Harry something. He said
he'd call again. But, darling, where were you, all this time?"

I was beginning to murmur about the library, homework,   54
when the phone rang. I answered, and it was Harry McGinnis, asking me to go to the movies with him the following
Saturday afternoon. I said of course, I'd love to, and I giggled
in a silly new way. But my giggle was one of relief; I was saved,
I was normal, after all. I belonged in the world of light, of
lightheartedness. Car Jones had not really touched me.

I spent the next day, Sunday, in alternating states of agita-   55
tion and anticipation.

On Monday, on my way to school, I felt afraid of seeing   56
Car, at the same time that I was both excited and shy at the
prospect of Harry McGinnis—a combination of emotions
that was almost too much for me, that dazzling, golden first
of May, and that I have not dealt with too successfully in later
life.

Harry paid even less attention to me than he had before;   57
it was a while before I realized that he was conspicuously not
looking in my direction, not teasing me, and that that in itself
was a form of attention, as well as being soothing to my
shyness.

I realized too, after a furtive scanning of the back row, that   58
Car Jones was *not at school* that day. Relief flooded through
my blood like oxygen, like spring air.

Absences among the truck children were so unremarkable,   59
and due to so many possible causes, that any explanation at
all for his was plausible. Of course it occurred to me, among
other imaginings, that he had stayed home out of shame for
what he did to me. Maybe he had run away to sea, had joined
the Navy or the Marines? Coldheartedly, I hoped so. In any
case, there was no way for me to ask.

Later that week the truth about Car Jones did come out—   60 at first as a drifting rumor, then confirmed, and much more remarkable than joining the Navy: Car Jones had gone to the principal's office, a week or so back, and had demanded to be tested for entrance (immediate) into high school, a request so unprecedented (usually only pushy academic parents would ask for such a change) and so dumbfounding that it was acceded to. Car took the test and was put into the sophomore high-school class, on the other side of town, where he by age and size—and intellect, as things turned out; he tested high—most rightfully belonged.

I went to a lot of Saturday movies with Harry McGinnis, where we clammily held hands, and for the rest of that spring, and into summer, I was teased about Harry. No one seemed to remember having teased me about Car Jones.

Considering the size of Hilton at that time, it seems surprising that I almost never saw Car again, but I did not, except for a couple of tiny glimpses, during the summer that I was still going to the movies with Harry. On both those occasions, seen from across the street, or on the other side of a dim movie house, Car was with an older girl, a high-school girl, with curled hair, and lipstick, all that. I was sure that his hands and teeth were clean.

By the time I had entered high school, along with all those others who were by now my familiar friends, Car was a freshman in the local university, and his family had moved into town. Then his name again was bruited about among us, but this time was an underground rumor: Car Jones was reputed to have "gone all the way"—to have "done it" with a pretty and most popular senior in our high school. (It must be remembered that this was more unusual among the young then than now.) The general (whispered) theory was that Car's status as a college boy had won the girl; traditionally, in Hilton, the senior high-school girls began to date the freshmen in the university, as many and as often as possible. But this was not necessarily true; maybe the girl was simply drawn to Car, his height and his shoulders, his stormy eyes. Or maybe they didn't do it after all.

The next thing I heard about Car, who was by then an authentic town person, a graduate student in the university, was that he had written a play which was to be produced by the campus dramatic society. (Maybe that is how he finally met his movie star, as a playwright? The column didn't say.) I think I read this item in the local paper, probably in a clipping forwarded to me by my mother; her letters were always thick with clippings, thin with messages of a personal nature. ⁶⁴

My next news of Car came from my uncle, the French professor, a violent, enthusiastic partisan in university affairs, especially in their more traditional aspects. In scandalized tones, one family Thanksgiving, he recounted to me and my mother, that a certain young man, a graduate student in English, named Carstairs Jones, had been offered a special sort of membership in D.K.E., his own beloved fraternity, and "Jones had *turned it down*." My mother and I laughed later and privately over this; we were united in thinking my uncle a fool, and I am sure that I added, Well, good for him. But I did not, at that time, reconsider the whole story of Car Jones, that most unregenerate and wicked of the truck children. ⁶⁵

But now, with this fresh news of Carstairs Jones, and his wife the movie star, it occurs to me that we two, who at a certain time and place were truly misfits, although quite differently—we both have made it: what could be more American dream-y, more normal, than marriage to a lovely movie star? Or, in my case, marriage to the successful surgeon? ⁶⁶

And now maybe I can reconstruct a little of that time; specifically, can try to see how it really was for Car, back then. Maybe I can even understand that kiss. ⁶⁷

Let us suppose that he lived in a somewhat better than usual farmhouse; later events make this plausible—his family's move to town, his years at the university. Also, I wish him well. I will give him a dignified white house with a broad ⁶⁸

front porch, set back among pines and oaks, in the red clay countryside. The stability and size of his house, then, would have set Car apart from his neighbors, the other farm families, other truck children. Perhaps his parents too were somewhat "different," but my imagination fails at them; I can easily imagine and clearly see the house, but not its population. Brothers? sisters? Probably, but I don't know.

Car would go to school, coming out of his house at the honk of the stained and bulging, ugly yellow bus, which was crowded with his supposed peers, toward whom he felt both contempt and an irritation close to rage. Arrived at school, as one of the truck children, he would be greeted with a total lack of interest; he might as well have been invisible, or been black, *unless* he misbehaved in an outright, conspicuous way. And so he did: Car yawned noisily during history class, he hummed during study hall and after recess he dawdled around the playground and came in late. And for these and other assaults on the school's decorum he was punished in one way or another, and then, when all else failed to curb his ways, he would be *held back,* forced to repeat an already insufferably boring year of school.

One fall there was a minor novelty in school: a new girl (me), a Yankee, who didn't look much like the other girls, with long straight hair, instead of curled, and Yankee clothes, wool skirts and sweaters, instead of flowery cotton dresses worn all year round. A funny accent, a Yankee name: Emily Ames. I imagine that Car registered those facts about me, and possibly the additional information that I was almost as invisible as he, but without much interest.

Until the day of truth or consequences. I don't think Car was around on the playground while the game was going on; one of the girls would have seen him, and squealed out, "Oooh, there's Car, there *he is!*" I rather believe that some skinny little kid, an unnoticed truck child, overheard it all, and then ran over to where Car was lounging in one of the school buses, maybe peeling an orange and throwing the peel, in spirals, out the window. "Say, Car, that little Yankee girl, she says she'd like to kiss you."

"Aw, go on."   72

He is still not very interested; the little Yankee girl is as   73
dumb as the others are.

And then he hears me being teased, everywhere, and   74
teased with his name. "Emily would kiss Car Jones—Emily
Jones!" Did he feel the slightest pleasure at such notoriety?
I think he must have; a man who would marry a movie star
must have at least a small taste for publicity. Well, at that point
he began to write me those notes: "You are the prettiest one
of the girls" (which I was not). I think he was casting us both
in ill-fitting roles, me as the prettiest, defenseless girl, and
himself as my defender.

He must have soon seen that it wasn't working out that   75
way. I didn't need a defender, I didn't need him. I was having
a wonderful time, at his expense, if you think about it, and I
am pretty sure Car did think about it.

Interestingly, at the same time he had his perception of my   76
triviality, Car must have got his remarkable inspiration in
regard to his own life: there was a way out of those miserably
boring classes, the insufferable children who surrounded him.
He would demand a test, he would leave this place for the
high school.

Our trellis meeting must have occurred after Car had taken   77
the test, and had known that he did well. When he kissed me
he was doing his last "bad" thing in that school, was kissing
it off, so to speak. He was also insuring that I, at least, would
remember him; he counted on its being my first kiss. And he
may have thought that I was even sillier than I was, and that
I would tell, so that what had happened would get around
the school, waves of scandal in his wake.

For some reason, I would also imagine that Car is one of   78
those persons who never look back; once kissed, I was readily
dismissed from his mind, and probably for good. He could
concentrate on high school, new status, new friends. Just as,
now married to his movie star, he does not ever think of
having been a truck child, one of the deprived, the disappointed. In his mind there are no ugly groaning trucks, no
hopeless littered playground, no squat menacing school
building.

But of course I could be quite wrong about Car Jones. He 79 could be another sort of person altogether; he could be as haunted as I am by everything that ever happened in his life.

COMMENT ON "TRUTH OR CONSEQUENCES"

"Truth or Consequences" is an excellent illustration of how narration and description are used in short fiction. The catalyst for the story is the narrator's reading in a gossip column about Car Jones's marriage to a famous former movie star. His name sparks a memory, and the narrator (Emily) tries to reconstruct the events that occurred during her school years. The story is paced at two speeds: the opening is slow as Emily describes the various social divisions on the playground; the action speeds up once Emily says she would rather kiss Car Jones than be eaten by ants. The plot reaches its climax when Car Jones calls Emily's bluff and asks her to meet him by the trellis near the school. The story concludes as Emily (older and wiser?) continues to wonder about the "truth" and "consequences" of this brief encounter.

Narration and Description as a Writing Strategy

1. Recount the details of an accident or disaster in which you were a witness or a victim. You may wish to retell the events as a reporter would for a front-page story in the local newspaper, or you may recount the events from a more personal point of view, as Maya Angelou does in her description of the "disaster" in Mrs. Cullinan's kitchen. If you were a witness, consider the points of view of the other people involved so that you can give your readers an objective perspective on the event. If you were a victim, slow the pace of the major conflict, which probably occurred quickly, so you can show your readers its emotional impact.

2. Report an experience in which you had to commit an extremely difficult or distasteful deed. You may wish to begin, as George Orwell does, by telling your readers about the conditions you encountered before you confronted the problem of whether to commit the questionable act. Be sure to list all the options you considered before you acted, and conclude by reflecting on your attitude toward your choice. And, of course, make sure to plot your essay so that the *act* is given the central and most dramatic position.

3. In "Basketball Season," Donna Tartt recounts her experience as a young cheerleader, caught between the worlds of the *snobs* and the *sluts*. Study those paragraphs where Tartt describes the behavior of these two groups. Then make a list of other types of high school peer groups—such as those that exist among male students. Recount an experience in which you had to decide which group (if any) you wanted to join. Evoke the dramatic details of your attempt to make a decision.

4. Chronicle a significant event in your life that occurred during a major crisis in the life of the nation—the civil rights movement, the Persian Gulf War, some environmental disaster. Like Wakako Yamauchi, consider how the

personal experience of your family was affected by the *public* experience of the country.

5. Narrate your experience with another culture. Like Terry Tempest Williams, you may want to compare the way different cultures explain experiences (or people) that are different. Or you may want to describe how people who are different are treated within your own culture. For example, you may want to focus on a public ceremony— wedding, baptism, funeral—to illustrate how people deal with the problem of difference.

6. Demonstrate the effects of perception on values (how "seeing is believing"). All the writers in this section deal with this subject. Angelou demonstrates how white people's inability to "see" black people distorts their belief about them. Tartt describes how the social codes of high school shape students' attitudes about gender and class. Williams reveals how words such as *normal* and *handicapped* encourage people to form opinions about people who are different. Yamauchi explains how stories about her parents' homeland can create a "Fantasy Island." Orwell shows how seeing the crowd's mocking faces convinces him to shoot the elephant. And Emily Ames, the narrator in Alice Adams's short story, tells how her concern for social acceptance made her misread the actions of someone who was different.

PROCESS
ANALYSIS

⁓

A **process** is an operation that moves through a series of steps to bring about a desired result. You can call almost any procedure a process, whether it is getting out of bed in the morning or completing a transaction on the stock exchange. A useful way to identify a particular kind of process is by its principal function. A process can be *natural* (the birth of a baby), *mechanical* (starting a car engine), *physical* (dancing), or *mental* (reading).

Analysis is an operation that divides something into its parts in order to understand the whole more clearly. For example, poetry readers analyze the lines of a poem to find meaning. Doctors analyze a patient's symptoms to prescribe

treatment. Politicians analyze the opinions of individual voters and groups of voters to plan campaigns.

If you want to write a process-analysis essay, you need to
go through three steps: (1) divide the process you are going
to explain into its individual steps; (2) show the movement
of the process, step by step, from beginning to end; and (3)
explain how each step works, how it ties into other steps in
the sequence, and how it brings about the desired result.

PURPOSE

Usually you will write a process analysis to accomplish two
purposes: *to give directions* and *to provide information*. Sometimes you might find it difficult to separate the two purposes.
After all, when you give directions about how to do something (hit a baseball), you also have to provide information
on how the whole process works (rules of the game—strike
zone, walks, hits, base running, outs, scoring). But usually
you can separate the two because you're trying to accomplish
different goals. When you give directions, you want to help
your readers do something (change a tire). When you give
information, you want to satisfy your readers' curiosity about
some process they'd like to know about but are unlikely to
perform (pilot a space shuttle).

You might also write a process analysis to demonstrate that
(1) a task that looks difficult is really easy or (2) a task that
looks easy is really quite complex. For instance, you might
want to show that selecting a specific tool can simplify a
complex process (using a microwave oven to cook a six-
course dinner). You might also want to show why it's important to have a prearranged plan to make a process seem simple
(explaining the preparations for an informal television interview).

AUDIENCE

When you write a process-analysis essay, you must think carefully about who your audience will be. First, you need to

decide whether you're writing *to* an audience (giving directions) or writing *for* an audience (providing information). If you are writing *to* an audience, you can address directly readers who are already interested in your subject: "If you want to plant a successful garden, you must follow these seven steps." If you are writing *for* an audience, you can write from a more detached point of view, but you have to find a way to catch the interest of more casual readers: "Although many Americans say they are concerned about nuclear power, few understand how a nuclear power plant works."

Second, you have to determine how wide the knowledge gap is between you and your readers. Writing about a process suggests you are something of an expert in that area. If you can be sure your readers are also experts, you can make certain assumptions as you write your analysis. For instance, if you're outlining courtroom procedure to a group of fellow law students, you can assume you don't have to define the special meaning of the word *brief.*

On the other hand, if you feel sure your intended audience knows almost nothing about a process (or has only general knowledge), you can take nothing for granted. If you are explaining how to operate a VCR to readers who have never used one, you will have to define special terms and explain all procedures. If you assume your readers are experts when they are not, you will confuse or annoy them. If you assume they need to be told everything when they don't, you will bore or antagonize them. And, finally, remember that to analyze a process effectively, you must either research it carefully or have firsthand knowledge of its operation. It's risky to try to explain something you don't really understand.

STRATEGIES

The best way to write a process analysis is to organize your essay according to five parts:

> Overview
> Special terms

Sequence of steps

Examples

Results

The first two parts help your readers understand the process, the next two show the process in action, and the last one evaluates the worth of the completed process.

Begin your analysis with an *overview* of the whole process. To make such an overview, you take these four steps:

1. Define the objective of the process
2. Identify (and number) the steps in the sequence
3. Group some small steps into larger units
4. Call attention to the most important steps or units

For example, Edward Hoagland begins his analysis of the jury system by pointing out that the jurists' objective was to be fair, "to be better than themselves." Nikki Giovanni makes her recommendations for black students in sequence and then goes on to illustrate some of the common problems that occur with each recommendation.

Each process has its own *special terms* to describe tools, tasks, and methods, and you will have to define those terms for your readers. You can define them at the beginning so your readers will understand the terms when you use them, but often you do better to define them as you use them. Your readers may have trouble remembering specialized language out of context, so it's often practical to define your terms throughout the course of the essay, pausing to explain their special meaning or use the first time you introduce them. Tom and Ray Magliozzi follow this strategy in "Inside the Engine" by describing the oil pump, crankcase, journals, and bearings inside the engine and then describing the warning lights on the dashboard.

When you write a process-analysis essay, you must present the *sequence of steps* clearly and carefully. As you do so, give the reason for each step and, where appropriate, provide these reminders:

1. *Do not omit any steps.* A sequence is a sequence because all steps depend on one another. Nikki Giovanni explains the importance of going to class to establish "a consistent presence in the classroom."
2. *Do not reverse steps.* A sequence is a sequence because each step must be performed according to a necessary and logical pattern. Lars Eighner reminds readers that if they start eating something before they have inspected it, they are likely to discover moldy bread or sour milk after they have put it into their mouth.
3. *Suspend certain steps.* Occasionally, a whole series of steps must be suspended and another process completed before the sequence can resume. Tom and Ray Magliozzi warn readers that before they can shut off an overheated car, they must "Use all necessary caution and get the thing over to the breakdown lane."
4. *Do not overlook steps within steps.* Each sequence is likely to have a series of smaller steps buried within each step. Edward Hoagland reminds his readers that selecting a jury may involve another procedure—agreeing to plea bargain.
5. *Avoid certain steps.* It is often tempting to insert steps that are not recommended but that appear "logical." Philip Weiss warns his readers not to try a procedure that looks logical when the trunk is open but may prove ineffective when the trunk is closed.

You may want to use several kinds of examples to explain the steps in a sequence:

1. *Pictures.* You can use graphs, charts, and diagrams to illustrate the operation of the process. Although none of the writers in this section uses pictures, the Magliozzis do discuss the warning lights that signal the overheated, glowing-red engine.
2. *Anecdotes.* Since you're claiming some level of expertise by writing a process analysis, you can clarify your explanation by using examples from your own experience. Eighner uses this method when he describes his experience selecting

discarded pizzas and waiting for the "junk" that will be pitched at the end of a semester.

3. *Variants.* You can mention alternative steps to show that the process may not be as rigid or simplistic as it often appears. Weiss's primary purpose is to demonstrate his method for opening a trunk, but since it works only 60 percent of the time, he acknowledges the need for alternative methods.

4. *Comparisons.* You can use comparisons to help your readers see that a complex process is similar to a process they already know. Hoagland uses this strategy when he compares jury duty to other universal experiences "like getting married or having a child, like voting."

Although you focus on the movement of the process when you write a process-analysis essay, finally you should also try to evaluate the *results* of that process. You can move to this last part by asking two questions: How do you know it's done? How do you know it's good? Sometimes the answer is simple: the car starts; the trunk opens. At other times, the answer is not so clear: the student may need further instruction; the jury may have difficulty reaching a decision.

USING PROCESS ANALYSIS IN PARAGRAPHS

Here are two process-analysis paragraphs. The first is written by a professional writer and is followed by an analysis. The second is written by a student writer and is followed by questions.

SCOTT RUSSELL SANDERS
from "Digging Limestone"

Dealing with the stone itself involves a whole new set of machines. Great mobile engines called channelers, powered by electricity, chug on rails

Topic sentence
predicts content

from one side of the bed to the other, chiseling   Names special
ten-foot-deep slots. Hammering and puffing   tools
along, they look and sound and smell like small
locomotives. By shifting rails, the quarriers even-
tually slice the bed into a grid of blocks. The first   Identifies first
of these to be removed is called the keyblock, and   step
it always provokes a higher than usual proportion
of curses. There is no way to get to the base of
this first block to cut it loose, so it must be   Describes sub-
wedged, hacked, splintered and worried at, until   sequent steps
something like a clean hole has been excavated.
Men can then climb down and, by drilling holes
and driving wedges, split the neighboring block   Makes compari-
free at its base, undoing in an hour a three-   son (earth's
hundred-million-year-old cement job.   crust to cement
                                                   job)

Comment This paragraph, excerpted from "Digging Limestone," analyzes the complicated process of removing large
slabs of limestone from the earth. The opening sentences
name the special machines required to begin the work. Sand-
ers makes sure his readers understand the importance of
removing the keyblock. Only after this slice of stone is removed can the workers proceed with the rest of the process,
"undoing in an hour a three-hundred-million-year-old cement job."

SARA TEMPLE
Making Stained Glass

Before you begin making stained glass, you will
need to purchase the right tools—most of which
you can find at your local hardware store. First,
select a glass cutter. It looks like a steel fork with
a wheel at one end. The wheel is the blade that
allows you to cut out the shape of each piece of
glass. Second, you will need another tool to
"break" the glass along the line you have scored

with your cutter. I've always called this object "the tool." Tell the hardware clerk what you want and she'll show you what you need. Third, pick out a glass grinder to polish each piece of glass to the right size. Finally, buy a soldering iron to fuse the various pieces of glass into your design. These last two tools can be "pricey," so you may want to find a partner to share the cost. In the process, you may discover that your stained glass will become more creative when you design it with a friend.

1. How does Temple list and describe the special tools needed in the process?
2. What advice does Temple provide about how to purchase and use the "pricey" tools?

PROCESS ANALYSIS

Points to Remember

1. Arrange the steps in your process in an orderly sequence.
2. Identify and explain the purpose of each of the steps in the process.
3. Describe the special tools, terms, and tasks needed to complete the process.
4. Provide warnings, where appropriate, about the consequences of omitting, reversing, or overlooking certain steps.
5. Supply illustrations and personal anecdotes to help clarify aspects of the process.

Tom (b. 1939) and Ray (b. 1949) Magliozzi—
better known as Click and Clack, the Tappet
Brothers—were born in East Cambridge, Massachusetts; both were educated at Massachusetts Institute of Technology. Tom earned additional
degrees from Northeastern University and Boston
University before working in marketing. Ray was
a VISTA volunteer, taught junior high school, and
worked in the Massachusetts State Consumer Affairs Department. In 1973, the brothers opened a
"do-it-yourself" garage in Cambridge called Good
News Garage. In 1976, they started a local radio
show in which they answered questions about auto
repair. This hilarious and informative show, "Car
Talk," was syndicated on National Public Radio in
1987. A sampling of their most amusing conversations appears in their book *Car Talk* (1991). In
"Inside the Engine," Tom and Ray explain how
an engine works and what the warning lights
mean.

Inside the Engine

A CUSTOMER OF OURS had an old Thunderbird that he 1
used to drive back and forth to New York to see a
girlfriend every other weekend. And every time he made the
trip he'd be in the shop the following Monday needing to
get something fixed because the car was such a hopeless piece
of trash. One Monday he failed to show up and Tom said,
"Gee, that's kind of unusual." I said jokingly, "Maybe he
blew the car up."

Well, what happened was that he was on the Merritt Park- 2
way in Connecticut when he noticed that he had to keep the

gas pedal all the way to the floor just to go 30 m.p.h., with this big V-8 engine, and he figured something was awry.

So he pulled into one of those filling stations where they 3 sell gasoline and chocolate-chip cookies and milk. And he asked the attendant to look at the engine and, of course, the guy said, "I can't help you. All I know is cookies and milk." But the guy agreed to look anyway since our friend was really desperate. His girlfriend was waiting for him and he needed to know if he was going to make it. Anyway, the guy threw open the hood and jumped back in terror. The engine was glowing red. Somewhere along the line, probably around

---

What makes the engines of today superior is not only the design and the metallurgy, but the lubricants.

Hartford, he must have lost all of his motor oil. The engine kept getting hotter and hotter, but like a lot of other things in the car that didn't work, neither did his oil pressure warning light. As a result, the engine got so heated up that it fused itself together. All the pistons melted, and the cylinder heads deformed, and the pistons fused to the cylinder walls, and the bearings welded themselves to the crankshaft—oh, it was a terrible sight! When he tried to restart the engine, he just heard a *click, click, click* since the whole thing was seized up tighter than a drum.

That's what can happen in a case of extreme engine ne- 4 glect. Most of us wouldn't do that, or at least wouldn't do it knowingly. Our friend didn't do it knowingly either, but he learned a valuable lesson. He learned that his girlfriend wouldn't come and get him if his car broke down. Even if he offered her cookies and milk.

The oil is critical to keeping things running since it not 5 only acts as a lubricant, but it also helps to keep the engine cool. What happens is that the oil pump sucks the oil out of what's called the sump (or the crankcase or the oil pan), and it pushes that oil, under pressure, up to all of the parts that need lubrication.

The way the oil works is that it acts as a cushion. The molecules of oil actually separate the moving metal parts from one another so that they don't directly touch; the crankshaft *journals,* or the hard parts of the crankshaft, never touch the soft connecting-rod *bearings* because there's a film of oil between them, forced in there under pressure. From the pump.

It's pretty high pressure too. When the engine is running at highway speed, the oil, at 50 or 60 pounds or more per square inch (or about 4 bars, if you're of the metric persuasion—but let's leave religion out of this), is coursing through the veins of the engine and keeping all these parts at safe, albeit microscopic, distances from each other.

But if there's a lot of dirt in the oil, the dirt particles get embedded in these metal surfaces and gradually the dirt acts as an abrasive and wears away these metal surfaces. And pretty soon the engine is junk.

It's also important that the motor oil be present in sufficient quantity. In nontechnical terms, that means there's got to be enough of it in there. If you have too little oil in your engine, there's not going to be enough of it to go around, and it will get very hot, because four quarts will be doing the work of five, and so forth. When that happens, the oil gets overheated and begins to burn up at a greater than normal rate. Pretty soon, instead of having four quarts, you have three and a half quarts, then three quarts doing the work of five. And then, next thing you know, you're down to two quarts and your engine is glowing red, just like that guy driving to New York, and it's chocolate-chip cookie time.

In order to avoid this, some cars have gauges and some have warning lights; some people call them "idiot lights." Actually, we prefer to reverse it and call them "idiot gauges." I think gauges are bad. When you drive a car—maybe I'm weird about this—I think it's a good idea to look at the road most of the time. And you can't look at the road if you're

busy looking at a bunch of gauges. It's the same objection
we have to these stupid radios today that have so damn many
buttons and slides and digital scanners and so forth that you
need a copilot to change stations. Remember when you just
turned a knob?

Not that gauges are bad in and of themselves. I think if   11
you have your choice, what you want is idiot lights—or what
we call "genius lights"—and gauges too. It's nice to have a
gauge that you can kind of keep an eye on for an overview
of what's going on. For example, if you know that your
engine typically runs at 215 degrees and on this particular
day, which is not abnormally hot, it's running at 220 or 225,
you might suspect that something is wrong and get it looked
at before your radiator boils over.

On the other hand, if that gauge was the only thing you   12
had to rely on and you didn't have a light to alert you when
something was going wrong, then you'd look at the thing all
the time, especially if your engine had melted on you once.
In that case, why don't you take the bus? Because you're not
going to be a very good driver, spending most of your time
looking at the gauges.

Incidentally, if that oil warning light ever comes on, shut   13
the engine off! We don't mean that you should shut it off in
rush-hour traffic when you're in the passing lane. Use all
necessary caution and get the thing over to the breakdown
lane. But don't think you can limp to the next exit, because
you can't. Spend the money to get towed and you may save
the engine.

It's a little-known fact that the oil light does *not* signify   14
whether or not you have oil in the engine. The oil warning
light is really monitoring the oil *pressure*. Of course, if you
have no oil, you'll have no oil pressure, so the light will be
on. But it's also possible to have plenty of oil and an oil pump
that's not working for one reason or another. In this event,
a new pump would fix the problem, but if you were to drive

the car (saying, "It must be a bad light, I just checked the oil!") you'd melt the motor.

So if the oil warning light comes on, even if you just had 15
an oil change and the oil is right up to the full mark on the dipstick and is nice and clean—don't drive the car!

Here's another piece of useful info. When you turn the key 16
to the "on" position, all the little warning lights *should light up:* the temperature light, the oil light, whatever other lights you may have. Because that is the *test mode* for these lights. If those lights *don't* light up when you turn the key to the "on" position (just before you turn it all the way to start the car), does that mean you're out of oil? No. It means that something is wrong with the warning light itself. If the light doesn't work then, it's not going to work at all. Like when you need it, for example.

One more thing about oil: overfilling is just as bad as 17
underfilling. Can you really have too much of a good thing? you ask. Yes. If you're half a quart or even a quart overfilled, it's not a big deal, and I wouldn't be afraid to drive the car under those circumstances. But if you're a quart and a half or two quarts or more overfilled, you could have so much oil in the crankcase that the spinning crankshaft is going to hit the oil and turn it into suds. It's impossible for the pump to pump suds, so you'll ruin the motor. It's kind of like a front-loading washing machine that goes berserk and spills suds all over the floor when you put too much detergent in. That's what happens to your motor oil when you overfill it.

With all this talk about things that can go wrong, let's not 18
forget that modern engines are pretty incredible. People always say, "You know, the cars of yesteryear were wonderful. They built cars rough and tough and durable in those days."

Horsefeathers. 19

The cars of yesteryear were nicer to look at because they 20
were very individualistic. They were all different, and some were even beautiful. In fact, when I was a kid, you could tell

the year, make, and model of a car from a hundred paces just by looking at the taillights or the grille.

Nowadays, they all look the same. They're like jellybeans on wheels. You can't tell one from the other. But the truth is, they've never made engines as good as they make them today. Think of the abuse they take! None of the cars of yesteryear was capable of going 60 or 70 miles per hour all day long and taking it for 100,000 miles.

Engines of today—and by today I mean from the late '60s on up—are far superior. What makes them superior is not only the design and the metallurgy, but the lubricants. The oil they had thirty years ago was lousy compared to what we have today. There are magic additives and detergents and long-chain polymers and what-have-you that make them able to hold dirt in suspension and to neutralize acids and to lubricate better than oils of the old days.

There aren't too many things that will go wrong, because the engines are made so well and the tolerances are closer. And aside from doing stupid things like running out of oil or failing to heed the warning lights or overfilling the thing, you shouldn't worry.

But here's one word of caution about cars that have timing belts: Lots of cars these days are made with overhead cam-shafts. The camshaft, which opens the valves, is turned by a gear and gets its power from the crankshaft. Many cars today use a notched rubber *timing belt* to connect the two shafts instead of a chain because it's cheaper and easy to change. And here's the caveat: *if you don't change it and the belt breaks, it can mean swift ruin to the engine.* The pistons can hit the valves and you'll have bent valves and possibly broken pistons.

So you can do many hundreds of dollars' worth of damage by failing to heed the manufacturer's warning about changing the timing belt in a timely manner. No pun intended. For most cars, the timing belt replacement is somewhere between $100 and $200. It's not a big deal.

I might add that there are many cars that have rubber timing belts that will *not* cause damage to the engine when they break. But even if you have one of those cars, make sure that you get the belt changed, at the very least, when the manufacturer suggests it. If there's no specific recommendation and you have a car with a rubber belt, we would recommend that you change it at 60,000 miles. Because even if you don't do damage to the motor when the belt breaks, you're still going to be stuck somewhere, maybe somewhere unpleasant. Maybe even Cleveland! So you want to make sure that you don't fall into that situation.

Many engines that have rubber timing belts also use the belt to drive the water pump. On these, don't forget to change the water pump when you change the timing belt, because the leading cause of premature belt failure is that the water pump seizes. So if you have a timing belt that drives the water pump, get the water pump out of there at the same time. You don't want to put a belt in and then have the water pump go a month later, because it'll break the new belt and wreck the engine. 27

The best way to protect all the other pieces that you can't get to without spending a lot of money is through frequent oil changes. The manufacturers recommend oil changes somewhere between seven and ten thousand miles, depending upon the car. We've always recommended that you change your oil at 3,000 miles. We realize for some people that's a bit of an inconvenience, but look at it as cheap insurance. And change the filter every time too. 28

And last but not least, I want to repeat this because it's important: Make sure your warning lights work. The oil pressure and engine temperature warning lights are your engine's lifeline. Check them every day. You should make it as routine as checking to see if your zipper's up. You guys should do it at the same time. 29

What you do is, you get into the car, check to see that your zipper's up, and then turn the key on and check to see if your oil pressure and temperature warning lights come on. 30

I don't know what women do. 31

For Study and Discussion

QUESTIONS FOR RESPONSE

1. What is your attitude toward cars? For example, do you see them as beautiful objects, mechanical conveniences, financial obligations, or technological puzzles?
2. What is your attitude toward car mechanics? How do you respond to their analysis of your car and its special parts?

QUESTIONS ABOUT PURPOSE

1. What parts of this essay *provide information* about the purpose of engines, oil, and gauges?
2. What parts of this essay *give directions* about how to avoid engine breakdown?

QUESTIONS ABOUT AUDIENCE

1. What assumptions do Tom and Ray make about the technical knowledge of their readers?
2. How do their direct commands—"Don't drive the car"—reveal their knowledge of their readers' behavior?

QUESTIONS ABOUT STRATEGIES

1. How do Tom and Ray use the opening example of the Thunderbird to demonstrate the consequences of extreme neglect?
2. How do they use analogies (cushion, veins, suds) to clarify their analysis of how oil helps an engine work?

QUESTIONS FOR DISCUSSION

1. Why is Tom and Ray's use of humor so effective in helping readers understand and follow instructions? For example, what is the zipper test? Can you think of a test women could use?
2. What is Tom and Ray's attitude toward modern technology? To what extent would the average car owner or car mechanic agree with their opinion?

Lars Eighner was born in 1948 in Corpus Christi, Texas, and attended the University of Texas at Austin. He held a series of jobs, including work as an attendant at the state mental hospital in Austin, before he became homeless. For five years he drifted between Austin and Hollywood, living on the streets and in abandoned buildings. Then he began to contribute essays to the *Threepenny Review*; these writings are collected in his memoir, *Travels with Lizabeth* (1993). In one of these essays, "My Daily Dives in the Dumpster," Eighner analyzes the "predictable series of stages that a person goes through in learning to scavenge."

My Daily Dives in the Dumpster

I BEGAN DUMPSTER DIVING about a year before I became homeless. 1

I prefer the term "scavenging" and use the word "scrounging" when I mean to be obscure. I have heard people, evidently meaning to be polite, use the word "foraging," but I prefer to reserve that word for gathering nuts and berries and such which I do also, according to the season and opportunity. 2

I like the frankness of the word "scavenging." I live from the refuse of others. I am a scavenger. I think it a sound and honorable niche, although if I could I would naturally prefer to live the comfortable consumer life, perhaps—and only perhaps—as a slightly less wasteful consumer owing to what I have learned as a scavenger. 3

Except for jeans, all my clothes come from Dumpsters. 4
Boom boxes, candles, bedding, toilet paper, medicine, books,

a typewriter, a virgin male love doll, change sometimes amounting to many dollars: All came from Dumpsters. And, yes, I eat from Dumpsters too.

There are a predictable series of stages that a person goes   5 through in learning to scavenge. At first the new scavenger is filled with disgust and self-loathing. He is ashamed of being seen and may lurk around trying to duck behind things, or he may try to dive at night. (In fact, this is unnecessary, since

---

*Scavenging, more than most other pursuits,
tends to yield returns in some proportion
to the effort and the intelligence brought
to bear.*

---

most people instinctively look away from scavengers.)

Every grain of rice seems to be a maggot. Everything   6 seems to stink. The scavenger can wipe the egg yolk off the found can, but he cannot erase the stigma of eating garbage from his mind.

This stage passes with experience. The scavenger finds a   7 pair of running shoes that fit and look and smell brand-new. He finds a pocket calculator in perfect working order. He finds pristine ice cream, still frozen, more than he can eat or keep. He begins to understand: People do throw away perfectly good stuff, a lot of perfectly good stuff.

At this stage he may become lost and never recover. All   8 the Dumpster divers I have known come to the point of trying to acquire everything they touch. Why not take it, they reason, it is all free. This is, of course, hopeless, and most divers come to realize that they must restrict themselves to items of relatively immediate utility.

The finding of objects is becoming something of an urban   9 art. Even respectable, employed people will sometimes find something tempting sticking out of a Dumpster or standing beside one. Quite a number of people, not all of them of the bohemian type, are willing to brag that they found this or that piece in the trash.

But eating from Dumpsters is the thing that separates the   10
dilettanti from the professionals. Eating safely involves three principles: using the senses and common sense to evaluate the condition of the found materials; knowing the Dumpsters of a given area and checking them regularly; and seeking always to answer the question, Why was this discarded?

Perhaps everyone who has a kitchen and a regular supply   11
of groceries has, at one time or another, eaten half a sandwich before discovering mold on the bread, or has gotten a mouthful of milk before realizing the milk had turned. Nothing of the sort is likely to happen to a Dumpster diver because he is constantly reminded that most food is discarded for a reason.

Yet perfectly good food can be found in Dumpsters.   12
Canned goods, for example, turn up fairly often in the Dumpsters I frequent. All except the most phobic people would be willing to eat from a can even if it came from a Dumpster. I have few qualms about dry foods such as crackers, cookies, cereal, chips, and pasta if they are free of visible contaminants and still dry and crisp. Raw fruits and vegetables with intact skins seem perfectly safe to me, excluding, of course, the obviously rotten. Many are discarded for minor imperfections that can be pared away. Chocolate is often discarded only because it has become discolored as the cocoa butter de-emulsified.

I began scavenging by pulling pizzas out of the Dumpster   13
behind a pizza delivery shop. In general, prepared food requires caution, but in this case I knew what time the shop closed and went to the Dumpster as soon as the last of the help left.

Because the workers at these places are usually inexperi-   14
enced, pizzas are often made with the wrong topping, baked

incorrectly, or refused on delivery for being cold. The products to be discarded are boxed up because inventory is kept
by counting boxes: A boxed pizza can be written off; an
unboxed pizza does not exist. So I had a steady supply of
fresh, sometimes warm pizza.

The area I frequent is inhabited by many affluent college   15
students. I am not here by chance; the Dumpsters are very
rich. Students throw out many good things, including food,
particularly at the end of the semester and before and after
breaks. I find it advantageous to keep an eye on the academic
calendar.

A typical discard is a half jar of peanut butter—though   16
non-organic peanut butter does not require refrigeration and
is unlikely to spoil in any reasonable time. Occasionally I find
a cheese with a spot of mold, which, of course, I just pare
off, and because it is obvious why the cheese was discarded,
I treat it with less suspicion than an apparently perfect cheese
found in similar circumstances. One of my favorite finds is
yogurt—often discarded, still sealed, when the expiration
date has passed—because it will keep for several days, even in
warm weather.

I avoid ethnic foods I am unfamiliar with. If I do not know 17
what it is supposed to look or smell like when it is good, I
cannot be certain I will be able to tell if it is bad.

No matter how careful I am I still get dysentery at least   18
once a month, oftener in warm weather. I do not want to
paint too romantic a picture. Dumpster diving has serious
drawbacks as a way of life.

Though I have a proprietary feeling about my Dumpsters,   19
I don't mind my direct competitors, other scavengers, as
much as I hate the soda-can scroungers.

I have tried scrounging aluminum cans with an able-   20
bodied companion, and afoot we could make no more than
a few dollars a day. I can extract the necessities of life from
the Dumpsters directly with far less effort than would be
required to accumulate the equivalent value in aluminum.
Can scroungers, then, are people who *must* have small
amounts of cash—mostly drug addicts and winos.

I do not begrudge them the cans, but can scroungers tend   21
to tear up the Dumpsters, littering the area and mixing the
contents. There are precious few courtesies among scavengers, but it is a common practice to set aside surplus items:
pairs of shoes, clothing, canned goods, and such. A true
scavenger hates to see good stuff go to waste, and what he
cannot use he leaves in good condition in plain sight. Can
scroungers lay waste to everything in their path and will stir
one of a pair of good shoes to the bottom of a Dumpster to
be lost or ruined in the muck. They become so specialized
that they can see only cans and earn my contempt by passing
up change, canned goods, and readily hockable items.

Can scroungers will even go through individual garbage   22
cans, something I have never seen a scavenger do. Going
through individual garbage cans without spreading litter is
almost impossible, and litter is likely to reduce the public's
tolerance of scavenging. But my strongest reservation about
going through individual garbage cans is that this seems to
me a very personal kind of invasion, one to which I would
object if I were a homeowner.

Though Dumpsters seem somehow less personal than gar-   23
bage cans, they still contain bank statements, bills, correspondence, pill bottles, and other sensitive information. I avoid
trying to draw conclusions about the people who dump in
the Dumpsters I frequent. I think it would be unethical to
do so, although I know many people will find the idea of
scavenger ethics too funny for words.

Occasionally a find tells a story. I once found a small paper   24
bag containing some unused condoms, several partial tubes
of flavored sexual lubricant, a partially used compact of birth
control pills, and the torn pieces of a picture of a young man.
Clearly, the woman was through with him and planning to
give up sex altogether.

Dumpster things are often sad—abandoned teddy bears,   25
shredded wedding albums, despaired-of sales kits. I find dia-
ries and journals. College students also discard their papers;
I am horrified to discover the kind of paper that now merits
an A in an undergraduate course.

Dumpster diving is outdoor work, often surprisingly pleas-   26
ant. It is not entirely predictable; things of interest turn up
every day, and some days there are finds of great value. I am
always very pleased when I can turn up exactly the thing I
most wanted to find. Yet in spite of the element of chance,
scavenging, more than most other pursuits, tends to yield
returns in some proportion to the effort and intelligence
brought to bear.

I think of scavenging as a modern form of self-reliance.   27
After ten years of government service, where everything is
geared to the lowest common denominator, I find work that
rewards initiative and effort refreshing. Certainly I would be
happy to have a sinecure again, but I am not heartbroken to
be without one.

I find from the experience of scavenging two rather deep   28
lessons. The first is to take what I can use and let the rest go.
I have come to think that there is no value in the abstract. A
thing I cannot use or make useful, perhaps by trading, has
no value, however fine or rare it may be. (I mean useful in
the broad sense—some art, for example, I would think valuable.)

The second lesson is the transience of material being. I do   29
not suppose that ideas are immortal, but certainly they are
longer-lived than material objects.

The things I find in Dumpsters, the love letters and rag   30
dolls of so many lives, remind me of this lesson. Many times
in my travels I have lost everything but the clothes on my
back. Now I hardly pick up a thing without envisioning
the time I will cast it away. This, I think, is a healthy state of
mind. Almost everything I have now has already been cast
out at least once, proving that what I own is valueless to
someone.

I find that my desire to grab for the gaudy bauble has been   31
largely sated. I think this is an attitude I share with the very
wealthy—we both know there is plenty more where whatever
we have came from. Between us are the rat-race millions who
have confounded their selves with the objects they grasp and

who nightly scavenge the cable channels looking for they know not what.

I am sorry for them. 32

For Study and Discussion

QUESTIONS FOR RESPONSE

1. What assumptions do you make about someone sorting through a Dumpster?
2. What things that you throw away in the weekly garbage might others find valuable?

QUESTIONS ABOUT PURPOSE

1. Why does Eighner prefer the term *scavenging* to *scrounging* or *foraging* to characterize the process he analyzes?
2. In what ways does Eighner's analysis demonstrate that Dumpster diving is "a sound and honorable niche"?

QUESTIONS ABOUT AUDIENCE

1. How does Eighner anticipate his audience's reaction to his subject by presenting the "predictable series of stages that a person goes through in learning to scavenge"?
2. How do Eighner's "scavenger ethics" enhance his standing with his readers?

QUESTIONS ABOUT STRATEGIES

1. How does Eighner use the example of pizza to illustrate the three principles of eating from a Dumpster?
2. How does Eighner's analysis of the process of "soda-can scrounging" help distinguish that process from "scavenging"?

QUESTIONS FOR DISCUSSION

1. How do the two lessons Eighner has learned demonstrate that his "work" rewards initiative and effort?
2. What attitudes toward consumption and waste does Eighner claim he shares with the very wealthy? Why does he feel sorry for "the rat-race millions"?

Nikki Giovanni was born in 1943 in Knoxville, Tennessee, and was educated at Fisk University, the University of Pennsylvania, and Columbia University. She has taught creative writing at Rutgers University and Virginia Tech and worked for the Ohio Humanities Council and the Appalachian Community Fund. Her poems have appeared in the collections *My House* (1972), *The Women and the Men* (1975), and *Those Who Ride the Night Winds* (1983). Her nonfiction work appears in books such as *Gemini: An Extended Autobiographical Statement on My First Twenty-five Years Being a Black Poet* (1971), *Sacred Cows . . . and Other Edibles* (1988), and *Racism 101* (1994). In "Racism 101," Giovanni tells black students how to succeed at predominantly white colleges.

Campus Racism 101

T HERE IS A bumper sticker that reads: TOO BAD IGNO- 1
RANCE ISN'T PAINFUL. I like that. But ignorance is. We just seldom attribute the pain to it or even recognize it when we see it. Like the postcard on my corkboard. It shows a young man in a very hip jacket smoking a cigarette. In the background is a high school with the American flag waving. The caption says: "Too cool for school. Yet too stupid for the real world." Out of the mouth of the young man is a bubble enclosing the words "Maybe I'll start a band." There could be a postcard showing a jock in a uniform saying, "I don't need school. I'm going to the NFL or NBA." Or one showing a young man or woman studying and a group of young

people saying, "So you want to be white." Or something
equally demeaning. We need to quit it.

I am a professor of English at Virginia Tech. I've been here   2
for four years, though for only two years with academic rank.
I am tenured, which means I have a teaching position for life,
a rarity on a predominantly white campus. Whether from
malice or ignorance, people who think I should be at a
predominantly Black institution will ask, "Why are you at
Tech?" Because it's here. And so are Black students. But even
if Black students weren't here, it's painfully obvious that this
nation and this world cannot allow white students to go

---

*Your job is not to educate white people; it is
to obtain an education.*

---

through higher education without interacting with Blacks in
authoritative positions. It is equally clear that predominantly
Black colleges cannot accommodate the numbers of Black
students who want and need an education.

Is it difficult to attend a predominantly white college?   3
Compared with what? Being passed over for promotion because you lack credentials? Being turned down for jobs because you are not college-educated? Joining the armed forces
or going to jail because you cannot find an alternative to the
streets? Let's have a little perspective here. Where can you go
and what can you do that frees you from interacting with the
white American mentality? You're going to interact; the only
question is, will you be in some control of yourself and your
actions, or will you be controlled by others? I'm going to
recommend self-control.

What's the difference between prison and college? They   4
both prescribe your behavior for a given period of time.
They both allow you to read books and develop your writing.
They both give you time alone to think and time with your

peers to talk about issues. But four years of prison doesn't give you a passport to greater opportunities. Most likely that time only gives you greater knowledge of how to get back in. Four years of college gives you an opportunity not only to lift yourself but to serve your people effectively. What's the difference when you are called nigger in college from when you are called nigger in prison? In college you can, though I admit with effort, follow procedures to have those students who called you nigger kicked out or suspended. You can bring issues to public attention without risking your life. But mostly, college is and always has been the future. We, neither less nor more than other people, need knowledge. There are discomforts attached to attending predominantly white colleges, though no more so than living in a racist world. Here are some rules to follow that may help:

Go to class. No matter how you feel. No matter how you 5 think the professor feels about you. It's important to have a consistent presence in the classroom. If nothing else, the professor will know you care enough and are serious enough to be there.

Meet your professors. Extend your hand (give a firm hand- 6 shake) and tell them your name. Ask them what you need to do to make an A. You may never make an A, but you have put them on notice that you are serious about getting good grades.

Do assignments on time. Typed or computer-generated. 7 You have the syllabus. Follow it, and turn those papers in. If for some reason you can't complete an assignment on time, let your professor know before it is due and work out a new due date—then meet it.

Go back to see your professor. Tell him or her your name 8 again. If an assignment received less than an A, ask why, and find out what you need to do to improve the next assignment.

Yes, your professor is busy. So are you. So are your parents 9 who are working to pay or help with your tuition. Ask early what you need to do if you feel you are starting to get into academic trouble. Do not wait until you are failing.

Understand that there will be professors who do not like you; 10

there may even be professors who are racist or sexist or both. You must discriminate among your professors to see who will give you the help you need. You may not simply say, "They are all against me." They aren't. They mostly don't care. Since you are the one who wants to be educated, find the people who want to help.

Don't defeat yourself. Cultivate your friends. Know your   11
enemies. You cannot undo hundreds of years of prejudicial thinking. Think for yourself and speak up. Raise your hand in class. Say what you believe no matter how awkward you may think it sounds. You will improve in your articulation and confidence.

Participate in some campus activity. Join the newspaper   12
staff. Run for office. Join a dorm council. Do something that involves you on campus. You are going to be there for four years, so let your presence be known, if not felt.

You will inevitably run into some white classmates who are   13
troubling because they often say stupid things, ask stupid questions—and expect an answer. Here are some comebacks to some of the most common inquiries and comments:

Q: What's it like to grow up in a ghetto?   14
A: I don't know.   15

Q (from the teacher): Can you give us the Black perspective   16
on Toni Morrison, Huck Finn, slavery, Martin Luther King, Jr., and others?
A: I can give you *my* perspective. (Do not take the burden   17
of 22 million people on your shoulders. Remind everyone that you are an individual, and don't speak for the race or any other individual within it.)

Q: Why do all the Black people sit together in the dining   18
hall?
A: Why do all the white students sit together?   19

Q: Why should there be an African-American studies course?   20
A: Because white Americans have not adequately studied the   21

contributions of Africans and African-Americans. Both Black and white students need to know our total common history.

Q: Why are there so many scholarships for "minority" students?   22

A: Because they wouldn't give my great-grandparents their forty acres and the mule.   23

Q: How can whites understand Black history, culture, literature, and so forth?   24

A: The same way we understand white history, culture, literature, and so forth. That is why we're in school: to learn.   25

Q: Should whites take African-American studies courses?   26

A: Of course. We take white-studies courses, though the universities don't call them that.   27

Comment: When I see groups of Black people on campus, it's really intimidating.   28

Comeback: I understand what you mean. I'm frightened when I see white students congregating.   29

Comment: It's not fair. It's easier for you guys to get into college than for other people.   30

Comeback: If it's so easy, why aren't there more of us?   31

Comment: It's not our fault that America is the way it is.   32

Comeback: It's not our fault, either, but both of us have a responsibility to make changes.   33

It's really very simple. Educational progress is a national concern; education is a private one. Your job is not to educate white people; it is to obtain an education. If you take the racial world on your shoulders, you will not get the job done. Deal with yourself as an individual worthy of respect, and make everyone else deal with you the same way. College is a little like playing grown-up. Practice what you want to be. You have been telling your parents you are grown. Now is your chance to act like it.   34

For Study and Discussion

QUESTIONS FOR RESPONSE

1. How have you responded to situations in which you were convinced that your teacher did not like you?
2. How have you felt when a teacher or fellow student placed you in a group (characterized by stereotypes) and then asked you to speak *for* that group?

QUESTIONS ABOUT PURPOSE

1. How does Giovanni explain her reasons for teaching at a predominantly white school?
2. In what ways does the issue of control, particularly self-control, explain the purpose of her advice?

QUESTIONS ABOUT AUDIENCE

1. How do the examples in the first paragraph and the advice in the last paragraph identify Giovanni's primary audience?
2. How does Giovanni's status as professor at a predominantly white college establish her authority to address her audience on "Racism 101"?

QUESTIONS ABOUT STRATEGIES

1. How does Giovanni arrange her advice? Why is her first suggestion—"Go to class"—her *first* suggestion? Why is her last suggestion—"Participate in some campus activity"—her *last* suggestion?
2. How does she use sample questions and answers to illustrate the experience of learning on a white campus?

QUESTIONS FOR DISCUSSION

1. What does Giovanni's attitude toward *individual* as opposed to *group* perspective suggest about the nature of "racism"?
2. How might white students learn as much as black students from following her advice?

Philip Weiss was born in Boston, Massachusetts, in 1955 and educated at Harvard University. He began his career as a reporter with the Philadelphia *Daily News* and worked for a series of alternative weekly newspapers before assuming his position as contributing editor to *Harper's* and *Esquire*. He has published articles in the *New York Times Magazine* and writes a column for the *New York Observer*. In "How to Get Out of a Locked Trunk," reprinted from *Harper's*, Weiss describes the procedure he has discovered for getting out of a "sticky situation."

How to Get Out of a Locked Trunk

O N A HOT Sunday last summer my friend Tony and I   1
drove my rental car, a '91 Buick, from St. Paul to the small town of Waconia, Minnesota, forty miles southwest. We each had a project. Waconia is Tony's boyhood home, and his sister had recently given him a panoramic postcard of Lake Waconia as seen from a high point in the town early in the century. He wanted to duplicate the photograph's vantage point, then hang the two pictures together in his house in Frogtown. I was hoping to see Tony's father, Emmett, a retired mechanic, in order to settle a question that had been nagging me: Is it possible to get out of a locked car trunk?

We tried to call ahead to Emmett twice, but he wasn't   2
home. Tony thought he was probably golfing but that there was a good chance he'd be back by the time we got there. So we set out.

I parked the Buick, which was a silver sedan with a red   3

interior, by the graveyard near where Tony thought the picture had been taken. He took his picture and I wandered
among the headstones, reading the epitaphs. One of them
was chillingly anti-individualist. It said, "Not to do my will,
but thine."

Trunk lockings had been on my mind for a few weeks. It   4
seemed to me that the fear of being locked in a car trunk had
a particular hold on the American imagination. Trunk lockings occur in many movies and books—from *Goodfellas* to
Thelma and Louise to *Humboldt's Gift*. And while the high-
brow national newspapers generally shy away from trunk

---

*Every culture comes up with tests of
a person's ability to get out of a
sticky situation.*

---

lockings, the attention they receive in local papers suggests a
widespread anxiety surrounding the subject. In an afternoon
at the New York Public Library I found numerous stories
about trunk lockings. A Los Angeles man is discovered,
bloodshot, banging the trunk of his white Eldorado following a night and a day trapped inside; he says his captors went
on joyrides and picked up women. A forty-eight-year-old
Houston doctor is forced into her trunk at a bank ATM and
then the car is abandoned, parked near the Astrodome. A
New Orleans woman tells police she gave birth in a trunk
while being abducted to Texas. Tests undermine her story,
the police drop the investigation. But so what if it's a fantasy?
That only shows the idea's hold on us.

Every culture comes up with tests of a person's ability to   5
get out of a sticky situation. The English plant mazes. Tropi-
cal resorts market those straw finger-grabbers that tighten
their grip the harder you pull on them, and Viennese intel-

lectuals gave us the concept of childhood sexuality—figure it out, or remain neurotic for life.

At least you could puzzle your way out of those predicaments. When they slam the trunk, though, you're helpless unless someone finds you. You would think that such a common worry should have a ready fix, and that the secret of getting out of a locked trunk is something we should all know about.   6

I phoned experts but they were very discouraging.   7

"You cannot get out. If you got a pair of pliers and bat's eyes, yes. But you have to have a lot of knowledge of the lock," said James Foote at Automotive Locksmiths in New York City.   8

Jim Frens, whom I reached at the technical section of *Car and Driver* in Detroit, told me the magazine had not dealt with this question. But he echoed the opinion of experts elsewhere when he said that the best hope for escape would be to try and kick out the panel between the trunk and the backseat. That angle didn't seem worth pursuing. What if your enemies were in the car, crumpling beer cans and laughing at your fate? It didn't make sense to join them.   9

The people who deal with rules on auto design were uncomfortable with my scenarios. Debra Barclay of the Center for Auto Safety, an organization founded by Ralph Nader, had certainly heard of cases, but she was not aware of any regulations on the matter. "Now, if there was a defect involved—" she said, her voice trailing off, implying that trunk locking was all phobia. This must be one of the few issues on which she and the auto industry agree. Ann Carlson of the Motor Vehicle Manufacturers Association became alarmed at the thought that I was going to play up a non-problem: "In reality this very rarely happens. As you say, in the movies it's a wonderful plot device," she said. "But in reality apparently this is not that frequent an occurrence. So they have not designed that feature into vehicles in a specific way."   10

When we got to Emmett's one-story house it was full of people. Tony's sister, Carol, was on the floor with her two   11 small children. Her husband, Charlie, had one eye on the golf tournament on TV, and Emmett was at the kitchen counter, trimming fat from meat for lunch. I have known Emmett for fifteen years. He looked better than ever. In his retirement he had sharply changed his diet and lost a lot of weight. He had on shorts. His legs were tanned and muscular. As always, his manner was humorous, if opaque.

Tony told his family my news: I was getting married in three weeks. Charlie wanted to know where my fiancée was. Back East, getting everything ready. A big-time hatter was fitting her for a new hat. 12

Emmett sat on the couch, watching me. "Do you want my advice?" 13

"Sure." 14

He just grinned. A gold tooth glinted. Carol and Charlie pressed him to yield his wisdom. 15

Finally he said, "Once you get to be thirty, you make your own mistakes." 16

He got out several cans of beer, and then I brought up what was on my mind. 17

Emmett nodded and took off his glasses, then cleaned them and put them back on. 18

We went out to his car, a Mercury Grand Marquis, and Emmett opened the trunk. His golf clubs were sitting on top of the spare tire in a green golf bag. Next to them was a toolbox and what he called his "burglar tools," a set of elbowed rods with red plastic handles he used to open door locks when people locked their keys inside. 19

Tony and Charlie stood watching. Charlie is a banker in Minneapolis. He enjoys gizmos and is extremely practical. I would describe him as unflappable. That's a word I always wanted to apply to myself, but my fiancée had recently informed me that I am high-strung. Though that surprised me, I didn't quarrel with her. 20

For a while we studied the latch assembly. The lock closed in much the same way that a lobster might clamp on to a pencil. The claw portion, the jaws of the lock, was mounted inside the trunk lid. When you shut the lid, the jaws locked 21 on to the bend of a U-shaped piece of metal mounted on the body of the car. Emmett said my best bet would be to unscrew the bolts. That way the U-shaped piece would come loose and the lock's jaws would swing up with it still in their grasp.

"But you'd need a wrench," he said. 22

It was already getting too technical. Emmett had an air of 23 endless patience, but I felt defeated. I could only imagine bloodied fingers, cracked teeth. I had hoped for a simple trick.

Charlie stepped forward. He reached out and squeezed the 24 lock's jaws. They clicked shut in the air, bound together by heavy springs. Charlie now prodded the upper part of the left-hand jaw, the thicker part. With a rough flick of his thumb, he was able to force the jaws to snap open. Great.

Unfortunately, the jaws were mounted behind a steel plate 25 the size of your palm in such a way that while they were accessible to us, standing outside the car, had we been inside the trunk the plate would be in our way, blocking the jaws.

This time Emmett saw the way out. He fingered a hole in 26 the plate. It was no bigger than the tip of your little finger. But the hole was close enough to the latch itself that it might be possible to angle something through the hole from inside the trunk and nudge the jaws apart. We tried with one of my keys. The lock jumped open.

It was time for a full-dress test. Emmett swung the clubs 27 out of the trunk, and I set my can of Schmidt's on the rear bumper and climbed in. Everyone gathered around, and Emmett lowered the trunk on me, then pressed it shut with his meaty hands. Total darkness. I couldn't hear the people outside. I thought I was going to panic. But the big trunk felt comfortable. I was pressed against a sort of black carpet that softened the angles against my back.

I could almost stretch out in the trunk, and it seemed to 28 me I could make them sweat if I took my time. Even Emmett, that sphinx, would give way to curiosity. Once I was out he'd ask how it had been and I'd just grin. There were some things you could only learn by doing.

It took a while to find the hole. I slipped the key in and   29
angled it to one side. The trunk gasped open.

Emmett motioned the others away, then levered me out   30
with his big right forearm. Though I'd only been inside for
a minute, I was disoriented—as much as anything because
someone had moved my beer while I was gone, setting it
down on the cement floor of the garage. It was just a little
thing, but I could not be entirely sure I had gotten my own
beer back.

Charlie was now raring to try other cars. We examined the   31
latch on his Toyota, which was entirely shielded to the trunk
occupant (i.e., no hole in the plate), and on the neighbor's
Honda (ditto). But a 1991 Dodge Dynasty was doable. The
trunk was tight, but its lock had a feature one of the mechanics I'd phoned described as a "tailpiece": a finger-like extension of the lock mechanism itself that stuck out a half inch
into the trunk cavity; simply by twisting the tailpiece I could
free the lock. I was even faster on a 1984 Subaru that had a
little lever device on the latch.

We went out to my rental on Oak Street. The Skylark was   32
in direct sun and the trunk was hot to the touch, but when
we got it open we could see that its latch plate had a perfect
hole, a square in which the edge of the lock's jaw appeared
like a face in a window.

The trunk was shallow and hot. Emmett had to push my   33
knees down before he could close the lid. This one was a little
suffocating. I imagined being trapped for hours, and even
before he had got it closed I regretted the decision with a
slightly nauseous feeling. I thought of Edgar Allan Poe's live
burials, and then about something my fiancée had said more
than a year and a half before. I had been on her case to get
married. She was divorced, and at every opportunity I would
reissue my proposal—even during a commercial. She'd interrupted one of these chirps to tell me, in a cold, throaty voice,
that she had no intention of ever going through another
divorce: "This time, it's death out." I'd carried those words
around like a lump of wet clay.

As it happened, the Skylark trunk was the easiest of all. 34
The hole was right where it was supposed to be. The trunk
popped open, and I felt great satisfaction that we'd been able
to figure out a rule that seemed to apply about 60 percent of
the time. If we publicized our success, it might get the attention it deserved. All trunks would be fitted with such a hole.
Kids would learn about it in school. The grip of the fear
would relax. Before long a successful trunk-locking scene
would date a movie like a fedora dates one today.

When I got back East I was caught up in wedding prepa- 35
rations. I live in New York, and the wedding was to take place
in Philadelphia. We set up camp there with five days to go.
A friend had lent my fiancée her BMW, and we drove it south
with all our things. I unloaded the car in my parents' drive-
way. The last thing I pulled out of the trunk was my fiancée's
hat in its heavy cardboard shipping box. She'd warned me I
was not allowed to look. The lid was free but I didn't open
it. I was willing to be surprised.

When the trunk was empty it occurred to me I might hop 36
in and give it a try. First I looked over the mechanism. The
jaws of the BMW's lock were shielded, but there seemed to
be some kind of cable coming off it that you might be able
to manipulate so as to cause the lock to open. The same cable
that allowed the driver to open the trunk remotely . . .

I fingered it for a moment or two but decided I didn't 37
need to test out the theory.

For Study and Discussion

QUESTIONS FOR RESPONSE

1. What kind of "sticky situations" have you encountered?
2. How have you responded to the situation? Did you panic, retain
   your poise, work patiently to solve the problem?

QUESTIONS ABOUT PURPOSE

1. What sort of evidence does Weiss present to justify his research into the question that has been nagging him: "Is it possible to get out of a locked car trunk?"
2. What does he predict will be the outcome of his successful experiments?

QUESTIONS ABOUT AUDIENCE

1. How does Weiss's theory that "the fear of being locked in a car trunk [has] a particular hold on the American imagination" identify his audience?
2. How do the experts Weiss consults—mechanics, designers, Emmett, Charlie—provide a test audience for this theory?

QUESTIONS ABOUT STRATEGIES

1. How does Weiss's description of the lobster claw, the bolt, the plate, and the hole clarify the problem he is trying to solve?
2. What makes the process he discovers "un-doable" on some cars?

QUESTIONS FOR DISCUSSION

1. Offer some other examples of Weiss's premise that "There were some things you could only learn by doing." Explain the reasons for your choice.
2. Why does Weiss decide that he doesn't need to test his theory on his fiancée's friend's BMW?

Edward Hoagland was born in New York City in 1932 and was educated at Harvard University. Although he has written several novels and books on travel, Hoagland considers himself a personal essayist, a writer who is concerned with expressing "what I think" and "what I am." He has published essays in *Commentary, Newsweek,* the *Village Voice,* and the *New York Times* on an intriguing range of subjects such as tugboats, turtles, circuses, city life in Cairo, and his own stutter. His essays have been collected in books such as *The Courage of Turtles* (1971), *The Edward Hoagland Reader* (1979), *Notes from the Century Before: A Journal from British Columbia* (1982), and *Balancing Acts* (1992). He has also published a collection of stories, *City Tales/Wyoming Stories* (1986), with Gretel Ehrlich. In "In the Toils of the Law," reprinted from *Walking the Dead Diamond River* (1973), Hoagland uses his own experience to explain the process of being selected for and serving on a jury.

In the Toils of the Law

L ATELY PEOPLE SEEM to want to pigeonhole themselves ("I'm 'into' this," "I'm 'into' that"), and the anciently universal experiences like getting married or having a child, like voting or jury duty, acquire a kind of poignancy. We hardly believe that our vote will count, we wonder whether the world will wind up uninhabitable for the child, but still we do vote with a rueful fervor and look at new babies with undimmed tenderness, because who knows what will become of these old humane responsibilities? . . .

Jury duty. Here one sits listening to evidence: thumbs up   2 for a witness or thumbs down. It's unexpectedly moving; everybody tries so hard to be fair. For their two weeks of service people really try to be better than themselves. In Manhattan eighteen hundred are called each week from the voters' rolls, a third of whom show up and qualify. Later this third is divided into three groups of two hundred, one for the State Supreme Court of New York County, one for the Criminal Court, and one for the Civil Court. At Civil Court, 111 Centre Street, right across from the Tombs, there are jury rooms on the third and eleventh floors, and every Monday a new pool goes to one or the other. The building is relatively modern, the chairs upholstered as in an airport lounge, and the two hundred people sit facing forward like a school of fish until the roll is called. It's like waiting six or seven hours a day for an unscheduled flight to leave. They read and watch the clock, go to the drinking fountain, strike up a conversation, dictate business letters into the pay telephones. When I served, one man in a booth was shouting, "I'll knock your teeth down your throat! I don't want to hear, I don't want to know!"

. . . There are lots of retired men and institutional employ-   3
ees from banks, the Post Office or the Transit Authority whose bosses won't miss them, as well as people at loose ends who welcome the change. But some look extremely busy,

---

Jury duty is unexpectedly moving; everybody tries so hard to be fair.

---

rushing back to the office when given a chance or sitting at the tables at the front of the room, trying to keep up with their work. They'll write payroll checks, glancing to see if you notice how important they are, or pore over statistical charts or contact sheets with a magnifying glass, if they are in public relations or advertising. Once in a while a clerk emerges to rotate a lottery box and draw the names of jurors, who go into one of the challenge rooms—six jurors, six alternates—to be interviewed by the plaintiff's and defendant's lawyers. Unless the damages asked are large, in civil cases the jury has six members, only five of whom must agree on a decision, and since no one is going to be sentenced to jail, the evidence for a decision need merely seem preponderant, not "beyond a reasonable doubt."

The legal fiction is maintained that the man or woman you see as defendant is actually going to have to pay, but the defense attorneys are generally insurance lawyers from a regular battery which each big company keeps at the courthouse to handle these matters, or from the legal corps of the City of New York, Con Edison, Hertz Rent A Car, or whoever. If so, they act interchangeably and you may see a different face in court than you saw in the challenge room, and still another during the judge's charge. During my stint most cases I heard about went back four or five years, and the knottiest problem for either side was producing witnesses who were still willing to testify. In negligence cases, so many of which involve automobiles, there are several reasons why the insurers haven't settled earlier. They've waited for the plaintiff to lose hope or greed, and to see what cards each contestant will finally hold in his hands when the five years have passed. More significantly, it's a financial matter. The straight-arrow companies that do right by a sufferer and promptly pay him off lose the use as capital of that three thousand dollars or so meanwhile—multiplied perhaps eighty thousand times, for all the similar cases they have.

Selecting a jury is the last little battle of nerves between the two sides. By now the opposing attorneys know who will testify and have obtained pretrial depositions; this completes the hand each of them holds. Generally they think they know what will happen, so to save time and costs they settle the case either before the hearing starts or out of the jury's earshot during the hearing with the judge's help. Seeing a good sober jury waiting to hear them attempt to justify a bad case greases the wheels.

In the challenge room, though, the momentum of con- 6
frontation goes on. With a crowded court calendar, the judge
in these civil cases is not present, as a rule. It's a small room,
and there's an opportunity for the lawyers to be folksy or
emotional in ways not permitted them later on. For example,
in asking the jurors repeatedly if they will "be able to convert
pain and suffering into dollars and cents" the plaintiff's attorney is preparing the ground for his more closely supervised
presentation in court. By asking them if they own any stock
in an insurance company he can get across the intelligence,
which is otherwise *verboten,* that not the humble "defendant"
but some corporation is going to have to pay the tab. His
opponent will object if he tells too many jokes and wins too
many friends, but both seek not so much a sympathetic jury
as a jury that is free of nuts and grudge-holders, a jury
dependably ready to give everybody "his day in court"—a
phrase one hears over and over. The questioning we were
subjected to was so polite as to be almost apologetic, however, because of the danger of unwittingly offending any of
the jurors who remained. Having to size up a series of strangers, on the basis of some monosyllabic answers and each
fellow's face, profession and address, was hard work for these
lawyers. Everybody was on his best behavior, the jurors too,
because the procedure so much resembled a job interview,
and no one wanted to be considered less than fair-minded,
unfit to participate in the case; there was a vague sense of
shame about being excused.

The six alternates sat listening. The lawyers could look at 7
them and draw any conclusions they wished, but they could
neither question them until a sitting juror had been challenged, nor know in advance which one of the alternates
would be substituted first. Each person was asked about his
work, about any honest bias or special knowledge he might
have concerning cases of the same kind, or any lawsuits he
himself might have been involved in at one time. Some questions were probably partly designed to educate us in the
disciplines of objectivity, lest we think it was all too easy, and
one or two lawyers actually made an effort to educate us in

the majesty of the law, since, as they said, the judges sometimes are "dingbats" and don't. We were told there should
be no opprobrium attached to being excused, that we must
not simply assume a perfect impartiality in ourselves but
should help them to examine us. Jailhouse advocates, or
Spartan types who might secretly believe that the injured
party should swallow his misfortune and grin and bear a
stroke of bad luck, were to be avoided, of course, along with
the mingy, the flippant, the grieved and the wronged, as well
as men who might want to redistribute the wealth of the
world by finding for the plaintiff, or who might not limit their
deliberations to the facts of the case, accepting the judge's
interpretation of the law as law. We were told that our common sense and experience of life was what was wanted to sift
out the likelihood of the testimony we heard.

Most dismissals were caused just by a lawyer's hunch—or 8
figuring the percentages as baseball managers do. After the
first day's waiting in the airport lounge, there wasn't anybody
who didn't want to get on a case; even listening as an alternate in the challenge room was a relief. I dressed in a suit and
tie and shined my shoes. I'd been afraid that when I said I
was a novelist no lawyer would have me, on the theory that
novelists favor the underdog. On the contrary, I was accepted
every time; apparently a novelist was considered ideal, having
no allegiances at all, no expertise, no professional link to the
workaday world. I stutter and had supposed that this too
might disqualify me [but] these lawyers did not think it so.
What they seemed to want was simply a balanced group,
because when a jury gets down to arguing there's no telling
where its leadership will arise. The rich man from Sutton
Place whom the plaintiff's lawyer almost dismissed, fearing
he'd favor the powers that be, may turn out to be a fighting
liberal whose idea of what constitutes proper damages is
much higher than what the machinist who sits next to him
has in mind. In one case I heard about, a woman was clonked
by a Christmas tree in a department store and the juror whose
salary was lowest suggested an award of fifty dollars, and the
man who earned the most, fifty thousand dollars (they

rounded it off to fifteen hundred dollars). These were the kind of cases Sancho Panza did so well on when he was governor of Isle Barataria, and as I was questioned about my prejudices, and solemnly looking into each lawyer's eyes, shook my head—murmuring, No, I had no prejudices—all the time my true unreliable quirkiness filled my head. All I could do was resolve to try to be fair.

By the third day, we'd struck up shipboard friendships. 9 There was a babbling camaraderie in the jury pool, and for lunch we plunged into that old, eclipsed, ethnic New York near City Hall—Chinese roast ducks hanging in the butcher's windows on Mulberry Street next door to an Italian store selling religious candles. We ate at Cucina Luna and Giambone's. Eating at Ping Ching's, we saw whole pigs, blanched white, delivered at the door. We watched an Oriental funeral with Madame Nhu the director waving the limousines on. The deceased's picture, heaped with flowers, was in the lead car, and all his beautiful daughters wept with faces disordered and long black hair streaming down. One of the Italian bands which plays on feast days was mourning over a single refrain—two trumpets, a clarinet, a mellophone and a drum.

As an alternate I sat in on the arguments for a rent-a-car 10 crash case, with four lawyers, each of whom liked to hear himself talk, representing the different parties. The theme was that we were New Yorkers and therefore streetwise and no fools. The senior fellow seemed to think that all his years of trying these penny-ante negligence affairs had made him very good indeed, whereas my impression was that the reason he was still trying them was because he was rather bad. The same afternoon I got on a jury to hear the case of a cleaning woman, sixty-four, who had slipped on the floor of a Harlem ballroom in 1967 and broken her ankle. She claimed the floor was overwaxed. She'd obviously been passed from hand to hand within the firm that had taken her case and had wound up with an attractive young man who was here cutting his teeth. What I liked about her was her abusive manner, which expected no justice and made no distinction at all between her own lawyer and that of the ballroom owner, though she was confused by the fact that the judge was black. He was from the Supreme Court, assigned to help cut through this backlog, had a clerk with an Afro, and was exceedingly brisk and effective.

The porter who had waxed the floor testified—a man of 11 good will, long since at another job. The ballroom owner had operated the hall for more than thirty years, and his face was fastidious, Jewish, sensitive, sad, like that of a concertgoer who is not unduly pleased with his life. He testified, and it was not *his* fault. Nevertheless the lady had hurt her ankle and been out of pocket and out of work. It was a wedding reception, and she'd just stepped forward, saying, "Here comes the bride!"

The proceedings were interrupted while motions were 12 heard in another case, and we sat alone in a jury room, trading reading material, obeying the injunction not to discuss the case, until after several hours we were called back and thanked by the judge. "They also serve who stand and wait." He said that our presence next door as a deliberative body, passive though we were, had pressured a settlement. It was for seven hundred and fifty dollars, a low figure to me (the court attendant told me that there had been a legal flaw in the plaintiff's case), but some of the other jurors thought she'd deserved no money; they were trying to be fair to the ballroom man. Almost always that's what the disputes boiled down to: one juror trying to be fair to one person, another to another.

On Friday of my first week I got on a jury to hear the 13 plight of a woman who had been standing at the front of a bus and had been thrown forward and injured when she stooped to pick up some change that had spilled from her purse. The bus company's lawyer was a ruddy, jovial sort. "Anybody here have a bone to pick with our New York City buses?" We laughed and said, no, we were capable of sending her away without any award if she couldn't prove negligence. Nevertheless, he settled with her attorney immediately after we left the challenge room. (These attorneys did not necessarily run to type. There was a Transit Authority man who shouted like William Kunstler; five times the judge had an officer make him sit down, and once threatened to have the chap bound to his chair.)

I was an alternate for another car crash. With cases in progress all over the building, the jury pool had thinned out, so that no sooner were we dropped back into it than our names were called again. Even one noteworthy white-haired fellow who was wearing a red velvet jump suit, a dragon-colored coat and a dangling gold talisman had some experiences to talk about. I was tabbed for a panel that was to hear from a soft-looking, tired, blond widow of fifty-seven who, while walking home at night five years before from the shop where she worked, had tripped into an excavation only six inches deep but ten feet long and three feet wide. She claimed that the twists and bumps of this had kept her in pain and out of work for five months. She seemed natural and truthful on the witness stand, yet her testimony was so brief and flat that one needed to bear in mind how much time had passed. As we'd first filed into the courtroom she had watched us with the ironic gravity that a person inevitably would feel who has waited five years for a hearing and now sees the cast of characters who will decide her case. This was a woeful low point of her life, but the memory of how badly she'd felt was stale.

The four attorneys on the case were straightforward youngsters getting their training here. The woman's was properly aggressive; Con Edison's asked humorously if we had ever quarreled with Con Edison over a bill; the city's, who was an idealist with shoulder-length hair, asked with another laugh if we disliked New York; and the realty company's, whether we fought with our landlords. Of course, fair-minded folk that we were, we told them no. They pointed out that just as the code of the law provides that a lone woman, fifty-seven, earning a hundred dollars a week, must receive the same consideration in court as a great city, so must the city be granted an equal measure of justice as that lone woman was.

Our panel included a bank guard, a lady loan officer, a

young black Sing Sing guard, a pale, slim middle-aged executive from Coca-Cola, a hale fellow who sold package tours
from an airline and looked like the Great Gildersleeve, and
me. If her attorney had successfully eliminated Spartans from
the jury, we'd surely award her something; the question was
how much. I wondered about the five months. No bones
broken—let's say, being rather generous, maybe two months
of rest. But couldn't the remainder be one of those dead-still
intermissions that each of us must stop and take once or twice
in a life, not from any single blow but from the accumulating
knocks and scabby disappointments that pile up, the harsh-
ness of winning a living, and the rest of it—for which the
government in its blundering wisdom already makes some
provision through unemployment insurance?

But there were no arguments. The judge had allowed the   17
woman to testify about her injuries on the condition that her
physician appear. When, the next day, he didn't, a mistrial
was declared.

For Study and Discussion

QUESTIONS FOR RESPONSE

1. What preconceptions do you have about the American jury system? What is the source of these preconceptions—television,
   books, movies?
2. What aspects of Hoagland's description of jury duty would encourage or discourage you from serving on a jury?

QUESTIONS ABOUT PURPOSE

1. Does Hoagland's analysis suggest that jury duty is a simple or a
   complex process? What do the first few sentences in paragraph 2
   suggest about the process? What does the rest of the essay demonstrate?
2. In what ways does Hoagland's analysis support or contradict his
   theories about contemporary attitudes toward "anciently universal experiences"?

QUESTIONS ABOUT AUDIENCE

1. How does Hoagland's use of the pronoun "we" in the first paragraph identify his audience?
2. How does Hoagland's description of his fellow jurors show his readers the difficulties a jury faces when it tries to arrive at a fair decision?

QUESTIONS ABOUT STRATEGIES

1. How does Hoagland use the lawyers' questions to illustrate the selection process? What kind of people are these questions designed to eliminate?
2. How does Hoagland use the five cases he heard as examples to illustrate different problems with the jury process? For example, what problem does the jury face in the last case?

QUESTIONS FOR DISCUSSION

1. Hoagland argues that jurors "really try to be better than themselves." What does this assertion suggest about how we judge people in our everyday lives?
2. Hoagland is assigned to Civil Court, where most of the cases are at least five years old. Having read Hoagland's testimony about these cases, how would you evaluate the effectiveness of the American legal system?

Elizabeth Winthrop was born in 1948 in Washington, D.C., and educated at Sarah Lawrence College. She worked for Harper and Row editing "Harper Junior Books" before she began her own career as author of books for children. She has written more than thirty such books, including *Bunk Beds* (1972), *Potbellied Possums* (1977), *In My Mother's House* (1988), and *The Battle for the Castle* (1993). Winthrop has twice won the PEN Syndicated Fiction Contest, once in 1985 with her story "Bad News" and again in 1990 with "The Golden Darters." In the latter story, reprinted from *American Short Fiction,* a young girl betrays her father by using their creation for the wrong purpose.

The Golden Darters

I WAS TWELVE YEARS old when my father started tying flies. It was an odd habit for a man who had just undergone a serious operation on his upper back, but, as he remarked to my mother one night, at least it gave him a world over which he had some control.

The family grew used to seeing him hunched down close to his tying vise, hackle pliers in one hand, thread bobbin in the other. We began to bandy about strange phrases—foxy quills, bodkins, peacock hurl. Father's corner of the living room was off limits to the maid with the voracious and destructive vacuum cleaner. Who knew what precious bit of calf's tail or rabbit fur would be sucked away never to be seen again?

Because of my father's illness, we had gone up to our summer cottage on the lake in New Hampshire a month

early. None of my gang of friends ever came till the end of
July, so in the beginning of that summer I hung around home
watching my father as he fussed with the flies. I was the only
child he allowed to stand near him while he worked. "Your
brothers bounce," he muttered one day as he clamped the
vise onto the curve of a model-perfect hook. "You can stay
and watch if you don't bounce."

So I took great care not to bounce or lean or even breathe   4
too noisily on him while he performed his delicate maneu-
vers, holding back hackle with one hand as he pulled off the
final flourish of a whip finish with the other. I had never been
so close to my father for so long before, and while he studied
his tiny creations, I studied him. I stared at the large pores
of his skin, the sleek black hair brushed straight back from
the soft dip of his temples, the jaw muscles tightening and
slackening. Something in my father seemed always to be
ticking. He did not take well to sickness and enforced
confinement.

When he leaned over his work, his shirt collar slipped down   5
to reveal the recent scar, a jagged trail of disrupted tissue.
The tender pink skin gradually paled and then toughened
during those weeks when he took his prescribed afternoon
nap, lying on his stomach on our little patch of front lawn.
Our house was one of the closest to the lake and it seemed
to embarrass my mother to have him stretch himself out on
the grass for all the swimmers and boaters to see.

"At least sleep on the porch," she would say. "That's why   6
we set the hammock up there."

"Why shouldn't a man sleep on his own front lawn if he   7
so chooses?" he would reply. "I have to mow the bloody
thing. I might as well put it to some use."

And my mother would shrug and give up.   8

At the table when he was absorbed, he lost all sense of   9
anything but the magnified insect under the light. Often
when he pushed his chair back and announced the comple-
tion of his latest project to the family, there would be a bit
of down or a tuft of dubbing stuck to the edge of his lip. I

did not tell him about it but stared, fascinated, wondering how long it would take to blow away. Sometimes it never did, and I imagine he discovered the fluff in the bathroom mirror when he went upstairs to bed. Or maybe my mother plucked it off with one of those proprietary gestures of hers that irritated my brothers so much.

In the beginning, Father wasn't very good at the fly-tying. He was a large, thick-boned man with sweeping gestures, a robust laugh, and a sudden terrifying temper. If he had not loved fishing so much, I doubt he would have persevered with the fussy business of the flies. After all, the job required tools normally associated with woman's work. Thread and bobbins, soft slippery feathers, a magnifying glass, and an instruction manual that read like a cookbook. It said things like, "Cut off a bunch of yellowtail. Hold the tip end with the left hand and stroke out the short hairs." [10]

But Father must have had a goal in mind. You tie flies because one day, in the not-too-distant future, you will attach them to a tippet, wade into a stream, and lure a rainbow trout out of his quiet pool. [11]

There was something endearing, almost childish, about his stubborn nightly ritual at the corner table. His head bent under the standing lamp, his fingers trembling slightly, he would whisper encouragement to himself, talk his way through some particularly delicate operation. Once or twice I caught my mother gazing silently across my brothers' heads at him. When our eyes met, she would turn away and busy herself in the kitchen. [12]

Finally, one night, after weeks of allowing me to watch, he told me to take his seat. "Why, Father?" [13]

"Because it's time for you to try one." [14]

"That's all right. I like to watch." [15]

"Nonsense, Emily. You'll do just fine." [16]

He had stood up. The chair was waiting. Across the room, my mother put down her knitting. Even the boys, embroiled in a noisy game of double solitaire, stopped their wrangling for a moment. They were all waiting to see what I would do. It was my fear of failing him that made me hesitate. I knew [17] that my father put his trust in results, not in the learning process.

"Sit down, Emily." [18]

I obeyed, my heart pounding. I was a cautious, secretive [19] child, and I could not bear to have people watch me doing things. My piano lesson was the hardest hour in the week. The teacher would sit with a resigned look on her face while my fingers groped across the keys, muddling through a sonata that I had played perfectly just an hour before. The difference was that then nobody had been watching.

"—so we'll start you off with a big hook." He had been [20] talking for some time. How much had I missed already?

"Ready?" he asked. [21]

I nodded. [22]

"All right then, clamp this hook into the vise. You'll be [23] making the golden darter, a streamer. A big flashy fly, the kind that imitates a small fish as it moves underwater."

Across the room, my brothers had returned to their game, [24] but their voices were subdued. I imagined they wanted to hear what was happening to me. My mother had left the room.

"Tilt the magnifying glass so you have a good view of the [25] hook. Right. Now tie on with the bobbin thread."

It took me three tries to line the thread up properly on the [26] hook, each silken line nesting next to its neighbor. "We're going to do it right, Emily, no matter how long it takes."

"It's hard," I said quietly. [27]

Slowly I grew used to the tiny tools, to the oddly enlarged [28] view of my fingers through the magnifying glass. They looked as if they didn't belong to me anymore. The feeling in their tips was too small for their large, clumsy movements. Despite my father's repeated warnings, I nicked the floss once against the barbed hook. Luckily it did not give way.

"It's Emily's bedtime," my mother called from the [29] kitchen.

"Hush, she's tying in the throat. Don't bother us now." [30]

I could feel his breath on my neck. The mallard barbules [31] were stubborn, curling into the hook in the wrong direction.

Behind me, I sensed my father's fingers twisting in imitation of my own.

"You've almost got it," he whispered, his lips barely moving. "That's right. Keep the thread slack until you're all the way around." 32

I must have tightened it too quickly. I lost control of the feathers in my left hand, the clumsier one. First the gold mylar came unwound and then the yellow floss. 33

"Damn it all, now look what you've done," he roared, and for a second I wondered whether he was talking to me. He sounded as if he were talking to a grown-up. He sounded the way he had just the night before when an antique teacup had slipped through my mother's soapy fingers and shattered against the hard surface of the sink. I sat back slowly, resting my aching spine against the chair for the first time since we'd begun. 34

"Leave it for now, Gerald," my mother said tentatively from the kitchen. Out of the corner of my eye, I could see her sponging the kitchen counter with small, defiant sweeps of her hand. "She can try again tomorrow." 35

"What happened?" called a brother. They both started across the room toward us but stopped at a look from my father. 36

"We'll start again," he said, his voice once more under control. "Best way to learn. Get back on the horse." 37

With a flick of his hand, he loosened the vise, removed my hook, and threw it into the wastepaper basket. 38

"From the beginning?" I whispered. 39

"Of course," he replied. "There's no way to rescue a mess like that." 40

My mess had taken almost an hour to create. 41

"Gerald," my mother said again. "Don't you think—" 42

"How can we possibly work with all these interruptions?" he thundered. I flinched as if he had hit me. "Go on upstairs, all of you. Emily and I will be up when we're done. Go on, for God's sake. Stop staring at us." 43

At a signal from my mother, the boys backed slowly away and crept up to their room. She followed them. I felt all 44 alone, as trapped under my father's piercing gaze as the hook in the grip of its vise.

We started again. This time my fingers were trembling so much that I ruined three badger hackle feathers, stripping off the useless webbing at the tip. My father did not lose his temper again. His voice dropped to an even, controlled monotone that scared me more than his shouting. After an hour of painstaking labor, we reached the same point with the stubborn mallard feathers curling into the hook. Once, twice, I repinched them under the throat, but each time they slipped away from me. Without a word, my father stood up and leaned over me. With his cheek pressed against my hair, he reached both hands around and took my fingers in his. I longed to surrender the tools to him and slide away off the chair, but we were so close to the end. He captured the curling stem with the thread and trapped it in place with three quick wraps. 45

"Take your hands away carefully," he said. "I'll do the whip finish. We don't want to risk losing it now." 46

I did as I was told, sat motionless with his arms around me, my head tilted slightly to the side so he could have the clear view through the magnifying glass. He cemented the head, wiped the excess glue from the eye with a waste feather, and hung my golden darter on the tackle box handle to dry. When at last he pulled away, I breathlessly slid my body back against the chair. I was still conscious of the havoc my clumsy hands or an unexpected sneeze could wreak on the table, which was cluttered with feathers and bits of fur. 47

"Now, that's the fly you tied, Emily. Isn't it beautiful?" 48

I nodded. "Yes, Father." 49

"Tomorrow, we'll do another one. An olive grouse. Smaller hook but much less complicated body. Look. I'll show you in the book." 50

As I waited to be released from the chair, I didn't think he meant it. He was just trying to apologize for having lost his temper, I told myself, just trying to pretend that our time together had been wonderful. But the next morning when I came down, late for breakfast, he was waiting for me with the 51 materials for the olive grouse already assembled. He was ready to start in again, to take charge of my clumsy fingers with his voice and talk them through the steps.

That first time was the worst, but I never felt comfortable 52 at the fly-tying table with Father's breath tickling the hair on my neck. I completed the olive grouse, another golden darter to match the first, two muddler minnows, and some others. I don't remember all the names anymore.

Once I hid upstairs, pretending to be immersed in my 53 summer reading books, but he came looking for me.

"Emily," he called. "Come on down. Today we'll start the 54 lead-winged coachman. I've got everything set up for you."

I lay very still and did not answer. 55

"Gerald," I heard my mother say. "Leave the child alone. 56 You're driving her crazy with those flies."

"Nonsense," he said, and started up the dark, wooden 57 stairs, one heavy step at a time.

I put my book down and rolled slowly off the bed so that 58 by the time he reached the door of my room, I was on my feet, ready to be led back downstairs to the table.

Although we never spoke about it, my mother became 59 oddly insistent that I join her on trips to the library or the general store.

"Are you going out again, Emily?" my father would call 60 after me. "I was hoping we'd get some work done on this minnow."

"I'll be back soon, Father," I'd say. "I promise." 61

"Be sure you do," he said. 62

And for a while I did. 63

Then at the end of July, my old crowd of friends from 64 across the lake began to gather and I slipped away to join them early in the morning before my father got up.

The girls were a gang. When we were all younger, we'd 65 held bicycle relay races on the ring road and played down at the lakeside together under the watchful eyes of our mothers. Every July, we threw ourselves joyfully back into each other's lives. That summer we talked about boys and smoked illicit cigarettes in Randy Kidd's basement and held leg-shaving parties in her bedroom behind a safely locked door. Randy was the ringleader. She was the one who suggested we pierce our ears.

"My parents would die," I said. "They told me I'm not   66
allowed to pierce my ears until I'm seventeen."

"Your hair's so long, they won't even notice," Randy said.   67
"My sister will do it for us. She pierces all her friends' ears at college."

In the end, only one girl pulled out. The rest of us sat in   68
a row with the obligatory ice cubes held to our ears, waiting for the painful stab of the sterilized needle.

Randy was right. At first my parents didn't notice. Even   69
when my ears became infected, I didn't tell them. All alone in my room, I went through the painful procedure of twisting the gold studs and swabbing the recent wounds with alcohol. Then on the night of the club dance, when I had changed my clothes three times and played with my hair in front of the mirror for hours, I came across the small plastic box with dividers in my top bureau drawer. My father had given it to me so that I could keep my flies in separate compartments, untangled from one another. I poked my finger in and slid one of the golden darters up along its plastic wall. When I held it up, the mylar thread sparkled in the light like a jewel. I took out the other darter, hammered down the barbs of the two hooks, and slipped them into the raw holes in my ear-lobes.

Someone's mother drove us all to the dance, and Randy   70
and I pushed through the side door into the ladies' room. I put my hair up in a ponytail so the feathered flies could twist and dangle above my shoulders. I liked the way they made me look—free and different and dangerous, even. And they made Randy notice.

"I've never seen earrings like that," Randy said. "Where   71
did you get them?"

"I made them with my father. They're flies. You know, for   72
fishing."

"They're great. Can you make me some?"   73

I hesitated. "I have some others at home I can give you," 74
I said at last. "They're in a box in my bureau."

"Can you give them to me tomorrow?" she asked. 75

"Sure," I said with a smile. Randy had never noticed 76
anything I'd worn before. I went out to the dance floor,
swinging my ponytail in time to the music.

My mother noticed the earrings as soon as I got home. 77

"What has gotten into you, Emily? You know you were 78
forbidden to pierce your ears until you were in college. This
is appalling."

I didn't answer. My father was sitting in his chair behind 79
the fly-tying table. His back was better by that time, but he
still spent most of his waking hours in that chair. It was as if
he didn't like to be too far away from his flies, as if something
might blow away if he weren't keeping watch.

I saw him look up when my mother started in with me. 80
His hands drifted ever so slowly down to the surface of the
table as I came across the room toward him. I leaned over so
that he could see my earrings better in the light.

"Everybody loved them, Father. Randy says she wants a 81
pair, too. I'm going to give her the muddler minnows."

"I can't believe you did this, Emily," my mother said in a 82
loud, nervous voice. "It makes you look so cheap."

"They don't make me look cheap, do they, Father?" I 83
swung my head so he could see how they bounced, and my
hip accidentally brushed the table. A bit of rabbit fur floated
up from its pile and hung in the air for a moment before it
settled down on top of the foxy quills.

"For God's sake, Gerald, speak to her," my mother said 84
from her corner.

He stared at me for a long moment as if he didn't know 85
who I was anymore, as I were a trusted associate who had
committed some treacherous and unspeakable act. "That is
not the purpose for which the flies were intended," he said.

"Oh, I know that," I said quickly. "But they look good 86
this way, don't they?"

He stood up and considered me in silence for a long time   87
across the top of the table lamp.

"No, they don't," he finally said. "They're hanging upside   88
down."

Then he turned off the light and I couldn't see his face   89
anymore.

COMMENT ON "THE GOLDEN DARTERS"

"The Golden Darters" questions the purpose of learning a particular process. Emily's father decides to tie fishing flies to help him recuperate from back surgery. Although he is clumsy at first, he masters the tools, the procedure, and the artistry of tying. He has a goal in mind—to "attach [the flies] to a tippet, wade into a stream, and lure a rainbow trout out of his quiet pool." Emily's father decides to teach her what he has learned, even though his presence makes her nervous and her mistakes complicate the work process. Emily eventually escapes his obsession and joins her girlfriends to learn other procedures—smoking, leg-shaving, ear-piercing. The last procedure enables Emily to experiment—to wear two yellow darters as earrings to the club dance. Although she dazzles her friends, she disappoints her father, who sees her experiment as a betrayal.

Process Analysis as a Writing Strategy

1. Write an essay for the readers of a magazine such as *Popular Mechanics* in which you give directions on how to solve a simple mechanical problem. Like Tom and Ray Magliozzi, you may want to analyze how the process is supposed to work before you give directions on how to correct the process once it goes wrong. You may also want to present the worst-case results if your readers don't take care of this simple problem.

2. Provide information for the members of your writing class on the steps you followed to complete an educational project such as writing a research paper. Like Nikki Giovanni, you may want to explain these steps to a particular group of students.

3. Lars Eighner's "My Daily Dives in the Dumpster" raises significant questions about how our culture views the processes of consuming, disposing, and conserving. Construct a portrait of a conscientious consumer, and then analyze the processes he or she would use to maintain an ethically responsible relationship to the environment.

4. Analyze the various steps in a political process (casting a vote) or economic process (purchasing stock). Assume that your audience watches a lot of television. Explain how the process you are analyzing (selecting a jury) differs from the process they see represented on the tube.

5. Analyze a cultural process that tests "a person's ability to get out of a sticky situation." Illustrate how the process serves as a metaphor for the culture. Like Philip Weiss, you may want to cite evidence from the movies or local news stories to support your theory.

6. Analyze a process that confuses or intimidates people, particularly when other people are watching. Elizabeth Winthrop's short story "The Golden Darters" is obviously a good source for this assignment. Your job is to describe the intricate steps of the physical tasks and to speculate on why the presence of the observer (a teacher, a relative, a friend) makes the task so difficult.

COMPARISON AND CONTRAST

Technically speaking, when you **compare** two or more things, you're looking for similarities; and when you **contrast** them, you're looking for differences. In practice, of course, the operations are opposite sides of the same coin, and one implies the other. When you look for what's similar, you will also notice what is different. You can compare things at all levels, from the trivial (plaid shoelaces and plain ones) to the really serious (the differences between a career in medicine and one in advertising). Often when you compare things at a serious level, you do so to make a choice. That's why it's helpful to know how to organize your thinking so that you can analyze similarities and differences in a systematic, useful way that brings out significant differences. It's particularly helpful to have such a system when you are going to write a comparison-and-contrast essay.

PURPOSE

You can take two approaches to writing comparison-and-contrast essays; each has a different purpose. You can make a *strict* comparison, exploring the relationship between things in the same class, or you can do a *fanciful* comparison, looking at the relationship among things from different classes.

When you write a *strict* comparison, you compare only things that are truly alike—actors with actors, musicians with musicians, but *not* actors with musicians. You're trying to find similar information about both your subjects. For instance, what are the characteristics of actors, whether they are movie or stage actors? How are jazz musicians and classical musicians alike, even if their music is quite different? In a strict comparison, you probably also want to show how two things in the same class are different in important ways. Often when you focus your comparison on differences, you do so in order to make a judgment and, finally, a choice. That's one of the main reasons people make comparisons, whether they're shopping or writing.

When you write a *fanciful* comparison, you try to set up an imaginative, illuminating comparison between two things that don't seem at all alike, and you do it for a definite reason: to help explain and clarify a complex idea. For instance, the human heart is often compared to a pump—a fanciful and useful comparison that enables one to envision the heart at work. You can use similar fanciful comparisons to help your readers see new dimensions to events. For instance, you can compare the astronauts landing on the moon to Columbus discovering the New World, or you can compare the increased drug use among young people to an epidemic spreading through part of our culture.

You may find it difficult to construct an entire essay around a fanciful comparison—such attempts tax the most creative energy and can quickly break down. Probably you can use this method of comparison most effectively as a device for enlivening your writing and highlighting dramatic similarities. When you're drawing fanciful comparisons, you're not very likely to be comparing to make judgments or recommend choices. Instead, your purpose in writing a fanciful comparison is to catch your readers' attention and show new connections between unlike things.

AUDIENCE

As you plan a comparison-and-contrast essay, think ahead about what your readers already know and what they're going to expect. First, ask yourself what they know about the items or ideas you're going to compare. Do they know a good deal about both—for instance, two popular television programs? Do they know very little about either item—for instance, Buddhism and Shintoism? Or do they know quite a bit about one but little about the other—for instance, football and rugby?

If you're confident that your readers know a lot about both items (the television programs), you can spend a little time pointing out similarities and concentrate on your reasons for making the comparison. When readers know little about either (Eastern religions), you'll have to define each, using concepts they are familiar with before you can point out important contrasts. If readers know only one item in a pair (football and rugby), then use the known to explain the unknown. Emphasize what is familiar to them about football, and explain how rugby is like it but also how it is different.

As you think about what your readers need, remember they want your essay to be fairly balanced, not 90 percent about Buddhism and 10 percent about Shintoism, or two paragraphs about football and nine or ten about rugby. When your focus seems so unevenly divided, you appear to be using one element in the comparison only as a springboard to talk about the other. Such an imbalance can disappoint your readers, who expect to learn about both.

STRATEGIES

You can use two basic strategies for organizing a comparison-and-contrast essay. The first is the *divided* or *subject-by-subject* pattern. The second is the *alternating* or *point-by-point* pattern.

When you use the *divided* pattern, you present all your information on one topic before you bring in information on the other topic. Mark Twain uses this method in "Two Views of the River." First he gives an apprentice's poetic view, emphasizing the beauty of the river; then he gives the pilot's practical view, emphasizing the technical problems the river poses.

When you use the *alternating* pattern, you work your way through the comparison point by point, giving information first on one aspect of the topic, then on the other. If Mark Twain had used an alternating pattern, he would have given the apprentice's poetic view of a particular feature of the river, then the pilot's pragmatic view of that same feature. He would have followed that pattern throughout, commenting on each feature—the wind, the surface of the river, the sunset, the color of the water—by alternating between the apprentice's and the pilot's points of view.

Although both methods are useful, you'll find that each has benefits and drawbacks. The divided pattern lets you present each part of your essay as a satisfying whole. It works especially well in short essays, such as Twain's, where you're presenting only two facets of a topic and your reader can easily keep track of the points you want to make. Its drawback is that sometimes you slip into writing what seems like two separate essays. When you're writing a long comparison essay about a complex topic, you may have trouble organizing your material clearly enough to keep your readers on track.

The alternating pattern works well when you want to show the two subjects you're comparing side by side, emphasizing the points you're comparing. You'll find it particularly good for longer essays, such as Edward T. Hall's "The Arab World," when you want to show many complex points of comparison and need to help your readers see how those points match up. The drawback of the alternating pattern is that you may reduce your analysis to an exercise. If you use it for making only a few points of comparison in a short essay on a simple topic, your essay sounds choppy and disconnected, like a simple list.

Often you can make the best of both worlds by *combining strategies*. For example, you can start out using a divided pattern to give an overall, unified view of the topics you're going to compare. Then you can shift to an alternating pattern to show how many points of comparison you've found between your subjects. Deborah Tannen uses a version of this strategy in "Rapport-Talk and Report-Talk." She begins by establishing the difference between private conversations and public speaking; then she uses an alternating pattern within each category to demonstrate the contrasts between the speaking styles of men and women.

When you want to write a good comparison-and-contrast analysis, keep three guidelines in mind: (1) *balance parts*, (2) *include reminders*, and (3) *supply reasons*. Look, for example, at how David McCullough arranges his comparison of Franklin Delano Roosevelt and Harry Truman so that he provides the same kind of information on each man. He also uses transitional phrases to show readers when he is discussing the presidents' differences and when he is analyzing their similarities. Finally, several times in the essay, he gives his rationale for highlighting "the little man from Missouri" at the expense of the legendary man from Hyde Park.

Bill McKibben uses similar strategies when he contrasts his firsthand experience with nature and his secondhand experience with nature by means of television, catalogs the various ways television distorts the way we think about nature, and reasons that our reliance on such images makes it difficult for us to understand and accept nature on its own terms.

USING COMPARISON AND CONTRAST IN PARAGRAPHS

Here are two comparison-and-contrast paragraphs. The first is written by a professional writer and is followed by an analysis. The second is written by a student writer and is followed by questions.

BRUCE CATTON
from "Grant and Lee: A Study in Contrasts"

So Grant and Lee were in complete contrast, representing two diametrically opposed elements in American life. Grant was the modern man emerging; beyond him, ready to come on the stage, was the great age of steel and machinery, of crowded cities and a restless, burgeoning vitality. Lee might have ridden down from the old age of chivalry, lance in hand, silken banner fluttering over his head. Each man was the perfect champion of his cause, drawing both his strengths and his weaknesses from the people he led.

Side notes: Uses alternating pattern 1. Grant (modern man) — Topic sentence establishes differences — 2. Lee (chivalric man) — Evokes similarity

Comment This paragraph demonstrates how comparisons can work on several levels at the same time. Catton not only contrasts Grant and Lee but also uses these famous generals to contrast two "diametrically opposed elements in American life"—the modern man and the chivalric man. Catton concludes his contrast by evoking a major similarity between the two men: each embodied the strengths and weaknesses of "the people he led."

NATHAN M. HARMS
Howard and Rush

Howard [Stern] and Rush [Limbaugh] seem like the ying and yang of talk radio. Howard is thin and shaggy and loves to bash entrenched, stodgy Republicans. Rush is fat and dapper and loves to bash traditional liberal Democrats. Howard, the defender of individual freedom, wants to sleep with every woman in America. Rush, the defender of family values, wants every American woman to stay home and take care of the kids. Although they may think the world works in different ways, Howard and Rush work in the world in the same way. They focus their shows on controversy, belittle those who disagree with them, package their "philosophies" in best-selling books, and thrive on their ability to create publicity and fame for themselves.

1. What specific points of differences does Harms see between Howard Stern and Rush Limbaugh?
2. What major personality trait does Harms suspect they share?

COMPARISON AND CONTRAST

Points to Remember

1. Decide whether you want the pattern of your comparison to focus on complete units (*divided*) or specific features (*alternating*).
2. Consider the possibility of combining the two patterns.
3. Determine which subject should be placed in the first position and why.
4. Arrange the points of your comparison in a logical, balanced, and dramatic sequence.
5. Make sure you introduce and clarify the reasons for making your comparison.

Mark Twain (the pen name of Samuel Clemens, 1835–1910) was born in Florida, Missouri, and grew up in the river town of Hannibal, Missouri, where he watched the comings and goings of the steamboats he would eventually pilot. Twain spent his young adult life working as a printer, a pilot on the Mississippi, and a frontier journalist. After the Civil War, he began a career as a humorist and storyteller, writing such classics as *The Adventures of Tom Sawyer* (1876), *Life on the Mississippi* (1883), *The Adventures of Huckleberry Finn* (1885), and *A Connecticut Yankee in King Arthur's Court* (1889). His place in American writing was best characterized by editor William Dean Howells, who called Twain the "Lincoln of our literature." In "Two Views of the River," taken from *Life on the Mississippi,* Twain compares the way he saw the river as an innocent apprentice to the way he saw it as an experienced pilot.

Two Views of the River

N OW WHEN I had mastered the language of this water, and had come to know every trifling feature that bordered the great river as familiarly as I knew the letters of the alphabet, I had made a valuable acquisition. But I had lost something, too. I had lost something which could never be restored to me while I lived. All the grace, the beauty, the poetry, had gone out of the majestic river! I still keep in mind a certain wonderful sunset which I witnessed when steamboating was new to me. A broad expanse of the river was turned to blood; in the middle distance the red hue brightened into gold, through which a solitary log came floating

1

black and conspicuous; in one place a long, slanting mark lay sparkling upon the water; in another the surface was broken by boiling, tumbling rings that were as many-tinted as an opal; where the ruddy flush was faintest, was a smooth spot that was covered with graceful circles and radiating lines, ever so delicately traced; the shore on our left was densely wooded, and the somber shadow that fell from this forest was broken in one place by a long, ruffled trail that shone like silver; and high above the forest wall a clean-stemmed dead tree waved a single leafy bough that glowed like a flame in the unobstructed splendor that was flowing from the sun.

When I mastered the language of the river,
I made a valuable acquisition, but I lost
something too.

There were graceful curves, reflected images, woody heights, soft distances; and over the whole scene, far and near, the dissolving lights drifted steadily, enriching it every passing moment with new marvels of coloring.

I stood like one bewitched. I drank it in, in a speechless rapture. The world was new to me, and I had never seen anything like this at home. But as I have said, a day came when I began to cease from noting the glories and the charms which the moon and the sun and the twilight wrought upon the river's face; another day came when I ceased altogether to note them. Then, if that sunset scene had been repeated, I should have looked upon it without rapture, and should have commented upon it, inwardly, after this fashion: "This sun means that we are going to have wind to-morrow; that floating log means that the river is rising, small thanks to it; that slanting mark on the water refers to a bluff reef which is going to kill somebody's steamboat one of these nights, if it keeps on stretching out like that; those tumbling 'boils' show

2

a dissolving bar and a changing channel there; the lines and circles in the slick water over yonder are a warning that that troublesome place is shoaling up dangerously; that silver streak in the shadow of the forest is the 'break' from a new snag, and he has located himself in the very best place he could have found to fish for steamboats; that tall dead tree, with a single living branch, is not going to last long, and then how is a body ever going to get through this blind place at night without the friendly old landmark?"

No, the romance and beauty were all gone from the river.   3 All the value any feature of it had for me now was the amount of usefulness it could furnish toward compassing the safe piloting of a steamboat. Since those days, I have pitied doctors from my heart. What does the lovely flush in a beauty's cheek mean to a doctor but a "break" that ripples above some deadly disease? Are not all her visible charms sown thick with what are to him the signs and symbols of hidden decay? Does he ever see her beauty at all, or doesn't he simply view her professionally, and comment upon her unwholesome condition all to himself? And doesn't he sometimes wonder whether he has gained most or lost most by learning his trade?

For Study and Discussion

QUESTIONS FOR RESPONSE

1. Mark Twain is one of America's most famous historical personalities. Which of his books or stories have you read? What ideas and images from this selection do you associate with his other works?
2. Do you agree with Twain when he argues that an appreciation of beauty depends on ignorance of danger? Explain your answer.

QUESTIONS ABOUT PURPOSE

1. What does Twain think he has gained and lost by learning the river?

2. What does Twain accomplish by *dividing* the two views of the river rather than *alternating* them beneath several headings?

QUESTIONS ABOUT AUDIENCE

1. Which attitude—poetic or pragmatic—does Twain anticipate his readers have toward the river? Explain your answer.
2. How does he expect his readers to answer the questions he raises in paragraph 3?

QUESTIONS ABOUT STRATEGIES

1. What sequence does Twain use to arrange the points of his comparison?
2. Where does Twain use transitional phrases and sentences to match up the parts of his comparison?

QUESTIONS FOR DISCUSSION

1. Besides the pilot and the doctor, can you identify other professionals who lose as much as they gain by learning their trade?
2. How would people whose job is to create beauty—writers, painters, musicians, architects, gardeners—respond to Twain's assertion that knowledge of their craft destroys their ability to appreciate beauty?

David McCullough was born in 1933 in Pittsburgh, Pennsylvania, and educated at Yale University. He began his career with Time, Inc., writing
for a new magazine, *Sports Illustrated,* before
moving on to the United States Information
Agency, where his love of research prompted him
to begin writing for *American Heritage.* He is one
of America's most prominent historical writers.
Among his works are *The Johnstown Flood* (1968),
The Great Bridge (1972), and *The Path between the
Seas: The Creation of the Panama Canal, 1870–
1914* (1978). In "FDR and Truman," excerpted
from his Pulitzer Prize–winning biography *Truman* (1992), McCullough compares the public
images of the two presidents with their private
lives.

FDR *and* Truman

O N TUESDAY, AUGUST 18, 1944, in the shade of a magnolia tree said to have been planted by Andrew Jackson, Franklin Roosevelt and Harry Truman had lunch on the
South Lawn of the White House. Because of the heat,
Roosevelt suggested they take off their jackets. So it was in
their shirtsleeves, seated at a small round table set with crystal
and silver from the Coolidge years, that the two men posed
together for photographers for the first time.

In background, interests, personality, in everything from
the sounds of their voices to the kind of company they enjoyed to the patterns of their careers, they could not have
been much more dissimilar. Roosevelt was now in his twelfth
year in office. He had been President for so long and through
such trying, stirring times that it seemed to many Americans,

including the junior Senator from Missouri, that he was virtually the presidency itself. His wealth, education, the social position he had known since boyhood were everything Harry Truman never had. Life and customs at the Roosevelt family estate on the upper Hudson River were as far removed from Jackson County, Missouri, as some foreign land. Roosevelt fancied himself a farmer. To Truman, Roosevelt was the kind of farmer who had never pulled a weed, never known debt, or crop failure, or a father's call to roll out of bed at 5:30 on a bitter cold morning.

Truman, with his Monday night poker games, his Masonic   3

---

*Roosevelt had been given things all of his
life—Truman had been given
almost nothing.*

---

ring and snappy bow ties, the Main Street pals, the dry Missouri voice, was entirely, undeniably middle American. He had only to open his mouth and his origins were plain. It wasn't just that he came from a particular part of the country, geographically, but from a specific part of the American experience, an authentic pioneer background, and a specific place in the American imagination. His Missouri, as he loved to emphasize, was the Missouri of Mark Twain and Jesse James. In manner and appearance, he might have stepped from a novel by Sinclair Lewis, an author Truman is not known to have read. To anyone taking him at face value, this might have been George F. Babbitt having lunch with the President under the Jackson magnolia.

Roosevelt, on the other hand, was from the world of Edith   4
Wharton stories and drawings by Charles Dana Gibson. He was the authentic American patrician come to power, no matter that he loved politics or a night of poker with "the boys" quite as much as the Senator from Missouri, or that

he, too, was a Mason and chose a bow tie as many mornings as not, including this one. Roosevelt had been given things all of his life—houses, furniture, servants, travels abroad. Truman had been given almost nothing. He had never had a house to call his own. He had been taught from childhood, and by rough experience, that what he became would depend almost entirely on what he did. Roosevelt had always known the possibilities open to him—indeed, how much was expected of him—because of who he was.

Both were men of exceptional determination, with great reserves of personal courage and cheerfulness. They were alike too in their enjoyment of people. (The human race, Truman once told a reporter, was an "excellent outfit.") Each had an active sense of humor and was inclined to be dubious of those who did not. But Roosevelt, who loved stories, loved also to laugh at his own, while Truman was more of a listener and laughed best when somebody else told "a good one." Roosevelt enjoyed flattery, Truman was made uneasy by it. Roosevelt loved the subtleties of human relations. He was a master of the circuitous solution to problems, of the pleasing if ambiguous answer to difficult questions. He was sensitive to nuances in a way Harry Truman never was and never would be. Truman, with his rural Missouri background, and partly, too, because of the limits of his education, was inclined to see things in far simpler terms, as right or wrong, wise or foolish. He dealt little in abstractions. His answers to questions, even complicated questions, were nearly always direct and assured, plainly said, and followed often by a conclusive "And that's all there is to it," an old Missouri expression, when in truth there may have been a great deal more "to it."

Each of them had been tested by his own painful struggle, Roosevelt with crippling polio, Truman with debt, failure, obscurity, and the heavy stigma of the Pendergasts. Roosevelt liked to quote the admonition of his old headmaster at Groton, Dr. Endicott Peabody: "Things in life will not always run smoothly. Sometimes we will be rising toward the heights—then all will seem to reverse itself and start downward. The great fact to remember is that the trend of civili-

zation is forever upward. . . ." Assuredly Truman would have
subscribed to the same vision. They were two optimists at
heart, each in his way faithful to the old creed of human
progress. But there had been nothing in Roosevelt's experience like the night young Harry held the lantern as his
mother underwent surgery, nothing like the Argonne, or   *WWI*
Truman's desperate fight for political survival in 1940.

Roosevelt, as would be said, was a kind of master conjurer.   7
He had imagination, he was theatrical. If, as his cousins saw
him, Harry Truman was Horatio, then Franklin Roosevelt
was Prospero.

Truman was often called a simple man, which he was not.   8
"I wonder why we are made so that what we really think and
feel we cover up," he had once confided to Bess, and some
who knew him well would, in retrospect, feel he had withheld
too much of himself from public view, and that this was
among his greatest limitations. But in contrast to Franklin
Roosevelt—and it was Truman's destiny from this point forward to be forever contrasted to Roosevelt—he was truly
uncomplicated, open, and genuine. In private correspondence Truman could be extremely revealing, whereas
Roosevelt never dropped the mask, never poured his heart
out on paper as did Truman in hundreds of letters and notes
to himself, even after it was clear that he was to be a figure
in history.

To many Americans, Truman would always be the "little   9
man from Missouri." Roosevelt was larger than life, even in
a wheelchair. He had that force of personality that Truman
so admired in a leader and to a degree rarely equaled in the
ranks of the presidency. This, too, was something Truman
knew he did not have himself, as he knew he had no exceptional intellectual prowess, as had, say, Henry Wallace. "I am
not a deep thinker as you are," he had told Wallace only a
day earlier when asking Wallace for his help in the campaign
ahead. Yet Truman, as Republican Congressman Joe Martin
would write, was "smarter by far than most people realized."

In some ways Truman would have felt more in common,   10
more at ease, with the earlier Roosevelt, Theodore, had he

been host for the lunch. They were much more alike in temperament. They could have talked books, Army life, or the boyhood handicap of having to meet the world wearing thick spectacles. Or possibly the old fear of being thought a sissy. Like Theodore Roosevelt, and unlike Franklin, Truman had never known what it was to be glamorous.

The contrast in appearance between the President and his 11 new running mate was striking. Truman looked robust, younger than his age. The President, though only two years older, seemed a haggard old man. He had returned only the day before from his long mission to the Pacific, and from the sag of his shoulders, the ashen circles under his eyes, it was clear the trip had taken its toll. Truman, who had not seen the President in more than a year, was stunned by how he looked. Even the famous voice seemed to have no energy or resonance.

The lunch was sardines on toast. The conversation dealt 12 mainly with the campaign ahead and was not very private or revealing, since the President's daughter, Anna Roosevelt Boettiger, joined them. Truman would later repeat only one remark of Roosevelt's. The President told him not to travel by airplane, because it was important that one of them stay alive.

To his dismay, Truman noticed that Roosevelt's hand 13 shook so badly he was unable to pour cream in his coffee.

"The President looked fine and ate a bigger lunch than I 14 did," Truman told reporters afterward, already becoming party to the fiction of a steady hand at the helm. To Bess and Margaret, who were still in Independence, he described how Roosevelt had given him two roses, one for each of them. "You should have seen your Pa walking down Connecticut Avenue . . . with his hat blown up by the wind (so he looked like a college boy—gray hair and all) and two rosebuds in hand," he wrote, as if he hadn't a worry in the world. But arriving at his Senate office, he appeared noticeably upset. He was greatly concerned about the President, he told Harry Vaughan, and described how Roosevelt's hand had trembled so pouring his cream in his coffee that he put more in the saucer than in the cup. "His hands were shaking and he talks with considerable difficulty. . . . It doesn't seem to be any mental lapse of any kind," Truman said, "but physically he's just going to pieces."

In September, Truman took Eddie McKim to a White House reception, where McKim was so shocked by the President's appearance he wondered if Roosevelt would live long enough to be inaugurated, if Henry Wallace might become President after all. On the way out, as they were walking through the gate, McKim told Truman to turn and look back, because that was where he would be living before long. "I'm afraid you're right, Eddie," Truman said. "And it scares the hell out of me." 15

To his cousin Laura Delano, Roosevelt would later remark that he liked Harry Truman. "Harry is a fine man, intelligent, able, and has integrity. He doesn't know much about foreign affairs, but he's learning fast . . ." 16

How Truman honestly felt about Roosevelt can be deduced only from odd remarks to friends or in his private notes and correspondence, and the picture that emerges, though incomplete, is not complimentary. He called him Santa Claus. He called him a prima donna and a fakir. Writing about Bernard Baruch, whom he disliked, Truman would say, "There never was a greater egotist unless it was Franklin D." Another time, describing Roosevelt to Bess, he wrote, "He's so damn afraid that he won't have all the power and glory that he won't let his friends help as it should be done." 17

There was little subtle about Truman. He was never remote, rarely ever evasive. He had been raised on straight answers by people who nearly always meant what they said. Roosevelt wasn't that way. "You know how it is when you see the President," Truman once told Allen Drury. "He does all the talking, and he talks about what he wants to talk about, and he never talks about anything you want to talk about, so there isn't much you can do." 18

To Republican Owen Brewster, Truman said he had but one objection to the President and that was "he lies." 19

Such feelings, however, would never be publicly expressed, 20 not by Senator Harry Truman of his President, his Commander in Chief and leader of the Democratic Party. That would be unthinkably disloyal, not to say politically unwise and unprofessional. On occasion Truman could also rise to Roosevelt's defense and in a manner not unlike that of his father. At a meeting in Boston in a room at the Ritz-Carlton Hotel that fall, halfway through the campaign, Joe Kennedy began vilifying Roosevelt. "Harry, what the hell are you doing campaigning for that crippled son-of-a-bitch that killed my son Joe?" Kennedy said, referring to his oldest son, who had died in the war. Kennedy went on, saying Roosevelt had caused the war. Truman, by his later account, stood all he could, then told Kennedy to keep quiet or he would throw him out the window. Bob Hannegan had to step in and take Truman aside to remind him of how important Kennedy's money was to the Democratic Party.

For Study and Discussion

QUESTIONS FOR RESPONSE

1. Have you ever been compared constantly to someone else—a relative, a friend, a former student or employee? How did you respond?
2. How have you reacted to comparisons of American presidents—for example, Kennedy and Nixon, Reagan and Bush, Carter and Clinton?

QUESTIONS ABOUT PURPOSE

1. McCullough demonstrates that in almost every respect Roosevelt and Truman were different. What traits does he find the two men share?
2. How do the last two paragraphs of this selection illustrate McCullough's thesis that Truman was more complex than his public image indicated?

QUESTIONS ABOUT AUDIENCE

1. What assumption does McCullough make about his audience when he consistently discusses Roosevelt first and Truman second?

2. What does he assume about his readers when he compares Truman to a character in Sinclair Lewis and Roosevelt to a character in Edith Wharton?

QUESTIONS ABOUT STRATEGIES

1. How do McCullough's characterizations of Truman as Horatio, Hamlet's faithful friend, and Roosevelt as Prospero, the magician-ruler in Shakespeare's *The Tempest*, clarify their personalities?

2. How does McCullough compare Roosevelt's assessment of Truman and Truman's assessment of Roosevelt?

QUESTIONS FOR DISCUSSION

1. What does McCullough mean when he suggests that Truman probably had more in common with Theodore Roosevelt than with Franklin Roosevelt?

2. What are the advantages and disadvantages for a public or private citizen of seeing the world in simple terms and saying exactly what he or she thinks?

Deborah Tannen was born in 1945 in Brooklyn, New York, and was educated at the State University of New York at Binghamton, Wayne State University, and the University of California at Berkeley. She has taught English at the Hellenic American Union in Athens, Greece; Herbert H. Lehman College of the City University of New York; and Georgetown University. She has contributed articles on language to numerous scholarly books, including *Language and Social Identity* (1982) and *Languages and Linguistics in Context* (1986), and she has written several books on language and gender, including *Gender and Discourse* (1994) and *Talking from 9 to 5* (1994). Tannen's *That's Not What I Meant! How Conversational Style Makes or Breaks Your Relations with Others* (1986) attracted national attention because of its engaging study of the breakdown of communication between the sexes. In "Rapport-Talk and Report-Talk," excerpted from *You Just Don't Understand* (1989), Tannen compares the public and private conversational styles of men and women.

Rapport-Talk and Report-Talk

W HO TALKS MORE, then, women or men? The seemingly contradictory evidence is reconciled by the difference between what I call *public* and *private speaking*. More men feel comfortable doing "public speaking," while more women feel comfortable doing "private" speaking. Another way of capturing these differences is by using the terms *report-talk* and *rapport-talk*.

For most women, the language of conversation is primarily   2 a language of rapport: a way of establishing connections and negotiating relationships. Emphasis is placed on displaying similarities and matching experiences. From childhood, girls criticize peers who try to stand out or appear better than others. People feel their closest connections at home, or in settings where they *feel* at home—with one or a few people they feel close to and comfortable with—in other words, during private speaking. But even the most public situations can be approached like private speaking.

For most men, talk is primarily a means to preserve independence and negotiate and maintain status in a hierarchical

3

To men, talk is for information. To women, talk is for interaction.

---

social order. This is done by exhibiting knowledge and skill, and by holding center stage through verbal performance such as story-telling, joking, or imparting information. From childhood, men learn to use talking as a way to get and keep attention. So they are more comfortable speaking in larger groups made up of people they know less well—in the broadest sense, "public speaking." But even the most private situations can be approached like public speaking, more like giving a report than establishing rapport.

PRIVATE SPEAKING: THE WORDY WOMAN AND THE MUTE MAN

What is the source of the stereotype that women talk a lot? Dale Spender suggests that most people feel instinctively (if not consciously) that women, like children, should be seen and not heard, so any amount of talk from them seems like too much. Studies have shown that if women and men talk equally in a group, people think the women talked more. So

4

there is truth to Spender's view. But another explanation is that men think women talk a lot because they hear women talking in situations where men would not: on the telephone; or in social situations with friends, when they are not discussing topics that men find inherently interesting; or, like the couple at the women's group, at home alone—in other words, in private speaking.

Home is the setting for an American icon that features the   5
silent man and the talkative woman. And this icon, which grows out of the different goals and habits I have been describing, explains why the complaint most often voiced by women about the men with whom they are intimate is "He doesn't talk to me"—and the second most frequent is "He doesn't listen to me."

A woman who wrote to Ann Landers is typical: 6

> *My husband never speaks to me when he comes home from work. When I ask, "How did everything go today?" he says, "Rough . . ." or "It's a jungle out there." (We live in Jersey and he works in New York City.)*
>
> *It's a different story when we have guests or go visiting. Paul is the gabbiest guy in the crowd—a real spellbinder. He comes up with the most interesting stories. People hang on every word. I think to myself, "Why doesn't he ever tell me these things?"*
>
> *This has been going on for 38 years. Paul started to go quiet on me after 10 years of marriage. I could never figure out why. Can you solve the mystery?*
> —THE INVISIBLE WOMAN

Ann Landers suggests that the husband may not want to talk because he is tired when he comes home from work. Yet women who work come home tired too, and they are nonetheless eager to tell their partners or friends everything that happened to them during the day and what these fleeting, daily dramas made them think and feel.

Sources as lofty as studies conducted by psychologists, as 7 down to earth as letters written to advice columnists, and as sophisticated as movies and plays come up with the same insight: Men's silence at home is a disappointment to women. Again and again, women complain, "He seems to have everything to say to everyone else, and nothing to say to me."

The film *Divorce American Style* opens with a conversation 8 in which Debbie Reynolds is claiming that she and Dick Van Dyke don't communicate, and he is protesting that he tells her everything that's on his mind. The doorbell interrupts their quarrel, and husband and wife compose themselves before opening the door to greet their guests with cheerful smiles.

Behind closed doors, many couples are having conversa- 9 tions like this. Like the character played by Debbie Reynolds, women feel men don't communicate. Like the husband played by Dick Van Dyke, men feel wrongly accused. How can she be convinced that he doesn't tell her anything, while he is equally convinced he tells her everything that's on his mind? How can women and men have such different ideas about the same conversations?

When something goes wrong, people look around for a 10 source to blame: either the person they are trying to communicate with ("You're demanding, stubborn, self-centered") or the group that the other person belongs to ("All women are demanding"; "All men are self-centered"). Some generous-minded people blame the relationship ("We just can't communicate"). But underneath, or overlaid on these types of blame cast outward, most people believe that something is wrong with them.

If individual people or particular relationships were to 11 blame, there wouldn't be so many different people having the same problems. The real problem is conversational style. Women and men have different ways of talking. Even with the best intentions, trying to settle the problem through talk can only make things worse if it is ways of talking that are causing trouble in the first place.

BEST FRIENDS

Once again, the seeds of women's and men's styles are sown   12
in the ways they learn to use language while growing up. In
our culture, most people, but especially women, look to their
closest relationships as havens in a hostile world. The center
of a little girl's social life is her best friend. Girls' friendships
are made and maintained by telling secrets. For grown
women too, the essence of friendship is talk, telling each
other what they're thinking and feeling, and what happened
that day: who was at the bus stop, who called, what they said,
how that made them feel. When asked who their best friends
are, most women name other women they talk to regularly.
When asked the same question, most men will say it's their
wives. After that, many men name other men with whom they
do things such as play tennis or baseball (but never just sit
and talk) or a chum from high school whom they haven't
spoken to in a year.

When Debbie Reynolds complained that Dick Van Dyke   13
didn't tell her anything, and he protested that he did, both
were right. She felt he didn't tell her anything because he
didn't tell her the fleeting thoughts and feelings he experienced throughout the day—the kind of talk she would have
with her best friend. He didn't tell her these things because
to him they didn't seem like anything to tell. He told her
anything that seemed important—anything he would tell his
friends.

Men and women often have very different ideas of what's   14
important—and at what point "important" topics should be
raised. A woman told me, with lingering incredulity, of a
conversation with her boyfriend. Knowing he had seen his
friend Oliver, she asked, "What's new with Oliver?" He replied, "Nothing." But later in the conversation it came out
that Oliver and his girlfriend had decided to get married.
"That's nothing?" the woman gasped in frustration and disbelief.

For men, "Nothing" may be a ritual response at the start   15
of a conversation. A college woman missed her brother but

rarely called him because she found it difficult to get talk going. A typical conversation began with her asking, "What's up with you?" and his replying, "Nothing." Hearing his "Nothing" as meaning "There is nothing personal I want to talk about," she supplied talk by filling him in on her news and eventually hung up in frustration. But when she thought back, she remembered that later in the conversation he had mumbled, "Christie and I got into another fight." This came so late and so low that she didn't pick up on it. And he was probably equally frustrated that she didn't.

Many men honestly do not know what women want, and women honestly do not know why men find what they want so hard to comprehend and deliver.   16

"TALK TO ME!"

Women's dissatisfaction with men's silence at home is cap-   17
tured in the stock cartoon setting of a breakfast table at which a husband and wife are sitting: He's reading a newspaper; she's glaring at the back of the newspaper. In a Dagwood strip, Blondie complains, "Every morning all he sees is the newspaper! I'll bet you don't even know I'm here!" Dagwood reassures her, "Of course I know you're here. You're my wonderful wife and I love you very much." With this, he unseeingly pats the paw of the family dog, which the wife has put in her place before leaving the room. The cartoon strip shows that Blondie is justified in feeling like the woman who wrote to Ann Landers: invisible.

Another cartoon shows a husband opening a newspaper   18
and asking his wife, "Is there anything you would like to say to me before I begin reading the newspaper?" The reader knows that there isn't—but that as soon as he begins reading the paper, she will think of something. The cartoon highlights the difference in what women and men think talk is for: To him, talk is for information. So when his wife interrupts his reading, it must be to inform him of something that he needs to know. This being the case, she might as well tell

him what she thinks he needs to know before he starts reading. But to her, talk is for interaction. Telling things is a way to show involvement, and listening is a way to show interest and caring. It is not an odd coincidence that she always thinks of things to tell him when he is reading. She feels the need for verbal interaction most keenly when he is (unaccountably, from her point of view) buried in the newspaper instead of talking to her.

Yet another cartoon shows a wedding cake that has, on top, in place of the plastic statues of bride and groom in tuxedo and gown, a breakfast scene in which an unshaven husband reads a newspaper across the table from his disgruntled wife. The cartoon reflects the enormous gulf between the romantic expectations of marriage represented by the plastic couple in traditional wedding costume, and the often disappointing reality represented by the two sides of the newspaper at the breakfast table—the front, which he is reading, and the back, at which she is glaring. 19

These cartoons, and many others on the same theme, are funny because people recognize their own experience in them. What's not funny is that many women are deeply hurt when men don't talk to them at home, and many men are deeply frustrated by feeling they have disappointed their partners, without understanding how they failed or how else they could have behaved. 20

Some men are further frustrated because, as one put it, "When in the world am I supposed to read the morning paper?" If many women are incredulous that many men do not exchange personal information with their friends, this man is incredulous that many women do not bother to read the morning paper. To him, reading the paper is an essential part of his morning ritual, and his whole day is awry if he doesn't get to read it. In his words, reading the newspaper in the morning is as important to him as putting on makeup in the morning is to many women he knows. Yet many women, he observed, either don't subscribe to a paper or don't read it until they get home in the evening. "I find this very puzzling," he said. "I can't tell you how often I have 21 picked up a woman's morning newspaper from her front door in the evening and handed it to her when she opened the door for me."

To this man (and I am sure many others), a woman who objects to his reading the morning paper is trying to keep him from doing something essential and harmless. It's a violation of his independence—his freedom of action. But when a woman who expects her partner to talk to her is disappointed that he doesn't, she perceives his behavior as a failure of intimacy: He's keeping things from her; he's lost interest in her; he's pulling away. A woman I will call Rebecca, who is generally quite happily married, told me that this is the one source of serious dissatisfaction with her husband, Stuart. Her term for his taciturnity is *stinginess of spirit*. She tells him what she is thinking, and he listens silently. She asks him what he is thinking, and he takes a long time to answer, "I don't know." In frustration she challenges, "Is there nothing on your mind?"

For Rebecca, who is accustomed to expressing her fleeting thoughts and opinions as they come to her, *saying* nothing means *thinking* nothing. But Stuart does not assume that his passing thoughts are worthy of utterance. He is not in the habit of uttering his fleeting ruminations, so just as Rebecca "naturally" speaks her thoughts, he "naturally" dismisses his as soon as they occur to him. Speaking them would give them more weight and significance than he feels they merit. All her life she has had practice in verbalizing her thoughts and feelings in private conversations with people she is close to; all his life he has had practice in dismissing his and keeping them to himself. . . .

PUBLIC SPEAKING: THE TALKATIVE MAN AND THE SILENT WOMAN

So far I have been discussing the private scenes in which many men are silent and many women are talkative. But there are other scenes in which the roles are reversed. Returning to Rebecca and Stuart, we saw that when they are home alone,

22

23

24

Rebecca's thoughts find their way into words effortlessly, whereas Stuart finds he can't come up with anything to say. The reverse happens when they are in other situations. For example, at a meeting of the neighborhood council or the parents' association at their children's school, it is Stuart who stands up and speaks. In that situation, it is Rebecca who is silent, her tongue tied by an acute awareness of all the negative reactions people could have to what she might say, all the mistakes she might make in trying to express her ideas. If she musters her courage and prepares to say something, she needs time to formulate it and then waits to be recognized by the chair. She cannot just jump up and start talking the way Stuart and some other men can.

Eleanor Smeal, president of the Fund for the Feminist   25
Majority, was a guest on a call-in radio talk show, discussing abortion. No subject could be of more direct concern to women, yet during the hour-long show, all the callers except two were men. Diane Rehm, host of a radio talk show, expresses puzzlement that although the audience for her show is evenly split between women and men, 90 percent of the callers to the show are men. I am convinced that the reason is not that women are uninterested in the subjects discussed on the show. I would wager that women listeners are bringing up the subjects they heard on *The Diane Rehm Show* to their friends and family over lunch, tea, and dinner. But fewer of them call in because to do so would be putting themselves on display, claiming public attention for what they have to say, catapulting themselves onto center stage.

I myself have been the guest on innumerable radio and   26
television talk shows. Perhaps I am unusual in being completely at ease in this mode of display. But perhaps I am not unusual at all, because, although I am comfortable in the role of invited expert, I have never called in to a talk show I was listening to, although I have often had ideas to contribute. When I am the guest, my position of authority is granted before I begin to speak. Were I to call in, I would be claiming that right on my own. I would have to establish my credibility by explaining who I am, which might seem self-aggrandizing,

or not explain who I am and risk having my comments ignored or not valued. For similar reasons, though I am comfortable lecturing to groups numbering in the thousands, I rarely ask questions following another lecturer's talk, unless I know both the subject and the group very well.

My own experience and that of talk show hosts seems to 27 hold a clue to the difference in women's and men's attitudes toward talk: Many men are more comfortable than most women in using talk to claim attention. And this difference lies at the heart of the distinction between report-talk and rapport-talk.

REPORT-TALK IN PRIVATE

Report-talk, or what I am calling public speaking, does not 28 arise only in the literally public situation of formal speeches delivered to a listening audience. The more people there are in a conversation, the less well you know them, and the more status differences among them, the more a conversation is *like* public speaking or report-talk. The fewer the people, the more intimately you know them, and the more equal their status, the more it is like private speaking or rapport-talk. Furthermore, women feel a situation is more "public"—in the sense that they have to be on good behavior—if there are men present, except perhaps for family members. Yet even in families, the mother and children may feel their home to be "backstage" when Father is not home, "on-stage" when he is: Many children are instructed to be on good behavior when Daddy is home. This may be because he is not home often, or because Mother—or Father—doesn't want the children to disturb him when he is.

The difference between public and private speaking also 29 explains the stereotype that women don't tell jokes. Although some women are great raconteurs who can keep a group spellbound by recounting jokes and funny stories, there are fewer such personalities among women than among men. Many women who do tell jokes to large groups of people come from ethnic backgrounds in which verbal performance is highly valued. For example, many of the great women stand-up comics, such as Fanny Brice and Joan Rivers, came from Jewish backgrounds.

Although it's not true that women don't tell jokes, it is true that many women are less likely than men to tell jokes in large groups, especially groups including men. So it's not surprising that men get the impression that women never tell jokes at all. Folklorist Carol Mitchell studied joke telling on a college campus. She found that men told most of their jokes to other men, but they also told many jokes to mixed groups and to women. Women, however, told most of their jokes to other women, fewer to men, and very few to groups that included men as well as women. Men preferred and were more likely to tell jokes when they had an audience: at least two, often four or more. Women preferred a small audience of one or two, rarely more than three. Unlike men, they were reluctant to tell jokes in front of people they didn't know well. Many women flatly refused to tell jokes they knew if there were four or more in the group, promising to tell them later in private. Men never refused the invitation to tell jokes.

All of Mitchell's results fit in with the picture I have been drawing of public and private speaking. In a situation in which there are more people in the audience, more men, or more strangers, joke telling, like any other form of verbal performance, requires speakers to claim center stage and prove their abilities. These are the situations in which many women are reluctant to talk. In a situation that is more private, because the audience is small, familiar, and perceived to be members of a community (for example, other women), they are more likely to talk.

The idea that telling jokes is a kind of self-display does not imply that it is selfish or self-centered. The situation of joke telling illustrates that status and connection entail each other. Entertaining others is a way of establishing connections with them, and telling jokes can be a kind of gift giving, where the joke is a gift that brings pleasure to receivers. The key issue is asymmetry: One person is the teller and the others are the audience. If these roles are later exchanged— for example, if the joke telling becomes a round in which one person after another takes the role of teller—then there is symmetry on the broad scale, if not in the individual act. However, if women habitually take the role of appreciative audience and never take the role of joke teller, the asymmetry of the individual joke telling is diffused through the larger interaction as well. This is a hazard for women. A hazard for men is that continually telling jokes can be distancing. This is the effect felt by a man who complained that when he talks to his father on the phone, all his father does is tell him jokes. An extreme instance of a similar phenomenon is the class clown, who, according to teachers, is nearly always a boy.

RAPPORT-TALK IN PUBLIC

Just as conversations that take place at home among friends   33
can be like public speaking, even a public address can be like private speaking: for example, by giving a lecture full of personal examples and stories.

At the executive committee of a fledgling professional   34
organization, the outgoing president, Fran, suggested that the organization adopt the policy of having presidents deliver a presidential address. To explain and support her proposal, she told a personal anecdote: Her cousin was the president of a more established professional organization at the time that Fran held the same position in this one. Fran's mother had been talking to her cousin's mother on the telephone. Her cousin's mother told Fran's mother that her daughter was preparing her presidential address, and she asked when Fran's presidential address was scheduled to be. Fran was embarrassed to admit to her mother that she was not giving one. This made her wonder whether the organization's professional identity might not be enhanced if it emulated the more established organizations.

Several men on the committee were embarrassed by Fran's   35
reference to her personal situation and were not convinced by her argument. It seemed to them not only irrelevant but unseemly to talk about her mother's telephone conversations

at an executive committee meeting. Fran had approached the meeting—a relatively public context—as an extension of the private kind. Many women's tendency to use personal experience and examples, rather than abstract argumentation, can be understood from the perspective of their orientation to language as it is used in private speaking.

A study by Celia Roberts and Tom Jupp of a faculty meeting at a secondary school in England found that the women's arguments did not carry weight with their male colleagues because they tended to use their own experience as evidence, or argue about the effect of policy on individual students. The men at the meeting argued from a completely different perspective, making categorical statements about right and wrong. 36

The same discussion is found in discussions at home. A man told me that he felt critical of what he perceived as his wife's lack of logic. For example, he recalled a conversation in which he had mentioned an article he had read in *The New York Times* claiming that today's college students are not as idealistic as students were in the 1960s. He was inclined to accept this claim. His wife questioned it, supporting her argument with the observation that her niece and her niece's friends were very idealistic indeed. He was incredulous and scornful of her faulty reasoning; it was obvious to him that a single personal example is neither evidence nor argumentation—it's just anecdote. It did not occur to him that he was dealing with a different logical system, rather than a lack of logic. 37

The logic this woman was employing was making sense of the world as a more private endeavor—observing and integrating her personal experience and drawing connections to the experiences of others. The logic the husband took for granted was a more public endeavor—more like gathering information, conducting a survey, or devising arguments by rules of formal logic as one might in doing research. 38

Another man complained about what he and his friends call women's "shifting sands" approach to discussion. These men feel that whereas they try to pursue an argument logically, step by step, until it is settled, women continually 39 change course in mid-stream. He pointed to the short excerpt from *Divorce American Style* quoted above as a case in point. It seemed to him that when Debbie Reynolds said, "I can't argue now. I have to take the French bread out of the oven," she was evading the argument because she had made an accusation—"All you do is criticize"—that she could not support.

This man also offered an example from his own experience.   40 His girlfriend had told him of a problem she had because her boss wanted her to do one thing and she wanted to do another. Taking the boss's view for the sake of argumentation, he pointed out a negative consequence that would result if she did what she wanted. She countered that the same negative consequence would result if she did what the boss wanted. He complained that she was shifting over to the other field of battle—what would happen if she followed her boss's will—before they had made headway with the first—what would happen if she followed her own.

For Study and Discussion

QUESTIONS FOR RESPONSE

1. How would you characterize your own conversational style?
2. How does context affect the way you talk? What situations make you shift styles?

QUESTIONS ABOUT PURPOSE

1. What does Tannen want to demonstrate about the relationship between communication failure and conversational style?
2. How do size (the number of people) and status (those people claiming authority) contribute to Tannen's comparison of rapport-talk and report-talk?

QUESTIONS ABOUT AUDIENCE

1. What assumptions does Tannen make about the probable gender of most of her readers?

2. How does Tannen assume her audience can benefit from her analysis?

QUESTIONS ABOUT STRATEGIES

1. How does Tannen use advice columns, movies, and cartoons to illustrate the problems of domestic communication?
2. How does Tannen use her own experience as a lecturer to compare the way men and women talk in public?

QUESTIONS FOR DISCUSSION

1. Do the men and women you know construct arguments according to Tannen's format? How many men use personal experience as evidence? How many women make categorical assertions?
2. To what extent do conversational styles depend on innate skill (personality type) or learned behavior (acquired habits)? To what extent is it possible (or desirable) to change styles?

Bill McKibben was born in 1960 in Palo Alto, California, and educated at Harvard University. He began his career as a staff writer for *The New Yorker*, focusing on environmental issues. In *The End of Nature* (1989) he assesses the ecological disasters that will occur if the industrialized world does not change its habits. In *The Age of Missing Information* (1992) he speculates on how television has changed our lives. In "Nature and Televised Nature," excerpted from the latter book, McKibben argues that television's representation of certain forms of nature destroys our understanding of the larger context of environmental systems.

Nature and Televised Nature

UNABLE THOUGH I was to forecast the weather, I retained sufficient mother wit to recognize that it had turned into a gorgeous day, and so I set out to climb Blackberry Mountain, Crow's smaller neighbor.

From the pond I followed a brook down to the valley between the peaks—it is a mossy cool trickle in the summer, and instead of clambering over deadfall along the banks you can hop easily from rock to rock down the creek. I stopped occasionally at the small clear pools to admire the water striders, their legs dimpling the tense surface, their small bodies casting impressive shadows on the creek bottom as they went about their inscrutable business.

When I reached the valley between the mountains, I could look up at the open cliffs at the top of Blackberry. Since there's no trail to the summit, I just hit out along a compass bearing through the woods. The bottom slopes have been logged in the last couple of decades—the sun pours into the clearings, which of course are luxuriant with thorny berry cane. I fought my way through, and after twenty minutes or so, as the slope steepened, rock patches began to appear—the trees were fewer and bigger, and in the shade of one hemlock I lay down to rest. After about ten minutes, at least a dozen small birds began to resume the activity I had interrupted with my noisy arrival. They were mostly small thrushes, and they flew in and out of the branches in what looked like a

When you get most of your information about nature through television, the "real" nature around you begins to seem dull.

high-speed game of tag, over and over, lighting now on a swaying bough, then launching themselves off into the air once more.

After my rest I climbed the remaining distance to Blackberry's long summit ridge, and walked out along the top of the steep cliffs that faced back to Crow. The wind was blowing below—I could hear it rush like white water and see where it was riffling the maple tops in the mountain valley— but up on top it was still, and the sun baked the fragrant pine needles. I was sitting, drinking from my canteen, when I saw a vulture appear way below in the draw between the mountains. He circled slowly and methodically up, holding his wings in a stiff, lacquered bow, never flapping, always soaring. Eventually, after perhaps a half hour, he was directly above me on the cliffs, perhaps a hundred feet in the air, still circling. He was joined there by four, then five, finally six others, circling so close I could count feathers. When they passed directly overhead it was nearly unbearable—almost erotic— this feeling of being watched. At moments I felt small and vulnerable, like prey; if they disappeared from view for a

4

minute I wanted to know where they were. But by the time I finally rose to go back to my tent on Crow, I felt almost protected, watched over. It had been thrilling—my heart was beating hard.

Still and all, by the standards of television nature, the water striders and the thrushes and even the vultures were hardly worth mentioning. I had not been gored, chased, or even roared at. I had failed to tranquilize anything with a dart; no creature had inflated stupendous air sacs in a curious and ancient mating ritual, or eaten its young, or done any of the other prodigious tricks that happen around the clock on nature television. You could spend nearly the whole day watching nothing but nature documentaries, and if you did you would emerge exhausted. Nature on TV is the job of a man named Graham or Ian or Nigel who makes every announcement ("Using his incisors like a comb, the marmot attends to his thick underfleece") sound like Churchill in wartime. The point of the show can be that, say, elephants are all but exterminated in a certain African refuge, but you can be sure that our host will find one. Not one—dozens. "I think there's a jolly good chance of sketching this lot," the host is saying as he piles out of his Land-Rover. "There's the matriarch—she's the one to watch. I'd be crazy to get too close to her. If I can reach that anthill I can get some good sketches. She's accompanied by uncles and aunties of all ages—the young males get kicked out because they get stroppy." On the voiceover, the narrator may be confessing the boring truth: "Lions are lazy—the males are the worst. They'll sleep twenty hours a day if they get the chance." But on the screen the lions are training their young by chasing jackals and other exotic game—Oooh, so much for that zebra. The man in the jeep, obligatory spare tire on the hood, tracks the lion pack toward a watering hole, never losing sight of them. He spies some ostriches: "Ostriches mean water, and water means life—and the lion feels an ancient urge. Perhaps she's come upon a place to start a pride." Oooh—lion sex! Cubs come tumbling out after a two- or three-minute gestation, full of play, and the timeless predatory cycle repeats—

5

Oooh, poor wildebeest. Switch the channel and someone is releasing a seal from a California aquarium. He starts to travel north, but suddenly a killer whale is on his tail. A brief respite in a kelp bed ("It's the life of Riley, lying on your back and eating crab so fresh it tries to walk away") and then our seal resumes his trip up the coast to the Pribilofs, where the breeding beach is a great heaving mass of flippers. At the precise moment our hero washes ashore, the men appear with the baseball bats for the annual fur harvest; fortunately he retreats to the safety of the ocean before they can get him, still alive for the documentaries that will surely follow.

It would be churlish to complain about these gorgeous   6
films. It would be even more churlish to quote from a recent interview in *Entertainment Weekly* with Wolfgang Bayer. An acclaimed nature photographer who's made dozens of TV films, he tells of hoisting tame, declawed jaguars into trees for action scenes, and spray-painting pet-shop ferrets till they're ringers for the nearly extinct black-footed variety, and starving piranhas so they'll attack with more ferocity. He once did a show on an Amazonian tarantula that occasionally eats birds. How often does it eat birds, asked the reporter? "As often as you throw them to him," he says. It would be churlish because TV nature films have without any question done an immense amount of good—species exist today that would be fossil records if Philo Farnsworth hadn't invented the picture tube. Your can of tuna has a little "dolphin-safe" symbol on it because in 1963 Chuck Connors starred in a film called *Flipper,* which gave birth to a TV show of the same name. The movie version was shown on May 3—in the month of May alone it was on the Disney Channel five times and on Cinemax twice, so presumably each new generation sees the boy battle his stern, old-fashioned father, who actually believes dolphins are a threat to his fishery. "If they come, we'll kill them. We have no choice," the father says. The rise of environmental consciousness over the intervening three decades can be felt in just how shocking this attitude now seems. Some fishermen still kill dolphins, but they try to hide their work because nearly everyone agrees it is a sick waste;

in 1963, obviously, *not* killing dolphins was regarded as revolutionary, and *Flipper* is a key reason for the change.

In 1963, too, the sperm-whale kill reached its peak, claiming about thirty thousand of the great beasts. We think of whaling as being at its height in the last century, when Nantucket men and Gloucester men and Mystic men and the men of a dozen other ports that are now pricy tourist attractions sailed the globe in search of lamp oil. But the slaughter continued, except of those species that were already reduced below commercial levels, until about the time that a slight Frenchman took to the TV screens. On any given time that day you can see Jacques Cousteau, the John Muir of the deep, two or three times—here he is in the sea grass beds of Australia, a safe pasture for sea cows now threatened by sand-mining; here he is working to "cweate a weef, shimmawing with life." His son Michel is apparently taking over the family trade, and has perfected the sad Gallic intonations of his dad. He is swimming next to a giant grouper—"I hardly ever see a fish so large anymore, which were my constant companions when I began diving. I cannot resist reaching out to this veteran of living, as if to touch the past, the time when big fish were nothing more than that." Cousteau's success can be measured in the sea, where remnant populations of some species survive because of great human efforts, and even more in the popular mind—a four-year-old boy just spent the weekend with us, and his conversation rarely strayed from the topic of killer whales, a species that until quite recently stirred loathing and not love.

Still, measured in the largest terms, such appeals aren't working. That is, virtually everyone in the industrialized world has a television and has presumably, if only by accident, seen many hours of gorgeous nature films—seen a more diverse and wondrous natural world than man could ever have seen before. And yet we're still not willing to do anything very drastic to save that world. We'll buy dolphin-safe tuna if it doesn't cost much extra, but we won't cut back on driving and consuming electricity and doing the other things that lead to global warming, even though the world now loses

as much as 5 percent of its coral reefs annually due to higher
water temperatures likely caused by the greenhouse effect.
Species continue to disappear, and at an accelerating rate;
presidents continue to propose, say, drilling for oil in the
Arctic National Wildlife Refuge, square in the middle of an
enormous caribou herd. Why can't Graham and Ian and
Nigel stop this?

They can't, I think, because for all their dart guns and   9
millions of feet of film they actually get across remarkably
little information—much less than you'd acquire almost unconsciously from a good long hike. Half the time they spe-
cialize in misinformation, undercutting their message with
their pictures. The Englishman is telling you that this great
flightless bird is on the edge of extinction, but for half an
hour he is showing you endless pictures of this great flightless
bird, so how bad could it be? The actual numbers of surviving
big mammals are astoundingly small—grizzly bears in the
lower forty-eight states can be counted in the hundreds. In
fact, you've probably seen a large fraction of them at one time
or another, wandering slowly through the telephoto field of
a Yellowstone camera. But they appear so often they seem
numerous. No one shows film of the weeks in camp waiting
for the damned gorillas to appear—a documentary of trees
that used to be inhabited by the ancient manlike primates but
no longer are is a documentary people wouldn't watch,
though that void is the true revelation about an awful lot of
the world.

Something even more insidious happens when you get   10
most of your nature through television, though—the "real"
nature around you, even when it's intact, begins to seem dull.
Mr. Bayer, the man with the spray-painted ferrets, said, "If
we showed viewers only natural, unadulterated filmmaking,
wildlife filmmakers would be out of business in a year, it'd be
so boring." So, instead, nature films are like the highlight
clips they show on the evening sportscast, all rim-bending
slam dunks and bleachers-clearing home runs and knee-
crumpling knockout punches. If you'd been raised on a
steady diet of such footage and then you went to a game,

you'd feel cheated—what is all this business with singles and pop flies? Why do the hockey players skate around for so long between fights? The highlights films erode appreciation for the various beauties of the game, some of which are small and patient.

The problem is even more severe with the natural world, where the ratio of observable high drama is much lower. A movie like *Benji the Hunted,* which was on the Disney Channel, presents the forest as a place where, in the space of a day, you encounter and must vanquish mountain lions, wolves, grizzlies, badgers, and so on right down Noah's list—it is a car-chase flick with animals. (And as impossible in its outcome as most car chases—Benji, a domesticated dog, has somehow retained the instinct necessary to outwit every predatory mammal of the North American continent, while acquiring a remarkably un-Darwinian compassion for the young of other species.) How disappointing, then, to go for a walk in a healthy Eastern woods and see so few bared claws. In many years hiking in the East I've happened across bears twice. Once, in Maine, I rounded a corner in a trail and there, three feet away, as lost in thought as I had been, sat a black bear. One look at me and she dived for the bushes—total contact time perhaps four seconds. A few years later, walking near my house with my wife, I heard a noise in a treetop and all of a sudden another black bear, roughly the size and shape of a large sofa, dropped to the ground a few yards away. She glowered in our direction and then lit out the opposite way. Time of engagement: maybe seven seconds. Those were grand encounters, and they've spiced every other day I've spent in the woods—on the way up Blackberry Mountain, for instance, I sang as I waded through the berry bushes, aware that this is where any bear with a stomach would be. But if I counted as dramatic only those days when I actually saw a big fierce mammal, I would think the forest a boring place indeed.

Big animals are fairly scarce in the best of conditions, and understandably shy—an Adirondack hunter last fall shot a bear that biologists, studying his teeth, determined was forty-

three years old. That is, he'd been hiding out up here since
before Truman beat Dewey. When you do see large animals
it's usually at a pretty good distance, not right up close as on
TV—you can rarely sneak up on, say, a heron the way you
can with a zoom lens. (On the other hand, you need a big,
natural field of vision to get a sense of the graceful spookiness
with which they glide.) But even if you did see a rare animal,
and somehow managed to creep up real close, chances are it
wouldn't be doing anything all that amazing. Chances are it
would be lying in the sun, or perhaps grooming itself, or
maybe, like the duck on the pond, swimming back and forth.
A lot of animals are remarkably good at sitting still (especially
when they suspect they're under surveillance), and this is
something TV never captures. The nature documentaries are
as absurdly action-packed as the soap operas, where a life's
worth of divorce, adultery, and sudden death are crammed
into a week's worth of watching—trying to understand "nature" from watching *Wild Kingdom* is as tough as trying to
understand "life" from watching *Dynasty*.

This is particularly true because, even at its best, TV covers   13
only a small slice of the natural world. There are perhaps ten
million (some say thirty million) species on earth; of those
that we know about and have catalogued, only a few meet
the requirements for extensive television coverage—cuteness
(or grotesqueness so complete it borders on the cute), great
amiability or ferocity, accessibility (it lives on grassland plains
or beaches, not in the deep ocean, badly lit caves, or rain-
forest canopies), correct size to show up well on camera, and
so on. Species with these characteristics seem to exist in
roughly the same ratio as human television actors to the
general population, and they are as consistently overexposed.
But even the most unengaging, hard-to-get-at, drab little
animal has a great advantage over any plant except a Venus's-
flytrap, and that is mobility. In its immense fear that we might
grow bored, TV has not yet acquired the courage necessary
to show an unmoving picture for very long, and so the only
hope of star-struck vegetation is time-lapse photography,
which works okay for orchids but doesn't do much for, say,

evergreens. Someone sent me a "working treatment" recently for a television program celebrating trees that is being made by a leading wildlife filmmaker. The "tease opening" features "intercutting of striking tree images with interview characters expressing

> Wonder
>
> Concern
>
> Reverence

followed by opening credits over breathtaking images of trees and forests" against an *"engaging mix of forest sounds, rain, and music."* The film covers rain forest, swamps, and the autumn blaze of color; it looks at furniture and at musical instruments made from wood; it covers bonsai and the Yellowstone fires, all in forty-seven and a half minutes, leaving twelve and a half for commercials. Beautiful, no doubt, but perhaps the wrong way to nurture appreciation for trees, whose most glorious characteristic is that they stay in the same place forever. Any time spent in a real forest gives you this information: a tree is of a piece with the soil from which it grows and the sky it rises into, part and parcel of the insect that eats at its middle and the bird that eats the insect, inseparable from the forest of other trees and yet perfect in its humped and gnarly isolation. And yet this is so hard to show—much easier to flash a sequoia on the screen and say this counts because it's big.

The upshot of a nature education by television is a deep fondness for certain species and a deep lack of understanding of systems, or of the policies that destroy those systems. For instance, one of the ads that may come on during this celebration of trees, as it did several times on May 3, is paid for by the Forest Products Council. "Today we have more trees than we did back in 1920," it says, "thanks in part to something our forest products companies do three million times a day—plant a tree." The visuals accompanying this reassuring voice are stunning—from the air we see a bend in a wilderness river with a rich and exuberant old forest spilling forth to the bank. There's a lot less of this kind of forest than there was in 1920, thanks in part (in whole, really) to something else the forest products companies do every day, which is cut down virgin stands of climax forest, the biologically diverse, marvelously complex ancient forest that covered much of this country when Europeans arrived. The forest products companies *do* plant trees. They plant them in nice straight rows, every sapling the same age and the same height and the same species, and then they drop herbicides from helicopters to keep down undesirable varieties; they create, in other words, sterile plantations for growing timber and pulp. And the forest products companies often perform this public service on public lands, under the guidance of government employees. The great national forests, which cover so much of the western part of the nation, are mostly managed as timber farms; the trees, in many cases old-growth forests, are sold to lumber companies and then cut down. One of these public servants is Smokey Bear, whose commercials run all day and night. We all grew up believing Smokey hated forest fires because they fried Bambi's kin, but the truth is Smokey doesn't want you to burn the forest down because his employer, the Forest Service, wants to cut it down instead. You don't see this when you drive through a national forest, because the government employs an enormous corps of landscape architects whose whole job is to make sure the clearcuts are invisible. And you don't see it on TV because it's political, and a tree is a tree, and it's time to look at the fur seals again.

In 1990, according to the *New York Times,* the not-to-be-lived-without accessory was the "personal meadow, a mini-expanse of green grass growing ever-so-sweetly out of a gently rusticated plywood box." "They couldn't walk by without coming in to touch it," said one florist. "It's such a fresh look. People have very strong reactions to it." An interior designer who changes the sod in his foyer every two weeks when it begins to yellow says, "I see it as Eastern in its concept."

Like urban living, TV cuts us off from context—stops us 16
from understanding plants and animals as parts of systems,
from grounding them in ideas larger than "fresh" or fierce or
cute. And so we don't know what to make of them. We are
still pulled toward this natural world, with a tug so strong it
must be primal, but TV helps turn it into a zoo; hence most
of our responses are artificial. Animals amble across the screen
all day and night—I saw the same squad of marching fla-
mingos twice during the day on different networks. ("They're
stupid," said the handler on one of the programs. "It took
me six months to get them to walk in formation.") CNN, in
just a few hours, reported on a new virus that was spreading
among macaws, parrots, and cockatoos; an orphanage that
had been established for African elephants whose mothers
had been killed by poachers; a group of manatees in the
waterways of Florida who were being gouged by outboard
propellers; a white tiger being born in a zoo; some home
videos of dolphins dying in the tuna nets that a man had
risked his life to take; a debate about whether people should
be permitted to swim in tanks with dolphins; some "doomsday dolphins" that might be trained for ordnance work; and
a Navy plan to kill thirty-five thousand feral goats on San
Clemente island. The day's main animal feature was a constantly repeated story on the abuses of puppy breeders, a
story that also appeared on virtually every network's broadcast. The Humane Society had issued a report that morning—most pet store dogs, it turns out, come from breeders
in six Midwestern states, who in many cases raise them in
such horrid conditions that they sicken and die after purchase. Two big dogs and their owner came on the *Today* show
to chat with Bryant Gumbel about the problem; other networks aired film of puppies crowded together in wire cages.
"Her ear canal has been inflamed so long there's no longer
any hole in there," said one vet. "Her skin is dry, cracking,
bleeding in spots. Boy—I can imagine how uncomfortable
she is."

We all can. That's the marvelous thing about pets—our 17
visceral and natural affection for them offers an easy door for

human minds to enter into a larger than normal world, a
world where our preoccupations count for less. A dog or a
cat or a rabbit is a constant reminder that there is more than
us out there—our love for them is a healthy recognition of
that more. But when that love lacks a larger context, the
relationship turns mawkish. Everyone knows about pet ceme-
teries, but CNN carried the story of a cemetery where people
could be buried *with* their pets. The Fox affiliate offered news
of a New York company that will freeze-dry your dead pet so
you can keep him in your living room. A twenty-pound dog
will run you $1,200—"We charge by the pound, but on birds
we've got a flat price"—and take four months to prepare.
"After we got him back, we'd just put him in his normal
position, and people would walk up to him, pet him, joke
with him, and then notice he was dead," said one satisfied
owner. "Archie was our whole life. Everything we did was for
Archie. . . . Even though he wasn't going to be living, we
could still stroke him, still tell him how much we loved him."

The healthier relationships always had some content to   18
them—one of the local channels, for instance, carried a fine
report about the members of the Fairfax County police K-9
squad, German shepherds who live at the homes of their
handlers. "You get very used to grabbing the dog and loving
him up," said one cop. But it's a relationship based more on
respect—on an appreciation of a dog's nature, his gifts—than
on sentiment. "When he gets in the cruiser his personality
changes. You can actually see the transition. He has a little
dance he does—a twirl like 'Let's get rolling.'" One of the
German shepherds, Jake, was stabbed seven times but kept
on going—he collared the criminal despite his fatal wounds.
"They become such a part of you—it's like losing an arm or
a leg or a baby," said his distraught handler. But there was
no suggestion that Jake should be freeze-dried—he was too
real for that.

In somewhat the same way, the men on a few of the   19
angling programs showed some real connection with their
catch—they were both competitors and, in a strange sense,
colleagues. "This fish is exhausted beyond any of our beliefs,

it's fought so hard," said one hip-booted host of *Fish'n Can-ada.* "It's your duty as an angler to wait till she's fully revived before releasing her." Don Meissner, the host of *Rod 'n' Reel Streamside,* caught a big old brookie: "I tell you, my heart's just a poundin'. Holy cow, oh, oh, holy cow, look at that fish. . . . Since I got older, my feelings on fishing have changed tremendously. It's just to be out there. Not to kill something. Oh my—I'm shaking like a leaf." Now, you could argue that there's something perverse about catching a fish and letting him go, and you could argue that if people really *admired* a fish they wouldn't stick a barb through its lip and pull on it for a quarter of an hour. And if you argued any of those things you might be right. Still, there is an echo of something here, of the traditional respectful relationship between hunters and their quarry.

Even in the most civilized, that tug remains. A Cousteau 20 special on the Turner Broadcasting System showed crowds of Australians climbing off buses to wade along a beach where dolphins lolled in the surf. Some of the people were painfully stupid—sticking their fingers down the dolphin's blowhole. But most seemed genuinely filled with

> Wonder
>
> Concern
>
> Reverence

"In ze welcome of ze dolphins lies ze test of human wisdom," said Cousteau, right as usual. Do we appreciate dolphins for the tricks they can perform, for being like limited humans?— the trainer at a Hawaii dolphin show said that she knew her charge was "smart" because "he wants something for noth-ing." Do we appreciate them as an economic and recreational "resource," like the striped bass described by a hatchery director on *Virginia Wildlife?* (Captured fish are weighed to determine how much hormone, collected from the pituitaries of pregnant women, to inject them with—"Fish in captivity tend to hold back on their eggs, but this overrides that.") Or do we begin to understand again what once was common knowledge—that they're marvelous for their own reasons, that they matter independently of us?

That piece of information can come only when you accept [21] nature and its component parts on their own terms—small and placid and dull and parts of systems, as well as big and flashy and fierce and soulful. Alone on a mountain you do start slowly to learn this lesson—it's inevitable if you lie on your back for hours and watch the hawks just circle, or lie on your stomach and watch the ducks just swim. They are not there for you—they are there because the world belongs to them too. Learn this lesson too well and you are in trouble, for in our current world it will mostly bring pain, mostly breed hysteria. Even on television this pain occasionally surfaces. HBO was showing Diane Fossey's story, *Gorillas in the Mist*—it is the story of a kook, driven mad by her understanding of what was happening around her. On paper her actions look insane—she kidnaps poachers, imprisons them. But watching the gorillas, tugged by that old tug, you know why she did what she did. The gorillas so clearly *belong*. An even better film, and more remarkable considering it was made way back in 1958, is John Huston's *The Roots of Heaven,* an elephant story starring Errol Flynn that aired on the American Movie Channel. "Anyone who's seen the great herds on the march across the last free spaces knows it is something the world can't afford to lose," says the Flynn character, and of course he is right.

But the world *is* losing them—CNN is filled with the [22] pictures of dying elephants and of a dozen other creatures. This is perhaps the ultimate loss of information—too sophisticated to burn books, we burn the planet. Each day information leaks away—some branch of life that evolved for millions of years is gone, and the next day two more, and six the day after that. The world grows stupider, less substantial. And those of us who would fight have little ground on which to stand, for the tug at our hearts from the sad picture on the screen is no substitute for the deep and lifelong understandings we've let slip away.

For Study and Discussion

QUESTIONS FOR RESPONSE

1. What kind of "nature stories" do you watch on television?
2. What aspect of the show—the scenery, the animals, the plot, the narrator—engages your attention?

QUESTIONS ABOUT PURPOSE

1. Why does McKibben admit that "It would be churlish to complain about these gorgeous films?"
2. What thesis does he attempt to prove about the difference between "real nature" and televised nature?

QUESTIONS ABOUT AUDIENCE

1. What assumptions does McKibben make about his readers' "environmental consciousness"?
2. What assumptions does he make about their television viewing habits?

QUESTIONS ABOUT STRATEGIES

1. How does McKibben use the first four paragraphs to demonstrate the *complexity* of his experience with nature and its *inappropriateness* for a television show?
2. How do McKibben's comparisons of nature films with sports-highlight films, car-crash flicks, and soap operas clarify the purpose of his essay?

QUESTIONS FOR DISCUSSION

1. In what ways does "televised nature" provide us with "fondness for certain species" and a "lack of understanding of systems"?
2. Why does "televised nature" prevent us from understanding "what was once common knowledge" about "real nature"?

Edward T(witchell) Hall was born in 1914 in
Webster Groves, Missouri, and was educated at
Pomona College, the University of Denver, the
University of Arizona, and Columbia University.
An anthropologist, he has taught at the University
of Denver, Bennington College, and Illinois Institute of Technology, and since 1967 he has been
professor of anthropology at Northwestern University. His books include *Beyond Culture* (1976),
a study of the effects of physical settings on human
behavior; *The Hidden Dimension* (1977); *The
Dance of Life: The Other Dimension of Time*
(1983), an exploration of the concept of time from
many vantage points; *Understanding Cultural
Differences* (1990), a cross-cultural study of industrial management; and *West of the Thirties* (1994),
an account of his discoveries among the Navajo
and Hopi Indians. In "The Arab World," reprinted from *The Hidden Dimension,* Hall analyzes
the hidden assumptions and attitudes that divide
the Arab and Western worlds.

The Arab World

I N SPITE OF over two thousand years of contact, Western-   1
ers and Arabs still do not understand each other. Proxemic research reveals some insights into this difficulty.
Americans in the Middle East are immediately struck by two
conflicting sensations. In public they are compressed and
overwhelmed by smells, crowding, and high noise levels; in
Arab homes Americans are apt to rattle around, feeling exposed and often somewhat inadequate because of too much
space! (The Arab houses and apartments of the middle and

upper classes which Americans stationed abroad commonly occupy are much larger than the dwellings such Americans usually inhabit.) Both the high sensory stimulation which is experienced in public places and the basic insecurity which comes from being in a dwelling that is too large provide Americans with an introduction to the sensory world of the Arab.

BEHAVIOR IN PUBLIC

Pushing and shoving in public places is characteristic of Middle Eastern culture. Yet it is not entirely what Americans think it is (being pushy and rude) but stems from a different set of

---

Americans instinctively avoid touching others in public; to Arabs, there is no such thing as an intrusion in public.

---

assumptions concerning not only the relations between people but how one experiences the body as well. Paradoxically, Arabs consider northern Europeans and Americans pushy, too. This was very puzzling to me when I started investigating these two views. How could Americans who stand aside and avoid touching be considered pushy? I used to ask Arabs to explain this paradox. None of my subjects was able to tell me specifically what particulars of American behavior were responsible, yet they all agreed that the impression was widespread among Arabs. After repeated unsuccessful attempts to gain insight into the cognitive world of the Arab on this particular point, I filed it away as a question that only time would answer. When the answer came, it was because of a seemingly inconsequential annoyance.

While waiting for a friend in a Washington, D.C., hotel lobby and wanting to be both visible and alone, I had seated

myself in a solitary chair outside the normal stream of traffic.
In such a setting most Americans follow a rule, which is all
the more binding because we seldom think about it, that can
be stated as follows: as soon as a person stops or is seated in
a public place, there balloons around him a small sphere of
privacy which is considered inviolate. The size of the sphere
varies with the degree of crowding, the age, sex, and the
importance of the person, as well as the general surroundings.
Anyone who enters this zone and stays there is intruding. In
fact, a stranger who intrudes, even for a specific purpose,
acknowledges the fact that he has intruded by beginning his
request with "Pardon me, but can you tell me . . . ?"

To continue, as I waited in the deserted lobby, a stranger   4
walked up to where I was sitting and stood close enough so
that not only could I easily touch him but I could even hear
him breathing. In addition, the dark mass of his body filled
the peripheral field of vision on my left side. If the lobby had
been crowded with people, I would have understood his
behavior, but in an empty lobby his presence made me exceedingly uncomfortable. Feeling annoyed by this intrusion,
I moved my body in such a way as to communicate annoyance. Strangely enough, instead of moving away, my actions
seemed only to encourage him, because he moved even
closer. In spite of the temptation to escape the annoyance, I
put aside thoughts of abandoning my post, thinking, "To hell
with it. Why should I move? I was here first and I'm not
going to let this fellow drive me out even if he is a boor."
Fortunately, a group of people soon arrived whom my tor-
mentor immediately joined. Their mannerisms explained his
behavior, for I knew from both speech and gestures that they
were Arabs. I had not been able to make this crucial identification by looking at my subject when he was alone because
he wasn't talking and he was wearing American clothes.

In describing the scene later to an Arab colleague, two   5
contrasting patterns emerged. My concept and my feelings
about my own circle of privacy in a "public" place immediately struck my Arab friend as strange and puzzling. He said,
"After all, it's a public place, isn't it?" Pursuing his line of
inquiry, I found that in Arab thought I had no rights what-

soever by virtue of occupying a given spot; neither my place nor my body was inviolate! For the Arab, there is no such thing as an intrusion in public. Public means public. With this insight, a great range of Arab behavior that had been puzzling, annoying, and sometimes even frightening began to make sense. I learned, for example, that if *A* is standing on a street corner and *B* wants his spot, *B* is within his rights if he does what he can to make *A* uncomfortable enough to move. In Beirut only the hardy sit in the last row in a movie theater, because there are usually standees who want seats and who push and shove and make such a nuisance that most people give up and leave. Seen in this light, the Arab who "intruded" on my space in the hotel lobby had apparently selected it for the very reason I had: it was a good place to watch two doors and the elevator. My show of annoyance, instead of driving him away, had only encouraged him. He thought he was about to get me to move.

Another silent source of friction between Americans and Arabs is in an area that Americans treat very informally—the manners and rights of the road. In general, in the United States we tend to defer to the vehicle that is bigger, more powerful, faster, and heavily laden. While a pedestrian walking along a road may feel annoyed he will not think it unusual to step aside for a fast-moving automobile. He knows that because he is moving he does not have the right to the space around him that he has when he is standing still (as I was in the hotel lobby). It appears that the reverse is true with the Arabs, who apparently *take on rights to space as they move*. For someone else to move into a space an Arab is also moving into is a violation of his rights. It is infuriating to an Arab to have someone else cut in front of him on the highway. It is the American's cavalier treatment of moving space that makes the Arab call him aggressive and pushy.

CONCEPTS OF PRIVACY

The experience described above and many others suggested to me that Arabs might actually have a wholly contrasting set of assumptions concerning the body and the rights associated with it. Certainly the Arab tendency to shove and push each other in public and to feel and pinch women in public conveyances would not be tolerated by Westerners. It appeared to me that they must not have any concept of a private zone outside the body. This proved to be precisely the case.

In the Western world, the person is synonymous with an   8
individual inside a skin. And in northern Europe generally, the skin and even the clothes may be inviolate. You need permission to touch either if you are a stranger. This rule applies in some parts of France, where the mere touching of another person during an argument used to be legally defined as assault. For the Arab the location of the person in relation to the body is quite different. The person exists somewhere down inside the body. The ego is not completely hidden, however, because it can be reached very easily with an insult. It is protected from touch but not from words. The dissociation of the body and the ego may explain why the public amputation of a thief's hand is tolerated as standard punishment in Saudi Arabia. It also sheds light on why an Arab employer living in a modern apartment can provide his servant with a room that is a boxlike cubicle approximately 5 by 10 by 4 feet in size that is not only hung from the ceiling to conserve floor space but has an opening so that the servant can be spied on.

As one might suspect, deep orientations toward the self   9
such as the one just described are also reflected in the language. This was brought to my attention one afternoon when an Arab colleague who is the author of an Arab-English dictionary arrived in my office and threw himself into a chair in a state of obvious exhaustion. When I asked him what had been going on, he said: "I have spent the entire afternoon trying to find the Arab equivalent of the English word 'rape.' There is no such word in Arabic. All my sources, both written and spoken, can come up with no more than an approximation, such as 'He took her against her will.' There is nothing in Arabic approaching your meaning as it is expressed in that one word."

Differing concepts of the placement of the ego in relation   10 to the body are not easily grasped. Once an idea like this is accepted, however, it is possible to understand many other facets of Arab life that would otherwise be difficult to explain. One of these is the high population density of Arab cities like Cairo, Beirut, and Damascus. According to the animal studies described in the earlier chapters,[1] the Arabs should be living in a perpetual behavioral sink. While it is probable that Arabs are suffering from population pressures, it is also just as possible that continued pressure from the desert has resulted in a cultural adaptation to high density which takes the form described above. Tucking the ego down inside the body shell not only would permit higher population densities but would explain why it is that Arab communications are stepped up as much as they are when compared to northern European communication patterns. Not only is the sheer noise level much higher, but the piercing look of the eyes, the touch of the hands, and the mutual bathing in the warm moist breath during conversation represent stepped-up sensory inputs to a level which many Europeans find unbearably intense.

The Arab dream is for lots of space in the home, which unfortunately many Arabs cannot afford. Yet when he has space, it is very different from what one finds in most American homes. Arab spaces inside their upper middle-class homes are tremendous by our standards. They avoid partitions because Arabs *do not like to be alone*. The form of the home is such as to hold the family together inside a single protective shell, because Arabs are deeply involved with each other. Their personalities are intermingled and take nourishment from each other like the roots and soil. If one is not with people and actively involved in some way, one is deprived of life. An old Arab saying reflects this value: "Paradise without people should not be entered because it is Hell." Therefore, Arabs in the United States often feel socially and sensorially deprived and long to be back where there is human warmth and contact.

Since there is no physical privacy as we know it in the Arab

11

12

---

[1]I.e., earlier chapters of *The Hidden Dimension*.

family, not even a word for privacy, one could expect that the Arabs might use some other means to be alone. Their way to be alone is to stop talking. Like the English, an Arab who shuts himself off in this way is not indicating that anything is wrong or that he is withdrawing, only that he wants to be alone with his own thoughts or does not want to be intruded upon. One subject said that her father would come and go for days at a time without saying a word, and no one in the family thought anything of it. Yet for this very reason, an Arab exchange student visiting a Kansas farm failed to pick up the cue that his American hosts were mad at him when they gave him the "silent treatment." He only discovered something was wrong when they took him to town and tried forcibly to put him on a bus to Washington, D.C., the headquarters of the exchange program responsible for his presence in the U.S.

ARAB PERSONAL DISTANCES

Like everyone else in the world, Arabs are unable to formu-   13
late specific rules for their informal behavior patterns. In fact, they often deny that there are any rules, and they are made anxious by suggestions that such is the case. Therefore, in order to determine how the Arab sets distances, I investigated the use of each sense separately. Gradually, definite and distinctive behavioral patterns began to emerge.

Olfaction occupies a prominent place in the Arab life. Not   14
only is it one of the distance-setting mechanisms, but it is a vital part of a complex system of behavior. Arabs consistently breathe on people when they talk. However, this habit is more than a matter of different manners. To the Arab, good smells are pleasing and a way of being involved with each other. To smell one's friend is not only nice but desirable, for to deny him your breath is to act ashamed. Americans, on the other hand, trained as they are not to breathe in people's faces, automatically communicate shame in trying to be polite. Who would expect that when our highest diplomats are putting on their best manners they are also communicating

shame? Yet this is what occurs constantly, because diplomacy is not only "eyeball to eyeball" but breath to breath.

By stressing olfaction, Arabs do not try to eliminate all the body's odors, only to enhance them and use them in building human relationships. Nor are they self-conscious about telling others when they don't like the way they smell. A man leaving his house in the morning may be told by his uncle, "Habib, your stomach is sour and your breath doesn't smell too good. Better not talk too close to people today." Smell is even considered in the choice of a mate. When couples are being matched for marriage, the man's go-between will sometimes ask to smell the girl, who may be turned down if she doesn't "smell nice." Arabs recognize that smell and disposition may be linked. 15

In a word, the olfactory boundary performs two roles in Arab life. It enfolds those who want to relate and separates those who don't. The Arab finds it essential to stay inside the olfactory zone as a means of keeping tab on changes in emotion. What is more, he may feel crowded as soon as he smells something unpleasant. While not much is known about "olfactory crowding," this may prove to be as significant as any other variable in the crowding complex because it is tied directly to the body chemistry and hence to the state of health and emotions. . . . It is not surprising, therefore, that the olfactory boundary constitutes for the Arabs an informal distance-setting mechanism in contrast to the visual mechanisms of the Westerner. 16

FACING AND NOT FACING

One of my earliest discoveries in the field of intercultural communication was that the position of the bodies of people in conversation varies with the culture. Even so, it used to puzzle me that a special Arab friend seemed unable to walk and talk at the same time. After years in the United States, he could not bring himself to stroll along, facing forward while talking. Our progress would be arrested while he edged ahead, cutting slightly in front of me and turning sideways 17 so we could see each other. Once in this position, he would stop. His behavior was explained when I learned that for the Arabs to view the other person peripherally is regarded as impolite, and to sit or stand back-to-back is considered very rude. You must be involved when interacting with Arabs who are friends.

One mistaken American notion is that Arabs conduct all conversations at close distances. This is not the case at all. On social occasions, they may sit on opposite sides of the room and talk across the room to each other. They are, however, apt to take offense when Americans use what are to them ambiguous distances, such as the four- to seven-foot social-consultative distance. They frequently complain that Americans are cold or aloof or "don't care." This was what an elderly Arab diplomat in an American hospital thought when the American nurses used "professional" distance. He had the feeling that he was being ignored, that they might not take good care of him. Another Arab subject remarked, referring to American behavior, "What's the matter? Do I smell bad? Or are they afraid of me?"

Arabs who interact with Americans report experiencing a certain flatness traceable in part to a very different use of the eyes in private and in public as well as between friends and strangers. Even though it is rude for a guest to walk around the Arab home eying things, Arabs look at each other in ways which seem hostile or challenging to the American. One Arab informant said that he was in constant hot water with Americans because of the way he looked at them without the slightest intention of offending. In fact, he had on several occasions barely avoided fights with American men who apparently thought their masculinity was being challenged because of the way he was looking at them. As noted earlier, Arabs look each other in the eye when talking with an intensity that makes most Americans highly uncomfortable.

INVOLVEMENT

As the reader must gather by now, Arabs are involved with each other on many different levels simultaneously. Privacy in a public place is foreign to them. Business transactions in the bazaar, for example, are not just between buyer and seller, but are participated in by everyone. Anyone who is standing around may join in. If a grownup sees a boy breaking a window, he must stop him even if he doesn't know him. Involvement and participation are expressed in other ways as well. If two men are fighting, the crowd must intervene. On the political level, *to fail to intervene* when trouble is brewing is to take sides, which is what our State Department always seems to be doing. Given the fact that few people in the world today are even remotely aware of the cultural mold that forms their thoughts, it is normal for Arabs to view *our* behavior as though it stemmed from *their* own hidden set of assumptions.

FEELINGS ABOUT ENCLOSED SPACES

In the course of my interviews with Arabs the term "tomb" kept cropping up in conjunction with enclosed space. In a word, Arabs don't mind being crowded by people but hate to be hemmed in by walls. They show a much greater overt sensitivity to architectural crowding than we do. Enclosed space must meet at least three requirements that I know of if it is to satisfy the Arabs: there must be plenty of unobstructed space in which to move around (possibly as much as a thousand square feet); very high ceilings—so high in fact that they do not normally impinge on the visual field; and, in addition, there must be an unobstructed view. It was spaces such as these in which the Americans referred to earlier felt so uncomfortable. One sees the Arab's need for a view expressed in many ways, even negatively, for to cut off a neighbor's view is one of the most effective ways of spiting him. In Beirut one can see what is known locally as the "spite house." It is nothing more than a thick, four-story wall, built at the end of a long fight between neighbors, on a narrow strip of land for the express purpose of denying a view of the Mediterranean to any house built on the land behind. According to one of my informants, there is also a house on a small plot of land between Beirut and Damascus which is completely surrounded by a neighbor's wall built high enough to cut off the view from all windows!

BOUNDARIES

Proxemic patterns tell us other things about Arab culture.   22
For example, the whole concept of the boundary as an abstraction is almost impossible to pin down. In one sense, there are no boundaries. "Edges" of towns, yes, but permanent boundaries out in the country (hidden lines), no. In the course of my work with Arab subjects I had a difficult time translating our concept of a boundary into terms which could be equated with theirs. In order to clarify the distinctions between the two very different definitions, I thought it might be helpful to pinpoint acts which constituted trespass. To date, I have been unable to discover anything even remotely resembling our own legal concept of trespass.

Arab behavior in regard to their own real estate is apparently an extension of, and therefore consistent with, their approach to the body. My subjects simply failed to respond whenever trespass was mentioned. They didn't seem to understand what I meant by this term. This may be explained by the fact that they organize relationships with each other according to closed social systems rather than spatially. For thousands of years Moslems, Marinites, Druses, and Jews have lived in their own villages, each with strong kin affiliations. Their hierarchy of loyalties is: first to one's self, then to kinsman, townsman, or tribesman, co-religionist and/or countryman. Anyone not in these categories is a stranger. Strangers and enemies are very closely linked, if not synonymous, in Arab thought. Trespass in this context is a matter of who you are, rather than a piece of land or a space with a boundary that can be denied to anyone and everyone, friend and foe alike.   23

In summary, proxemic patterns differ. By examining them   24
it is possible to reveal hidden cultural frames that determine the structure of a given people's perceptual world. Perceiving the world differently leads to differential definitions of what

constitutes crowded living, different interpersonal relations, and a different approach to both local and international politics. . . .

For Study and Discussion

QUESTIONS FOR RESPONSE

1. What characteristics of the Arab world appeal to you? What characteristics would make it impossible for you to feel at home in such a world?
2. What questions would you like to ask Hall about his research methodology? For example, how did a Western anthropologist uncover the "hidden dimension" of the Arab culture?

QUESTIONS ABOUT PURPOSE

1. What is Hall's primary purpose—to describe the unique features of the Arab world, to compare the behavior of Arabs and Westerners, or to demonstrate how hidden cultural frames determine perception? Explain your answer.
2. What connection does Hall establish between the way in which Westerners and Arabs define the ego and the way in which they behave toward one another in public?

QUESTIONS ABOUT AUDIENCE

1. How much does Hall assume his readers know about Arab culture? How much space does he devote to his discussion of Arab culture and how much to his discussion of American (or Western) culture?
2. What assumptions does Hall make about his readers' ability to "formulate specific rules for their informal behavior patterns"? How is this essay designed to improve his readers' competence in this area?

QUESTIONS ABOUT STRATEGIES

1. Hall does not rigidly adhere to either the subject-by-subject or the point-by-point strategy. In what parts of his essay does he

use each method? How do his subject and purpose determine which strategy he uses?
2. How does Hall use the senses of smell and sight to explain the difference between Arab and American social etiquette?

QUESTIONS FOR DISCUSSION

1. Why do Americans place such high value on privacy? Why do Arabs hate to be alone? How do you respond to the old Arab saying "Paradise without people should not be entered because it is Hell"?
2. Hall says that Arabs avoid partitions in their homes, build walls for spite, and fail to understand the concept of boundary. How might these cultural attitudes explain the political difficulties in the Arab world?

Alice Walker was born in 1944 in Eatonton, Georgia, attended Spelman College in Atlanta, and graduated from Sarah Lawrence College. She then became active in the civil rights movement, helping to register voters in Georgia, teaching in the Head Start program in Mississippi, and working on the staff of the New York City welfare department. In subsequent years, she began her own writing career while teaching at Wellesley College, the University of California at Berkeley, and Brandeis University. Her writing reveals her interest in the themes of sexism and racism, themes she embodies in her widely acclaimed novels: *The Third Life of Grange Copeland* (1970), *Meridian* (1976), *The Color Purple* (1982), and *Possessing the Secret Joy* (1992). Her stories, collected in *In Love and Trouble: Stories of Black Women* (1973) and *You Can't Keep a Good Woman Down* (1981), and essays, found in *Living by the Word* (1988) and *The Temple of My Familiar* (1989), examine the complex experiences of black women. "Everyday Use," reprinted from *In Love and Trouble,* focuses on a reunion that reveals two contrasting attitudes toward family heritage.

Everyday Use
for your grandmama

I WILL WAIT for her in the yard that Maggie and I made so clean and wavy yesterday afternoon. A yard like this is more comfortable than most people know. It is not just a yard. It is like an extended living room. When the hard clay

1

is swept clean as a floor and the fine sand around the edges lined with tiny, irregular grooves anyone can come and sit and look up into the elm tree and wait for the breezes that never come inside the house.

Maggie will be nervous until after her sister goes: she will   2
stand hopelessly in corners homely and ashamed of the burn scars down her arms and legs, eyeing her sister with a mixture of envy and awe. She thinks her sister has held life always in the palm of one hand, that "no" is a word the world never learned to say to her.

You've no doubt seen those TV shows where the child who   3
has "made it" is confronted, as a surprise, by her own mother and father, tottering in weakly from backstage. (A pleasant surprise, of course: What would they do if parent and child came on the show only to curse out and insult each other?) On TV mother and child embrace and smile into each other's faces. Sometimes the mother and father weep, the child wraps them in her arms and leans across the table to tell how she would not have made it without their help. I have seen these programs.

Sometimes I dream a dream in which Dee and I are sud-   4
denly brought together on a TV program of this sort. Out of a dark and soft-seated limousine I am ushered into a bright room filled with many people. There I meet a smiling, gray, sporty man like Johnny Carson who shakes my hand and tells me what a fine girl I have. Then we are on the stage and Dee is embracing me with tears in her eyes. She pins on my dress a large orchid, even though she has told me once that she thinks orchids are tacky flowers.

In real life I am a large, big-boned woman with rough,   5
man-working hands. In the winter I wear flannel nightgowns to bed and overalls during the day. I can kill and clean a hog as mercilessly as a man. My fat keeps me hot in zero weather. I can work all day, breaking ice to get water for washing. I can eat pork liver cooked over the open fire minutes after it comes steaming from the hog. One winter I knocked a bull calf straight in the brain between the eyes with a sledge

hammer and had the meat hung up to chill before nightfall. But of course all this does not show on television. I am the way my daughter would want me to be: a hundred pounds lighter, my skin like an uncooked barley pancake. My hair glistens in the hot bright lights. Johnny Carson has much to do to keep up with my quick and witty tongue.

But that is a mistake. I know even before I wake up. Who 6 ever knew a Johnson with a quick tongue? Who can even imagine me looking a strange white man in the eye? It seems to me I have talked to them always with one foot raised in flight, with my head turned in whichever way is farthest from them. Dee, though. She would always look anyone in the eye. Hesitation was no part of her nature.

"How do I look, Mama?" Maggie says, showing just 7 enough of her thin body enveloped in pink skirt and red blouse for me to know she's there, almost hidden by the door.

"Come out into the yard," I say. 8

Have you ever seen a lame animal, perhaps a dog run over 9 by some careless person rich enough to own a car, sidle up to someone who is ignorant enough to be kind to him? That is the way my Maggie walks. She has been like this, chin on chest, eyes on ground, feet in shuffle, ever since the fire that burned the other house to the ground.

Dee is lighter than Maggie, with nicer hair and a fuller 10 figure. She's a woman now, though sometimes I forget. How long ago was it that the other house burned? Ten, twelve years? Sometimes I can still hear the flames and feel Maggie's arm sticking to me, her hair smoking and her dress falling off her in little black papery flakes. Her eyes seemed stretched open, blazed open by the flames reflected in them. And Dee. I see her standing off under the sweet gum tree she used to dig gum out of; a look of concentration on her face as she watched the last dingy gray board of the house fall in toward the red-hot brick chimney. Whe don't you do a dance around the ashes? I'd wanted to ask her. She had hated the house that much.

I used to think she hated Maggie, too. But that was before 11 we raised the money, the church and me, to send her to Augusta to school. She used to read to us without pity; forcing words, lies, other folks' habits, whole lives upon us two, sitting trapped and ignorant underneath her voice. She washed us in a river of make-believe, burned us with a lot of knowledge we didn't necessarily need to know. Pressed us to her with the serious way she read, to shove us away at just the moment, like dimwits, we seemed about to understand.

Dee wanted nice things. A yellow organdy dress to wear to her graduation from high school; black pumps to match a green suit she'd made from an old suit somebody gave me. She was determined to stare down any disaster in her efforts. Her eyelids would not flicker for minutes at a time. Often I fought off the temptation to shake her. At sixteen she had a style of her own: and knew what style was.   12

I never had an education myself. After second grade the school was closed down. Don't ask me why: in 1927 colored asked fewer questions than they do now. Sometimes Maggie reads to me. She stumbles along good-naturedly but can't see well. She knows she is not bright. Like good looks and money, quickness passed her by. She will marry John Thomas (who has mossy teeth in an earnest face) and then I'll be free to sit here and I guess just sing church songs to myself. Although I never was a good singer. Never could carry a tune. I was always better at a man's job. I used to love to milk till I was hoofed in the side in '49. Cows are soothing and slow and don't bother you, unless you try to milk them the wrong way.   13

I have deliberately turned my back on the house. It is three rooms, just like the one that burned, except the roof is tin; they don't make shingle roofs any more. There are no real windows, just some holes cut in the sides, like the portholes in a ship, but not round and not square, with rawhide holding the shutters up on the outside. This house is in a pasture, too, like the other one. No doubt when Dee sees it she will want to tear it down. She wrote me once that no matter   14

where we "choose" to live, she will manage to come see us.
But she will never bring her friends. Maggie and I thought
about this and Maggie asked me, "Mama, when did Dee ever
have any friends?"

She had a few. Furtive boys in pink shirts hanging about   15
on washday after school. Nervous girls who never laughed.
Impressed with her they worshiped the well-turned phrase,
the cute shape, the scalding humor that erupted like bubbles
in lye. She read to them.

When she was courting Jimmy T she didn't have much   16
time to pay to us, but turned all her faultfinding power on
him. He *flew* to marry a cheap gal from a family of ignorant
flashy people. She hardly had time to recompose herself.

When she comes I will meet—but there they are!   17

Maggie attempts to make a dash for the house, in her   18
shuffling way, but I stay her with my hand. "Come back
here," I say. And she stops and tries to dig a well in the sand
with her toe.

It is hard to see them clearly through the strong sun. But   19
even the first glimpse of leg out of the car tells me it is Dee.
Her feet were always neat-looking, as if God himself had
shaped them with a certain style. From the other side of the
car comes a short, stocky man. Hair is all over his head a foot
long and hanging from his chin like a kinky mule tail. I hear
Maggie suck in her breath. "Uhnnnh," is what it sounds like.
Like when you see the wriggling end of a snake just in front
of your foot on the road. "Uhnnnh."

Dee next. A dress down to the ground, in this hot weather.   20
A dress so loud it hurts my eyes. There are yellows and
oranges enough to throw back the light of the sun. I feel my
whole face warming from the heat waves it throws out. Earrings, too, gold and hanging down to her shoulders. Bracelets
dangling and making noises when she moves her arm up to
shake the folds of the dress out of her armpits. The dress is
loose and flows, and as she walks closer, I like it. I hear
Maggie go "Uhnnnh" again. It is her sister's hair. It stands
straight up like the wool on a sheep. It is black as night and

around the edges are two long pigtails that rope about like small lizards disappearing behind her ears.

"Wa-su-zo-Tean-o!" she says, coming on in that gliding   21
way the dress makes her move. The short stocky fellow with the hair to his navel is all grinning and he follows up with "Asalamalakim, my mother and sister!" He moves to hug Maggie but she falls back, right up against the back of my chair. I feel her trembling there and when I look up I see the perspiration falling off her chin.

"Don't get up," says Dee. Since I am stout it takes some-   22
thing of a push. You can see me trying to move a second or two before I make it. She turns, showing white heels through her sandals, and goes back to the car. Out she peeks next with a Polaroid. She stoops down quickly and lines up picture after picture of me sitting there in front of the house with Maggie cowering behind me. She never takes a shot without making sure the house is included. When a cow comes nibbling around the edge of the yard she snaps it and me and Maggie *and* the house. Then she puts the Polaroid in the back seat of the car, and comes up and kisses me on the forehead.

Meanwhile Asalamalakim is going through the motions   23
with Maggie's hand. Maggie's hand is limp as a fish, and probably as cold, despite the sweat, and she keeps trying to pull it back. It looks like Asalamalakim wants to shake hands but wants to do it fancy. Or maybe he don't know how people shake hands. Anyhow, he soon gives up on Maggie.

"Well," I say. "Dee."   24

"No, Mama," she says. "Not 'Dee,' Wangero Leewanika   25
Kemanjo!"

"What happened to 'Dee'?" I wanted to know.   26

"She's dead," Wangero said. "I couldn't bear it any longer   27
being named after the people who oppress me."

"You know as well as me you was named after your aunt   28
Dicie," I said. Dicie is my sister. She named Dee. We called her "Big Dee" after Dee was born.

"But who was *she* named after," asked Wangero.   29

"I guess after Grandma Dee," I said.   30

"And who was she named after?" asked Wangero.   31

"Her mother," I said, and saw Wangero getting tired. 32
"That's about as far back as I can trace it," I said. Though,
in fact, I probably could have carried it back beyond the Civil
War through the branches.

"Well," said Asalamalakim, "there you are." 33

"Uhnnnh," I heard Maggie say. 34

"There I was not," I said, "before 'Dicie' cropped up in 35
our family, so why should I try to trace it that far back?"

He just stood there grinning, looking down on me like 36
somebody inspecting a Model A car. Every once in a while
he and Wangero sent eye signals over my head.

"How do you pronounce this name?" I asked. 37

"You don't have to call me by it if you don't want to," 38
said Wangero.

"Why shouldn't I?" I asked. "If that's what you want us 39
to call you, we'll call you."

"I know it might sound awkward at first," said Wangero. 40

"I'll get used to it," I said. "Ream it out again." 41

Well, soon we got the name out of the way. Asalamalakim 42
had a name twice as long **and th**ree times as hard. After I
tripped over it two or three times he told me to just call him
Hakim-a-barber. I wanted to ask him was he a barber, but I
didn't really think he was, so I didn't ask.

"You must belong to those beef-cattle peoples down the 43
road," I said. They said "Asalamalakim" when they met you,
too, but they didn't shake hands. Always too busy: feeding
the cattle, fixing the fences, putting up salt-lick shelters,
throwing down hay. When the white folks poisoned some of
the herd the men stayed up all night with rifles in their hands,
I walked a mile and half just to see the sight.

Hakim-a-barber said, "I accept some of their doctrines, 44
but farming and raising cattle is not my style." (They didn't
tell me, and I didn't ask, whether Wangero [Dee] had really
gone and married him.)

We sat down to eat and right away he said he didn't eat 45
collards and pork was unclean. Wangero, though, went on
through the chitlins and corn bread, the greens and everything else. She talked a blue streak over the sweet potatoes.

Everything delighted her. Even the fact that we still used the benches her daddy made for the table when we couldn't afford to buy chairs.

"Oh, Mama!" she cried. Then turned to Hakim-a-barber.   46
"I never knew how lovely these benches are. You can feel the rump prints," she said, running her hands underneath her and along the bench. Then she gave a sigh and her hand closed over Grandma Dee's butter dish. "That's it!" she said. "I knew there was something I wanted to ask you if I could have." She jumped up from the table and went over in the corner where the churn stood, the milk in its clabber by now. She looked at the churn and looked at it.

"This churn top is what I need," she said. "Didn't Uncle   47
Buddy whittle it out of a tree you all used to have?"

"Yes," I said.   48

"Uh huh," she said happily. "And I want the dasher, too."   49

"Uncle Buddy whittle that, too?" asked the barber.   50

Dee (Wangero) looked up at me.   51

"Aunt Dee's first husband whittled the dash," said Maggie   52
so low you almost couldn't hear her. "His name was Henry, but they called him Stash."

"Maggie's brain is like an elephant's," Wangero said,   53
laughing. "I can use the churn top as a centerpiece for the alcove table," she said, sliding a plate over the churn, "and I'll think of something artistic to do with the dasher."

When she finished wrapping the dasher the handle stuck   54
out. I took it for a moment in my hands. You didn't even have to look close to see where hands pushing the dasher up and down to make butter had left a kind of sink in the wood. In fact, there were a lot of small sinks; you could see where thumbs and fingers had sunk into the wood. It was beautiful light yellow wood, from a tree that grew in the yard where Big Dee and Stash had lived.

After dinner Dee (Wangero) went to the trunk at the foot   55
of my bed and started rifling through it. Maggie hung back in the kitchen over the dishpan. Out came Wangero with two quilts. They had been pieced by Grandma Dee and then Big Dee and me had hung them on the quilt frames on the front

porch and quilted them. One was in the Lone Star pattern.
The other was Walk Around the Mountain. In both of them
were scraps of dresses Grandma Dee had worn fifty and more
years ago. Bits and pieces of Grandpa Jarrell's Paisley shirts.
And one teeny faded blue piece, about the size of a penny
matchbox, that was from Great Grandpa Ezra's uniform that
he wore in the Civil War.

"Mama," Wangero said sweet as a bird. "Can I have these   56
old quilts?"

I heard something fall in the kitchen, and a minute later   57
the kitchen door slammed.

"Why don't you take one or two of the others?" I asked.   58
"These old things was just done by me and Big Dee from
some tops your grandma pieced before she died."

"No," said Wangero. "I don't want those. They are   59
stitched around the borders by machine."

"That's make them last better," I said.   60

"That's not the point," said Wangero. "These are all pieces   61
of dresses Grandma used to wear. She did all this stitching by
hand. Imagine!" She held the quilts securely in her arms,
stroking them.

"Some of the pieces, like those lavender ones, come from   62
old clothes her mother handed down to her," I said, moving
up to touch the quilts. Dee (Wangero) moved back just
enough so that I couldn't reach the quilts. They already
belonged to her.

"Imagine!" she breathed again, clutching them closely to   63
her bosom.

"The truth is," I said, "I promised to give them quilts to   64
Maggie, for when she marries John Thomas."

She gasped like a bee had stung her.   65

"Maggie can't appreciate these quilts!" she said. "She'd   66
probably be backward enough to put them to everyday use."

"I reckon she would," I said. "God knows I been saving   67
'em for long enough with nobody using 'em. I hope she
will!" I didn't want to bring up how I had offered Dee
(Wangero) a quilt when she went away to college. Then she
had told me they were old-fashioned, out of style.

"But they're *priceless!*" she was saying now, furiously; for   68
she has a temper. "Maggie would put them on the bed and
in five years they'd be in rags. Less than that!"

"She can always make some more," I said. "Maggie knows   69
how to quilt."

Dee (Wangero) looked at me with hatred. "You just will   70
not understand. The point is these quilts, *these* quilts!"

"Well," I said, stumped. "What would *you* do with them?"   71

"Hang them," she said. As if that was the only thing you   72
could do with quilts.

Maggie by now was standing in the door. I could almost   73
hear the sound her feet made as they scraped over each other.

"She can have them, Mama," she said, like somebody used   74
to never winning anything, or having anything reserved for
her. "I can 'member Grandma Dee without the quilts."

I looked at her hard. She had filled her bottom lip with   75
checkerberry snuff and it gave her face a kind of dopey,
hangdog look. It was Grandma Dee and Big Dee who taught
her how to quilt herself. She stood there with her scarred
hands hidden in the folds of her skirt. She looked at her sister
with something like fear but she wasn't mad at her. This was
Maggie's portion. This was the way she knew God to work.

When I looked at her like that something hit me in the   76
top of my head and ran down to the soles of my feet. Just
like when I'm in church and the spirit of God touches me
and I get happy and shout. I did something I never had done
before: hugged Maggie to me, then dragged her on into the
room, snatched the quilts out of Miss Wangero's hands and
dumped them into Maggie's lap. Maggie just sat there on my
bed with her mouth open.

"Take one or two of the others," I said to Dee.   77

But she turned without a word and went out to Hakim-   78
a-barber.

"You just don't understand," she said, as Maggie and I   79
came out to the car.

"What don't I understand?" I wanted to know.   80

"Your heritage," she said. And then she turned to Maggie,   81
kissed her and said, "You ought to try to make something of

yourself, too, Maggie. It's really a new day for us. But from the way you and Mamma still live you'd never know it."

She put on some sunglasses that hid everything above the tip of her nose and her chin.   82

Maggie smiled; maybe at the sunglasses. But a real smile, not scared. After we watched the car dust settle I asked Maggie to bring me a dip of snuff. And then the two of us sat there just enjoying, until it was time to go in the house and go to bed.   83

COMMENT ON "EVERYDAY USE"

Alice Walker's "Everyday Use" sets up a comparison between a mother and her visiting daughter over their heritage. For Mama and her daughter Maggie, heritage is a matter of everyday living, of "everyday use." For Mama's other daughter, Dee (Wangero), however, heritage is a matter of style, a fashionable obsession with one's roots. These comparisons are revealed first in Walker's description of the physical appearance of the characters. Mama is fat and manly, and Maggie bears the scars from a fire. By contrast, Dee (Wangero) is beautiful and striking in her brightly colored African dress, earrings, sunglasses, and Afro hair style. Next, Walker compares the characters' skills. Mama can butcher a hog or break ice to get water, and Maggie is able to make beautiful quilts. Dee (Wangero), on the other hand, thinks of herself as outside this domestic world, educated by books to understand the cultural significance of her heritage. The problem posed by the debate over family possessions is whether heritage is an object to be preserved, like a priceless painting, or a process, to be learned, like the creation of a quilt.

Comparison and Contrast as a Writing Strategy

1. Select a place in your childhood neighborhood—perhaps a garden, a playground, or a movie theater. Then, in an essay addressed to your writing class, write a short comparison of the way the place used to be and the way it is now. Consider the example of Mark Twain's "Two Views of the River" as you compare your childhood and adult visions. Consider also what you have learned about the place or about yourself by making the comparison. That lesson should help control your decisions about purpose and audience.

2. Select two people who embody admirable characteristics— grandparents, teachers, public figures. Then, like David McCullough, compare and contrast their strengths and weaknesses. Include information on how they might see each other. Cite biographical information that accounts for their similarities and differences.

3. Conduct some research on the conversational patterns in your home (or dormitory) and in your classroom. Keep track of who talks, what they talk about, and how they use conversation—for example, to make friends, to report information, to win approval. Keep track of who doesn't talk and in what situations they are likely to stay silent. Then write an essay in which you compare the patterns of home and school conversation.

4. In "Nature and Televised Nature" Bill McKibben contrasts what he learned from observing the world firsthand and from watching it on television. Select a subject you know well—your job, your hometown, your favorite sport or hobby—and then compare your firsthand experience with the subject with the way it is represented on television.

5. Write an essay comparing the way two magazines or newspapers cover the same story. You could select magazines that have opposing political philosophies or newspapers that are published in different parts of the country. Or, like

Edward T. Hall, you may wish to analyze how two cultures see the same problem. For example, compare American and Libyan statements on terrorism, American and Russian views on economic aid, or American and Mexican policies on immigration.

6. Compare and contrast arguments on both sides of a controversial issue such as welfare reform or gun control. Such issues produce controversy because there are legitimate arguments on each side. They also produce controversy because people can simplify them in slogans (Reading is good; television is bad). Select two slogans that present the opposing sides of the controversy you are writing about. Compare and contrast the assumptions, evidence, and logic of both slogans. Like Deborah Tannen, avoid choosing sides. Maintain a neutral tone as you assess the motives, methods, and reasons for each argument.

DIVISION
AND
CLASSIFICATION

༄

Division and **classification** are mental processes that often work together. When you *divide*, you separate something (a college, a city) into sections (departments, neighborhoods). When you *classify*, you place examples of something (restaurants, jobs) into categories or classes (restaurants: moderately expensive, very expensive; jobs: unskilled, semiskilled, and skilled).

When you divide, you move downward from a concept to the subunits of that concept. When you classify, you move upward from specific examples to classes or categories that share a common characteristic. For example, you could *divide* a television news program into subunits such as news, features, editorials, sports, and weather. And you could *classify*

some element of that program—such as the editorial commentator on the six o'clock news—according to his or her
style, knowledge, and trustworthiness. You can use either
division or classification singly, depending on your purpose,
but most of the time you will probably use them together
when you are writing a classification essay. First you might
identify the subunits in a college sports program—football,
basketball, hockey, volleyball, tennis; then you could classify
them according to their budgets—most money budgeted for
football, the least budgeted for volleyball.

PURPOSE

When you write a classification essay, your chief purpose is to
explain. You might want to explain an established method for
organizing information, such as the Library of Congress system, or a new plan for arranging data such as the Internal
Revenue Service's latest schedule for itemizing tax deduc-
tions. On one level, your purpose in such an essay is simply
to show how the system works. At a deeper level, your purpose is to define, analyze, and justify the organizing principle
that underlies the system.

You can also write a classification essay to *entertain* or to
persuade. If you classify to entertain, you have an opportunity
to be clever and witty. If you classify to persuade, you have a
chance to be cogent and forceful. If you want to entertain,
you might concoct an elaborate scheme for classifying fools,
pointing out the distinguishing features of each category and
giving particularly striking examples of each type. But if you
want to persuade, you could explain how some new or controversial plan, such as the metric system or congressional
redistricting, is organized, pointing out how the schemes use
new principles to identify and organize information. Again,
although you may give your readers a great deal of information in such an essay, your main purpose is to persuade them
that the new plan is better than the old one.

AUDIENCE

As with any writing assignment, when you write a classification essay, you need to think carefully about what your readers already know and what they need to get from your writing. If you're writing on a new topic (social patterns in a primitive society) or if you're explaining a specialized system of classification (the botanist's procedure for identifying plants), your readers need precise definitions and plenty of illustrations for each subcategory. If your readers already know about your subject and the system it uses for classification (the movies' G, PG, PG–13, R, and NC–17 rating codes), then you don't need to give them an extensive demonstration. In that kind of writing situation, you might want to sketch the system briefly to refresh your readers' memories but then move on, using examples of specific movies to analyze whether the system really works.

You also need to think about how your readers might use the classification system that you explain in your essay. If you're classifying rock musicians, your readers are probably going to regard the system you create as something self-enclosed—interesting and amusing, perhaps something to quibble about, but not something they're likely to use in their everyday lives. On the other hand, if you write an essay classifying stereo equipment, your readers may want to use your system when they shop. For the first audience, you can use an informal approach to classification, dividing your subject into interesting subcategories and illustrating them with vivid examples. For the other audience, you need to be careful and strict in your approach, making sure you divide your topic into all its possible classes and illustrating each class with concrete examples.

STRATEGIES

When you write a classification essay, your basic strategy for organization should be to *divide your subject* into major categories that exhibit a common trait, then subdivide those categories into smaller units. Next, *arrange your categories into a sequence that shows a logical or a dramatic progression.* Finally, *define each of your categories.* First, show how each category is different from the others; then discuss its most vivid examples.

To make this strategy succeed, you must be sure that your classification system is *consistent, complete, emphatic,* and *significant.* Here is a method for achieving this goal. First, when you divide your subject into categories, *apply the same principle of selection to each class.* You may find this hard to do if you're trying to explain a system that someone else has already established but that is actually inconsistent. You have undoubtedly discovered that record stores use overlapping and inconsistent categories. Linda Ronstadt albums, for example, may be found in sections labeled *country, rock, pop, standards,* and *female vocal.* You can avoid such tangles if you create and control your own classification system.

For instance, in "The Extendable Fork" Calvin Trillin classifies eaters by how they eat off other people's plates. Russell Baker follows a similar strategy in "The Plot Against People" when he classifies objects by their ability to "resist man and ultimately to defeat him." By contrast, the other three writers in this section explain existing systems of classification. In "Shades of Black" Mary Mebane classifies the arbitrary and unfair assessment of students by color and class. In "Territorial Behavior" Desmond Morris classifies people by the way they define and mark territorial boundaries. And Gail Sheehy classifies human development in terms of "predictable crises of adulthood."

After you have divided your subject into separate and consistent categories, *make sure your division is complete.* The simplest kind of division separates a subject into two categories: A and Not-A (for example, conformists and nonconformists). This kind of division, however, is rarely encouraged. It allows you to tell your readers about category A (conformists), but you won't tell them much about Not-A (nonconformists). For this reason, you should try to "exhaust" your subject by finding at least three separate categories and by acknowledging any examples that don't fit into the system. When an author writes a formal classification essay, like Sheehy's in this section, he or she tries to be definitive—to include everything significant. Even when authors are writing less formal classification essays, such as Trillin's and Baker's, they try to set up a reasonably complete system.

Once you have completed your process of division, *arrange your categories and examples in an emphatic order.* Sheehy arranges her categories of human development chronologically, from the rebellion of eighteen-year-olds to the mellowing of fifty-year-olds. Morris arranges his classification of territory into increasingly smaller areas of space. Mebane arranges her categories into increasingly subtle codes of class and color. The authors of these essays reveal the principal purpose underlying their classification schemes: to show variety in similarity, to point out how concepts change, and to challenge the arbitrariness of an established system.

Finally, *you need to show the significance of your system of classification.* The strength of the classification process is that you can use it to analyze a subject in any number of ways. Its weakness is that you can use it to subdivide a subject into all kinds of trivial or pointless categories. You can classify people by their educational backgrounds, their work experience, or their significant achievements. You can also classify them by their shoe size, the kind of socks they wear, or their tastes in ice cream. Notice that when Mary Mebane explains her classification system, she questions the social and psychological impact it has on self-esteem. Even a writer who chooses a subject that doesn't seem particularly significant—such as Calvin Trillin's eaters or Russell Baker's objects—must convince readers that his or her *system* counts in some way, if only because it lays out and demonstrates, consistently and completely, the significant subdivisions of the subject.

USING DIVISION AND CLASSIFICATION IN PARAGRAPHS

Here are two division-and-classification paragraphs. The first is written by a professional writer and is followed by an analysis. The second is written by a student writer and is followed by questions.

HERBERT J. GANS
from *Deciding What's News*

Identifies principles of division (suitability)

The *New York Times* announces every day that it contains "All the News That's Fit to Print." The wording is arrogant, but the phrase makes the point that the news consists of suitable stories. To determine story suitability, journalists employ a large number of suitability considerations, all of which are interrelated. These can be divided into three categories: substantive considerations judge story content and the newsworthiness of what sources supply; product considerations evaluate the "goodness" of stories; and competitive considerations test stories for their ability to serve in the continuing rivalry among news organizations to provide the most suitable news.

Establishes three categories: (1) substantive, (2) product, (3) competitive

Comment In this excerpt from his study of the media, Herbert J. Gans divides the suitability of news stories into three categories. Although he admits that the categories are "interrelated," Gans suggests that journalists classify a story by three types of considerations: (1) substantive—whether the story is newsworthy; (2) product—whether the story is "good"; and (3) competitive—whether the story improves the paper's standing against other newspapers.

GARETH TUCKER
"Gentlemen! Start Your Engines"

On a typical weekend, most couch potatoes can channel-surf past about a dozen car races. As they watch brightly colored machines circling the track again and again, like images on some manic video game, they may conclude that a race is a race is a race. Actually automobile racing is divided into many subtle subcategories. For example, the three most popular forms can be identified by the image of the car and driver. Stock cars are perceived as souped-up versions of "stock" cars driven by "good ole boys" who talk as if they have just outrun the local police. Indy cars are perceived as masterpieces of engineering driven by "test pilots" who speak the technobabble of rocket scientists. Formula One cars are almost as technologically advanced as Indy cars, but they still retain the image of the European "Grand Prix" car—the sports car driven by some count who talks as if he's just finished a jolly little tour through the countryside.

1. What principle does Tucker use to establish his three categories?
2. How does his characterization of the race car driver help clarify each category?

DIVISION AND CLASSIFICATION

Points to Remember

1. Determine whether you want to (a) explain an existing system of classification or (b) create your own system.
2. Divide your subject into smaller categories by applying the same principle of selection to each category.
3. Make sure that your division is complete by establishing separate and consistent types of categories.
4. Arrange your categories (and the examples you use to illustrate each category) in a logical and emphatic sequence.
5. Demonstrate the significance of your system by calling your readers' attention to its significance.

Calvin Trillin was born in Kansas City, Missouri, in 1935 and was educated at Yale University. He began his career by working as a reporter for *Time* magazine, then as a columnist for *The New Yorker*. In recent years, he has written a national newspaper column and staged a one-man show off-Broadway. His writing includes two novels, *Runestruck* (1977) and *Floater* (1980); several collections of reporting, *U.S. Journal* (1971), *Killings* (1982), and *American Stories* (1991); a best selling memoir, *Remembering Denny* (1993); and numerous books of humor. In "The Extendable Fork," reprinted from his syndicated column, Trillin classifies eaters by how they eat off of other people's plates.

The Extendable Fork

IN OUR HOUSE, news that the extendable fork had been invented was greeted with varying degrees of enthusiasm. I think it's fair to say that I was the most enthusiastic of all. I eat off of other people's plates. My wife was mildly enthusiastic. She figures that if I use an extendable fork I'm less likely to come away from the table with gravy on my cuff.

People who eat off of other people's plates can be categorized in four types—The Finisher, The Waif, The Researcher and The Simple Thief. I might as well admit right here at the beginning that I am all four.

The Finisher demonstrates concern that food may be left uneaten even though the starving children your mother told you about are still hungry. Once the pace of eating begins to slacken off a bit, he reaches across to spear a roast potato off of someone's plate a nanosecond after saying, "If you're not planning to finish these . . ."

The long-reach eater I think of as The Waif often doesn't 4 order much himself at a restaurant, claiming that he's not terribly hungry or that he's trying to lose weight. Then, he gazes at his dinner companions' plates, like a hungry urchin who has his nose pressed up against the window of a restaurant where enormously fat rich people are slurping oysters and shoveling down mounds of boeuf bourguignon. Occasionally, he murmurs something like, "That looks delicious." Answering "Actually, it's not all that good" does not affect

---

People who eat off other people's plates come in four categories: The Finisher, The Waif, The Researcher, and The Simple Thief.

---

him—although it may slow down the Researcher, who, as he extends his fork usually says something like, "I'm curious how they do these fried onions."

The Simple Thief simply waits for his dining companions 5 to glance away, then confidently grabs what he wants. If he's desperate, he may actually take measures to distract them, saying something like, "Is it my imagination, or could that be Michael Jackson and Lisa Marie Presley at the table over by the door?"

That sort of subterfuge is not necessary, by the way, if the 6 plate I have singled out as a target is my wife's. She does not object to my sampling—a reflection, I've always thought, of her generous heart. In fact, I have said in the past that if a young groom on his honeymoon reaches over for the first time to sample his bride's fettuccine only to be told "Don't you like what you're having?" or "There really isn't that much of this," he knows he's in for a long haul.

Actually, my wife might be called a Finisher herself. If 7

we're having fried chicken, she will stare at what's on my plate after I have indeed finished. "Look at all the chicken you left," she'll say. Or "There's a ton of meat still on that chicken."

Oddly enough, this is precisely the sort of thing that I   8
heard from my mother, who was also fond of saying that I didn't "do a good job" on the chicken. The way my wife eats chicken is to eat every speck of meat off the bones, so that the chicken looks as if it had been staked out on an anthill by a tribe of crazed chicken torturers. She treats a lobster the same way.

I eat more the way a shark eats—tearing off whatever   9
seems exposed and easy to get at. I have suggested, in fact, that in fried-chicken or lobster restaurants we could economize by getting only one order, which I could start and my wife could finish.

My wife's approach to finishing does not, of course, re-   10
quire an extendable fork, but I intend to be an early customer myself. According to an item in the *New York Times,* the fork is nearly two feet long when fully opened. It's being marketed under the name of Alan's X-Tenda Fork.

I might have chosen another name, but this one is,   11
I'll admit, evocative. For me, it conjures up visions of a Limbaugh-sized man named Alan sitting in a restaurant with friends and family. He seems to be engaging in normal conversation, but his tiny eyes dart from plate to plate; occasionally, with a fork as quick as the strike of an adder, he helps with the finishing.

In fact, I can imagine Alan inventing other needed imple-   12
ments—a sort of vacuum tube, for instance, that can suck up french fries from three feet away. I can see him improving on Alan's X-Tenda Fork. He might install a tiny tape recorder in it, so when you pulled it out to its full length and moved it quickly across the table a voice said, "If you're not planning to finish these . . ."

For Study and Discussion

QUESTIONS FOR RESPONSE

1. How do you respond when someone eats off your plate?
2. What explanations do you offer when you want to sample something from someone else's plate?

QUESTIONS ABOUT PURPOSE

1. How does Trillin use the news of the invention of the "extendable fork" to justify his classification of eaters?
2. What purpose does Trillin accomplish by admitting that he fits into all four categories?

QUESTIONS ABOUT AUDIENCE

1. What assumptions does Trillin make about the eating habits of his readers?
2. How do his comments about his wife's and mother's behavior clarify his attitude toward his readers?

QUESTIONS ABOUT STRATEGIES

1. What principle does Trillin use to divide and identify his four types of eaters?
2. How does he use dialogue to illustrate the strategies of each eater?

QUESTIONS FOR DISCUSSION

1. What do books of etiquette say about the practice of eating from another's plate?
2. How does the concept of finishing fit into our cultural attitudes toward efficiency and economy?

Russell Baker was born in 1925 in rural Loudoun County, Virginia; graduated from Johns Hopkins University; and served in the navy during World War II. He began his newspaper career in 1947, covering the State Department, White House, and Congress for the *New York Times* until, as he recounts, "I just got bored. I had done enough reporting." The *Times* offered him a thrice-weekly column, which came to be called "Observer" and which Baker continues to write today. Many of his columns have been collected in book form: *Poor Russell's Almanac* (1972), *So This Is Depravity* (1980), *The Rescue of Miss Yaskell and Other Pipe Dreams* (1983), and *There's a Country in My Cellar* (1990). His autobiography, *Growing Up* (1982), was awarded the Pulitzer Prize. *The Good Times* (1989) continues his reminiscences. In "The Plot Against People," Baker employs his wry humor to classify inanimate objects into three categories.

The Plot Against People

I NANIMATE OBJECTS ARE classified into three major categories—those that don't work, those that break down and those that get lost.   1

The goal of all inanimate objects is to resist man and ultimately to defeat him, and the three major classifications are based on the method each object uses to achieve its purpose. As a general rule, any object capable of breaking down at the moment when it is most needed will do so. The automobile is typical of the category.   2

With the cunning typical of its breed, the automobile never breaks down while entering a filling station with a large staff of idle mechanics. It waits until it reaches a downtown inter-   3 section in the middle of the rush hour, or until it is fully loaded with family and luggage on the Ohio Turnpike.

Thus it creates maximum misery, inconvenience, frustra- 4 tion and irritability among its human cargo, thereby reducing its owner's life span.

Washing machines, garbage disposals, lawn mowers, light 5 bulbs, automatic laundry dryers, water pipes, furnaces, electrical fuses, television tubes, hose nozzles, tape recorders, slide projectors—all are in league with the automobile to take

---

The goal of all inanimate objects is to defeat man; their strategies are to break down, not work, or get lost.

---

their turn at breaking down whenever life threatens to flow smoothly for their human enemies.

Many inanimate objects, of course, find it extremely diffi- 6 cult to break down. Pliers, for example, and gloves and keys are almost totally incapable of breaking down. Therefore, they have had to evolve a different technique for resisting man.

They get lost. Science has still not solved the mystery of 7 how they do it, and no man has ever caught one of them in the act of getting lost. The most plausible theory is that they have developed a secret method of locomotion which they are able to conceal the instant a human eye falls upon them.

It is not uncommon for a pair of pliers to climb all the way 8 from the cellar to the attic in its single-minded determination to raise its owner's blood pressure. Keys have been known to burrow three feet under mattresses. Women's purses, despite their great weight, frequently travel through six or seven rooms to find hiding space under a couch.

Scientists have been struck by the fact that things that 9 break down virtually never get lost, while things that get lost hardly ever break down.

A furnace, for example, will invariably break down at the 10 depth of the first winter cold wave, but it will never get lost.

A woman's purse, which after all does have some inherent capacity for breaking down, hardly ever does; it almost invariably chooses to get lost.

Some persons believe this constitutes evidence that inanimate objects are not entirely hostile to man, and that a negotiated peace is possible. After all, they point out, a furnace could infuriate a man even more thoroughly by getting lost than by breaking down, just as a glove could upset him far more by breaking down than by getting lost.   11

Not everyone agrees, however, that this indicates a conciliatory attitude among inanimate objects. Many say it merely proves that furnaces, gloves and pliers are incredibly stupid.   12

The third class of objects—those that don't work—is the most curious of all. These include such objects as barometers, car clocks, cigarette lighters, flashlights and toy-train locomotives. It is inaccurate, of course, to say that they never work. They work once, usually for the first few hours after being brought home, and then quit. Thereafter, they never work again.   13

In fact, it is widely assumed that they are built for the purpose of not working. Some people have reached advanced ages without ever seeing some of these objects—barometers, for example—in working order.   14

Science is utterly baffled by the entire category. There are many theories about it. The most interesting holds that the things that don't work have attained the highest state possible for an inanimate object, the estate to which things that break down and things that get lost can still only aspire.   15

They have truly defeated man by conditioning him never to expect anything of them, and in return they have given man the only peace he receives from inanimate society. He does not expect his barometer to work, his electric locomotive to run, his cigarette lighter to light or his flashlight to illuminate, and when they don't, it does not raise his blood pressure.   16

He cannot attain that peace with furnaces and keys and cars and women's purses as long as he demands that they work for their keep.   17

For Study and Discussion

QUESTIONS FOR RESPONSE

1. What experiences have you had with objects that don't work, break down, or get lost?
2. How does Baker's title, "The Plot Against People," prepare you for the subject of this classification of things?

QUESTIONS ABOUT PURPOSE

1. How do Baker's introduction of his first category (paragraph 2) and his illustrative example (paragraph 3) demonstrate that his primary purpose is to entertain?
2. In what ways do Baker's repeated references to science reinforce or alter his purpose?

QUESTIONS ABOUT AUDIENCE

1. How does Baker's use of examples reveal his assumptions about the common experience of his audience?
2. How does Baker expect his readers to use his classification system? Look particularly at paragraphs 11, 12, and 16.

QUESTIONS ABOUT STRATEGIES

1. What is the principle by which Baker divides objects into three categories?
2. What does Baker accomplish by scrambling the sequence of categories he presents in his opening sentence?

QUESTIONS FOR DISCUSSION

1. What evidence can you supply to confirm Baker's thesis that "the highest state possible for an inanimate object" occurs when it conditions people not to expect anything from it?
2. What evidence can you suggest to defeat Baker's thesis? How would you support the argument that objects do *not* defeat people but provide them with ways to extend their creative powers?

Mary Mebane was born in 1933 in Durham, North Carolina, and educated at North Carolina Central University and the University of North Carolina. She taught in the public schools of North Carolina before moving on to teaching writing at the University of South Carolina and the University of Wisconsin. She has written essays for the *New York Times;* a two-act play, *Take a Sad Song* (1975); and two volumes of her autobiography, *Mary: An Autobiography* (1981) and *Mary, Wayfarer* (1983). In "Shades of Black," excerpted from the first autobiographical volume, Mebane reveals how class and color have been used to classify members of the African-American community.

Shades of Black

D URING MY FIRST week of classes as a freshman, I was stopped one day in the hall by the chairman's wife, who was indistinguishable in color from a white woman. She wanted to see me, she said.

This woman had no official position on the faculty, except that she was an instructor in English; nevertheless, her summons had to be obeyed. In the segregated world there were (and remain) gross abuses of authority because those at the pinnacle, and even their spouses, felt that the people "under" them had no recourse except to submit—and they were right except that sometimes a black who got sick and tired of it would go to the whites and complain. This course of action was severely condemned by the blacks, but an interesting thing happened—such action always got positive results. Power was thought of in negative terms: I can deny someone something, I can strike at someone who can't strike back, I can ride someone down; that proves I am powerful. The concept of power as a force for good, for affirmative response to people or situations, was not in evidence.

When I went to her office, she greeted me with a big smile. 3 "You know," she said, "you made the highest mark on the verbal part of the examination." She was referring to the examination that the entire freshman class took upon entering the college. I looked at her but I didn't feel warmth, for in spite of her smile her eyes and tone of voice were saying, "How could this black-skinned girl score higher on the verbal than some of the students who've had more advantages than she? It must be some sort of fluke. Let me talk to her." I felt it, but I managed to smile my thanks and back off. For here at North Carolina College at Durham, as it had been since the beginning, social class and color were the primary criteria used in determining status on the campus.

First came the children of doctors, lawyers, and college 4 teachers. Next came the children of public-school teachers, businessmen, and anybody else who had access to more money than the poor black working class. After that came the

---

At my college, social class and color were the primary criteria in determining status on campus.

---

bulk of the student population, the children of the working class, most of whom were the first in their families to go beyond high school. The attitude toward them was: You're here because we need the numbers, but in all other things defer to your betters.

The faculty assumed that light-skinned students were more 5 intelligent, and they were always a bit nonplussed when a dark-skinned student did well, especially if she was a girl.

They had reason to be appalled when they discovered that I planned to do not only well but better than my light-skinned peers.

I don't know whether African men recently transported to the New World considered themselves handsome or, more important, whether they considered African women beautiful in comparison with Native American Indian women or immigrant European women. It is a question that I have never heard raised or seen research on. If African men considered African women beautiful, just when their shift in interest away from black black women occurred might prove to be an interesting topic for researchers. But one thing I know for sure: by the twentieth century, really black skin on a woman was considered ugly in this country. This was particularly true among those who were exposed to college.   6

Hazel, who was light brown, used to say to me, "You are *dark*, but not *too* dark." The saved commiserating with the damned. I had the feeling that if nature had painted one more brushstroke on me, I'd have had to kill myself.   7

Black skin was to be disguised at all costs. Since a black face is rather hard to disguise, many women took refuge in ludicrous makeup. Mrs. Burry, one of my teachers in elementary school, used white face powder. But she neglected to powder her neck and arms, and even the black on her face gleamed through the white, giving her an eerie appearance. But she did the best she could.   8

I observed all through elementary and high school that for various entertainments the girls were placed on the stage in order of color. And very black ones didn't get into the front row. If they were past caramel-brown, to the back row they would go. And nobody questioned the justice of these decisions—neither the students nor the teachers.   9

One of the teachers at Wildwood School, who was from the Deep South and was just as black as she could be, had been a strict enforcer of these standards. That was another irony—that someone who had been judged outside the realm   10 of beauty herself because of her skin tones should have adopted them so wholeheartedly and applied them herself without question.

One girl stymied that teacher, though. Ruby, a black cherry of a girl, not only got off the back row but off the front row as well, to stand alone at stage center. She could outsing, outdance, and outdeclaim everyone else, and talent proved triumphant over pigmentation. But the May Queen and her Court (and in high school, Miss Wildwood) were always chosen from among the lighter ones. 11

When I was a freshman in high school, it became clear that a light-skinned sophomore girl named Rose was going to get the "best girl scholar" prize for the next three years, and there was nothing I could do about it, even though I knew I was the better. Rose was caramel-colored and had shoulder-length hair. She was highly favored by the science and math teacher, who figured the averages. I wasn't. There was only one prize. Therefore, Rose would get it until she graduated. I was one year behind her, and I would not get it until after she graduated. 12

To be held in such low esteem was painful. It was difficult not to feel that I had been cheated out of the medal, which I felt that, in a fair competition, I perhaps would have won. Being unable to protest or do anything about it was a traumatic experience for me. From then on I instinctively tended to avoid the college-exposed, dark-skinned male, knowing that when he looked at me he saw himself and, most of the time, his mother and sister as well, and since he had rejected his blackness, he had rejected theirs and mine. 13

Oddly enough, the lighter-skinned black male did not seem to feel so much prejudice toward the black black woman. It was no accident, I felt, that Mr. Harrison, the eighth-grade teacher, who was reddish-yellow himself, once protested to the science and math teacher about the fact that he always assigned sweeping duties to Doris and Ruby Lee, two black black girls. Mr. Harrison said to them one day, right in the other teacher's presence, "You must be some bad 14 girls. Every day I come down here ya'll are sweeping." The science and math teacher got the point and didn't ask them to sweep anymore.

Uneducated black males, too, sometimes related very well   15
to the black black woman. They had been less firmly indoc-
trinated by the white society around them and were more securely rooted in their own culture.

Because of the stigma attached to having dark skin, a black   16
black woman had to do many things to find a place for herself. One possibility was to attach herself to a light-skinned woman, hoping that some of the magic would rub off on her. A second was to make herself sexually available, hoping to attract a mate. Third, she could resign herself to a more chaste life-style—either (for the professional woman) teaching and work in established churches or (for the uneducated woman) domestic work and zealous service in the Holy and Sanctified churches.

Even as a young girl, Lucy had chosen the first route. Lucy   17
was short, skinny, short-haired, and black black, and thus unacceptable. So she made her choice. She selected Patricia, the lightest-skinned girl in the school, as her friend, and followed her around. Patricia and her friends barely tolerated Lucy, but Lucy smiled and doggedly hung on, hoping that some who noticed Patricia might notice her, too. Though I felt shame for her behavior, even then I understood.

As is often the case of the victim agreeing with and adopt-   18
ing the attitudes of oppressor, so I have seen it with black black women. I have seen them adopt the oppressor's attitude that they are nothing but "sex machines," and their suppos-
edly superior sexual performance becomes their sole reason for being and for esteeming themselves. Such women learn early that in order to make themselves attractive to men they have somehow to shift the emphasis from physical beauty to some other area—usually sexual performance. Their constant talk is of their desirability and their ability to gratify a man sexually.

I knew two such women well—both of them black black.   19
To hear their endless talk of sexual conquests was very sad. I

have never seen the category that these women fall into described anywhere. It is not that of promiscuity or nymphomania. It is the category of total self-rejection: "Since I am black, I am ugly, I am nobody. I will perform on the level that they have assigned to me." Such women are the pitiful results of what not only white America but also, and more important, black America has done to them.

Some, not taking the sexuality route but still accepting 20 black society's view of their worthlessness, swing all the way across to intense religiosity. Some are staunch, fervent workers in the more traditional Southern churches—Baptist and Methodist—and others are leaders and ministers in the lower status, more evangelical Holiness sects.

Another avenue open to the black black woman is excel- 21 lence in a career. Since in the South the field most accessible to such women is education, a great many of them prepared to become teachers. But here, too, the black black woman had problems. Grades weren't given to her lightly in school, nor were promotions on the job. Consequently, she had to prepare especially well. She had to pass examinations with flying colors or be left behind; she knew that she would receive no special consideration. She had to be overqualified for a job because otherwise she didn't stand a chance of getting it—and she was competing only with other blacks. She had to have something to back her up: not charm, not personality—but training.

The black black woman's training would pay off in the 22 1970's. With the arrival of integration the black black woman would find, paradoxically enough, that her skin color in an integrated situation was not the handicap it had been in an all-black situation. But it wasn't until the middle and late 1960s, when the post-1945 generation of black males arrived on college campuses, that I noticed any change in the situation at all. *He* wore an afro and *she* wore an afro, and sometimes the only way you could tell them apart was when his afro was taller than hers. Black had become beautiful, and the really black girl was often selected as queen of various campus activities. It was then that the dread I felt at dealing with the college-educated black male began to ease. Even now, though, when I have occasion to engage in any type of transaction with a college-educated black man, I gauge his age. If I guess he was born after 1945, I feel confident that the transaction will turn out all right. If he probably was born before 1945, my stomach tightens, I find myself taking shallow breaths, and I try to state my business and escape as soon as possible.

For Study and Discussion

QUESTIONS FOR RESPONSE

1. How do you respond when you or your friends are judged by some physical feature—weight, height, hair?
2. How do you and your friends identify various social classes? What assumptions do you make about people in each class?

QUESTIONS ABOUT PURPOSE

1. Why does Mebane use the concept of power to introduce her classification?
2. How does Mebane use her essay to explain the impulse of the victim to adopt the attitudes of the oppressor?

QUESTIONS ABOUT AUDIENCE

1. Does Mebane envision her readers as primarily black or primarily white, primarily men or primarily women? Explain your answer.
2. In what way do you think Mebane's system may apply to the attitudes of today's African-American students? Explain your answer.

QUESTIONS ABOUT STRATEGIES

1. How does Mebane classify her college classmates by color and class? What assumptions do her teachers make about black black working-class women?

2. What options does Mebane suggest are available to black black women? How are these options enforced?

QUESTIONS FOR DISCUSSION

1. How did the civil rights movement of the 1950s and black consciousness movement of the 1960s change the African-American community's definition of beauty?
2. Do subtle judgments about class and color still control the power structure of the African-American community? In what way?

Desmond Morris was born in 1928 in Purton, Wiltshire, England, and educated at Birmingham University and Oxford University. After receiving his doctorate, Morris was briefly a researcher in Oxford's department of zoology before going to work for the Zoological Society of London. He directed the society's television and film unit for several years, served as the society's curator of mammals, and then, striking out in an apparently new direction, became the director of London's Institute of Contemporary Arts. In 1950 he exhibited his own paintings in a one-man show. Since 1968 he has held a research fellowship at Oxford and devoted much of his time to writing. Although he has written many books about animals (chiefly for children), his major writing has focused on human behavior. Two of his books on that subject, *The Naked Ape* (1967) and *The Human Zoo* (1968), received much critical and popular acclaim. In "Territorial Behaviour," reprinted from *Manwatching* (1974), Morris identifies three kinds of territories that people define and defend.

Territorial Behaviour

A TERRITORY IS a defended space. In the broadest sense, there are three kinds of human territory: tribal, family and personal.

It is rare for people to be driven to physical fighting in defense of these "owned" spaces, but fight they will, if pushed to the limit. The invading army encroaching on national territory, the gang moving into a rival district, the trespasser climbing into an orchard, the burglar breaking into a house, the bully pushing to the front of a queue, the driver trying to steal a parking space, all of these intruders are liable to be met with resistance varying from the vigorous to the savagely violent. Even if the law is on the side of the intruder, the urge to protect a territory may be so strong that otherwise peaceful citizens abandon all their usual controls and inhibitions. Attempts to evict families from their homes, no matter how socially valid the reasons, can lead to siege conditions reminiscent of the defence of a medieval fortress.

The fact that these upheavals are so rare is a measure of the success of Territorial Signals as a system of dispute pre- 3

To defend our territory, we employ visual signals at three levels: tribal, family, and personal.

---

vention. It is sometimes cynically stated that "all property is theft," but in reality it is the opposite. Property, as owned space which is *displayed* as owned space, is a special kind of sharing system which reduces fighting much more than it causes it. Man is a co-operative species, but he is also competitive, and his struggle for dominance has to be structured in some way if chaos is to be avoided. The establishment of territorial rights is one such structure. It limits dominance geographically. I am dominant in my territory and you are dominant in yours. In other words, dominance is shared out spatially, and we all have some. Even if I am weak and unintelligent and you can dominate me when we meet on neutral ground, I can still enjoy a thoroughly dominant role as soon as I retreat to my private base. Be it ever so humble, there is no place like a home territory.

Of course, I can still be intimidated by a particularly domi- 4
nant individual who enters my home base, but his encroachment will be dangerous for him and he will think twice about

it, because he will know that here my urge to resist will be dramatically magnified and my usual subservience banished. Insulted at the heart of my own territory, I may easily explode into battle—either symbolic or real—with a result that may be damaging to both of us.

In order for this to work, each territory has to be plainly advertised as such. Just as a dog cocks its leg to deposit its personal scent on the trees in its locality, so the human animal cocks its leg symbolically all over his home base. But because we are predominantly visual animals we employ mostly visual signals, and it is worth asking how we do this at the three levels: tribal, family and personal.

First: the Tribal Territory. We evolved as tribal animals, living in comparatively small groups, probably of less than a hundred, and we existed like that for millions of years. It is our basic social unit, a group in which everyone knows everyone else. Essentially, the tribal territory consisted of a home base surrounded by extended hunting grounds. Any neighbouring tribe intruding on our social space would be repelled and driven away. As these early tribes swelled into agricultural super-tribes, and eventually into industrial nations, their territorial defence systems became increasingly elaborate. The tiny, ancient home base of the hunting tribe became the great capital city, the primitive war-paint became the flags, emblems, uniforms and regalia of the specialized military, and the war-chants became national anthems, marching songs and bugle calls. Territorial boundary-lines hardened into fixed borders, often conspicuously patrolled and punctuated with defensive structures—forts and lookout posts, checkpoints and great walls, and, today, customs barriers.

Today each nation flies its own flag, a symbolic embodiment of its territorial status. But patriotism is not enough. The ancient tribal hunter lurking inside each citizen finds himself unsatisfied by membership of such a vast conglomeration of individuals, most of whom are totally unknown to him personally. He does his best to feel that he shares a common territorial defence with them all, but the scale of the operation has become inhuman. It is hard to feel a sense of belonging with a tribe of fifty million or more. His answer is to form sub-groups, nearer to his ancient pattern, smaller and more personally known to him—the local club, the teenage gang, the union, the specialist society, the sports association, the political party, the college fraternity, the social clique, the protest group, and the rest. Rare indeed is the individual who does not belong to at least one of these splinter groups, and take from it a sense of tribal allegiance and brotherhood. Typical of all these groups is the development of Territorial Signals—badges, costumes, headquarters, banners, slogans, and all the other displays of group identity. This is where the action is, in terms of tribal territorialism, and only when a major war breaks out does the emphasis shift upwards to the higher group level of the nation.

Each of these modern pseudo-tribes sets up its own special   8 kind of home base. In extreme cases non-members are totally excluded, in others they are allowed in as visitors with limited rights and under a control system of special rules. In many ways they are like miniature nations, with their own flags and emblems and their own border guards. The exclusive club has its own "customs barrier": the doorman who checks your "passport" (your membership card) and prevents strangers from passing in unchallenged. There is a government: the club committee; and often special displays of the tribal elders: the photographs or portraits of previous officials on the walls. At the heart of the specialized territories there is a powerful feeling of security and importance, a sense of shared defence against the outside world. Much of the club chatter, both serious and joking, directs itself against the rottenness of everything outside the club boundaries—in that "other world" beyond the protected portals.

In social organizations which embody a strong class sys-   9 tem, such as military units and large business concerns, there are many territorial rules, often unspoken, which interfere with the official hierarchy. High-status individuals, such as officers or managers, could in theory enter any of the regions occupied by the lower levels in the peck order, but they limit this power in a striking way. An officer seldom enters a sergeant's mess or a barrack room unless it is for a formal inspection. He respects those regions as alien territories even though he has the power to go there by virtue of his dominant role. And in businesses, part of the appeal of unions, over and above their obvious functions, is that with their officials, headquarters and meetings they add a sense of territorial power for the staff workers. It is almost as if each military organization and business concern consists of two warring tribes: the officers versus the other ranks, and the management versus the workers. Each has its special home base within the system, and the territorial defence pattern thrusts itself into what, on the surface, is a pure social hierarchy. Negotiations between managements and unions are tribal battles fought out over the neutral ground of a boardroom table, and are as much concerned with territorial display as they are with resolving problems of wages and conditions. Indeed, if one side gives in too quickly and accepts the other's demands, the victors feel strangely cheated and deeply suspicious that it may be a trick. What they are missing is the protracted sequence of ritual and counter-ritual that keeps alive their group territorial identity.

Likewise, many of the hostile displays of sports fans and   10
teenage gangs are primarily concerned with displaying their group image to rival fan-clubs and gangs. Except in rare cases, they do not attack one another's headquarters, drive out the occupants, and reduce them to a submissive, subordinate condition. It is enough to have scuffles on the borderlands between the two rival territories. This is particularly clear at football matches, where the fan-club headquarters becomes temporarily shifted from the club-house to a section of the stands, and where minor fighting breaks out at the unofficial boundary line between the massed groups of rival supporters. Newspaper reports play up the few accidents and injuries which do occur on such occasions, but when these are studied in relation to the total numbers of displaying fans involved it is clear that the serious incidents represent only a tiny fraction of the overall group behaviour. For every actual punch or kick

there are a thousand war-cries, war-dances, chants and gestures.

Second: the Family Territory. Essentially, the family is a 11 breeding unit and the family territory is a breeding ground. At the centre of this space, there is the nest—the bedroom— where, tucked up in bed, we feel at our most territorially secure. In a typical house the bedroom is upstairs, where a safe nest should be. This puts it farther away from the entrance hall, the area where contact is made, intermittently, with the outside world. The less private reception rooms, where intruders are allowed access, are the next line of defence. Beyond them, outside the walls of the building, there is often a symbolic remnant of the ancient feeding grounds— a garden. Its symbolism often extends to the plants and animals it contains, which cease to be nutritional and become merely decorative—flowers and pets. But like a true territorial space it has a conspicuously displayed boundary-line, the garden fence, wall, or railings. Often no more than a token barrier, this is the outer territorial demarcation, separating the private world of the family from the public world beyond. To cross it puts any visitor or intruder at an immediate disadvantage. As he crosses the threshold, his dominance wanes, slightly but unmistakably. He is entering an area where he senses that he must ask permission to do simple things that he would consider a right elsewhere. Without lifting a finger, the territorial owners exert their dominance. This is done by all the hundreds of small ownership "markers" they have deposited on their family territory: the ornaments, the "possessed" objects positioned in the rooms and on the walls; the furnishings, the furniture, the colours, the patterns, all owner-chosen and all making this particular home base unique to them.

It is one of the tragedies of modern architecture that there 12 has been a standardization of these vital territorial living-units. One of the most important aspects of a home is that it should be similar to other homes only in a general way, and that in detail it should have many differences, making it a

particular home. Unfortunately, it is cheaper to build a row
of houses, or a block of flats, so that all the family living-units
are identical, but the territorial urge rebels against this trend
and house-owners struggle as best they can to make their
mark on their mass-produced properties. They do this with
garden-design, with front-door colours, with curtain patterns, with wallpaper and all the other decorative elements
that together create a unique and different family environment. Only when they have completed this nest-building do
they feel truly "at home" and secure.

When they venture forth as a family unit they repeat the   13
process in a minor way. On a day-trip to the seaside, they load
the car with personal belongings and it becomes their temporary, portable territory. Arriving at the beach they stake out
a small territorial claim, marking it with rugs, towels, baskets
and other belongings to which they can return from their
seaboard wanderings. Even if they all leave it at once to bathe,
it retains a characteristic territorial quality and other family
groups arriving will recognize this by setting up their own
"home" bases at a respectful distance. Only when the whole
beach has filled up with these marked spaces will newcomers
start to position themselves in such a way that the inter-base
distance becomes reduced. Forced to pitch between several
existing beach territories they will feel a momentary sensation
of intrusion, and the established "owners" will feel a similar
sensation of invasion, even though they are not being directly
inconvenienced.

The same territorial scene is being played out in parks and   14
fields and on riverbanks, wherever family groups gather in
their clustered units. But if rivalry for spaces creates mild
feelings of hostility, it is true to say that, without the territorial
system of sharing and space-limited dominance, there would
be chaotic disorder.

Third: the Personal Space. If a man enters a waiting-room   15
and sits at one end of a long row of empty chairs, it is possible
to predict where the next man to enter will seat himself. He
will not sit next to the first man, nor will he sit at the far end,
right away from him. He will choose a position about halfway

between these two points. The next man to enter will take the largest gap left, and sit roughly in the middle of that, and so on, until eventually the latest newcomer will be forced to select a seat that places him right next to one of the already seated men. Similar patterns can be observed in cinemas, public urinals, aeroplanes, trains and buses. This is a reflection of the fact that we all carry with us, everywhere we go, a portable territory called a Personal Space. If people move inside this space, we feel threatened. If they keep too far outside it, we feel rejected. The result is a subtle series of spatial adjustments, usually operating quite unconsciously and producing ideal compromises as far as this is possible. If a situation becomes too crowded, then we adjust our reactions accordingly and allow our personal space to shrink. Jammed into an elevator, a rush-hour compartment, or a packed room, we give up altogether and allow body-to-body contact, but when we relinquish our Personal Space in this way, we adopt certain special techniques. In essence, what we do is to convert these other bodies into "nonpersons." We studiously ignore them, and they us. We try not to face them if we can possibly avoid it. We wipe all expressiveness from our faces, letting them go blank. We may look up at the ceiling or down at the floor, and we reduce body movements to a minimum. Packed together like sardines in a tin, we stand dumbly still, sending out as few social signals as possible.

Even if the crowding is less severe, we still tend to cut 16 down our social interactions in the presence of large numbers. Careful observations of children in play groups revealed that if they are high density groupings there is less social interaction between the individual children, even though there is theoretically more opportunity for such contacts. At the same time, the high-density groups show a higher frequency of aggressive and destructive behaviour patterns in their play. Personal Space—"elbow room"—is a vital commodity for the human animal, and one that cannot be ignored without risking serious trouble.

Of course, we all enjoy the excitement of being in a crowd, 17 and this reaction cannot be ignored. But there are crowds and crowds. It is pleasant enough to be in a "spectator crowd," but not so appealing to find yourself in the middle of a rush-hour crush. The difference between the two is that the spectator crowd is all facing in the same direction and concentrating on a distant point of interest. Attending a theatre, there are twinges of rising hostility toward the stranger who sits down immediately in front of you or the one who squeezes into the seat next to you. The shared armrest can become a polite, but distinct, territorial boundary-dispute region. However, as soon as the show begins, these invasions of Personal Space are forgotten and the attention is focused beyond the small space where the crowding is taking place. Now, each member of the audience feels himself spatially related, not to his cramped neighbours, but to the actor on the stage, and this distance is, if anything, too great. In the rush-hour crowd, by contrast, each member of the pushing throng is competing with his neighbours all the time. There is no escape to a spatial relation with a distant actor, only the pushing, shoving bodies all around.

Those of us who have to spend a great deal of time in crowded conditions become gradually better able to adjust, but no one can ever become completely immune to invasions of Personal Space. This is because they remain forever associated with either powerful hostile or equally powerful loving feelings. All through our childhood we will have been held to be loved and held to be hurt, and anyone who invades our Personal Space when we are adults is, in effect, threatening to extend his behaviour into one of these two highly charged areas of human interaction. Even if his motives are clearly neither hostile nor sexual, we still find it hard to suppress our reactions to his close approach. Unfortunately, different countries have different ideas about exactly how close is close. It is easy enough to test your own "space reaction": when you are talking to someone in the street or in any open space, reach out with your arm and see where the nearest point on his body comes. If you hail from western Europe, you will find that he is at roughly fingertip distance from you. In other words, as you reach out, your fingertips will just about make contact with his shoulder. If you come from eastern Europe you will find you are standing at "wrist distance." If you come from the Mediterranean region you will find that you are much closer to your companion, at little more than "elbow distance."

Trouble begins when a member of one of these cultures [19] meets and talks to one from another. Say a British diplomat meets an Italian or an Arab diplomat at an embassy function. They start talking in a friendly way, but soon the fingertips man begins to feel uneasy. Without knowing quite why, he starts to back away gently from his companion. The companion edges forward again. Each tries in this way to set up a Personal Space relationship that suits his own background. But it is impossible to do. Every time the Mediterranean diplomat advances to a distance that feels comfortable for him, the British diplomat feels threatened. Every time the Briton moves back, the other feels rejected. Attempts to adjust this situation often lead to a talking pair shifting slowly across a room, and many an embassy reception is dotted with western-European fingertip-distance men pinned against the walls by eager elbow-distance men. Until such differences are fully understood, and allowances made, these minor differences in "body territories" will continue to act as an alienation factor which may interfere in a subtle way with diplomatic harmony and other forms of international transaction.

If there are distance problems when engaged in conversation, then there are clearly going to be even bigger difficulties [20] where people must work privately in a shared space. Close proximity of others, pressing against the invisible boundaries of our personal body-territory, makes it difficult to concentrate on non-social matters. Flatmates, students sharing a study, sailors in the cramped quarters of a ship, and office staff in crowded workplaces, all have to face this problem. They solve it by "cocooning." They use a variety of devices to shut themselves off from the others present. The best possible cocoon, of course, is a small private room—a den, a private office, a study or a studio—which physically obscures the presence of other nearby territory-owners. This is the ideal situation for non-social work, but the space-sharers cannot enjoy this luxury. Their cocooning must be symbolic. They may, in certain cases, be able to erect small physical barriers, such as screens and partitions, which give substance to their invisible Personal Space boundaries, but when this cannot be done, other means must be sought. One of these is the "favoured object." Each space-sharer develops a preference, repeatedly expressed until it becomes a fixed pattern, for a particular chair, or table, or alcove. Others come to respect this, and friction is reduced. This system is often formally arranged (this is my desk, that is yours), but even where it is not, favoured places soon develop. Professor Smith has a favourite chair in the library. It is not formally his, but he always uses it and others avoid it. Seats around a mess-room table, or a boardroom table, become almost personal property for specific individuals. Even in the home, father has his favourite chair for reading the newspaper or watching television. Another device is the blinkers-posture. Just as a horse that over-reacts to other horses and the distractions of the noisy race-course is given a pair of blinkers to shield its eyes, so people studying privately in a public place put on pseudo-blinkers in the form of shielding hands. Resting their elbows on the table, they sit with their hands screening their eyes from the scene on either side.

A third method of reinforcing the body-territory is to use personal markers. Books, papers and other personal belongings are scattered around the favoured site to render it more privately owned in the eyes of companions. Spreading out one's belongings is a well-known trick in public-transport situations, where a traveller tries to give the impression that seats next to him are taken. In many contexts carefully arranged personal markers can act as an effective territorial display, even in the absence of the territory owner. Experiments in a library revealed that placing a pile of magazines on the table in one seating position successfully reserved that place for an average of 77 minutes. If a sports-jacket was added, draped over the chair, then the "reservation effect" lasted for over two hours.

In these ways, we strengthen the defences of our Personal   22
Spaces, keeping out intruders with the minimum of open
hostility. As with all territorial behaviour, the object is to
defend space with signals rather than with fists and at all three
levels—the tribal, the family and the personal—it is a remarkably efficient system of space-sharing. It does not always seem
so, because newspapers and newscasts inevitably magnify the
exceptions and dwell on those cases where the signals have
failed and wars have broken out, gangs have fought, neighbouring families have feuded, or colleagues have clashed, but
for every territorial signal that has failed, there are millions of
others that have not. They do not rate a mention in the news,
but they nevertheless constitute a dominant feature of human
society—the society of a remarkably territorial animal.

For Study and Discussion

QUESTIONS FOR RESPONSE

1. How do you define your personal space? What markers do you
   use to identify the boundaries of this space?
2. What special techniques (or tricks) do you use when you are
   forced to live or work in a crowded space?

QUESTIONS ABOUT PURPOSE

1. What is Morris attempting to prove about the human need for
   dominance? How do the concepts of threat, safety, rejection, and
   ritual relate to his thesis?
2. Why is territorial behavior defined and controlled by "advertising"? In addition to "visual signals," what other factors define
   "defended space"? Make a list of the signals Morris mentions that
   are not visual. How do people discover these signs?

QUESTIONS ABOUT AUDIENCE

1. How does Morris's style suggest that he is writing for the readers
   of "coffee-table" books? For example, how does he manipulate
   point of view in paragraph 3 to appeal to the common experience
   of his readers?

2. In what ways does Morris anticipate that his readers will adjust his definitions of tribal, family, and personal space to their own experiences? Cite examples in each of his three categories.

QUESTIONS ABOUT STRATEGIES

1. How does Morris use the interior design and external landscape of a house to define family territory? How does the family make their territory portable?
2. How does Morris illustrate the need for flexibility in defining his third category? For example, what kind of territorial adjustments do people have to make when they enter a crowded elevator or rush-hour traffic?

QUESTIONS FOR DISCUSSION

1. How does the concept of hierarchy complicate Morris's analysis of territory? For example, what is the difference between the concepts of class and tribe? Examine Morris's analysis of business and the military in paragraph 9.
2. According to Morris, "different countries have different ideas" about personal space. How might contrasting ideas about personal space help explain contrasting notions of political space? How does paragraph 19 explain why diplomatic conversations could end in military conflicts?

Gail Sheehy was born in 1937, attended the University of Vermont and Columbia University Journalism School, and worked as contributing editor for *New York* magazine for ten years. Her writing has appeared in *Esquire, McCall's, Ms.,* and *Rolling Stone*. Although Sheehy's first book was a novel, *Lovesounds* (1970), she soon turned to nonfiction, writing *Panthermania: The Clash of Black Against Black in One American City* (1971), *Hustling: Prostitution in Our Wide Open Society* (1973), and her best-selling *Passages: Predictable Crises of Adult Life* (1976). Her more recent books include *The Spirit of Survival* (1986), a history of Cambodia; *The Silent Passage* (1992), a study of the social and psychological effects of menopause; and *New Passages* (1995), an analysis of adult behavior beyond the age of fifty. In "Predictable Crises of Adulthood," excerpted from the second chapter of *Passages,* Sheehy identifies six stages that most adults experience between the ages of eighteen and fifty.

Predictable Crises of Adulthood

WE ARE NOT unlike a particularly hardy crustacean. The lobster grows by developing and shedding a series of hard, protective shells. Each time it expands from within, the confining shell must be sloughed off. It is left exposed and vulnerable until, in time, a new covering grows to replace the old.

With each passage from one stage of human growth to the next we, too, must shed a protective structure. We are left exposed and vulnerable—but also yeasty and embryonic again, capable of stretching in ways we hadn't known before. These sheddings may take several years or more. Coming out of each passage, though, we enter a longer and more stable period in which we can expect relative tranquillity and a sense of equilibrium regained. . . .

As we shall see, each person engages the steps of develop-   3
ment in his or her own characteristic *step-style*. Some people never complete the whole sequence. And none of us "solves" with one step—by jumping out of the parental home into a job or marriage, for example—the problems in separating from the caregivers of childhood. Nor do we "achieve" autonomy once and for all by converting our dreams into concrete goals, even when we attain those goals. The central

---

On the developmental ladder, the mastery of one set of tasks may fortify us for the next period and the next set of challenges.

---

issues or tasks of one period are never fully completed, tied up, and cast aside. But when they lose their primacy and the current life structure has served its purpose, we are ready to move on to the next period.

Can one catch up? What might look to others like listless-   4
ness, contrariness, a maddening refusal to face up to an ob-vious task may be a person's own unique detour that will bring him out later on the other side. Developmental gains won can later be lost—and rewon. It's plausible, though it can't be proven, that the mastery of one set of tasks fortifies us for the next period and the next set of challenges. But it's important not to think too mechanistically. Machines work by units. The bureaucracy (supposedly) works step by step. Human beings, thank God, have an individual inner dynamic that can never be precisely coded.

Although I have indicated the ages when Americans are   5

likely to go through each stage, and the differences between men and women where they are striking, do not take the ages too seriously. The stages are the thing, and most particularly the sequence.

Here is the briefest outline of the developmental ladder. 6

PULLING UP ROOTS

Before 18, the motto is loud and clear: "I have to get away 7 from my parents." But the words are seldom connected to action. Generally still safely part of our families, even if away at school, we feel our autonomy to be subject to erosion from moment to moment.

After 18, we begin Pulling Up Roots in earnest. College, 8 military service, and short-term travels are all customary vehicles our society provides for the first round trips between family and a base of one's own. In the attempt to separate our view of the world from our family's view, despite vigorous protestations to the contrary—"I know exactly what I want!"—we cast about for any beliefs we can call our own. And in the process of testing those beliefs we are often drawn to fads, preferably those most mysterious and inaccessible to our parents.

Whatever tentative memberships we try out in the world, 9 the fear haunts us that we are really kids who cannot take care of ourselves. We cover that fear with acts of defiance and mimicked confidence. For allies to replace our parents, we turn to our contemporaries. They become conspirators. So long as their perspective meshes with our own, they are able to substitute for the sanctuary of the family. But that doesn't last very long. And the instant they diverge from the shaky ideals of "our group," they are seen as betrayers. Rebounds to the family are common between the ages of 18 and 22.

The tasks of this passage are to locate ourselves in a peer 10 group role, a sex role, an anticipated occupation, an ideology or world view. As a result, we gather the impetus to leave home physically and the identity to *begin* leaving home emotionally.

Even as one part of us seeks to be an individual, another   11
part longs to restore the safety and comfort of merging with
another. Thus one of the most popular myths of this passage
is: We can piggyback our development by attaching to a
Stronger One. But people who marry during this time often
prolong financial and emotional ties to the family and relatives that impede them from becoming self-sufficient.

A stormy passage through the Pulling Up Roots years will   12
probably facilitate the normal progression of the adult life
cycle. If one doesn't have an identity crisis at this point, it
will erupt during a later transition, when the penalties may
be harder to bear.

THE TRYING TWENTIES

The Trying Twenties confront us with the question of how   13
to take hold in the adult world. Our focus shifts from the
interior turmoils of late adolescence—"Who am I?" "What is
truth?"—and we become almost totally preoccupied with
working out the externals. "How do I put my aspirations into
effect?" "What is the best way to start?" "Where do I go?"
"Who can help me?" "How did *you* do it?"

In this period, which is longer and more stable compared   14
with the passage that leads to it, the tasks are as enormous as
they are exhilarating: To shape a Dream, that vision of ourselves which will generate energy, aliveness, and hope. To
prepare for a lifework. To find a mentor if possible. And to
form the capacity for intimacy, without losing in the process
whatever consistency of self we have thus far mustered. The
first test structure must be erected around the life we choose
to try.

Doing what we "should" is the most pervasive theme of   15
the twenties. The "shoulds" are largely defined by family
models, the press of the culture, or the prejudices of our
peers. If the prevailing cultural instructions are that one
should get married and settle down behind one's own door,
a nuclear family is born. If instead the peers insist that one
should do one's own thing, the 25-year-old is likely to har-

ness himself onto a Harley-Davidson and burn up Route 66 in the commitment to have no commitments.

One of the terrifying aspects of the twenties is the inner   16 conviction that the choices we make are irrevocable. It is largely a false fear. Change is quite possible, and some altera- tion of our original choices is probably inevitable.

Two impulses, as always, are at work. One is to build a   17 firm, safe structure for the future by making strong commit- ments, to "be set." Yet people who slip into a ready-made form without much self-examination are likely to find them- selves *locked in.*

The other urge is to explore and experiment, keeping any   18 structure tentative and therefore easily reversible. Taken to the extreme, these are people who skip from one trial job and one limited personal encounter to another, spending their twenties in the *transient* state.

Although the choices of our twenties are not irrevocable,   19 they do set in motion a Life Pattern. Some of us follow the locked-in pattern, others the transient pattern, the wun- derkind pattern, the caregiver pattern, and there are a number of others. Such patterns strongly influence the particular questions raised for each person during each passage. . . .

Buoyed by powerful illusions and belief in the power of   20 the will, we commonly insist in our twenties that what we have chosen to do is the one true course in life. Our backs go up at the merest hint that we are like our parents, that two decades of parental training might be reflected in our current actions and attitudes.

"Not me," is the motto, "I'm different."   21

CATCH-30

Impatient with devoting ourselves to the "shoulds," a new   22 vitality springs from within as we approach 30. Men and women alike speak of feeling too narrow and restricted. They blame all sorts of things, but what the restrictions boil down to are the outgrowth of career and personal choices of the twenties. They may have been choices perfectly suited to that stage. But now the fit feels different. Some inner aspect that was left out is striving to be taken into account. Important new choices must be made, and commitments altered or deepened. The work involves great change, turmoil, and often crisis—a simultaneous feeling of rock bottom and the urge to bust out.

One common response is the tearing up of the life we spent   23
most of our twenties putting together. It may mean striking out on a secondary road toward a new vision or converting a dream of "running for president" into a more realistic goal. The single person feels a push to find a partner. The woman who was previously content at home with children chafes to venture into the world. The childless couple reconsiders children. And almost everyone who is married, especially those married for seven years, feels a discontent.

If the discontent doesn't lead to a divorce, it will, or   24
should, call for a serious review of the marriage and of each partner's aspirations in the Catch-30 condition. The gist of that condition was expressed by a 29-year-old associate with a Wall Street law firm:

"I'm considering leaving the firm. I've been there four   25
years now; I'm getting good feedback, but I have no clients of my own. I feel weak. If I wait much longer, it will be too late, too close to that fateful time of decision on whether or not to become a partner. I'm success-oriented. But the concept of being 55 years old and stuck in a monotonous job drives me wild. It drives me crazy now, just a little bit. I'd say that 85 percent of the time I thoroughly enjoy my work. But when I get a screwball case, I come away from court saying, 'What am I doing here?' It's a *visceral* reaction that I'm wasting my time. I'm trying to find some way to make a social contribution or a slot in city government. I keep saying, 'There's something more.'"

Besides the push to broaden himself professionally, there   26
is a wish to expand his personal life. He wants two or three more children. "The concept of a home has become very meaningful to me, a place to get away from troubles and relax. I love my son in a way I could not have anticipated. I never could live alone."

Consumed with the work of making his own critical life- 27
steering decisions, he demonstrates the essential shift at this
age: an absolute requirement to be more self-concerned. The
self has new value now that his competency has been proved.

His wife is struggling with her own age-30 priorities. She 28
wants to go to law school, but he wants more children. If she
is going to stay home, she wants him to make more time for
the family instead of taking on even wider professional commitments. His view of the bind, of what he would most like
from his wife, is this:

"I'd like not to be bothered. It sounds cruel, but I'd like 29
not to have to worry about what she's going to do next week.
Which is why I've told her several times that I think she
should do something. Go back to school and get a degree in
social work or geography or whatever. Hopefully that would
fulfill her, and then I wouldn't have to worry about her line
of problems. I want her to be decisive about herself."

The trouble with his advice to his wife is that it comes out 30
of concern with *his* convenience, rather than with *her* development. She quickly picks up on this lack of goodwill: He is
trying to dispose of her. At the same time, he refuses her the
same latitude to be "selfish" in making an independent decision to broaden her own horizons. Both perceive a lack of
mutuality. And that is what Catch-30 is all about for the
couple.

ROOTING AND EXTENDING

Life becomes less provisional, more rational and orderly in 31
the early thirties. We begin to settle down in the full sense.
Most of us begin putting down roots and sending out new
shoots. People buy houses and become very earnest about
climbing career ladders. Men in particular concern themselves with "making it." Satisfaction with marriage generally
goes downhill in the thirties (for those who have remained together) compared with the highly valued, vision-supporting
marriage of the twenties. This coincides with the couple's
reduced social life outside the family and the in-turned focus
on raising their children.

THE DEADLINE DECADE

In the middle of the thirties we come upon a crossroads. We 32
have reached the halfway mark. Yet even as we are reaching
our prime, we begin to see there is a place where it finishes.
Time starts to squeeze.

The loss of youth, the faltering of physical powers we have 33
always taken for granted, the fading purpose of stereotyped
roles by which we have thus far identified ourselves, the
spiritual dilemma of having no absolute answers—any or all
of these shocks can give this passage the character of crisis.
Such thoughts usher in a decade between 35 and 45 that can
be called the Deadline Decade. It is a time of both danger
and opportunity. All of us have the chance to rework the
narrow identity by which we defined ourselves in the first half
of life. And those of us who make the most of the opportunity
will have a full-out authenticity crisis.

To come through this authenticity crisis, we must reexam- 34
ine our purposes and reevaluate how to spend our resources
from now on. "Why am I doing all this? What do I really
believe in?" No matter what we have been doing, there will
be parts of ourselves that have been suppressed and now need
to find expression. "Bad" feelings will demand acknowledgment along with the good.

It is frightening to step off onto the treacherous footbridge 35
leading to the second half of life. We can't take everything
with us on this journey through uncertainty. Along the way,
we discover that we are alone. We no longer have to ask
permission because we are the providers of our own safety.
We must learn to give ourselves permission. We stumble upon
feminine or masculine aspects of our natures that up to this
time have usually been masked. There is grieving to be done
because an old self is dying. By taking in our suppressed and
even our unwanted parts, we prepare at the gut level for the
reintegration of an identity that is ours and ours alone—not
some artificial form put together to please the culture or our
mates. It is a dark passage at the beginning. But by disassem-

bling ourselves, we can glimpse the light and gather our parts into a renewal.

Women sense this inner crossroads earlier than men do. The time pinch often prompts a woman to stop and take an all-points survey at age 35. Whatever options she has already played out, she feels a "my last chance" urgency to review those options she has set aside and those that aging and biology will close off in the *now foreseeable* future. For all her qualms and confusion about where to start looking for a new future, she usually enjoys an exhilaration of release. Assertiveness begins rising. There are so many firsts ahead.   36

Men, too, feel the time push in the mid-thirties. Most men respond by pressing down harder on the career accelerator. It's "my last chance" to pull away from the pack. It is no longer enough to be the loyal junior executive, the promising young novelist, the lawyer who does a little *pro bono* work on the side. He wants now to become part of top management, to be recognized as an established writer, or an active politician with his own legislative program. With some chagrin, he discovers that he has been too anxious to please and too vulnerable to criticism. He wants to put together his own ship.   37

During this period of intense concentration on external advancement, it is common for men to be unaware of the more difficult, gut issues that are propelling them forward. The survey that was neglected at 35 becomes a crucible at 40. Whatever rung of achievement he has reached, the man of 40 usually feels stale, restless, burdened, and unappreciated. He worries about his health. He wonders, "Is this all there is?" He may make a series of departures from well-established lifelong base lines, including marriage. More and more men are seeking second careers in midlife. Some become self-destructive. And many men in their forties experience a major shift of emphasis away from pouring all their energies into their own advancement. A more tender, feeling side comes into play. They become interested in developing an ethical self.   38

RENEWAL OR RESIGNATION

Somewhere in the mid-forties, equilibrium is regained. A new   39
stability is achieved, which may be more or less satisfying.

If one has refused to budge through the midlife transition,   40
the sense of staleness will calcify into resignation. One by one,
the safety and supports will be withdrawn from the person
who is standing still. Parents will become children; children
will become strangers; a mate will grow away or go away; the
career will become just a job—and each of these events will
be felt as an abandonment. The crisis will probably emerge
again around 50. And although its wallop will be greater, the
jolt may be just what is needed to prod the resigned middle-
ager toward seeking revitalization.

On the other hand . . .   41

If we have confronted ourselves in the middle passage and   42
found a renewal of purpose around which we are eager to
build a more authentic life structure, these may well be the
best years. Personal happiness takes a sharp turn upward for
partners who can now accept the fact: "I cannot expect
anyone to fully understand me." Parents can be forgiven for
the burdens of our childhood. Children can be let go without
leaving us in collapsed silence. At 50, there is a new warmth
and mellowing. Friends become more important than ever,
but so does privacy. Since it is so often proclaimed by people
past midlife, the motto of this stage might be "No more
bullshit."

For Study and Discussion

QUESTIONS FOR RESPONSE

1. Does it reassure or infuriate you when what you assume is your
   own idiosyncratic behavior is classified as "normal" for your age?
   Explain your answer.
2. How much confidence do you have in Sheehy's system? What
   kinds of evidence do you think she used to organize it?

QUESTIONS ABOUT PURPOSE

1. What is Sheehy's purpose—to define the various stages of human development or to analyze the process of moving (or the consequences of not moving) from one stage to another?
2. What do the words *predictable* and *crisis* contribute to Sheehy's purpose?

QUESTIONS ABOUT AUDIENCE

1. Who does Sheehy imagine as the readers of her essay: general readers, psychologists, people who are stuck in one stage, or people who have successfully navigated the passage from stage to stage?
2. How does Sheehy use the pronoun *we* to establish a relationship with her readers?

QUESTIONS ABOUT STRATEGIES

1. How does Sheehy use the opening metaphor of the lobster shedding its shell to clarify the system of development she intends to classify?
2. How effective are the headings Sheehy uses to identify the six stages of development?

QUESTIONS FOR DISCUSSION

1. What assumptions about growth does Sheehy make by stopping her system at age fifty? Suggest some crises (and stages) for the years after fifty.
2. What problems do psychologists encounter when they try to make generalizations about human behavior? For example, how does Sheehy's classification system compare with those designed for early childhood and adolescence?

FLANNERY O'CONNOR

Flannery O'Connor (1925–1964) was born in Savannah, Georgia, and was educated at the Women's College of Georgia and the University of Iowa. She returned to her mother's farm near Milledgeville, Georgia, when she discovered that she had contracted lupus erythematosus, the systemic disease that had killed her father and of which she herself was to die. For the last fourteen years of her life, she lived a quiet, productive life on the farm—raising peacocks, painting, and writing the extraordinary stories and novels that won her worldwide acclaim. Her novels, *Wise Blood* (1952), which was adapted for film in 1979, and *The Violent Bear It Away* (1960), deal with fanatical preachers. Her thirty-one carefully crafted stories, combining grotesque comedy and violent tragedy, appear in *A Good Man Is Hard to Find* (1955), *Everything That Rises Must Converge* (1965), and *The Complete Stories* (1971), which won the National Book Award. "Revelation" dramatizes the ironic discoveries a woman makes about how different classes of people fit into the order of things.

Revelation

THE DOCTOR'S WAITING room, which was very small, was almost full when the Turpins entered and Mrs. Turpin, who was very large, made it look even smaller by her presence. She stood looming at the head of the magazine table set in the center of it, a living demonstration that the room was inadequate and ridiculous. Her little bright black eyes took in all the patients as she sized up the seating situ-

1

ation. There was one vacant chair and a place on the sofa occupied by a blond child in a dirty blue romper who should have been told to move over and make room for the lady. He was five or six, but Mrs. Turpin saw at once that no one was going to tell him to move over. He was slumped down in the seat, his arms idle at his sides and his eyes idle in his head; his nose ran unchecked.

Mrs. Turpin put a firm hand on Claud's shoulder and said in a voice that included anyone who wanted to listen, "Claud, you sit in that chair there," and gave him a push down into the vacant one. Claud was florid and bald and sturdy, somewhat shorter than Mrs. Turpin, but he sat down as if he were accustomed to doing what she told him to.

Mrs. Turpin remained standing. The only man in the room besides Claud was a lean stringy old fellow with a rusty hand spread out on each knee, whose eyes were closed as if he were asleep or dead or pretending to be so as not to get up and offer her his seat. Her gaze settled agreeably on a well-dressed gray-haired lady whose eyes met hers and whose expression said: if that child belonged to me, he would have some manners and move over—there's plenty of room there for you and him too.

Claud looked up with a sigh and made as if to rise.

"Sit down," Mrs. Turpin said. "You know you're not supposed to stand on that leg. He has an ulcer on his leg," she explained.

Claud lifted his foot onto the magazine table and rolled his trouser leg up to reveal a purple swelling on a plump marble-white calf.

"My!" the pleasant lady said. "How did you do that?"

"A cow kicked him," Mrs. Turpin said.

"Goodness!" said the lady.

Claud rolled his trouser leg down.

"Maybe the little boy would move over," the lady suggested, but the child did not stir.

"Somebody will be leaving in a minute," Mrs. Turpin said. She could not understand why a doctor—with as much money as they made charging five dollars a day to just stick their head in the hospital door and look at you—couldn't afford a decent-sized waiting room. This one was hardly bigger than a garage. The table was cluttered with limp-looking magazines and at one end of it there was a big green glass ash tray full of cigarette butts and cotton wads with little blood spots on them. If she had had anything to do with the running of the place, that would have been emptied every so often. There were no chairs against the wall at the head of the room. It had a rectangular-shaped panel in it that permitted a view of the office where the nurse came and went and the secretary listened to the radio. A plastic fern in a gold pot sat in the opening and trailed its fronds down almost to the floor. The radio was softly playing gospel music.

Just then the inner door opened and a nurse with the highest stack of yellow hair Mrs. Turpin had ever seen put her face in the crack and called for the next patient. The woman sitting beside Claud grasped the two arms of her chair and hoisted herself up; she pulled her dress free from her legs and lumbered through the door where the nurse had disappeared. 13

Mrs. Turpin eased into the vacant chair, which held her tight as a corset. "I wish I could reduce," she said, and rolled her eyes and gave a comic sigh. 14

"Oh, *you* aren't fat," the stylish lady said. 15

"Ooooo I am too," Mrs. Turpin said. "Claud he eats all he wants to and never weighs over one hundred and seventy-five pounds, but me I just look at something good to eat and I gain some weight," and her stomach and shoulders shook with laughter. "You can eat all you want to, can't you, Claud?" she asked, turning to him. 16

Claud only grinned. 17

"Well, as long as you have such a good disposition," the stylish lady said, "I don't think it makes a bit of difference what size you are. You just can't beat a good disposition." 18

Next to her was a fat girl of eighteen or nineteen, scowling into a thick blue book which Mrs. Turpin saw was entitled *Human Development*. The girl raised her head and directed her scowl at Mrs. Turpin as if she did not like her looks. She 19 appeared annoyed that anyone should speak while she tried to read. The poor girl's face was blue with acne and Mrs. Turpin thought how pitiful it was to have a face like that at that age. She gave the girl a friendly smile but the girl only scowled the harder. Mrs. Turpin herself was fat but she had always had good skin, and, though she was forty-seven years old, there was not a wrinkle in her face except around her eyes from laughing too much.

Next to the ugly girl was the child, still in exactly the same position, and next to him was a thin leathery old woman in a cotton print dress. She and Claud had three sacks of chicken feed in their pump house that was in the same print. She had seen from the first that the child belonged with the old woman. She could tell by the way they sat—kind of vacant and white-trashy, as if they would sit there until Doomsday if nobody called and told them to get up. And at right angles but next to the well-dressed pleasant lady was a lank-faced woman who was certainly the child's mother. She had on a yellow sweat shirt and wine-colored slacks, both gritty-looking, and the rims of her lips were stained with snuff. Her dirty yellow hair was tied behind with a little piece of red paper ribbon. Worse than niggers any day, Mrs. Turpin thought.

The gospel hymn playing was, "When I looked up and He looked down," and Mrs. Turpin, who knew it, supplied the last line mentally, "And wona these days I know I'll weear a crown."

Without appearing to, Mrs. Turpin always noticed people's feet. The well-dressed lady had on red and gray suede shoes to match her dress. Mrs. Turpin had on her good black patent leather pumps. The ugly girl had on Girl Scout shoes and heavy socks. The old woman had on tennis shoes and the white-trashy mother had on what appeared to be bedroom slippers, black straw with gold braid threaded through them—exactly what you would have expected her to have on.

Sometimes at night when she couldn't go to sleep, Mrs. Turpin would occupy herself with the question of who she would have chosen to be if she couldn't have been herself. If Jesus had said to her before he made her, "There's only two places available for you. You can either be a nigger or white-trash," what would she have said? "Please, Jesus, please," she would have said, "just let me wait until there's another place available," and he would have said, "No, you have to go right now and I have only those two places so make up your mind." She would have wiggled and squirmed and begged and pleaded but it would have been no use and finally she would have said, "All right, make me a nigger then—but that don't mean a trashy one." And he would have made her a neat clean respectable Negro woman, herself but black.

Next to the child's mother was a red-headed youngish woman, reading one of the magazines and working a piece of chewing gum, hell for leather, as Claud would say. Mrs. Turpin could not see the woman's feet. She was not white-trash, just common. Sometimes Mrs. Turpin occupied herself at night naming the classes of people. On the bottom of the heap were most colored people, not the kind she would have been if she had been one, but most of them; then next to them—not above, just away from—were the white-trash; then above them were the home-owners, and above them the home-and-land-owners, to which she and Claud belonged. Above she and Claud were people with a lot of money and much bigger houses and much more land. But here the complexity of it would begin to bear in on her, for some of the people with a lot of money were common and ought to be below she and Claud and some of the people who had good blood had lost their money and had to rent and then there were colored people who owned their homes and land as well. There was a colored dentist in town who had two red Lincolns and a swimming pool and a farm with registered white-face cattle on it. Usually by the time she had fallen asleep all the classes of people were moiling and roiling around in her head, and she would dream they were all crammed in together in a box car, being ridden off to be put in a gas oven.

"That's a beautiful clock," she said and nodded to her   25

24

right. It was a big wall clock, the face encased in a brass sunburst.

"Yes, it's very pretty," the stylish lady said agreeably. "And right on the dot too," she added, glancing at her watch. 26

The ugly girl beside her cast an eye upward at the clock, smirked, then looked directly at Mrs. Turpin and smirked again. Then she returned her eyes to her book. She was obviously the lady's daughter because, although they didn't look anything alike as to disposition, they both had the same shape of face and the same blue eyes. On the lady they sparkled pleasantly but in the girl's seared face they appeared alternately to smolder and to blaze. 27

What if Jesus had said, "All right, you can be white-trash or a nigger or ugly"! 28

Mrs. Turpin felt an awful pity for the girl, though she thought it was one thing to be ugly and another to act ugly. 29

The woman with the snuff-stained lips turned around in her chair and looked up at the clock. Then she turned back and appeared to look a little to the side of Mrs. Turpin. There was a cast in one of her eyes. "You want to know wher you can get you one of themther clocks?" she asked in a loud voice. 30

"No, I already have a nice clock," Mrs. Turpin said. Once somebody like her got a leg in the conversation, she would be all over it. 31

"You can get you one with green stamps," the woman said. "That's most likely wher he got hisn. Save you up enough, you can get you most anythang. I got me some joo'ry." 32

Ought to have got you a wash rag and some soap, Mrs. Turpin thought. 33

"I get contour sheets with mine," the pleasant lady said. 34

The daughter slammed her book shut. She looked straight in front of her, directly through Mrs. Turpin and on through the yellow curtain and the plate glass window which made the wall behind her. The girl's eyes seemed lit all of a sudden with a peculiar light, an unnatural light like night road signs give. Mrs. Turpin turned her head to see if there was anything going on outside that she should see, but she could not see 35 anything. Figures passing cast only a pale shadow through the curtain. There was no reason the girl should single her out for her ugly looks.

"Miss Finley," the nurse said, cracking the door. The 36 gum-chewing woman got up and passed in front of her and Claud and went into the office. She had on red high-heeled shoes.

Directly across the table, the ugly girl's eyes were fixed on 37 Mrs. Turpin as if she had some very special reason for disliking her.

"This is wonderful weather, isn't it?" the girl's mother said. 38

"It's good weather for cotton if you can get the niggers 39 to pick it," Mrs. Turpin said, "but niggers don't want to pick cotton any more. You can't get the white folks to pick it and now you can't get the niggers—because they got to be right up there with the white folks."

"They gonna *try* anyways," the white-trash woman said, 40 leaning forward.

"Do you have one of the cotton-picking machines?" the 41 pleasant lady asked.

"No," Mrs. Turpin said, "they leave half the cotton in the 42 field. We don't have much cotton anyway. If you want to make it farming now, you have to have a little of everything. We got a couple of acres of cotton and a few hogs and chickens and just enough white-face that Claud can look after them himself."

"One thang I don't want," the white-trash woman said, 43 wiping her mouth with the back of her hand. "Hogs. Nasty stinking things, a-gruntin and a-rootin all over the place."

Mrs. Turpin gave her the merest edge of her attention. 44 "Our hogs are not dirty and they don't stink," she said. "They're cleaner than some children I've seen. Their feet never touch the ground. We have a pig-parlor—that's where you raise them on concrete," she explained to the pleasant lady, "and Claud scoots them down with the hose every afternoon and washes off the floor." Cleaner by far than that child right there, she thought. Poor nasty little thing. He had not moved except to put the thumb of his dirty hand into his mouth.

The woman turned her face away from Mrs. Turpin. "I 45
know I wouldn't scoot down no hog with no hose," she said
to the wall.

You wouldn't have no hog to scoot down, Mrs. Turpin 46
said to herself.

"A-gruntin and a-rootin and a-groanin," the woman mut- 47
tered.

"We got a little of everything," Mrs. Turpin said to the 48
pleasant lady. "It's no use in having more than you can handle
yourself with help like it is. We found enough niggers to pick
our cotton this year but Claud he has to go after them and
take them home again in the evening. They can't walk that
half a mile. No they can't. I tell you," she said and laughed
merrily, "I sure am tired of buttering up niggers, but you got
to love em if you want em to work for you. When they come
in the morning, I run out and I say, 'Hi yawl this morning?'
and when Claud drives them off to the field I just wave to
beat the band and they just wave back." And she waved her
hand rapidly to illustrate.

"Like you read out of the same book," the lady said, 49
showing she understood perfectly.

"Child, yes," Mrs. Turpin said. "And when they come in 50
from the field, I run out with a bucket of icewater. That's the
way it's going to be from now on," she said. "You may as
well face it."

"One thang I know," the white-trash woman said. "Two 51
thangs I ain't going to do: love no niggers or scoot down no
hog with no hose." And she let out a bark of contempt.

The look that Mrs. Turpin and the pleasant lady exchanged 52
indicated they both understood that you had to *have* certain
things before you could *know* certain things. But every time
Mrs. Turpin exchanged a look with the lady, she was aware
that the ugly girl's peculiar eyes were still on her, and she had
trouble bringing her attention back to the conversation.

"When you got something," she said, "you got to look 53
after it." And when you ain't got a thing but breath and
britches, she added to herself, you can afford to come to town
every morning and just sit on the Court House coping and
spit.

A grotesque revolving shadow passed across the curtain   54
behind her and was thrown palely on the opposite wall. Then
a bicycle clattered down against the outside of the building.
The door opened and a colored boy glided in with a tray from
the drugstore. It had two large red and white paper cups on
it with tops on them. He was a tall, very black boy in discolored white pants and a green nylon shirt. He was chewing
gum slowly, as if to music. He set the tray down in the office
opening next to the fern and stuck his head through to look
for the secretary. She was not in there. He rested his arms on
the ledge and waited, his narrow bottom stuck out, swaying
to the left and right. He raised a hand over his head and
scratched the base of his skull.

"You see that button there, boy?" Mrs. Turpin said. "You   55
can punch that and she'll come. She's probably in the back
somewhere."

"Is thas right?" the boy said agreeably, as if he had never   56
seen the button before. He leaned to the right and put his
finger on it. "She sometime out," he said and twisted around
to face his audience, his elbows behind him on the counter.
The nurse appeared and he twisted back again. She handed
him a dollar and he rooted in his pocket and made the change
and counted it out to her. She gave him fifteen cents for a tip
and he went out with the empty tray. The heavy door swung
to slowly and closed at length with the sound of suction. For
a moment no one spoke.

"They ought to send all them niggers back to Africa," the   57
white-trash woman said. "That's wher they come from in the
first place."

"Oh, I couldn't do without my good colored friends," the   58
pleasant lady said.

"There's a heap of things worse than a nigger," Mrs.   59
Turpin agreed. "It's all kinds of them just like it's all kinds of
us."

"Yes, and it takes all kinds to make the world go round,"   60
the lady said in her musical voice.

As she said it, the raw-complexioned girl snapped her teeth   61
together. Her lower lip turned downwards and inside out,

revealing the pale pink inside of her mouth. After a second it rolled back up. It was the ugliest face Mrs. Turpin had ever seen anyone make and for a moment she was certain that the girl had made it at her. She was looking at her as if she had known and disliked her all her life—all of Mrs. Turpin's life, it seemed too, not just all the girl's life. Why, girl, I don't even know you, Mrs. Turpin said silently.

She forced her attention back to the discussion. "It wouldn't be practical to send them back to Africa," she said. "They wouldn't want to go. They got it too good here." 62

"Wouldn't be what they wanted—if I had anythang to do with it," the woman said. 63

"It wouldn't be a way in the world you could get all the niggers back over there," Mrs. Turpin said. "They'd be hiding out and lying down and turning sick on you and wailing and hollering and raring and pitching. It wouldn't be a way in the world to get them over there." 64

"They got over here," the trashy woman said. "Get back like they got over." 65

"It wasn't so many of them then," Mrs. Turpin explained. 66

The woman looked at Mrs. Turpin as if here was an idiot indeed but Mrs. Turpin was not bothered by the look, considering where it came from. 67

"Nooo," she said, "they're going to stay here where they can go to New York and marry white folks and improve their color. That's what they all want to do, every one of them, improve their color." 68

"You know what comes of that, don't you?" Claud asked. 69

"No, Claud, what?" Mrs. Turpin said. 70

Claud's eyes twinkled. "White-faced niggers," he said with never a smile. 71

Everybody in the office laughed except the white-trash and the ugly girl. The girl gripped the book in her lap with white fingers. The trashy woman looked around her from face to face as if she thought they were all idiots. The old woman in the feed sack dress continued to gaze expressionless across the floor at the high-top shoes of the man opposite her, the one who had been pretending to be asleep when the Turpins 72

came in. He was laughing heartily, his hands still spread out
on his knees. The child had fallen to the side and was lying
now almost face down in the old woman's lap.

While they recovered from their laughter, the nasal chorus   73
on the radio kept the room from silence.

> *"You go to blank blank*
> *And I'll go to mine*
> *But we'll all blank along*
> *To-geth-ther,*
> *And all along the blank*
> *We'll hep eachother out*
> *Smile-ling in any kind of*
> *Weath-ther!"*

Mrs. Turpin didn't catch every word but she caught   74
enough to agree with the spirit of the song and it turned her
thoughts sober. To help anybody out that needed it was her
philosophy of life. She never spared herself when she found
somebody in need, whether they were white or black, trash
or decent. And of all she had to be thankful for, she was most
thankful that this was so. If Jesus had said, "You can be high
society and have all the money you want and be thin and
svelte-like, but you can't be a good woman with it," she
would have had to say, "Well don't make me that then. Make
me a good woman and it don't matter what else, how fat or
how ugly or how poor!" Her heart rose. He had not made
her a nigger or white-trash or ugly! He had made her herself
and given her a little of everything. Jesus, thank you! she said.
Thank you thank you thank you! Whenever she counted her
blessings she felt as buoyant as if she weighed one hundred
and twenty-five pounds instead of one hundred and eighty.

"What's wrong with your little boy?" the pleasant lady   75
asked the white-trashy woman.

"He has a ulcer," the woman said proudly. "He ain't give   76
me a minute's peace since he was born. Him and her are just
alike," she said, nodding at the old woman, who was running
her leathery fingers through the child's pale hair. "Look like
I can't get nothing down them two but Co' Cola and candy."

That's all you try to get down em, Mrs. Turpin said to   77
herself. Too lazy to light the fire. There was nothing you
could tell her about people like them that she didn't know
already. And it was not just that they didn't have anything.
Because if you gave them everything, in two weeks it would
all be broken or filthy or they would have chopped it up for
lightwood. She knew all this from her own experience. Help
them you must, but help them you couldn't.

All at once the ugly girl turned her lips inside out again.   78
Her eyes fixed like two drills on Mrs. Turpin. This time there
was no mistaking that there was something urgent behind
them.

Girl, Mrs. Turpin exclaimed silently, I haven't done a thing   79
to you! The girl might be confusing her with somebody else.
There was no need to sit by and let herself be intimidated.
"You must be in college," she said boldly, looking directly at
the girl. "I see you reading a book there."

The girl continued to stare and pointedly did not answer.   80

Her mother blushed at this rudeness. "The lady asked you   81
a question, Mary Grace," she said under her breath.

"I have ears," Mary Grace said.   82

The poor mother blushed again. "Mary Grace goes to   83
Wellesley College," she explained. She twisted one of the
buttons on her dress. "In Massachusetts," she added with a
grimace. "And in the summer she just keeps right on studying. Just reads all the time, a real book worm. She's done real
well at Wellesley; she's taking English and Math and History
and Psychology and Social Studies," she rattled on, "and I
think it's too much. I think she ought to get out and have
fun."

The girl looked as if she would like to hurl them all   84
through the plate glass window.

"Way up north," Mrs. Turpin murmured and thought,   85
well, it hasn't done much for her manners.

"I'd almost rather to have him sick," the white-trash   86
woman said, wrenching the attention back to herself. "He's
so mean when he ain't. Look like some children just take
natural to meanness. It's some gets bad when they get sick
but he was the opposite. Took sick and turned good. He

don't give me no trouble now. It's me waitin to see the doctor," she said.

If I was going to send anybody back to Africa, Mrs. Turpin 87 thought, it would be your kind, woman. "Yes, indeed," she said aloud, but looking up at the ceiling, "it's a heap of things worse than a nigger." And dirtier than a hog, she added to herself.

"I think people with bad dispositions are more to be pitied 88 than anyone on earth," the pleasant lady said in a voice that was decidedly thin.

"I thank the Lord he has blessed me with a good one," 89 Mrs. Turpin said. "The day has never dawned that I couldn't find something to laugh at."

"Not since she married me anyways," Claud said with a 90 comical straight face.

Everybody laughed except the girl and the white-trash. 91

Mrs. Turpin's stomach shook. "He's such a caution," she 92 said, "that I can't help but laugh at him."

The girl made a loud ugly noise through her teeth. 93

Her mother's mouth grew thin and tight. "I think the 94 worst thing in the world," she said, "is an ungrateful person. To have everything and not appreciate it. I know a girl," she said, "who has parents who would give her anything, a little brother who loves her dearly, who is getting a good education, who wears the best clothes, but who can never say a kind word to anyone, who never smiles, who just criticizes and complains all day long."

"Is she too old to paddle?" Claud asked. 95

The girl's face was almost purple. 96

"Yes," the lady said, "I'm afraid there's nothing to do but 97 leave her to her folly. Some day she'll wake up and it'll be too late."

"It never hurt anyone to smile," Mrs. Turpin said. "It just 98 makes you feel better all over."

"Of course," the lady said sadly, "but there are just some 99 people you can't tell anything to. They can't take criticism."

"If it's one thing I am," Mrs. Turpin said with feeling, "it's 100 grateful. When I think who all I could have been besides myself and what all I got, a little of everything, and a good disposition besides, I just feel like shouting, 'Thank you, Jesus, for making everything the way it is!' It could have been different!" For one thing, somebody else could have got Claud. At the thought of this, she was flooded with gratitude and a terrible pang of joy ran through her. "Oh thank you, Jesus, Jesus, thank you!" she cried aloud.

The book struck her directly over her left eye. It struck 101 almost at the same instant that she realized the girl was about to hurl it. Before she could utter a sound, the raw face came crashing across the table toward her, howling. The girl's fingers sank like clamps into the soft flesh of her neck. She heard the mother cry out and Claud shout, "Whoa!" There was an instant when she was certain that she was about to be in an earthquake.

All at once her vision narrowed and she saw everything as 102 if it were happening in a small room far away, or as if she were looking at it through the wrong end of a telescope. Claud's face crumpled and fell out of sight. The nurse ran in, then out, then in again. Then the gangling figure of the doctor rushed out of the inner door. Magazines flew this way and that as the table turned over. The girl fell with a thud and Mrs. Turpin's vision suddenly reversed itself and she saw everything large instead of small. The eyes of the white-trashy woman were staring hugely at the floor. There the girl, held down on one side by the nurse and on the other by her mother, was wrenching and turning in their grasp. The doctor was kneeling astride her, trying to hold her arm down. He managed after a second to sink a long needle into it.

Mrs. Turpin felt entirely hollow except for her heart which 103 swung from side to side as if it were agitated in a great empty drum of flesh.

"Somebody that's not busy call for the ambulance," the 104 doctor said in the off-hand voice young doctors adopt for terrible occasions.

Mrs. Turpin could not have moved a finger. The old man 105 who had been sitting next to her skipped nimbly into the office and made the call, for the secretary still seemed to be gone.

"Claud!" Mrs. Turpin called. 106

He was not in his chair. She knew she must jump up and   107
find him but she felt like some one trying to catch a train in
a dream, when everything moves in slow motion and the
faster you try to run the slower you go.

"Here I am," a suffocated voice, very unlike Claud's, said.   108

He was doubled up in the corner on the floor, pale as   109
paper, holding his leg. She wanted to get up and go to him
but she could not move. Instead, her gaze was drawn slowly
downward to the churning face on the floor, which she could
see over the doctor's shoulder.

The girl's eyes stopped rolling and focused on her. They   110
seemed a much lighter blue than before, as if a door that had
been tightly closed behind them was now open to admit light
and air.

Mrs. Turpin's head cleared and her power of motion re-   111
turned. She leaned forward until she was looking directly into
the fierce brilliant eyes. There was no doubt in her mind that
the girl did know her, knew her in some intense and personal
way, beyond time and place and condition. "What you got
to say to me?" she asked hoarsely and held her breath, waiting, as for a revelation.

The girl raised her head. Her gaze locked with Mrs. Tur-   112
pin's. "Go back to hell where you came from, you old wart
hog," she whispered. Her voice was low but clear. Her eyes
burned for a moment as if she saw with pleasure that her
message had struck its target.

Mrs. Turpin sank back in her chair.   113

After a moment the girl's eyes closed and she turned her   114
head wearily to the side.

The doctor rose and handed the nurse the empty syringe.   115
He leaned over and put both hands for a moment on the
mother's shoulders, which were shaking. She was sitting on
the floor, her lips pressed together, holding Mary Grace's
hand in her lap. The girl's fingers were gripped like a baby's
around her thumb. "Go on to the hospital," he said. "I'll call
and make the arrangements."

"Now let's see that neck," he said in a jovial voice to Mrs.   116
Turpin. He began to inspect her neck with his first two

fingers. Two little moon-shaped lines like pink fish bones were indented over her windpipe. There was the beginning of an angry red swelling above her eye. His fingers passed over this also.

"Lea' me be," she said thickly and shook him off. "See about Claud. She kicked him." 117

"I'll see about him in a minute," he said and felt her pulse. He was a thin gray-haired man, given to pleasantries. "Go home and have yourself a vacation the rest of the day," he said and patted her on the shoulder. 118

Quit your pattin me, Mrs. Turpin growled to herself. 119

"And put an ice pack over that eye," he said. Then he went and squatted down beside Claud and looked at his leg. After a moment he pulled him up and Claud limped after him into the office. 120

Until the ambulance came, the only sounds in the room were the tremulous moans of the girl's mother, who continued to sit on the floor. The white-trash woman did not take her eyes off the girl. Mrs. Turpin looked straight ahead at nothing. Presently the ambulance drew up, a long dark shadow, behind the curtain. The attendants came in and set the stretcher down beside the girl and lifted her expertly onto it and carried her out. The nurse helped the mother gather up her things. The shadow of the ambulance moved silently away and the nurse came back in the office. 121

"That ther girl is going to be a lunatic, ain't she?" the white-trash woman asked the nurse, but the nurse kept on to the back and never answered her. 122

"Yes, she's going to be a lunatic," the white-trash woman said to the rest of them. 123

"Po' critter," the old woman murmured. The child's face was still in her lap. His eyes looked idly out over her knees. He had not moved during the disturbance except to draw one leg up under him. 124

"I thank Gawd," the white-trash woman said fervently, "I ain't a lunatic." 125

Claud came limping out and the Turpins went home. 126

As their pick-up truck turned into their own dirt road and 127 made the crest of the hill, Mrs. Turpin gripped the window ledge and looked out suspiciously. The land sloped gracefully down through a field dotted with lavender weeds and at the start of the rise their small yellow frame house, with its little flower beds spread out around it like a fancy apron, sat primly in its accustomed place between two giant hickory trees. She would not have been startled to see a burnt wound between two blackened chimneys.

Neither of them felt like eating so they put on their house clothes and lowered the shade in the bedroom and lay down, Claud with his leg on a pillow and herself with a damp washcloth over her eye. The instant she was flat on her back, the image of a razor-backed hog with warts on its face and horns coming out behind its ears snorted into her head. She moaned, a low quiet moan.   128

"I am not," she said tearfully, "a wart hog. From hell." But the denial had no force. The girl's eyes and her words, even the tone of her voice, low but clear, directed only to her, brooked no repudiation. She had been singled out for the message, though there was trash in the room to whom it might justly have been applied. The full force of this fact struck her only now. There was a woman there who was neglecting her own child but she had been overlooked. The message had been given to Ruby Turpin, a respectable, hard-working, church-going woman. The tears dried. Her eyes began to burn instead with wrath.   129

She rose on her elbow and the washcloth fell into her hand. Claud was lying on his back, snoring. She wanted to tell him what the girl had said. At the same time, she did not wish to put the image of herself as a wart hog from hell into his mind.   130

"Hey, Claud," she muttered and pushed his shoulder.   131

Claud opened one pale baby blue eye.   132

She looked into it warily. He did not think about any thing. He just went his way.   133

"Wha, whasit?" he said and closed the eye again.   134

"Nothing," she said. "Does your leg pain you?"   135

"Hurts like hell," Claud said.   136

"It'll quit terreckly," she said and lay back down. In a   137

moment Claud was snoring again. For the rest of the afternoon they lay there. Claud slept. She scowled at the ceiling.
Occasionally she raised her fist and made a small stabbing
motion over her chest as if she was defending her innocence
to invisible guests who were like the comforters of Job, rea-
sonable-seeming but wrong.

About five-thirty Claud stirred. "Got to go after those   138
niggers," he sighed, not moving.

She was looking straight up as if there were unintelligible   139
handwriting on the ceiling. The protuberance over her eye
had turned a greenish-blue. "Listen here," she said.

"What?"   140

"Kiss me."   141

Claud leaned over and kissed her loudly on the mouth. He   142
pinched her side and their hands interlocked. Her expression
of ferocious concentration did not change. Claud got up,
groaning and growling, and limped off. She continued to
study the ceiling.

She did not get up until she heard the pick-up truck   143
coming back with the Negroes. Then she rose and thrust her
feet in her brown oxfords, which she did not bother to lace,
and stumped out onto the back porch and got her red plastic
bucket. She emptied a tray of ice cubes into it and filled it
half full of water and went out into the back yard. Every
afternoon after Claud brought the hands in, one of the boys
helped him put out hay and the rest waited in the back of the
truck until he was ready to take them home. The truck was
parked in the shade under one of the hickory trees.

"Hi yawl this evening?" Mrs. Turpin asked grimly, appear-   144
ing with the bucket and the dipper. There were three women
and a boy in the truck.

"Us doin nicely," the oldest woman said. "Hi you doin?"   145
and her gaze stuck immediately on the dark lump on Mrs.
Turpin's forehead. "You done fell down, ain't you?" she
asked in a solicitous voice. The old woman was dark and
almost toothless. She had on an old felt hat of Claud's set
back on her head. The other two women were younger and
lighter and they both had new bright green sunhats. One of

them had hers on her head; the other had taken hers off and the boy was grinning beneath it.

Mrs. Turpin set the bucket down on the floor of the truck. "Yawl hep yourselves," she said. She looked around to make sure Claud had gone. "No, I didn't fall down," she said, folding her arms. "It was something worse than that."   146

"Ain't nothing bad happen to you!" the old woman said. She said it as if they all knew that Mrs. Turpin was protected in some special way by Divine Providence. "You just had you a little fall."   147

"We were in town at the doctor's office for where the cow kicked Mr. Turpin," Mrs. Turpin said in a flat tone that indicated they could leave off their foolishness. "And there was this girl there. A big fat girl with her face all broke out. I could look at that girl and tell she was peculiar but I couldn't tell how. And me and her mama was just talking and going along and all of a sudden WHAM! She throws this big book she was reading at me and . . ."   148

"Naw!" the old woman cried out.   149

"And then she jumps over the table and commences to choke me."   150

"Naw!" they all exclaimed, "naw!"   151

"Hi come she do that?" the old woman asked. "What ail her?"   152

Mrs. Turpin only glared in front of her.   153

"Somethin ail her," the old woman said.   154

"They carried her off in an ambulance," Mrs. Turpin continued, "but before she went she was rolling on the floor and they were trying to hold her down to give her a shot and she said something to me." She paused. "You know what she said to me?"   155

"What she say?" they asked.   156

"She said," Mrs. Turpin began, and stopped, her face very dark and heavy. The sun was getting whiter and whiter, blanching the sky overhead so that the leaves of the hickory tree were black in the face of it. She could not bring forth the words. "Something real ugly," she muttered.   157

"She sho shouldn't said nothin ugly to you," the old woman said. "You so sweet. You the sweetest lady I know."   158

"She pretty too," the one with the hat on said.   159

"And stout," the other one said. "I never knowed no 160
sweeter white lady."

"That's the truth befo' Jesus," the old woman said.   161
"Amen! You des as sweet and pretty as you can be."

Mrs. Turpin knew exactly how much Negro flattery was   162
worth and it added to her rage. "She said," she began again
and finished this time with a fierce rush of breath, "that I was
an old wart hog from hell."

There was an astounded silence.   163

"Where she at?" the youngest woman cried in a piercing   164
voice.

"Lemme see her. I'll kill her!"   165

"I'll kill her with you!" the other one cried.   166

"She b'long in the sylum," the old woman said emphati-   167
cally. "You the sweetest white lady I know."

"She pretty too," the other two said. "Stout as she can be   168
and sweet. Jesus satisfied with her!"

"Deed he is," the old woman declared.   169

Idiots! Mrs. Turpin growled to herself. You could never   170
say anything intelligent to a nigger. You could talk at them
but not with them. "Yawl ain't drunk your water," she said
shortly. "Leave the bucket in the truck when you're finished
with it. I got more to do than just stand around and pass the
time of day," and she moved off and into the house.

She stood for a moment in the middle of the kitchen. The   171
dark protuberance over her eye looked like a miniature tor-
nado cloud which might any moment sweep across the horizon of her brow. Her lower lip protruded dangerously. She
squared her massive shoulders. Then she marched into the
front of the house and out the side door and started down
the road to the pig parlor. She had the look of a woman going
single-handed, weaponless, into battle.

The sun was a deep yellow now like a harvest moon and   172
was riding westward very fast over the far tree line as if it
meant to reach the hogs before she did. The road was rutted
and she kicked several good-sized stones out of her path as
she strode along. The pig parlor was on a little knoll at the
end of a lane that ran off from the side of the barn. It was a

square of concrete as large as a small room, with a board fence about four feet high around it. The concrete floor sloped slightly so that the hog wash could drain off into a trench where it was carried to the field for fertilizer. Claud was standing on the outside, on the edge of the concrete, hanging onto the top board, hosing down the floor inside. The hose was connected to the faucet of a water trough nearby.

Mrs. Turpin climbed up beside him and glowered down   173
at the hogs inside. There were seven long-snouted bristly shoats in it—tan with liver-colored spots—and an old sow a few weeks off from farrowing. She was lying on her side grunting. The shoats were running about shaking themselves like idiot children, their little slit pig eyes searching the floor for anything left. She had read that pigs were the most intelligent animal. She doubted it. They were supposed to be smarter than dogs. There had even been a pig astronaut. He had performed his assignment perfectly but died of a heart attack afterwards because they left him in his electric suit, sitting upright throughout his examination when naturally a hog should be on all fours.

A-gruntin and a-rootin and a-groanin.   174

"Gimme that hose," she said, yanking it away from Claud.   175
"Go on and carry them niggers home and then get off that leg."

"You look like you might have swallowed a mad dog,"   176
Claud observed, but he got down and limped off. He paid no attention to her humors.

Until he was out of earshot, Mrs. Turpin stood on the side   177
of the pen, holding the hose and pointing the stream of water at the hind quarters of any shoat that looked as if it might try to lie down. When he had had time to get over the hill, she turned her head slightly and her wrathful eyes scanned the path. He was nowhere in sight. She turned back again and seemed to gather herself up. Her shoulders rose and she drew in her breath.

"What do you send me a message like that for?" she said   178
in a low fierce voice, barely above a whisper but with the force of a shout in its concentrated fury. "How am I a hog and me

both? How am I saved and from hell too?" Her free fist was knotted and with the other she gripped the hose, blindly pointing the stream of water in and out of the eye of the old sow whose outraged squeal she did not hear.

The pig parlor commanded a view of the back pasture 179 where their twenty beef cows were gathered around the hay-bales Claud and the boy had put out. The freshly cut pasture sloped down to the highway. Across it was their cotton field and beyond that a dark green dusty wood which they owned as well. The sun was behind the wood, very red, looking over the paling of trees like a farmer inspecting his own hogs.

"Why me?" she rumbled. "It's no trash around here, black 180 or white, that I haven't given to. And break my back to the bone every day working. And do for the church."

She appeared to be the right size woman to command the 181 arena before her. "How am I a hog?" she demanded. "Exactly how am I like them?" and she jabbed the stream of water at the shoats. "There was plenty of trash there. It didn't have to be me.

"If you like trash better, go get yourself some trash then," 182 she railed. "You could have made me trash. Or a nigger. If trash is what you wanted why didn't you make me trash?" She shook her fist with the hose in it and a watery snake appeared momentarily in the air. "I could quit working and take it easy and be filthy," she growled. "Lounge about the sidewalks all day drinking root beer. Dip snuff and spit in every puddle and have it all over my face. I could be nasty.

"Or you could have made me a nigger. It's too late for me 183 to be a nigger," she said with deep sarcasm, "but I could act like one. Lay down in the middle of the road and stop traffic. Roll on the ground."

In the deepening light everything was taking on a myste- 184 rious hue. The pasture was growing a peculiar glassy green and the streak of highway had turned lavender. She braced herself for a final assault and this time her voice rolled out over the pasture. "Go on," she yelled, "call me a hog! Call me a hog again. From hell. Call me a wart hog from hell. Put that bottom rail on top. There'll still be a top and bottom!"

A garbled echo returned to her.   185

A final surge of fury shook her and she roared, "Who do   186
you think you are?"

The color of everything, field and crimson sky, burned for   187
a moment with a transparent intensity. The question carried
over the pasture and across the highway and the cotton field
and returned to her clearly like an answer from beyond the
wood.

She opened her mouth but no sound came out of it.   188

A tiny truck, Claud's, appeared on the highway, heading   189
rapidly out of sight. Its gears scraped thinly. It looked like a
child's toy. At any moment a bigger truck might smash into
it and scatter Claud's and the niggers' brains all over the road.

Mrs. Turpin stood there, her gaze fixed on the highway,   190
all her muscles rigid, until in five or six minutes the truck
reappeared, returning. She waited until it had had time to
turn into their own road. Then like a monumental statue
coming to life, she bent her head slowly and gazed, as if
through the very heart of mystery, down into the pig parlor
at the hogs. They had settled all in one corner around the
old sow who was grunting softly. A red glow suffused them.
They appeared to pant with a secret life.

Until the sun slipped finally behind the tree line, Mrs.   191
Turpin remained there with her gaze bent to them as if she
were absorbing some abysmal life-giving knowledge. At last
she lifted her head. There was only a purple streak in the sky,
cutting through a field of crimson and leading, like an extension of the highway, into the descending dusk. She raised her
hands from the side of the pen in a gesture hieratic and
profound. A visionary light settled in her eyes. She saw the
streak as a vast swinging bridge extending upward from the
earth through a field of living fire. Upon it a vast horde of
souls were rumbling toward heaven. There were whole companies of white-trash, clean for the first time in their lives, and
bands of black niggers in white robes, and battalions of freaks
and lunatics shouting and clapping and leaping like frogs.
And bringing up the end of the procession was a tribe of
people whom she recognized at once as those who, like

herself and Claud, had always had a little of everything and the God-given wit to use it right. She leaned forward to observe them closer. They were marching behind the others with great dignity, accountable as they had always been for good order and common sense and respectable behavior. They alone were on key. Yet she could see by their shocked and altered faces that even their virtues were being burned away. She lowered her hands and gripped the rail of the hog pen, her eyes small but fixed unblinkingly on what lay ahead. In a moment the vision faded but she remained where she was, immobile.

At length she got down and turned off the faucet and made her slow way on the darkening path to the house. In the woods around her the invisible cricket choruses had struck up, but what she heard were the voices of the souls climbing upward into the starry field and shouting hallelujah.

192

COMMENT ON "REVELATION"

Ruby Turpin, the central character in Flannery O'Connor's "Revelation," is obsessed with the classification process. At night she occupies herself "naming the classes of people": most "colored people" are on the bottom; "next to them— not above, just away from—are the white trash"; and so on. Mrs. Turpin puzzles about the exceptions to her system—the black dentist who owns property and the decent white folks who have lost their money—but for the most part she is certain about her system and her place in it. In the doctor's waiting room, she sizes up the other patients, placing them in their appropriate classes. But her internal and external dialogue reveals the ironies and inconsistencies in her rigid system. Self-satisfied, pleased that Jesus is on her side, she is not prepared for the book on *Human Development* that is thrown at her or the events that follow—the transparent flattery of the black workers, her cleaning of the pig parlor, and finally her vision of the highway to heaven that reveals her real place in God's hierarchy.

Division and Classification as a Writing Strategy

1. Write a column for your local newspaper in which you develop a system for classifying a concept such as trash. You may decide to interpret this word literally, developing a scheme to categorize the type of objects people throw away. Or you may decide to interpret the word figuratively, focusing on things that some people consider worthless— gossip columns, romance magazines, game shows. As Russell Baker did, develop a clever thesis about the subject you are classifying. Here are a few possibilities: although people throw trash away, it won't go away; people's distaste for trash is the cause of its creation; people are so saturated by trash that they accept it as part of their culture with its own subtle subcategories.

2. In an essay addressed to a psychology class, classify various kinds of eaters. Instead of writing a humorous essay like Calvin Trillin's, you may want to write a serious essay that classifies people by what they eat, how fast they eat, or when they eat.

3. Mary Mebane argues that the system of class and color is used to impose power in a negative way. Consider some other system that uses power in a positive way. For example, you may want to classify people by the various ways they empower others.

4. Analyze Gail Sheehy's essay from the perspective of gender. Does her use of the pronoun *we,* her description of examples, and her concepts of growth and adulthood suggest that she is outlining "predictable crises" for both men and women? Reconsider her six stages by pointing out how each one may need substantial revision when seen from a woman's point of view.

5. Classify a job you have held according to its various work environments. Use Desmond Morris's suggestions for identifying and claiming work space. Your purpose is to demonstrate that (a) controlling your work space contrib-

uted to your success at that particular job and (b) understanding the boundaries that marked the work space of
others helped you move up in the work hierarchy. Focus
on a simple work situation like a restaurant. How do the
waiter, maître d', and cashier define and defend their territories? What part did your ability to recognize or mimic
such behavior play in your promotion from waiter to cashier?

6. Using Gail Sheehy's crisis/growth model, write an essay
in which you classify the predictable crises of a college
education. Although you may divide the period into the
traditional four years (ages eighteen to twenty-one), remember that the average student takes six years to complete a college education and that the nontraditional
student population is the fastest-growing group within the
university. Use this information to expand and enrich your
classification system. But use your system, as Sheehy does,
to illustrate some theory of intellectual development. What
are the factors that permit or prevent students from moving from stage to stage?

DEFINITION

༒

As a writer, both in and out of college, you're likely to spend a good deal of time writing definitions. In an astronomy class, you may be asked to explain what the Doppler effect is or what a white dwarf star is. In a literature class, you may be asked to define a sonnet and identify its different forms. If you become an engineer, you may write to define problems your company proposes to solve or to define a new product your company has developed. If you become a business executive, you may have to write a brochure to describe a new service your company offers or draft a letter that defines the company's policy on credit applications.

Writers use definitions to establish boundaries, to show the essential nature of something, and to explain the special qualities that identify a purpose, place, object, or concept and distinguish it from others similar to it. Writers often write extended definitions—definitions that go beyond the one-sentence or one-paragraph explanations that you find in a dictionary or encyclopedia to expand on and examine the essential qualities of a policy, an event, a group, or a trend. Sometimes an extended definition becomes an entire book. Some books are written to define the good life; others are written to define the ideal university or the best kind of government. In fact, many of the books on any current nonfiction best-seller list are primarily definitions. The essays in this section of *The Riverside Reader* are all extended definitions.

PURPOSE

When you write, you can use definitions in several ways. For instance, you can define to *point out the special nature* of something. You may want to show the special flavor of San Francisco that makes it different from other major cities in the world, or you may want to describe the unique features that make the Macintosh computer different from other personal computers.

You can also define to *explain*. In an essay about cross-country skiing, you might want to show your readers what the sport is like and point out why it's less hazardous and less expensive than downhill skiing but better exercise. You might also define to *entertain*—to describe the essence of what it means to be a "good old boy," for instance. Often you define to *inform;* that is what you are doing in college papers when you write about West Virginia folk art or postmodern architecture. Often you write to *establish a standard,* perhaps for a good exercise program, a workable environmental policy, or even the ideal pair of running shoes. Notice that when you define to set a standard, you may also be defining to *persuade,* to convince your reader to accept the ideal you describe. Many definitions are essentially arguments.

Sometimes you may even write to *define yourself.* That is

what you are doing when you write an autobiographical statement for a college admissions officer or a scholarship committee, or when you write a job application letter. You hope to give your readers the special information that will distinguish you from all other candidates. When that is your task, you'll profit by knowing the common strategies for defining and by recognizing how other writers have used them.

AUDIENCE

When you're going to use definition in your writing, you can benefit by thinking ahead of time about what your readers expect from you. Why are they reading, and what questions will they want you to answer? You can't anticipate all their questions, but you should plan on responding to at least two kinds of queries.

First, your readers are likely to ask, "What distinguishes what you're writing about? What's typical or different about it? How do I know when I see one?" For example, if you were writing about the Olympic games, your readers would probably want to know the difference between today's Olympic games and the original games in ancient Greece. With a little research, you could tell them about several major differences.

Second, for more complex topics you should expect that your readers will also ask, "What is the basic character or the essential nature of what you're writing about? What do you mean when you say 'alternative medicine,' 'Marxist theory,' or 'white-collar crime?'" Answering questions such as these is more difficult, but if you're going to use terms like these in an essay, you have an obligation to define them, using as many strategies as you need to clarify your terms. To define white-collar crime, for instance, you could specify that it is nonviolent, likely to happen within businesses, and involves illegal manipulation of funds or privileged information. You should also strengthen your definition by giving examples that your readers might be familiar with.

STRATEGIES

You can choose from a variety of strategies for defining and use them singly or in combination. A favorite strategy for all of us is *giving examples,* a technique as natural as pointing to a certain kind of automobile or to the picture of a horse in a children's book. Writers use the same method when they describe a scene or an event to help readers get a visual image. Every writer in this section defines by giving examples, but in "The Hoax" John Berendt uses the greatest number in the shortest article as he describes impostors, forgeries, frauds, and fake radio broadcasts. Kathleen Norris relies on examples to illustrate what she means by *gossip.* And Raymond Carver's short story "What We Talk About When We Talk About Love" also focuses on defining through examples.

You can define by *analyzing qualities* to show what features distinguish your topic. When you do that, you pick out particular qualities that you want your readers to associate with the person, concept, or object you're defining. Rose del Castillo Guilbault depends on this strategy in "Americanization Is Tough on 'Macho'" as she shows that in its original context *macho* means "responsible, hardworking, . . . patriarchal" but in its Americanized context has come to mean "chauvinist, a brute, uncouth." Berendt also analyzes qualities when he says, "To qualify as a hoax, a prank must have magic in it."

A similar strategy is *attributing characteristics.* Alison Lurie does this in "Folktale Liberation" when she describes the elements of fairy tales that support the ideas of women's liberation. Francine du Plessix Gray uses this strategy when she identifies the special characteristics that we need in our friends: trust and selflessness.

Gray's essay also demonstrates *defining negatively,* the important technique of saying what something is not. She points out that friendship, unlike romantic love, is not possessive or jealous. Raymond Carver defines negatively when his main character insists that love is *not* dragging someone around by her hair. Another way to define is by *using analogies,* a favorite strategy of many writers. Gray begins her essay "On Friendship" saying, "I saw Madame Bovary at Bloomingdale's the other morning," thus drawing an analogy between the shallow heroine of Flaubert's novel and the modern woman caught up in consumerism and romantic fiction.

You can also define by *giving functions.* Sometimes the most significant fact about a person, object, or institution is what he, she, or it does. In "The Holy Use of Gossip," Kathleen Norris's main assertion is that gossip serves an essential function in communities: it strengthens communal bonds, provides comic relief, and helps people express solidarity. In "Folktale Liberation," Alison Lurie claims that one of the main functions of fairy tales in their original forms was to help children cope with problems in their lives.

COMBINING STRATEGIES

Even when you're writing an article or essay that is primarily a definition, you're not limited to the strategies we've just mentioned. You may want to combine definition with other patterns, as most professional writers do. For example, in "Rapport-Talk and Report-Talk" (see page 176) Deborah Tannen defines men's and women's different communication styles, then argues that many of the problems between men and woman grow out of these differences. In "A Chinaman's Chance" (page 462) Eric Liu gives his own definition of the American Dream, then argues that young people who feel they have no chance to achieve the dream are mistaken.

Some writers also use narration and description as a way of defining. Maya Angelou defines a certain kind of racist attitude in her narrative "My Name Is Margaret" (see page 29), and Donna Tartt tells stories about her year as a cheerleader to define the male-dominated sports culture of her high school (page 37).

As you read essays in this section, and especially as you reread them, keep part of your mind alert to spot the strategies the writer is using. You may want to incorporate some of them into your own writing. You may want to define through anecdotes, as the writers do in "The Hoax" and

"The Holy Use of Gossip." Or you want to define differences between items by means of comparison and contrast as the author of "Americanization Is Tough on 'Macho'" does.

USING DEFINITION IN PARAGRAPHS

Here are two definition paragraphs. The first is written by a professional writer and is followed by an analysis. The second is written by a student writer and is followed by questions.

AMY TAN
From "Watching China"

Wonders how Chinese people define democracy

I try to imagine what democracy means to people in China who dream of it. I don't think they are envisioning electoral colleges, First Amendment rights or civil lawsuits. I imagine their dream of democracy begins with a feeling in the chest, one that has been restrained for so long it grows larger and more insistent, until it bursts forth with a shout. Democracy is the right to shout, "Listen to us."

Instead believes they have an urge that must be let out

For them, democracy must be the right to be listened to

Doesn't think they think of this as abstraction

Comment In this skillfully written paragraph from an article in *Glamour,* the Chinese-American author of *The Joy Luck Club* uses her novelist's skills to quickly reduce the large abstraction "democracy" to something very personal. She makes us think about what people who can only dream of democracy must want. She defines negatively at first, suggesting that they probably don't think of democratic institutions in the same lofty terms as we do, who are used to freedom; rather their yearning for democracy is a gut feeling, a plea. In her final, powerful sentence she defines democracy at its most basic: the right to shout "Listen to us."

JASON UTESCH
Personality

"She has a great personality." Translation: she goes to bed early to watch the shopping channel.

"He has a great <u>personality</u>." Translation: he tells dirty jokes at funerals. The "p" word is troublesome not only because all the great personalities we've been told about have proved disappointing, but also because all the great personalities we know don't seem to measure up to other people's expectations. Even the old song suggests that <u>personality</u> is a complicated quality to define because to have it a person has to have a special <u>walk</u>, <u>talk</u>, <u>smile</u>, <u>charm</u>, <u>love</u>, and PLUS she (or he) has to have a great big <u>heart</u>.

1. What do you see as Utesch's purpose in listing so many contradictions in the way people define *personality*?
2. What does the writer imply by using the phrase "The 'p' word"?

DEFINITION

Points to Remember

1. Remember that you are obligated to define key terms that you use in your writing—such as Marxism, alternative medicine, nontraditional student.
2. Understand your purpose in defining: to explain, to entertain, to persuade, to set boundaries, or to establish a standard.
3. Understand how writers construct an argument from a definition. For example, by defining the good life or good government, they argue for that kind of life or government.
4. Know the several ways of defining: giving examples, analyzing qualities, attributing characteristics, defining negatively, using analogies, and showing function.
5. Learn to use definition in combination with other strategies, as a basis on which to build an argument, or as supporting evidence.

John Berendt was born in Syracuse, New York, in 1939 and was educated at Harvard University. He began his writing career as an associate editor at *Esquire,* before editing *Holiday Magazine* and writing and producing television programs such as *The David Frost Show* and *The Dick Cavett Show.* In 1979, he returned to *Esquire* as a columnist and began contributing articles to periodicals such as *New York Magazine.* In 1993, he published his first book, *Midnight in the Garden of Good and Evil,* a "nonfiction novel" about a controversial murder in Savannah, Georgia. In "The Hoax," reprinted from *Esquire,* Berendt defines the magical ingredients of a hoax.

The Hoax

WHEN THE HUMORIST Robert Benchley was an under- 1
graduate at Harvard eighty years ago, he and a couple of friends showed up one morning at the door of an elegant Beacon Hill mansion, dressed as furniture repairmen. They told the housekeeper they had come to pick up the sofa. Five minutes later they carried the sofa out the door, put it on a truck, and drove it three blocks away to another house, where, posing as deliverymen, they plunked it down in the parlor. That evening, as Benchley well knew, the couple living in house A were due to attend a party in house B. Whatever the outcome—and I'll get to that shortly—it was guaranteed to be a defining example of how proper Bostonians handle social crises. The wit inherent in Benchley's practical joke elevated it from the level of prank to the more respectable realm of hoax.

To qualify as a hoax, a prank must have magic in it—the 2

word is derived from *hocus-pocus,* after all. Daring and irony are useful ingredients, too. A good example of a hoax is the ruse perpetrated by David Hampton, the young black man whose pretense of being Sidney Poitier's son inspired John Guare's *Six Degrees of Separation.* Hampton managed to insinuate himself into two of New York's most sophisticated households—one headed by the president of the public-television station WNET, the other by the dean of the Columbia School of Journalism. Hampton's hoax touched a number of sensitive themes: snobbery, class, race, and sex, all of which playwright Guare deftly exploited.

Hampton is a member of an elite band of famous impostors that includes a half-mad woman who for fifty years claimed to be Anastasia, the lost daughter of the assassinated   3

To qualify as a hoax, a prank must have magic in it. . . .

---

czar Nicholas II; and a man named Harry Gerguson, who became a Hollywood restaurateur and darling of society in the 1930s and 1940s as the ersatz Russian prince Mike Romanoff.

Forgeries have been among the better hoaxes. Fake Vermeers painted by an obscure Dutch artist, Hans van Meegeren, were so convincing that they fooled art dealers, collectors, and museums. The hoax came to light when Van Meegeren was arrested as a Nazi collaborator after the war. To prove he was not a Nazi, he admitted he had sold a fake Vermeer to Hermann Göring for $256,000. Then he owned up to having created other "Vermeers," and to prove he could do it, he painted *Jesus in the Temple* in the style of Vermeer while under guard in jail.   4

In a bizarre twist, a story much like Van Meegeren's became the subject of the book *Fake!,* by Clifford Irving, who   5 in 1972 attempted to pull off a spectacular hoax of his own: a wholly fraudulent "authorized" biography of Howard Hughes. Irving claimed to have conducted secret interviews with the reclusive Hughes, and McGraw-Hill gave him a big advance. Shortly before publication, Hughes surfaced by telephone and denied that he had ever spoken with Irving. Irving had already spent $100,000 of the advance; he was convicted of fraud and sent to jail.

As it happens, we are used to hoaxes where I come from.   6
I grew up just a few miles down the road from Cardiff, New York—a town made famous by the Cardiff Giant. As we learned in school, a farmer named Newell complained, back in 1889, that his well was running dry, and while he and his neighbors were digging a new one, they came upon what appeared to be the fossilized remains of a man twelve feet tall. Before the day was out, Newell had erected a tent and posted a sign charging a dollar for a glimpse of the "giant"—three dollars for a longer look. Throngs descended on Cardiff. It wasn't long before scientists determined that the giant had been carved from a block of gypsum. The hoax came undone fairly quickly after that, but even so—as often happens with hoaxes—the giant became an even bigger attraction *because* it was a hoax. P. T. Barnum offered Newell a fortune for the giant, but Newell refused, and it was then that he got his comeuppance. Barnum simply made a replica and put it on display as the genuine Cardiff Giant. Newell's gig was ruined.

The consequences of hoaxes are what give them spice.   7
Orson Welles's lifelike 1938 radio broadcast of H. G. Wells's *War of the Worlds* panicked millions of Americans, who were convinced that martians had landed in New Jersey. The forged diary of Adolf Hitler embarrassed historian Hugh Trevor-Roper, who had vouched for its authenticity, and *Newsweek* and *The Sunday Times* of London, both of which published excerpts in 1983 shortly before forensic tests proved that there were nylon fibers in the paper it was written on, which wouldn't have been possible had it originated before 1950. The five-hundred-thousand-year-old remains of Piltdown man, found in 1912, had anthropologists confused

about human evolution until 1953, when fluoride tests exposed the bones as an elaborate modern hoax. And as for Robert Benchley's game on Beacon Hill, no one said a word about the sofa all evening, although there it sat in plain sight. One week later, however, couple A sent an anonymous package to couple B. It contained the sofa's slipcovers.

For Study and Discussion

QUESTIONS FOR RESPONSE

1. What hoaxes do you know about or have you been involved in? Which of them had elements that might be described as daring or witty?
2. What's your reaction to those incidents in Berendt's account that involve criminal fraud? How do you explain that reaction?

QUESTIONS ABOUT PURPOSE

1. How do you think Berendt wants you to respond to the tricksters he describes in his essay? To what extent did you respond that way?
2. Berendt's examples of people duped by hoaxes include scientists, a historian, a college president, an eminent publisher, and curators of several museums. What does he accomplish by telling stories about such a wide range of dupes?

QUESTIONS ABOUT AUDIENCE

1. This essay originally appeared in *Esquire* magazine. What traits and attitudes do you think a writer for *Esquire* assumes characterize its readers? (If necessary, browse through an issue of *Esquire* in the library to get a feel for its audience.)
2. Berendt seems to assume that everyone enjoys stories about tricksters getting the best of their victims. In your case, is the assumption justified? Why or why not?

QUESTIONS ABOUT STRATEGIES

1. What does the writer achieve by opening and closing the essay with the anecdote about the sofa?
2. How would you characterize the tone of this essay? What attitude of the writer toward his subject do you think the tone reflects? Do you find that attitude engaging or off-putting?

QUESTIONS FOR DISCUSSION

1. Which of Berendt's anecdotes do you find the most entertaining? Why?
2. When would you say a deception ceases to be a hoax and turns into something else? What examples can you think of?

ROSE DEL CASTILLO GUILBAULT

Rose del Castillo Guilbault was born in 1952 in Sonora, Mexico, and was educated at San Jose State University in California. For the past fourteen years she has worked as director of editorial and public affairs for KGO-TV, the ABC affiliate in San Francisco. For two years, she wrote a column called "Hispanic USA," which appeared in *This World,* a weekly magazine of the *San Francisco Chronicle.* In one of these columns, "Americanization Is Tough on 'Macho,'" Guilbault defines American and Hispanic attitudes toward the connotations of the word *macho.*

Americanization Is Tough on "Macho"

W HAT IS *MACHO?* That depends which side of the border you come from. 1

Although it's not unusual for words and expressions to lose their subtlety in translation, the negative connotations of *macho* in this country are troublesome to Hispanics. 2

Take the newspaper descriptions of alleged mass murderer Ramon Salcido. That an insensitive, insanely jealous, hard-drinking, violent Latin male is referred to as *macho* makes Hispanics cringe. 3

"*Es muy macho,*" the women in my family nod approvingly, describing a man they respect. But in the United States, when women say, "He's so macho," it's with disdain. 4

The Hispanic *macho* is manly, responsible, hardworking, a man in charge, a patriarch. A man who expresses strength 5

through silence. What the Yiddish language would call a
mensch.

The American *macho* is a chauvinist, a brute, uncouth,   6
selfish, loud, abrasive, capable of inflicting pain, and sexually
promiscuous.

Quintessential *macho* models in this country are Sylvester   7
Stallone, Arnold Schwarzenegger and Charles Bronson. In
their movies, they exude toughness, independence, masculinity. But a closer look reveals their machismo is really violence
masquerading as courage, sullenness disguised as silence, and
irresponsibility camouflaged as independence.

If the Hispanic ideal of *macho* were translated to American   8

The misuse of macho *hints at a deeper*
cultural misunderstanding that extends
beyond mere word definitions.

---

screen roles, they might be Jimmy Stewart, Sean Connery
and Laurence Olivier.

In Spanish, *macho* ennobles Latin males. In English, it   9
devalues them. This pattern seems consistent with the
conflicts ethnic minority males experience in this country.
Typically the cultural traits other societies value don't translate as desirable characteristics in America.

I watched my own father struggle with these cultural am-   10
biguities. He worked on a farm for twenty years. He laid
down miles of irrigation pipe, carefully plowed long, neat
rows in fields, hacked away at recalcitrant weeds and drove
tractors through whirlpools of dust. He stoically worked
twenty-hour days during harvest season, accepting the long
hours as part of agricultural work. When the boss complained
or upbraided him for minor mistakes, he kept quiet, even
when it was obvious the boss had erred.

He handled the most menial tasks with pride. At home he   11 was a good provider, helped out my mother's family in Mexico without complaint, and was indulgent with me. Arguments between my mother and him generally had to do with money, or with his stubborn reluctance to share his troubles. He tried to work them out in his own silence. He didn't want to trouble my mother—a course that backfired, because the imagined is always worse than the reality.

Americans regarded my father as decidedly un-*macho*. His character was interpreted as nonassertive, his loyalty non-ambition, and his quietness ignorance. I once overheard the boss's son blame him for plowing crooked rows in a field. My father merely smiled at the lie, knowing the boy had done it, but didn't refute it, confident his good work was well known. But the boss instead ridiculed him for being "stupid" and letting a kid get away with a lie. Seeing my embarrassment, my father dismissed the incident, saying, "They're the dumb ones. Imagine, me fighting with a kid."   12

I tried not to look at him with American eyes because sometimes the reflection hurt.   13

Listening to my aunts' clucks of approval, my vision focused on the qualities America overlooked. "He's such a hard worker. So serious, so responsible." My aunts would secretly compliment my mother. The unspoken comparison was that he was not like some of their husbands, who drank and womanized. My uncles represented the darker side of *macho*.   14

In a patriarchal society, few challenge their roles. If men drink, it's because it's the manly thing to do. If they gamble, it's because it's how men relax. And if they fool around, well, it's because a man simply can't hold back so much man! My aunts didn't exactly meekly sit back, but they put up with these transgressions because Mexican society dictated this was their lot in life.   15

In the United States, I believe it was the feminist movement of the early '70s that changed *macho*'s meaning. Perhaps my generation of Latin women was in part responsible. I recall Chicanos complaining about the chauvinistic nature of Latin men and the notion they wanted their women bare-   16

foot, pregnant and in the kitchen. The generalization that
Latin men embodied chauvinistic traits led to this interesting
twist of semantics. Suddenly a word that represented something positive in one culture became a negative prototype in
another.

The problem with the use of *macho* today is that it's   17
become an accepted stereotype of the Latin male. And like
all stereotypes, it distorts truth.

The impact of language in our society is undeniable. And   18
the misuse of *macho* hints at a deeper cultural misunderstanding that extends beyond mere word definitions.

For Study and Discussion

QUESTIONS FOR RESPONSE

1. How have you heard the word *macho* used in conversation? From
your point of view, does the word have primarily positive or
negative connotations? Why do you think it carries those connotations?
2. If you have Hispanic friends or your family is Hispanic, to what
extent does their use of *macho* correspond to the definition
Guilbault gives? How much general agreement do you see about
the definition among Hispanics?

QUESTIONS ABOUT PURPOSE

1. According to Guilbault, why is the Hispanic culture troubled by
the term *macho* having acquired negative connotations?
2. What does Guilbault suggest are the hazards involved in making
an important term from one culture a part of another culture's
slang?

QUESTIONS ABOUT AUDIENCE

1. Guilbault wrote this essay for her column "Hispanic USA,"
which appeared in the Sunday magazine of the *San Francisco
Chronicle*. Who does she assume her primary audience to be—
Hispanics or Anglo-Americans? How do you know?

2. From what sources does Guilbault assume that her Anglo-American readers have gotten their idea of *macho*? How powerful are those sources in creating attitudes? Why?

QUESTIONS ABOUT STRATEGIES

1. How does Guilbault use movie stars to establish the contrast between American and Hispanic definitions of *macho*? Why does she choose such a strategy?
2. How does Guilbault's use of her father as an exemplar of *macho* strengthen her argument?

QUESTIONS FOR DISCUSSION

1. With the help of others in the class, identify some other characteristics that are honored in other cultures but devalued by Americans. For instance, what traits do you know of that are honored by many people from Asian and Arab countries but are not considered especially valuable by Americans?
2. In what ways is the "machismo" problem complicated by issues of gender and class? For instance, how do men and women use the word *macho* differently? How might those who think of themselves as Chicano use the word differently from those who think of themselves as Hispanic?

Kathleen Norris was born in 1947 in Washington, D.C., and educated at Bennington College. She worked for a brief period as program secretary for the Academy of American Poets in New York before moving to South Dakota, where she became affiliated with Leaves of Grass, Inc. She has contributed poems and essays to *Dragonfly, Sumac,* and *Tennessee Poetry Journal,* published two collections of poetry, *Falling Off* (1971) and *Middle of the World* (1981), and written the widely praised *Dakota: A Spiritual Geography* (1993). In "The Holy Use of Gossip," reprinted from *Dakota,* Norris defines the various uses of gossip in a small town.

The Holy Use of Gossip

It is the responsibility of writers to listen to gossip and pass it on.
It is the way all storytellers learn about life.
— GRACE PALEY

If there's anything worth calling theology, it is listening to
people's stories, listening to them and cherishing them.
— MARY PELLAUER

I ONCE SCANDALIZED a group of North Dakota teenagers who had been determined to scandalize me. Working as an artist-in-residence in their school for three weeks, I happened to hit prom weekend. Never much for proms in high school, I helped decorate, cutting swans out of posterboard and sprinkling them with purple glitter as the school gym was festooned with lavender and silver crepe paper streamers.

On Monday morning a group of the school outlaws was

gossiping in the library, just loud enough for me to hear, about the drunken exploits that had taken place at a prairie party in the wee hours after the dance: kids meeting in some remote spot, drinking beer and listening to car stereos turned up loud, then, near dawn, going to one girl's house for breakfast. I finally spoke up and said, "See, it's like I told you: the party's not over until you've told the stories. That's where all writing starts." They looked up at me, pretending that it bothered them that I'd heard.

"And," I couldn't resist adding, "everyone knows you 3 don't get piss-drunk and then eat scrambled eggs. If you

---

At its deepest level, small-town gossip is about how we face matters of life and death.

---

didn't know it before, you know it now." "You're not going to write about *that*, are you?" one girl said, her eyes wide. "I don't know," I replied, "I might. It's all grist for the mill."

When my husband and I first moved to Dakota, people 4 were quick to tell us about an eccentric young man who came from back East and gradually lost his grip on reality. He shared a house with his sheep until relatives came and took him away. "He was a college graduate," someone would always add, looking warily at us as if to say, we know what can happen to Easterners who are too well educated. This was one of the first tales to go into my West River treasure-house of stories. It was soon joined by the story of the man who shot himself to see what it felt like. He hit his lower leg and later said that while he didn't feel anything for a few seconds, after that it hurt like hell.

There was Rattlesnake Bill, a cowboy who used to carry 5 rattlers in a paper sack in his pickup truck. If you didn't believe him, he'd put his hand in without looking and take one out to show you. One night Bill limped into a downtown bar on crutches. A horse he was breaking had dragged him for about a mile, and he was probably lucky to be alive. He'd been knocked out, he didn't know for how long, and when he regained consciousness he had crawled to his house and changed clothes to come to town. Now Bill thought he'd drink a little whiskey for the pain. "Have you been to a doctor?" friends asked. "Nah, whiskey'll do."

Later that night at the steak house I managed to get Bill   6
to eat something—most of my steak, as it turned out, but he needed it more than I. The steak was rare, and that didn't sit well with Bill. A real man eats his steak well done. But when I said, "What's the matter, are you too chicken to eat rare meat?" he gobbled it down. He slept in his pickup that night, and someone managed to get him to a doctor the next day. He had a broken pelvis.

There was another cowboy who had been mauled by a   7
bobcat in a remote horse barn by the Grand River. The animal had leapt from a hayloft as he tied up a horse, and he had managed to grab a rifle and shoot her. He felt terrible afterwards, saying, "I should have realized the only reason she'd have attacked like that was because she was protecting young." He found her two young cubs, still blind, in the loft. In a desperate attempt to save them he called several veterinarians in the hope that they might know of a lactating cat who had aborted. Such a cat was found, but the cubs lived just a few more days.

There was the woman who nursed her husband through   8
a long illness. A dutiful farm daughter and ranch wife, she had never experienced life on her own. When she was widowed, all the town spoke softly about "poor Ida." But when "poor Ida" kicked up her heels and, entering a delayed adolescence in her fifties, dyed her hair, dressed provocatively, and went dancing more than once a week at the steak house, the sympathetic cooing of the gossips turned to outrage. The woman at the center of the storm hadn't changed; she was still an innocent, bewildered by the calumny now directed at her. She lived it down and got herself a steady boyfriend, but

she still dyes her hair and dresses flashy. I'm grateful for the color she adds to the town.

Sometimes it seems as if the whole world is fueled by gossip. Much of what passes for hard news today is the Hollywood fluff that was relegated to pulp movie magazines when I was a girl. From the Central Intelligence Agency to *Entertainment Tonight,* gossip is big business. But in small towns, gossip is still small-time. And as bad as it can be—venal, petty, mean—in the small town it also stays closer to the roots of the word. If you look up gossip in the *Oxford English Dictionary* you find that it is derived from the words for God and sibling, and originally meant "akin to God." It was used to describe one who has contracted spiritual kinship by acting as a sponsor at baptism; one who helps "give a name to." Eric Partridge's *Origins,* a dictionary of etymology, tells you simply to "see God," and there you find that the word's antecedents include gospel, godspell, *sippe* (or consanguinity) and "*sabha,* a village community—notoriously inter-related." 9

We are interrelated in a small town, whether or not we're related by blood. We know without thinking about it who owns what car; inhabitants of a town as small as a monastery learn to recognize each other's footsteps in the hall. Story is a safety valve for people who live as intimately as that; and I would argue that gossip done well can be a holy thing. It can strengthen communal bonds. 10

Gossip provides comic relief for people under tension. Candidates at one monastery are told of a novice in the past who had such a hot temper that the others loved to bait him. Once when they were studying he closed a window and the other monks opened it; once, twice. When he got up to close the window for the third time, he yelled at them, "Why are you making me sin with this window?" 11

Gossip can help us give a name to ourselves. The most revealing section of the weekly *Lemmon Leader* is the personal column in the classified ads, where people express thanks to those who helped with the bloodmobile, a 4-H booth at the county fair, a Future Homemakers of America fashion show, 12 a benefit for a family beset by huge medical bills. If you've been in the hospital or have suffered a death in the family, you take out an ad thanking the doctor, ambulance crew, and wellwishers who visited, sent cards, offered prayers, or brought gifts of food.

Often these ads are quite moving, written from the heart. The parents of a small boy recently thanked those who had remembered their son with   13

> *prayers, cards, balloons, and gifts, and gave moral support to the rest of the family when Ty underwent surgery. . . . It's great to be home again in this caring community, and our biggest task now is to get Ty to eat more often and larger amounts. Where else but Lemmon would we find people who would stop by and have a bedtime snack and milk with Ty or provide good snacks just to help increase his caloric intake, or a school system with staff that take the time to make sure he eats his extra snacks. May God Bless all of you for caring about our "special little" boy—who is going to gain weight!*

No doubt it is the vast land surrounding us, brooding on the edge of our consciousness, that makes it necessary for us to call such attention to human activity. Publicly asserting, as do many of these ads, that we live in a caring community helps us keep our hopes up in a hard climate or hard times, and gives us a sense of identity.   14

Privacy takes on another meaning in such an environment, where you are asked to share your life, humbling yourself before the common wisdom, such as it is. Like everyone else, you become public property and come to accept things that city people would consider rude. A young woman using the pay phone in a West River café is scrutinized by several older women who finally ask her, "Who are you, anyway?" On discovering that she is from a ranch some sixty miles south, they question her until, learning her mother's maiden name,   15 they are satisfied. They know her grandparents by reputation; good ranchers, good people.

The *Leader* has correspondents in rural areas within some 16 fifty miles of Lemmon—Bison, Chance, Duck Creek, Howe, Morristown, Rosebud (on the Grand River), Shadehill, Spring Butte, Thunder Hawk, White Butte—as well as at the local nursing home and in the town of Lemmon itself, who report on "doings." If you volunteer at the nursing home's weekly popcorn party and sing-along, your name appears. If you host a card party at your home, this is printed, along with the names of your guests. If you have guests from out of town, their names appear. Many notices would baffle an outsider, as they require an intimate knowledge of family relationships to decipher. One recent column from White Butte, headed "Neighbors Take Advantage of Mild Winter Weather to Visit Each Other," read in part: "Helen Johanssen spent several afternoons with Gaylene Francke; Mavis Merdahl was a Wednesday overnight guest at the Alvera Ellis home."

Allowing yourself to be a subject of gossip is one of the 17 sacrifices you make, living in a small town. And the pain caused by the loose talk of ignorant people is undeniable. One couple I know, having lost their only child to a virulent pneumonia (a robust thirty-five years old, he was dead in a matter of days) had to endure rumors that he had died of suicide, AIDS, and even anthrax. But it's also true that the gossips don't know all that they think they know, and often misread things in a comical way. My husband was once told that he was having an affair with a woman he hadn't met, and I still treasure the day I was encountered by three people who said, "Have you sold your house yet?" "When's the baby due?" and, "I'm sorry to hear your mother died."

I could trade the sources of the first two rumors: we'd 18 helped a friend move into a rented house, and I'd bought baby clothes downtown when I learned that I would soon become an aunt. The third rumor was easy enough to check; I called my mother on the phone. The flip side, the saving grace, is that despite the most diligent attentions of the die-hard gossips, it is possible to have secrets.

Of course the most important things can't be hidden: 19
birth, sickness, death, divorce. But gossip is essentially democratic. It may be the plumber and his wife who had a screaming argument in a bar, or it could be the bank president's
wife who moved out and rented a room in the motel; everyone is fair game. And although there are always those who
take delight in the misfortunes of others, and relish a juicy
story at the expense of truth and others' feelings, this may be
the exception rather than the rule. Surprisingly often, gossip
is the way small-town people express solidarity.

I recall a marriage that was on the rocks. The couple had   20
split up, and gossip ran wild. Much sympathy was expressed
for the children, and one friend of the couple said to me,
"The worst thing she could do is to take him back too soon.
This will take time." Those were healing words, a kind of
prayer. And when the family did reunite, the town breathed
a collective sigh of relief.

My own parents' marriage was of great interest in Lem-   21
mon back in the 1930s. My mother, the town doctor's only
child, eloped with another Northwestern University student;
a musician, of all things. A poor preacher's kid. "This will
bear watching," one matriarch said. My parents fooled her.
As time went on, the watching grew dull. Now going on
fifty-five years, their marriage has outlasted all the gossip.

Like the desert tales that monks have used for centuries as   22
a basis for a theology and way of life, the tales of small-town
gossip are often morally instructive, illustrating the ways ordinary people survive the worst that happens to them; or,
conversely, the ways in which self-pity, anger, and despair can
overwhelm and destroy them. Gossip is theology translated
into experience. In it we hear great stories of conversion, like
the drunk who turns his or her life around, as well as stories
of failure. We can see that pride really does go before a fall,
and that hope is essential. We watch closely those who retire,
or who lose a spouse, lest they lose interest in living. When
we gossip we are also praying, not only for them but for
ourselves.

At its deepest level, small-town gossip is about how we face   23 matters of life and death. We see the gossip of earlier times, the story immortalized in ballads such as "Barbara Allen," lived out before our eyes as a young man obsessively in love with a vain young woman nearly self-destructs. We also see how people heal themselves. One of the bravest people I know is a young mother who sewed and embroidered exquisite baptismal clothes for her church with the memorial money she received when her first baby died. When she gave birth to a healthy girl a few years later, the whole town rejoiced.

My favorite gossip takes note of the worst and the best that is in us. Two women I know were diagnosed with terminal cancer. One said, "If I ever get out of this hospital, I'm going to look out for Number One." And that's exactly what she did. Against overwhelming odds, she survived, and it made her mean. The other woman spoke about the blessings of a life that had taken some hard blows: her mother had killed herself when she was a girl, her husband had died young. I happened to visit her just after she'd been told that she had less than a year to live. She was dry-eyed, and had been reading the Psalms. She was entirely realistic about her illness and said to me, "The one thing that scares me is the pain. I hope I die before I turn into an old bitch." I told her family that story after the funeral, and they loved it; they could hear in it their mother's voice, the way she really was. 24

For Study and Discussion

QUESTIONS FOR RESPONSE

1. What stories similar to those Norris tells can you relate about your own community? That community can be an organization or an extended family as well as a town.
2. Norris stresses the positive effects of gossip. What are some of the negative effects that you have witnessed? Overall, how would you describe the balance between positive and negative gossip in your community?

QUESTIONS ABOUT PURPOSE

1. What common attitude about gossip does Norris hope to counteract?
2. What kind of picture of her small town does Norris seek to create? What common beliefs about small towns does she seek to overcome?

QUESTIONS ABOUT AUDIENCE

1. What assumptions do you think Norris makes about the way most people react to stories? How do you yourself feel about stories?
2. Although today relatively few people live in a small town like the one Norris describes, she suggests that her audience should see that her generalizations apply to larger communities. To what extent do you think she is warranted in that assumption?

QUESTIONS ABOUT STRATEGIES

1. How does Norris expand the definition of gossip into something that goes beyond the ordinary use of the term? Why is it important for her to do this?
2. What common themes in the stories Norris tells support her assertions about gossip as a benevolent force in a community?

QUESTIONS FOR DISCUSSION

1. Many magazines, newspaper columns, and radio and television shows make big profits by reporting or even sometimes creating gossip about celebrities. What do you see as some of the consequences of such activity?
2. What purpose do you feel that gossip, as Norris defines it, fills in your life and your community?

Alison Lurie was born in Chicago in 1926 and was educated in New York, Connecticut, and at Radcliffe College. Her first novel, *Love and Friendship,* was published in 1962. The title of the book was borrowed from an early Jane Austen novel, and over the years reviewers have pointed to similarities between the two writers. Lurie's tendency to write about the closed community she knows best—the wealthy and educated segment of American society—is also reminiscent of Austen. Her fifth novel, *The War Between the Tates* (1974), was the first to find a sizable audience. Her seventh novel, *Foreign Affairs* (1984), was awarded a Pulitzer Prize. Alison Lurie has also published several collections of stories for children; a witty social history of apparel, *The Language of Clothes* (1981); and a study of children's literature, *Don't Tell the Grown-ups* (1990). In "Folktale Liberation," excerpted from this last work, Lurie defines the "most subversive texts in children's literature"— fairy tales.

Folktale Liberation

FOLKTALES ARE THE oldest and most widely known form 1 of literature for children. "Beauty and the Beast" was told in classical Greece and ancient India; "Hansel and Gretel" has been collected in the West Indies, in African villages, and among the American Indians.

These tales also have another distinction: they are among 2 the most subversive texts in children's literature. Often, though usually in disguised form, they support the rights of disadvantaged members of the population—children, women, and the poor—against the establishment. Law and order are not always respected: the master thief fools the count and the parson, and Jack kills the giant and steals his treasure. Rich people are often unlucky, afflicted, or helpless: kings and queens cannot have children or suffer from strange illnesses, while the poor are healthy and enterprising and fortunate.

As long as these stories remained part of an oral culture,   3 related to small audiences of unimportant people, they were largely overlooked by the literary and educational establishment. But as soon as they began to surface in printed texts

---

Fairy tales portrayed a society in which women were as competent and active as men.

---

there were outcries of horror and disapproval; cries that have continued to this day.

The late-eighteenth-century author and educational   4 authority Sarah Trimmer cautioned parents against allowing their children to hear or read fairy tales, which she considered immoral because they taught ambition, violence, a love of wealth, and the desire to marry above one's station. Cinderella, she wrote, "paints some of the worst passions that can enter into the human breast, and of which little children should, if possible, be totally ignorant; such as envy, jealousy, a dislike of step-mothers and half-sisters, vanity, a love of dress, etc." Other critics complained that these tales were unscientific and confused truth with fiction, and that they wasted time that would be better spent learning facts, skills, and good manners.

More than 150 years later it was still believed in high-   5 minded progressive circles that fairy tales were unsuitable for children. "Does not 'Cinderella' interject a social and eco-

nomic situation which is both confusing and vicious? . . .
Does not 'Jack and the Beanstalk' delay a child's rationalizing
of the world and leave him longer than is desirable without
the beginnings of scientific standards?" as one child education
expert, Lucy Sprague Mitchell, put it in the introduction to
her *Here and Now Story Book,* which I received for my fifth
birthday. It would be much better, she and her colleagues
thought, for children to read simple, pleasant, realistic tales
that would help to prepare us for the adult world.

Mrs. Mitchell's own contribution to literature was a squat   6
volume, sunny orange in color, with an idealized city scene
on the cover. Inside I could read about the Grocery Man
("This is John's Mother. Good morning, Mr. Grocery Man")
and How Spot Found a Home. The children and parents in
these stories were exactly like the ones I knew, only more
boring. They never did anything really wrong, and nothing
dangerous or surprising ever happened to them—no more
than it did to Dick and Jane, whom I and my friends were
soon to meet in first grade.

After we grew up, of course, we found out how unrealistic   7
these stories had been. The simple, pleasant adult society they
had prepared us for did not exist. As we had suspected, the
fairy tales had been right all along—the world was full of
hostile, stupid giants and perilous castles and people who
abandoned their children in the nearest forest. To succeed in
this world you needed some special skill or patronage, plus
remarkable luck; and it didn't hurt to be very good-looking.
The other qualities that counted were wit, boldness, stubborn persistence, and an eye for the main chance. Kindness
to those in trouble was also advisable—you never knew who
might be useful to you later on.

The fairy tales were also way ahead of Mrs. Mitchell with   8
respect to women's liberation. In her stories men drove wag-
ons and engines and boats, built skyscrapers, worked in
stores, and ran factories; women did nothing except keep
house, look after children, and go shopping. Fairy tales, on
the other hand, portrayed a society in which women were as
competent and active as men, at every age and in every class.

Gretel, not Hansel, defeated the witch; and for every clever youngest son there was a youngest daughter equally resourceful. The contrast continued in maturity, when women were often more powerful than men. Real help for the hero or heroine came most often from a fairy godmother or wise woman, and real trouble from a witch or wicked stepmother. With a frequency that recalls current feminist polemics, the significant older male figures were either dumb macho giants or malevolent little dwarfs.

Yet in spite of this, some contemporary feminists have   9
joined the chorus of critics and attacked fairy tales as a male chauvinist form of literature: they believe that giving children stories like "Cinderella" and "Snow White" is a sort of brainwashing, intended to convince them that all little girls must be gentle, obedient, passive, and domestic while they wait patiently for their princes to come.

In a way these objections are understandable, since some   10
of the tales we know best—those that have been popularized by Walt Disney, for instance—do have this kind of heroine. But from the point of view of European (and world) folklore, such stories are highly unrepresentative. The traditional tale, in fact, is exactly the sort of subversive literature of which a feminist should approve.

For one thing, these stories are in a literal sense women's   11
literature. Charles Perrault, who was one of the first to write them down, called them "old wives' tales, governesses' and grannies' tales." Later, throughout Europe (except in Ireland), the storytellers from whom the Grimm brothers and their followers collected their material were most often women; in some areas, they were all women. For hundreds of years, while written literature was almost exclusively in the hands of men, these tales were being invented and passed on orally by women.

In content too fairy tales are women's literature. Writers   12
like Robert Graves have seen them as survivals of an older, matriarchal culture and faith; but whether they are right or not, it is women who most often are the central characters in many of these stories, and women who have the supernatural

power. In the Grimms' original *Children's and Household Tales* (1812), there are sixty-one women and girl characters who have magic powers as against only twenty-one men and boys: and these men are usually dwarfs and not humans.

Another thing that separates the folktale from the printed literature of its time is that it is a middle- and working-class genre. The world it portrays and the problems it deals with are those of farmers, artisans, shopkeepers, and the working poor: survival, employment, family unity. The heroes and heroines of these tales are often very badly off, while the supernatural villains—the giants and ogres and witches—are rich. "Kings" and "queens," who lack supernatural powers and have human problems—infertility, exterior enemies, serious illness—seem from internal evidence to be merely well-to-do farmers. Literary retellings of the tales, however, from Perrault to the present, usually give their royalty a convincingly aristocratic setting.

The handful of folktales that most readers today know are not typical of the genre. They are the result of a more insidious sort of critical attack than that mounted by Sarah Trimmer and her heirs: the skewed selection and silent revision of subversive texts. At first this selection and revision were open and acknowledged. Perrault rewrote the stories he had heard from his "old wives" in elegant seventeenth-century French, adding witty morals in verse and turning the wise women of folk tradition into pretty fairies in court dress with sparkling wands and butterfly wings. In midnineteenth-century England, George Cruikshank made his four favorite tales into temperance tracts—at Cinderella's wedding, he reported, a great bonfire was made of all the bottles of wine and spirits in the castle. Even the Grimm brothers openly bowdlerized their stories to make them "suitable for childhood," and, as time went on, altered them in other ways. In each subsequent edition of the tales, for instance, women were given less to say and do.

Most compilers of books of fairy tales, unfortunately, have been less direct. For nearly two hundred years tales have been omitted and unacknowledged changes made in the original texts. The stories we know best today reflect the taste of the literary men who edited the first popular collections of fairy stories for children during the nineteenth century. They read the hundreds of folktales that had been gathered by scholars, chose the ones that most appealed to them as conventional upper-middle-class Victorians, and then rewrote these tales to make them suitable for Victorian children.

By the late nineteenth century a canon had been estab- 16 lished, and the dozen or so tales these editors had liked best were reprinted again and again. "Sleeping Beauty" was retold over and over, always without its original ending, in which the heroine gives birth to two children as the result of the prince's passionate awakening of her. Meanwhile, "The Sleeping Prince," a parallel story about a passive hero rescued from enchantment by an active heroine, was forgotten.

Folktales recorded in the field are full of everything the 17 Victorian editors left out: sex, death, low humor, and especially female initiative. In some more recent and comprehensive books of tales—as well as in Andrew Lang's famous fairy books named after colors, the later volumes of which were largely compiled and revised by his wife—there are more active heroines. They travel to the world's end, cross oceans on a wild goose's back, climb mountains of glass, enter giants' castles and steal magic objects, outwit false suitors, and defeat all kinds of supernatural enemies. They work for years to release their lovers or relatives from enchantments and help them to escape from witches and ogres. They are in effect liberated women who have courage, intelligence, resourcefulness, endurance, and kind hearts.

For Study and Discussion

QUESTIONS FOR RESPONSE

1. What folktales do you know: "Hansel and Gretel," "Beauty and the Beast," "Aladdin and the Magic Lamp"? In what ways do you think these or other fairy stories —perhaps "Jack and the

Beanstalk"—"support the rights of disadvantaged members of the population—children, women, and the poor—against the establishment," as Lurie suggests?

2. Today's young people often encounter folktales in the form of movies or television cartoons. If that is the form most familiar to you, to what extent do you think such tales still give the liberating effect that Lurie sees in the originals?

QUESTIONS ABOUT PURPOSE

1. What function does Lurie think stories about enchantment and magical powers can serve in the lives of the children who read them?
2. Lurie seems to be suggesting to parents and others who read to children that they go back to reading the original tales and avoid the sanitized and often sentimental movie versions. What does she think that change would achieve?

QUESTIONS ABOUT AUDIENCE

1. This essay comes from Lurie's book *Don't Tell the Grown-ups,* a textbook for courses on teaching children's literature. What experiences with modern children's books does Lurie assume her readers have had?
2. How much of a role did fairy tales and folktales from books play in your childhood? What do you particularly remember about them? To what extent do those experiences make you agree or disagree with Lurie's claims?

QUESTIONS ABOUT STRATEGIES

1. What early appeal does Lurie make to the rebellious adolescent streak that she assumes most of her readers share with her?
2. What evidence does Lurie present to support her claim that folktales and fairy tales are essentially a literature of women's liberation? How do you respond to that claim?

QUESTIONS FOR DISCUSSION

1. What elements in the lives of many of today's children would help them make connections between the kinds of things that

happen in folktales and their own experiences? How could such
connections help them?

2. Whom does Lurie see as responsible for the changes in fairy
   stories from their original forms to the censored Victorian versions and the Disney versions of today? What does she see as the
   major motives for changing the stories?

Francine du Plessix Gray was born in 1930 in Warsaw, Poland, and came to the United States in 1941. She was educated at Bryn Mawr, Black Mountain, and Barnard colleges. She worked as a reporter for UPI, an editorial assistant for *Realities,* a book editor for *Art in America,* and a staff writer for *The New Yorker.* She has also taught writing at Yale University and Columbia University. Her articles, stories, and reviews have appeared in *Vogue, The New Yorker,* and the *New York Times Book Review.* Her nonfiction includes *Divine Disobedience: Profiles in Catholic Radicalism* (1970), *Adam and Eve and the City* (1987), and *Soviet Women: Walking the Tightrope* (1990). She has also written three novels: *Lovers and Tyrants* (1976), *World Without End* (1981), and *October Blood* (1985). "On Friendship," reprinted from *Adam and Eve and the City,* defines the central role of friendship in achieving human happiness.

On Friendship

I SAW MADAME BOVARY at Bloomingdale's the other morning, or rather, I saw many incarnations of her. She was hovering over the cosmetic counters, clutching the current issue of *Cosmopolitan,* whose cover line read "New Styles of Coupling, Including Marriage." Her face already ablaze with numerous products advertised to make her irresistible to the opposite sex, she looked anguished, grasping, overwrought, and terribly lonely. And I thought to myself: Poor girl! With all the reams of literature that have analyzed her plight (victimized by double standards, by a materialistic middle-class

1

glutting on the excesses of romantic fiction), notwithstanding all these diagnoses, one fact central to her tragic fate has never been stressed enough: Emma Bovary had a faithful and boring husband and a couple of boring lovers—not so intolerable a condition—but she did not have a friend in the world. And when I think of the great solitude which the original Emma and her contemporaries exude, one phrase jumps to my mind. It comes from an essay by Francis Bacon, and it is one of the finest statements ever penned about the human need for friendship: "Those who have no friends to open themselves unto are cannibals of their own hearts."

In the past years the theme of friendship has been increasingly prominent in our conversations, in our books and films, 2

Friendship is the bond least affected by striving for power, physical pleasure, or material profit.

---

even in our college courses. It is evident that many of us are yearning with new fervor for this form of bonding. And our yearning may well be triggered by the same disillusionment with the reign of Eros that destroyed Emma Bovary. Emma was eating her heart out over a fantasy totally singular to the Western world, and only a century old at that: the notion that sexual union between men and women who believe that they are passionately in love, a union achieved by free choice and legalized by marriage, tends to offer a life of perpetual bliss and is the most desirable human bond available on earth. It is a notion bred in the same frenzied climate of the romantic epoch that caused countless young Europeans to act like the characters of their contemporary literature. Goethe's *Werther* is said to have triggered hundreds of suicides. Numerous wives glutted on the fantasies of George Sand's heroines demanded separations because their husbands were unpoetic. And Emma Bovary, palpitating from that romantic fiction which precurses our current sex manuals in its outlandish hopes for the satiation of desire, muses in the third week of her marriage: Where is "the felicity, the passion, the intoxication" that had so enchanted her in the novels of Sir Walter Scott?

This frenzied myth of love which has also led to the downfall of Cleopatra, Juliet, Romeo, and King Kong continues to breed, in our time, more garbled thinking, wretched verse, and nonsensical jingles than any emotion under the sun: "All You Need Is Love," or as we heard it in our high-school days, "Tell me you'll love me forever, if only tonight." As Flaubert put it, we are all victims of romanticism. And if we still take for granted its cult of heterosexual passion, it is in part because we have been victimized, as Emma was, by the propaganda machine of the Western novel. It was the power and the genius of the novel form to fuse medieval notions of courtly love with the idealization of marriage that marked the rise of the eighteenth-century middle class. (By "romantic love," I mean an infatuation that involves two major ingredients: a sense of being "enchanted" by another person through a complex process of illusion, and a willingness to totally surrender to that person.) 3

One hardly needs a course in anthropology to realize that this alliance of marriage and romantic love is restricted to a small segment of the Western world, and would seem sheer folly in most areas of this planet. The great majority of humans—be it in China, Japan, Africa, India, the Moslem nations—still engage in marriages prearranged by their elders or dictated by pragmatic reasons of money, land, tribal politics, or (as in the Socialist countries) housing shortages. Romantically motivated marriage as the central ingredient of the good life is almost as novel in our own West. In popular practice, it remained restricted to a narrow segment of the middle class until the twentieth century. And on the level of philosophical reflection, it was always friendship between members of the same sex, never any bonding of sexual affection, which from Greek times to the Enlightenment was held 4

to be the cornerstone of human happiness. Yet this central
role allotted to friendship for two thousand years has been
progressively eroded by such factors as the nineteenth century exaltation of instinct; science's monopoly on our theories of human sentiment; the massive eroticizing of society;
and that twentieth-century celebration of the body that
reaches its peak in the hedonistic solitude of the multiple
orgasm.

To Aristotle, friendship can be formed only by persons of 5
virtue: A man's capacity for friendship is the most accurate
measure of his virtue; it is the foundation of the state, for
great legislators care even more for friendship than they care
for justice. To Plato, as we know, passionate affection un-
tainted by physical relations is the highest form of human
bonding. To Cicero, *Amicitia* is more important than either
money, power, honors, or health because each of these gifts
can bring us only one form of pleasure, whereas the pleasures
of friendship are marvelously manifold; and friendship being
based on equity, the tyrant is the man least capable of forming
that bond because of his need to wield power over others.
Montaigne's essay, along with Bacon's, is the most famous of
many that glorify our theme in the Renaissance. And like the
ancients, he stresses the advantages of friendship over any
kind of romantic and physical attachment. Love for members
of the opposite sex, in Montaigne's words, is "an impetuous
and fickle flame, undulating and variable, a fever flame subject
to fits and lulls." Whereas the fire of friendship produces "a
general and universal warmth, moderate and even," and will
always forge bonds superior to those of marriage because
marriage's continuance is "constrained and forced, depending on factors other than our free will."

A century later, even La Rochefoucauld, that great cynic 6
who described the imperialism of the ego better than any
other precursor of Freud, finds that friendship is the only
human bond in which the tyrannical cycle of our self-love
seems broken, in which "we can love each other even more
than love ourselves." One of the last classic essays on friend-

ship I can think of before it loses major importance as a philosophical theme is by Ralph Waldo Emerson. And it's interesting to note that by mid-nineteenth century, the euphoric absolutes which had previously described this form of bonding are sobered by many cautious qualifications. A tinge of modern pragmatism sets in. Emerson tends to distrust any personal friendship unless it functions for the purpose of some greater universal fraternity.

Yet however differently these thinkers focused on our theme, they all seemed to reach a consensus on the qualities of free will, equity, trust, and selflessness unique to the affection of friendship. They cannot resist comparing it to physical passion, which yearns for power over the other, seeks possession and the state of being possessed, seeks to devour, breeds on excess, can easily become demonic, is closely allied to the death wish, and is often a form of agitated narcissism quite unknown to the tranquil, balanced rule of friendship. And rereading the sagas of Tristan and Iseult, Madame Bovary, and many other romantic lovers, it is evident that their passions tend to breed as much on a masturbatory excitement as on a longing for the beloved. They are in love with love, their delirium is involved with a desire for self-magnification through suffering, as evidenced in Tristan's words, "Eyes with joy are blinded. I myself am the world." There is confrontation, turmoil, aggression, in the often militaristic language of romantic love: Archers shoot fatal arrows or unerring shafts; the male enemy presses, pursues, and conquers; women surrender after being besieged by amorous assaults. Friendship on the other hand is the most pacifist species in the fauna of human emotions, the most steadfast and sharing. No wonder then that the finest pacifist ideology in the West was devised by a religious group—the Quakers—which takes as its official name the Religious Society of Friends; the same temperate principle of fraternal bonding informs that vow demanded by the Benedictine Order—the Oath of Stability—which remains central to the monastic tradition to this day. No wonder, also, that the kind of passionate friendship shared by David and Jonathan has inspired very few masterpieces of literature, which seem to thrive on tension and illicitness. For until they were relegated to the dissecting rooms of the social sciences, our literary views of friendship tended to be expressed in the essay form, a cool, reflective mode that never provided friendship with the motive, democratic, propagandistic force found by Eros in novel, verse, and stage. To this day, friendship totally resists commercial exploitation, unlike the vast businesses fueled by romantic love that support the couture, perfume, cosmetic, lingerie, and pulp-fiction trades.

One should note, however, that most views of friendship 8 expressed in the past twenty centuries of Western thought have dealt primarily with the male's capacity for affection. And they tend to be extremely dubious about the possibility of women ever being able to enjoy genuine friendships with members of their own sex, not to speak of making friends with male peers. Montaigne expressed a prejudice that lasts well into our day when he wrote, "The ordinary capacity of women is inadequate for that communion and fellowship which is the nurse of that sacred bond, nor does their soul feel firm enough to endure the strain of so tight and durable a knot." It is shocking, though not surprising, to hear prominent social scientists paraphrase that opinion in our own decades. Konrad Lorenz and Lionel Tiger, for instance, seem to agree that women are made eminently unsociable by their genetic programming; their bondings, in Lorenz's words, "must be considered weak imitations of the exclusively male associations." Given the current vogue for sociobiology, such assertions are often supported by carefully researched papers on the courtship patterns of Siberian wolves, the prevalence of eye contact among male baboons, and the vogue for gang-banging among chimpanzees.

Our everyday language reflects the same bias: "Fraternity" 9 is a word that goes far beyond its collegiate context and embraces notions of honor, dignity, loyalty. "Sorority" is something we might have belonged to as members of the University of Oklahoma's bowling team in the early 1950s. So I think it is high time that the same feminist perspective that has begun to correct the biases of art history and psychoanalysis should be brought to bear on this area of anthropology. We have indeed been deprived of those official, dramatically visible rites offered to men in pub, poolroom, Elks, hunting ground, or football league. And having been brought up in a very male world, I'm ashamed to say it took me a decade of feminist consciousness to realize that the few bonding associations left to twentieth-century women—garden clubs, church suppers, sewing circles (often derided by men because they do not deal with power)—have been activities considerably more creative and life-enhancing than the competition of the poolroom, the machismo of beer drinking, or the bloodshed of hunting.

Among both sexes, the rites and gestures of friendship seemed to have been decimated in the Victorian era, which brought a fear of homosexuality unprecedented in the West. (They also tended to decrease as rites of heterosexual coupling became increasingly permissive.) Were Dr. Johnson and James Boswell gay, those two men who constantly exhibited their affection for each other with kisses, tears, and passionate embraces? I suspect they were as rabidly straight as those tough old soldiers described by Tacitus begging for last kisses when their legion broke up. Since Freud, science has tended to dichotomize human affection along lines of deviance and normalcy, genitality and platonic love, instead of leaving it as a graduated spectrum of emotion in which love, friendship, sensuality, sexuality, can freely flow into each other as they did in the past. This may be another facet of modern culture that has cast coolness and self-consciousness on our gestures of friendship. The 1960s brought us some hope for change, both in its general emotional climate and in our scientists' tendency to relax their definitions of normalcy and deviance. For one of the most beautiful signs of that decade's renewed yearning for friendship and community, particularly evident among the groups who marched in civil-rights or antiwar demonstrations, was the sight of men clutching, kissing, embracing each other as unabashedly as Dr. Johnson and James Boswell.

10

Which leads me to reflect on the reasons why I increasingly   11
turn to friendship in my own life: In a world more and more
polluted by the lying of politicians and the illusions of the
media, I occasionally crave to hear and to tell the truth. To
borrow a beautiful phrase from Friedrich Nietzsche, I look
upon my friend as "the beautiful enemy" who alone is able
to offer me total candor. I look for the kind of honest friend
Emma Bovary needed: one who could have told her that her
lover was a jerk.

Friendship is by its very nature freer of deceit than any   12
other relationship we can know because it is the bond least
affected by striving for power, physical pleasure, or material
profit, most liberated from any oath of duty or of constancy.
With Eros the *body* stands naked, in friendship our *spirit* is
denuded. Friendship, in this sense, is a human condition
resembling what may be humanity's most beautiful and necessary lie—the promise of an afterlife. It is an almost celestial
sphere in which we most resemble that society of angels
offered us by Christian theology, in which we can sing the
truth of our inner thoughts in relative freedom and abun-
dance. No wonder then that the last contemporary writers
whose essays on friendship may remain classics are those
religiously inclined, scholars relatively unaffected by positiv-
ism or behaviorism, or by the general scientificization of
human sentiment. That marvelous Christian maverick, C. S.
Lewis, tells us: "Friendship is unnecessary, like philosophy,
like art, like the universe itself (since God did not *need* to
create). It has no survival value; rather it is one of those things
that give value to survival." And the Jewish thinker Simone
Weil focuses on the classic theme of free consent when she
writes: "Friendship is a miracle by which a person consents
to view from a certain distance, and without coming any
nearer, the very being who is necessary to him as food."

The quality of free consent and self-determination inher-   13
ent in friendship may be crucial to the lives of twentieth-
century women beginning their vocations. But in order to
return friendship to an absolutely central place in our lives,
we might have to wean ourselves in part from the often
submissive premises of romantic passion. I suspect that we

shall always need some measure of swooning and palpitating, of ecstasy and trembling, of possessing and being possessed. But, I also suspect that we've been bullied and propagandized into many of these manifestations by the powerful modern organism that I call the sexual-industrial complex and that had an antecedent in the novels that fueled Emma Bovary's deceitful fantasies. For one of the most treacherous aspects of the cult of romantic love has been its complex idealization and exploitation of female sexuality. There is now a new school of social scientists who are militantly questioning the notion that Western romantic love is the best foundation for human bonding, and their criticism seems much inspired by feminist perspectives. The Australian anthropologist Robert Brain, for instance, calls romantic love "a lunatic relic of medieval passions . . . the handmaiden of a moribund capitalistic culture and of an equally dead Puritan ethic."

What exactly would happen if we women remodeled our 14 concepts of ideal human bonding on the ties of friendship and abandoned the premises of enchantment and possession? Such a restructuring of our ideals of happiness could be extremely subversive. It might imply a considerable de-eroticizing of society. It could bring about a minor revolution against the sexual-industrial complex that brings billions of dollars to thousands of men by brainwashing us into the roles of temptress and seductress, and estranges us from the plain and beautiful Quaker ideal of being a sister to the world. How topsy-turvy the world would be! Dalliance, promiscuity, all those more sensationalized aspects of the Women's Movement that were once seen as revolutionary might suddenly seem most bourgeois and old-fashioned activities. If chosen in conditions of rigorous self-determination, the following values, considered up to now as reactionary, could suddenly become the most radical ones at hand: Virginity. Celibacy. Monastic communities. And that most endangered species of all, fidelity in marriage, which has lately become so exotically rare that it might soon become very fashionable, and provide the cover story for yet another publication designed to alleviate the seldom-admitted solitude of swinging singles: "Mick Jagger Is into Fidelity."

For Study and Discussion

QUESTIONS FOR RESPONSE

1. How do you respond to Montaigne's sixteenth-century point of view that women don't have the capacity for real friendship or to the assertion of twentieth-century social scientist Konrad Lorenz that women's friendships are weak imitations of men's? How does your own experience jibe with those statements?
2. Many women feel that the women's movement has helped to change the way in which women relate to each other, creating more bonding and less competition. Drawing on your own experiences, explain how you would respond to that claim.

QUESTIONS ABOUT PURPOSE

1. How does Gray want to change her readers' view of romantic love? Do you think she is talking primarily to women or to men? How can you tell?
2. This writer argues that we should focus more on friendship and less on erotic love. Which of these goals do you think is more important for her? What about the essay makes you think so?

QUESTIONS ABOUT AUDIENCE

1. What influences and elements in our society make nearly every American reader familiar with what the writer calls "the sexual-industrial complex"? How does a department store like Bloomingdale's epitomize many elements in that complex?
2. What value do you think an audience of college readers puts on romantic love? What experiences might they have had with romantic love that would affect the way they respond to Gray's argument?

QUESTIONS ABOUT STRATEGIES

1. Why do you think the writer starts her essay with "I saw Madame Bovary at Bloomingdale's the other morning"? What is the immediate picture you get? How does the writer go on to reach readers who may not have read *Madame Bovary*?
2. What effect does the writer get by pointing out the militaristic

language of romantic love in paragraph 7? How does this effect serve her purpose?

QUESTIONS FOR DISCUSSION

1. Describe the elements of Gray's "sexual-industrial complex." How powerful do you think it is? Who is most affected by it?
2. What changes in our society could come about if it were "de-eroticized," as the writer puts it? How would you feel about such changes?

Raymond Carver (1938–1988) was born in Clatskanie, Oregon, and educated at Humboldt State College (now California State University at Arcata) and at the University of Iowa. Carver worked as an editor for Science Research Associates before accepting positions as lecturer in creative writing at the University of California at Berkeley, at the Writing Workshop at the University of Iowa, and at the University of Texas at El Paso. In 1980 he became a professor of English at Syracuse University. He died in the summer of 1988 at the age of fifty at his home in Port Angeles, Washington. Carver contributed poems and stories to many literary periodicals and national magazines such as *Esquire* and *Harper's*. His poems are collected in *Near Klamath* (1968), *Winter Insomnia* (1970), and *At Night the Salmon Move* (1976). His stories, which received many awards, are collected in *Will You Please Be Quiet, Please?* (1976), *Furious Seasons* (1977), *What We Talk About When We Talk About Love* (1981), *Cathedral* (1983), *The Stories of Raymond Carver* (1985), and *Where I'm Calling From,* completed shortly before his death. In "What We Talk About When We Talk About Love," Carver records a "kitchen-table symposium" on the subject of love.

What We Talk About When We Talk About Love

M Y FRIEND MEL McGinnis was talking. Mel McGinnis is a cardiologist, and sometimes that gives him the right.

The four of us were sitting around his kitchen table drink-   2
ing gin. Sunlight filled the kitchen from the big window
behind the sink. There were Mel and me and his second wife,
Teresa—Terri, we called her—and my wife, Laura. We lived
in Albuquerque then. But we were all from somewhere else.

There was an ice bucket on the table. The gin and the   3
tonic water kept going around, and we somehow got on the
subject of love. Mel thought real love was nothing less than
spiritual love. He said he'd spent five years in a seminary
before quitting to go to medical school. He said he still
looked back on those years in the seminary as the most
important years in his life.

Terri said the man she lived with before she lived with Mel   4
loved her so much he tried to kill her. Then Terri said, "He
beat me up one night. He dragged me around the living
room by my ankles. He kept saying, 'I love you, I love you,
you bitch.' He went on dragging me around the living room.
My head kept knocking on things." Terri looked around the
table. "What do you do with love like that?"

She was a bone-thin woman with a pretty face, dark eyes,   5
and brown hair that hung down her back. She liked necklaces
made of turquoise, and long pendant earrings.

"My God, don't be silly. That's not love, and you know   6
it," Mel said. "I don't know what you'd call it, but I sure
know you wouldn't call it love."

"Say what you want to, but I know it was," Terri said. "It   7
may sound crazy to you, but it's true just the same. People
are different, Mel. Sure, sometimes he may have acted crazy.
Okay. But he loved me. In his own way maybe, but he loved
me. There was love there, Mel. Don't say there wasn't."

Mel let out his breath. He held his glass and turned to   8
Laura and me. "The man threatened to kill me," Mel said.
He finished his drink and reached for the gin bottle. "Terri's
a romantic. Terri's of the kick-me-so-I'll-know-you-love-me
school. Terri, hon, don't look that way." Mel reached across
the table and touched Terri's cheek with his fingers. He
grinned at her.

"Now he wants to make up," Terri said.   9

"Make up what?" Mel said. "What is there to make up? I   10
know what I know. That's all."

"How'd we get started on this subject, anyway?" Terri   11
said. She raised her glass and drank from it. "Mel always has
love on his mind," she said. "Don't you, honey?" She smiled.
And I thought that was the last of it.

"I just wouldn't call Ed's behavior love. That's all I'm   12
saying, honey," Mel said. "What about you guys?" Mel said
to Laura and me. "Does that sound like love to you?"

"I'm the wrong person to ask," I said. "I didn't even know   13
the man. I've only heard his name mentioned in passing. I
wouldn't know. You'd have to know the particulars. But I
think what you're saying is that love is an absolute."

Mel said, "The kind of love I'm talking about is. The kind   14
of love I'm talking about, you don't try to kill people."

Laura said, "I don't know anything about Ed, or anything   15
about the situation. But who can judge anyone else's situation?"

I touched the back of Laura's hand. She gave me a quick   16
smile. I picked up Laura's hand. It was warm, the nails polished, perfectly manicured. I encircled the broad wrist with
my fingers, and I held her.

"When I left, he drank rat poison," Terri said. She clasped   17
her arms with her hands. "They took him to the hospital in
Santa Fe. That's where we lived then, about ten miles out.
They saved his life. But his gums went crazy from it. I mean
they pulled away from his teeth. After that, his teeth stood
out like fangs. My God," Terri said. She waited a minute,
then let go of her arms and picked up her glass.

"What people won't do!" Laura said.   18

"He's out of the action now," Mel said. "He's dead."   19

Mel handed me the saucer of limes. I took a section,   20
squeezed it over my drink, and stirred the ice cubes with my
finger.

"It gets worse," Terri said. "He shot himself in the mouth.   21
But he bungled that too. Poor Ed," she said. Terri shook her
head.

"Poor Ed nothing," Mel said. "He was dangerous."   22

Mel was forty-five years old. He was tall and rangy with   23 curly soft hair. His face and arms were brown from the tennis he played. When he was sober, his gestures, all his movements, were precise, very careful.

"He did love me though, Mel. Grant me that," Terri said. 24 "That's all I'm asking. He didn't love me the way you love me. I'm not saying that. But he loved me. You can grant me that, can't you?"

"What do you mean, he bungled it?" I said. 25

Laura leaned forward with her glass. She put her elbows 26 on the table and held her glass in both hands. She glanced from Mel to Terri and waited with a look of bewilderment on her open face, as if amazed that such things happened to people you were friendly with.

"How'd he bungle it when he killed himself?" I said. 27

"I'll tell you what happened," Mel said. "He took this 28 twenty-two pistol he'd bought to threaten Terri and me with. Oh, I'm serious, the man was always threatening. You should have seen the way we lived in those days. Like fugitives. I even bought a gun myself. Can you believe it? A guy like me? But I did. I bought one for self-defense and carried it in the glove compartment. Sometimes I'd have to leave the apartment in the middle of the night. To go to the hospital, you know? Terri and I weren't married then, and my first wife had the house and kids, the dog, everything, and Terri and I were living in this apartment here. Sometimes, as I say, I'd get a call in the middle of the night and have to go in to the hospital at two or three in the morning. It'd be dark out there in the parking lot, and I'd break into a sweat before I could even get to my car. I never knew if he was going to come up out of the shrubbery or from behind a car and start shooting. I mean, the man was crazy. He was capable of wiring a bomb, anything. He used to call my service at all hours and say he needed to talk to the doctor, and when I'd return the call, he'd say, 'Son of a bitch, your days are numbered.' Little things like that. It was scary, I'm telling you."

"I still feel sorry for him," Terri said. 29

"It sounds like a nightmare," Laura said. "But what exactly 30 happened after he shot himself?"

Laura is a legal secretary. We'd met in a professional ca- 31 pacity. Before we knew it, it was a courtship. She's thirty-five, three years younger than I am. In addition to being in love, we like each other and enjoy one another's company. She's easy to be with.

"What happened?" Laura said. 32

Mel said, "He shot himself in the mouth in his room. 33
Someone heard the shot and told the manager. They came in with a passkey, saw what had happened, and called an ambulance. I happened to be there when they brought him in, alive but past recall. The man lived for three days. His head swelled up to twice the size of a normal head. I'd never seen anything like it, and I hope I never do again. Terri wanted to go in and sit with him when she found out about it. We had a fight over it. I didn't think she should see him like that. I didn't think she should see him, and I still don't."

"Who won the fight?" Laura said. 34

"I was in the room with him when he died," Terri said. 35
"He never came up out of it. But I sat with him. He didn't have anyone else."

"He was dangerous," Mel said. "If you call that love, you 36
can have it."

"It was love," Terri said. "Sure, it's abnormal in most 37
people's eyes. But he was willing to die for it. He did die for it."

"I sure as hell wouldn't call it love," Mel said. "I mean, 38
no one knows what he did it for. I've seen a lot of suicides, and I couldn't say anyone ever knew what they did it for."

Mel put his hands behind his neck and tilted his chair back. 39
"I'm not interested in that kind of love," he said. "If that's love, you can have it."

Terri said, "We were afraid. Mel even made a will out and 40
wrote to his brother in California who used to be a Green Beret. Mel told him who to look for if something happened to him."

Terri drank from her glass. She said, "But Mel's right—we 41
lived like fugitives. We were afraid. Mel was, weren't you, honey? I even called the police at one point, but they were

no help. They said they couldn't do anything until Ed actually did something. Isn't that a laugh?" Terri said.

She poured the last of the gin into her glass and waggled 42 the bottle. Mel got up from the table and went to the cupboard. He took down another bottle.

"Well, Nick and I know what love is," Laura said. "For us, 43 I mean," Laura said. She bumped my knee with her knee. "You're supposed to say something now," Laura said, and turned her smile on me.

For an answer, I took Laura's hand and raised it to my lips. 44 I made a big production out of kissing her hand. Everyone was amused.

"We're lucky," I said. 45

"You guys," Terri said. "Stop that now. You're making me 46 sick. You're still on the honeymoon, for God's sake. You're still gaga, for crying out loud. Just wait. How long have you been together now? How long has it been? A year? Longer than a year?"

"Going on a year and a half," Laura said, flushed and 47 smiling.

"Oh, now," Terri said. "Wait awhile." 48

She held her drink and gazed at Laura. 49

"I'm only kidding," Terri said. 50

Mel opened the gin and went around the table with the 51 bottle.

"Here, you guys," he said. "Let's have a toast. I want to 52 propose a toast. A toast to love. To true love," Mel said.

We touched glasses. 53

"To love," we said. 54

Outside in the backyard, one of the dogs began to bark. 55 The leaves of the aspen that leaned past the window ticked against the glass. The afternoon sun was like a presence in this room, the spacious light of ease and generosity. We could have been anywhere, somewhere enchanted. We raised our glasses again and grinned at each other like children who had agreed on something forbidden.

"I'll tell you what real love is," Mel said. "I mean, I'll give   56
you a good example. And then you can draw your own
conclusions." He poured more gin into his glass. He added
an ice cube and a sliver of lime. We waited and sipped our
drinks. Laura and I touched knees again. I put a hand on her
warm thigh and left it there.

"What do any of us really know about love?" Mel said. "It   57
seems to me we're just beginners at love. We say we love each
other and we do, I don't doubt it. I love Terri and Terri loves
me, and you guys love each other too. You know the kind of
love I'm talking about now. Physical love, that impulse that
drives you to someone special, as well as love of the other
person's being, his or her essence, as it were. Carnal love and,
well, call it sentimental love, the day-to-day caring about the
other person. But sometimes I have a hard time accounting
for the fact that I must have loved my first wife too. But I
did, I know I did. So I suppose I am like Terri in that regard.
Terri and Ed." He thought about it and then he went on.
"There was a time when I thought I loved my first wife more
than life itself. But now I hate her guts. I do. How do you
explain that? What happened to that love? What happened to
it, is what I'd like to know. I wish someone could tell me.
Then there's Ed. Okay, we're back to Ed. He loves Terri so
much he tries to kill her and he winds up killing himself."
Mel stopped talking and swallowed from his glass. "You guys
have been together eighteen months and you love each other.
It shows all over you. You glow with it. But you both loved
other people before you met each other. You've both been
married before, just like us. And you probably loved other
people before that too, even. Terri and I have been together
five years, been married for four. And the terrible thing, the
terrible thing is, but the good thing too, the saving grace,
you might say, is that if something happened to one of us—
excuse me for saying this—but if something happened to one
of us tomorrow, I think the other one, the other person,
would grieve for a while, you know, but then the surviving
party would go out and love again, have someone else soon
enough. All this, all of this love we're talking about, it would

just be a memory. Maybe not even a memory. Am I wrong?
Am I way off base? Because I want you to set me straight if
you think I'm wrong. I want to know. I mean, I don't know
anything, and I'm the first one to admit it."

"Mel, for God's sake," Terri said. She reached out and   58
took hold of his wrist. "Are you getting drunk? Honey? Are
you drunk?"

"Honey, I'm just talking," Mel said. "All right? I don't   59
have to be drunk to say what I think. I mean, we're all just
talking, right?" Mel said. He fixed his eyes on her.

"Sweetie, I'm not criticizing," Terri said.   60

She picked up her glass.   61

"I'm not on call today," Mel said. "Let me remind you of   62
that. I am not on call," he said.

"Mel, we love you," Laura said.   63

Mel looked at Laura. He looked at her as if he could not   64
place her, as if she was not the woman she was.

"Love you too, Laura," Mel said. "And you, Nick, love   65
you too. You know something?" Mel said. "You guys are our
pals," Mel said.

He picked up his glass.   66

Mel said, "I was going to tell you about something. I   67
mean, I was going to prove a point. You see, this happened
a few months ago, but it's still going on right now, and it
ought to make us feel ashamed when we talk like we know
what we're talking about when we talk about love."

"Come on now," Terri said. "Don't talk like you're drunk   68
if you're not drunk."

"Just shut up for once in your life," Mel said very quietly.   69
"Will you do me a favor and do that for a minute? So as I
was saying, there's this old couple who had this car wreck out
on the interstate. A kid hit them and they were all torn to
shit and nobody was giving them much chance to pull
through."

Terri looked at us and then back at Mel. She seemed   70
anxious, or maybe that's too strong a word.

Mel was handing the bottle around the table.   71

"I was on call that night," Mel said. "It was May or maybe   72
it was June. Terri and I had just sat down to dinner when the
hospital called. There'd been this thing out on the interstate.
Drunk kid, teenager, plowed his dad's pickup into this
camper with this old couple in it. They were up in their
mid-seventies, that couple. The kid—eighteen, nineteen,
something—he was DOA. Taken the steering wheel through
his sternum. The old couple, they were alive, you understand.
I mean, just barely. But they had everything. Multiple frac-
tures, internal injuries, hemorrhaging, contusions, lacera-
tions, the works, and they each of them had themselves
concussions. They were in a bad way, believe me. And, of
course, their age was two strikes against them. I'd say she was
worse off than he was. Ruptured spleen along with everything
else. Both kneecaps broken. But they'd been wearing their
seatbelts and, God knows, that's what saved them for the
time being."

"Folks, this is an advertisement for the National Safety   73
Council," Terri said. "This is your spokesman, Dr. Melvin R.
McGinnis, talking." Terri laughed. "Mel," she said, "some-
times you're just too much. But I love you, hon," she said.

"Honey, I love you," Mel said.   74

He leaned across the table. Terri met him halfway. They   75
kissed.

"Terri's right," Mel said as he settled himself again. "Get   76
those seatbelts on. But seriously, they were in some shape,
those oldsters. By the time I got down there, the kid was
dead, as I said. He was off in a corner, laid out on a gurney.
I took one look at the old couple and told the ER nurse to
get me a neurologist and an orthopedic man and a couple of
surgeons down there right away."

He drank from his glass. "I'll try to keep this short," he   77
said. "So we took the two of them up to the OR and worked
like fuck on them most of the night. They had these incredible reserves, those two. You see that once in a while. So we
did everything that could be done, and toward morning
we're giving them a fifty-fifty chance, maybe less than that

for her. So here they are, still alive the next morning. So, okay, we move them into the ICU, which is where they both kept plugging away at it for two weeks, hitting it better and better on all the scopes. So we transfer them out to their own room."

Mel stopped talking. "Here," he said, "let's drink this cheapo gin the hell up. Then we're going to dinner, right? Terri and I know a new place. That's where we'll go, to this new place we know about. But we're not going until we finish up this cut-rate, lousy gin." 78

Terri said, "We haven't actually eaten there yet. But it looks good. From the outside, you know." 79

"I like food," Mel said. "If I had it to do all over again, I'd be a chef, you know? Right, Terri?" Mel said. 80

He laughed. He fingered the ice in his glass. 81

"Terri knows," he said. "Terri can tell you. But let me say this. If I could come back again in a different life, a different time and all, you know what? I'd like to come back as a knight. You were pretty safe wearing all that armor. It was all right being a knight until gunpowder and muskets and pistols came along." 82

"Mel would like to ride a horse and carry a lance," Terri said. 83

"Carry a woman's scarf with you everywhere," Laura said. 84

"Or just a woman," Mel said. 85

"Shame on you," Laura said. 86

Terri said, "Suppose you came back as a serf. The serfs didn't have it so good in those days," Terri said. 87

"The serfs never had it good," Mel said. "But I guess even the knights were vessels to someone. Isn't that the way it worked? But then everyone is always a vessel to someone. Isn't that right? Terri? But what I liked about knights, besides their ladies, was that they had that suit of armor, you know, and they couldn't get hurt very easy. No cars in those days, you know? No drunk teenagers to tear into your ass." 88

"Vassals," Terri said. 89

"What?" Mel said. 90

"Vassals," Terri said. "They were called vassals, not ves-   91
sels."

"Vassals, vessels," Mel said, "what the fuck's the differ-   92
ence? You knew what I meant anyway. All right," Mel said.
"So I'm not educated. I learned my stuff. I'm a heart surgeon, sure, but I'm just a mechanic. I go in and I fuck around
and I fix things. Shit," Mel said.

"Modesty doesn't become you," Terri said.   93

"He's just a humble sawbones," I said. "But sometimes   94
they suffocated in all that armor, Mel. They'd even have heart
attacks if it got too hot and they were too tired and worn
out. I read somewhere that they'd fall off their horses and
not be able to get up because they were too tired to stand
with all that armor on them. They got trampled by their own
horses sometimes."

"That's terrible," Mel said. "That's a terrible thing, Nicky.   95
I guess they'd just lay there and wait until somebody came
along and made a shish kebab out of them."

"Some other vessel," Terri said.   96

"That's right," Mel said. "Some vassal would come along   97
and spear the bastard in the name of love. Or whatever the
fuck it was they fought over in those days."

"Same things we fight over these days," Terri said.   98

Laura said, "Nothing's changed."   99

The color was still high in Laura's cheeks. Her eyes were   100
bright. She brought her glass to her lips.

Mel poured himself another drink. He looked at the label   101
closely as if studying a long row of numbers. Then he slowly
put the bottle down on the table and slowly reached for the
tonic water.

"What about the old couple?" Laura said. "You didn't   102
finish that story you started."

Laura was having a hard time lighting her cigarette. Her   103
matches kept going out.

The sunshine inside the room was different now, changing,   104
getting thinner. But the leaves outside the window were still
shimmering, and I stared at the pattern they made on the

panes and on the Formica counter. They weren't the same patterns, of course.

"What about the old couple?" I said. 105

"Older but wiser," Terri said. 106

Mel stared at her. 107

Terri said, "Go on with your story, hon. I was only kidding. Then what happened?" 108

"Terri, sometimes," Mel said. 109

"Please Mel," Terri said. "Don't always be so serious, sweetie. Can't you take a joke?" 110

"Where's the joke?" Mel said. 111

He held his glass and gazed steadily at his wife. 112

"What happened?" Laura said. 113

Mel fastened his eyes on Laura. He said, "Laura, if I didn't have Terri and if I didn't love her so much, and if Nick wasn't my best friend, I'd fall in love with you. I'd carry you off, honey," he said. 114

"Tell your story," Terri said. "Then we'll go to that new place, okay?" 115

"Okay," Mel said. "Where was I?" he said. He stared at the table and then he began again. 116

"I dropped in to see each of them every day, sometimes twice a day if I was up doing other calls anyway. Casts and bandages, head to foot, the both of them. You know, you've seen it in the movies. That's just the way they looked, just like in the movies. Little eye-holes and nose-holes and mouth-holes. And she had to have her legs slung up on top of it. Well, the husband was very depressed for the longest while. Even after he found out that his wife was going to pull through, he was still very depressed. Not about the accident, though. I mean, the accident was one thing, but it wasn't everything. I'd get up to his mouth-hole, you know, and he'd say no, it wasn't the accident exactly but it was because he couldn't see her through his eye-holes. He said that was what was making him feel so bad. Can you imagine? I'm telling you, the man's heart was breaking because he couldn't turn his goddamn head and *see* his goddamn wife." 117

Mel looked around the table and shook his head at what he was going to say. 118

"I mean, it was killing the old fart just because he couldn't   119
look at the fucking woman."

We all looked at Mel.   120

"Do you see what I'm saying?" he said.   121

Maybe we were a little drunk by then. I know it was hard   122
keeping things in focus. The light was draining out of the
room, going back through the window where it had come
from. Yet nobody made a move to get up from the table to
turn on the overhead light.

"Listen," Mel said. "Let's finish this fucking gin. There's   123
about enough left here for one shooter all around. Then let's
go eat. Let's go to the new place."

"He's depressed," Terri said. "Mel, why don't you take a   124
pill?"

Mel shook his head. "I've taken everything there is."   125

"We all need a pill now and then," I said.   126

"Some people are born needing them," Terri said.   127

She was using her finger to rub at something on the table.   128
Then she stopped rubbing.

"I think I want to call my kids," Mel said. "Is that all right 129
with everybody? I'll call my kids," he said.

Terri said, "What if Marjorie answers the phone? You guys,   130
you've heard us on the subject of Marjorie? Honey, you know
you don't want to talk to Marjorie. It'll make you feel even
worse."

"I don't want to talk to Marjorie," Mel said. "But I want   131
to talk to my kids."

"There isn't a day goes by that Mel doesn't say he wishes   132
she'd get married again. Or else die," Terri said. "For one
thing," Terri said, "she's bankrupting us. Mel says it's just to
spite him that she won't get married again. She has a boyfriend who lives with her and the kids, so Mel is supporting
the boyfriend too."

"She's allergic to bees," Mel said. "If I'm not praying she'll 133
get married again, I'm praying she'll get herself stung to
death by a swarm of fucking bees."

"Shame on you," Laura said.   134

"Bzzzzzzz," Mel said, turning his fingers into bees and   135
buzzing them at Terri's throat. Then he let his hands drop
all the way to his sides.

"She's vicious," Mel said. "Sometimes I think I'll go up   136
there dressed like a beekeeper. You know, that hat that's like
a helmet with the plate that comes down over your face, the
big gloves, and the padded coat? I'll knock on the door and
let loose a hive of bees in the house. But first I'd make sure
the kids were out, of course."

He crossed one leg over the other. It seemed to take him   137
a lot of time to do it. Then he put both feet on the floor and
leaned forward, elbows on the table, his chin cupped in his
hands.

"Maybe I won't call the kids, after all. Maybe it isn't such   138
a hot idea. Maybe we'll just go eat. How does that sound?"

"Sounds fine to me," I said. "Eat or not eat. Or keep   139
drinking. I could head right on out into the sunset."

"What does that mean, honey?" Laura said.   140

"It just means what I said," I said. "It means I could just   141
keep going. That's all it means."

"I could eat something myself," Laura said. "I don't think   142
I've ever been so hungry in my life. Is there something to
nibble on?"

"I'll put out some cheese and crackers," Terri said.   143

But Terri just sat there. She did not get up to get anything.   144

Mel turned his glass over. He spilled it out on the table.   145

"Gin's gone," Mel said.   146

Terri said, "Now what?"   147

I could hear my heart beating. I could hear everyone's   148
heart. I could hear the human noise we sat there making, not
one of us moving, not even when the room went dark.

COMMENT ON "WHAT WE TALK ABOUT WHEN WE TALK ABOUT LOVE"

In "What We Talk About When We Talk About Love,"
Carver creates a kitchen-table symposium on love. The

participants are familiar ones in our society—two couples who have been divorced and remarried but who still seem to believe in romantic love as much as did the knights of chivalry whom Mel admires. All of them, but particularly Mel, keep trying to figure out what it is we mean when we talk about love, and, not surprisingly, they use the most common of definition strategies: they give examples, positive and negative. Love is physical attraction like Nick and Laura's; love is a romantic ideal like the knight fighting for his lady; it's the pity Terri felt for her dying husband. Most of all, for Mel, it's the devotion of the elderly couple together in the hospital room. Love is *not*, he insists, physical violence and abuse of someone you claim to love. Toward the end of the story, Carver hints that Mel's compulsion to define love may be a symptom of his desperate search for real love. Whatever love is, he doesn't seem to have found it. He's drinking heavily, and he's depressed even though, as he says, "I've taken everything there is."

Definition as a Writing Strategy

1. Reread the strategies section on pages 310–311. Then for your classmates and instructor, write a definition essay about your high school that will give your audience a vivid idea of what that high school was like. What was valued most in the school? Describe some of the admired students. What were the most important activities? Define by giving examples, analyzing qualities, attributing characteristics, drawing analogies when possible, and telling stories about particular individuals that illustrate the flavor and character of the school. This kind of assignment provides a great opportunity to tell stories about people.

2. For a challenging assignment focusing on a person, pick someone you find especially interesting—an athlete such as Nancy Kerrigan, a businessperson such as Bill Gates or Michael Dell, an entertainment personality such as Oprah Winfrey or Barbra Streisand, a public figure such as Al Gore or Hillary Rodham Clinton. Through a computer search, locate several magazine articles on that person, and read them. Be sure to use substantial articles, not just items from gossip columns. Write a definition essay in which you describe the person—his or her professional activities and personal interests—trying to bring out the unique traits that have made the person successful. Remember that anecdotes are useful in this kind of essay. Your hypothetical audience could be readers of a magazine such as *Parade* or *Esquire*.

3. If as a child you enjoyed fairy stories or books such as *The Wizard of Oz*, the Nancy Drew books, or the Baby Sitter books, reread some of the fairy stories or two or three of the books and take notes. If you didn't read such fiction, find current examples of stories that constitute a modern folk literature: popular soap operas like *All My Children* or *As the World Turns* or popular television sitcoms like *The Cosby Show, Northern Exposure,* or *The Simpsons.* Watch a

few episodes of these and take notes. Then write an essay similar to Alison Lurie's "Folktale Liberation" in which you analyze how the stories you have chosen present men and women, workers and executives, the powerful and the weak, children and adults. Describe the social system they portray and the values of that system.

4. Choose a term that interests you—for example, *camaraderie, sportsmanship, sex appeal, gutsiness, good taste*—and for your campus newspaper write a guest column defining that term with examples and anecdotes. What are the necessary characteristics of someone who has the quality? What is the opposite quality? Who epitomizes the term for you?

5. Reread Francine du Plessix Gray's essay "On Friendship," focusing on her comments on the "sexual-industrial complex" (paragraphs 13 and 14 and the references to Bloomingdale's in paragraph 1) and its effects on women. Browse through several magazines directed principally toward girls and women—for instance, *Seventeen, Cosmopolitan, Elle, Mademoiselle, Vanity Fair.* Examine the articles, especially the ads, and then write an essay defining the "sexual-industrial complex" that Gray describes in the last sentence of paragraph 7 as "vast businesses fueled by romantic love that support the couture, perfume, cosmetic, lingerie, and pulp-fiction trades." What does the "sexual-industrial complex" sell? How does it sell? What are its goals? What definitions of women does it promote? What values does it emphasize? Your audience for this article could be your classmates, or you could write a guest editorial column for your student newspaper.

6. Writers and speakers often argue from definition, trying to get their audiences to agree with or approve of something by defining it positively (for example, a good education) or to criticize something by defining it negatively (for example, a bad grading policy). Drawing on material and information you are getting in one of your courses, write a paper suitable for that course defining a concept, policy,

theory, or event either negatively or positively. For a course in early childhood development, you could define a good day-care center. For a chemistry course, you could do a process paper on how to set up a good laboratory experiment. For a government course, you could define a well-run local campaign. For a speech course, you could define an effective speaking style.

CAUSE
AND
EFFECT

᨜

If you are like most people, you were born curious and will stay that way all your life, always wondering why things happen, wanting to know reasons. You want to know why the wind blows or what makes some young people dye their hair green, but you also want to know how to control your life and your environment. You can't have that control unless you understand **causes.** That is why so much writing is cause-and-effect writing. You need it to help you understand more about your world so you can improve it. Writing about causes plays an important role in almost all the professions, and it certainly figures prominently in writing in college.

You also want to know about **effects.** Will A lead to B? And also to C, D, and E? Such questions also arise partly from pure curiosity—a youngster will pull any string or push any button just to find out what will happen—but they stem too from a need to regulate your life, to understand how your acts affect the lives of others. You want to predict consequences so you can manage your existence in ways that other creatures cannot manage theirs. You see an effect and look for explanations, usually in writing; and when you try to explain an effect to someone else, you often do it in writing.

PURPOSE

When you write cause-and-effect essays, you're likely to have one of three purposes. Frequently, you will write *to explain*. You want your readers to know how and why things happen, to satisfy their curiosity or to educate them on some issue. You could write a paper in science or economics to lay out logical explanations and show connections for your readers. At other times, you might use a cause-and-effect pattern simply *to speculate* about an interesting topic—for example, to theorize about why a new style has become popular or what the effects will be of a new "no pass/no play" law for high school athletes.

You can also use cause-and-effect writing *to argue*. That may be the way you will use it most often, particularly when you are making an argument to pragmatic people who will pay attention to practical, common-sense reasons. When you cannot get someone to listen to arguments that something is right or wrong, you may be able to persuade by arguing not that a policy is wrong but that it is foolish or impractical—that it will have bad effects.

AUDIENCE

You can assume that cause-and-effect arguments appeal to most audiences because the pattern is such a natural one that readers are used to seeing it. Whether they are teachers, lawyers, parents, doctors, or politicians, your readers will expect you to explain and argue from cause and effect.

When you are thinking about your readers for such arguments, you will find that it helps greatly to think about them as jurors for whom you are going to present a case. You can make up a list of questions about your readers just as a lawyer would to help him or her formulate an argument. Here are some suggested questions: How ready are your readers to hear your arguments? Do you need to give them background information to prepare them? How skeptical are they likely to be? How much evidence will they require? What kind of evidence will they require: factual, statistical? Are your readers bright and well informed, likely to see the connections you want them to make, or will you have to spell everything out? Like a lawyer, you're trying to establish *probable* cause-and-effect sequences. You have the best chance of doing that if you think ahead of time about the expectations, questions, and doubts your readers will have.

STRATEGIES

When you make a cause-and-effect argument, you want your readers to accept your analysis—to agree that when A occurs, then B will probably follow. Thus Cathy Young argues in "Keeping Women Weak" that radical feminists weaken rather than empower women when they claim that women need to be protected by special regulations and conduct codes. She develops her essay by drawing an analogy between paranoia and suspicion in the Soviet Union, where she grew up, and the radical feminists' tendency to see sexism and oppression in virtually all male-female relationships. You could use the same kind of argument if you wanted to write a primarily cause-and-effect paper claiming that a culture that glorifies competition, particularly in bruising sports like football and hockey, shouldn't be surprised at gangs and street violence among young males. You could support your claims with articles you find by using the key words *sports, violence,* and *gangs* for a computerized search.

When you are arguing about effects, you want your readers to accept your analysis of a situation and agree that activity

X has been a major contributor to problem Y. William Raspberry uses this kind of pattern in his essay "The Decline of
Marriage." He argues that the rising rate of illegitimacy in
America and its accompaniment, more and more children
living in poverty, is being caused by the decline of marriage—
increasingly, young unmarried mothers have no in-laws or
extended family to help them. You could use the same kind
of pattern if you wanted to write about why so many ordinary
families are buying bulky, expensive-to-run, four-wheel-drive
sports vehicles that seem impractical for their needs. You
would have to do considerable reading in auto magazines and
the business pages to frame your hypothesis, but it could be
fun, especially if you're a car buff.

Some of the strategies you can use for cause-and-effect
papers resemble those used by lawyers in making an argument. For instance, it's a good idea to *state your claim early*
and then *show the connection* you're setting up. Then *present
supporting evidence*—past experience, research findings,
documentation, personal observation, expert testimony, and
so on. Pay special attention to establishing links between the
claim and the evidence. It's crucial to establish that connection. Stephen Jay Gould uses this approach in "Carrie Buck's
Daughter."

You don't have to write every cause-and-effect paper to
prove something or as if you were conducting a major court
case. You can also write interesting speculative papers in
which you theorize about certain trends—for instance, wearing baseball caps backward or athletic shoes with the laces
untied—and try to find who initiated the trends and why. Or
you could write satirically about some of the annoyances in
our culture—for instance, the 800 "help" numbers that keep
you on hold forever.

POTENTIAL PITFALLS IN CAUSE-AND-EFFECT PAPERS

Although cause and effect is a powerful writing strategy, it
can also be a hazardous one. When it comes to dealing with

the difficult, ongoing problems of people and societies, you can almost never prove simple cause-and-effect relationships. Many serious human problems really have no good, single solutions because our lives and cultures are so complex. Thus, to keep from looking naive or poorly informed, avoid hasty statements such as "I know what causes X, and we can fix it if we just do Y." To avoid such pitfalls, you should observe the following cautions in writing about cause and effect.

First, as in all expository writing, be careful about how much you claim. Instead of insisting that if A happens, B is inevitable, write, "I believe if A occurs, B is very likely to happen" or "B will probably follow if A happens." For instance, you might feel absolutely sure that if the university opened a child-care center for students' children, attendance at classes would be higher, but you can't absolutely prove it. You would gain more credibility with university administrators if you were careful not to overstate your case.

Second, be careful not to oversimplify cause-and-effect connections. Experienced writers and observers know that most major problems and important events have not one cause but several. Daniel Goleman makes this clear in "Peak Performance: Why Records Fall" when he points out that many elements have contributed to better performance among athletes—better coaching, improved equipment, and more knowledge about physiology. Nevertheless, he points out, intensive, longer practicing seems to be the major cause of better performance in most activities.

A less complicated, because more easily analyzed, effect that one might explore is the significant decline in deaths from heart disease in the United States in the last thirty years. There are many reasons for this decline, not just one or two. Increasingly, people smoke less, eat healthier foods, exercise more, and try to control their blood pressure. New treatments for heart problems also make a difference. Similarly, when major events occur, such as the disintegration of socialism in eastern Europe or the Los Angeles riots of May, 1992, knowledgeable observers know that they have multiple and complex causes. Thus, prudent writers qualify their claims about causes and effects by using phrases such as "a major cause," "an important result," or "an immediate effect."

You should also take care to distinguish between immediate, obvious causes for something and more remote, less apparent causes. You may feel that the immediate cause of the distressing rise in teenage pregnancies in the United States is movies and television programs that are much more sexually explicit than those of fifteen years ago, but it's important to recognize that there are more far-reaching, long-term reasons, such as poor sex education programs, many taboos on dispensing birth control information, and the increased focus on sexuality in ads.

Third, avoid confusing coincidence or simple sequence for cause and effect. Just because X follows Y doesn't mean Y causes X—that assumption is the basis of superstitions. If an increase in the automobile accident rate follows a drop in gasoline prices, you can't conclude there is a necessary connection between the two events. There might be, but a prudent investigator would want much more data before drawing such a conclusion. If you jump to quick conclusions about causes and effects, you risk falling into the "false cause" or "after this, therefore because of this" fallacy.

So working with cause and effect in a paper can be tricky and complex. That doesn't mean, however, that you should refrain from using cause-and-effect explanations or arguments until you are absolutely sure of your ground. You can't always wait for certainty to make an analysis or a forecast. The best you can do is observe carefully, speculate intelligently, and add qualifications.

USING CAUSE AND EFFECT IN PARAGRAPHS

Here are two cause-and-effect paragraphs. The first is written by a professional writer and is followed by an analysis. The second is written by a student writer and is followed by questions.

CORNEL WEST
from *Race Matters*

Effect: The L.A. riots in 1992

Cause: Sense of powerlessness in American society

Reasons he thinks it was not caused by race or class issues

What happened in Los Angeles in April of 1992 was neither a race riot nor a class rebellion. Rather, this monumental upheaval was a multiracial, trans-class, and largely male display of justified social rage. For all its ugly, xenophobic resentment, its air of adolescent carnival, and its downright barbaric behavior, it signified the sense of powerlessness in American society. Glib attempts to reduce its meaning to the pathologies of the black underclass, the criminal actions of hoodlums, or the political revolt of the oppressed urban masses miss the mark. Of those arrested, only 36 percent were black, more than a third had full-time jobs, and most claimed to shun political affiliation. What we witnessed in Los Angeles was the consequence of a lethal linkage of economic decline, cultural decay, and political lethargy in American life. Race was the visible catalyst, not the underlying cause.

Sees riots as the consequence of longtime neglect in American life

Comment In this paragraph from his 1993 book, West, a professor of religion and African-American studies at Howard University, starts by asserting that the 1992 Los Angeles riots were *not* caused by either race or class issues; he believes such analyses are glib and oversimplified, and he gives the facts to back up his statement. Rather, he claims, the riots were caused by the "sense of powerlessness in American society," powerlessness that grew out of "a lethal linkage of economic decline, cultural decay, and political lethargy in American life." Race was only the catalyst that set things off. West is pointing out that we need to be careful not to reach for easy explanations for major upheavals in our society—they're almost always caused by deep and complex causes that have been building for a long time. His phrases "adolescent car-

nival," "barbaric behavior," and "lethal linkage" are particularly forceful.

EMILY LINDERMAN
Barrier-Free Design

Many merchants view the Americans with Disabilities Act as expensive social engineering. They
have established an attractive and affordable
space for their businesses. Their customers seem
satisfied. Then the federal government requires
them to provide accessible ramps and elevators,
wider doorways and halls, larger bathrooms, and
lower drinking fountains. Seen from another perspective, however, making these changes may pay
off in the long run. How many times have you
tried to move furniture into a building or up to
the third floor? How many times have you tried
to find a place for your packages in a cramped
bathroom stall? And how many times have you
had to lift your little brother up to the fountain
to get a drink? All customers, not simply disabled
customers, will benefit from and reward merchants who invest in these barrier-free buildings.

1. Whom do you think Linderman is addressing with her argument
   for the benefits of barrier-free buildings?
2. How does the significance of the extra benefits that Linderman
   mentions compare with the significance of the benefits that the
   Disabilities Act was designed to provide?

CAUSE AND EFFECT

Points to Remember

1. Remember that in human events you can almost never prove direct, simple, cause-and-effect relationships. Qualify your claims.
2. Be careful not to oversimplify your cause-and-effect statements; be cautious about saying that a cause always produces a certain effect or that a remedy never succeeds.
3. Distinguish between the immediate, obvious cause of something and more long-range, less apparent causes for that effect.
4. Avoid confusing coincidence or simple sequence with cause and effect; because B follows A doesn't mean that A caused B.
5. Build your cause-and-effect argument as a trial lawyer would. Present as much evidence as you can and argue for your hypothesis.

William Raspberry was born in 1935 in Okolona, Mississippi, and was educated at Indiana Central College. In 1956, he began his career as a journalist working for a black weekly, the *Indianapolis Recorder.* In 1962, he joined the staff of the *Washington Post* as a teletypist and moved up to reporter and then to assistant city editor before beginning his column in 1966. He has shaped the column to fit his own interests, focusing on local topics once a week while treating broader themes in his two syndicated columns. He has also published a collection of his columns, *Looking Backward at Us* (1991). In "The Decline of Marriage: A Bad Omen," a 1994 column, Raspberry suggests the reasons why "that little piece of paper" (a marriage license) makes a difference.

The Decline of Marriage: A Bad Omen

> They are our enemies, and so we marry them.
> — ZULU SAYING

O NE OF THE remarkable—if seldom remarked—benefits of marriage is that it makes kinsmen out of strangers. It unites kingdoms, settles wars, links cultures and builds relationships that are all but impossible without marriage. 1

It's a thought that occurs to me when I think of family—of the vast diversity of individuals who have become special to me because they marry a relative of mine. Suddenly our educational and cultural differences shrink to insignificance. They have a call on my resources, and I on theirs, not because 2 of any special deservedness but because they are family. Even relatives of these new relatives become special through the sacrament of marriage.

David W. Murray, an anthropologist, says that what I have experienced in my own life is a phenomenon that cuts across cultures, across time and across geography. But he says something else: that the decline of marriage in America betokens impending doom. 3

"Cultures differ in many ways, but all societies that survive are built on marriage," he writes in the spring 1994 issue of *Policy Review*. "Marriage is a society's cultural infrastructure, 4

Marriage matters, and so does the fact that we are forgetting how much it matters.

---

its bridges of social connectedness. The history of human society shows that when people stop marrying, their continuity as a culture is in jeopardy."

Murray's piece is titled "Poor Suffering Bastards"—not to be mean but to make a point. The out-of-wedlock child has, throughout history, been a luckless child, with no claim on his father or his father's family—and with no responsibility to them. That, says Murray, is the reason the word "bastard" has come to denote someone who is heartless, or cruel, or a cheat. The man with no relatives to be shamed by his dishonor has fewer constraints against dishonorable behavior. 5

To the extent that the treatment of "illegitimate" children is a matter of attitude, it can be solved merely by deciding to be kinder. That, in fact, is what we've done for a generation. Any number of social policies have been altered in the name of kindness. We no longer kick pregnant girls out of school, or require them to beg for readmittance to church. We have abandoned the term "bastard" (except in its derivative sense) and refuse even to describe children born out of wedlock as 6 "illegitimate." We don't want to stigmatize them for reasons utterly beyond their control.

Murray's point, though, is that attitude is only a part of it.   7
Children of people who have married into my family have a claim on me that other, perhaps more deserving, children simply do not have. Helping family is different from charity. Or, as Murray, who taught at Brandeis before becoming a Bradley Scholar at the Heritage Foundation, puts it:

"Marriage is the act of creating formal kinsmen who are   8
bound to help us, and the ceremony of marrying, itself, helps to create in us moral sentiments of commitment and formal responsibility. The absence of marriage is not only a major reason why single parents are found so often in poverty, but why their children so often become solitary victims and vic-timizers."

It's easy enough to point to "fatherless" children who, far   9
from being victims or victimizers, have become important contributors to society. It is also true that the victimization and victimizing are often a byproduct of stigmatism.

Still, marriage and legitimacy matter in ways that we hardly   10
think of until Murray points them out. Married couples, more than single parents, can count on their own parents and grandparents for economic backup.

Or this. "Having a car helps in finding and keeping a job,   11
but only 18 percent (of the inner-city underclass) have access to one. People with kin networks 'branch out' and find sup-port from relatives, who lend, repair or help buy an automo-bile. The married, having more relatives, gain better access to transportation, and are more likely to have steady work."

It simply isn't true, as some insist, that "that little piece of   12
paper doesn't make any difference." It makes a tremendous difference. Just think of how differently you would regard an appeal for help from (a) your daughter's boyfriend or (b) your son-in-law. Think of the differing degrees to which you could count on help from someone with the means to provide it if that someone were the brother of your son's father-in-law or merely a relative of the girl your boy had a baby by. Marriage matters, and so does the fact that we are forgetting how much it matters.

Robert Frost once described home as "the place where,   13
when you have to go there, they have to take you in." By
that token, relatives—including those we acquire by marriage—are the folk who, when you have to ask them for help,
they have to give it.

For Study and Discussion

QUESTIONS FOR RESPONSE

1. Drawing on your own experience and that of people you know,
   how would you reply to Raspberry's claims about the value of
   marriage if you were to write him a letter?
2. In your experience, how does being married affect the way a
   couple manages their relationship? For instance, are they more
   or less likely to be able to work out problems, manage their
   finances, and so on?

QUESTIONS ABOUT PURPOSE

1. What attitudes or beliefs do you think Raspberry is challenging?
   What evidence can you give that the attitudes he deplores are
   common?
2. How does the well-being of children figure into Raspberry's
   argument?

QUESTIONS ABOUT AUDIENCE

1. What knowledge about trends in parenting in the United States
   does Raspberry assume his readers bring to this article?
2. How, if at all, do you think readers' ages would affect the way
   they respond to this article?

QUESTIONS ABOUT STRATEGIES

1. What is the effect of Raspberry's quoting an anthropologist to
   support his argument?
2. What everyday experiences that most people can identify with
   does Raspberry use to reinforce his argument?

QUESTIONS FOR DISCUSSION

1. What groups or cultures do you know of in which family honor acts as a powerful force for controlling behavior? Explain how that force operates. How would such constraints work in our society?
2. Raspberry is an African-American. How do you think his experience with the importance of the family and relatives compares with that of other ethnic groups?

Cathy Young was born in 1963 in Moscow, in the former Soviet Union, and was educated at Rutgers University. After writing a weekly column for the college newspaper, she began contributing articles to the *New York Times* and *American Spectator.* One year after graduating from Rutgers, she published *Growing Up in Moscow: Memoirs of a Soviet Girlhood* (1989). She is currently at work on *The Virgin of Terror: A Biography of Charlotte Corday,* a book on the political activism of women in Russia. In "Keeping Women Weak," reprinted from *NEXT: Young American Writers on the New Generation* (1994), Young analyzes the effects of feminism on her generation's attitudes toward women's liberation.

Keeping Women Weak

NOT LONG AGO, I attended a conference on women's 1
research and activism in the nineties, attended by dozens of feminist academics, writers, and public figures. At the wrap-up session, a middle-aged history professor from the Midwest introduced a discordant note into the spirit of celebration. "The fact," she said, "is that young women just aren't interested in feminism or feminist ideas, even though they are leading feminist lives—planning to become lawyers, doctors, professionals. What is it about feminism, and about our approach, that puts young women off?"

In response, some blamed "the backlash," others "homo- 2
phobia." One woman protested that there *were* young feminists out there, citing sexual harassment lawsuits filed by high-school girls—apparently a greater accomplishment than merely preparing for a career. Another declared that what

feminist educators needed to give their students was "an understanding of the power dynamic," not "quote-unquote objectivity." (Could it be something about comments like these that turns female students off?) Missing from this picture was any serious discussion of what modern feminism has to offer modern young women.

Feminism meant a great deal to me when I came to the   3 United States thirteen years ago, after a childhood spent in the Soviet Union. Indeed, one of the things that elated me the most about America was women's liberation.

The society in which I had grown up was one that officially   4 proclaimed sexual equality and made it a point of great pride

---

The new radical feminism seeks to regulate personal relationships to a degree unprecedented since the Puritans roamed the earth.

---

yet stereotyped men and women in ways reminiscent of the American fifties. At school, we had mandatory home economics for girls and shop for boys, a practice no one thought of challenging. At the music school for the gifted where my mother taught piano, to say that someone played "like a girl"—pleasantly, neatly, and without substance—was a commonly used putdown; in literary reviews, the highest compliment to be paid a woman writer or poet was that she wrote like a man.

As I approached college age, I learned that there was tacit   5 but widely known discrimination against women in the college-entrance exams, on the assumption that a less-capable male would in the end be a more valuable asset than a bright female, who would have boys and makeup and marriage on her mind. And all too many smart, ambitious girls seemed to accept this injustice as inevitable, assuming simply that they had to be twice as good as the boys to prove themselves.

It was just as unquestioningly accepted that housework,   6
including the arduous task of Soviet shopping, was women's
work; when the problem of women's excessive double burden at home and on the job was mentioned at all, the proposed solution was always for men to be paid more and for
women to spend more time at home, not for men to pitch
in with domestic chores. And although my parents' relationship was an uncommonly equal one, my father still quoted
to me the dictum (coming from Karl Marx, a thinker he
generally did not regard as much of an authority) that
"woman's greatest strength is her weakness."

My discovery of America was also a discovery of femi-   7
nism—not only *Ms.* magazine and *The Feminine Mystique* but
also the open and straightforward manner of young American
women I met. This was in stark contrast to the style that so
many Russian women reverently equated with "femininity"—
a more-or-less affected air of capriciousness and frailty, a
flirtatious deference to men. I admired the easy camaraderie
between boys and girls on American college campuses, the
independence and self-confidence of young women who invited guys on dates and picked up the tab, drove when they
were out with male companions, and wouldn't let anyone
treat them like frail, helpless little things.

Those early impressions may have been too optimistic,   8
perhaps somewhat superficial, perhaps incomplete. But I
don't think they were wrong.

Becoming an American as a teenager in 1980, I joined the   9
first generation of American women who had grown up assuming not only that they would work most of their lives but
also that they were the equals of men and that they could be
anything they wanted to be (except maybe a full-time home-
maker). This was also the first generation, really, to have
grown up after the sexual revolution—at a time when, at least
among the educated, the nice-girls-don't sexual standard
vanished almost completely. In a somewhat dizzying reversal
of traditional norms, many girls felt embarrassed telling their
first lovers that they were virgins (at least that's how I felt).

Of course new choices meant new pressures. I never   10
thought a world of sexual equality would be a utopia of peace

and harmony. I did believe that our generation of women, and men, was on its way to achieving a world in which people were judged as individuals and not on the basis of their gender; a world in which men and women worked and loved in equal partnership—even if, inevitably, they continued every so often to make each other miserable and furious.

And then something funny happened on the way to that   11
feminist future. We were told that we were victims, with little control over our lives and our choices; we were told that we needed to be protected.

When the right said that women were victimized by career   12
opportunities and sexual freedom, it didn't matter much—at least to the middle-class, college-educated women who were the main beneficiaries of these new opportunities. Who, in those social circles, was going to listen to people who said that wives should obey their husbands and stick to the kitchen and nursery—to Phyllis Schlafly or Jerry Falwell, notorious reactionaries with little impact on mass culture?

But the message of victimhood also came from the feminist   13
left. Everywhere around us, we were told, was a backlash seeking to snatch from us the freedoms we had gained. We were told that we were the targets of a hidden war and had better start acting like one, searching for subtle signs of enemy forays everywhere. If we believed that we had never experienced gender-based injustice and had never felt particularly restricted by our gender, we were not just naive but dangerous: we were turning our backs on feminism and fostering the myth that its major battles had been won.

Whenever a campus study has shown that young people of   14
both sexes increasingly share the same values and aspirations and that most college women are quite confident of their ability to succeed in the workplace and to combine family and career, older feminists seem far from pleased. Their warnings—oh, just wait until these young women get a taste of the real world and find that they still face prejudice and discrimination—can sound almost gleeful.

Older feminists talk a good line about empowering young   15
women and letting them speak in their own voices; but that

goes only as long as these voices say all the approved things. At a university workshop on peer sexual harassment in schools I attended in the spring of 1993, some of the panelists complained that many girls didn't seem to understand what sexual harassment was; when boys made passes or teased them sexually they just shrugged it off, or they thought it was funny and actually liked it. "They need to be educated," one speaker said earnestly, "that the boys aren't just joking around with you, that it's harassment."

Ignored in all this discussion was intriguing evidence of the assertive, even aggressive sexuality of many of today's teenage girls, who apparently do a bit of harassing of their own. If girls seemed to revel in sexual attention, that could only be a sign of "low self-esteem" or inability to say no.   16

Judging by all those complaints about the unraised consciousness of the young, the preoccupation with the sexual and other victimization of high-school and college females is not coming, by and large, from young women themselves. Most of them, I believe, tend to regard all the extreme rhetoric as a sort of background noise; if they think about feminism at all, they often decide that they want no part of it—even if they're all for equal rights. The kind of feminists they usually see in their midst may further contribute to this alienation.   17

When I was still in college, I began to notice, alongside the spirited, independent, ambitious young women I admired, a different product of the feminist age: the ever-vigilant watchdog on the alert for signs of sexism. Occasionally, she made a good point; when our environmental science professor blamed overpopulation in part on Third World women "choosing" to have lots of babies, a student spoke up to note that for most Third World women, childbearing was hardly a matter of choice.   18

More typical, alas, was the young woman in my human sexuality class who was constantly pouncing on the professor for saying something like "People who suffer from premature ejaculation . . ." ("Are you implying that only men are people?"). When he had the audacity to cite data indicating that   19 some rapists were motivated primarily by hatred of women and the desire to dominate them but others were driven primarily by sexual impulses, she went ballistic: "The ONLY thing that causes rape is men wanting to control and terrorize women, and you're trying to make it SEXY!" Later, this person bragged about having caused the poor prof "a lot of trouble" by filing a complaint with the dean.

Paranoid is a red-flag word to many feminists—under- 20
standably so, since it has been used all too often to dismiss women's rightful concerns about sexism. But what other word can come to mind when a woman claims that her writing instructor's selection of a sample of bad writing—a conservative Christian screed linking pornography and com-munism—was a personal insult directed at her, since she had sometimes worn a Women Against Pornography button in school?

And what can one expect when Naomi Wolf, a writer 21
hailed as a trailblazer of a new "Third Wave" of feminism for the younger generation, urges women to undertake—and men, to gracefully (and gratefully) second—"the arduous, often boring, nonnegotiable *daily chore of calling attention to sexism*" (emphasis mine)? In the essay "Radical Heterosexu-ality, or, How to Love a Man and Save Your Feminist Soul" (published in the twentieth-anniversary issue of *Ms.*), Wolf describes how even well-intentioned men tend to be blind to the horrific things women have to put up with:

> Recently, I walked down a New York City avenue with a woman friend, X, and a man friend, Y. I pointed out to Y the leers, hisses, and invitations to sit on faces. Each woman saw clearly what the other woman saw, but Y was baffled. . . . A passerby makes kissy-noises with his tongue while Y is scrutinizing the menu of the nearest bistro. "There, there! Look! Listen!" we cried. "What? Where? Who?" wailed poor Y, valiantly, uselessly spinning.

Like poor Y, I am baffled. God knows, I've been taking 22
walks in Manhattan at least once or twice a week for nearly

thirteen years now, and not a single invitation to sit on a face, not even a single hiss as far as I recall—nothing more dramatic than the occasional "You look gorgeous today" or "That's a pretty outfit," and certainly nothing like the constant barrage Wolf describes. Even the time I wore a new dress that exposed much more cleavage than I realized, all it cost me was one fairly tame remark (as I was stepping into a subway car, a man who was stepping off stared at my bosom and muttered, "Very nice"). Applied to everyday life and interpersonal relations, "eternal vigilance is the price of liberty" strikes me as a rather disastrous motto to adopt.

Like all would-be revolutionaries, the radical feminists seek   23
to subordinate private life to ideology—an endeavor that I find, quite simply, frightening. You don't have to spend part of your life under a totalitarian system (though maybe it helps) to realize that social and political movements that subordinate life to ideology have a nasty way of turning coercive, whether it's the mass violence of communism or the neo-Puritan controls of "P.C."

This is not to say that there is no room for rethinking   24
traditional attitudes, on things ranging from who picks up the check in the restaurant to who takes care of the baby. Millions of women and men are grappling with these issues at home and in the workplace, some more successfully than others. But that doesn't mean they have to walk around with their eyes glued to a microscope.

Eternal vigilance is a tempting trap for post-baby-boomer   25
feminists. It has been often remarked that women of earlier generations had to struggle against visible and overt barriers, such as being denied admission to law school, or told that only men need apply for certain jobs or that married women shouldn't work. It seemed that once such barriers dropped, equality would come quickly. It didn't quite turn out that way; there were other, more insidious roadblocks, from a working mother's guilt over taking a business trip to a professor's unconscious tendency to call on the boys in the class. The problem, however, is that subtle sexism is an elusive target, with plenty of room for error and misinterpretation. If you complain to your professor that you find the course

work too difficult and he says, "Well, I've always thought girls didn't belong in this class anyway," there's not a shadow of a doubt that he's a sexist pig. But suppose he says, "Hey, start working harder or drop the class, but don't come whining to me." Is he being insensitive to you as a woman? (An incident of this sort figured in a recent sex-discrimination suit at the University of Minnesota.) Or is he simply a blunt fellow who believes people should stand on their own two feet and who would have treated a male student exactly the same? And if he had been tough on a man but sensitive and solicitous toward a woman student, wouldn't that have been exactly the kind of paternalism feminists used to oppose?

But then, certain aspects of cutting-edge feminism do   26
smack of a very old-fashioned paternalism, a sort of chivalry without the charm. At some campus meetings, it is considered P.C. for men who are first in line for the microphone to cede their place to a woman in order to ensure that female speakers—apparently too timid to just get up and get in line—get a proper hearing. Ladies first?

Definitions of "hostile environment" sexual harassment   27
often seem like a throwback to prefeminist, if not positively Victorian, standards of how to treat a lady: no off-color jokes, no sexual remarks, no swearing and, God forbid, no improper advances. Surveys purporting to gauge the prevalence of harassment lump together sexual blackmail—demands for sex as a condition of promotion, good grades, or other rewards—with noncoercive advances from coworkers or fellow students, with sexual jokes or innuendo, "improper staring" or "winking."

Well, guess what: women too make off-color jokes and   28
risqué comments, and even sexual advances. Sure, many women at one time or another also have to deal with obnoxious, lecherous, and/or sexist jerks. But in most cases, especially if the man is not a superior, they're perfectly capable of putting a jerk back in his place. Of course, radical feminists such as Catharine MacKinnon tell us that there is *always* an imbalance of power between a man and a woman: even if you're studying for an MBA and have a prestigious job lined

up, you're still powerless. Now there's a message guaranteed to build up self-confidence and self-esteem.

A video on sexual harassment, broadcast on public televi- 29 sion twice in January 1993 and available free through an 800 number, includes a segment on a university experiment in which unwitting male students are assigned to supervise the computer work of an attractive girl. Before leaving them alone, the male research assistant pretends to take small liberties with the young woman (putting a hand on her shoulder, bending closely over her) while explaining the work process, and in most cases the male student proceeds to imitate this behavior or even push it a little further.

Then, the young woman—who, of course, has known 30 what's been going on the whole time—talks on camera about how the experience has helped her understand what it's like to feel powerless. But doesn't this powerlessness have at least something to do with the fact that she was undoubtedly instructed not to show displeasure? Is it such a good idea to teach young women that, short of legal intervention, they have no way of dealing with such annoyances?

I don't believe that our views or our allegiances are deter- 31 mined solely or primarily by age. Still, one might have expected our generation to articulate a feminism rooted in the experience of women who have never felt subordinated to men, have never felt that their options were limited by gender in any significant way or that being treated as sexual beings diminished their personhood. This is not, of course, the experience of all young women; but it is the experience of many, and an experience that should be taken as a model. Perhaps those of us who have this positive view of our lives and our relationships with men have not lived up to our responsibility to translate that view into a new feminist vision.

In an *Esquire* article about sexual politics and romantic 32 love on campus in the nineties, Janet Viggiani, then–assistant dean for coeducation at Harvard, was quoted as saying, "I think young women now are very confused. . . . They don't have many models for how to be strong females and feminine. Many of their models are victim models—passive, weak, endangered." In recent years, feminist activism has focused almost entirely on negatives, from eating disorders to sexual violence and abuse. Sadly, these problems are all too real, and they certainly should be confronted; what they should not be is the central metaphor for the female condition or for relations between women and men, or for feminism. What does it mean when the only time young women and girls think of feminism is not when they think of achievement but when they think of victimization?

The emphasis on victimhood has had an especially dra- 33 matic effect on attitudes toward sexuality. We didn't revel in our sexual freedom for too long; as if the shadow of AIDS weren't bad enough, sex was suddenly fraught with danger and violence as much as possibilities of pleasure, or even more so. A cartoon in the *Nation* shows a girl grooming herself before a mirror, with the caption, "Preparing for a date"— and in the next frame, a boy doing the same, with the caption, "Preparing for a date rape." Pamphlets on sexual assault warn that one out of every five dates ends in a rape, and that up to 25 percent of college women become victims: "Since you can't tell who has the potential for rape by simply looking, be on your guard with every man."

If these numbers are true, women would be well advised 34 either to forswear dating altogether or to carry a can of Mace on every date. But what about these numbers? When one looks at how they are obtained, and how rape is defined, it becomes clear that the acquaintance-rape hysteria not only gives young women an exaggerated picture of the dangers they face in the company of men but essentially demeans women, absolving or stripping them of all responsibility for their behavior.

The question is not whether a woman's provocative dress, 35 flirtatious behavior, or drinking justifies sexual assault; that attitude is now on the wane, for which the women's movement certainly deserves credit. It's not even a question of whether a woman should have to fight back and risk injury to prove that she did not consent to sex. The latest crusade makes a woman a victim of rape if she did not rebuff a man's

sexual advances because she was too shy or didn't want to
hurt his feelings, or if she had sex while drunk (not passed
out, just sufficiently intoxicated so that her inhibitions were
loosened) and felt bad about it afterwards. In a typical sce-
nario, a couple is making out and then the woman pulls back
and says, "I really think we shouldn't," and the man draws
her back toward him, *nonforcibly,* and continues to fondle
her, or says, "Oh come on, you know you want it," and
eventually they end up having sex. If the woman feels that
the intercourse was "unwanted," she can—according to the
anti-date-rape activists—claim to be a victim, no different
from the woman who's attacked at knifepoint in a dark,
empty parking lot.

A few years ago, I was at the apartment of an ex-boyfriend   36
with whom I was still on friendly terms; after a couple of
beers, we started kissing. When his hand crept under my skirt,
I suddenly sobered up and thought of several good reasons
why I should not go to bed with the guy. I wriggled out of
his arms, got up, and said, "That's enough." Undaunted, he
came up from behind and squeezed my breasts. I rammed
my elbow into his chest, forcefully enough to make the point,
and snapped, "Didn't you hear me? I said, enough."

Some people might say that I overreacted (my ex-   37
boyfriend felt that way), but the logic of modern-day radical
feminists suggests the opposite: that I displayed a heroism
that cannot be required of any woman in a situation like that
because she could expect the guy to beat her up, to maim
her, even if he hadn't made any threats or shown any violent
tendencies. A "reasonable" woman would have passively sub-
mitted and then cried rape.

Even "no means no" is no longer enough; some activists   38
want to say that yes means no, or at least the absence of an
explicit yes means no. Feminist legal theorist MacKinnon
suggests that much of what our society regards as consensual
sex hardly differs from rape and that, given women's oppression, it is doubtful "whether consent is a meaningful concept" at all. Which is to say that, like underage children and
the mentally retarded, women are to be presumed incapable

of valid consent. MacKinnon's frequent ally, polemicist An-
drea Dworkin, states bluntly that all intercourse is rape.

This reasoning is still very far from mainstream acceptance.   39
Even MacKinnon only expresses such views when addressing
fairly narrow and converted audiences, not when she's interviewed on TV. Yet a 1992 report by the Harvard Date Rape
Task Force recommended that university guidelines define
rape as "any act of sexual intercourse that occurs without the
expressed consent of the person." What does this mean—that
a consent form must be signed before a date? Or that, as a
couple moves toward the bed after passionate and mutual
heavy petting, the man should ask the woman if she's quite
sure she wants to? (A friend who just graduated from college
tells me that some men are actually beginning to act that
way.) And perhaps he has to keep asking every time: the
couple's prior sexual relationship, the advocates say, makes
no difference whatsoever.

Clearly, this vision leaves no room for spontaneity, for   40
ambiguity, for passionate, wordless, animal sex. What's more,
it is, in the end, deeply belittling to women, who apparently
cannot be expected to convey their wishes clearly or to show
a minimum of assertiveness. It also perpetuates a view of
woman as the passive and reticent partner who may or may
not want sex and man as the pursuer who is naturally presumed to want it: *she* is not required to ask for *his* consent
(even though, given some current definitions, plenty of
women must have committed rape at least a few times in their
lives; I'm sure I have). Sex is something men impose on
women. We're back full circle to fragile, chaste, nineteenth-
century womanhood.

And some people think that's good. Recently, I got into a   41
discussion with a conservative Catholic male who vehemently
argued that the campaign against date rape was nothing more
than a distorted expression of women's legitimate rejection
of sexual freedom, a thing so contrary to their chaste natures.
Casual sex, he said, makes women (but not men) feel cheap
and used, and what they're doing now is using the extreme
language of rape to describe this exploitation; things were

really better under the much-maligned double standard, when women were expected to say no to sex, and thus accorded more protection from male lust. To some conservatives, the outcry about sexual harassment confirms what conservatives have known all along: women want to be put on a pedestal and treated like ladies; they find sexual advances insulting because they are chaster than men.

I don't think that's true. Most young women have no wish   42
to return to the days when they were branded as sluts if they said yes. It may be, however, that this generation's confusion over sexual boundaries has to do with the pains of transition from one set of morals to another, of contradictory cultural messages: the traditional ones of chastity as the basis of female self-respect and reputation and the new ones of sexual liberation and female desire. Sometimes, we may not think we're "cheap" if we go to bed with a man we just met—at least, we're no worse than the guy is for going to bed with a woman he just met—yet when we wake up the next morning we may find that *he* thinks less of us but not of himself. And we may find, to our chagrin, that feminine coyness is not quite as extinct as we might like to think. The other day, a very liberated fortysomething friend of mine breezily said, "Oh, of course no modern woman says no when she means yes." Alas, recent studies (done by feminist researchers) show that *by their own admission,* about half of college women sometimes do.

But there may be another reason, too, for this generation's   43
susceptibility to the victim mentality: overconfidence in the perfectibility of life. The sexual-liberation rhetoric itself overlooked the complexity of human emotions and fostered the belief that sexual relationships could be free of all manipulation or unfair pressure. More generally, there is the idealistic arrogance of middle-class boys and girls who have grown up in a sheltered, affluent environment, accustomed to the notion that getting one's way is a basic right. The old cliché "Life isn't fair" is not only unpopular nowadays but profoundly suspect, seen as a smokescreen designed by the oppressors to keep the oppressed—women and minorities, in

particular—in their place. Yes, it has been used for such purposes often enough. But often it happens to be true, and to disregard that is to invite disastrous consequences—like the belief that anyone, male or female, is entitled to an an-noyance-free life.

The danger in the new radical feminism is not only that it legitimizes what is, deep down, an extremely retrograde view of women; it also seeks to regulate personal relationships to a degree unprecedented since the Puritans roamed the earth. If you feel that a man has enticed or pressured you into having unwanted sex, you don't confront him and call him a manip-ulative creep; you run to a campus grievance committee and demand redress. If you don't like the way a coworker has been putting his hand on your shoulder, you don't have to tell him to stop it—you can go and file a lawsuit instead. Courts and law-enforcement authorities are being asked to step into situations where, short of installing hidden cameras in every bedroom and every office hallway, they have no way of finding out on whose side the truth is. Of course, many millions of women and men remain relatively unaffected by this relentless politicization of the personal. Still, the damage is being done.

Again, it may be my Soviet background that makes me especially sensitive to the perils of this aggressive, paternalistic interventionism. In the Soviet *ancien régime*, it was not un-common to report one's unfaithful spouse to the Communist party bureau at his (or, less commonly, her) workplace, and conflicts between husband and wife—particularly if both were party members—were often settled at public meetings that satisfied both the voyeuristic and the viciously moralistic impulses of the other comrades.

What are we going to be, then? Assertive, strong women (and sometimes, surely, also needy and vulnerable, because we *are* human), seeing ourselves as no better or worse than men; aware of but not obsessed with sexism; interested in loving and equal relationships but with enough confidence in ourselves, and enough understanding of human foibles, to know better than to scrutinize every move we or our partners make for political incorrectness? Or full-time agents of the gender-crimes police?

Women's liberation is not yet a completed task. Sexism still   47
lingers and injustice toward women still exists, particularly in the distribution of domestic tasks. We are still working on new standards and values to guide a new, equal relationship between men and women. But "Third Wave" feminism, which tries to fight gender bias by defining people almost entirely in terms of gender, is not the way to go.

We need a "Third Way" feminism that rejects the excesses   48
of the gender fanatics *and* the sentimental traditionalism of the Phyllis Schlaflys; one that does not seek special protections for women and does not view us as too socially disadvantaged to take care of ourselves. Because on the path that feminism has taken in the past few years, we are allowing ourselves to be treated as frail, helpless little things—by our would-be liberators.

For Study and Discussion

QUESTIONS FOR RESPONSE

1. For women: Describe an incident with a man in which someone might have seen you as a victim. What was your own reaction to the incident?
2. For men: How do you distinguish for yourself between behavior you mean to be friendly and attentive and behavior that might be interpreted as sexist or patronizing?

QUESTIONS ABOUT PURPOSE

1. What changes in behavior and attitude among today's college students do you think Young wants to help bring about with this essay? How could those changes come about?
2. What does Young mean by claiming that the new radical feminism legitimizes an extremely retrograde view of women? See paragraph 44.

QUESTIONS ABOUT AUDIENCE

1. Most of us write for readers with whom we believe we share experiences and concerns. To what extent do you feel that you share Young's experiences and concerns, and how does that feeling affect the way you respond to her essay?
2. Assuming that Young realizes she is not likely to persuade the radical feminists she is criticizing, to what other groups do you think she directs her essay? Give some of their characteristics.

QUESTIONS ABOUT STRATEGIES

1. How does Young go about establishing her credentials as a modern young woman who is concerned about women's issues?
2. How does Young use material from her seventeen years in Russia to strengthen her argument? How well does the strategy work?

QUESTIONS FOR DISCUSSION

1. What do you see as the differences between pioneer feminists such as Gloria Steinem and Betty Friedan—often called radicals in their day—and those feminists of today whom Young calls "radical"?
2. What are some of the consequences for members of a group who become persuaded that they are victims?

DANIEL GOLEMAN

Daniel Goleman was born in 1946 in Stockton, California, and was educated at Amherst College and Harvard University. After working for several years as a professor of psychology, he began his career as an editor for *Psychology Today*. He has contributed more than fifty articles to psychology journals and has written a dozen books, including *The Meditative Mind* (1988), *The Creative Spirit* (1992), and *Mind, Body Medicine: How to Use Your Mind for Better Health* (1993). In "Peak Performance: Why Records Fall," reprinted from a 1994 *New York Times* article, Goleman analyzes how dedication to practice contributes to "peak performances."

Peak Performance:
Why Records Fall

THE OLD JOKE—How do you get to Carnegie Hall? Practice, practice, practice—is getting a scientific spin. Researchers are finding an unexpected potency from deliberate practice in world-class competitions of all kinds, including chess matches, musical recitals and sporting events. 1

Studies of chess masters, virtuoso musicians and star athletes show that the relentless training routines of those at the top allows them to break through ordinary limits in memory and physiology, and so perform at levels that had been thought impossible. 2

World records have been falling inexorably over the last century. For example, the marathon gold medalist's time in the 1896 Olympics Games was, by 1990, only about as good as the qualifying time for the Boston Marathon. 3

"Over the last century Olympics have become more and
more competitive, and so athletes steadily have had to put in
more total lifetime hours of practice," said Dr. Michael Mahoney, a psychologist at the University of North Texas in
Denton, who helps train the United States Olympic weight-
lifting team. "These days you have to live your sport."

That total dedication is in contrast to the relatively leisurely
attitude taken at the turn of the century, when even world-
class athletes would train arduously for only a few months
before their competition.

"As competition got greater, training extended to a whole
season," said Dr. Anders Ericsson, a psychologist at Florida

---

*Through their hours of practice, elite
performers of all kinds master shortcuts
that give them an edge.*

State University in Tallahassee who wrote an article on the
role of deliberate practice for star performance recently in the
journal *American Psychologist*. "Then it extended through the
year, and then for several years. Now the elite performers start
their training in childhood. There is a historical trend toward
younger starting ages, which makes possible a greater and
greater total number of hours of practice time."

To be sure, there are other factors at work: coaching methods have become more sophisticated, equipment has improved and the pool of people competing has grown. But
new studies are beginning to reveal the sheer power of training itself.

Perhaps the most surprising data show that extensive practice can break through barriers in mental capacities, particularly short-term memory. In short-term memory, information
is stored for the few seconds that it is used and then fades, as
in hearing a phone number which one forgets as soon as it is
dialed.

The standard view, repeated in almost every psychology 9
textbook, is that the ordinary limit on short-term memory is
for seven or so bits of information—the length of a phone
number. More than that typically cannot be retained in short-
term memory with reliability unless the separate units are
"chunked," as when the numbers in a telephone prefix are
remembered as a single unit.

But, in a stunning demonstration of the power of sheer 10
practice to break barriers in the mind's ability to handle
information, Dr. Ericsson and associates at Carnegie-Mellon
University have taught college students to listen to a list of
as many as 102 random digits and then recite it correctly.
After 50 hours of practice with differing sets of random digits,
four students were able to remember up to 20 digits after a
single hearing. One student, a business major not especially
talented in mathematics, was able to remember 102 digits.
The feat took him more than 400 hours of practice.

The ability to increase memory in a particular domain is 11
at the heart of a wide range high-level performance, said Dr.
Herbert Simon, professor of computer science and psychol-
ogy at Carnegie-Mellon University and a Nobel laureate. Dr.
Ericsson was part of a team studying expertise led by Dr.
Simon.

"Every expert has acquired something like this memory 12
ability" in his or her area of expertise, said Dr. Simon. "Memory is like an index; experts have approximately 50,000
chunks of familiar units of information they recognize. For a
physician, many of those chunks are symptoms."

A similar memory training effect, Dr. Simon said, seems 13
to occur with many chess masters. The key skill chess players
rehearse in practicing is, of course, selecting the best move.
They do so by studying games between two chess masters
and guessing the next move from their own study of the
board as the game progresses.

Repeated practice results in a prodigious memory for chess 14
positions. The ability of some chess masters to play blind-
folded, while simply told what moves their opponents make,
has long been known; in the 1940's Adrian DeGroot, himself
a Dutch grandmaster, showed that many chess masters are

able to look at a chess board in midgame for as little as five seconds and then repeat the position of every piece on the board.

Later systematic studies by Dr. Simon's group showed that 15 the chess masters' memory feat was limited to boards used in actual games; they had no such memory for randomly placed pieces. "They would see a board and think, that reminds me of Spassky versus Lasker," said Dr. Simon.

This feat of memory was duplicated by a college student 16 who knew little about chess, but was given 50 hours of training in remembering chess positions by Dr. Ericsson in a 1990 study.

Through their hours of practice, elite performers of all 17 kinds master shortcuts that give them an edge. Dr. Bruce Abernathy, a researcher at the University of Queensland in Australia, has found that the most experienced players in racquet sports like squash and tennis are able to predict where a serve will land by cues in the server's posture before the ball is hit.

A 1992 study of baseball greats like Hank Aaron and Rod 18 Carew by Thomas Hanson, then a graduate student at the University of Virginia in Charlottesville, found that the all-time best hitters typically started preparing for games by studying films of the pitchers they would face, to spot cues that would tip off what pitch was about to be thrown. Using such fleeting cues demands rehearsing so well that the response to them is automatic, cognitive scientists have found.

The maxim that practice makes perfect has been borne out 19 through research on the training of star athletes and artists. Dr. Anthony Kalinowski, a researcher at the University of Chicago, found that swimmers who achieved the level of national champion started their training at an average age of 10, while those who were good enough to make the United States Olympic teams started on average at 7. This is the same age difference found for national and international chess champions in a 1987 study.

Similarly, the best violinists of the 20th century, all with 20 international careers as soloists for more than 30 years, were found to have begun practicing their instrument at an average age of 5, while violinists of only national prominence, those affiliated with the top music academy in Berlin, started at 8, Dr. Ericsson found in research reported last year in *The Psychological Review*.

Because of limits on physical endurance and mental alertness, world-class competitors—whether violinists or weight lifters—typically seem to practice arduously no more than four hours a day, Dr. Ericsson has found from studying a wide variety of training regimens.   21

"When we train Olympic weight lifters, we find we often have to throttle back the total time they work out," said Dr. Mahoney. "Otherwise you find a tremendous drop in mood, and a jump in irritability, fatigue and apathy."   22

Because their intense practice regimen puts them at risk for burnout or strain injuries, most elite competitors also make rest part of their training routine, sleeping a full eight hours and often napping a half-hour a day, Dr. Ericsson found.   23

Effective practice focuses not just on the key skills involved, but also systematically stretches the person's limits. "You have to tweak the system by pushing, allowing for more errors at first as you increase your limits," said Dr. Ericsson. "You don't get benefits from mechanical repetition, but by adjusting your execution over and over to get closer to your goal."   24

Violin virtuosos illustrate the importance of starting early in life. In his 1993 study Dr. Ericsson found that by age 20 top-level violinists in music academies had practiced a lifetime total of about 10,000 hours, while those who were slightly less accomplished had practiced an average of about 7,500 hours.   25

A study of Chinese Olympic divers, done by Dr. John Shea of Florida State University, found that some 11-year-old divers had spent as many hours in training as had 21-year-old American divers. The Chinese divers started training at age 4.   26

"It can take 10 years of extensive practice to excel in   27 anything," said Dr. Simon. "Mozart was 4 when he started composing, but his world-class music started when he was about 17."

Total hours of practice may be more important than time   28
spent in competition, according to findings not yet published by Dr. Neil Charness, a colleague of Dr. Ericsson at Florida State University. Dr. Charness, comparing the rankings of 107 competitors in the 1993 Berlin City Tournament, found that the more time they spent practicing alone, the higher their ranking as chess players. But there was no relationship between the chess players' rankings and the time they spent playing others.

As has long been known, the extensive training of an elite   29
athlete molds the body to fit the demands of a given sport. What has been less obvious is the extent of these changes.

"The sizes of hearts and lungs, joint flexibility and bone   30
strength all increase directly with hours of training," said Dr. Ericsson. "The number of capillaries that supply blood to trained muscles increases."

And the muscles themselves change, Dr. Ericsson said.   31
Until very recently, researchers believed that the percentage of muscle fiber types was more than 90 percent determined by heredity. Fast-twitch muscles, which allow short bursts of intense effort, are crucial in sports like weight lifting and sprinting, while slow-twitch muscles, richer in red blood cells, are essential for endurance sports like marathons. "Muscle fibers in those muscles can change from fast twitch to slow twitch, as the sport demands," said Dr. Ericsson.

Longitudinal studies show that years of endurance training   32
at champion levels leads athletes' hearts to increase in size well beyond the normal range for people their age.

Such physiological changes are magnified when training   33
occurs during childhood, puberty and adolescence. Dr. Ericsson thinks this may be one reason virtually all top athletes today began serious practice as children or young adolescents, though some events, like weight training, may be exceptions because muscles need to fully form before intense lifting begins.

The most contentious claim made by Dr. Ericsson is that   34 practice alone, not natural talent, makes for a record-breaking performance. "Innate capacities have very little to do with becoming a champion," said his colleague, Dr. Charness. "What's key is motivation and temperament, not a skill specific to performance. It's unlikely you can get just any child to apply themselves this rigorously for so long."

But many psychologists argue that the emphasis on practice alone ignores the place of talent in superb performance. "You can't assume that random people who practice a lot will rise to the top," said Dr. Howard Gardner, a psychologist at Harvard University. Dr. Ericsson's theories "leave out the question of who selects themselves—or are selected—for intensive training," adding, "It also leaves out what we most value in star performance, like innovative genius in a chess player or emotional expressiveness in a concert musician." 35

Dr. Gardner said: "I taught piano for many years, and there's an enormous difference between those who practice dutifully and get a little better every week, and those students who break away from the pack. There's plenty of room for innate talent to make a difference over and above practice time. Mozart was not like you and me." 36

For Study and Discussion

QUESTIONS FOR RESPONSE

1. Think of some top performers who started very young—for instance, violinist Midori, chess prodigy Bobby Fisher, or tennis player Jennifer Capriati. What do you know about their subsequent lives? To what extent can you generalize about such individuals?
2. If you hope to be a top performer in your chosen field, does this essay encourage you or discourage you? Explain why.

QUESTIONS ABOUT PURPOSE

1. What message do you think the experts quoted in this essay are giving to young people who want to excel in something? What do you see as the impact of that message?

2. What role do you think science plays in sports these days? What is your feeling about that role?

QUESTIONS ABOUT AUDIENCE

1. What groups of readers do you see as people who would particularly benefit from learning about the research reported here? In what way would they benefit?
2. How would the value system of a reader—that is, the complex of things that the reader thinks is important—affect the way he or she responds to this essay?

QUESTIONS ABOUT STRATEGIES

1. What is the impact of Goleman's pointing out that the marathon runner who won an Olympic gold medal a hundred years ago could barely qualify for the Boston Marathon today?
2. How does Goleman's use of diverse authorities strengthen his essay?

QUESTIONS FOR DISCUSSION

1. What impact do you think the new realities about becoming a winner will have on the families of young artists and athletes? How might it differ among families?
2. What factors in a competitor's performance that are not discussed here might affect his or her achievement? How important are those elements?

DIANE ACKERMAN

Diane Ackerman was born in 1948 in Waukegan, Illinois, and was educated at Pennsylvania State University and Cornell University. She has worked as a social worker in New York City, as a professor of English at the University of Pittsburgh, and as a writer-in-residence at William and Mary College, Columbia University, and Cornell University. In addition to contributing her poems and essays to numerous magazines, she currently is on staff at *The New Yorker.* Her books include several collections of poems, *The Planets: A Cosmic Pastoral* (1976), *Lady Faustus* (1985), *Jaguar of Sweet Laughter* (1990); a memoir, *On Extended Wings: An Adventure in Flight* (1985); and three extraordinary works of nonfiction, *A Natural History of the Senses* (1990), *Moon by Whale Light* (1991), and *A Natural History of Love* (1993). In "The Face of Beauty," excerpted from *A Natural History of the Senses,* Ackerman analyzes the causes of our obsession with beauty.

The Face of Beauty

I N A STUDY in which men were asked to look at photographs of pretty women, it was found they greatly preferred pictures of women whose pupils were dilated. Such pictures caused the pupils of the men's eyes to dilate as much as 30 percent. Of course, this is old news to women of the Italian Renaissance and Victorian England alike, who used to drop belladonna (a poisonous plant in the nightshade family, whose name means "beautiful woman") into their eyes to enlarge their pupils before they went out with gentlemen. Our pupils expand involuntarily when we're aroused or excited; thus, just seeing a pretty woman with dilated pupils signaled the men that she found them attractive, and that made their pupils begin a body-language tango in reply. When I was on shipboard recently, traveling through the ferocious winds and waves of Drake Passage and the sometimes bouncy waters around the Antarctic peninsula, the South Orkneys, South Georgia, and the Falklands, I noticed that many passengers wore a scopolamine patch behind one ear to combat seasickness. Greatly dilated pupils, a side effect of the patch, began to appear a few days into the trip; everybody one met had large, welcoming eyes, which no doubt

---

Beauty can be powerful enough to cause the downfall of great leaders and change the career of empires.

---

encouraged the feeling of immediate friendship and camaraderie. Some people grew to look quite zombielike, as they drank in wide gulps of light, but most seemed especially open and warm. Had they checked, the women would have discovered that their cervixes were dilated, too. In professions where emotion or sincere interests need to be hidden, such as gambling or jade-dealing, people often wear dark glasses to hide intentions visible in their telltale pupils.

We may pretend that beauty is only skin deep, but Aristotle was right when he observed that "beauty is a far greater recommendation than any letter of introduction." The sad truth is that attractive people do better in school, where they receive more help, better grades, and less punishment; at work, where they are rewarded with higher pay, more pres-

---

*An alkaloid extracted from henbane and various other plants of the nightshade family, scopolamine has also been used as truth serum. What a perfect cocktail for a cruise: large pupils continuously signaling interest in everyone they see, and a strong urge to be uninhibited and open to persuasion.

tigious jobs, and faster promotions; in finding mates, where they tend to be in control of the relationships and make most of the decisions; and among total strangers, who assume them to be interesting, honest, virtuous, and successful. After all, in fairy tales, the first stories most of us hear, the heroes are handsome, the heroines are beautiful, and the wicked sots are ugly. Children learn implicitly that good people are beautiful and bad people are ugly, and society restates that message in many subtle ways as they grow older. So perhaps it's not surprising that handsome cadets at West Point achieve a higher rank by the time they graduate, or that a judge is more likely to give an attractive criminal a shorter sentence. In a 1968 study conducted in the New York City prison system, men with scars, deformities, and other physical defects were divided into three groups. The first group received cosmetic surgery, the second intensive counseling and therapy, and the third no treatment at all. A year later, when the researchers checked to see how the men were doing, they discovered that those who had received cosmetic surgery had adjusted the best and were less likely to return to prison. In experiments conducted by corporations, when different photos were attached to the same résumé, the more attractive person was hired. Prettier babies are treated better than homelier ones, not just by strangers but by the baby's parents as well. Mothers snuggle, kiss, talk to, play more with their baby if it's cute; and fathers of cute babies are also more involved with them. Attractive children get higher grades on their achievement tests, probably because their good looks win praise, attention, and encouragement from adults. In a 1975 study, teachers were asked to evaluate the records of an eight-year-old who had a low IQ and poor grades. Every teacher saw the same records, but to some the photo of a pretty child was attached, and to others that of a homely one. The teachers were more likely to recommend that the homely child be sent to a class for retarded children. The beauty of another can be a valuable accessory. One particularly interesting study asked people to look at a photo of a man and a woman, and to evaluate only the man. As it turned out, if the woman on the man's arm was pretty, the man was thought to be more intelligent and successful than if the woman was unattractive.

Shocking as the results of these and similar experiments   3
might be, they confirm what we've known for ages: Like it or not, a woman's face has always been to some extent a commodity. A beautiful woman is often able to marry her way out of a lower class and poverty. We remember legendary beauties like Cleopatra and Helen of Troy as symbols of how beauty can be powerful enough to cause the downfall of great leaders and change the career of empires. American women spend millions on makeup each year; in addition, there are the hairdressers, the exercise classes, the diets, the clothes. Handsome men do better as well, but for a man the real commodity is height. One study followed the professional lives of 17,000 men. Those who were at least six feet tall did much better—received more money, were promoted faster, rose to more prestigious positions. Perhaps tall men trigger childhood memories of looking up to authority—only our parents and other adults were tall, and they had all the power to punish or protect, to give absolute love, set our wishes in motion, or block our hopes.

The human ideal of a pretty face varies from culture to   4
culture, of course, and over time, as Abraham Cowley noted in the seventeenth century:

> *Beauty, thou wild fantastic ape*
> *Who dost in every country change thy shape!*

But in general what we are probably looking for is a combination of mature and immature looks—the big eyes of a child, which make us feel protective, the high cheekbones and other features of a fully developed woman or man, which make us feel sexy. In an effort to look sexy, we pierce our noses, elongate our earlobes or necks, tattoo our skin, bind our feet, corset our ribs, dye our hair, have the fat liposuctioned from our thighs, and alter our bodies in countless other ways. Throughout most of western history, women were expected to be curvy, soft, and voluptuous, real earth mothers radiant with sensuous fertility. It was a preference with a strong evolutionary basis: A plump woman had a greater store of body fat and the nutrients needed for pregnancy, was more likely to survive during times of hunger, and would be able to protect her growing fetus and breast-feed it once it was born. In many areas of Africa and India, fat is considered not only beautiful but prestigious for both men and women. In the United States, in the Roaring Twenties and also in the Soaring Seventies and Eighties, when ultrathin was in, men wanted women to have the figures of teenage boys, and much psychological hay could be made from how this reflected the changing role of women in society and the work place. These days, most men I know prefer women to have a curvier, reasonably fit body, although most women I know would still prefer to be "too" thin.

But the face has always attracted an admirer's first glances, especially the eyes, which can be so smoldery and eloquent, and throughout the ages people have emphasized their facial features with makeup. Archaeologists have found evidence of Egyptian perfumeries and beauty parlors dating to 4,000 B.C., and makeup paraphernalia going back to 6,000 B.C. The ancient Egyptians preferred green eye shadow topped with a glitter made from crushing the iridescent carapaces of certain beetles; kohl eye liner and mascara; blue-black lipstick; red rouge; and fingers and feet stained with henna. They shaved their eyebrows and drew in false ones. A fashionable Egyptian woman of those days outlined the veins on her breasts in blue and coated her nipples with gold. Her nail polish signaled social status, red indicating the highest. Men also indulged in elaborate potions and beautifiers; and not only for a night out: Tutankhamen's tomb included jars of makeup and beauty creams for his use in the afterlife. Roman men adored cosmetics, and commanders had their hair coiffed and perfumed and their nails lacquered before they went into battle. Cosmetics appealed even more to Roman women, to one of whom Martial wrote in the first century A.D., "While you remain at home, Galla, your hair is at the hairdresser's; you take out your teeth at night and sleep tucked away in a hundred cosmetic boxes—even your face does not sleep with you. Then you wink at men under an eyebrow you took out of a drawer that same morning." A second-century Roman physician invented cold cream, the formula for which has changed little since then. We may remember from the Old Testament that Queen Jezebel painted her face before embarking on her wicked ways, a fashion she learned from the high-toned Phoenicians in about 850 B.C. In the eighteenth century, European women were willing to eat Arsenic Complexion Wafers to make their skin whiter; it poisoned the hemoglobin in the blood so that they developed a fragile, lunar whiteness. Rouges often contained such dangerous metals as lead and mercury, and when used as lip-stain they went straight into the bloodstream. Seventeenth-century European women and men sometimes wore beauty patches in the shape of hearts, suns, moons, and stars, applying them to their breasts and face, to draw an admirer's eye away from any imperfections, which, in that era, too often included smallpox scars.

Studies conducted recently at the University of Louisville   6 asked college men what they considered to be the ideal components in a woman's face, and fed the results into a computer. They discovered that their ideal woman had wide cheekbones; eyes set high and wide apart; a smallish nose; high eyebrows; a small neat chin; and a smile that could fill half of the face. On faces deemed "pretty," each eye was one-fourteenth as high as the face, and three-tenths its width; the nose didn't occupy more than five percent of the face; the distance from the bottom lip to the chin was one fifth the height of the face, and the distance from the middle of the eye to the eyebrow was one-tenth the height of the face. Superimpose the faces of many beautiful women onto these computer ratios, and none will match up. What this geometry of beauty boils down to is a portrait of an ideal mother—a young, healthy woman. A mother had to be fertile, healthy, and energetic to protect her young and continue to bear lots of children, many of whom might die in infancy. Men drawn to such women had a stronger chance of their genes surviving. Capitalizing on the continuing subtleties of that appeal, plastic surgeons sometimes advertise with extraordinary bluntness. A California surgeon, Dr. Vincent Forshan, once ran an eight-page color ad in *Los Angeles* magazine showing a gorgeous young woman with a large, high bosom, flat stomach, high, tight buttocks, and long sleek legs posing beside a red Ferrari. The headline over the photo ran: "Automobile by Ferrari . . . *body by Forshan.*" Question: What do those of us who aren't tall, flawlessly sculpted adolescents do? Answer: Console ourselves with how relative beauty can be. Although it wins our first praise and the helpless gift of our attention, it can curdle before our eyes in a matter of moments. I remember seeing Omar Sharif in *Doctor Zhivago* and *Lawrence of Arabia,* and thinking him astoundingly handsome. When I saw him being interviewed on television some months later, and heard him declare that his only interest in life was playing bridge, which is how he spent most of his spare time, to my great amazement he was transformed before my eyes into an unappealing man. Suddenly his eyes seemed rheumy and his chin stuck out too much and none of the pieces of his anatomy fell together in the right proportions. I've watched this alchemy work in reverse, too, when a not-particularly-attractive stranger opened his mouth to speak and became ravishing. Thank heavens for the arousing qualities of zest, intelligence, wit, curiosity, sweetness, passion, talent, and grace. Thank heavens that, though good looks may rally one's attention, a lasting sense of a person's beauty reveals itself in stages. Thank heavens, as Shakespeare puts it in *A Midsummer Night's Dream:* "Love looks not with the eyes, but with the mind."

For Study and Discussion

QUESTIONS FOR RESPONSE

1. What is your first response to this essay? Does it anger you, reinforce your own biases, make you want to argue with the author? Why do you think you respond that way?
2. If you know someone who is very beautiful or handsome, how

do you think that person's looks have affected his or her life?
What is your own reaction to that person?

QUESTIONS ABOUT PURPOSE

1. What is the purpose of a biological explanation for the power of
   beauty?
2. In the last few sentences of the essay, the author introduces some
   cautions about being impressed by beauty. Why do you think she
   includes those warnings, particularly so late in the essay?

QUESTIONS ABOUT AUDIENCE

1. In what ways do you think men and women might respond
   differently to this essay? Why?
2. What groups of people are likely to respond negatively to the
   essay? What would be the basis of their disagreement?

QUESTIONS ABOUT STRATEGIES

1. Ackerman quotes data and makes assertions from a broad array
   of authorities. How convincing do you find her evidence? Why?
2. What do Ackerman's abundant historical references add to the
   essay?

QUESTIONS FOR DISCUSSION

1. What reservations do you have about the power of beauty? What
   experiences, beliefs, or influences have led to those reservations?
2. What interests in our society seem to you to have a stake in
   perpetuating the importance of good looks? How do they promote their interests? For instance, read what Francine du Plessix
   Gray says in "On Friendship" (see page 349) about the sexual-
   industrial complex.

Stephen Jay Gould was born in New York City in 1941 and attended Antioch College and Columbia University. Trained as a paleontologist, Gould has been a professor of geology at Harvard University since 1967. Throughout his teaching and writing career he has been known for his ability to translate challenging scientific theories into understandable terms. His books include *The Panda's Thumb: More Reflections in Natural History* (1980), *Hen's Teeth and Horse's Toes: Further Reflections in Natural History* (1983), *The Flamingo's Smile: Reflections in Natural History* (1985), *An Urchin in the Storm: Essays About Books and Ideas* (1987), *Bully for Brontosaurus* (1991), and *Eight Little Piggies* (1993). Several of these books are collections of his monthly column for *Natural History* magazine, "This View of Life." In "Carrie Buck's Daughter," reprinted from *The Flamingo's Smile*, Gould traces the tragic consequences of a simplistic assessment of the chain of cause and effect.

Carrie Buck's Daughter

T HE LORD REALLY put it on the line in his preface to that prototype of all prescription, the Ten Commandments:

> *. . . for I, the Lord thy God, am a jealous God, visiting the iniquity of the fathers upon the children unto the third and fourth generation of them that hate me (Exod. 20:5).*

The terror of this statement lies in its patent unfairness—its   2
promise to punish guiltless offspring for the misdeeds of their
distant forebears.

A different form of guilt by genealogical association at-   3
tempts to remove this stigma of injustice by denying a cherished premise of Western thought—human free will. If
off-spring are tainted not simply by the deeds of their parents
but by a material form of evil transferred directly by biological
inheritance, then "the iniquity of the fathers" becomes a
signal or warning for probable misbehavior of their sons.
Thus Plato, while denying that children should suffer directly

---

Carrie Buck's case was never about mental
deficiency; she was persecuted for supposed
sexual immorality and social deviance.

---

for the crimes of their parents, nonetheless defended the
banishment of a personally guiltless man whose father, grandfather, and great-grandfather had all been condemned to
death.

It is, perhaps, merely coincidental that both Jehovah and   4
Plato chose three generations as their criterion for establishing different forms of guilt by association. Yet we maintain
a strong folk, or vernacular, tradition for viewing triple oc-
currences as minimal evidence of regularity. Bad things, we
are told, come in threes. Two may represent an accidental
association; three is a pattern. Perhaps, then, we should not
wonder that our own century's most famous pronouncement
of blood guilt employed the same criterion—Oliver Wendell
Holmes's defense of compulsory sterilization in Virginia (Supreme Court decision of 1927 in *Buck v. Bell*): "three generations of imbeciles are enough."

Restrictions upon immigration, with national quotas set to   5
discriminate against those deemed mentally unfit by early

versions of IQ testing, marked the greatest triumph of the American eugenics movement—the flawed hereditarian doctrine, so popular earlier in our century and by no means extinct today, that attempted to "improve" our human stock by preventing the propagation of those deemed biologically unfit and encouraging procreation among the supposedly worthy. But the movement to enact and enforce laws for compulsory "eugenic" sterilization had an impact and success scarcely less pronounced. If we could debar the shiftless and the stupid from our shores, we might also prevent the propagation of those similarly afflicted but already here.

The movement for compulsory sterilization began in earnest during the 1890s, abetted by two major factors—the rise of eugenics as an influential political movement and the perfection of safe and simple operations (vasectomy for men and salpingectomy, the cutting and tying of Fallopian tubes, for women) to replace castration and other socially unacceptable forms of mutilation. Indiana passed the first sterilization act based on eugenic principles in 1907 (a few states had previously mandated castration as a punitive measure for certain sexual crimes, although such laws were rarely enforced and usually overturned by judicial review). Like so many others to follow, it provided for sterilization of afflicted people residing in the state's "care," either as inmates of mental hospitals and homes for the feeble-minded or as inhabitants of prisons. Sterilization could be imposed upon those judged insane, idiotic, imbecilic, or moronic, and upon convicted rapists or criminals when recommended by a board of experts. 6

By the 1930s, more than thirty states had passed similar laws, often with an expanded list of so-called hereditary defects, including alcoholism and drug addiction in some states, and even blindness and deafness in others. These laws were continually challenged and rarely enforced in most states; only California and Virginia applied them zealously. By January 1935, some 20,000 forced "eugenic" sterilizations had been performed in the United States, nearly half in California. 7

No organization crusaded more vociferously and success- 8

fully for these laws than the Eugenics Record Office, the semiofficial arm and repository of data for the eugenics movement in America. Harry Laughlin, superintendent of the Eugenics Record Office, dedicated most of his career to a tireless campaign of writing and lobbying for eugenic sterilization. He hoped, thereby, to eliminate in two generations the genes of what he called the "submerged tenth"—"the most worthless one-tenth of our present population." He proposed a "model sterilization law" in 1922, designed

> to prevent the procreation of persons socially inadequate from defective inheritance, by authorizing and providing for eugenical sterilization of certain potential parents carrying degenerate hereditary qualities.

This model bill became the prototype for most laws passed   9
in America, although few states cast their net as widely as Laughlin advised. (Laughlin's categories encompassed "blind, including those with seriously impaired vision; deaf, including those with seriously impaired hearing; and dependent, including orphans, ne'er-do-wells, the homeless, tramps, and paupers.") Laughlin's suggestions were better heeded in Nazi Germany, where his model act inspired the infamous and stringently enforced *Erbgesundheitsrecht*, leading by the eve of World War II to the sterilization of some 375,000 people, most for "congenital feeble-mindedness," but including nearly 4,000 for blindness and deafness.

The campaign for forced eugenic sterilization in America   10
reached its climax and height of respectability in 1927, when the Supreme Court, by an 8–1 vote, upheld the Virginia sterilization bill in *Buck v. Bell*. Oliver Wendell Holmes, then in his mid-eighties and the most celebrated jurist in America, wrote the majority opinion with his customary verve and power of style. It included the notorious paragraph, with its chilling tag line, cited ever since as the quintessential statement of eugenic principles. Remembering with pride his own

distant experiences as an infantryman in the Civil War, Holmes wrote:

> *We have seen more than once that the public welfare may call upon the best citizens for their lives. It would be strange if it could not call upon those who already sap the strength of the state for these lesser sacrifices. . . . It is better for all the world, if instead of waiting to execute degenerate offspring for crime, or to let them starve for their imbecility, society can prevent those who are manifestly unfit from continuing their kind. The principle that sustains compulsory vaccination is broad enough to cover cutting the Fallopian tubes. Three generations of imbeciles are enough.*

Who, then, were the famous "three generations of imbeciles," and why should they still compel our interest? 11

When the state of Virginia passed its compulsory sterilization law in 1924, Carrie Buck, an eighteen-year-old white woman, lived as an involuntary resident at the State Colony for Epileptics and Feeble-Minded. As the first person selected for sterilization under the new act, Carrie Buck became the focus for a constitutional challenge launched, in part, by conservative Virginia Christians who held, according to eugenical "modernists," antiquated views about individual preferences and "benevolent" state power. (Simplistic political labels do not apply in this case, and rarely in general for that matter. We usually regard eugenics as a conservative movement and its most vocal critics as members of the left. This alignment has generally held in our own decade. But eugenics, touted in its day as the latest in scientific modernism, attracted many liberals and numbered among its most vociferous critics groups often labeled as reactionary and antiscientific. If any political lesson emerges from these shifting allegiances, we might consider the true inalienability of certain human rights.) 12

But why was Carrie Buck in the State Colony and why was   13
she selected? Oliver Wendell Holmes upheld her choice as
judicious in the opening lines of his 1927 opinion:

> *Carrie Buck is a feeble-minded white woman who*
> *was committed to the State Colony. . . . She is the*
> *daughter of a feeble-minded mother in the same in-*
> *stitution, and the mother of an illegitimate feeble-*
> *minded child.*

In short, inheritance stood as the crucial issue (indeed as   14
the driving force behind all eugenics). For if measured mental
deficiency arose from malnourishment, either of body or
mind, and not from tainted genes, then how could sterilization be justified? If decent food, upbringing, medical care,
and education might make a worthy citizen of Carrie Buck's
daughter, how could the State of Virginia justify the severing
of Carrie's Fallopian tubes against her will? (Some forms of
mental deficiency are passed in inheritance in family lines, but
most are not—a scarcely surprising conclusion when we consider the thousand shocks that beset us all during our lives,
from abnormalities in embryonic growth to traumas of birth,
malnourishment, rejection, and poverty. In any case, no fair-
minded person today would credit Laughlin's social criteria
for the identification of hereditary deficiency—ne'er-do-
wells, the homeless, tramps, and paupers—although we shall
soon see that Carrie Buck was committed on these grounds.)
When Carrie Buck's case emerged as the crucial test of   15
Virginia's law, the chief honchos of eugenics understood that
the time had come to put up or shut up on the crucial issue
of inheritance. Thus, the Eugenics Record Office sent Arthur
H. Estabrook, their crack fieldworker, to Virginia for a
"scientific" study of the case. Harry Laughlin himself provided a deposition, and his brief for inheritance was presented
at the local trial that affirmed Virginia's law and later worked
its way to the Supreme Court as *Buck v. Bell.*
Laughlin made two major points to the court. First, that   16
Carrie Buck and her mother, Emma Buck, were feeble-

minded by the Stanford-Binet test of IQ then in its own infancy. Carrie scored a mental age of nine years, Emma of seven years and eleven months. (These figures ranked them technically as "imbeciles" by definitions of the day, hence Holmes's later choice of words—though his infamous line is often misquoted as "three generations of idiots." Imbeciles displayed a mental age of six to nine years; idiots performed worse, morons better, to round out the old nomenclature of mental deficiency.) Second, that most feeble-mindedness resides ineluctably in the genes, and that Carrie Buck surely belonged with this majority. Laughlin reported:

> *Generally, feeble-mindedness is caused by the inheritance of degenerate qualities; but sometimes it might be caused by environmental factors which are not hereditary. In the case given, the evidence points strongly toward the feeble-mindedness and moral delinquency of Carrie Buck being due, primarily, to inheritance and not to environment.*

Carrie Buck's daughter was then, and has always been, the pivotal figure of this painful case. I noted in beginning this essay that we tend (often at our peril) to regard two as potential accident and three as an established pattern. The supposed imbecility of Emma and Carrie might have been an unfortunate coincidence, but the diagnosis of similar deficiency for Vivian Buck (made by a social worker, as we shall see, when Vivian was but six months old) tipped the balance in Laughlin's favor and led Holmes to declare the Buck lineage inherently corrupt by deficient heredity. Vivian sealed the pattern—*three* generations of imbeciles are enough. Besides, had Carrie not given illegitimate birth to Vivian, the issue (in both senses) would never have emerged. 17

Oliver Wendell Holmes viewed his work with pride. The man so renowned for his principle of judicial restraint, who had proclaimed that freedom must not be curtailed without "clear and present danger"—without the equivalent of falsely yelling "fire" in a crowded theater—wrote of his judgment 18 in *Buck v. Bell:* "I felt that I was getting near the first principle of real reform."

And so *Buck v. Bell* remained for fifty years, a footnote to   19
a moment of American history perhaps best forgotten. Then, in 1980, it reemerged to prick our collective conscience, when Dr. K. Ray Nelson, then director of the Lynchburg Hospital where Carrie Buck had been sterilized, researched the records of his institution and discovered that more than 4,000 sterilizations had been performed, the last as late as 1972. He also found Carrie Buck, alive and well near Charlottesville, and her sister Doris, covertly sterilized under the same law (she was told that her operation was for appendicitis), and now, with fierce dignity, dejected and bitter because she had wanted a child more than anything else in her life and had finally, in her old age, learned why she had never conceived.

As scholars and reporters visited Carrie Buck and her sister,   20
what a few experts had known all along became abundantly clear to everyone. Carrie Buck was a woman of obviously normal intelligence. For example, Paul A. Lombardo of the School of Law at the University of Virginia, and a leading scholar of *Buck v. Bell,* wrote in a letter to me:

> *As for Carrie, when I met her she was reading newspapers daily and joining a more literate friend to assist at regular bouts with the crossword puzzles. She was not a sophisticated woman, and lacked social graces, but mental health professionals who examined her in later life confirmed my impressions that she was neither mentally ill nor retarded.*

On what evidence, then, was Carrie Buck consigned to the   21
State Colony for Epileptics and Feeble-Minded on January 23, 1924? I have seen the text of her commitment hearing; it is, to say the least, cursory and contradictory. Beyond the bald and undocumented say-so of her foster parents, and her own brief appearance before a commission of two doctors and a justice of the peace, no evidence was presented. Even

the crude and early Stanford-Binet test, so fatally flawed as a measure of innate worth (see my book *The Mismeasure of Man,* although the evidence of Carrie's own case suffices) but at least clothed with the aura of quantitative respectability, had not yet been applied.

When we understand why Carrie Buck was committed in January 1924, we can finally comprehend the hidden meaning of her case and its message for us today. The silent key, again as from the first, is her daughter Vivian, born on March 28, 1924, and then but an evident bump on her belly. Carrie Buck was one of several illegitimate children borne by her mother, Emma. She grew up with foster parents, J. T. and Alice Dobbs, and continued to live with them as an adult, helping out with chores around the house. She was raped by a relative of her foster parents, then blamed for the resulting pregnancy. Almost surely, she was (as they used to say) committed to hide her shame (and her rapist's identity), not because enlightened science had just discovered her true mental status. In short, she was sent away to have her baby. Her case never was about mental deficiency; Carrie Buck was persecuted for supposed sexual immorality and social deviance. The annals of her trial and hearing reek with the contempt of the well-off and well-bred for poor people of "loose morals." Who really cared whether Vivian was a baby of normal intelligence; she was the illegitimate child of an illegitimate woman. Two generations of bastards are enough. Harry Laughlin began his "family history" of the Bucks by writing: "These people belong to the shiftless, ignorant and worthless class of anti-social whites of the South."

We know little of Emma Buck and her life, but we have no more reason to suspect her than her daughter Carrie of true mental deficiency. Their supposed deviance was social and sexual; the charge of imbecility was a cover-up, Mr. Justice Holmes notwithstanding.

We come then to the crux of the case, Carrie's daughter, Vivian. What evidence was ever adduced for her mental deficiency? This and only this: At the original trial in late 1924, when Vivian Buck was seven months old, a Miss

Wilhelm, social worker for the Red Cross, appeared before the court. She began by stating honestly the true reason for Carrie Buck's commitment:

> *Mr. Dobbs, who had charge of the girl, had taken her when a small child, had reported to Miss Duke [the temporary secretary of Public Welfare for Albemarle County] that the girl was pregnant and that he wanted to have her committed somewhere—to have her sent to some institution.*

Miss Wilhelm then rendered her judgment of Vivian Buck   25
by comparing her with the normal granddaughter of Mrs. Dobbs, born just three days earlier:

> *It is difficult to judge probabilities of a child as young as that, but it seems to me not quite a normal baby. In its appearance—I should say that perhaps my knowledge of the mother may prejudice me in that regard, but I saw the child at the same time as Mrs. Dobbs' daughter's baby, which is only three days older than this one, and there is a very decided difference in the development of the babies. That was about two weeks ago. There is a look about it that is not quite normal, but just what it is, I can't tell.*

This short testimony, and nothing else, formed all the   26
evidence for the crucial third generation of imbeciles. Cross-examination revealed that neither Vivian nor the Dobbs grandchild could walk or talk, and that "Mrs. Dobbs' daughter's baby is a very responsive baby. When you play with it or try to attract its attention—it is a baby that you can play with. The other baby is not. It seems very apathetic and not responsive." Miss Wilhelm then urged Carrie Buck's sterilization: "I think," she said, "it would at least prevent the propagation of her kind." Several years later, Miss Wilhelm denied that she had ever examined Vivian or deemed the child feeble-minded.

Unfortunately, Vivian died at age eight of "enteric colitis"   27 (as recorded on her death certificate), an ambiguous diagnosis that could mean many things but may well indicate that she fell victim to one of the preventable childhood diseases of poverty (a grim reminder of the real subject in *Buck v. Bell*). She is therefore mute as a witness in our reassessment of her famous case.

When *Buck v. Bell* resurfaced in 1980, it immediately struck me that Vivian's case was crucial and that evidence for the mental status of a child who died at age eight might best be found in report cards. I have therefore been trying to track down Vivian Buck's school records for the past four years and have finally succeeded. (They were supplied to me by Dr. Paul A. Lombardo, who also sent other documents, including Miss Wilhelm's testimony, and spent several hours answering my questions by mail and Lord knows how much time playing successful detective *in re* Vivian's school records. I have never met Dr. Lombardo; he did all this work for kindness, collegiality, and love of the game of knowledge, not for expected reward or even requested acknowledgment. In a profession—academics—so often marred by pettiness and silly squabbling over meaningless priorities, this generosity must be recorded and celebrated as a sign of how things can and should be.)

Vivian Buck was adopted by the Dobbs family, who had raised (but later sent away) her mother, Carrie. As Vivian Alice Elaine Dobbs, she attended the Venable Public Elementary School of Charlottesville for four terms, from September 1930 until May 1932, a month before her death. She was a perfectly normal, quite average student, neither particularly outstanding nor much troubled. In those days before grade inflation, when C meant "good, 81–87" (as defined on her report card) rather than barely scraping by, Vivian Dobbs received A's and B's for deportment and C's for all academic subjects but mathematics (which was always difficult for her, and where she scored D) during her first term in Grade 1A, from September 1930 to January 1931. She improved during her second term in 1B, meriting an A in deportment, C in mathematics, and B in all other academic subjects; she was placed on the honor roll in April 1931. Promoted to 2A, she had trouble during the fall term of 1931, failing mathematics and spelling but receiving A in deportment, B in reading, and C in writing and English. She was "retained to 2A" for the next term—or "left back" as we used to say, and scarcely a sign of imbecility as I remember all my buddies who suffered a similar fate. In any case, she again did well in her final term, with B in deportment, reading, and spelling, and C in writing, English, and mathematics during her last month in school. This daughter of "lewd and immoral" women excelled in deportment and performed adequately, although not brilliantly, in her academic subjects.

In short, we can only agree with the conclusion that Dr.   30 Lombardo has reached in his research on *Buck v. Bell*—there were no imbeciles, not a one, among the three generations of Bucks. I don't know that such correction of cruel but forgotten errors of history counts for much, but I find it both symbolic and satisfying to learn that forced eugenic sterilization, a procedure of such dubious morality, earned its official justification (and won its most quoted line of rhetoric) on a patent falsehood.

Carrie Buck died last year. By a quirk of fate, and not by   31 memory or design, she was buried just a few steps from her only daughter's grave. In the umpteenth and ultimate verse of a favorite old ballad, a rose and a brier—the sweet and the bitter—emerge from the tombs of Barbara Allen and her lover, twining about each other in the union of death. May Carrie and Vivian, victims in different ways and in the flower of youth, rest together in peace.

For Study and Discussion

QUESTIONS FOR RESPONSE

1. What do you know about the Nazis' attempts to create a "master race" through the study of eugenics? If you have heard about that program, how does it affect the way you respond to this essay?
2. Gould wrote this essay almost sixty years after the decision in the

case of *Bell v. Buck*. How do you think today's public, including the groups of people you feel most comfortable with, would respond to same issues if they were raised today? How much have attitudes changed since 1927?

QUESTIONS ABOUT PURPOSE

1. Chief Justice Oliver Wendell Holmes is probably the most famous, most revered, and most frequently quoted of all Supreme Court justices. What does Gould accomplish by showing the role he played in the Carrie Buck decision?
2. What attitudes of the society in which Carrie Buck was reared does Gould want his readers to analyze and evaluate? Why?

QUESTIONS ABOUT AUDIENCE

1. What knowledge about the racial policies of the Nazi regime in Germany in the 1930s does Gould count on his readers having? To what extent is he warranted in assuming that knowledge in an audience of today's college-educated readers? Why?
2. How does Gould connect the analysis of why Carrie Buck was sterilized to his readers' knowledge of contemporary social problems?

QUESTIONS ABOUT STRATEGIES

1. What evidence does Gould bring in to support his belief that Carrie Buck's treatment was motivated by prejudice and shame, not by concern over her mental abilities?
2. In what paragraphs do you notice Gould's own feelings surfacing? How do you think his showing those feelings affects the impact of the essay?

QUESTIONS FOR DISCUSSION

1. Now, nearly seventy years after the event, in what ways can or should the case of *Bell v. Buck* still compel our interest and be worth discussing? What issues about it are timeless?
2. Do the men and women in your class have different responses to this essay? How do they differ, how strong are the differences, and how do you account for those differences?

SANDRA CISNEROS

Sandra Cisneros was born in 1954 in Chicago and spent much of her childhood living in Chicago and Mexico City. A graduate of the University of Iowa Writer's Workshop, she has taught writing at the University of California at Berkeley and the University of Michigan. She has also taught in the San Antonio Public Schools and worked as literary director of the Guadalupe Cultural Arts Center. She has contributed stories and poems to periodicals such as *Imagine, Contact II,* and *Revista Chicano-Riquena.* Her poems appear in *Bad Boys* (1980), *The Rodrigo Poems* (1985), and *My Wicked, Wicked Ways* (1987); her stories are collected in *Woman Hollering Creek* (1991). Cisneros's book for young adults, *The House on Mango Street* (1983), won the American Book Award. In "One Holy Night," reprinted from *Woman Hollering Creek,* Cisneros's narrator analyzes the impact of her "holy night" with a man who claims he is descended from Mayan kings.

One Holy Night

About the truth, if you give it to a person, then he has power over you. And if someone gives it to you, then they have made themselves your slave. It is a strong magic. You can never take it back.
—CHAQ UXMAL PALOQUÍN

H E SAID HIS name was Chaq. Chaq Uxmal Paloquín. That's what he told me. He was of an ancient line of Mayan kings. Here, he said, making a map with the heel of

1

his boot, this is where I come from, the Yucatán, the ancient cities. This is what Boy Baby said.

It's been eighteen weeks since Abuelita chased him away with the broom, and what I'm telling you I never told nobody, except Rachel and Lourdes, who know everything. He said he would love me like a revolution, like a religion. Abuelita burned the pushcart and sent me here, miles from home, in this town of dust, with one wrinkled witch woman who rubs my belly with jade, and sixteen nosy cousins.

I don't know how many girls have gone bad from selling cucumbers. I know I'm not the first. My mother took the crooked walk too, I'm told, and I'm sure my Abuelita has her own story, but it's not my place to ask.

Abuelita says it's Uncle Lalo's fault because he's the man of the family and if he had come home on time like he was supposed to and worked the pushcart on the days he was told to and watched over his goddaughter, who is too foolish to look after herself, nothing would've happened, and I wouldn't have to be sent to Mexico. But Uncle Lalo says if they had never left Mexico in the first place, shame enough would have kept a girl from doing devil things.

I'm not saying I'm not bad. I'm not saying I'm special. But I'm not like the Allport Street girls, who stand in doorways and go with men into alleys.

All I know is I didn't want it like that. Not against the bricks or hunkering in somebody's car. I wanted it to come undone like gold thread, like a tent full of birds. The way it's supposed to be, the way I knew it would be when I met Boy Baby.

But you must know, I was no girl back then. And Boy Baby was no boy. Chaq Uxmal Paloquín. Boy Baby was a man. When I asked him how old he was he said he didn't know. The past and the future are the same thing. So he seemed boy and baby and man all at once, and the way he looked at me, how do I explain?

I'd park the pushcart in front of the Jewel food store Saturdays. He bought a mango on a stick the first time. Paid for it with a new twenty. Next Saturday he was back. Two

mangoes, lime juice, and chili powder, keep the change. The
third Saturday he asked for a cucumber spear and ate it slow.
I didn't see him after that till the day he brought me Kool-Aid
in a plastic cup. Then I knew what I felt for him.

Maybe you wouldn't like him. To you he might be a bum.   9
Maybe he looked it. Maybe. He had broken thumbs and
burnt fingers. He had thick greasy fingernails he never cut
and dusty hair. And all his bones were strong ones like a
man's. I waited every Saturday in my same blue dress. I sold
all the mango and cucumber, and then Boy Baby would come
finally.

What I knew of Chaq was only what he told me, because   10
nobody seemed to know where he came from. Only that he
could speak a strange language that no one could understand,
said his name translated into boy, or boy-child, and so it was
the street people nicknamed him Boy Baby.

I never asked about his past. He said it was all the same   11
and didn't matter, past and the future all the same to his
people. But the truth has a strange way of following you, of
coming up to you and making you listen to what it has to
say.

Night time. Boy Baby brushes my hair and talks to me in   12
his strange language because I like to hear it. What I like to
hear him tell is how he is Chaq, Chaq of the people of the
sun, Chaq of the temples, and what he says sounds sometimes
like broken clay, and at other times like hollow sticks, or like
the swish of old feathers crumbling into dust.

He lived behind Esparza & Sons Auto Repair in a little   13
room that used to be a closet—pink plastic curtains on a
narrow window, a dirty cot covered with newspapers, and a
cardboard box filled with socks and rusty tools. It was there,
under one bald bulb, in the back room of the Esparza garage,
in the single room with pink curtains, that he showed me the
guns—twenty-four in all. Rifles and pistols, one rusty musket,
a machine gun, and several tiny weapons with mother-of-
pearl handles that looked like toys. So you'll see who I am,
he said, laying them all out on the bed of newspapers. So
you'll understand. But I didn't want to know.

The stars foretell everything, he said. My birth. My son's. The boy-child who will bring back the grandeur of my people from those who have broken the arrows, from those who have pushed the ancient stones off their pedestals. 14

Then he told how he had prayed in the Temple of the Magician years ago as a child when his father had made him promise to bring back the ancient ways. Boy Baby had cried in the temple dark that only the bats made holy. Boy Baby who was man and child among the great and dusty guns lay down on the newspaper bed and wept for a thousand years. When I touched him, he looked at me with the sadness of stone. 15

You must not tell anyone what I am going to do, he said. And what I remember next is how the moon, the pale moon with its one yellow eye, the moon of Tikal, and Tulum, and Chichén, stared through the pink plastic curtains. Then something inside bit me, and I gave out a cry as if the other, the one I wouldn't be anymore, leapt out. 16

So I was initiated beneath an ancient sky by a great and mighty heir—Chaq Uxmal Paloquín. I, Ixchel, his queen. 17

The truth is, it wasn't a big deal. It wasn't any deal at all. I put my bloody panties inside my T-shirt and ran home hugging myself. I thought about a lot of things on the way home. I thought about all the world and how suddenly I became a part of history and wondered if everyone on the street, the sewing machine lady and the *panadería* saleswomen and the woman with two kids sitting on the bus bench didn't all know. *Did I look any different? Could they tell?* We were all the same somehow, laughing behind our hands, waiting the way all women wait, and when we find out, we wonder why the world and a million years made such a big deal over nothing. 18

I know I was supposed to feel ashamed, but I wasn't ashamed. I wanted to stand on top of the highest building, the top-top floor, and yell, *I know.* 19

Then I understood why Abuelita didn't let me sleep over at Lourdes's house full of too many brothers, and why the 20

Roman girl in the movies always runs away from the soldier, and what happens when the scenes in love stories begin to fade, and why brides blush, and how it is that sex isn't simply a box you check *M* or *F* on in the test we get at school.

I was wise. The corner girls were still jumping into their   21
stupid little hopscotch squares. I laughed inside and climbed the wooden stairs two by two to the second floor rear where me and Abuelita and Uncle Lalo live. I was still laughing when I opened the door and Abuelita asked, Where's the pushcart?

And then I didn't know what to do.   22

It's a good thing we live in a bad neighborhood. There   23
are always plenty of bums to blame for your sins. If it didn't happen the way I told it, it really could've. We looked and looked all over for the kids who stole my pushcart. The story wasn't the best, but since I had to make it up right then and there with Abuelita staring a hole through my heart, it wasn't too bad.

For two weeks I had to stay home. Abuelita was afraid the   24
street kids who had stolen the cart would be after me again. Then I thought I might go over to the Esparza garage and take the pushcart out and leave it in some alley for the police to find, but I was never allowed to leave the house alone. Bit by bit the truth started to seep out like a dangerous gasoline.

First the nosy woman who lives upstairs from the laundro-   25
mat told my Abuelita she thought something was fishy, the pushcart wheeled into Esparza & Sons every Saturday after dark, how a man, the same dark Indian one, the one who never talks to anybody, walked with me when the sun went down and pushed the cart into the garage, that one there, and yes we went inside, there where the fat lady named Concha, whose hair is dyed a hard black, pointed a fat finger.

I prayed that we would not meet Boy Baby, and since the   26
gods listen and are mostly good, Esparza said yes, a man like that had lived there but was gone, had packed a few things and left the pushcart in a corner to pay for his last week's rent.

We had to pay $20 before he would give us our pushcart   27 back. Then Abuelita made me tell the real story of how the cart had disappeared, all of which I told this time, except for that one night, which I would have to tell anyway, weeks later, when I prayed for the moon of my cycle to come back, but it would not.

When Abuelita found out I was going to *dar a luz,* she 28 cried until her eyes were little, and blamed Uncle Lalo, and Uncle Lalo blamed this country, and Abuelita blamed the infamy of men. That is when she burned the cucumber push-cart and called me a *sinvergüenza* because I *am* without shame.

Then I cried too—Boy Baby was lost from me—until my 29 head was hot with headaches and I fell asleep. When I woke up, the cucumber pushcart was dust and Abuelita was sprinkling holy water on my head.

Abuelita woke up early every day and went to the Esparza 30 garage to see if news about that *demonio* had been found, had Chaq Uxmal Paloquín sent any letters, any, and when the other mechanics heard that name they laughed, and asked if we had made it up, that we could have some letters that had come for Boy Baby, no forwarding address, since he had gone in such a hurry.

There were three. The first, addressed "Occupant," de- 31 manded immediate payment for a four-month-old electric bill. The second was one I recognized right away—a brown envelope fat with cake-mix coupons and fabric-softener sam-ples—because we'd gotten one just like it. The third was addressed in a spidery Spanish to a Señor C. Cruz, on paper so thin you could read it unopened by the light of the sky. The return address a convent in Tampico.

This was to whom my Abuelita wrote in hopes of finding 32 the man who could correct my ruined life, to ask if the good nuns might know the whereabouts of a certain Boy Baby—and if they were hiding him it would be of no use because God's eyes see through all souls.

We heard nothing for a long time. Abuelita took me out 33 of school when my uniform got tight around the belly and said it was a shame I wouldn't be able to graduate with the other eighth graders.

Except for Lourdes and Rachel, my grandma and Uncle   34
Lalo, nobody knew about my past. I would sleep in the big bed I share with Abuelita same as always. I could hear Abuelita and Uncle Lalo talking in low voices in the kitchen as if they were praying the rosary, how they were going to send me to Mexico, to San Dionisio de Tlaltepango, where I have cousins and where I was conceived and would've been born had my grandma not thought it wise to send my mother here to the United States so that neighbors in San Dionisio de Tlaltepango wouldn't ask why her belly was suddenly big.

I was happy. I liked staying home. Abuelita was teaching   35
me to crochet the way she had learned in Mexico. And just when I had mastered the tricky rosette stitch, the letter came from the convent which gave the truth about Boy Baby— however much we didn't want to hear.

He was born on a street with no name in a town called   36
Miseria. His father, Eusebio, is a knife sharpener. His mother, Refugia, stacks apricots into pyramids and sells them on a cloth in the market. There are brothers. Sisters too of which I know little. The youngest, a Carmelite, writes me all this and prays for my soul, which is why I know it's all true.

Boy Baby is thirty-seven years old. His name is Chato   37
which means fat-face. There is no Mayan blood.

I don't think they understand how it is to be a girl. I don't   38
think they know how it is to have to wait your whole life. I count the months for the baby to be born, and it's like a ring of water inside me reaching out and out until one day it will tear from me with its own teeth.

Already I can feel the animal inside me stirring in his own   39
uneven sleep. The witch woman says it's the dreams of weasels that make my child sleep the way he sleeps. She makes me eat white bread blessed by the priest, but I know it's the ghost of him inside me that circles and circles, and will not let me rest.

Abuelita said they sent me here just in time, because a little later Boy Baby came back to our house looking for me, and she had to chase him away with the broom. The next thing we hear, he's in the newspaper clippings his sister sends. A picture of him looking very much like stone, police hooked on either arm . . . *on the road to* Las Grutas de Xtacumbilxuna, *the Caves of the Hidden Girl . . . eleven female bodies . . . the last seven years . . .*

Then I couldn't read but only stare at the little black-and-white dots that make up the face I am in love with.

All my girl cousins here either don't talk to me, or those who do, ask questions they're too young to know *not* to ask. What they want to know really is how it is to have a man, because they're too ashamed to ask their married sisters.

They don't know what it is to lay so still until his sleep breathing is heavy, for the eyes in the dim dark to look and look without worry at the man-bones and the neck, the man-wrist and man-jaw thick and strong, all the salty dips and hollows, the stiff hair of the brow and sour swirl of sideburns, to lick the fat earlobes that taste of smoke, and stare at how perfect is a man.

I tell them, "It's a bad joke. When you find out you'll be sorry."

I'm going to have five children. Five. Two girls. Two boys. And one baby.

The girls will be called Lisette and Maritza. The boys I'll name Pablo and Sandro.

And my baby. My baby will be named Alegre, because life will always be hard.

Rachel says that love is like a big black piano being pushed off the top of a three-story building and you're waiting on the bottom to catch it. But Lourdes says it's not that way at all. It's like a top, like all the colors in the world are spinning so fast they're not colors anymore and all that's left is a white hum.

There was a man, a crazy who lived upstairs from us when   49
we lived on South Loomis. He couldn't talk, just walked around all day with this harmonica in his mouth. Didn't play it. Just sort of breathed through it, all day long, wheezing, in and out, in and out.

This is how it is with me. Love I mean.   50

COMMENT ON "ONE HOLY NIGHT"

In her story "One Holy Night" Sandra Cisneros uses a first-person narrative to take us into the mind of a fourteen-year-old girl who has romanticized her seduction—really rape—by a stranger into "one holy night," a night that leaves her pregnant. Sure that she is better than the girls who slip into alleys with boys, the girl imagines her first sexual experience will be as if something will "come undone like gold thread, like a tent full of birds." And because her seducer convinces her that he is like a god, the descendant of an ancient line of Mayan kings, and that his son will be the boy-child who will bring back the grandeur of his people, she thinks of losing her virginity as an initiation "beneath an ancient sky" that makes her his queen. Her romanticism and her longing to be someone special betray her into giving herself to a man she really knows nothing about.

Reality takes over when she is sent away to relatives to have her baby, still mooning over the child's father and convinced she's still in love with him. The truth about that father is stark, even dangerous. He was a thirty-seven-year-old man from nowhere with no trace of Mayan blood, much less royal blood. It's also probable that he has killed and hidden the bodies of eleven women. But at the end, we're still not quite sure if the title "One Holy Night" is ironic or if the girl will always look back on her sex with a stranger as "one holy night."

Cause and Effect as a Writing Strategy

1. In his essay "The Decline of Marriage" William Raspberry argues that major changes in our attitudes about marriage in the past few decades have created serious problems in our society, leaving many young parents and children in trouble because they don't have the solid support of a family behind them. Write an essay in which you identify another major change in our society in the past several years and discuss some of the effects that it has had. Changes you might write about are looser standards about portraying sex in movies, television shows, and advertising; the rise of radio talk shows in which people can express extreme opinions; the growth of journalism that seeks to expose every detail of celebrities' and politicians' lives; or the greatly increased involvement of church groups in political campaigns. Like Raspberry, use specific examples to illustrate your points; don't just generalize. Write the essay for your classmates and instructor.

2. For an editorial in your campus newspaper, write an essay of between 300 and 500 words about an incident on your campus that involved allegations of racist or sexist behavior. In your editorial, take sides. In your opinion, were the people who claimed they had been discriminated against justified in their accusations? Were they indeed victims, and if so, what should their response have been? If you don't think they were justified in the complaint, explain why. Conclude with a suggestion about how such incidents might be avoided in the future.

3. You may strongly disagree with one of the cause-and-effect essays in this section and want to refute what the author is saying or at least argue against a part of his or her thesis. If so, develop a paper by supposing that the writer has appeared as a speaker in your college's Ideas and Issues lecture series and has given his or her essay as a talk. Write your counterargument as a guest editorial for your campus

newspaper, assuming that your readers will be other students and the college faculty.

Here are some of the strategies you might use for your argument:

a. Challenge the cause-and-effect relationships that the author claims.

b. Citing information you have from different sources or from your experience, argue that the writer's conclusions are faulty.

c. Challenge the accuracy of some of the writer's evidence, or show weak links in his or her reasoning.

d. Show that the writer has failed to take certain things into account about his or her readers or their situation and has thus weakened the thesis of the essay.

e. Demonstrate that the writer has let his or her biases distort the argument.

f. Show that the writer claims too much, more than the evidence warrants.

Keep in mind how skillfully the writers in this section of the book use facts and examples to support their essays, and be sure you do the same.

4. Write an essay for your classmates telling why you have chosen the profession you currently plan to go into. What are your reasons? Why do you think it will be rewarding? What caused you to choose this profession? Whom do you know in the profession, and how have their experiences affected your choice? What kind of training and education will be necessary, and what sacrifices, both financial and personal, might be involved? What kind of conflicts, if any, do you think you might experience between your personal and professional lives? What effects do you think those conflicts might have on you?

5. Write a personal essay telling a story from your past or present about someone whose looks didn't conform to the model of beauty approved at that time and place and who suffered as a consequence. For example, you could write about someone who was constantly teased about being

very tall or very short and the effects that teasing had. Or you could write about a person who was considered beautiful or handsome and what effect that assessment had on the person's life. For instance, you may have known a model who felt that no one saw past her looks to appreciate her for herself or who had no friends because people were jealous of her. Conclude with a reflection about how such encounters have affected you and what they say about our culture. A good hypothetical audience for such a paper would be a young person's magazine, perhaps *Scholastic* or *Seventeen*.

6. In "Carrie Buck's Daughter," Stephen Jay Gould argues that Carrie Buck was sterilized not because she, her mother, and her daughter were feeble-minded but because of a combination of injustices inflicted on her both by individuals and by the community. In an essay written to be shared with your classmates and instructor, write a paper analyzing what you perceive those injustices to be and theorizing about what real issues were hidden behind the public excuses. If you know of similar kinds of injustices that have occurred within your own social group or subculture, you might bring them in as modern-day examples of such practices.

PERSUASION
AND
ARGUMENT

Intuitively, you already know a good deal about **argument.** For one thing, you use it all the time as you go through the day talking or writing and making claims and giving reasons. But you also live surrounded by arguments. They come not only from people you talk to and deal with in everyday personal or business situations, but also from television, radio, newspapers, subway posters, billboards, and signs and brochures of all kinds. Any time someone is trying to persuade you to buy something, contribute money, take action, make a judgment, or change your mind about anything, that person is arguing with you.

People write entire books showing how to argue effectively, how to analyze arguments, and how to refute them.

Colleges offer complete courses in the subject. Obviously, then, the subject is too complex and extensive for us to do more than skim the surface in this brief discussion. This introduction offers a quick overview of some important argument theory, tips about the kinds of arguments you can make, some concerns and strategies to keep in mind as you write arguments, and a reminder about pitfalls to avoid. If you want to learn more about making better arguments and criticizing them effectively, you can find useful books in your college bookstore or library or take an argumentation course in your speech department.

In college writing, you're not likely to spend time writing arguments about matters of taste—that is, debates in which you're saying little more than "I like it" or "I don't like it." You may enjoy talking with friends about whether you'd rather watch soccer or rugby, but mere preferences don't make workable topics for writing arguments in college. Nor do matters of fact, such as whether Mount Hood or Mount Whitney is the highest peak in the United States. Such disputes can be quickly settled by research and aren't worth the time it takes to write about them.

But in college you will probably write a wide variety of other kinds of arguments, ranging from strong personal opinion essays to closely reasoned position statements. At one extreme, in the personal opinion essays, you may make emotional claims and support them with moving and colorful language. At the other extreme, in the position statements, you try to make strictly logical claims and support them with factual, research-based data. Traditionally, your emotional argument would be classified as *persuasive,* and your logical argument would be classified as *rational.* In practice, however, most arguments mix emotion and reason in various degrees. In this section, the argumentative essays are arranged along a continuum; the more emotional, opinion-focused essays appear at the beginning, and the more objective, fact-focused essays are at the end of the section.

It's also important to remember that writing that is primarily rational isn't necessarily better than writing that is mainly emotional. Some occasions call for appeals to pride, loyalty, or compassion; for using vivid metaphors that reach the senses; and for strong language that touches the passions. When someone is speaking at a political rally or graduation ceremony or giving a eulogy, the audience wants not statistics and intellectual reasoning but emotional satisfaction and inspiration. The kind of writing done for such occasions is called *ceremonial discourse*, and often it is successful precisely because it is emotional.

When you write arguments for college instructors or your fellow students, however, you should assume that you face a skeptical audience, one that wants explanations and good reasons. Thus you need to write primarily rational arguments built mostly on evidence and logical appeal, although at times you might bring in emotional elements. You can take your cue from lawyers pleading a courtroom case. You should argue as persuasively as you can, but you should also make reasonable claims and support them with strong evidence.

PURPOSE

When you hear the term *argument*, you may automatically connect it with controversy and conflict. That's not necessarily the case, however, particularly in academic writing. There—and at other times too—you may have many purposes other than winning a dispute.

Sometimes you may argue *to support a cause*. For instance, you might write an editorial in favor of subsidized child care on your campus. You may also argue *to urge people to action* or *to promote change*—for instance, when you write a campaign brochure or a petition to reduce student fees. Sometimes you may argue *to refute a theory*—perhaps a history paper claiming that antislavery sentiment was not the chief cause of the Civil War. You can also write arguments *to arouse sympathy*—for better laws against child abuse, for example; *to stimulate interest*—for more participation in student government; *to win agreement*—to get condominium residents to agree to abolish regulations against pets; and *to provoke anger*—to arouse outrage against a proposed tax. And, of course, you might incorporate several of these purposes into one piece of writing.

AUDIENCE

When you write arguments, you must think about your readers. Who are they, what do they know, what do they believe, and what do they expect? Unless you can answer these questions at least partially, you cannot expect to write an effective argument. There simply is no such thing as a good argument in the abstract, separated from its purpose and its audience. Any argument you write is a good one only if it does what you want it to do with the particular readers who are going to read it. So by no later than the second draft of any argument you write, you need to know why you are writing and for whom you are writing.

Often it's not easy to analyze your readers. You have to work partly by instinct. Sometimes you adjust the tone of your writing almost automatically to suit a particular group of readers, and often you know intuitively that certain strategies won't work with certain readers. But you don't have to depend only on hunches. Working through a set of questions as part of your preparation to write will yield important information about your readers and will help you gradually form a sense of audience to guide you as you write and revise.

If you are trying to choose an audience for your paper, ask yourself the following questions:

1. Who is likely to be interested in what I am writing about?
2. What groups could make the changes I'm arguing for?

When you know the answers to these questions, you can direct your writing to readers to whom you have something to say—otherwise, there's little point in writing.

Once you have settled on your audience, ask yourself these questions:

1. What do my readers already know about my topic?
   a. What experience and knowledge do they have that I can use?
   b. Can I use specialized language? Should I?
   c. How can I teach them something they want to know?
2. How do my readers feel about my topic?
   a. What shared values can I appeal to?
   b. What prejudices or preconceptions must I pay attention to?
   c. What kind of approach will work best with them—casual or formal, objective or personal, factual or anecdotal?
3. What questions will my readers want me to answer?

You may find it especially useful to write out the answers to that last question.

When you have worked your way through all of these questions, either as a brainstorming exercise or in a prewriting group discussion, you'll have a stronger sense of who your readers are and how you can appeal to them.

STRATEGIES

When you are writing arguments, you can use a wide range of strategies, but most of them will fall into one of these three categories: *emotional appeal, logical appeal,* or *ethical appeal.*

Emotional Appeal

You argue by emotional or nonlogical appeal when you appeal to the emotions, the senses, and to personal biases or prejudices. You incorporate such appeals into your writing when you use *connotative language* that elicits feelings or reactions—words like *melancholy, crimson, slovenly,* or *villainous.* Usually you're also using nonlogical appeal when you use *figurative language*—metaphors, allusions, or colorful phrases that make the reader draw comparisons or make associations. Phrases like "environmental cancer" or "industrial Goliath" evoke images and comparisons and play on the emotions.

Creating a tone is also a nonlogical strategy and an important one. The tone you choose can exert a powerful force on your readers, catching their attention, ingratiating you into their favor, conveying an air of authority and confidence. You can establish a friendly, close-to-your-reader tone by using contractions and the pronouns *I, we,* and *you.* You can create a relaxed tone by bringing in humor or personal anecdote, or you can give your writing an air of authority and detachment by avoiding personal pronouns and writing as objectively as possible.

All the writers in this section use emotional appeal, but those who rely on it most heavily are Martin Luther King, Jr., and Brigid Brophy. In "I Have a Dream" King appeals to the feelings and hopes of his listeners through the extensive use of metaphor and impassioned language. In "The Rights of Animals" Brophy appeals to her readers' compassion and sense of fairness through her vivid descriptions of animal suffering and her frequent use of words like "sacrifice," "torture," and "exploit." In "A Chinaman's Chance" Eric Liu also makes an emotional appeal through his stories and through phrases like "a nation of second chances" and "freedom and opportunity"; his language, however, is more restrained than King's and Brophy's.

Logical Appeal

You argue with logical or rational strategies when you appeal mainly to your readers' intelligence, reason, and common sense. Here you depend heavily on *making claims* and *using supporting evidence.* Like a lawyer arguing a case, you may *bring in testimony* (including statistics and reports), *cite authorities,* and *argue from precedent.* You *make comparisons* and *use analogies* to strengthen your presentation, and you *theorize about cause and effect.* You also *de-emphasize personal feelings,* although you may not eliminate them completely, and *focus on facts and research.*

Wendell Berry's "The Problem of Tobacco" and William Styron's "The Habit" are the most apparently logical in this section, relying heavily on statistics and cause-and-effect reasoning. But both of them also incorporate considerable emotional appeal, particularly Berry when he argues for his vision of the good life. Styron even starts his essay with a highly emotional statement: "The lamentable history of the cigarette is that of a mortally corrupting addiction having been embraced by millions of people in the spirit of childlike innocence." Berry appeals to the emotions through his stories about a pleasant boyhood spent among tobacco farmers.

In "The Coming White Underclass" Charles Murray makes a logical appeal by using statistics to indicate the dimensions of the illegitimacy problem, then suggesting that there is a rational solution: stop subsidizing unwed mothers, and the births will stop. Nevertheless, emotional appeal runs throughout the essay in his phrasing: "wrong-headed social policy," "degraded cultural and social norms," and "Dickensian barracks," for example. Rosemary Bray uses logic and evidence in "So How Did I Get Here?" Arguing forcefully from statistics and history, she demolishes the common misconceptions about welfare. But the factual account of her family's years on welfare has great emotional impact, and the tone of her article is strong and angry when she attacks the patriarchal attitudes that perpetuate stereotypes.

Ethical Appeal

An ethical appeal is the most subtle and often the most powerful because it comes from character and reputation, not words. As a writer your ethical appeal stems from your ability to convince your readers that you are a reliable, intelligent person who knows what you're talking about and cares about the issues. Building this kind of appeal into your argument isn't easy. You have to know your readers and respect them, and you have to show that you've done your homework. For most readers, you also have to be careful not to exaggerate or make excessive claims; otherwise, you'll destroy your credibility.

Most of the writers in this section demonstrate strong ethical appeal, partly because they all have excellent credentials in their fields, but also because they show respect for their readers and have done their homework. Martin Luther King's ethical appeal is the strongest because it rests on his record as a fighter for civil rights and his own history of being willing to sacrifice for his beliefs. In the companion essay, "A Chinaman's Chance," Eric Liu's ethical appeal comes from his family's experience as aliens in the United States and his thoughtful analysis of how the American Dream has affected him. Rosemary Bray's ethical appeal comes from the dramatic story of her family's struggle during their years on welfare. Charles Murray's ethical appeal seems mixed. It may be strong for readers of the *Wall Street Journal,* his original audience, who might feel he's making a sensible argument about a serious problem, but it may lack authenticity for other readers, who feel he shows little empathy for or knowledge of the people he's talking about.

Ultimately, ethical appeal is the strongest of all argument strategies because it comes from the image and presence that the writer projects to her or his audience. If you show your readers that you are honest, knowledgeable, thoughtful, and genuinely committed to your position, your arguments are likely to be well received.

POTENTIAL PITFALLS IN ARGUMENT

This brief introduction to argument cannot point out all the things that can go wrong in arguments—the so-called logical fallacies—but adhering to the following guidelines should keep you from getting into too much trouble.

1. *Don't claim too much.* Avoid suggesting that the proposal you're arguing for will solve all the problems involved—for instance, implying that legalizing drugs would get rid of drug-related crimes or that openly paying football players would eliminate recruitment scandals. Settle for suggesting that your ideas may be worth considering or that you have thought of a new approach.

2. *Don't oversimplify complex issues.* Usually when an issue is serious enough and interesting enough for you to spend your time writing about it, it's a complicated matter with a tangled history and involves difficult issues. If you try to reduce it to simplistic terms and come up with an easy solution, you'll lose credibility quickly. Instead, acknowledge that the matter defies easy analysis but suggest that some things could be done.

3. *Support your arguments with concrete evidence and specific proposals, not with generalizations and conventional sentiments.* Always assume you are arguing for skeptical readers who expect you to demonstrate your case and won't be impressed by opinion alone. You can hold their interest and gain their respect only if you teach them something as you argue and present an old problem in a new light.

As you read the essays in this section, try to identify how these writers are arguing and what strategies they are using to convince you. As you get in the habit of reading arguments analytically and appreciatively, you will move toward writing arguments more easily and effectively. None of these strategies is new, after all, and seeing what other writers have done can give you an idea of what is possible.

USING PERSUASION AND ARGUMENT IN PARAGRAPHS

Here are two persuasive paragraphs. The first is written by a professional writer and is followed by an analysis. The second is written by a student and is followed by questions.

PETE HAMILL
from "End Game"

Claim: American
civil society be-
ing destroyed by
negation, self-
pity, confronta-
tion, vulgarity,
and hatred

Supporting
details, cynical
politics,
obstruction

Good men leav-
ing, degrading
pop culture

Specifics

American civil society, long founded on the notion of "from many, one" *e pluribus unum,* is
being swept away by a poisonous flood of negation, sectarianism, self-pity, confrontation, vulgarity, and flat-out, old-fashioned hatred. Politics
is an ice jam of accusation and obstruction, the
hardest vulgarians honored for their cynicism, its
good men fleeing to tend private gardens. Pop
culture both feeds and reflects the larger society,
and as evidence of collapse, is chilling. Snoop
Doggy Dogg and Al D'Amato have triumphed
over Wynton Marsalis and George Mitchell.
Good taste lies up the block with an ax in its
back.

Final nega-
tive image

Comment In this paragraph from a postelection essay in the
December 1994 issue of *Esquire,* Pete Hamill, a long-time
commentator on social trends in the United States, contrasts
the hopeful attitude of compromise and unity symbolized by
e pluribus unum, the slogan on all U.S. coins, to the angry,
hate-filled, political mood that he believes surfaced in the
midterm election. He deplores the recent political styles of
obstruction and confrontation and says that our vulgar, taste-
less pop culture simply reflects the nasty, self-pitying mood
of the country. He feels all sense of community has collapsed.

Hamill's argument is angry and despairing. He sees "good
men" no longer willing to run for office and all sense of
community collapsing. For proof, he compares the abrasive
music of Snoop Doggy Dogg to the exquisite music of Wynton Marsalis and the demagoguery of Senator Alfonse
D'Amato to the statemanship of former Senator George
Mitchell. A final dramatic image crowns the argument of the
paragraph: "Good taste lies up the block with an ax in its
back."

The argument is primarily emotional, depending heavily

on strong language and images, but Hamill is also careful to give examples to make his point. Also, he depends on his readers' bringing with them fresh knowledge of the negative, vindictive campaign of 1994. His purpose, here and in the full essay, is to persuade his readers that unless the country as a whole moves back from its anger and divisiveness, we will lose the essence of our country, the ability of many different races and religions to live together harmoniously.

JIM F. SALOMAN
Genetic Engineering

We need to regulate experiments in genetic engineering. Scientists can reconfigure the genetic makeup of an organism. They can literally change life. But without appropriate controls, such tampering can lead to unpredictable and violent results. What would happen if scientists were able to resurrect an extinct species that would reverse the order of natural selection? And what would happen if they produced a superior organism that destroyed the balance of our present ecosystem? And what would happen if they started "creating" people for particular tasks? They could design aggressive men to fight wars and passive women to breed children. Whole new social classes could be created, some genetically advanced, some genetically restricted. If we are to protect the rights of individuals and prevent evolutionary chaos, we must create a thoughtful public policy that protects us from our own scientific experiments.

1. How might Saloman go on to develop this paragraph into a full-length persuasive essay?
2. Saloman gives several examples of what he calls "unpredictable and violent results." How would you evaluate the persuasive value of the several generalizations that he gives as examples of such results?

ARGUMENT AND PERSUASION

Points to Remember

1. Remember that in order to argue well, you must understand your audience and know your purpose.
2. Understand the three principal kinds of appeal: emotional appeal, the appeal to feelings and senses; logical appeal, the appeal to intelligence and reason; and ethical appeal, the appeal from the character and competence of the author. The most effective arguments combine all three.
3. Construct an argument as a lawyer would construct a case to present to a jury; state your assertions and back them up with evidence and reason, appealing to your readers' intellect and feelings.
4. Always assume your audience is intelligent, although some members of it may be uninformed on a particular issue.
5. Avoid three common pitfalls: (a) don't overstate your claims; (b) be careful not to oversimplify complex issues; and (c) support your arguments with concrete evidence, not generalizations.

Martin Luther King, Jr. (1929–1968) was born in
Atlanta, Georgia, and was educated at Morehouse
College, Crozer Theological Seminary, and Boston University. Ordained a Baptist minister in his
father's church in 1947, King soon became involved in civil rights activities in the South. In
1957 he founded the Southern Christian Leadership Conference and established himself as America's most prominent spokesman for nonviolent
racial integration. In 1963 he was named *Time*
magazine's Man of the Year; in 1964 he was given
the Nobel Peace Prize. In 1968 he was assassinated in Memphis, Tennessee. His writing includes *Letter from Birmingham City Jail* (1963),
Why We Can't Wait (1964), and *Where Do We Go
from Here: Chaos or Community?* (1967). "I Have
a Dream" is the famous speech King delivered at
the Lincoln Memorial at the end of the "March
on Washington" in 1963 to commemorate the
one hundredth anniversary of the Emancipation
Proclamation. King argues that realization of the
dream of freedom for all American citizens is long
overdue.

I Have a Dream

FIVE SCORE YEARS ago, a great American, in whose sym-   1
bolic shadow we stand, signed the Emancipation Proclamation. This momentous decree came as a great beacon
light of hope to millions of Negro slaves who had been seared
in the flames of withering injustice. It came as a joyous
daybreak to end the long night of captivity.

But one hundred years later, we must face the tragic fact   2 that the Negro is still not free. One hundred years later, the life of the Negro is still sadly crippled by the manacles of segregation and the chains of discrimination. One hundred years later, the Negro lives on a lonely island of poverty in the midst of a vast ocean of material prosperity. One hundred years later, the Negro is still languishing in the corners of American society and finds himself an exile in his own land. So we have come here today to dramatize an appalling condition.

In a sense we have come to our nation's Capitol to cash a   3
check. When the architects of our republic wrote the magnificent words of the Constitution and the Declaration of

---

There will be neither rest nor tranquility in America until the Negro is granted his citizenship rights.

Independence, they were signing a promissory note to which every American was to fall heir. This note was a promise that all men would be guaranteed the unalienable rights of life, liberty, and the pursuit of happiness.

It is obvious today that America has defaulted on this   4
promissory note insofar as her citizens of color are concerned. Instead of honoring this sacred obligation, America has given the Negro people a bad check; a check which has come back marked "insufficient funds." But we refuse to believe that the bank of justice is bankrupt. We refuse to believe that there are insufficient funds in the great vaults of opportunity of this nation. So we have come to cash this check—a check that will give us upon demand the riches of freedom and the security of justice. We have also come to this hallowed spot to remind America of the fierce urgency of *now*. This is no time to engage in the luxury of cooling off or to take the tranquilizing drug of gradualism. *Now* is the time to make real the

promises of Democracy. *Now* is the time to rise from the dark and desolate valley of segregation to the sunlit path of racial justice. *Now* is the time to open the doors of opportunity to all of God's children. *Now* is the time to lift our nation from the quicksands of racial injustice to the solid rock of brotherhood.

It would be fatal for the nation to overlook the urgency of the moment and to underestimate the determination of the Negro. This sweltering summer of the Negro's legitimate discontent will not pass until there is an invigorating autumn of freedom and equality. 1963 is not an end, but a beginning. Those who hope that the Negro needed to blow off steam and will now be content will have a rude awakening if the nation returns to business as usual. There will be neither rest nor tranquility in America until the Negro is granted his citizenship rights. The whirlwinds of revolt will continue to shake the foundations of our nation until the bright day of justice emerges.

5

Very good use of metaphor

But there is something I must say to my people who stand on the warm threshold which leads into the palace of justice. In the process of gaining our rightful place we must not be guilty of wrongful deeds. Let us not seek to satisfy our thirst for freedom by drinking from the cup of bitterness and hatred. We must forever conduct our struggle on the high plane of dignity and discipline. We must not allow our creative protest to degenerate into physical violence. Again and again we must rise to the majestic heights of meeting physical force with soul force. The marvelous new militancy which has engulfed the Negro community must not lead us to a distrust of all white people, for many of our white brothers, as evidenced by their presence here today, have come to realize that their destiny is tied up with our destiny and their freedom is inextricably bound to our freedom. We cannot walk alone.

6

even for Black as white as white

And as we walk, we must make the pledge that we shall march ahead. We cannot turn back. There are those who are asking the devotees of civil rights, "When will you be satisfied?" We can never be satisfied as long as the Negro is the victim of the unspeakable horrors of police brutality. We

7

can never be satisfied as long as our bodies, heavy with the fatigue of travel, cannot gain lodging in the motels of the highways and the hotels of the cities. We cannot be satisfied as long as the Negro's basic mobility is from a smaller ghetto to a larger one. We can never be satisfied as long as a Negro in Mississippi cannot vote and a Negro in New York believes he has nothing for which to vote. No, no, we are not satisfied, and we will not be satisfied until justice rolls down like waters and righteousness like a mighty stream.

I am not unmindful that some of you have come here out 8 of great trials and tribulations. Some of you have come fresh from narrow jail cells. Some of you have come from areas where your quest for freedom left you battered by the storms of persecution and staggered by the winds of police brutality. You have been the veterans of creative suffering. Continue to work with the faith that unearned suffering is redemptive.

Go back to Mississippi, go back to Alabama, go back to 9 South Carolina, go back to Georgia, go back to Louisiana, go back to the slums and ghettoes of our northern cities, knowing that somehow this situation can and will be changed. Let us not wallow in the valley of despair.

I say to you today, my friends, that in spite of the difficul- 10 ties and frustrations of the moment I still have a dream. It is a dream deeply rooted in the American dream.

I have a dream that one day this nation will rise up and 11 live out the true meaning of its creed: "We hold these truths to be self-evident; that all men are created equal."

I have a dream that one day on the red hills of Georgia 12 the sons of former slaves and the sons of former slaveowners will be able to sit down together at the table of brotherhood.

I have a dream that the state of Mississippi, a desert state 13 sweltering with the heat of injustice and oppression, will be transformed into an oasis of freedom and justice.

I have a dream that my four little children will one day live 14 in a nation where they will not be judged by the color of their skin but by the content of their character.

I have a dream today. 15

I have a dream that the state of Alabama, whose governor's 16 lips are presently dripping with the words of interposition and nullification, will be transformed into a situation where little black boys and black girls will be able to join hands with little white boys and white girls and walk together as sisters and brothers.

I have a dream today.   17

I have a dream that one day every valley shall be exalted,   18
every hill and mountain shall be made low, the rough places will be made plain, and the crooked places will be made straight, and the glory of the Lord shall be revealed, and all flesh shall see it together.

This is our hope. This is the faith with which I return to   19
the South. With this faith we will be able to hew out of the mountain of despair a stone of hope. With this faith we will be able to transform the jangling discords of our nation into a beautiful symphony of brotherhood. With this faith we will be able to work together, to pray together, to struggle together, to go to jail together, to stand up for freedom together, knowing that we will be free one day.

This will be the day when all of God's children will be able   20
to sing with new meaning.

> *My country, 'tis of thee*
> *Sweet land of liberty,*
> *Of thee I sing:*
> *Land where my fathers died,*
> *Land of the pilgrims' pride,*
> *From every mountainside*
> *Let freedom ring.*

And if America is to be a great nation this must become   21
true. So let freedom ring from the prodigious hilltops of New Hampshire. Let freedom ring from the mighty mountains of New York. Let freedom ring from the heightening Alleghenies of Pennsylvania!

Let freedom ring from the snowcapped Rockies of Colo-   22
rado!

Let freedom ring from the curvaceous peaks of California!   23

But not only that; let freedom ring from Stone Mountain   24
of Georgia!

Let freedom ring from Lookout Mountain of Tennessee!   25

Let freedom ring from every hill and molehill of Missis-   26
sippi. From every mountainside, let freedom ring.

When we let freedom ring, when we let it ring from every   27
village and every hamlet, from every state and every city, we
will be able to speed up that day when all of God's children,
black men and white men, Jews and Gentiles, Protestants and
Catholics, will be able to join hands and sing in the words of
the old Negro spiritual, "Free at last! free at last! thank God
almighty, we are free at last!"

For Study and Discussion

QUESTIONS FOR RESPONSE

1. What experiences of injustice have you had (or perhaps witnessed,
   read about, or seen in a movie) that help you to identify with
   King's dreams and feel the force of his speech?
2. What did you already know about the life of King and of his place
   in modern U.S. history that prepared you for reading "I Have a
   Dream"? How well did the speech live up to what you expected
   of it?

QUESTIONS ABOUT PURPOSE

1. King has at least two strong messages. One message is local and
   immediate; the other one is national and long-range. How would
   you summarize those two messages?
2. How does King use his speech to reinforce his belief in nonvio-
   lence as the appropriate tool in the struggle for civil rights?

QUESTIONS ABOUT AUDIENCE

1. King gave this speech to a huge live audience that had come to
   Washington for a march for freedom and civil rights. How much

larger is the national audience he is addressing, and why is that audience also important?

2. This speech is one of the most widely anthologized of modern speeches. What audiences does it continue to appeal to and why?

QUESTIONS ABOUT STRATEGIES

1. How does King draw on metaphor to engage his listeners' feelings of injustice and give them hope for a new day? What are some of the most powerful metaphors?
2. In what way do King's talents as a minister serve his purposes in the speech? What African-American leader today do you think most resembles King in style and in mission?

QUESTIONS FOR DISCUSSION

1. If King were alive today, more than thirty years after this speech, how much of his dream do you think he would feel has come true? Look particularly at the visions he speaks of in paragraph 7 and paragraphs 11 through 16.
2. What elements in the speech reveal those qualities that contributed to King's power as a major civil rights leader, effective with whites as well as with blacks?

Eric Liu was born in Poughkeepsie, New York, in 1968, and was educated at Yale University. He worked as a legislative aide for Senator David Boren of Oklahoma and then as a speechwriter for Secretary of State Warren Christopher and President Bill Clinton. He is currently the publisher and editor of *The Next Progressive,* a journal of opinion, and the editor of *NEXT: Young American Writers on the New Generation* (1994). In "A Chinaman's Chance: Reflections on the American Dream," reprinted from *NEXT,* Liu argues that the American Dream is more about seizing opportunity than about claiming prosperity.

A Chinaman's Chance: Reflections on the American Dream

A LOT OF PEOPLE my age seem to think that the American Dream is dead. I think they're dead wrong. 1

Or at least only partly right. It is true that for those of us in our twenties and early thirties, job opportunities are scarce. There looms a real threat that we will be the first American generation to have a lower standard of living than our parents. 2

But what is it that we mean when we invoke the American Dream? 3

In the past, the American Dream was something that held people of all races, religions, and identities together. As James Comer has written, it represented a shared aspiration among all Americans—black, white, or any other color—"to provide well for themselves and their families as valued members of a 4 democratic society." Now, all too often, it seems the American Dream means merely some guarantee of affluence, a birthright of wealth.

At a basic level, of course, the American Dream is about 5 prosperity and the pursuit of material happiness. But to me, its meaning extends beyond such concerns. To me, the dream is not just about buying a bigger house than the one I grew up in or having shinier stuff now than I had as a kid. It also represents a sense of opportunity that binds generations together in commitment, so that the young inherit not only property but also perseverance, not only money but also a

---

I want to prove that a Chinaman's chance is as good as anyone else's.

---

mission to make good on the strivings of their parents and grandparents.

The poet Robert Browning once wrote that "a man's reach 6 must exceed his grasp—else what's a heaven for?" So it is in America. Every generation will strive, and often fail. Every generation will reach for success, and often miss the mark. But Americans rely as much on the next generation as on the next life to prove that such struggles and frustrations are not in vain. There may be temporary setbacks, cutbacks, recessions, depressions. But this is a nation of second chances. So long as there are young Americans who do not take what they have—or what they can do—for granted, progress is always possible.

My conception of the American Dream does not take 7 progress for granted. But it does demand the *opportunity* to achieve progress—and values the opportunity as much as the achievement. I come at this question as the son of immigrants. I see just as clearly as anyone else the cracks in the idealist vision of fulfillment for all. But because my parents came here with virtually nothing, because they did build something, I see the enormous potential inherent in the ideal.

I happen still to believe in our national creed: freedom and opportunity, and our common responsibility to uphold them. This creed is what makes America unique. More than any demographic statistic or economic indicator, it animates the American Dream. It infuses our mundane struggles—to plan a career, do good work, get ahead—with purpose and possibility. It makes America the only country that could produce heroes like Colin Powell—heroes who rise from nothing, who overcome the odds. 8

I think of the sacrifices made by my own parents. I appreciate the hardship of the long road traveled by my father— one of whose first jobs in America was painting the yellow line down a South Dakota interstate—and by my mother— whose first job here was filing pay stubs for a New York restaurant. From such beginnings, they were able to build a comfortable life and provide me with a breadth of resources—through arts, travel, and an Ivy League education. It was an unspoken obligation for them to do so. 9

I think of my boss in my first job after college, on Capitol Hill. George is a smart, feisty, cigar-chomping, take-no-shit Greek-American. He is about fifteen years older than I, has different interests, a very different personality. But like me, he is the son of immigrants, and he would joke with me that the Greek-Chinese mafia was going to take over one day. He was only half joking. We'd worked harder, our parents doubly harder, than almost anyone else we knew. To people like George, talk of the withering of the American Dream seems foreign. 10

It's undeniable that principles like freedom and opportunity, no matter how dearly held, are not enough. They can inspire a multiracial March on Washington, but they can not bring black salaries in alignment with white salaries. They can draw wave after wave of immigrants here, but they can not provide them the means to get out of our ghettos and barrios and Chinatowns. They are not sufficient for fulfillment of the American Dream. 11

But they are necessary. They are vital. And not just to the 12
children of immigrants. These ideals form the durable thread
that weaves us all in union. Put another way, they are one of
the few things that keep America from disintegrating into a
loose confederation of zip codes and walled-in communities.

What alarms me is how many people my age look at our 13
nation's ideals with a rising sense of irony. What good is such
a creed if you are working for hourly wages in a dead-end
job? What value do such platitudes have if you live in an urban
war zone? When the only apparent link between homeboys
and housepainters and bike messengers and investment bankers is pop culture—MTV, the NBA, movies, dance music—
then the social fabric is flimsy indeed.

My generation has come of age at a time when the country 14
is fighting off bouts of defeatism and self-doubt, at a time
when racism and social inequities seem not only persistent
but intractable. At a time like this, the retreat to one's own
kind is seen by more and more of my peers as an advance.
And that retreat has given rise again to the notion that there
are essential and irreconcilable differences among the races—
a notion that was supposed to have disappeared from American discourse by the time my peers and I were born in the
sixties.

Not long ago, for instance, my sister called me a "banana." 15

I was needling her about her passion for rap and hip-hop 16
music. Every time I saw her, it seemed, she was jumping and
twisting to Arrested Development or Chubb Rock or some
other funky group. She joked that despite being the daughter
of Chinese immigrants, she was indeed "black at heart." And
then she added, lightheartedly, "You, on the other hand—
well, you're basically a banana." Yellow on the outside, but
white inside.

I protested, denied her charge vehemently. But it was too 17
late. She was back to dancing. And I stood accused.

Ever since then, I have wondered what it means to be 18
black, or white, or Asian "at heart"—particularly for my
generation. Growing up, when other kids would ask whether
I was Chinese or Korean or Japanese, I would reply, a little

petulantly, "American." Assimilation can still be a sensitive subject. I recall reading about a Korean-born Congressman who had gone out of his way to say that Asian-Americans should expect nothing special from him. He added that he was taking speech lessons "to get rid of this accent." I winced at his palpable self-hate. But then it hit me: Is this how my sister sees me?

There is no doubt that minorities like me can draw   19
strength from our communities. But in today's environment, anything other than ostentatious tribal fealty is taken in some communities as a sign of moral weakness, a disappointing dilution of character. In times that demand ever-clearer think-ing, it has become too easy for people to shut off their brains: "It's a black/Asian/Latino/white thing," says the variable T-shirt. "You wouldn't understand." Increasingly, we don't.

The civil-rights triumphs of the sixties and the cultural   20
revolutions that followed made it possible for minorities to celebrate our diverse heritages. I can appreciate that. But I know, too, that the sixties—or at least, my generation's grainy, hazy vision of the decade—also bequeathed to young Americans a legacy of near-pathological race consciousness.

Today's culture of entitlement—and of race entitlement in   21
particular—tells us plenty about what we get if we are black or white or female or male or old or young.

It is silent, though, on some other important issues. For   22
instance: What do we "get" for being American? And just as importantly, What do we owe? These are questions around which young people like myself must tread carefully, since talk of common interests, civic culture, responsibility, and inte-gration sounds a little too "white" for some people. To the new segregationists, the "American Dream" is like the old myth of the "Melting Pot": an oppressive fiction, an opiate for the unhappy colored masses.

How have we allowed our thinking about race to become   23
so twisted? The formal obstacles and the hateful opposition to civil rights have long faded into memory. By most external measures, life for minorities is better than it was a quarter century ago. It would seem that the opportunities for toler-

ance and cooperation are commonplace. Why, then, are so many of my peers so cynical about our ability to get along with one another?

The reasons are frustratingly ambiguous. I got a glimpse 24 of this when I was in college. It was late in my junior year, and as the editor of a campus magazine, I was sitting on a panel to discuss "The White Press at Yale: What Is to Be Done?" The assembly hall was packed, a diverse and noisy crowd. The air was heavy, nervously electric.

Why weren't there more stories about "minority issues" in 25 the Yale *Daily News?* Why weren't there more stories on Africa in my magazine, the foreign affairs journal? How many "editors of color" served on the boards of each of the major publications? The questions were volleyed like artillery, one round after another, punctuated only by the applause of an audience spoiling for a fight. The questions were not at all unfair. But it seemed that no one—not even those of us on the panel who *were* people of color—could provide, in this context, satisfactory answers.

Toward the end of the discussion, I made a brief appeal 26 for reason and moderation. And afterward, as students milled around restlessly, I was attacked: for my narrowmindedness— How dare you suggest that Yale is not a fundamentally prejudiced place!—for my simplemindedness—Have you, too, been co-opted?

And for my betrayal—Are you just white inside? 27

My eyes were opened that uncomfortably warm early sum- 28 mer evening. Not only to the cynical posturing and the combustible opportunism of campus racial politics. But more importantly, to the larger question of identity—my identity— in America. Never mind that the aim of many of the loudest critics was to generate headlines in the very publications they denounced. In spite of themselves—against, it would seem, their true intentions—they got me to think about who I am.

In our society today, and especially among people of my 29 generation, we are congealing into clots of narrow commonality. We stick with racial and religious comrades. This tribal consciousness-raising can be empowering for some. But while

America was conceived in liberty—the liberty, for instance, to associate with whomever we like—it was never designed to be a mere collection of subcultures. We forget that there is in fact such a thing as a unique American identity that transcends our sundry tribes, sets, gangs, and cliques.

I have grappled, wittingly or not, with these questions of identity and allegiance all my life. When I was in my early teens, I would invite my buddies overnight to watch movies, play video games, and beat one another up. Before too long, my dad would come downstairs and start hamming it up— telling stories, asking gently nosy questions, making corny jokes, all with his distinct Chinese accent. I would stand back, quietly gauging everyone's reaction. Of course, the guys loved it. But I would feel uneasy.   30

What was then cause for discomfort is now a source of strength. Looking back on such episodes, I take pride in my father's accented English; I feel awe at his courage to laugh loudly in a language not really his own.   31

It was around the same time that I decided that continued attendance at the community Chinese school on Sundays was uncool. There was no fanfare; I simply stopped going. As a child, I'd been too blissfully unaware to think of Chinese school as anything more than a weekly chore, with an annual festival (dumplings and spring rolls, games and prizes). But by the time I was a peer-pressured adolescent, Chinese school seemed like a badge of the woefully unassimilated. I turned my back on it.   32

Even as I write these words now, it feels as though I am revealing a long-held secret. I am proud that my ancestors— scholars, soldiers, farmers—came from one of the world's great civilizations. I am proud that my grandfather served in the Chinese Air Force. I am proud to speak even my clumsy brand of Mandarin, and I feel blessed to be able to think idiomatically in Chinese, a language so much richer in nuance and subtle poetry than English.   33

Belatedly, I appreciate the good fortune I've had to be the son of immigrants. As a kid, I could play Thomas Jefferson in the bicentennial school play one week and the next week   34 play the poet Li Bai at the Chinese school festival. I could come home from an afternoon of teen slang at the mall and sit down to dinner for a rollicking conversation in our family's hybrid of Chinese and English. I understood, when I went over to visit friends, that my life was different. At the time, I just never fully appreciated how rich it was.

Yet I know that this pride in my heritage does not cross 35 into prejudice against others. What it reflects is pride in what my country represents. That became clear to me when I went through Marine Corps Officer Candidates' School. During the summers after my sophomore and junior years of college, I volunteered for OCS, a grueling boot camp for potential officers in the swamps and foothills of Quantico, Virginia.

And once I arrived—standing 5'4", 135 pounds, bespec- 36 tacled, a Chinese Ivy League Democrat—I was a target straight out of central casting. The wiry, raspy-voiced drill sergeant, though he was perhaps only an inch or two taller than I, called me "Little One" with as much venom as can be squeezed into such a moniker. He heaped verbal abuse on me, he laughed when I stumbled, he screamed when I hesi- tated. But he also never failed to remind me that just because I was a little shit didn't mean I shouldn't run farther, climb higher, think faster, hit harder than anyone else.

That was the funny thing about the Marine Corps. It is, 37 ostensibly, one of the most conservative institutions in the United States. And yet, for those twelve weeks, it represented the kind of color-blind equality of opportunity that the rest of society struggles to match. I did not feel uncomfortable at OCS to be of Chinese descent. Indeed, I drew strength from it. My platoon was a veritable cross section of America: forty young men of all backgrounds, all regions, all races, all levels of intelligence and ability, displaced from our lives (if only for a few weeks) with nowhere else to go.

Going down the list of names—Courtemanche, Dough- 38 erty, Grella, Hunt, Liu, Reeves, Schwarzman, and so on— brought to mind a line from a World War II documentary I once saw, which went something like this: The reason why it seemed during the war that America was as good as the rest of the world put together was that America *was* the rest of the world put together.

Ultimately, I decided that the Marines was not what I wanted to do for four years and I did not accept the second lieutenant's commission. But I will never forget the day of the graduation parade: bright sunshine, brisk winds, the band playing Sousa as my company passed in review. As my mom and dad watched and photographed the parade from the rafters, I thought to myself: this is the American Dream in all its cheesy earnestness. I felt the thrill of truly being part of something larger and greater than myself. 39

I do know that American life is not all Sousa marches and flag-waving. I know that those with reactionary agendas often find it convenient to cloak their motives in the language of Americanism. The "American Party" was the name of a major nativist organization in the nineteenth century. "America First" is the siren song of the isolationists who would withdraw this country from the world and expel the world from this country. I know that our national immigration laws were once designed explicitly to cut off the influx from Asia. 40

I also know that discrimination is real. I am reminded of a gentle old man who, after Pearl Harbor, was stripped of his possessions without warning, taken from his home, and thrown into a Japanese internment camp. He survived, and by many measures has thrived, serving as a community leader and political activist. But I am reluctant to share with him my wide-eyed patriotism. 41

I know the bittersweet irony that my own father—a strong and optimistic man—would sometimes feel when he was alive. When he came across a comically lost cause—if the Yankees were behind 14–0 in the ninth, or if Dukakis was down ten points in the polls with a week left—he would often joke that the doomed party had "a Chinaman's chance" of success. It was one of those insensitive idioms of a generation ago, and it must have lodged in his impressionable young mind when he first came to America. It spoke of a perceived stacked deck. 42

I know, too, that for many other immigrants, the dream simply does not work out. Fae Myenne Ng, the author of 43

Bone, writes about how her father ventured here from China under a false identity and arrived at Angel Island, the detention center outside the "Gold Mountain" of San Francisco. He got out, he labored, he struggled, and he suffered "a bitter no-luck life" in America. There was no glory. For him, Ng suggests, the journey was not worth it.

But it is precisely because I know these things that I want   44
to prove that in the long run, over generations and across ethnicities, it *is* worth it. For the second-generation American, opportunity is obligation. I have seen and faced racism. I understand the dull pain of dreams deferred or unmet. But I believe still that there is so little stopping me from building the life that I want. I was given, through my parents' labors, the chance to bridge that gap between ideals and reality. Who am I to throw away that chance?

Plainly, I am subject to the criticism that I speak too much   45
from my own experience. Not everyone can relate to the second-generation American story. When I have spoken like this with some friends, the issue has been my perspective. *What you say is fine for you. But unless you grew up where I did, unless you've had people avoid you because of the color of your skin, don't talk to me about common dreams.*

But are we then to be paralyzed? Is respect for different   46
experiences supposed to obviate the possibility of shared aspirations? Does the diversity of life in America doom us to a fractured understanding of one another? The question is basic: Should the failure of this nation thus far to fulfill its stated ideals incapacitate its young people, or motivate us?

Our country was built on, and remains glued by, the idea   47
that everybody deserves a fair shot and that we must work together to guarantee that opportunity—the original American Dream. It was this idea, in some inchoate form, that drew every immigrant here. It was this idea, however sullied by slavery and racism, that motivated the civil-rights movement. To write this idea off—even when its execution is spotty—to let American life descend into squabbles among separatist tribes would not just be sad. It would be a total mishandling of a legacy, the squandering of a great historical inheritance.

Mine must not be the first generation of Americans to lose   48

America. Just as so many of our parents journeyed here to find their version of the American Dream, so must young Americans today journey across boundaries of race and class to rediscover one another. We are the first American generation to be born into an integrated society, and we are accustomed to more race mixing than any generation before us. We started open-minded, and it's not too late for us to stay that way.

Time is of the essence. For in our national political culture today, the watchwords seem to be *decline* and *end*. Apocalyptic visions and dark millennial predictions abound. The end of history. The end of progress. The end of equality. Even something as ostensibly positive as the end of the Cold War has a bittersweet tinge, because for the life of us, no one in America can get a handle on the big question, "What Next?" 49

For my generation, this fixation on endings is particularly enervating. One's twenties are supposed to be a time of widening horizons, of bright possibilities. Instead, America seems to have entered an era of limits. Whether it is the difficulty of finding jobs from some place other than a temp agency, or the mountains of debt that darken our future, the message to my peers is often that this nation's time has come and gone; let's bow out with grace and dignity. 50

A friend once observed that while the Chinese seek to adapt to nature and yield to circumstance, Americans seek to conquer both. She meant that as a criticism of America. But I interpreted her remark differently. I *do* believe that America is exceptional. And I believe it is up to my generation to revive that spirit, that sense that we do in fact have control over our own destiny—as individuals and as a nation. 51

If we are to reclaim a common destiny, we must also reach out to other generations for help. It was Franklin Roosevelt who said that while America can't always build the future for its youth, it can—and must—build its youth for the future. That commitment across generations is as central to the American Dream as any I have enunciated. We are linked, black and white, old and young, one and inseparable. 52

I know how my words sound. I am old enough to perceive 53

my own naïveté but young enough still to cherish it. I realize that I am coming of age just as the American Dream is showing its age. Yet I still have faith in this country's unique destiny—to create generation after generation of hyphenates like me, to channel this new blood, this resilience and energy into an ever more vibrant future for *all* Americans.

And I want to prove—for my sake, for my father's sake, and for my country's sake—that a Chinaman's chance is as good as anyone else's.

54

For Study and Discussion

QUESTIONS FOR RESPONSE

1. Do you endorse or discount Liu's argument? How do you think your family background and history affect your response?
2. How would you define the American Dream? To what extent do you think it has been or will be fulfilled for you?

QUESTIONS ABOUT PURPOSE

1. To what criticisms *about* his generation is Liu responding? To what criticisms *from* his generation is he responding?
2. What specific attitudes among young people does Liu challenge?

QUESTIONS ABOUT AUDIENCE

1. Liu wrote this essay for a 1994 book titled *NEXT: Young American Writers on the New Generation,* a book he conceived of and also edited. What kind of readers do you think he envisioned for the book? How do you think you fit into that group?
2. What do you think Liu's appeal might be to generations older than his? Why?

QUESTIONS ABOUT STRATEGIES

1. What is the impact of Liu's writing about his parents' experience?
2. Liu was once one of President Clinton's speechwriters. What

strategies does he use that he might have learned through that experience?

QUESTIONS FOR DISCUSSION

1. What evidence, if any, do you see that students are splitting into separate groups on your campus? What is your view of such splits? Why?
2. What factors in Liu's life and experiences do you think played a significant part in his success in college and beyond? How would those factors affect his outlook on life?

Brigid Brophy was born in London, England, in 1929 and attended St. Paul's Girls' School and St. Hugh's College at Oxford University. Quick-witted and keenly intelligent, she soon became a writer, following the family tradition established by her father, novelist John Brophy. Her novels include *Hackenfeller's Ape* (1954), *Flesh* (1962), and *Palace Without Chairs* (1978). Her nonfiction includes works as diverse as *Mozart the Dramatist: A New View of Mozart's Operas and His Age* (1964), *The Rights of Animals* (1969), and *Baroque 'n' Roll and Other Essays* (1987). A regular contributor to the *New Statesman, London Magazine,* and the *Times Literary Supplement,* Brophy is an impassioned defender of her moral and political opinions. In "The Rights of Animals," reprinted from *Don't Never Forget: Collected Views and Reviews* (1966), she argues one of her favorite causes—the responsibility of the superior species (human beings) to behave decently toward the inferior species (animals).

The Rights of Animals

WERE IT ANNOUNCED tomorrow that anyone who fancied it might, without risk of reprisals or recriminations, stand at a fourth-storey window, dangle out of it a length of string with a metal (labelled "Free") on the end, wait till a chance passer-by took a bite and then, having entangled his cheek or gullet on a hook hidden in the food, haul him up to the fourth floor and there batter him to death with a knobkerry, I do not think there would be many takers. 1

Most sane adults would, I imagine, sicken at the mere 2

thought. Yet sane adults do the equivalent to fish every day: not in panic, sexual jealousy, ideological frenzy or even greed—many of our freshwater fish are virtually inedible, and not one of them constitutes a threat to the life, love or ideology of a human on the bank—but for amusement. Civilisation is not outraged at their behaviour. On the contrary: that a person's hobby is fishing is often read as a guarantee of his sterling and innocent character.

The relationship of *homo sapiens* to the other animals is 3 one of unremitting exploitation. We employ their work; we eat and wear them. We exploit them to serve our superstitions: whereas we used to sacrifice them to our gods and tear

Where animals are concerned, humanity seems to have switched off its morals and aesthetics—indeed, its very imagination.

out their entrails in order to foresee the future, we now sacrifice them to Science and experiment on their entrails in the hope—or on the mere off chance—that we might thereby see a little more clearly into the present. When we can think of no pretext for causing their death and no profit to turn it to, we often cause it nonetheless, wantonly, the only gain being a brief pleasure for ourselves, which is usually only marginally bigger than the pleasure we could have had without killing anything; we could quite well enjoy our marksmanship or crosscountry galloping without requiring a real dead wild animal to shew for it at the end.

It is rare for us to leave wild animals alive; when we do, 4 we often do not leave them wild. Some we put on display in a prison just large enough for them to survive, but not in any full sense to live, in. Others we trundle about the country in their prisons, pausing every now and then to put them on public exhibition performing, like clockwork, "tricks" we

have "trained" into them. However, animals are not clockwork but instinctual beings. Circus "tricks" are spectacular
or risible as the case may be precisely *because* they violate the
animals' instinctual nature—which is precisely why they
ought to violate both our moral and our aesthetic sense.

But where animals are concerned humanity seems to have   5
switched off its morals and aesthetics—indeed, its very imagination. Goodness knows those faculties function erratically
enough in our dealings with one another. But at least we
recognise their faultiness. We spend an increasing number of
our cooler moments trying to forestall the moral and aesthetic breakdowns which are liable, in a crisis, to precipitate
us into atrocities against each other. We have bitter demarcation disputes about where the rights of one man end and
those of the next man begin, but most men now acknowledge
that there are such things as the rights of the next man. Only
in relation to the next animal can civilised humans persuade
themselves that they have absolute and arbitrary rights—that
they may do anything whatever that they can get away with.

The reader will have guessed in some detail by now what   6
sort of person he confronts in me: a sentimentalist; probably
a killjoy; a person with no grasp on economic realities; a twee
anthropomorphist, who attributes human feelings (and no
doubt human names and clothes as well) to animals, and yet
actually prefers animals to humans and would sooner succour
a stray cat than an orphan child; a latter-day version of those
folklore English spinsters who in the nineteenth century excited the ridicule of the natives by walking round Florence
requesting them not to ill-treat their donkeys; and *par excellence*, of course, a crank.

Well. To take the last item first: if by "crank" you mean   7
"abnormal," yes. My views are shared by only a smallish (but
probably not so small as you think) part of the citizenry—as
yet. Still, that proves nothing either way about the validity of
our views. It is abnormal to be a lunatic convinced you are
Napoleon, but equally (indeed, numerically considered,
probably even more) abnormal to be a genius. The test of a
view is its rationality, not the number of people who endorse

it. It would have been cranky indeed in the ancient world to raise the question of the rights of slaves—so cranky that scarcely a voice went on record as doing so. To us it seems incredible that the Greek philosophers should have scanned so deep into right and wrong and yet never *noticed* the immorality of slavery. Perhaps three thousand years from now it will seem equally incredible that we do not notice the immorality of our oppression of animals.

Slavery was the ancient world's patch of moral and aesthetic insensitivity. Indeed, it was not until the eighteenth and nineteenth centuries of our own era that the human conscience was effectively and universally switched on in that respect. Even then, we went on with economic and social exploitations which stopped short of slavery only in constitutional status, and people were found to justify them. But by then the exploiters had at least been forced onto the defensive and felt obliged to produce the feeble arguments that had never even been called for in the ancient world. Perhaps it is a sign that our conscience is about to be switched on in relation to animals that some animal-exploiters are now seeking to justify themselves. When factory farmers tell us that animals kept in "intensive" (i.e. concentration) camps are being kindly spared the inclemency of a winter outdoors, and that calves do not mind being tethered for life on slats because they have never known anything else, an echo should start in our historical consciousness: do you remember how childlike blackamoors were kindly spared the harsh responsibilities of freedom, how the skivvy didn't feel the hardship of scrubbing all day because she was used to it, how the poor didn't mind their slums because they had never known anything else? 8

The first of the factory farmers' arguments is, of course, an argument for ordinary farms to make better provision for animals in winter, not for ordinary farms to be replaced by torture chambers. As for the one about the animals' never having known anything else, I still shan't believe it valid but I shall accept that the factory farmers genuinely believe it themselves when they follow out its logic by using their 9 profits to finance the repatriation of every circus and zoo animal that was caught in the wild, on the grounds that those *have* known something else.

Undismayed by being a crank, I will make you a free gift 10 of another stick to beat me with, by informing you that I am a vegetarian. Now, surely, you have me. Not only am I a more extreme crank, a member of an even smaller minority, than you had realised; surely I *must*, now, be a killjoy. Yet which, in fact, kills more joy: the killjoy who would deprive you of your joy in eating steak, which is just one of the joys open to you, or the kill-animal who puts an end to all the animal's joys along with its life?

Beware, however (if we may now take up the first item in 11 your Identikit portrait of me), how you call me a sentimentalist in this matter. I may be less of one than you are. I won't kill an animal in order to eat it, but I am no respecter of dead bodies as such. If our chemists discovered (as I'm sure they quickly would were there a demand) how to give tenderness and hygiene to the body of an animal which had died of old age, I would willingly eat it; and in principle that goes for human animals, too. In practice I suspect I should choke on a rissole which I knew might contain bits of Great-Aunt Emily (whether through love for or repulsion from her I am not quite sure), and I admit I might have to leave rational cannibalism to future generations brought up without my irrational prejudice (which is equally irrational whether prompted by love or by repulsion for the old lady). But you were accusing me, weren't you, of sentimentality and ignorance of economic realities. Have you thought how much of the world's potential food supply *you* unrealistically let go waste because of your sentimental compunction about eating your fellow citizens after they have lived out their natural lives?

If we are going to rear and kill animals for our food, I think 12 we have a moral obligation to spare them pain and terror in both processes, simply because they are sentient. I can't *prove* they are sentient; but then I have no proof *you* are. Even though you are articulate, whereas an animal can only scream or struggle, I have no assurance that your "It hurts" expresses anything like the intolerable sensations I experience in pain. I know, however, that when I visit my dentist and say "It hurts," I am grateful that he gives me the benefit of the doubt.

I don't myself believe that, even when we fulfill our mini-   13
mum obligation not to cause pain, we have the right to kill animals. I know I would have no right to kill you, however painlessly, just because I liked your flavour, and I am not in a position to judge that your life is worth more to you than the animal's to it. If anything, you probably value yours less; unlike the animal, you are capable of acting on an impulse to suicide. Christian tradition would permit me to kill the animal but not you, on the grounds that you have, and it hasn't, an immortal soul. I am not a Christian and do not avail myself of this licence; but if I were, I should in elementary justice see the soul theory as all the more reason to let the animal live out the one mortal life it has.

The only genuine moral problem is where there is a direct   14
clash between an animal's life and a human one. Our diet proposes no such clash, meat not being essential to a human life; I have sustained a very healthy one for ten years without. And in fact such clashes are much rarer in reality than in exam papers, where we are always being asked to rescue either our grandmother or a Rubens from a blazing house. . . .

The most genuine and painful clash is, of course, on the   15
subject of vivisection. To hold vivisection never justified is a hard belief. But so is its opposite. I believe it is never justified because I can see nothing (except our being able to get away with it) which lets us pick on animals that would not equally let us pick on idiot humans (who would be more useful) or, for the matter of that, on a few humans of any sort whom we might sacrifice for the good of the many. If we do permit vivisection, here if anywhere we are under the most stringent minimum obligations. The very least we must make sure of is that no experiment is ever duplicated, or careless, or done for mere teaching's sake or as a substitute for thinking. Know-ing how often, in every other sphere, pseudowork proliferates

in order to fill time and jobs, and how often activity substitutes for thought, and then reading the official statistics about vivisection, do you truly believe we *do* make sure? . . .

Our whole relation to animals is tinted by a fantasy—and a fallacy—about our toughness. We feel obliged to demonstrate we can take it; in fact, it is the animals who take it. So shy are we of seeming sentimental that we often disguise our humane impulses under "realistic" arguments: foxhunting is snobbish; factory-farmed food doesn't taste so nice. But foxhunting would still be an atrocity if it were done by authenticated, pedigreed proletarians, and so would factory-farming even if a way were found of making its corpses tasty. So, incidentally, would slavery, even if it were proved a hundred times more economically realistic than freedom. 16

The saddest and silliest of the superstitions to which we sacrifice animals is our belief that by killing them we ourselves somehow live more fully. We might live more fully by entering imaginatively into their lives. But shedding their blood makes us no more full-blooded. It is a mere myth, often connected with our myth about the *savoir vivre* and sexiness of the sunny south (which is how you manged to transform me into a frustrated British virgin in Florence). There is no law of nature which makes *savoir vivre* incompatible with "live and let live." The bullfighter who torments a bull to death and then castrates it of an ear has neither proved nor increased his own virility; he has merely demonstrated that he is a butcher with balletic tendencies. 17

Superstition and dread of sentimentality weight all our questions against the animals. We *don't* scrutinise vivisection rigorously—we somehow think it would be soft of us to do so, which we apparently think a worse thing to be than cruel. When, in February of this year, the House of Lords voted against a Bill banning animal acts from circuses, it was pointed out that animal-trainers would lose their jobs. (Come to think of it, many human-trainers must have lost theirs when it was decided to ban gladiator acts from circuses.) No one pointed out how many unemployed acrobats and jugglers would *get* jobs to replace the animals. (I'm not, you see 18 by the way, the sort of killjoy who wants to abolish the circus as such.) Similarly with the anthropomorphism argument, which works in both directions but is always wielded in one only. In the same House of Lords debate, Lady Summerskill, who had taken the humane side, was mocked by a noble lord on the grounds that were *she* shut up in a cage she would indeed suffer from mortification and the loss of her freedom, but an animal, not being human, wouldn't. Why did no one point out that a human, in such circumstances, dreadful as they are, would have every consolation of the human intellect and imagination, from reading books to analysing his circumstances and writing to the Home Secretary about them, whereas the animal suffers the raw terror of not comprehending what is being done to it?

In point of fact, I am the very opposite of an anthropomorphist. I don't hold animals superior or even equal to humans. The whole case for behaving decently to animals rests on the fact that we are the superior species. We are the species uniquely capable of imagination, rationality and moral choice—and that is precisely why we are under the obligation to recognise and respect the rights of animals.   19

For Study and Discussion

QUESTIONS FOR RESPONSE

1. How do you respond to Brophy's assertion that "The relationship of *homo sapiens* to other animals is one of unremitting exploitation"?
2. If you or any of your family hunts or fishes, how do you feel about Brophy's charge that such acts are immoral? What arguments can be made for hunting and fishing?

QUESTIONS ABOUT PURPOSE

1. What policies regarding animals would Brophy like to see outlawed in England and elsewhere? How could such policies be interpreted as exploitative?

2. Since Brophy is unlikely to persuade large numbers of people to stop eating meat, poultry, or fish, what changes in the ways such products are raised would she consider progress?

QUESTIONS ABOUT AUDIENCE

1. Brophy was writing for the British public. What do you know about British attitudes toward animals that might make the British public sympathetic to her arguments? To what extent do you think such attitudes can be found among Americans?
2. What knowledge about the way laboratory or farm animals are sometimes treated do you think an audience of college students is likely to share with Brophy?

QUESTIONS ABOUT STRATEGIES

1. How does Brophy go about getting her readers to put themselves in the situation of animals? How effective is her strategy?
2. Why does Brophy introduce a humorous tone in anticipating possible objections and accusations from her readers (see paragraphs 6, 7, 10, and 11)? What does she gain by this tactic?

QUESTIONS FOR DISCUSSION

1. What economic effects would follow in your region of the country if legislation were passed to adopt all or even some of Brophy's proposals about animal rights?
2. How do you react to the persona Brophy projects in this essay? Do you see her as a moral crusader, an admirable activist, a crackpot, or a sentimental idealist? Which, if any, of her reforms would you like to see go into effect?

Vicki Hearne was born in 1946 in Austin, Texas, and was educated at the University of California at Riverside and Stanford University. She has taught creative writing at the University of California at Davis and Yale University. Her own writing includes two volumes of poetry, *Nervous Horses* (1980) and *In Absence of Horses* (1984); a novel, *The White German Shepherd* (1988); and two extraordinary books of nonfiction, *Adam's Task: Calling Animals by Name* (1986) and *Bandit: Dossier of a Dangerous Dog* (1991)—all of which focus on the complicated relationship between humans and animals. An expert animal trainer, Hearne has established the National Pit Bull Terrier Defense Association and Literary Society. In "What's Wrong with Animal Rights?," reprinted from *Harper's*, Hearne argues that animal-rights activists have "got it all wrong" because they are preoccupied with the problems of animal suffering rather than the possibility of animal happiness.

What's Wrong with Animal Rights?

NOT ALL HAPPY animals are alike. A Doberman going over a hurdle after a small wooden dumbbell is sleek, all arcs of harmonious power. A basset hound cheerfully performing the same exercise exhibits harmonies of a more lugubrious nature. There are chimpanzees who love precision the way musicians or fanatical housekeepers or accomplished hypochondriacs do; others for whom happiness is a matter of invention and variation—chimp vaudevillians. There is a rhinoceros whose happiness, as near as I can make out, is in needing to be trained every morning, all over again, or else he "forgets" his circus routine, and in this you find a clue to the slow, deep, quiet chuckle of his happiness and to the glory of the beast. Happiness for Secretariat is in his ebullient bound, that joyful length of stride. For the draft horse or the weight-pull dog, happiness is of a different shape, more awesome and less obviously intelligent. When the pulling horse is at its most intense, the animal goes into himself, allocating all of the educated power that organizes his desire to dwell

---

Work is the foundation of the happiness a trainer and an animal discover together.

---

in fierce and delicate intimacy with that power, leans into the harness, and MAKES THAT SUCKER *MOVE*.

If we are speaking of human beings and use the phrase "animal happiness," we tend to mean something like "creature comforts." The emblems of this are the golden retriever rolling in the grass, the horse with his nose deep in the oats, the kitty by the fire. Creature comforts are important to animals—"Grub first, then ethics" is a motto that would describe many a wise Labrador retriever, and I have a pit bull named Annie whose continual quest for the perfect pillow inspires her to awesome feats. But there is something more to animals, a capacity for satisfactions that come from work in the fullest sense—what is known in philosophy and in this country's Declaration of Independence as "happiness." This is a sense of personal achievement, like the satisfaction felt by a good wood-carver or a dancer or a poet or an accomplished dressage horse. It is a happiness that, like the artist's, must come from something within the animal, something trainers call "talent." Hence, it cannot be imposed on the animal. But it is also something that does not come *ex nihilo*. If it had not been a fairly ordinary thing, in one part of the world, to teach young children to play the pianoforte, it is doubtful that Mozart's music would exist.

Happiness is often misunderstood as a synonym for pleasure or as an antonym for suffering. But Aristotle associated happiness with ethics—codes of behavior that urge us toward the sensation of getting it right, a kind of work that yields the "click" of satisfaction upon solving a problem or surmounting an obstacle. In his *Ethics,* Aristotle wrote, "If happiness is activity in accordance with excellence, it is reasonable that it should be in accordance with the highest excellence." Thomas Jefferson identified the capacity for happiness as one of the three fundamental rights on which all others are based: "life, liberty, and the pursuit of happiness." 3

I bring up this idea of happiness as a form of work because I am an animal trainer, and work is the foundation of the happiness a trainer and an animal discover together. I bring up these words also because they cannot be found in the lexicon of the animal-rights movement. This absence accounts for the uneasiness toward the movement of most people, who sense that rights advocates have a point but take it too far when they liberate snails or charge that goldfish at the county fair are suffering. But the problem with the animal-rights advocates is not that they take it too far, it's that they've got it all wrong. 4

Animal rights are built upon a misconceived premise that rights were created to prevent us from unnecessary suffering. You can't find an animal-rights book, video, pamphlet, or rock concert in which someone doesn't mention the Great Sentence, written by Jeremy Bentham in 1789. Arguing in favor of such rights, Bentham wrote: "The question is not, Can they *reason?* nor, can they *talk?* but, can they suffer?" 5

The logic of the animal-rights movement places suffering at the iconographic center of a skewed value system. The thinking of its proponents—given eerie expression in a virtually sado-pornographic sculpture of a tortured monkey that 6 won a prize for its compassionate vision—has collapsed into a perverse conundrum. Today the loudest voices calling for—demanding—the destruction of animals are the humane organizations. This is an inevitable consequence of the apotheosis of the drive to relieve suffering: Death is the ultimate release. To compensate for their contradictions, the humane movement has demonized, in this century and the last, those who made animal happiness their business: veterinarians, trainers, and the like. We think of Louis Pasteur as the man whose work saved you and me and your dog and cat from rabies, but antivivisectionists of the time claimed that rabies increased in areas where there were Pasteur Institutes.

An anti-rabies public-relations campaign mounted in England in the 1880s by the Royal Society for the Prevention of Cruelty to Animals and other organizations led to orders being issued to club any dog found not wearing a muzzle. England still has her cruel and unnecessary law that requires an animal to spend six months in quarantine before being allowed loose in the country. Most of the recent propaganda about pit bulls—the crazy claim that they "take hold with their front teeth while they chew away with their rear teeth" (which would imply, incorrectly, that they have double jaws) —can be traced to literature published by the Humane Society of the United States during the fall of 1987 and earlier. If your neighbors want your dog or horse impounded and destroyed because he is a nuisance—say the dog barks, or the horse attracts flies—it will be the local Humane Society to whom your neighbors turn for action.

In a way, everyone has the opportunity to know that the history of the humane movement is largely a history of miseries, arrests, prosecutions, and death. The Humane Society is the pound, the place with the decompression chamber or the lethal injections. You occasionally find worried letters about this in Ann Landers's column.

Animal-rights publications are illustrated largely with photographs of two kinds of animals—"Helpless Fluff" and "Agonized Fluff," the two conditions in which some people seem to prefer their animals, because any other version of an animal is too complicated for propaganda. In the introduction to his book *Animal Liberation,* Peter Singer says somewhat smugly that he and his wife have no animals and, in fact, don't much care for them. This is offered as evidence of his objectivity and ethical probity. But it strikes me as an odd, perhaps obscene, underpinning for an ethical project that encourages university and high school students to cherish their ignorance of, say, great bird dogs as proof of their devotion to animals.

I would like to leave these philosophers behind, for they are inept connoisseurs of suffering who might revere my Airedale for his capacity to scream when subjected to a blowtorch but not for his wit and courage, not for his natural good manners that are a gentle rebuke to ours. I want to celebrate the moment not long ago when, at his first dog show, my Airedale, Drummer, learned that there can be a public place where his work is respected. I want to celebrate his meticulousness, his happiness upon realizing at the dog show that no one would swoop down upon him and swamp him with the goo-goo excesses known as the "teddy-bear complex" but that people actually got out of his way, gave him room to work. I want to say, "There can be a six-and-a-half-month-old puppy who can care about accuracy, who can be fastidious, and whose fastidiousness will be a foundation for courage later." I want to say, "Leave my puppy alone!"

I want to leave the philosophers behind, but I cannot, in part because the philosophical problems that plague academicians of the animal-rights movement are illuminating. They wonder, do animals have rights or do they have interests? Or, if these rightists lead particularly unexamined lives, they dismiss that question as obvious (yes, of course, animals have rights, prima facie) and proceed to enumerate them, James Madison style. This leads to the issuance of bills of rights—the right to an environment, the right not to be used in medical experiments—and other forms of trivialization.

The calculus of suffering can be turned against the philosophers of festering flesh, even in the case of food animals, or exotic animals who perform in movies and circuses. It is true that it hurts to be slaughtered by man, but it doesn't hurt nearly as much as some of the cunningly cruel arrangements meted out by "Mother Nature." In Africa, 75 percent of the lions cubbed do not survive to the age of two. For those who make it to two, the average age at death is ten years. Asali, the movie and TV lioness, was still working at age twenty-one. There are fates worse than death, but twenty-one years of a close working relationship with Hubert Wells, Asali's trainer, is not one of them. Dorset sheep and polled Herefords would not exist at all were they not in a symbiotic relationship with human beings.

A human being living in the "wild"—somewhere, say,   13 without the benefits of medicine and advanced social organizations—would probably have a life expectancy of from thirty to thirty-five years. A human being living in "captivity"—in, say, a middle-class neighborhood of what the Centers for Disease Control call a Metropolitan Statistical Area—has a life expectancy of seventy or more years. For orangutans in the wild in Borneo and Malaysia, the life expectancy is thirty-five years; in captivity, fifty years. The wild is not a suffering-free zone or all that frolicsome a location.

The questions asked by animal-rights activists are flawed,   14 because they are built on the concept that the origin of rights is in the avoidance of suffering rather than in the pursuit of happiness. The question that needs to be asked—and that will put us in closer proximity to the truth—is not, do they have rights? or, what are those rights? but rather, what is a right?

Rights originate in committed relationships and can be   15 found, both intact and violated, wherever one finds such relationships—in social compacts, within families, between animals, and between people and nonhuman animals. This is as true when the nonhuman animals in question are lions or parakeets as when they are dogs. It is my Airedale whose excellencies have my attention at the moment, so it is with reference to him that I will consider the question, what is a right?

When I imagine situations in which it naturally arises that   16

A defends or honors or respects B's rights, I imagine situations in which the relationship between A and B can be indicated with a possessive pronoun. I might say, "Leave her alone, she's my daughter" or, "That's what she wants, and she is my daughter. I think I am bound to honor her wants." Similarly, "Leave her alone, she's my mother." I am more tender of the happiness of my mother, my father, my child, than I am of other people's family members; more tender of my friends' happiness than your friends' happinesses, unless you and I have a mutual friend.

Possession of a being by another has come into more and more disrepute, so that the common understanding of one person possessing another is slavery. But the important detail about the kind of possessive pronoun that I have in mind is reciprocity: If I have a friend, she has a friend. If I have a daughter, she has a mother. The possessive does not bind one of us while freeing the other; it cannot do that. Moreover, should the mother reject the daughter, the word that applies is "disown." The form of disowning that most often appears in the news is domestic violence. Parents abuse children; husbands batter wives. 17

Some cases of reciprocal possessives have built-in limitations, such as "my patient / my doctor" or "my student / my teacher" or "my agent / my client." Other possessive relations are extremely limited but still remarkably binding: "my neighor" and "my country" and "my president." 18

The responsibilities and the ties signaled by reciprocal possession typically are hard to dissolve. It can be as difficult to give up an enemy as to give up a friend, and often the one becomes the other, as though the logic of the possessive pronoun outlasts the forms it chanced to take at a given moment, as though we were stuck with one another. In these bindings, nearly inextricable, are found the origin of our rights. They imply a possessiveness but also recognize an acknowledgment by each side of the other's existence. 19

The idea of democracy is dependent on the citizens' having knowledge of the government; that is, realizing that the government exists and knowing how to claim rights against 20

it. I know this much because I get mail from the government
and see its "representatives" running about in uniforms.
Whether I actually have any rights in relationship to the
government is less clear, but the idea that I do is symbolized
by the right to vote. I obey the government, and, in theory,
it obeys me, by counting my ballot, reading the *Miranda*
warning to me, agreeing to be bound by the Constitution.
My friend obeys me as I obey her; the government "obeys"
me to some extent, and, to a different extent, I obey it.

What kind of thing can my Airedale, Drummer, have   21
knowledge of? He can know that I exist and through that
knowledge can claim his happiness, with varying degrees of
success, both with me and against me. Drummer can also
know about larger human or dog communities than the one
that consists only of him and me. There is my household—
the other dogs, the cats, my husband. I have had enough
dogs on campuses to know that he can learn that Yale exists
as a neighborhood or village. My older dog, Annie, not only
knows that Yale exists but can tell Yalies from townies, as I
learned while teaching there during labor troubles.

Dogs can have elaborate conceptions of human social   22
structures, and even of something like their rights and responsibilities within them, but these conceptions are never
elaborate enough to construct a rights relationship between
a dog and the state, or a dog and the Humane Society. Both
of these are concepts that depend on writing and memo-
randa, officers in uniform, plaques and seals of authority. All
of these are literary constructs, and all of them are beyond a
dog's ken, which is why the mail carrier who doesn't also
happen to be a dog's friend is forever an intruder—this is why
dogs bark at mailmen.

It is clear enough that natural rights relations can arise   23
between people and animals. Drummer, for example, can
insist, "Hey, let's go outside and do something!" if I have
been at my computer several days on end. He can both refuse
to accept various of my suggestions and tell me when he fears
for his life—such as the time when the huge, white flapping

flag appeared out of nowhere, as it seemed to him, on the town green one evening when we were working. I can (and do) say to him either, "Oh, you don't have to worry about that" or, "Uh oh, you're right, Drum, that guy looks dangerous." Just as the government and I—two different species of organism—have developed improvised ways of communicating, such as the vote, so Drummer and I have worked out a number of ways to make our expressions known. Largely through obedience, I have taught him a fair amount about how to get responses from me. Obedience is reciprocal; you cannot get responses from a dog to whom you do not respond accurately. I have enfranchised him in a relationship to me by educating him, creating the conditions by which he can achieve a certain happiness specific to a dog, maybe even specific to an Airedale, inasmuch as this same relationship has allowed me to plumb the happiness of being a trainer and writing this article.

Instructions in this happiness are given terms that are alien   24
to a culture in which liver treats, fluffy windup toys, and miniature sweaters are confused with respect and work. Jack Knox, a sheepdog trainer originally from Scotland, will shake his crook at a novice handler who makes a promiscuous move to praise a dog, and will call out in his Scottish accent, "Eh! Eh! Get back, get BACK! Ye'll no be abusin' the dogs like that in my clinic." America is a nation of abused animals, Knox says, because we are always swooping at them with praise, "no gi'ing them their freedom." I am reminded of Rainer Maria Rilke's account in which the Prodigal Son leaves—has to leave—because everyone loves him, even the dogs love him, and he has no path to the delicate and fierce truth of himself. Unconditional praise and love, in Rilke's story, disenfranchise us, distract us from what truly excites our interest.

In the minds of some trainers and handlers, praise is dis-   25
honesty. Paradoxically, it is a kind of contempt for animals that masquerades as a reverence for helplessness and suffering. The idea of freedom means that you do not, at least not while Jack Knox is nearby, helpfully guide your dog through

the motions of, say, herding over and over—what one trainer calls "explainy-wainy." This is rote learning. It works tolerably well on some handlers, because people have vast unconscious minds and can store complex pre-programmed behaviors. Dogs, on the other hand, have almost no unconscious minds, so they can learn only by thinking. Many children are like this until educated out of it.

If I tell my Airedale to sit and stay on the town green, and   26
someone comes up and burbles, "What a pretty thing you are," he may break his stay to go for a caress. I pull him back and correct him for breaking. Now he holds his stay because I have blocked his way to movement but not because I have punished him. (A correction blocks one path as it opens another for desire to work; punishment blocks desire and opens nothing.) He holds his stay now, and—because the stay opens this possibility of work, new to a heedless young dog— he watches. If the person goes on talking, and isn't going to gush with praise, I may heel Drummer out of his stay and give him an "Okay" to make friends. Sometimes something about the person makes Drummer feel that reserve is in order. He responds to an insincere approach by sitting still, going down into himself, and thinking, "This person has no business pawing me. I'll sit very still, and he will go away." If the person doesn't take the hint from Drummer, I'll give the pup a little backup by saying, "Please don't pet him, he's working," even though he was not under any command.

The pup reads this, and there is a flicker of a working trust   27
now stirring in the dog. Is the pup grateful? When the stranger leaves, does he lick my hand, full of submissive blandishments? This one doesn't. This one says nothing at all, and I say nothing much to him. This is a working trust we are developing, not a mutual-congratulation society. My backup is praise enough for him; the use he makes of my support is praise enough for me.

Listening to a dog is often praise enough. Suppose it is   28
just after dark and we are outside. Suddenly there is a shout from the house. The pup and I both look toward the shout and then toward each other: "What do you think?" I don't

so much as cock my head, because Drummer is growing up, and I want to know what he thinks. He takes a few steps toward the house, and I follow. He listens again and comprehends that it's just Holly, who at fourteen is much given to alarming cries and shouts. He shrugs at me and goes about his business. I say nothing. To praise him for this performance would make about as much sense as praising a human being for the same thing. Thus:

> A. *What's that?*
> B. *I don't know. [Listens] Oh, it's just Holly.*
> C. *What a goooooood human being!*
> B. *Huh?*

This is one small moment in a series of like moments that   29
will culminate in an Airedale who on a Friday will have the discrimination and confidence required to take down a man who is attacking me with a knife and on Saturday clown and play with the children at the annual Orange Empire Dog Club Christmas party.

People who claim to speak for animal rights are increas-   30
ingly devoted to the idea that the very keeping of a dog or a horse or a gerbil or a lion is in and of itself an offense. The more loudly they speak, the less likely they are to be in a rights relation to any given animal, because they are spending so much time in airplanes or transmitting fax announcements of the latest Sylvester Stallone anti-fur rally. In a 1988 *Harper's* forum, for example, Ingrid Newkirk, the national director of People for the Ethical Treatment of Animals, urged that domestic pets be spayed and neutered and ultimately phased out. She prefers, it appears, wolves—and wolves someplace else—to Airedales and, by a logic whose interior structure is both emotionally and intellectually forever closed to Drummer, claims thereby to be speaking for "animal rights."

She is wrong. I am the only one who can own up to my   31
Airedale's inalienable rights. Whether or not I do it perfectly at any given moment is no more refutation of this point than

whether I am perfectly my husband's mate at any given moment refutes the fact of marriage. Only people who know Drummer, and whom he can know, are capable of this relationship. PETA and the Humane Society and the ASPCA and the Congress and NOW—as institutions—do have the power to affect my ability to grant rights to Drummer but are otherwise incapable of creating conditions or laws or rights that would increase his happiness. Only Drummer's owner has the power to obey him—to obey who he is and what he is capable of—deeply enough to grant him his rights and open up the possibility of happiness.

For Study and Discussion

QUESTIONS FOR RESPONSE

1. What impression does the author of the essay make on you? How do you think her work as an animal trainer affects her attitudes toward animal-rights activists?
2. How do you respond to Hearne's belief that animals can have work in which they take satisfaction? If you can, give examples that might demonstrate such possibilities.

QUESTIONS ABOUT PURPOSE

1. What kinds of animal-rights activists is Hearne most critical of? Can you think of issues about animal rights that she doesn't address?
2. What kind of relationship between animals and their owners would Hearne like to see? How does that ideal relationship fit in with her ideas about animal rights?

QUESTIONS ABOUT AUDIENCE

1. What groups of people do you think are likely to respond positively to Hearne's essay? Why? To what extent do you fit into that group?
2. If you are or have been an animal owner, what experiences have

you had that would reinforce or contradict Hearne's claims about how animals should be treated?

QUESTIONS ABOUT STRATEGIES

1. Hearne's images and language in the first paragraph are highly anthropomorphic—that is, through her choice of language she attributes human qualities and emotions to the animals she describes. What effect do you think she is trying to achieve with her readers?
2. In paragraphs 9 and 30, Hearne uses a sarcastic tone and extreme examples to criticize certain animal-rights activists. What effect does this strategy have on you? What do you think she hopes to accomplish by using this approach?

QUESTIONS FOR DISCUSSION

1. What are the major differences between the kind of animal rights Brigid Brophy argues for in "The Rights of Animals" and the kind of animal rights Hearne is talking about in her essay? On what guidelines for dealing with animals do you think the two authors would be likely to agree?
2. What do you think of Hearne's argument that animals suffer in the wild more than they do in captivity?

WILLIAM STYRON

William Styron was born in 1925 in Newport News, Virginia, and was educated at Duke University. His first three novels—*Lie Down in Darkness* (1951), *The Long March* (1957), and *Set This House on Fire* (1960)—established him as one of the most gifted writers of his generation. With the publication of *The Confessions of Nat Turner* (1967), an account of the "only effective, sustained revolt in the annals of American Negro slavery," he became one of the most controversial. The novel was awarded the Pulitzer Prize, but it provoked considerable debate in the racially explosive atmosphere of the sixties. Styron's other work includes a play, *In the Clap Stick* (1973), a widely acclaimed novel, *Sophie's Choice* (1976), and a collection of stories, *Tidewater Morning* (1993). His nonfiction consists of a collection of essays, *This Quiet Dust and Other Writings* (1982), and a powerful memoir, *Darkness Visible: A Memoir of Madness* (1990). "The Habit" first appeared in *The New York Review of Books* on the occasion of the publication of *The Consumers Union Report on Smoking* (1963). Styron uses the "inescapable" evidence from that report to construct a persuasive argument for giving up a "mortally corrupting addiction."

The Habit

T HE LAMENTABLE HISTORY of the cigarette is that of a mortally corrupting addiction having been embraced by millions of people in the spirit of childlike innocence. It is a history which is also strikingly brief. Cigarettes began to be

he is against it

497

manufactured extensively around the turn of the century, but it was not until as recently as 1921 that cigarettes overtook chewing tobacco, as well as pipes and cigars, in per capita consumption, and the 1930s were well along before cigarette smoking became the accepted thing for ladies.

The popularity of cigarettes was inevitable and overwhelming. They were not offensive in close quarters, nor messy like pipes and cigars. They were easily portable. They did not look gross and unseemly in a lady's mouth. They were cheap to manufacture, and they were inhalable. Unlike the great majority of pipe and cigar smokers, whose pleasure is predominantly oral and contemplative, most cigarette smokers inhale

2

Only nuclear fallout exceeds cigarette smoking in gravity as a public health problem.

deep into their lungs with bladelike, rhythmic savagery, inflicting upon themselves in miniature a particularly abrasive form of air pollution. Further, the very fact of inhalation seems to enhance the cigarette's addictive power. Unhappily, few suspected the consequences in terms of health until long after cigarette smoking had gained its colossal momentum. That this type of auto-contamination is a major cause of lung cancer—that it is also a prime causative factor in deaths from coronary artery disease, bronchitis, asthma, emphysema, among other afflictions—was established, and for the first time well publicized, only a decade ago. The effect this knowledge has had upon the public consciousness may be suggested by the fact that sales this year reached the galactic sum of one-half trillion cigarettes—one hundred billion more than in 1953. There is something historically intimidating in the idea that cigarette smoking as a mass diversion and a raging increase in lung cancer have both come about during the lifetime of those who are now no more than fifty years old. It is the very *recentness* of the phenomenon which helps make it so shocking. The hard truth is that human beings have never in such a brief space of time, and in so grand and guileless a multitude, embraced a habit whose unwholesome effects not only would totally outweigh the meager satisfactions but would hasten the deaths of a large proportion of the people who indulged in it. Certainly (and there seems little doubt that the Surgeon General's report will make this clear) only nuclear fallout exceeds cigarette smoking in gravity as a public health problem.

For its lucid presentation of the medical evidence alone,   3 *The Consumers Union Report on Smoking* would be a valuable document. "The conclusion is inescapable," the *Report* begins, "and even spokesmen for the cigarette industry rarely seek to escape it: we are living in the midst of a major lung cancer epidemic. This epidemic hit men first and hardest, but has affected women as well. It cannot be explained away by such factors as improved diagnosis. And there is reason to believe that the worst is yet to come." Yet despite this minatory beginning the tone throughout is one of caution and reasonableness, and the authors—who manage an accomplished prose style rare in such collective undertakings—marshal their facts with such efficiency and persuasion that it is hard to imagine anyone but a fool or a tobacco lobbyist denying the close association between smoking and lung cancer. Yet, of course, not only lung cancer. The *Report* quotes, for instance, data based on an extensive study of smokers and non-smokers among English physicians, where the death rate *from all causes* was found to be doubled among heavy cigarette smokers in the group of men past 65, and quadrupled in the group 35 to 44. And the *Report* adds, with the modest and constructive irony that makes the book, if not exactly a joy, then agreeable to read: "These death rates among smokers are perhaps the least controversial of all the findings to date. For with respect to any particular disease there is always the possibility, however remote, that mistaken diagnosis and other conceivable errors may cast doubt on the statistics. But death is easily diagnosed."

In the end, however, what makes the *Report*'s message   4

supportable to those distracted souls among the millions of American smokers who may wish to kick the habit—or who, having kicked the habit, may wonder if it is not too late—is a kind of muted optimism. For all present evidence seems to indicate that the common cocktail party rationalization ("I've smoked too long to stop now, the damage is done") has no real basis in fact. In research carried out by the American Cancer Society, microscopic studies of the lung tissues of ex-smokers have shown a process in which precancerous cells are dying out instead of flourishing and reproducing as in the tissues of continuing smokers. Here the *Report* states, in regard to a carefully matched group composed in equal numbers of nonsmokers, ex-smokers and smokers: "Metaplastic cells with altered nuclei [i.e., precancerous cells] were found in 1.2 percent of the slides from the lungs of nonsmokers, as compared with 6.0 for ex-smokers—and *93.2 percent* for current smokers."

Certainly such evidence, combined with the fact that ex-   5
smokers have a lung cancer death rate which ranges down to one fifth of that of smokers who continue to smoke, should be of the greatest practical interest to anyone who ponders whether it may be worthwhile abandoning what is, after all, a cheerless, grubby, fumbling addiction. (Only the passion of a convert could provoke these last words. The *Report* was an aid to my stopping a two-pack-a-day habit which commenced in early infancy. Of course, stopping smoking may be in itself a major problem, one of psychological complexity. For myself, after two or three days of great flaccidity of spirit, an aimless oral yearning, aching moments of hunger at the pit of the stomach, and an awful intermittent urge to burst into tears, the problem resolved itself, and in less than a week all craving vanished. Curiously, for the first time in my life, I developed a racking cough, but this, too, disappeared. A sense of smugness, a kind of fatness of soul, is the reward for such a struggle. The intensity of the addiction varies, however, and some people find the ordeal fearfully difficult, if not next to impossible. I do have an urgent suspicion, though, that the greatest barrier to a termination of the habit is the

dread of some Faustian upheaval, when in fact that deprivation, while momentarily oppressive, is apt to prove not really
cruel at all.)

But if the *Report* is splendidly effective as a caveat, it may 6
be read for its sociological insights as well. Certainly the
history of commerce has few instances of such shameful ab-
dication of responsibility as that displayed by the cigarette
industry when in 1952 the "health scare," as it is so win-
somely known in the trade, brought about the crisis which
will reach a head in this month's report by the Surgeon
General. It seems clear that the industry, instead of trying to
forestall the inevitable with its lies and evasions, might have
acquitted itself with some honor had it made what the *Report*
calls the only feasible choices: to have urged caution on
smokers, to have given money to independent research organizations, to have avoided propaganda and controversy in
favor of unbiased inquiry. At the very least the industry might
have soft-pedaled or, indeed, silenced its pitch to young people. But panic and greed dominated the reaction, and during
the decade since the smoking–lung cancer link was made
public, the official position of the industry has been that, in
the matter of lung cancer, the villain is any and everything
but the cigarette. Even the American Cancer Society is in on
the evil plot and, in the words of one industry spokesman,
"relies almost wholly upon health scare propaganda to raise
millions of dollars from a gullible public."

Meanwhile, $200 million was spent last year on cigarette 7
ballyhoo, and during these last crucial ten years the annual
advertising expenditure has increased 134 percent—a vast
amount of it, of course, going to entice the very young. One
million of these young people, according to the American
Public Health Association, will die of smoking-induced lung
cancer before they reach the age of seventy years. "Between
the time a kid is eighteen and twenty-one, he's going to make
the basic decision to smoke or not to smoke," says L. W.
Bruff, advertising director of Liggett & Myers. "If he does
decide to smoke, we want to get him." I have never met Mr.
Bruff, but in my mind's eye I see him, poised like a cormorant

above those doomed minnows, and I am amused by the refinement, the weight of conscience, the delicate interplay of intellectual and moral alternatives which go into the making of such a prodigious thought. As the report demonstrates, however, Mr. Bruff is only typical of the leaders of an industry which last year received a bounty of $7 billion from 63 million American smokers. Perhaps the tragic reality is that neither this estimable report nor that of the Surgeon General can measurably affect, much less really change, such awesome figures.

For Study and Discussion

QUESTIONS FOR RESPONSE

1. In spite of the well-publicized dangers of smoking and the increasingly stringent regulations to restrict it, many young people continue to start smoking in high school or college. How do you account for their behavior?
2. How many people do you know who smoke? What generalizations can you make about them or about smokers in general? What might influence these smokers to quit the habit?

QUESTIONS ABOUT PURPOSE

1. What do you think Styron hopes to achieve by his attacks on the tobacco industry? What action does he want his readers to take?
2. What does he hope to accomplish with statistics in paragraphs 3 and 4?

QUESTIONS ABOUT AUDIENCE

1. Styron's readers fall into three groups: smokers, nonsmokers or former smokers, and tobacco industry employees and executives who may or may not smoke. How do you think their responses to this essay will differ?
2. Styron seems to assume that most readers who are still smokers would like to quit. In your experience, does that assumption seem justified? If it is, how would this essay appeal to them?

QUESTIONS ABOUT STRATEGIES

1. How does Styron use his own history as a smoker to strengthen his argument? How effective is this strategy?
2. Styron combines authoritative statistics and strong emotional appeal in this essay. How do they complement each other? Which do you find more persuasive?

QUESTIONS FOR DISCUSSION

1. When this essay was written, over thirty years ago, shortly before the Surgeon General's report on smoking appeared, Styron was not optimistic about many people giving up smoking. What do you know about how much smoking habits have changed since that time? What combination of factors has caused the change?
2. What do you know about current and recent activities of the tobacco industry? Considering that information, what do you think of Styron's analysis of the industry?

Wendell Berry was born in 1934 in Henry County, Kentucky, and was educated at the University of Kentucky. For the last thirty years he has taught English at the University of Kentucky and has written about the people and predicaments in his native landscape. His poems appear in several volumes—such as *Openings* (1968) and *Findings* (1969)—as well as in *Collected Poems 1957–1982* (1985), and his novels include *Remembering* (1988) and *Watch with Me* (1994). He is perhaps best known for his essays, which have appeared in collections such as *The Long-Legged House* (1969), *Continuous Harmony* (1972), *The Gift of Good Land* (1981), and *Sex, Economy, Freedom and Community* (1993). In "The Problem of Tobacco," reprinted from the last-named volume, Berry argues his way through the complicated issues involved in his support for the federal "tobacco program."

The Problem of Tobacco

THOUGH I WOULD just as soon get along without it, an humbling awareness of the complexity of moral issues is said to be a good thing. If such an awareness is, in fact, good—and if I, in fact, have it—I have tobacco to thank for it. To many people nowadays, there is nothing complex about the moral issue of tobacco. They are simply against it. They will sit in their large automobiles, spewing a miasma of toxic gas into the atmosphere, and they will thank you for not smoking a cigarette. They will sit in a smoke-free bar, drinking stingers and other lethal beverages, and wonder how smokers can have so little respect for their bodies. They will

1

complacently stand in the presence of a coal-fired power plant or a nuclear power plant or a bomb factory or a leaking chemical plant, and they will wonder how a tobacco farmer can have so little regard for public health. Well, as always, it matters whose ox is being gored. And tobacco, I am obliged to confess, is my ox.

I was born in tobacco country, into a family preoccupied with the cultivation, the economy, and the politics of tobacco. Many of my closest and dearest friends have been and are tobacco growers. I have worked in the crop from early childhood until now. I have liked and often enjoyed the work. I

2

We are inconsistent in condemning tobacco and excusing other, more damaging addictions.

---

love the crop in all its stages. I think tobacco is a beautiful plant. I love the lore and the conversation of tobacco growing. I love the smell of tobacco and of tobacco smoke.

Burley tobacco, as I first knew it, was produced with an intensity of care and a refinement of skill that far exceeded that given to any food crop that I know about. It was a handmade crop; between plant bed and warehouse, every plant, every leaf, was looked at, touched, appraised, lifted, and carried many times. The experience of growing up in a community in which virtually everybody was passionately interested in the quality of a local product was, I now see, a rare privilege. As a boy and a young man, I worked with men who were as fiercely insistent on the ways and standards of their discipline as artists—which is what they were. In those days, to be recognized as a "tobacco man" was to be accorded an honor such as other cultures bestowed on the finest hunters or warriors or poets. The accolade "He's a *tobacco* man!" would be accompanied by a shake of the head

3

to indicate that such surpassing excellence was, finally, a mystery; there was more to it than met the eye.

It is hardly too much to say that we were a tobacco culture. 4
Our nationality was more or less American. Our religion was nominally and sometimes approximately Christian. But our culture was largely determined by tobacco, just as the culture of the Plains Indians was determined by the horse. It was our staple crop, the cornerstone of our economy. Because of "the program"—the federal regulations that limited production in order to control price—the tobacco market was the only market on which the farmer was dependably not a victim. Though we practiced a diversified way of farming, our farming focused on tobacco. The rhythm of our farming year, as of our financial year, was set by the annual drama of the tobacco crop.

Because so much handwork was involved in the growing 5
of tobacco, it was a very sociable crop. "Many hands make light work," people said, and so one of the most attractive customs of our tobacco culture was "swapping work." The times of hardest work were "setting," in the spring, when the plants were moved from the beds to the patches; "cutting," in late summer, when the plants were harvested and hung in curing barns; and "stripping," in the fall and winter, when the cured leaves were removed from the stalks, graded, and tied in "hands" for the market. At these times, neighbors helped each other in order to bring together the many hands that lightened work. Thus, these times of hardest work were also times of big meals and of much talk, storytelling, and laughter.

To me, this was a good kind of life, and it provided excel- 6
lent experience for a boy. To work in the company of men and women who were superb workers, to learn their characters, to glean from their talk an intimate history of the people, farms, and fields that were one's true nationality—this was an education of inestimable value. To me, the tobacco patches and tobacco barns and stripping rooms of my native countryside have been an indispensable school. And so I cannot help but look on our tobacco culture with considerable affection and gratitude.

There is another, more practical benefit of tobacco that 7
must be mentioned. For a sloping, easily eroded countryside
such as I live in and such as comprises much of the "tobacco
belt," tobacco has been an ideal crop, because it has permitted significant income to be realized from small acreages,
thereby sparing us the inevitable damage of extensive plowing, and because it has conformed well to the pattern of
livestock farming. Tobacco, of course, has not been invariably
kind to the land; grown on steep hillsides, as it often was, it
was as damaging as any other row crop. But in general, I
believe that a considerable saving of soil can be attributed to
tobacco. If tobacco farmers had attempted to realize an
equivalent income from corn, neither they nor their fields
would have lasted long.

Perhaps nobody brought up as I was can speak of tobacco 8
without at least some affection. I have said as much good of
it as I know. But of course everything to be said about
tobacco is not good. There have always been people who
disliked it. There has long been a vague religious antipathy
to it, though in tobacco country, to date, churches have
generally been glad enough to receive their tithes from it.
Some have thought, and not without justification, that smoking or chewing or dipping is a "filthy habit." Though it was
often said, when I was a boy, that smoking would "stunt your
growth," we did not know any smokers who had been
stunted—unless, perhaps, they had been intended to be giants.

Tobacco became an authentic moral issue only within the 9
last thirty years and for two reasons: the case against it, as a
serious threat to health, became extremely persuasive; and in
spite of this widely recognized threat, tobacco has continued
to be grown, and tobacco products continue to be advertised
and sold. There is, in my opinion, no way to deny that this
is a most serious moral predicament and no way to evade the
questions raised by it or to lighten their gravity.

Because I have written a good bit about farmers who raise 10
tobacco and because I have often spoken in defense of the
tobacco program, I often fall into conversations on the subject with people who are indignant. These conversations are

always fragmentary because of the great complexity of the subject, and I have never been satisfied with any of them. And so I would like now to attempt something like a complete dialogue:

"Do you smoke? I am asked."   11
And I reply, "No."   12
"Did you ever smoke?"   13
"Yes, from about the age of fourteen until I was thirty."   14
"Why did you quit?"   15
"Two reasons. One, I had young children."   16
"So you do agree that smoking tobacco is unhealthy!"   17
"Yes, though I still have some questions on the subject.   18
Since, for example, there is nobody today whose lungs are polluted *only* with tobacco smoke, I would like to know what contribution other pollutants may make to 'tobacco-caused' diseases. And since nobody now smokes chemical-free tobacco, I would like to know the effect of the residues of agricultural chemicals in the tobacco. But, yes, I do believe that smoke inhalation is unhealthy."

"But most modern smoke is inhaled unwillingly. Why   19
would anyone willingly inhale smoke that is dangerous to health?"

"Well, to start with, sociability."   20
"Sociability?"   21
"Tobacco smoke is fragrant, and smoking at its best is   22
convivial or ceremonious and pleasant. Some would say it is a comfort. But you haven't asked me my second reason for quitting."

"What was your second reason?"   23
"Addiction. I didn't like being addicted. I had got so I   24
could smoke a cigarette without even knowing it. There was no pleasure in that."

"You're against addiction, then?"   25
"I'm against addiction to all things that are damaging and   26
unnecessary."

"Like what?"   27
"Speed, comfort, violence, usury."   28

"You didn't mention drugs."   29

"Those, too. Legal drugs, too. And then there are some   30
damaging things that are only necessary *because* we are addicted to them."

"For instance?"   31

"Petroleum. Most poisons. Automobiles."   32

"You're trying to change the subject, aren't you?"   33

"No, I'm just pointing to one of the dangers of the to-   34
bacco controversy."

"And what might that be?"   35

"That it is, to some extent, a red herring. In calling atten-   36
tion to the dangers of one kind of addiction, the tobacco
controversy distracts from the much greater danger that we
are an addictive society—that our people are rushing from
one expensive and dangerous fix to another, from drugs to
war to useless merchandise to various commercial thrills, and
that our corporate pushers are addicted to our addictions."

"But say we are an addictive society, does that make the   37
tobacco addiction right or excusable?"

"Of course not. It only means we ought to be aware of   38
our inconsistency in condemning tobacco and excusing other
damaging addictions, some of which are much more threatening than tobacco. Many people would like to think that
our diseases are caused by one simple thing, like tobacco,
which can be easily blamed on one group and fairly easily
given up. But of course they are fooling themselves. One
reason that people die of diseases is that they have grown old
enough to die of something; they are mortal, a fact that
modern humans don't like to face. Another reason is that as
a people we live unhealthy lives. We breathe unhealthy air,
drink unhealthy water, eat unhealthy food, eat too much, do
no physical work, and so forth."

"But the question remains, how can you have quit smok-   39
ing yourself because you recognize the danger and yet support the tobacco economy?"

"I don't support the tobacco economy, which involves   40
much that I don't like—seductive advertising, for one thing.
I support the tobacco program."

"What is that?"   41

"To risk oversimplification, it is an arrangement, spon-   42
sored by the federal government, voted for by the farmers,
by which they agree to limit production in order to secure a
livable return on investment and labor. This strategy of production control is commonplace in other productive indus-
tries but rare in farming. And the tobacco program has
worked well. In my part of the country, it has ensured the
survival of thousands of small farmers for more than half a
century."

"Why should these people receive a government subsidy   43
for growing a crop that the government acknowledges to be
dangerous to health?"

"It is not a subsidy. The tobacco that receives a top bid   44
that is less than the support price is placed under loan by the
program, the title to the crop remaining with the farmer until
its ultimate sale by the cooperative. The government supplies
the loan, which is repaid with interest and all expenses. And
for several years now, tobacco farmers and manufacturers
have been assessed one cent each per pound to pay administrative and other costs so that the program can be operated
at no net cost to taxpayers."

"But it's tobacco they're growing. To support the program   45
is to support tobacco and everything that goes with it."

"Well, let me ask *you* a question. Do you think everybody   46
is going to quit smoking?"

"I suppose, considering the failure of Prohibition and the   47
current popularity of illegal drugs, the answer probably is
no."

"And there is a probability, isn't there, that condemnations   48
and warnings, even proofs of danger, will make tobacco more
attractive to some people?"

"Yes, I suppose so."   49

"And if some people continue to use it, other people will   50
continue to grow it—is that not right?"

"I suppose it is."   51

"And so, if you destroyed the program, destroying in the   52 process the farmers who depend on the program, who would grow the tobacco?"

"I haven't thought much about that. Large corporate 53 growers under contract to the tobacco companies? Cheap laborers in Third World countries? I don't know."

"Most of the farmers who now grow it would, at any rate, 54 be out of business."

"Probably." 55

"And what would become of them?" 56

"They could move to the city." 57

"And into other work?" 58

"Maybe." 59

"Or they could go on welfare?" 60

"Maybe." 61

"But you don't know. You do admit that whatever hap- 62 pened, the loss of the program would be extremely painful, disorienting, and costly for many thousands of families?"

"Yes, I will admit that." 63

"So, you see, to support the program is only to say that if 64 tobacco is to be grown, you want it to be grown by the people who have always grown it—not by the sort for whom the failure of these people would be a 'window of opportunity.'"

"Now let me ask *you* something. If these people can't make 65 it on their own, if they must always be helped by some sort of program or other, why not let them fail? Is that not the way things should be—and, in fact, are? Adapt or die. The survival of the fittest. If they can't survive, they deserve to fail. And, yes, their failure then properly becomes a 'window of opportunity' for somebody else."

"Well, I would question the historical validity of that idea 66 and that attitude. I don't believe that any human community can be shown to have survived by the principle of all-out competition among its members, which the Bible (if that matters to you) explicitly forbids. And the implications for land use of that principle are absolutely ruinous. It makes impossible the establishment of a competent, long-lasting, soil-husbanding community on the land. Your 'fittest,' you know, would be the biggest or the wealthiest but not the best caretakers."

"The fact remains: you support the people who grow 67 tobacco that supports an addiction you say you don't support."

"You bet I do! They are my own people, who are as good 68 as other people."

"You can be a good person and grow tobacco?" 69

"Why don't you say what you really have in mind: Can 70 you be a good person and be a sinner? Our religious tradition certainly says you can. People have faults and they have virtues. Which they have the most of is a judgment we are not supposed to make, for the very good reason that none of us can be sure of having all the evidence."

"But our religious tradition also warns us again and again 71 of the danger of choosing a known evil over a known good."

"That's true. But for most tobacco farmers, the growing 72 of tobacco has not been so clearly a moral choice. They did not choose to grow tobacco in the same sense that David chose to send Uriah into battle. Many of them began growing tobacco before the moral issue arose. They were simply born to the crop, as were the generations before them, going back to the seventeenth century. The younger ones—the ones born, say, after the surgeon general's report of 1964—were either born to tobacco growing or they bought into it when they bought their farms. For them, tobacco growing came, literally, with the territory. In tobacco country, the choice not to grow tobacco (in the circumstances of the present agricultural economy) is tantamount to a choice not to farm."

"And yet now they all know the argument against tobacco. 73 Now it is an evil that they knowingly consent to."

"That is true. They consent to it in the same way that 74 people involved in the present energy economy consent to a whole array of toxic exhausts and other results that they know to be evil. They consent, they are guilty, and they can't see their way out."

"You are going on as if you expect to win this argument. 75 Do you?"

"Do I expect to argue my way to some uncontestable 76
justification of tobacco growing? No. I am arguing only that
tobacco growing is a complex, difficult issue. And I am explaining why I choose to stand with my people in their
dilemma."

"In other words, why you don't dissociate yourself from 77
this evil. Why don't you?"

"Why don't I dissociate myself from automobiles? Because 78
I don't see how to do it—not yet. And I don't want to
dissociate myself from the world."

"Well, I've heard you speak of some things—war, for in- 79
stance, and the nuclear power industry, and the use of throwaway containers—as if you would like to see those evils
stopped at once. Why not tobacco? If we can't stop people
from using it, why don't we immediately put an end to any
form of governmental approval of or support for its use?"

"Because that would destroy the program, which would 80
destroy many farmers. There are alternatives, you know, to
war, nuclear power, and throwaway containers."

"And tobacco farmers have no alternative to growing to- 81
bacco?"

"At present, none at all. That's why their 'choice' to grow 82
tobacco is not really a choice. They have had, as farmers,
nothing else to choose."

"What sort of alternative do they need?" 83

"They need a crop, or several crops, that can produce a 84
comparable income from comparable acreages, that can be
grown with family and neighborhood labor, and for which
there is a dependable market."

"They need to be growing food crops, you mean—fruits 85
and vegetables."

"I think so. Along with the meat and milk that they already 86
produce."

"I see you are still clinging to the idea of an agricultural 87
economy of diversified small farms that produce for local
markets and local consumers."

"Yes, I'm still clinging to it. I want people to continue to 88
eat. I want them to have, as dependably as possible, a local

supply of good food. I want their food budget to support a
thriving population of local farmers. That way, the land will
thrive."

"And you see the tobacco farmers as necessary to that?"   89

"I see *all* farmers—all that are left and, I hope, some   90
more—as necessary to that. Tobacco farmers are farmers and
among the best of them; their know-how is a great public
asset, if the public only recognized it. They are farming some
very good land. They should be growing food for the people
of their region, the people of neighboring cities—or they
should have a viable choice of doing so. The people who so
eagerly condemn them for growing tobacco should be just
as eager to help them find alternative crops. It is wrong to
condemn people for doing a thing and then offer no alternative but failure. A person could get mad about that."

"So you're not reconciled to your people's dependence on   91
tobacco?"

"Far from it."   92

"You see it as a problem to be solved?   93

I see it as a problem to be solved. And that means, too,   94
that I'm not reconciled to the general lack of interest in
solving it."

"You mean that in state government and the universities   95
there is no interest?"

"I would describe their interest, so far, as small—too small 96
to generate any real hope of a solution. But the difficulties
are enormous, and they had better be acknowledged. For one
thing, the idea of local food economies, or 'local food self-
sufficiency,' has few advocates and, so far as I know, no
powerful ones; it has been eclipsed by the 'global economy'
and the 'free market.' For another, most people are satisfied
so far with the present system of food supply—though it is a
satisfaction based on ignorance. And most difficult of all, if
we are to wean farmers from tobacco onto other crops, we
must somehow cause a local demand and a local supply to
come into existence simultaneously."

"Do you foresee no help with this from the federal gov-   97
ernment?"

"The federal government sponsors the tobacco program, 98
which is unusual behavior for the federal government, and
the program has always had to deal with the dangers implicit
in its unusualness. It has always had enemies, for in general
the federal government's agricultural policy has been exactly
the fight for survival that you were talking about: leave the
markets unregulated and production uncontrolled, and let
the farmers compete against each other year after year to
survive the overproduction that is the result of their competition; then, every year, the 'least efficient' farmers fail, and
their failure makes American agriculture stronger and better.
The government, so to speak, sees homicide as the perfect
cure—which it is, if you like homicide. Let me be plain with
you. I see no chance at all that the federal government will
soon take to heart the issue of the survival of tobacco farmers,
or of any other farmers, or the survival of the rural communities those farmers represent. It would be pleasant to hope
otherwise, but that would be to hope without reason. Nor
do I hope for much from state governments or universities.
The consensus seems to be that whoever or whatever fails
deserves to fail and that something better will inevitably be
built on such failures."

"You have, then, no hope?" 99

"To have given up illusory hope is not to be hopeless. I 100
see, simply, that the institutions that have most influenced
agriculture for the last forty or fifty years have demonstrated
an almost perfect lack of interest in the survival of farmers."

"And so what hope do you have?" 101

"When hope leaves government, it must go to the people. 102
So long as there is a demonstrable need and an imaginable
answer, there is hope. We need to make it possible for farmers
to choose not to grow tobacco and yet continue farming, and
we need a better, safer, fresher supply of food, which is to say
a *local* supply. And these two needs are, in fact, the same."

"You're going too fast. Why, necessarily, a *local* supply?" 103

"Well, the more local, the more fresh—there's no problem 104
with that, is there?"

"No." 105

"And as you shorten the distance between consumer and   106
producer, you increase the consumer's power to know and
influence the quality of food. Kentucky consumers, for instance, could influence Kentucky farmers much more easily
than they could influence California farmers."

"I can see that."   107

"Moreover, 'fresh' implies short distances and therefore   108
lower expenditures for transportation, packaging, refrigeration, national advertising campaigns, and so on. A local food
economy, in short, implies higher prices for farmers and lower
costs to consumers."

"And you think the government doesn't see this but the   109
people do?"

"Some people see it now. And more are going to see it,   110
for it is going to become easier to see. And those who see it
don't have to wait for the government to see it before they
do something."

"But what can they do?"   111

"They can start buying produce from local farmers."   112

"As individuals?"   113

"As individuals, if necessary. But groups can do it, too, and 114
can do it more effectively—conservation organizations, consumer groups, churches, local merchants, whoever is concerned. The government's approval is not necessary. In fact,
the process has already begun. Scattered all over the country,
there are farmers who are selling produce directly to urban
consumers. There have been consumer cooperatives for this
sort of dealing for a good many years. Local merchants sometimes stock local produce. If churches and conservation organizations—the two groups with most reason to be
concerned—would get involved, much more could be accomplished. But everything that is done demonstrates a possibility and suggests more that might be done. That is the
way it will grow."

"What are you talking about—some kind of revolution?"   115

"Not 'revolution.' I'm talking about economic secession—   116
just quietly forming the means of withdrawal, not only from

the tobacco economy but from the entire economy of exploi-
tive land use that is ruining both the countryside and the
country communities. The principle of this new economy
would simply be good use—the possibility, often demonstrated, that land and people can be used without being
destroyed. And this new economy would understand, first of
all, that the ruin of farmers solves *no* problem and makes
many."

For Study and Discussion

QUESTIONS FOR RESPONSE

1. What is your first reaction to Berry's defense of tobacco farmers?
   What do you think is the basis of that reaction?
2. How do you respond to Berry's claim that we are an addictive
   society? What do you think of the evidence he gives to back that
   claim?

QUESTIONS ABOUT PURPOSE

1. How does this essay move beyond the dilemma of tobacco farmers to issues that Berry sees as more important? What are those
   issues?
2. What does Berry hope to accomplish here not only for the
   tobacco farmers but for the other small farmers of America?

QUESTIONS ABOUT AUDIENCE

1. Berry, who writes most frequently about the environment, conservation, country living, and the simple life, has a faithful audience for that kind of writing. How do you think those readers
   might respond to his defense of tobacco farmers? To what extent
   do you think he has kept their reaction in mind in writing this
   essay?
2. What kinds of readers might be antagonized by Berry's arguments about this country's agricultural practices? What might
   their counterarguments be?

QUESTIONS ABOUT STRATEGIES

1. What does Berry achieve through constructing an extended dialogue to explain his points?
2. What does Berry achieve by starting out with his own experience of growing up in a tobacco culture?

QUESTIONS FOR DISCUSSION

1. How do you react to Berry's claim that as a people Americans lead unhealthy lives? What evidence can you think of to support or contradict his claim?
2. Which of Berry's arguments bring a positive response from you? Why do you think you are sympathetic to those arguments?

ROSEMARY L. BRAY

Rosemary L. Bray was born in Chicago in 1955
and was educated at Yale University. She has
worked as an editor for the *Wall Street Journal*,
Essence, *Ms.*, and the *New York Times Book Review*.
She has contributed articles to magazines such as
Redbook, *Savvy*, and *Glamour* and has written a
children's biography, *Martin Luther King* (1995).
She is currently at work on a political memoir,
Unafraid of the Dark. In "So How Did I Get
Here?," first printed in the *New York Times Magazine* in 1992, Bray uses her own experiences to
show how the "welfare question" has become "the
race question and the woman question in dis-
guise."

So How Did I Get Here?

G ROWING UP ON welfare was a story I had planned to 1
tell a long time from now, when I had children of my
own. My childhood on Aid to Families with Dependent
Children (A.F.D.C.) was going to be one of those stories I
would tell my kids about the bad old days, an urban legend
equivalent to Abe Lincoln studying by firelight. But I know
now I cannot wait, because in spite of a wealth of evidence
about the true nature of welfare and poverty in America, the
debate has turned ugly, vicious and racist. The "welfare question" has become the race question and the woman question
in disguise, and so far the answers bode well for no one.

In both blunt and coded terms, comfortable Americans 2
more and more often bemoan the waste of their tax money
on lazy black women with a love of copulation, a horror of
birth control and a lack of interest in marriage. Were it not
for the experiences of half my life, were I not black and female

and of a certain age, perhaps I would be like so many people who blindly accept the lies and distortions, half-truths and wrongheaded notions about welfare. But for better or worse, I do know better. I know more than I want to know about being poor. I know that the welfare system is designed to be inadequate, to leave its constituents on the edge of survival. I know because I've been there.

And finally, I know that perhaps even more dependent on   3 welfare than its recipients are the large number of Americans who would rather accept this patchwork of economic horrors than fully address the real needs of real people.

My mother came to Chicago in 1947 with a fourth-grade   4

The rage I feel about the welfare debate
comes from listening to a host of lies,
distortions, and exaggerations.

---

education, cut short by working in the Mississippi fields. She pressed shirts in a laundry for a while and later waited tables in a restaurant, where she met my father. Mercurial and independent, with a sixth-grade education, my Arkansas-born father worked at whatever came to hand. He owned a lunch wagon for a time and prepared food for hours in our kitchen on the nights before he took the wagon out. Sometimes he hauled junk and sold it in the open-air markets of Maxwell Street on Sunday mornings. Eight years after they met—seven years after they married—I was born. My father made her quit her job; her work, he told her, was taking care of me. By the time I was 4, I had a sister, a brother and another brother on the way. My parents, like most other American couples of the 1950's, had their own American dream—a husband who worked, a wife who stayed home, a family of smiling children. But as was true for so many African-American couples, their American dream was an illusion.

The house on the corner of Berkeley Avenue and 45th ⁵
Street is long gone. The other houses still stand, but today
the neighborhood is an emptier, bleaker place. When we
moved there, it was a street of old limestones with beveled
glass windows, all falling into vague disrepair. Home was a
four-room apartment on the first floor, in what must have
been the public rooms of a formerly grand house. The rent
was $110 a month. All of us kids slept in the big front room.
Because I was the oldest, I had a bed of my own, near a big
plate-glass window.

My mother and father had been married for several years ⁶
before she realized he was a gambler who would never stay
away from the track. By the time we moved to Berkeley
Avenue, Daddy was spending more time gambling, and
bringing home less and less money and more and more anger.
Mama's simplest requests were met with rage. They fought
once for hours when she asked for money to buy a tube of
lipstick. It didn't help that I always seemed to need a doctor.
I had allergies and bronchitis so severe that I nearly died one
Sunday after church when I was about 3.

It was around this time that my mother decided to sign ⁷
up for A.F.D.C. She explained to the caseworker that Daddy
wasn't home much, and when he was he didn't have any
money. Daddy was furious; Mama was adamant. "There were
times when we hardly had a loaf of bread in here," she told
me years later. "It was close. I wasn't going to let you all go
hungry."

Going on welfare closed a door between my parents that ⁸
never reopened. She joined the ranks of unskilled women
who were forced to turn to the state for the security their
men could not provide. In the sterile relationship between
herself and the State of Illinois, Mama found an autonomy
denied her by my father. It was she who could decide, at last,
some part of her own fate and ours. A.F.D.C. relegated
marginally productive men like my father to the ranks of
failed patriarchs who no longer controlled the destiny of their
families. Like so many of his peers, he could no longer afford
the luxury of a woman who did as she was told because her

economic life depended on it. Daddy became one of the shadow men who walked out back doors as caseworkers came in through the front. Why did he acquiesce? For all his anger, for all his frightening brutality, he loved us, so much that he swallowed his pride and periodically ceased to exist so that we might survive.

In 1960, the year my mother went on public aid, the 9 poverty threshold for a family of five in the United States was $3,560 and the monthly payment to a family of five from the State of Illinois was $182.56, a total of $2,190.72 a year. Once the $110 rent was paid, Mama was left with $72.56 a month to take care of all the other expenses. By any standard, we were poor. All our lives were proscribed by the narrow line between not quite and just enough.

What did it take to live? 10

It took the kindness of friends as well as strangers, the 11 charity of churches, low expectations, deprivation and patience. I can't begin to count the hours spent in long lines, long waits, long walks in pursuit of basic things. A visit to a local clinic (one housing doctors, a dentist and pharmacy in an incredibly crowded series of rooms) invariably took the better part of a day; I never saw the same doctor twice.

It took, as well, a turning of our collective backs on the 12 letter of a law that required reporting even a small and important miracle like a present of $5. All families have their secrets, but I remember the weight of an extra burden. In a world where caseworkers were empowered to probe into every nook and cranny of our lives, silence became defense. Even now, there are things I will not publicly discuss because I cannot shake the fear that we might be hounded by the state, eager to prosecute us for the crime of survival.

All my memories of our years on A.F.D.C. are seasoned 13 with unease. It's painful to remember how much every penny counted, how even a gap of 25 cents could make a difference in any given week. Few people understand how precarious life is from welfare check to welfare check, how the word "extra" has no meaning. Late mail, a bureaucratic mix-up . . . and a carefully planned method of survival lies in tatters.

What made our lives work as well as they did was my mother's genius at making do—worn into her by a childhood of rural poverty—along with her vivid imagination. She worked at home endlessly, shopped ruthlessly, bargained, cajoled, charmed. Her food store of choice was the one that stocked pork and beans, creamed corn, sardines, Vienna sausages and potted meat all at 10 cents a can. Clothing was the stuff of rummage sales, trips to Goodwill and bargain basements, where thin cotton and polyester reigned supreme. Our shoes came from a discount store that sold two pairs for $5. 14

It was an uphill climb, but there was no time for reflection; we were too busy with our everyday lives. Yet I remember how much it pained me to know that Mama, who recruited a neighbor to help her teach me how to read when I was 3, found herself left behind by her eldest daughter, then by each of us in turn. Her biggest worry was that we would grow up uneducated, so Mama enrolled us in parochial school. 15

When one caseworker angrily questioned how she could afford to send four children to St. Ambrose School, my mother, who emphatically declared "My kids need an education," told her it was none of her business. (In fact, the school had a volume discount of sorts; the price of tuition dropped with each child you sent. I still don't know quite how she managed it.) She organized our lives around church and school, including Mass every morning at 7:45. My brother was an altar boy; I laid out the vestments each afternoon for the next day's Mass. She volunteered as a chaperone for every class trip, sat with us as we did homework she did not understand herself. She and my father reminded us again and again and again that every book, every test, every page of homework was in fact a ticket out and away from the life we lived. 16

My life on welfare ended on June 4, 1976—a month after my 21st birthday, two weeks after I graduated from Yale. My father, eaten up with cancer and rage, lived just long enough to know the oldest two of us had graduated from college and were on our own. Before the decade ended, all of us had left the welfare rolls. The eldest of my brothers worked at the 17

post office, assumed support of my mother (who also went
to work, as a companion to an elderly woman) and earned
his master's degree at night. My sister married and got a job
at a bank. My baby brother parked cars and found a wife.
Mama's biggest job was done at last; the investment made in
our lives by the State of Illinois had come to fruition. Five
people on welfare for 18 years had become five working,
taxpaying adults. Three of us went to college, two of us
finished; one of us has an advanced degree; all of us can take
care of ourselves.

Ours was a best-case phenomenon, based on the synergy   18
of church and state, the government and the private sector
and the thousand points of light that we called friends and
neighbors. But there was something more: What fueled our
dreams and fired our belief that our lives could change for
the better was the promise of the civil rights movement and
the war on poverty—for millions of African-Americans the
defining events of the 1960's. Caught up in the heady atmosphere of imminent change, our world was filled not only with
issues and ideas but with amazing images of black people
engaged in the struggle for long-denied rights and freedoms.
We knew other people lived differently than we did, we knew
we didn't have much, but we didn't mind, because we knew
it wouldn't be long. My mother borrowed a phrase I had
read to her once from Dick Gregory's autobiography: Not
poor, just broke. She would repeat it often, as often as she
sang hymns in the kitchen. She loved to sing a spiritual
Mahalia Jackson had made famous: "Move On Up a Little
Higher." Like so many others, Mama was singing about earth
as well as heaven.

These are the things I remember every time I read another   19
article outlining America's welfare crisis. The rage I feel about
the welfare debate comes from listening to a host of lies,
distortions and exaggerations—and taking them personally.

I am no fool. I know of few women—on welfare or off—   20
with my mother's grace and courage and stamina. I know not
all women on welfare are cut from the same cloth. Some are
lazy; some are ground down. Some are too young; many are

without husbands. A few have made welfare fraud a lucrative career; a great many more have pushed the rules on outside income to their very limits.

I also know that none of these things justify our making welfare a test of character and worthiness, rather than an acknowledgment of need. Near-sainthood should not be a requirement for financial and medical assistance. 21

But all manner of sociologists and policy gurus continue to equate issues that simply aren't equivalent—welfare, race, rates of poverty, crime, marriage and childbirth—and to reach conclusions that serve to demonize the poor. More than one social arbiter would have us believe that we have all been mistaken for the last 30 years—that the efforts to relieve the most severe effects of poverty have not only failed but have served instead to increase and expand the ranks of the poor. In keeping women, children and men from starvation, we are told, we have also kept them from self-sufficiency. In our zeal to do good, we have undermined the work ethic, the family and thus, by association, the country itself. 22

So how did I get here? 23

Despite attempts to misconstrue and discredit the social programs and policies that changed—even saved—my life, certain facts remain. Poverty was reduced by 39 percent between 1960 and 1990, according to the Census Bureau, from 22.2 percent to 13.5 percent of the nation's population. That is far too many poor people, but the rate is considerably lower than it might have been if we had thrown up our hands and reminded ourselves that the poor will always be with us. Of black women considered "highly dependent," that is, on welfare for more than seven years, 81 percent of their daughters grow up to live productive lives off the welfare rolls, a 1992 Congressional report stated; the 19 percent who become second-generation welfare recipients can hardly be said to constitute an epidemic of welfare dependency. The vast majority of African-Americans are now working or middle class, an achievement that occurred in the past 30 years, most specifically between 1960 and 1973, the years of expansion in the very same social programs that it is so popular now to 24 savage. Those were the same years in which I changed from girl to woman, learned to read and think, graduated from high school and college, came to be a working woman, a taxpayer, a citizen.

In spite of all the successes we know of, in spite of the   25
reality that the typical welfare recipient is a white woman with young children, ideologues have continued to fashion from whole cloth the specter of the mythical black welfare mother, complete with a prodigious reproductive capacity and a galling laziness, accompanied by the uncaring and equally lazy black man in her life who will not work, will not marry her and will not support his family.

Why has this myth been promoted by some of the best   26
(and the worst) people in government, academia, journalism and industry? One explanation may be that the constant presence of poverty frustrates even the best-intentioned among us. It may also be because the myth allows for denial about who the poor in America really are and for denial about the depth and intransigence of racism regardless of economic status. And because getting tough on welfare is for some a first-class career move; what better way to win a position in the next administration than to trash those people least able to respond? And, finally, because it serves to assure white Americans that lazy black people aren't getting away with anything.

Many of these prescriptions for saving America from the   27
welfare plague not only reflect an insistent, if sometimes unconscious, racism but rest on the bedrock of patriarchy. They are rooted in the fantasy of a male presence as a path to social and economic salvation and in its corollary—the image of woman as passive chattel, constitutionally so afflicted by her condition that the only recourse is to transfer her care from the hands of the state to the hands of a man with a job. The largely ineffectual plans to create jobs for men in communities ravaged by disinvestment, the state-sponsored dragnets for men who cannot or will not support their children, the exhortations for women on welfare to find themselves a man and get married, all are the institutional

expressions of the same worn cultural illusion—that women and children without a man are fundamentally damaged goods. Men are such a boon, the reasoning goes, because they make more money than women do.

Were we truly serious about an end to poverty among women and children, we would take the logical next step. We would figure out how to make sure women who did a dollar's worth of work got a dollar's worth of pay. We would make sure that women could go to work with their minds at ease, knowing their children were well cared for. What women on welfare need, in large measure, are the things key to the life of every adult woman: economic security and autonomy. Women need the skills and the legitimate opportunity to earn a living for ourselves as well as for people who may rely on us; we need the freedom to make choices to improve our own lives and the lives of those dear to us.

"The real problem is not welfare," says Kathryn Edin, a professor of sociology at Rutgers University and a scholar in residence at the Russell Sage Foundation. "The real problem is the nature of low-wage work and lack of support for these workers—most of whom happen to be women raising their children alone."

Completing a five-year study of single mothers—some low-wage workers, some welfare recipients—Edin is quantifying what common sense and bitter experience have told millions of women who rotate off and on the welfare rolls: Women, particularly unskilled women with children, get the worst jobs available, with the least amount of health care, and are the most frequently laid off. "The workplace is not oriented toward people who have family responsibilities," she says. "Most jobs are set up assuming that someone else is minding the kids and doesn't need assistance."

But the writers and scholars and politicians who wax most rhapsodic about the need to replace welfare with work make their harsh judgments from the comfortable and supportive environs of offices and libraries and think tanks. If they need to go to the bathroom midsentence, there is no one timing their absence. If they take longer than a half-hour for lunch, there is no one waiting to dock their pay. If their baby sitter gets sick, there is no risk of someone having taken their place at work by the next morning. Yet these are conditions that low-wage women routinely face, which inevitably lead to the cyclical nature of their welfare histories. These are the realities that many of the most vocal and widely quoted critics of welfare routinely ignore. In his book *The End of Equality,* for example, Mickey Kaus discusses social and economic inequity, referring to David Ellwood's study on long-term welfare dependency without ever mentioning that it counts anyone who uses the services for at least one month as having been on welfare for the entire year.

In the heated atmosphere of the welfare debate, the larger   32
society is encouraged to believe that women on welfare have so violated the social contract that they have forfeited all rights common to those of us lucky enough not to be poor. In no area is this attitude more clearly demonstrated than in issues of sexuality and childbearing. Consider the following: A *Philadelphia Inquirer* editorial of Dec. 12, 1990, urges the use of Norplant contraceptive inserts for welfare recipients— in spite of repeated warnings from women's health groups of its dangerous side effects—in the belief that the drug "could be invaluable in breaking the cycle of inner-city poverty." (The newspaper apologized for the editorial after it met wide-spread criticism, both within and outside the paper.) A California judge orders a woman on welfare, convicted of abusing two of her four children, to use Norplant; the judge's decision was appealed. The Washington state legislature considers approving cash payments of up to $10,000 for women on welfare who agree to be sterilized. These and other proposals, all centering on women's reproductive capacities, were advanced in spite of evidence that welfare recipients have fewer children than those not on welfare.

The punitive energy behind these and so many other Dra-   33
conian actions and proposals goes beyond the desire to decrease welfare costs; it cuts to the heart of the nation's racial and sexual hysteria. Generated neither by law nor by fully informed public debate, these actions amount to social con-

trol over "those people on welfare"—a control many Americans feel they have bought and paid for every April 15. The question is obvious: If citizens were really aware of who receives welfare in America, however inadequate it is, if they acknowledged that white women and children were welfare's primary beneficiaries, would most of these things be happening?

Welfare has become a code word now. One that enables   34
white Americans to mask their sometimes malignant, sometimes benign racism behind false concerns about the suffering ghetto poor and their negative impact on the rest of us. It has become the vehicle many so-called tough thinkers use to undermine compassionate policy and engineer the reduction of social programs.

So how *did* I get here?   35

I kept my drawers up and my dress down, to quote my   36
mother. I didn't end up pregnant because I had better things to do. I knew I did because my uneducated, Southern-born parents told me so. Their faith, their focus on our futures are a far cry from the thesis of Nicholas Lemann, whose widely acclaimed book *The Promised Land* perpetuates the myth of black Southern sharecropping society as a primary source of black urban malaise. Most important, my family and I had every reason to believe that I had better things to do and that when I got older I would be able to do them. I had a mission, a calling, work to do that only I could do. And that is knowledge transmitted not just by parents, or school, or churches. It is a palpable thing, available by osmosis from the culture of the neighborhood and the world at large.

Add to this formula a whopping dose of dumb luck. It was   37
my sixth-grade teacher, Sister Maria Sarto, who identified in me the first signs of a stifling boredom and told my mother that I needed a tougher, more challenging curriculum than her school could provide. It was she who then tracked down the private Francis W. Parker School, which agreed to give me a scholarship if I passed the admissions test.

Had I been born a few years earlier, or a decade later, I   38
might now be living on welfare in the Robert Taylor Homes

or working as a hospital nurse's aide for $6.67 an hour. People who think such things could never have happened to me haven't met enough poor people to know better. The avenue of escape can be very narrow indeed. The hope and energy of the 1960's—fueled not only by a growing economy but by all the passions of a great national quest—is long gone. The sense of possibility I knew has been replaced with the popular cultural currency that money and those who have it are everything and those without are nothing.

Much has been made of the culture of the underclass, the culture of poverty, as though they were the free-floating illnesses of the African-American poor, rendering them immune to other influences: the widespread American culture of greed, for example, or of cynicism. It is a thinly veiled continuation of the endless projection of "dis-ease" onto black life, a convenient way to sidestep a more painful debate about the loss of meaning in American life that has made our entire nation depressed and dispirited. The malaise that has overtaken our country is hardly confined to African-Americans or the poor, and if both groups should disappear tomorrow, our nation would still find itself in crisis. To talk of the black "underclass threat" to the public sphere, as Mickey Kaus does, to demonize the poor among us and thus by association all of us—ultimately this does more damage to the body politic than a dozen welfare queens. 39

When I walk down the streets of my Harlem neighborhood, I see women like my mother, hustling, struggling, walking their children to school and walking them back home. And I also see women who have lost both energy and faith, talking loud, hanging out. I see the shadow men of a new generation, floating by with a few dollars and a toy, then drifting away to the shelters they call home. And I see, a dozen times a day, the little girls my sister and I used to be, the little boys my brothers once were. 40

Even the grudging, inadequate public help I once had is fading fast for them. The time and patience they will need to re-create themselves is vanishing under pressure for the big, 41 quick fix and the crushing load of blame being heaped upon them. In the big cities and the small towns of America, we have let theory, ideology and mythology about welfare and poverty overtake these children and their parents.

For Study and Discussion

QUESTIONS FOR RESPONSE

1. What beliefs about families on welfare did you bring to this essay? What effect do you think reading the essay has had on those beliefs?
2. How does talk about welfare reform focus on women? What is your response to that focus?

QUESTIONS ABOUT PURPOSE

1. What stereotypes about welfare recipients does Bray seek to break? What is the origin of those stereotypes?
2. What do you think Bray wants her readers to learn from her account of her family's struggle to achieve independence? What action would she like for them to take?

QUESTIONS ABOUT AUDIENCE

1. This article was first published in the *New York Times Magazine*. Why is the *New York Times* audience an important one for Bray to reach?
2. How do you think college readers differ from readers of the *New York Times*? How do you think college readers' responses might differ from those of *Times* readers?

QUESTIONS ABOUT STRATEGIES

1. Bray spends almost half the essay giving an account of her family's experiences on welfare. How does this strategy help her advance her argument?
2. How does Bray go about counteracting the myth she describes in paragraph 25?

QUESTIONS FOR DISCUSSION

1. Welfare is only one of many entitlement programs administered by the federal government. Some of the others are Social Security, farm subsidies, Medicare, and military and veterans' benefits. How do most of the public's feelings about these entitlement programs compare to their feelings about welfare? Why?
2. How is the welfare question "the race question and the woman question in disguise," as Bray asserts in the first paragraph of her essay?

Charles Murray was born in Newton, Iowa, in 1943 and was educated at Harvard University. Upon graduation, he worked in the Peace Corps in Thailand and as a research assistant for the American Institute for Research before attending Massachusetts Institute of Technology to complete his graduate studies. He returned to the American Institute for Research to supervise and evaluate federal welfare, urban education, and criminal justice programs. His assessment of this experience appears in books such as *Beyond Probation: Juvenile Corrections and the Chronic Delinquent* (1979) and *Safety Nets and the Truly Needy* (1982). The impact of these books encouraged Murray to conduct the research that produced two extremely controversial books, *Losing Ground: American Social Policy, 1950–1980* (1984) and *The Bell Curve: Intelligence and Class Structure in American Life* (1994). Murray currently works for the American Enterprise Institute. In "The Coming White Underclass," printed in the *Wall Street Journal* in 1993, he argues that the increasing number of white illegitimate children will have a severe social and economic impact on American culture.

The Coming White Underclass

E VERY ONCE IN a while the sky really is falling, and this seems to be the case with the latest national figures on illegitimacy. The unadorned statistic is that, in 1991, 1.2 million children were born to unmarried mothers, within a hair of 30% of all live births. How high is 30%? About four

1

percentage points higher than the black illegitimacy rate in the early 1960s that motivated Daniel Patrick Moynihan to write his famous memorandum on the breakdown of the black family.

The 1991 story for blacks is that illegitimacy has now 2 reached 68% of births to black women. In inner cities, the figure is typically in excess of 80%. Many of us have heard these numbers so often that we are inured. It is time to think about them as if we were back in the mid-1960s with the young Moynihan and asked to predict what would happen if the black illegitimacy rate were 68%.

Impossible, we would have said. But if the proportion of 3

Illegitimacy is the single most important social problem of our time because it drives everything else.

---

fatherless boys in a given community were to reach such levels, surely the culture must be *Lord of the Flies* writ large, the values of unsocialized male adolescents made norms—physical violence, immediate gratification and predatory sex. That is the culture now taking over the black inner city.

But the black story, however dismaying, is old news. The 4 new trend that threatens the U.S. is white illegitimacy. Matters have not yet quite gotten out of hand, but they are on the brink. If we want to act, now is the time.

In 1991, 707,502 babies were born to single white 5 women, representing 22% of white births. The elite wisdom holds that this phenomenon cuts across social classes, as if the increase in Murphy Browns were pushing the trendline. Thus, a few months ago, a Census Bureau study of fertility among all American women got headlines for a few days because it showed that births to single women with college degrees doubled in the last decade to 6% from 3%. This is an interesting trend, but of minor social importance. The real news of that study is that the proportion of single mothers with less than a high school education jumped to 48% from 35% in a single decade.

These numbers are dominated by whites. Breaking down the numbers by race (using data not available in the published version), women with college degrees contribute only 4% of white illegitimate babies, while women with a high school education or less contribute 82%. Women with family incomes of $75,000 or more contribute 1% of white illegitimate babies, while women with family incomes under $20,000 contribute 69%.

The National Longitudinal Study of Youth, a Labor Department study that has tracked more than 10,000 youths since 1979, shows an even more dramatic picture. For white women below the poverty line in the year prior to giving birth, 44% of births have been illegitimate, compared with only 6% for women above the poverty line. White illegitimacy is overwhelmingly a lower-class phenomenon.

This brings us to the emergence of a white underclass. In raw numbers, European-American whites are the ethnic group with the most people in poverty, most illegitimate children, most women on welfare, most unemployed men, and most arrests for serious crimes. And yet whites have not had an "underclass" as such, because the whites who might qualify have been scattered among the working class. Instead, whites have had "white trash" concentrated in a few streets on the outskirts of town, sometimes a Skid Row of unattached white men in the large cities. But these scatterings have seldom been large enough to make up a neighborhood. An underclass needs a critical mass, and white America has not had one.

But now the overall white illegitimacy rate is 22%. The figure in low-income, working-class communities may be twice that. How much illegitimacy can a community tolerate? Nobody knows, but the historical fact is that the trendlines on black crime, dropout from the labor force, and illegitimacy all shifted sharply upward as the overall black illegitimacy rate passed 25%.

The causal connection is murky—I blame the revolution

in social policy during that period, while others blame the sexual revolution, broad shifts in cultural norms, or structural changes in the economy. But the white illegitimacy rate is approaching that same problematic 25% region at a time when social policy is more comprehensively wrongheaded than it was in the mid-1960s, and the cultural and sexual norms are still more degraded.

The white underclass will begin to show its face in isolated ways. Look for certain schools in white neighborhoods to get a reputation as being unteachable, with large numbers of disruptive students and indifferent parents. Talk to the police; listen for stories about white neighborhoods where the incidence of domestic disputes and casual violence has been shooting up. Look for white neighborhoods with high concentrations of drug activity and large numbers of men who have dropped out of the labor force. Some readers will recall reading the occasional news story about such places already. 11

As the spatial concentration of illegitimacy reaches critical mass, we should expect the deterioration to be as fast among low-income whites in the 1990s as it was among low-income blacks in the 1960s. My proposition is that illegitimacy is the single most important social problem of our time—more important than crime, drugs, poverty, illiteracy, welfare or homelessness because it drives everything else. Doing something about it is not just one more item on the American policy agenda, but should be at the top. Here is what to do: 12

In the calculus of illegitimacy, the constants are that boys like to sleep with girls and that girls think babies are endearing. Human societies have historically channeled these elemental forces of human behavior via thick walls of rewards and penalties that constrained the overwhelming majority of births to take place within marriage. The past 30 years have seen those walls cave in. It is time to rebuild them. 13

The ethical underpinning for the policies I am about to describe is this: Bringing a child into the world is the most important thing that most human beings ever do. Bringing a child into the world when one is not emotionally or financially prepared to be a parent is wrong. The child deserves society's support. The parent does not. 14

The social justification is this: A society with broad legal freedoms depends crucially on strong nongovernmental institutions to temper and restrain behavior. Of these, marriage is paramount. Either we reverse the current trends in illegitimacy—especially white illegitimacy—or America must, willy-nilly, become an unrecognizably authoritarian, socially segregated, centralized state.

To restore the rewards and penalties of marriage does not require social engineering. Rather, it requires that the state stop interfering with the natural forces that have done the job quite effectively for millennia. Some of the changes I will describe can occur at the federal level; others would involve state laws. For now, the important thing is to agree on what should be done.

I begin with the penalties, of which the most obvious are economic. Throughout human history, a single woman with a small child has not been a viable economic unit. Not being a viable economic unit, neither have the single woman and child been a legitimate social unit. In small numbers, they must be a net drain on the community's resources. In large numbers, they must destroy the community's capacity to sustain itself. *Mirabile dictu,* communities everywhere have augmented the economic penalties of single parenthood with severe social stigma.

Restoring economic penalties translates into the first and central policy prescription: to end all economic support for single mothers. The AFDC (Aid to Families with Dependent Children) payment goes to zero. Single mothers are not eligible for subsidized housing or for food stamps. An assortment of other subsidies and in-kind benefits disappear. Since universal medical coverage appears to be an idea whose time has come, I will stipulate that all children have medical coverage. But with that exception, the signal is loud and unmistakable: From society's perspective, to have a baby that you cannot care for yourself is profoundly irresponsible, and the government will no longer subsidize it.

How does a poor young mother survive without government support? The same way she has since time immemorial. If she wants to keep a child, she must enlist support from her parents, boyfriend, siblings, neighbors, church or philanthropies. She must get support from somewhere, anywhere, other than the government. The objectives are threefold.

First, enlisting the support of others raises the probability   20
that other mature adults are going to be involved with the upbringing of the child, and this is a great good in itself.

Second, the need to find support forces a self-selection   21
process. One of the most short-sighted excuses made for current behavior is that an adolescent who is utterly unprepared to be a mother "needs someone to love." Childish yearning isn't a good enough selection device. We need to raise the probability that a young single woman who keeps her child is doing so volitionally and thoughtfully. Forcing her to find a way of supporting the child does this. It will lead many young women who shouldn't be mothers to place their babies for adoption. This is good. It will lead others, watching what happens to their sisters, to take steps not to get pregnant. This is also good. Many others will get abortions. Whether this is good depends on what one thinks of abortion.

Third, stigma will regenerate. The pressure on relatives   22
and communities to pay for the folly of their children will make an illegitimate birth the socially horrific act it used to be, and getting a girl pregnant something boys do at the risk of facing a shotgun. Stigma and shotgun marriages may or may not be good for those on the receiving end, but their deterrent effect on others is wonderful—and indispensable.

What about women who can find no support but keep the   23
baby anyway? There are laws already on the books about the right of the state to take a child from a neglectful parent. We have some 360,000 children in foster care because of them. Those laws would still apply. Society's main response, however, should be to make it as easy as possible for those mothers to place their children for adoption at infancy. To that end, state governments must strip adoption of the nonsense that has encumbered it in recent decades.

The first step is to make adoption easy for any married   24
couple who can show reasonable evidence of having the

resources and stability to raise a child. Lift all restrictions on interracial adoption. Ease age limitations for adoptive parents.

The second step is to restore the traditional legal principle   25
that placing a child for adoption means irrevocably relinquishing all legal rights to the child. The adoptive parents are parents without qualification. Records are sealed until the child reaches adulthood, at which time they may be unsealed only with the consent of biological child and parent.

Given these straightforward changes—going back to the   26
old way, which worked—there is reason to believe that some extremely large proportion of infants given up by their mothers will be adopted into good homes. This is true not just for flawless blue-eyed blond infants but for babies of all colors and conditions. The demand for infants to adopt is huge.

Some small proportion of infants and larger proportion of   27
older children will not be adopted. For them, the government should spend lavishly on orphanages. I am not recommending Dickensian barracks. In 1993, we know a lot about how to provide a warm, nurturing environment for children, and getting rid of the welfare system frees up lots of money to do it. Those who find the word "orphanages" objectionable may think of them as 24-hour-a-day preschools. Those who prattle about the importance of keeping children with their biological mothers may wish to spend some time in a patrol car or with a social worker seeing what the reality of life with welfare-dependent biological mothers can be like.

Finally, there is the matter of restoring the rewards of   28
marriage. Here, I am pessimistic about how much government can do and optimistic about how little it needs to do. The rewards of raising children within marriage are real and deep. The main task is to shepherd children through adolescence so that they can reach adulthood—when they are likely to recognize the value of those rewards—free to take on marriage and family. The main purpose of the penalties for single parenthood is to make that task easier.

One of the few concrete things that the government can   29
do to increase the rewards of marriage is make the tax code

favor marriage and children: Those of us who are nervous about using the tax code for social purposes can advocate making the tax code at least neutral.

A more abstract but ultimately crucial step in raising the 30 rewards of marriage is to make marriage once again the sole legal institution through which parental rights and responsibilities are defined and exercised.

Little boys should grow up knowing from their earliest 31 memories that if they want to have any rights whatsoever regarding a child that they sire—more vividly, if they want to grow up to be a daddy—they must marry. Little girls should grow up knowing from their earliest memories that if they want to have any legal claims whatsoever on the father of their children, they must marry. A marriage certificate should establish that a man and a woman have entered into a unique legal relationship. The changes in recent years that have blurred the distinctiveness of marriage are subtly but importantly destructive.

Together, these measures add up to a set of signals, some 32 with immediate and tangible consequences, others with long-term consequences, still others symbolic. They should be supplemented by others based on a re-examination of divorce law and its consequences.

That these policy changes seem drastic and unrealistic is a 33 peculiarity of our age, not of the policies themselves. With embellishments, I have endorsed the policies that were the uncontroversial law of the land as recently as John Kennedy's presidency. Then, America's elites accepted as a matter of course that a free society such as America's can sustain itself only through virtue and temperance in the people, that virtue and temperance depend centrally on the socialization of each new generation, and that the socialization of each generation depends on the matrix of care and resources fostered by marriage.

Three decades after that consensus disappeared, we face an 34 emerging crisis. The long, steep climb in black illegitimacy has been calamitous for black communities and painful for the nation. The reforms I have described will work for blacks as for whites, and have been needed for years. But the brutal truth is that American society as a whole could survive when illegitimacy became epidemic within a comparatively small ethnic minority. It cannot survive the same epidemic among whites.

For Study and Discussion

QUESTIONS FOR RESPONSE

1. What do you know firsthand of single white mothers like those Murray talks about or about divorced single mothers who are raising their children alone? What is your impression of how they manage their lives? To what extent does it correspond to Murray's impression?
2. Murray says in paragraph 4, "the black story, however dismaying, is old news." What is your response to that statement?

QUESTIONS ABOUT PURPOSE

1. What immediate actions does Murray hope to initiate among his readers? What long-range actions?
2. Why does Murray focus on white illegitimacy? How would his recommendations about single mothers affect all ethnic groups?

QUESTIONS ABOUT AUDIENCE

1. This article was first published in the *Wall Street Journal.* What do you know about its readers? What attitudes and concerns can Murray assume are likely to exist among these readers?
2. How do you think the experiences and attitudes of college readers at your institution compare with those of readers of the *Wall Street Journal*? What differences would those experiences make in their response?

QUESTIONS ABOUT STRATEGIES

1. What effect does Murray hope to achieve with the statistics he quotes in the first seven paragraphs?
2. Murray lays out a specific plan for reducing illegitimacy, saying

decisively, "Here is what to do." How do you think *Wall Street Journal* readers would react to this strategy and the remedies he proposes? How do you react to them? Why?

QUESTIONS FOR DISCUSSION

1. What issues do Murray's statements about adoption and orphanages (paragraphs 23 through 27) raise? How do you respond to the claims he makes in those paragraphs? Discuss his recommendations.
2. Read what Rosemary Bray says in paragraph 28 of "So How Did I Get Here?" To what extent do Murray's proposed solutions to illegitimacy problems resemble what she regards as a patriarchal fantasy? Explain.

Arthur C. Clarke was born in 1917 in Somerset, England. Although he was interested in science at an early age, building his first telescope at the age of thirteen, he could not afford a formal university education. During World War II, he was a radar specialist with the Royal Air Force. After the war he received educational assistance and entered King's College at the University of London, where in two years he graduated with honorary degrees in math and physics. He worked briefly as an editor for *Science Abstracts* but soon devoted his full attention to his lifetime vocation, writing about science. His nonfiction publications, such as *Interplanetary Flight* (1950), *The Exploration of Space* (1951), and *The Making of a Moon* (1957), explain space travel, but his science fiction is concerned with the complex effect of such travel on human emotions and values. His novels include *The Sounds of Mars* (1951) and *Rendezvous with Rama* (1974). His screenplay for Stanley Kubrick's film *2001: A Space Odyssey* is considered a classic. In "The Star," reprinted from *The Nine Billion Names of God* (1955), a Jesuit astronomer tells of a space journey that challenges his faith in God.

The Star

I T IS THREE thousand light-years to the Vatican. Once, I believed that space could have no power over faith, just as I believed that the heavens declared the glory of God's handiwork. Now I have seen that handiwork, and my faith is sorely troubled. I stare at the crucifix that hangs on the cabin wall above the Mark VI Computer, and for the first time in my life I wonder if it is no more than an empty symbol.

I have told no one yet, but the truth cannot be concealed. 2 The facts are there for all to read, recorded on the countless miles of magnetic tape and the thousands of photographs we are carrying back to Earth. Other scientists can interpret them as easily as I can, and I am not one who would condone that tampering with the truth which often gave my order a bad name in the olden days.

The crew were already sufficiently depressed: I wonder 3 how they will take this ultimate irony. Few of them have any religious faith, yet they will not relish using this final weapon in their campaign against me—that private, good-natured, but fundamentally serious war which lasted all the way from Earth. It amused them to have a Jesuit as chief astrophysicist: Dr. Chandler, for instance, could never get over it. (Why are medical men such notorious atheists?) Sometimes he would meet me on the observation deck, where the lights are always low so that the stars shine with undiminished glory. He would come up to me in the gloom and stand staring out of the great oval port, while the heavens crawled slowly around us as the ship turned end over end with the residual spin we had never bothered to correct.

"Well, Father," he would say at last, "it goes on forever 4 and forever, and perhaps *Something* made it. But how you can believe that Something has a special interest in us and our miserable little world—that just beats me." Then the argument would start, while the stars and nebulae would swing around us in silent, endless arcs beyond the flawlessly clear plastic of the observation port.

It was, I think, the apparent incongruity of my position 5 that caused most amusement to the crew. In vain I would point to my three papers in the *Astrophysical Journal*, my five in the *Monthly Notices of the Royal Astronomical Society*. I would remind them that my order has long been famous for its scientific works. We may be few now, but ever since the eighteenth century we have made contributions to astronomy and geophysics out of all proportion to our numbers. Will my report on the Phoenix Nebula end our thousand years of history? It will end, I fear, much more than that.

I do not know who gave the nebula its name, which seems 6 to me a very bad one. If it contains a prophecy, it is one that cannot be verified for several billion years. Even the word "nebula" is misleading: this is a far smaller object than those stupendous clouds of mist—the stuff of unborn stars—that are scattered throughout the length of the Milky Way. On the cosmic scale, indeed, the Phoenix Nebula is a tiny thing— a tenuous shell of gas surrounding a single star.

Or what is left of a star . . . 7

The Rubens engraving of Loyola seems to mock me as it 8 hangs there above the spectrophotometer tracings. What would *you*, Father, have made of this knowledge that has come into my keeping, so far from the little world that was all the Universe you knew? Would your faith have risen to the challenge, as mine has failed to do?

You gaze into the distance, Father, but I have traveled a 9 distance beyond any that you could have imagined when you founded our order a thousand years ago. No other survey ship has been so far from Earth: we are at the very frontiers of the explored Universe. We set out to reach the Phoenix Nebula, we succeeded, and we are homeward bound with our burden of knowledge. I wish I could lift that burden from my shoulders, but I call to you in vain across the centuries and the light-years that lie between us.

On the book you are holding the words are plain to read. 10 AD MAIOREM DEI GLORIAM, the message runs, but it is a message I can no longer believe. Would you still believe it, if you could see what we have found?

We knew, of course, what the Phoenix Nebula was. Every 11 year, in our Galaxy alone, more than a hundred stars explode, blazing for a few hours or days with thousands of times their normal brilliance before they sink back into death and obscurity. Such are the ordinary novae—the commonplace disasters of the Universe. I have recorded the spectrograms and light curves of dozens since I started working at the Lunar Observatory.

But three or four times in every thousand years occurs   12
something beside which even a nova pales into total insignificance.

When a star becomes a *supernova,* it may for a little while   13
outshine all the massed suns of the Galaxy. The Chinese
astronomers watched this happen in A.D. 1054, not knowing
what it was they saw. Five centuries later, in 1572, a supernova blazed in Cassiopeia so brilliantly that it was visible in
the daylight sky. There have been three more in the thousand
years that have passed since then.

Our mission was to visit the remnants of such a catastro-   14
phe, to reconstruct the events that led up to it, and, if possible, to learn its cause. We came slowly in through the
concentric shells of gas that had been blasted out six thousand
years before, yet were expanding still. They were immensely
hot, radiating even now with a fierce violet light, but were
far too tenuous to do us any damage. When the star had
exploded, its outer layers had been driven upward with such
speed that they had escaped completely from its gravitational
field. Now they formed a hollow shell large enough to engulf
a thousand solar systems, and at its center burned the tiny,
fantastic object which the star had now become—a White
Dwarf, smaller than the Earth, yet weighing a million times
as much.

The glowing gas shells were all around us, banishing the   15
normal night of interstellar space. We were flying into the
center of the cosmic bomb that had detonated millennia ago
and whose incandescent fragments were still hurtling apart.
The immense scale of the explosion, and the fact that the
debris already covered a volume of space many billions of
miles across, robbed the scene of any visible movement. It
would take decades before the unaided eye could detect any
motion in these tortured wisps and eddies of gas, yet the
sense of turbulent expansion was overwhelming.

We had checked our primary drive hours before, and were   16
drifting slowly toward the fierce little star ahead. Once it had
been a sun like our own, but it had squandered in a few hours
the energy that should have kept it shining for a million years.

Now it was a shrunken miser, hoarding its resources as if trying to make amends for its prodigal youth.

No one seriously expected to find planets. If there had   17
been any before the explosion, they would have been boiled
into puffs of vapor, and their substance lost in the greater
wreckage of the star itself. But we made the automatic search,
as we always do when approaching an unknown sun, and
presently we found a single small world circling the star at an
immense distance. It must have been the Pluto of this vanished Solar System, orbiting on the frontiers of the night. Too
far from the central sun ever to have known life, its remote-
ness had saved it from the fate of all its lost companions.

The passing fires had seared its rocks and burned away the   18
mantle of frozen gas that must have covered it in the days
before the disaster. We landed, and we found the Vault.

Its builders had made sure that we should. The monolithic   19
marker that stood above the entrance was now a fused stump,
but even the first long-range photographs told us that here
was the work of intelligence. A little later we detected the
continent-wide pattern of radioactivity that had been buried
in the rock. Even if the pylon above the vault had been
destroyed, this would have remained, an immovable and all
but eternal beacon calling to the stars. Our ship fell toward
this gigantic bull's-eye like an arrow into its target.

The pylon must have been a mile high when it was built,   20
but now it looked like a candle that had melted down into a
puddle of wax. It took us a week to drill through the fused
rock, since we did not have the proper tools for a task like
this. We were astronomers, not archaeologists, but we could
improvise. Our original purpose was forgotten: this lonely
monument, reared with such labor at the greatest possible
distance from the doomed sun, could have only one meaning.
A civilization that knew it was about to die had made its last
bid for immortality.

It will take us generations to examine all the treasures that 21
were placed in the Vault. They had plenty of time to prepare,
for their sun must have given its first warnings many years
before the final detonation. Everything that they wished to

preserve, all the fruit of their genius, they brought here to this distant world in the days before the end, hoping that some other race would find it and that they would not be utterly forgotten. Would we have done as well, or would we have been too lost in our own misery to give thought to a future we could never see or share?

If only they had had a little more time! They could travel freely enough between the planets of their own sun, but they had not yet learned to cross the interstellar gulfs, and the nearest Solar System was a hundred light-years away. Yet even had they possessed the secret of the Transfinite Drive, no more than a few millions could have been saved. Perhaps it was better thus. 22

Even if they had not been so disturbingly human as their sculpture shows, we could not have helped admiring them and grieving for their fate. They left thousands of visual records and the machines for projecting them, together with elaborate pictorial instructions from which it will not be difficult to learn their written language. We have examined many of these records, and brought to life for the first time in six thousand years the warmth and beauty of a civilization that in many ways must have been superior to our own. Perhaps they only showed us the best, and one can hardly blame them. But their worlds were very lovely, and their cities were built with a grace that matches anything of man's. We have watched them at work and play, and listened to their musical speech sounding across the centuries. One scene is still before my eyes—a group of children on a beach of strange blue sand, playing in the waves as children play on Earth. Curious whiplike trees line the shore, and some very large animal is wading in the shallows yet attracting no attention at all. 23

And sinking into the sea, still warm and friendly and life-giving, is the sun that will soon turn traitor and obliterate all this innocent happiness. 24

Perhaps if we had not been so far from home and so vulnerable to loneliness, we should not have been so deeply moved. Many of us had seen the ruins of ancient civilizations on other worlds, but they had never affected us so pro- 25 foundly. This tragedy was unique. It is one thing for a race to fail and die, as nations and cultures have done on Earth. But to be destroyed so completely in the full flower of its achievement, leaving no survivors—how could that be reconciled with the mercy of God?

My colleagues have asked me that, and I have given what 26 answers I can. Perhaps you could have done better, Father Loyola, but I have found nothing in the *Exercitia Spiritualia* that helps me here. They were not an evil people: I do not know what gods they worshiped, if indeed they worshiped any. But I have looked back at them across the centuries, and have watched while the loveliness they used their last strength to preserve was brought forth again into the light of their shrunken sun. They could have taught us much: why were they destroyed?

I know the answers that my colleagues will give when they 27 get back to Earth. They will say that the Universe has no purpose and no plan, that since a hundred suns explode every year in our Galaxy, at this very moment some race is dying in the depths of space. Whether that race has done good or evil during its lifetime will make no difference in the end: there is no divine justice, for there is no God.

Yet, of course, what we have seen proves nothing of the 28 sort. Anyone who argues thus is being swayed by emotion, not logic. God has no need to justify His actions to man. He who built the Universe can destroy it when He chooses. It is arrogance—it is perilously near blasphemy—for us to say what He may or may not do.

This I could have accepted, hard though it is to look upon 29 whole worlds and peoples thrown into the furnace. But there comes a point when even the deepest faith must falter, and now, as I look at the calculations lying before me, I know I have reached that point at last.

We could not tell, before we reached the nebula, how long 30 ago the explosion took place. Now, from the astronomical evidence and the record in the rocks of that one surviving planet, I have been able to date it very exactly. I know in what year the light of this colossal conflagration reached our Earth. I know how brilliantly the supernova whose corpse now dwindles behind our speeding ship once shone in terrestrial skies. I know how it must have blazed low in the east before sunrise, like a beacon in that oriental dawn.

There can be no reasonable doubt: the ancient mystery is   31
solved at last. Yet, oh God, there were so many stars you could have used. What was the need to give these people to the fire, that the symbol of their passing might shine above Bethlehem?

COMMENT ON "THE STAR"

The distressed narrator of this story is a Jesuit scientist who, on the basis of evidence that he cannot refute professionally or ethically, finds himself forced to acknowledge a scientific discovery that he fears may destroy his religious faith, the rock of his very existence. Two arguments are going on in the story. The first is a vocal one between the Jesuit and the crew, particularly a medical doctor who represents the traditional scientific view that although there may be order in the universe, there is no God who takes a special interest in the affairs of humans. The Jesuit represents the argument for faith in God and His concern for humankind. The second argument is the silent one that the Jesuit astrophysicist has seen building as his spaceship penetrated the outer reaches of space to investigate the origins of the Phoenix Nebula. He collects evidence from three sources: from the interstellar space debris that testifies to the explosion of a supernova; from irrefutable evidence left purposefully by a superior, cultured civilization that flourished on a lost planet several thousand years before; and, finally, from the evidence that allows him to calculate the date of the explosion that destroyed that planet. When he puts all the pieces together, the Jesuit sees the conclusion of the second argument. Ironically, it destroys the first argument but almost destroys the Jesuit also. God does indeed take special interest in the affairs of humans; the proof is that the date of the supernova that destroyed the beautiful lost civilization coincides precisely with the Star of Bethlehem announcing the birth of Jesus.

Persuasion and Argument as a Writing Strategy

1. Reread several of the essays in this section, and decide which one or two appeal to you most. Then analyze your response to those essays—to their topic, their tone, their vocabulary, their use of personal anecdotes or narratives, and to the kind of arguments the author presented. Why do you think you liked your one or two choices better than the rest or found them more convincing? What was it about them that appealed to you, a college student, even though you were not the intended reader for that essay? Finally, draw a general conclusion about what you think the author or authors have done that made their work effective for you and what lesson you could take for your own writing.

2. Reread "I Have a Dream" by Martin Luther King, Jr., and "A Chinaman's Chance" by Eric Liu. Write an essay comparing King's dreams and hopes for African-Americans with the American Dream that Liu wants to hang on to for his generation. What components of the two dreams are similar? To what extent do you think King and Liu would agree with each other? Conclude on a personal note by sketching out your own version of the American Dream and indicating how you hope to achieve it.

3. If you are interested in the welfare and rights of animals, visit your local humane society and see what kind of operation it is running. Talk to the administrators and to some of the citizens who hold nonpaying positions on its board of trustees or as volunteers. Find out what these people see as the chief problems for their organization and what they hope to achieve. Then write an editorial for your local newspaper in which you explain to the general public how the humane society operates, what its functions and goals are, and what it does for animals. If you are favorably impressed by the organization, argue for the city and the citizens to give it more support. If you are not favor-

ably impressed, argue for changes you think need to be
made.

4. Write a persuasive article for either your hometown newspaper or your campus newspaper in which you try to get
a local company or industry to contribute its support to a
civic project, either one that exists or one that you design.
Such a project might be restoring dilapidated homes for
people who need housing, sponsoring a literacy project, or
sponsoring a remodeling project for a public playground.
Be specific about how the company could help and how it
would benefit. You might reread the introduction to this
section to help you frame your argument and establish
your tone.

5. For an audience of your classmates and instructor, write
an essay in which you analyze how Rosemary Bray uses
narration and personal examples in "So How Did I Get
Here?" Citing several examples, show how this strategy
affects the appeal of her essay. Compare her primarily emotional and ethical appeal with Charles Murray's primarily
logical appeal in "The Coming White Underclass." Which
appeal do you find more effective and why?

6. Wendell Berry uses his essay "The Problem of Tobacco"
to illustrate, as he puts it, "the complexity of moral issues,"
and he uses his own experience and background to show
how tangled most issues become if we look at them thoroughly and thoughtfully. In the 1990s many public figures
make simplistic arguments about complex issues; welfare
and tobacco are just two of them. Drawing on your own
experience, choose an issue that is often argued about in
a simplistic way, and write an essay showing some of the
complexities of that issue. For example, if you grew up on
a farm or in a small town that depended on agriculture,
you know that doing away with farm subsidies is not as
simple as it sounds. Another complex issue is mandatory
prison sentences for certain crimes. Still another is banning
pornography from computer networks. Some other topics
that could generate spirited essays are withholding public
benefits from illegal aliens, capping tuition increases at

public universities, and making voter registration a condition of getting a driver's license. You might also choose a topic that is currently being discussed on your campus. Write your paper as an opinion piece for your local or campus paper.

RESOURCES
FOR
WRITING

ᏨᎦ

As you worked your way through this book, you discovered that you already possess many resources for reading and writing. You read essays on a wide variety of subjects. You encountered new and complicated information shaped by unusual and unsettling assertions. But you discovered experiences and feelings that you recognize—the challenge of learning, the ordeal of disappointment, the cost of achievement. As you examined these essays, you realized that you had something to say about your reading, something to contribute to the writers' interpretation of some complex subjects. Your reading revealed your resources for writing.

Your work with this book has also enabled you to identify and practice using patterns that at each stage of the writing process will help you transform your resources into writing. In the beginning, these patterns give rise to questions that you might ask about any body of information.

Suppose you want to write an essay on women's contributions to science. You might begin by asking why so few women are ranked among the world's great scientists. You might continue asking questions: What historical forces have discouraged women from becoming scientists (cause and effect)? How do women scientists define problems, analyze evidence, formulate conclusions (process analysis), and do they go about these processes in ways different from the ways used by men scientists (comparison and contrast)? If women scientists look at the world differently from the way men do, does this difference have an effect on the established notions of inquiry (argument)? Such questions work like the different lenses you attach to a camera: each lens gives you a slightly different perspective on your subject.

Your initial questions enable you to envision your subject from different perspectives. Answering one question encourages you to develop your subject according to a purpose associated with one of the common patterns of organization. For instance, if you decide to write about your first scuba dive, your choice of purpose seems obvious: to answer the question, What happened? You would then proceed to write a narrative essay. In drafting this essay, however, you may discover questions you had not anticipated, such as: What factors led to the development of scuba diving? How do you use scuba equipment? How is scuba diving similar to or different from swimming?

Responding to these new questions forces you to decide whether your new information develops or distorts your draft. The history of underwater diving—from diving bells to diving suits to self-contained equipment—may help your readers see a context for your narrative. On the other hand, such information may confuse them, distracting them from your original purpose: to tell what happened.

As you struggle with your new resources, you may decide

that your original purpose no longer drives your writing. You may decide to change your purpose and write a cause-and-effect essay. Instead of telling what happened on your first scuba dive, you might decide to use your personal experience, together with some reading, to write a more scientific essay analyzing the effects of underwater swimming on your senses of sight and hearing.

This book has helped you make such decisions by showing you how the common patterns of organization evoke different purposes, audiences, and strategies. In this final section, you will have the opportunity to make such decisions about a new collection of resources—an anthology of writing on the subject of health.

Before you begin reading these selections, take an initial inventory.

What kind of direct experience have you had with health?

Have you ever been sick?

Have you ever tried to manage your good health or heal an injury by diet, exercise, or stress management?

What kind of indirect experience have you had with health?

What sorts of illnesses have you seen among your friends and relatives?

What kind of medical practices have you seen portrayed in novels, on television, and in the movies?

What do you know about the American health system?

Who taught you how to live a healthy life?

Who taught you how to care for yourself when you became ill?

Where did you learn how to pay for your own medical expenses?

What is your attitude toward the current debate about health care?

What do you think about people who need health
care but can't pay for it?

What do you think about people who "cause"
their own illnesses?

What do you think about wealthy people over 65
who let Medicare pay for most of their medical
costs?

Thinking about such questions will remind you of the
extensive resources you bring to the subject of health. It is a
subject that touches all of our lives in some way. And it affects
our behavior in countless other ways—where we decide to
live, what we decide to eat, when we decide to consult a
doctor, how we spend our money, and whom we elect to
political office.

After you have made a preliminary inventory of your
knowledge and attitudes toward health, read the writings in
this section. You will notice that each selection asks you to
look at health from a different perspective:

1. *What happened? (narration and description).* Alice Stewart
   Trillin recounts her experience as a cancer patient and then
   describes how it changed the way she looks at the world.
2. *How do you do it? (process analysis).* Jane Brody analyzes
   the procedures for selecting the kind of exercise program
   best suited to your age, health, and fitness.
3. *How is it similar to or different from something else? (comparison and contrast).* Gerald Weissmann compares the
   kind of information that used to appear on a patient's
   medical charts with the data-based test results that are
   generated by computer. He compares both kinds of documents to the narratives of traditional and contemporary
   novels.
4. *What kind of subdivision does it contain? (division and
   classification).* Lewis Thomas divides medical technology
   into three classes and then assesses which class is the most
   efficient.
5. *How would you characterize it? (definition).* Richard Selzer

reflects on the difficulty of defining the source, intensity, and impact of pain without the use of metaphoric language.

6. *How did it happen? (cause and effect).* Norman Cousins analyzes how laughter (as well as all of life's positive emotions) can help heal disease.

7. *How can you prove it? (persuasion and argument).* Janice Castro presents compelling examples to demonstrate her assertion that dealing with our health problems requires thoughtful economic, political, and moral solutions.

The collection ends with Charles Johnson's short story "A Sorcerer's Apprentice" and student Ann Juralbal's essay "How to Avoid Second-Semester Burnout." The story focuses on a young man's attempt to learn the wisdom of an old conjure doctor. The student essay provides the kind of wisdom every student needs to avoid the physical and psychological distress of burnout.

Both selections raise questions that weave their way throughout the other writing in this section: How can I control my own health (or the health of others)? What habits or procedures do I need to learn to ensure good health? Why does my physical health depend on an enlightened attitude toward my emotional health?

As you examine these selections, keep track of how your reading expands your resources—provoking memories, adding information, and suggesting questions you had not considered when you made your initial inventory about health. Because this information will give you new ways to think about your original questions, you will want to explore your thinking in writing.

The assignments that follow each selection suggest several ways that you can use these resources for writing:

1. You can *respond* to the essay by shaping a similar experience according to its method of organization.

2. You can *analyze* the essay to discover how the writer uses

specific strategies to communicate a purpose to an audience.

3. You can use the essay as a springboard for an essay that *argues* a similar thesis in a different context.

4. You can *compare* the essay to other selections in the anthology that raise similar questions about health. At the end of each writing assignment, one or two selections are suggested as Resources for Comparison.

5. You can follow Ann Juralbal's example and explore some aspect of health by *combining* several writing strategies.

Drawing on your experience, reading, and familiarity with writing strategies, you are ready to work up a writing assignment on any subject.

Alice Stewart Trillin was born in 1938 in Rye, New York, and was educated at Wellesley College and Yale University. Trillin worked for several years as a college English teacher in New York City. That experience was the basis for her book about teaching underprepared students, *Teaching Basic Skills* (1980). She then began producing educational programming for public television. Her first series, *Writers Writing* (1985), is a dramatic portrayal of the writing process; her second, *Behind the Scenes* (1992), is a ten-part series presenting the arts to children. She first delivered "Of Dragons and Garden Peas" as a talk to medical students at both Cornell and Albert Einstein medical schools; she then published it in the *New England Journal of Medicine*. Using her own experience as a cancer patient, Trillin describes how her illness affected her attitude toward doctors, patients, friends, and family.

Of Dragons and Garden Peas
(Narration and Description)

WHEN I FIRST realized that I might have cancer, I felt   1
immediately that I had entered a special place, a place I came to call "The Land of the Sick People." The most disconcerting thing, however, was not that I found that place terrifying and unfamiliar, but that I found it so ordinary, so banal. I didn't feel different, didn't feel that my life had radically changed at the moment the word *cancer* became attached to it. The same rules still held. What had changed, however, was other people's perceptions of me. Uncon-

sciously, even with a certain amount of kindness, everyone—
with the single rather extraordinary exception of my husband—regarded me as someone who had been altered
irrevocably. I don't want to exaggerate my feeling of alienation or to give the impression that it was in any way dramatic.
I have no horror stories of the kind I read a few years ago in
the *New York Times;* people didn't move their desks away
from me at the office or refuse to let their children play with
my children at school because they thought that cancer was
catching. My friends are all too sophisticated and too sensitive
for that kind of behavior. Their distance from me was marked

*Our fear of death makes it essential to
maintain a distance between ourselves and
anyone who is threatened by death.*

most of all by their inability to understand the ordinariness,
the banality of what was happening to me. They marveled at
how well I was "coping with cancer." I had become special,
no longer like them. Their genuine concern for what had
happened to me, and their complete separateness from it,
expressed exactly what I had felt all my life about anyone I
had ever known who had experienced tragedy.

When asked to speak to a group of doctors and medical   2
students about what it was like to be a cancer patient, I
worried for a long time about what I should say. It was a
perfect opportunity—every patient's fantasy—to complain
about doctors' insensitivity, nurses who couldn't draw blood
properly, and perhaps even the awful food in hospitals. Or,
instead, I could present myself as the good patient, full of
uplifting thoughts about how much I had learned from having cancer. But, unlike many people, I had had very good
experiences with doctors and hospitals. And the role of the
brave patient troubled me, because I was afraid that all the

brave things I said might no longer hold if I got sick again. I had to think about this a great deal during the first two years after my operation as I watched my best friend live out my own worst nightmares. She discovered that she had cancer several months after I did. Several months after that, she discovered that it had metastasized; she underwent eight operations during the next year and a half before she died. All my brave talk was tested by her illness as it has not yet been tested by mine.

And so I decided not to talk about the things that separate   3
those of us who have cancer from those who do not. I decided that the only relevant thing for me to talk about was the one thing that we all have most in common. We are all afraid of dying.

Our fear of death makes it essential to maintain a distance   4
between ourselves and anyone who is threatened by death. Denying our connection to the precariousness of others' lives is a way of pretending that we are immortal. We need this deception—it is one of the ways we stay sane—but we also need to be prepared for the times when it doesn't work. For doctors, who confront death when they go to work in the morning as routinely as other people deal with balance sheets and computer printouts, and for me, to whom a chest x-ray or a blood test will never again be a simple, routine procedure, it is particularly important to face the fact of death squarely, to talk about it with one another.

Cancer connects us to one another because having cancer   5
is an embodiment of the existential paradox that we all experience: we feel that we are immortal, yet we know that we will die. To Tolstoy's Ivan Ilyich, the syllogism he had learned as a child, "'Caius is a man, men are mortal, therefore Caius is mortal,' had always seemed . . . correct as applied to Caius but certainly not as applied to himself." Like Ivan Ilyich, we all construct an elaborate set of defense mechanisms to separate ourselves from Caius. To anyone who has had cancer, these defense mechanisms become talismans that we invest with a kind of magic. These talismans are essential to our sanity, and yet they need to be examined.

First of all, we believe in the magic of doctors and medi- 6
cine. The purpose of a talisman is to give us control over the
things we are afraid of. Doctors and patients are accomplices
in staging a kind of drama in which we pretend that doctors
have the power to keep us well. The very best doctors—and
I have had the very best—share their power with their patients and try to give us the information that we need to
control our own treatment. Whenever I am threatened by
panic, my doctor sits me down and tells me something concrete. He draws a picture of my lung, or my lymph nodes; he
explains as well as he can how cancer cells work and what
might be happening in my body. Together, we approach my
disease intelligently and rationally, as a problem to be solved,
an exercise in logic to be worked out. Of course, through
knowledge, through medicine, through intelligence, we do
have some control. But at best this control is limited, and
there is always the danger that the disease I have won't behave
rationally and respond to the intelligent argument we have
constructed. Cancer cells, more than anything else in nature,
are likely to behave irrationally. If we think that doctors and
medicine can always protect us, we are in danger of losing
faith in doctors and medicine when their magic doesn't work.
The physician who fails to keep us well is like an unsuccessful
witch doctor; we have to drive him out of the tribe and look
for a more powerful kind of magic.

The reverse of this, of course, is that the patient becomes 7
a kind of talisman for the doctor. Doctors defy death by
keeping people alive. To a patient, it becomes immediately
clear that the best way to please a doctor is to be healthy. If
you can't manage that, the next best thing is to be well-
behaved. (Sometimes the difference between being healthy
and being well-behaved becomes blurred in a hospital, so that
it almost seems as if being sick were being badly behaved.) If
we get well, we help our doctors succeed; if we are sick, we
have failed. Patients often say that their doctors seem angry
with them when they don't respond to treatment. I think that
this phenomenon is more than patients' paranoia or the result

of overdeveloped medical egos. It is the fear of death again. It is necessary for doctors to become a bit angry with patients who are dying, if only as a way of separating themselves from someone in whom they have invested a good bit of time and probably a good bit of caring. We all do this to people who are sick. I can remember being terribly angry with my mother, who was prematurely senile, for a long time. Somehow I needed to think that it was her fault that she was sick, because her illness frightened me so much. I was also angry with my friend who died of cancer. I felt that she had let me down, that perhaps she hadn't fought hard enough. It was important for me to find reasons for her death, to find things that she might have done to cause it, as a way of separating myself from her and as a way of thinking that I would somehow have behaved differently, that I would somehow have been able to stay alive.

So, once we have recognized the limitations of the magic of doctors and medicine, where are we? We have to turn to our own magic, to our ability to "control" our bodies. For people who don't have cancer, this often takes the form of jogging and exotic diets and transcendental meditation. For people who have cancer, it takes the form of conscious development of the will to live. For a long time after I found out that I had cancer, I loved hearing stories about people who had simply decided that they would not be sick. I remember one story about a man who had a lung tumor and a wife with breast cancer and several children to support; he said, "I simply can't afford to be sick." Somehow the tumor went away. I think I suspected that there was a missing part to this story when I heard it, but there was also something that sounded right to me. I knew what he meant. I also found the fact that I had cancer unacceptable; the thought that my children might grow up without me was as ridiculous as the thought that I might forget to make appointments for their dental checkups and polio shots. I simply had to be there. Of course, doctors give a lot of credence to the power of the will over illness, but I have always suspected that the stories in

medical books about this power might also have missing
parts. My friend who died wanted to live more than anyone
I have ever known. The talisman of will didn't work for her.

The need to exert some kind of control over the irrational   9
forces that we imagine are loose in our bodies also results in
what I have come to recognize as the "brave act" put on by
people who have cancer. We all do it. The blood-count line
at Memorial Hospital can be one of the cheeriest places in
New York on certain mornings. It was on this line, during
my first visit to Memorial, that a young leukemia patient in
remission told me, "They treat lung cancer like the common
cold around here." (Believe me, that was the cheeriest thing
anyone had said to me in months.) While waiting for blood
counts, I have heard stories from people with lymphoma who
were given up for dead in other hospitals and who are feeling
terrific. The atmosphere in that line suggests a gathering of
knights who have just slain a bunch of dragons. But there are
always people in the line who don't say anything at all, and
I always wonder if they have at other times felt the exhilaration felt by those of us who are well. We all know, at least,
that the dragons are never quite dead and might at any time
be aroused, ready for another fight. But our brave act is
important. It is one of the ways we stay alive, and it is the
way that we convince those who live in "The Land of the
Well People" that we aren't all that different from them.

As much as I rely on the talisman of the will, I know that   10
believing in it too much can lead to another kind of deception. There has been a great deal written (mostly by psychia-
trists) about why people get cancer and which personality
types are most likely to get it. Susan Sontag has pointed out
that this explanation of cancer parallels the explanations for
tuberculosis that were popular before the discovery of the
tubercle bacillus. But it is reassuring to think that people get
cancer because of their personalities, because that implies that
we have some control over whether we get it. (On the other
hand, if people won't give up smoking to avoid cancer, I
don't see how they can be expected to change their personalities on the basis of far less compelling evidence.) The

trouble with this explanation of cancer is the trouble with any talisman: it is only useful when its charms are working. If I get sick, does that mean that my will to live isn't strong enough? Is being sick a moral and psychological failure? If I feel successful, as if I had slain a dragon, because I am well, should I feel guilty, as if I have failed, if I get sick?

One of the ways that all of us avoid thinking about death   11
is by concentrating on the details of our daily lives. The work that we do every day and the people we love—the fabric of our lives—convince us that we are alive and that we will stay alive. William Saroyan said in a recent book, "Why am I writing this book? To save my life, to keep from dying, of course. That is why we get up in the morning." Getting up in the morning seems particularly miraculous after having seriously considered the possibility that these mornings might be limited. A year after I had my lung removed, my doctors asked me what I cared about most. I was about to go to Nova Scotia, where we have a summer home, and where I had not been able to go the previous summer because I was having radiation treatments, and I told him that what was most important to me was garden peas. Not the peas themselves, of course, though they were particularly good that year. What was extraordinary to me after that year was that I could again think that peas were important, that I could concentrate on the details of when to plant them and how much mulch they would need instead of thinking about platelets and white cells. I cherished the privilege of thinking about trivia. Thinking about death can make the details of our lives seem unimportant, and so, paradoxically, they become a burden—too much trouble to think about. This is the real meaning of depression: feeling weighed down by the concrete, unable to make the effort to move objects around, overcome by ennui. It is the fear of death that causes that ennui, because the fear of death ties us too much to the physical. We think too much about our bodies, and our bodies become too concrete—machines not functioning properly.

The other difficulty with the talisman of the moment is   12
that it is often the very preciousness of these moments that

makes the thought of death so painful. As my friend got closer to death she became rather removed from those she loved the most. She seemed to have gone to some place where we couldn't reach her—to have died what doctors sometimes call a "premature death." I much preferred to think of her enjoying precious moments. I remembered the almost ritualistic way she had her hair cut and tied in satin ribbons before brain surgery, the funny, somehow joyful afternoon that we spent trying wigs on her newly shaved head. Those moments made it seem as if it wasn't so bad to have cancer. But of course it was bad. It was unspeakably bad, and toward the end she couldn't bear to speak about it or to be too close to the people she didn't want to leave. The strength of my love for my children, my husband, my life, even my garden peas has probably been more important than anything else in keeping me alive. The intensity of this love is also what makes me so terrified of dying.

For many, of course, a response to the existential paradox is religion—Kierkegaard's irrational leap toward faith. It is no coincidence that such a high number of conversions take place in cancer hospitals; there is even a group of Catholic nurses in New York who are referred to by other members of their hospital staff as "the death squad." I don't mean to belittle such conversions or any help that religion can give to anyone. I am at this point in my life simply unqualified to talk about the power of this particular talisman. 13

In considering some of the talismans we all use to deny death, I don't mean to suggest that these talismans should be abandoned. However, their limits must be acknowledged. Ernest Becker, in *The Denial of Death,* says that "skepticism is a more radical experience, a more manly confrontation of potential meaninglessness than mysticism." The most important thing I know now that I didn't know four years ago is that this "potential meaninglessness" can in fact be confronted. As much as I rely on my talismans—my doctors, my will, my husband, my children, and my garden peas—I know that from time to time I will have to confront what Conrad described as "the horror." I know that we can—all of us— 14 confront that horror and not be destroyed by it, even, to some extent, be enhanced by it. To quote Becker again: "I think that taking life seriously means something such as this: that whatever man does on this planet has to be done in the lived truth of the terror of creation, of the grotesque, of the rumble of panic underneath everything. Otherwise it is false."

It astonishes me that having faced the terror, we continue 15
to live, even to live with a great deal of joy. It is commonplace for people who have cancer—particularly those who feel as well as I do—to talk about how much richer their lives are because they have confronted death. Yes, my life is very rich. I have even begun to understand that wonderful line in *King Lear*, "Ripeness is all." I suppose that becoming ripe means finding out that none of the really important questions have answers. I wish that life had devised a less terrifying, less risky way of making me ripe. But I wasn't given any choice about this.

William Saroyan said recently, "I'm growing old! I'm fall- 16
ing apart! And it's VERY INTERESTING!" I'd be willing to bet that Mr. Saroyan, like me, would much rather be young and all in one piece. But somehow his longing for youth and wholeness doesn't destroy him or stop him from getting up in the morning and writing, as he says, to save his life. We will never kill the dragon. But each morning we confront him. Then we give our children breakfast, perhaps put a bit more mulch on the peas, and hope that we can convince the dragon to stay away for a while longer.

Topics for Writing
Narration and Description

1. *Respond.* In an essay for the Guest Opinion column of the journal of your state medical association (e.g., *The Journal of the Texas Medical Association*), tell your experience on some occasion when you were ill or had to visit a local doctor for a checkup. Describe how it felt to be a patient and how various members of the medical community (doctors, nurses, technicians) treated you. (*Resources for Comparison:* Terry Tempest Williams, "The Village Watchman," page 45; Nikki Giovanni, "Campus Racism 101," page 121)

2. *Analyze.* If you are interested in films and filmmaking, you may enjoy knowing that Alice Stewart Trillin has had considerable experience in making films. Write an essay for the members of a campus film club in which you analyze the various cinematic techniques she uses to set scenes and evoke the dramatic details in "Of Dragons and Garden Peas." You might also try to reconstruct the dramatics of the "scene" where Trillin first read this paper—an audience of doctors and medical students. How did she make them see their jobs in a different way? (*Resources for Comparison:* Flannery O'Connor, "Revelation," page 280; Stephen Jay Gould, "Carrie Buck's Daughter," page 417)

3. *Argue.* In a column for the newsletter of your church or your church's young people's organization, argue the merits of volunteering for your local hospice program. Point out that though many people want to detach themselves from friends and family who are seriously ill, the experience of volunteering can be very rich. You may want to interview the people who train Hospice volunteers, a Hospice volunteer, and a family who has used Hospice services to gather information for your argument. (*Resources for Comparison:* Francine du Plessix Gray, "On Friendship," page 341; Raymond Carver, "What We Talk About When We Talk About Love," page 352)

Jane Brody was born in 1941 in Brooklyn, New York, and was educated at Cornell University and the University of Wisconsin. She worked as a reporter for the *Minneapolis Tribune* before moving on to a job as science reporter for the *New York Times,* where she specialized in articles on medicine and biology. For the last thirty years, Brody has written a syndicated column, "Personal Health," which has established her as one of our country's foremost experts on health and nutrition. Her books include *Jane Brody's Nutrition Book* (1981), *Jane Brody's The New York Times Guide to Personal Health* (1982), and *Jane Brody's Good Food Book* (1985). In "Choosing an Exercise: What to Consider," reprinted from her *Guide to Personal Health,* Brody explains how to select the kind of exercise that is appropriate for you.

Choosing an Exercise: What to Consider
(Process Analysis)

. . . YOU CAN ACHIEVE total fitness in four minutes a day. . . . Jogging isn't enough; you have to *run* if you want to be really fit. . . . If you're over fifty, you should stick to walking. . . . If you can't exercise every day, you'd better not do it at all. . . . Swimming is the best exercise. . . . If you're thin (or muscular), you don't need to exercise. . . .

The list of myths and mistruths about exercise could go on and on. There are at least as many as there are miles in a marathoner's diary. For the millions of Americans who already have or eventually will succumb to the admonitions to get moving for the sake of their bodies and souls, the prevailing mythology has prompted confusion, anxiety, and inappropriate decisions on when and how to move.

Exercise can serve many purposes. It can enhance skills,   3 improve flexibility, build muscle strength and tone, relieve tension, help you lose weight and maintain the loss, and improve your body's general physiological condition, especially the ease with which your heart can supply oxygen to body tissues.

Different types of exercise may serve some of these functions, but not others. For example, bowling and golf can help   4

In choosing an exercise, it's important to know what you hope to get out of it.

---

you become more skillful at the game, strengthen certain muscles, and expend energy (calories), but they rarely involve enough continuous activity to condition your cardiovascular system. Isometric exercises (those which clamp down on muscles), such as weight lifting, water skiing, and arm wrestling, will promote strong muscles but are useless—in fact, countereffective—as cardiovascular conditioners and may actually be harmful to people with heart disease. On the other hand, brisk walking may do little for your athletic skills or muscle strength, but it can be highly beneficial to your heart and figure.

CONSIDER THE HEALTH VALUE

In choosing an exercise, it's important to know what you   5 hope to get out of it and whether that choice will help you achieve your goals.

Any type of exercise—from hanging laundry and scrubbing floors to badminton, skating, football, or long-distance   6 running—can help you control your weight. Weight gain represents an excess number of calories consumed over the number your body uses for energy. With any kind of motion, your body uses more calories than it does at rest. The more you move, the more calories you use. The heavier you are to start with, the more calories it takes to move yourself a given distance.

As an added benefit, moderate exercise improves the accuracy of your body's appetite control mechanism and usually decreases rather than increases appetite. It helps your body better adjust food intake to calorie expenditure.   7

You don't have to sweat or exercise strenuously to use energy. In fact, walking a mile uses approximately the same number of calories as running a mile. At moderate ranges of activity the difference, as far as calories are concerned, is that running a mile is faster and you may then have time to run a second mile and use up twice as many calories. In addition to the calories used while exercising, your body continues to use calories at a higher rate for many hours after you stop exercising.   8

Some activities are intense energy guzzlers, using eight or more times the amount of calories your body consumes at rest. These include running more than five and a half miles an hour, cycling thirteen or more miles an hour, playing squash and handball, and skipping rope. But you can use as many calories playing Ping-Pong or volleyball for an hour as you would running for half an hour.   9

This is not to say that Ping-Pong in any amount can be equivalent to running in total all-around exercise value. You are most likely to achieve a conditioning effect (fitness or endurance) if the activity uses the large muscles in a rhythmic, repetitive, continuous motion—so-called isotonic exercises. While the amount of energy (calories) used depends only on the amount of work your body does, conditioning is a function of both the amount of work and the vigor with which it is done.   10

A cardiovascular conditioning exercise must also be aerobic—that is, it promotes the use of oxygen and is capable of being sustained for at least two minutes at a time without   11 your getting out of breath. Walking, running, cycling, and swimming are aerobic exercises, but sprinting is not.

To condition the cardiovascular system, the exercise 12 should be performed at least three times a week for twenty minutes at a time during which the heart rate is within the individual's target zone. The target zone falls between 70 and 80 percent of the maximum rate your heart can achieve. The maximum heart rate (or pulse rate), counted as beats per minute, can be estimated for the average healthy adult by subtracting his or her age in years from 220; then taking 70 percent and 85 percent of that number. Between the two is the pulse rate range that is the target zone.

Thus, if you are forty-five years old, your maximal heart 13 rate would theoretically be 175, and the pulse rate to aim for—your target zone—in your exercise program would be between 122 and 148 beats per minute. There is little cardiac conditioning to be gained from exercise that falls much below or that exceeds this level.

To determine your heart rate while exercising, stop and 14 immediately take your pulse: Count the beats in ten seconds, and multiply by 6. As you become conditioned to a certain level of exercise, you may have to increase the rigor of your workout to keep your heart rate within the target zone. To avoid undue stress on your muscles and heart, every twenty-minute exercise session should be preceded by a five- to ten-minute warm-up and followed by a five- to ten-minute cool-down period of less intense exercise (if you're a jogger, you might walk briskly during your warm-up and cool-down). Stretching after exercise is important for preventing joint and muscle injuries and stiffness.

A conditioning exercise should be done regularly or the 15 benefits are rapidly lost. If you must stop for a week or more, resume at a lower-level workout and gradually build up again.

WHAT ELSE TO THINK ABOUT

Other factors to consider when you choose an exercise in- 16 clude the following:

Time available. Running or indoor stationary cycling can be 17
done at any time for thirty minutes or more. Organized
sports tend to be more time-consuming and restrictive. For
those short of time who can take the rigor of the activity, rope
jumping for ten minutes can provide a conditioning effect
equivalent to thirty minutes of jogging.

Cost and convenience. Tennis, for example, may involve driv- 18
ing miles to a court, paying high fees, searching for a partner,
and arranging schedules, all of which may discourage regular
participation. The cost of a bicycle (indoors or out) may be
prohibitive for some, but a jump rope can be purchased for
a dollar or two. For most people, sex is convenient and
inexpensive and uses a lot of calories, but to achieve a conditioning effect, the preorgasmic level of activity would have to
be maintained for at least twenty minutes.

Your body's capabilities. If you're uncoordinated, ball games 19
or rope jumping may prove very frustrating. If you're tight-
jointed, you may need flexibility-enhancing exercises (calis-
thenics) before you try running or tennis.

Age, health status, and present physical condition. Older peo- 20
ple need less rigorous activity to bring their heart rate into
the target zone. Beyond the age of thirty-five, you would be
wise to check with your doctor before starting a rigorous
exercise program. The doctor may recommend an exercise
stress test to see what level of activity your cardiovascular
system can tolerate.

Beyond fifty, condition yourself first through a walking 21
program before beginning more strenuous exercises. Beyond
sixty, most people would be wise to avoid the more taxing
exercises, such as jogging and competitive sports, and stick
instead to walking, swimming, and cycling, unless of course
they've been engaged in more vigorous activities for years. At
any age, if you have been sedentary for years or are out of
condition, start slowly and work up to more demanding
activities. Anyone with a chronic illness or muscle or joint

problems should consult a physician before starting to exercise.

Personal taste. You're more likely to stick with an exercise   22
that you enjoy, but you should give a new activity a trial of a
month or two before deciding you don't like it. Dr. Lenore
R. Zohman, an exercise cardiologist at Montefiore Hospital
in the Bronx, New York, advises that you think back to the
activities you enjoyed as a youngster for clues to what you
might like today.

"If you have an aversion to organized sports or strenuous   23
activity," she says, "brisk walking for twenty to thirty minutes
or climbing up twenty-five flights of stairs at a comfortable
pace during a day can help you achieve physical fitness."

Dr. Zohman points out that contrary to popular belief,   24
"there is no best exercise for everyone." Others recommend
that exercisers hone their skills at more than one activity. This
helps to develop muscle strength throughout the body, diminishes the chances of injury that can result when some
muscles are developed at the expense of others, and provides
alternative exercise possibilities if the main activity can't be
done at a particular time. When it rains, for example, someone who usually jogs or plays tennis can jump rope or ride a
stationary bicycle.

Topics for Writing
Process Analysis

1. *Respond.* Brody says that "The list of myths and mistruths about exercise could go on and on." For an article directed to the readers of a health and fitness magazine (you can easily find one at your local newsstand), write about an experience in your life in which you bought an exercise machine or invested in an exercise video or health club only to discover that you had been "sold." Analyze how the process was supposed to work, and assess the reasons it failed. (*Resources for Comparison:* Donna Tartt, "Basketball Season," page 37; John Berendt, "The Hoax," page 314)

2. *Analyze.* Although Brody suggests that "Exercise can serve many purposes," she is clearly interested in recommending exercise as a process for producing healthy citizens. In an essay to be shared and discussed with your fellow writing students, show how Brody's writing strategies serve her purpose. Analyze the way she tries to anticipate objections or suggest alternatives to those readers who find exercise tedious or inconvenient and how she goes about achieving her social goal: public compliance (that is, people agreeing to do something they ordinarily would not do). (*Resources for Comparison:* Philip Weiss, "How to Get Out of a Locked Trunk," page 127; William Styron, "The Habit," page 497)

3. *Argue.* Brody argues that exercise is essential to good health. Just for the fun of playing the Devil's Advocate, write an opinion column for your campus newspaper in which you argue for the alternative: exercise destroys good health. You might take the position that too much exercise produces excessive stress, stress that actually creates significant physical and psychological problems such as shin splints and losing friends. (*Resources for Comparison:* Elizabeth Winthrop, "The Golden Darters," page 145; Daniel Goleman, "Peak Performance: Why Records Fall," page 401)

Gerald Weissmann was born in Vienna, Austria, in 1930 and subsequently became a United States citizen. He received his bachelor's degree from Columbia University and his doctorate of medicine from New York University. He is currently professor of medicine at New York University Medical Center. Although his medical specialty is the diagnosis and treatment of arthritis, his avocation is writing about the growing division between the humanities and the sciences. His graceful essays, most of which were first published in *Hospital Practice*, treat subjects such as crime, bag ladies, plague, and nuclear weapons. They have been collected in *The Woods Hole Cantata: Essays on Science and Society* (1985) and *They All Laughed at Christopher Columbus: Tales of Medicine and the Art of Discovery* (1987). "The Chart of the Novel," reprinted from *The Woods Hole Cantata*, is a fanciful and provocative comparison of medical charts and novels.

The Chart of the Novel
(Comparison and Contrast)

L IKE OTHER PROFESSIONALS—football scouts, diplomats, and underwriters come to mind—doctors write many words, under pressure of time and for a limited audience. I refer, of course, to the medical charts of our patients. Most of these manuscripts (for even now this material is written almost entirely by hand) are rarely consulted by anyone other than doctors, nurses, or (Heaven forbid!) lawyers. I have always found the libraries of this literature, the record rooms

1

of hospitals, to contain a repository of human, as well as clinical, observations. On their tacky shelves, bound in buff cardboard and sometimes only partially decipherable, are stories of pluck and disaster, muddle and death. If well compressed and described, these *Brief Lives* are more chiseled than Aubrey's. Best of all, I love the conventional paragraph by which the story is introduced. Our tales invariably begin

> *We doctors seem to have exchanged the story of a single human for an impersonal checklist which describes a "case" with "problems."*

with the chief complaint that brought the patient to the hospital. Consider this sampling from three local hospitals:

> *This is the third MSH admission of a chronically wasted 64-year-old, 98-pound male Hungarian refugee composer, admitted from an unheated residential hotel with the chief complaint of progressive weakness (1945).* 2

> *This is the second SVH admission of a 39-year-old, obese Welsh male poet, admitted in acute coma after vomiting blood (1953).* 3

> *This is the first BH admission of a 22-year-old black, female activist transferred from the Women's House of Detention with chief complaints of sharp abdominal pains and an acutely inflamed knee (1968).* 4

How evocative of time, place, and person—and how different in tone and feeling from other sorts of opening lines! They certainly owe little to the news story: "Secretary 5 of State Schultz appeared today before the Foreign Relations Committee of the Senate to urge ratification of . . ." Nor does the description of a chief complaint owe its punch to any derivation from formal scientific prose: "Although the metabolism of arachidonic acid has been less studied in neutrophils than . . ."

The opening sequence of a medical record is unique, and 6 when well written, there's nothing quite like it. These lines localize a human being of defined sex, age, race, occupation, and physical appearance to a moment of extreme crisis: He or she has been "admitted." Attention must therefore be paid and everything recorded on that chart after the admitting note is a narrative account of that attention, of medical "care."

But this enthusiasm for the products of clinical prose may 7 be unwarranted. There may be other prose forms which, by their nature, tug at the reader with such firm hands: I have not found them. Now, my search has not been exhaustive— indeed, my inquiries are based on a sort of hunt-and-peck excursion amongst the yellowing survivors of my dated library. I must report, however, that no similar jabs of evocative prose hit me from the opening lines of biographer, of critic, of historian—not at all the kind of impact I was looking for. No, the real revelation came from the nineteenth-century novelist. I should not have been surprised:

> *Emma Woodhouse, handsome, clever and rich, with* 8
> *a comfortable home and happy disposition, seemed to*
> *unite some of her best blessings of existence, and had*
> *lived nearly twenty-one years in the world with very*
> *little to distress or vex her.*
> EMMA *Jane Austen*

> *Madame Vauquer (nee Deconflans) is an elderly* 9
> *person who for the past forty years has kept a lodging*
> *house in the Rue Neuve-Sainte-Genevieve, in the*
> *district that lies between the Latin Quarter and the*
> *Faubourg Saint-Marcel. Her house receives men and*

*women and no word has ever been breathed against
her respectable establishment.*
LE PÈRE GORIOT *Honoré de Balzac*

*Fyodor Pavlovitch Karamazov, a landowner well
known in our district in his own day, and still remembered among us owing to his mysterious and
tragic death, was a strange type, despicable and vicious, and at the same time absurd.*
THE BROTHERS KARAMAZOV *Fyodor Dostoyevsky*

10

Now, that sort of beginning is a little more like the opening
paragraphs of our charts. Does this mean that we've been
writing nineteenth-century novels all our professional lives,
but without knowing it? Do the white, pink, and blue sheets
which describe the events between admission and dis-
charge—between beginning and end—constitute a multi-
authored *roman à clef*? If we go on to the rest of the record,
it is more likely than not that other sources can be identified.
The "History of Present Illness," with its chronological list-
ings of coughs, grippes, and disability, owes much to the
novelist, but more to the diarist. But the "Past Medical History," drawn to the broader scale of social interactions, returns us again to the world of the novel, and the more
detailed "Family and Social History," which describes the
ailments of aunts and of nephews, which lists not only military service but the patient's choice of addiction, puts us into
the very middle of the realistic novel of 1860.

11

Now comes the "Physical Examination." Here the world
of the clinic or the laboratory intrudes: numbers, descriptions, and measurements. Indeed, from this point on, the
record is written in recognition of the debt medicine owes to
formal scientific exposition. In this portion of the chart, after
all the histories are taken, after the chest has been thumped
and the spleen has been fingered, after the white cells have
been counted and the potassium surveyed, the doctor can be
seen to abandon the position of recorder and to assume that
of the natural scientist. He arrives at a "Tentative Diagnosis,"

12

a hypothesis, so to speak, to be tested, as time, laboratory procedures, or responses to treatment confirm or deny the initial impression. The revisions of this hypothesis, together with accounts of how doctors and patients learn more about what is *really* wrong, constitute the bulk of our manuscript.

So we can argue that our records are an amalgam between   13
the observational norms of the nineteenth-century novelist and the causal descriptions of the physiologist. There is, per-haps, a connection between the two. If we agree that a novelist not only tells a story but weaves a plot, we imply by this the concept of causality. E. M. Forster, in *Aspects of the Novel,* draws the distinction nicely. He suggests that when a writer tells us, "The King dies, and then the Queen died," we are being told a story. When, however, the sentence is altered to read, "The King dies, and therefore the Queen died of grief," we are offered a plot—the notion of causality has been introduced. In much of our medical record keeping we are busy spinning a series of clinical plots: the temperature went down *because* antibiotics were given, etc.

Pick up a chart at random, and you will see what I mean.   14
The sixty-year-old taxi driver has been treated for eight days with antibiotics for his pneumonia. "Intern's Note: Fever down, sputum clearing, will obtain follow-up X-ray." A few days later: "X-ray shows round nodule near segment with resolving infiltrate. Have obtained permission for bron-choscopy and biopsy." Then, "JAR Note: Results of biopsy discussed with patient and family." Months intervene, and at the end of the readmission chart we find the dreary "Intern's Note: 4:00 A.M. Called to see patient . . ." Infection and tumor, hypothesis and test, beginning and end. And so we read these mixtures of story and plot, learning as much along the way about the sensibilities of the doctor as we do of the patient and his disease. The physician-narrator becomes as important to the tale as the unseen Balzac lurking in the boarding house of Madame Vauquer.

An optimistic attempt to reconcile both sources of our   15
clinical narratives, the novel and the scientist's notebook, was made by that great naturalist—and optimist—Emile Zola.

After an exhilarating dip into the work of Claude Bernard, Zola decided that the new modes of scientific description and their causal analyses might yield a *method* which would apply to the novel as well. Basing his argument on Bernard's *An Introduction to the Study of Experimental Medicine* (1865), Zola wrote an essay entitled *The Experimental Novel*. Zola explained that the novelist customarily begins with an experimental fact: He has observed—so to speak—the behavior of a fictional protagonist. Then, using the inference of character as a sort of hypothesis, the novelist invents a series of lifelike situations which test, as it were, whether the observations of behavior are concordant with the inference. The unfolding of the narrative, interpreted causally as plot, will then naturally, and inevitably, verify the hypothesis. How neat—and how reductionist!

But however simplified this scheme of Zola may appear to us today, it has the merit of suggesting how strong, indeed, is the base of scientific optimism upon which traditional clinical description rests. Our descriptions imply our confidence that detailed observation of individual responses to common disease have a permanent value, which can be used predictively. They reveal an upbeat conviction that causal relations, when appreciated, lead to therapeutic (or narrative) success. Recent views of medicine and the novel seem to challenge these assumptions. 16

If we look at the ways in which we have changed our records in the last decade from the "Problem-Oriented Patient Record," to the "Defined Data Base," we appear to have shifted from a view of patient and disease based on the human, novelistic approach of the last century to one based on the flow sheet of the electronic engineer or the punch card of the computer. No longer do our early narratives end in a tentative diagnosis, a testable hypothesis: we are left with a series of unconnected "problems." The stories dissolve into a sort of diagnostic litany—e.g., anemia, weight loss, fever, skin spots—without the unifying plot that ties these up with the causal thread of leukemia. Worse yet, these records are now frequently transformed into a series of checks scrawled 17 over preprinted sheets which carry in tedious detail a computer-generated laundry list of signs and symptoms. The anomie of impersonal, corporate personnel forms has crept into these records. Added to these forces, which have turned the doctor's prose into institutional slang, is the movement to eliminate reflections on sex preference, race, and social background. In the name of convenience and egalitarianism, we seem to have exchanged the story of the single sick human at a moment of crisis for an impersonal checklist which describes a "case" with "problems." When we fail at words, we fail to understand, we fail to feel.

But, I'm afraid that the new novelists have anticipated us   18
here, too. As the naturalistic novel has yielded to the stream of consciousness, to existential angst, and to flat introspection, the anomie of the clinic has been foreshadowed by that of the artist. The opening lines of our major modern novels sound the tones of disengagement as clearly as our clinical records.

> *Today, mother is dead. Or perhaps yesterday. I don't*   19
> *know. I received a telegram from the Home. "Mother*
> *dead. Funeral tomorrow. Best Wishes." It means*
> *nothing. Perhaps it was yesterday.*
> THE STRANGER *Albert Camus (1942)*

> *If only I could explain to you how changed I am since*   20
> *those days! Changed yet still the same, but now I can*
> *view my old preoccupation with a calm eye.*
> THE BENEFACTOR *Susan Sontag (1963)*

> *What makes Iago evil? Some people ask. I never ask.*   21
> PLAY IT AS IT LAYS *Joan Didion (1970)*

Perhaps as doctors we are now committed to acting as a   22
group of "benefactors" ministering to the sick "strangers"—
we cannot, or will not, be involved in the lives of those who
have come to us for care; we will now simply describe and
solve the problems of the case. We will play it as it lays.

Topics for Writing
Comparison and Contrast

1. *Respond.* Consider how you feel when your identity is summarized by a piece of paper—your driver's license, your grade report, medical tests, or a résumé. Then in a letter to an authority in the relevant area—a traffic judge, a college probations board, an insurance agent, a potential employer—explain why you are more capable or qualified than the piece of paper in question indicates. For example, explain to a traffic judge why you shouldn't have your license suspended even though you have acquired three moving violations. Be careful to keep in mind your audience's attitudes and concerns. (*Resources for Comparison:* Wendell Berry, "The Problem of Tobacco," page 504, Maya Angelou, "My Name is Margaret," page 29)
2. *Analyze.* Compare the kind of information Weissmann gives you about the characters described in excerpts from the medical charts and novels. Select the character you know the *most* about and the character you know the *least* about. Then in an essay to be shared with other students in your writing class, analyze the procedures you used to arrive at your decisions. (*Resources for Comparison:* Deborah Tannen, "Rapport-Talk and Report-Talk," page 176; Alison Lurie, "Folktale Liberation," page 333)
3. *Argue.* Weissmann argues that doctors have changed the way they write about their patients, shifting from "Problem-Oriented Patient Record" to the "Defined Data Base." For an audience that has a general interest in health-care issues—for example, readers of *Parade* magazine or *Reader's Digest*—write an essay that confirms Weissmann's conclusion that something important (the human relationship between doctor and patient) has been lost in this shift. Or counter Weissmann's assertion by arguing that the computer generates a valuable list of signs and symptoms that is precise and objective. (*Resources for Comparison:* David McCullough, "FDR and Truman," page 168; Diane Ackerman, "The Face of Beauty," page 409)

LEWIS THOMAS

Lewis Thomas (1913–1993) was born in Flushing, New York, and was educated at Princeton University and Harvard University Medical School. He held appointments at numerous research hospitals and medical schools before becoming president of the Sloan-Kettering Cancer Center in New York City. In 1971 he began contributing a popular column, "Notes of a Biology Watcher," to the *New England Journal of Medicine*. In 1974 his collection of these essays, *The Lives of a Cell: Notes of a Biology Watcher,* won the National Book Award for Arts and Letters. His other books include *The Medusa and the Snail: More Notes of a Biology Watcher (1979), The Youngest Science* (1983), *Late Night Thoughts on Listening to Mahler's Ninth Symphony* (1983), and *The Fragile Species* (1992). In "The Technology of Medicine," reprinted from *The Lives of a Cell,* Thomas classifies "three quite different levels of technology in medicine."

The Technology of Medicine
(Division and Classification)

TECHNOLOGY ASSESSMENT HAS become a routine exercise for the scientific enterprises on which the country is obliged to spend vast sums for its needs. Brainy committees are continually evaluating the effectiveness and cost of doing various things in space, defense, energy, transportation, and the like, to give advice about prudent investments for the future.

Somehow medicine, for all the $80-odd billion that it is

586

said to cost the nation, has not yet come in for much of this analytical treatment. It seems taken for granted that the technology of medicine simply exists, take it or leave it, and the only major technologic problem which policy-makers are interested in is how to deliver today's kind of health care, with equity, to all the people.

When, as is bound to happen sooner or later, the analysts get around to the technology of medicine itself, they will have to face the problem of measuring the relative cost and effectiveness of all the things that are done in the management of

---

There are three quite different levels of technology in medicine, so unlike each other as to seem altogether different undertakings.

---

disease. They make their living at this kind of thing, and I wish them well, but I imagine they will have a bewildering time. For one thing, our methods of managing disease are constantly changing—partly under the influence of new bits of information brought in from all corners of biologic science. At the same time, a great many things are done that are not so closely related to science, some not related at all.

In fact, there are three quite different levels of technology in medicine, so unlike each other as to seem altogether different undertakings. Practitioners of medicine and the analysts will be in trouble if they are not kept separate.

1. First of all, there is a large body of what might be termed "nontechnology," impossible to measure in terms of its capacity to alter either the natural course of disease or its eventual outcome. A great deal of money is spent on this. It is valued highly by the professionals as well as the patients. It consists of what is sometimes called "supportive therapy." It tides patients over through diseases that are not, by and large, understood. It is what is meant by the phrases "caring for"

and "standing by." It is indispensable. It is not, however, a technology in any real sense, since it does not involve measures directed at the underlying mechanism of disease.

It includes the large part of any good doctor's time that is 6
taken up with simply providing reassurance, explaining to patients who fear that they have contracted one or another lethal disease that they are, in fact, quite healthy.

It is what physicians used to be engaged in at the bedside 7
of patients with diphtheria, meningitis, poliomyelitis, lobar pneumonia, and all the rest of the infectious diseases that have since come under control.

It is what physicians must now do for patients with intrac- 8
table cancer, severe rheumatoid arthritis, multiple sclerosis, stroke, and advanced cirrhosis. One can think of at least twenty major diseases that require this kind of supportive medical care because of the absence of an effective technology. I would include a large amount of what is called mental disease, and most varieties of cancer, in this category.

The cost of this nontechnology is very high, and getting 9
higher all the time. It requires not only a great deal of time but also very hard effort and skill on the part of physicians; only the very best of doctors are good at coping with this kind of defeat. It also involves long periods of hospitalization, lots of nursing, lots of involvement of nonmedical professionals in and out of the hospital. It represents, in short, a substantial segment of today's expenditures for health.

2. At the next level up is a kind of technology best termed 10
"halfway technology." This represents the kinds of things that must be done after the fact, in efforts to compensate for the incapacitating effects of certain diseases whose course one is unable to do very much about. It is a technology designed to make up for disease, or to postpone death.

The outstanding examples in recent years are the trans- 11
plantations of hearts, kidneys, livers, and other organs, and the equally spectacular inventions of artificial organs. In the public mind, this kind of technology has come to seem like the equivalent of the high technologies of the physical sciences. The media tend to present each new procedure as

though it represented a breakthrough and therapeutic triumph, instead of the makeshift that it really is.

In fact, this level of technology is, by its nature, at the same 12
time highly sophisticated and profoundly primitive. It is the kind of thing that one must continue to do until there is a genuine understanding of the mechanisms involved in disease. In chronic glomerulonephritis, for example, a much clearer insight will be needed into the events leading to the destruction of glomeruli by the immunologic reactants that now appear to govern this disease, before one will know how to intervene intelligently to prevent the process, or turn it around. But when this level of understanding has been reached, the technology of kidney replacement will not be much needed and should no longer pose the huge problem of logistics, cost, and ethics that it poses today.

An extremely complex and costly technology for the man- 13
agement of coronary heart disease has evolved—involving specialized ambulances and hospital units, all kinds of electronic gadgetry, and whole platoons of new professional personnel—to deal with the end results of coronary thrombosis. Almost everything offered today for the treatment of heart disease is at this level of technology, with the transplanted and artificial hearts as ultimate examples. When enough has been learned to know what really goes wrong in heart disease, one ought to be in a position to figure out ways to prevent or reverse the process, and when this happens the current elaborate technology will probably be set to one side.

Much of what is done in the treatment of cancer, by 14
surgery, irradiation, and chemotherapy, represents halfway technology, in the sense that these measures are directed at the existence of already established cancer cells, but not at the mechanisms by which cells become neoplastic.

It is a characteristic of this kind of technology that it costs 15
an enormous amount of money and requires a continuing expansion of hospital facilities. There is no end to the need for new, highly trained people to run the enterprise. And there is really no way out of this, at the present state of knowledge. If the installation of specialized coronary-care

units can result in the extension of life for only a few patients with coronary disease (and there is no question that this technology is effective in a few cases), it seems to me an inevitable fact of life that as many of these as can be will be put together, and as much money as can be found will be spent. I do not see that anyone has much choice in this. The only thing that can move medicine away from this level of technology is new information, and the only imaginable source of this information is research.

3. The third type of technology is the kind that is so 16 effective that it seems to attract the least public notice; it has come to be taken for granted. This is the genuinely decisive technology of modern medicine, exemplified best by modern methods for immunization against diphtheria, pertussis, and the childhood virus diseases, and the contemporary use of antibiotics and chemotherapy for bacterial infections. The capacity to deal effectively with syphilis and tuberculosis represents a milestone in human endeavor, even though full use of this potential has not yet been made. And there are, of course, other examples: the treatment of endocrinologic disorders with appropriate hormones, the prevention of hemolytic disease of the newborn, the treatment and prevention of various nutritional disorders, and perhaps just around the corner the management of Parkinsonism and sickle-cell anemia. There are other examples, and everyone will have his favorite candidates for the list, but the truth is that there are nothing like as many as the public has been led to believe.

The point to be made about this kind of technology—the 17 real high technology of medicine—is that it comes as the result of a genuine understanding of disease mechanisms, and when it becomes available, it is relatively inexpensive, and relatively easy to deliver.

Offhand, I cannot think of any important human disease 18 for which medicine possesses the outright capacity to prevent or cure where the cost of the technology is itself a major problem. The price is never as high as the cost of managing the same diseases during the earlier stages of no-technology or halfway technology. If a case of typhoid fever had to be managed today by the best methods of 1935, it would run to a staggering expense. At, say, around fifty days of hospitalization, requiring the most demanding kind of nursing care, with the obsessive concern for details of diet that characterized the therapy of that time, with daily laboratory monitoring, and, on occasion, surgical intervention for abdominal catastrophe, I should think $10,000 would be a conservative estimate for the illness, as contrasted with today's cost of a bottle of chloramphenicol and a day or two of fever. The halfway technology that was evolving for poliomyelitis in the early 1950s, just before the emergence of the basic research that made the vaccine possible, provides another illustration of the point. Do you remember Sister Kenny, and the cost of those institutes for rehabilitation, with all those ceremonially applied hot fomentations, and the debates about whether the affected limbs should be totally immobilized or kept in passive motion as frequently as possible, and the masses of statistically tormented data mobilized to support one view or the other? It is the cost of that kind of technology, and its relative effectiveness, that must be compared with the cost and effectiveness of the vaccine.

Pulmonary tuberculosis had similar episodes in its history. 19 There was a sudden enthusiasm for the surgical removal of infected lung tissue in the early 1950s, and elaborate plans were being made for new and expensive installations for major pulmonary surgery in tuberculosis hospitals, and the INH and streptomycin came along and the hospitals themselves were closed up.

It is when physicians are bogged down by their incomplete 20 technologies, by the innumerable things they are obliged to do in medicine when they lack a clear understanding of disease mechanisms, that the deficiencies of the health-care system are most conspicuous. If I were a policy-maker, interested in saving money for health care over the long haul, I would regard it as an act of high prudence to give high priority to a lot more basic research in biologic science. This is the only way to get the full mileage that biology owes to the science of medicine, even though it seems, as used to be said in the days when the phrase still had some meaning, like asking for the moon.

Topics for Writing
Division and Classification

1. *Respond.* Write an article to appear in the newsletter of your health club or of the Physical Fitness Department of your university or on the weekly health page of your local newspaper. In it make a list of the machines you have encountered that measured your health (scales, stopwatches, x-rays, cardiovascular fitness evaluator). Describe your experience with one such machine that seemed to be consistently wrong. (*Resources for Comparison:* Tom and Ray Magliozzi, "Inside the Engine," page 105; Russell Baker, "The Plot Against People," page 244)

2. *Analyze.* For an essay written for the readers of a general magazine such as *Rolling Stone* or *Esquire,* list the diseases that Lewis Thomas uses to illustrate his three categories, and classify them according to how much attention they seem to get in the medium (television, newspapers, magazines, or radio) that you are most familiar with. For instance, look at feature stories on medical research, newspaper stories about medical breakthroughs, plots on TV hospital shows or soap operas, or segments on shows like *60 Minutes* or *20/20.* Analyze the reasons why some diseases seem to get more (and better) press than others, and show why you believe these priorities should be changed. (*Resources for Comparison:* Bill McKibben, "Nature and Televised Nature," page 191; Gail Sheehy, "Predictable Crises of Adulthood," page 269)

3. *Argue.* Thomas's reservations about "halfway technology" are that it is extremely expensive, rests on a partial understanding of the disease it treats, and requires extensive, costly research. Most of this research begins with laboratory animals, and, for many people, that raises issues about animal rights. For the editorial page of your local or campus newspaper, write a Guest Opinion column in which you argue either that human health should not be purchased with the death of animals or that human health

is more important than animal health so all laboratory experiments are justified. (*Resources for Comparison:* Vicki Hearne, "What's Wrong with Animal Rights?," page 484; Rosemary Bray, "So How Did I Get Here?" page 519)

Richard Selzer was born in Troy, New York, in 1928 and was educated at Union College and Albany Medical College. In 1960, after his internship and postdoctoral study, Selzer established a private practice in general surgery and became an associate professor of surgery at the Yale University medical school. His articles on various aspects of medicine have appeared in magazines such as *Harper's, Esquire, Redbook,* and *Mademoiselle,* and his books include a volume of short stories, *Rituals of Surgery* (1974), and several collections of essays, including *Mortal Lessons: Notes on the Art of Surgery* (1977), *Letters to a Young Doctor* (1983), *Taking the World In for Repairs* (1986), and two memoirs, *Down from Troy: A Doctor Comes of Age* (1992) and *Raising the Dead: A Doctor's Encounter with His Own Mortality* (1993). In "The Language of Pain," a 1994 essay from *The Wilson Quarterly,* Selzer describes the difficulties he has had as a doctor and a writer in trying to define *pain.*

The Language of Pain
(Definition)

WHY DO YOU write so much about pain? they ask me. 1 To give it a name, I reply. And I am not sure what I mean. I try again: In October, when the leaves have fallen from the trees, you can see farther into the forest. Now do you see? No? Well, what is your notion of pain? Pain is fire, a ravening, insatiable thing that insists upon utter domination; it is the occasion when the body reasserts itself over the mind; the universe contracts about the part that hurts; if the pain is not placated with analgesics, it will devour the whole organism. Only then will it too be snuffed. Still, pain is revelatory; in the blaze of it, one might catch a glimpse of the truth about human existence.

It was the poet Rilke who wrote that the events of the body 2
cannot be rendered in language. Surely this is so with pain as with its opposite, orgasm. These extremes of sensation remain beyond the power of language to express. Say that a doctor is examining a patient who is in pain. The doctor needs to know the exact location of the pain and its nature. Is the pain sharp or dull? Steady or intermittent? Does it throb or pulse? Is it stabbing? A heavy pressure? Crampy? Does it burn? Sting? All these questions the doctor asks of the patient. But there is no wholly adequate way for the sufferer to portray his pain other than to cry out. In order to convey his pain, the patient, like the writer, must resort to metaphor, simile, imagery: "You want to know what it's like? It's as if someone were digging in my ribs with a shovel." "It feels as if there's a heavy rock on my chest."

Years ago as a doctor and more recently as a writer, I 3
declared my faith in images—the human fact placed near a superhuman mystery, even if both are illusions of the senses.

In order to convey his pain, the patient, like the writer, must resort to metaphor, simile, and imagery.

Diagnosis, like writing, calls for the imagination and the skill to discover things not seen, things that hide themselves under the shadow of natural objects. It is the purpose of the writer and the doctor to fix these unseen phenomena in words, thereby presenting to plain sight what did not actually exist until he arrived. Much as a footprint hides beneath a foot until a step is taken.

By using metaphor and imagery, the patient brings the   4
doctor into a state of partial understanding of his pain. In
order to express it fully, he would have to cry out in a
language that is incomprehensible to anyone else. This language of pain has no consonants, but consists only of vowels:
ow! aiee! oy! oh! These are the sounds the sufferer makes,
each punctuated by grunts, hiccoughs, sobs, moans, gasps.
It is a self-absorbed language that might have been the first
ever uttered by prehistoric man. Perhaps it was learned from
animals. These howled vowels have the eloquence of the wild,
the uncivilized, the atavistic. Comprehension is instantane-
ous, despite the absence of what we call words. It is a mode
of expression beyond normal language. Nor could it be made
more passionate or revelatory by the most gifted writer. Not
even by Shakespeare.

But what is the purpose of these cries of pain? Wouldn't   5
silence be as eloquent? For one thing, the loud, unrestrained
pouring forth of vowels is useful in attracting the attention
of anyone within earshot who might come to the assistance
of the sufferer. Vowels carry farther than consonants and are
easier to mouth, requiring only the widely opened jaws, without the more complex involvement of tongue, teeth, and
palate that the speaking of consonants requires. Giuseppe
Verdi knew that and made his librettist write lines full of easily
singable vowels and diphthongs. It is the sung vowel that
carries to the last row of La Scala. The consonants are often
elided or faked by the singers who know that consonants are
confined to the immediate vicinity of the stage and are altogether less able to be infused with emotive force. It comes as
no surprise that the greatest opera singers are in the Italian
repertoire—Italian, a language dripping with vowels and in
which there is scarcely a word that does not end in one.
"Mille serpi divoranmi il petto," sings the anguished Alfredo
upon learning of the sacrifice made by his beloved Violetta
in *La Traviata*. The translation—"A thousand snakes are
eating my breast"—simply won't do.

One purpose of these cries of pain, then, might be to   6
summon help, to notify fellow members of the tribe of one's

predicament so that they will come running. But I think there is more to it than that. For the sufferer, these outcries have a kind of magical property of their own, offering not only an outlet for the emotion but a means of letting out the pain. Hollering, all by itself, gives a measure of relief. To cry out ow! or aiee! requires that the noise be carried away from the body on a cloud of warm, humid air that had been within the lungs of the sufferer. The expulsion of this air, and with it, the sound, is an attempt to exteriorize the pain, to dis-possess oneself of it, as though the vowels of pain were, in some magical way, the pain itself. It is not hard to see why the medieval church came to believe that a body, writhing and wracked and uttering unearthly, primitive cries, was pos-sessed by devils. Faced with such a sufferer, authorities of the church deemed exorcism both necessary and compassionate.

Go ahead and holler," says the nurse to the patient. "You'll   7
feel better. Don't hold it in." It is wise advice that has been passed down through the millennia of human suffering. But even these ululations cannot really convey to the reader what the sufferer is feeling, for they are not literature. To write *ow* or *aiee* on a page is not an art. The language of pain, then, is the most exclusive of tongues, spoken and understood by an elite of one. Hearing it, we shudder, out of sympathy for the sufferer, but just as much out of the premonition that each of us shall know this language in our time. Our turn will come. It is a fact that within moments of having been relieved of this pain, sufferers are no longer fluent in this language. They have already forgotten it, all but an inkling or two, and are left with a vague sense of dread, a recollection that the pain was awful, a fear that it might return.

In lieu of language, the doctor seems to diagnose by ex-   8
amining the body and its secretions—urine, blood, spinal fluid—and by using a number of ingenious photographic instruments. A last resort would be the laying open of the body for exploratory surgery. Fifty years ago, it was to the corpse that the doctor went for answers. Ironic that life should have provided concealment and death be revelatory.

Even now, it is only in the autopsy room that the true courage of the human body is apparent, the way it carries on in the face of all odds: arteriosclerosis, calculi, pulmonary fibrosis, softening of the brain. And still the body goes on day after day, bearing its burdens, if not jauntily, at least with acceptance and obedience until at last it must sink beneath the weight of those burdens and come to the morgue where its faithfulness can be observed and granted homage.

There is about pain that which exhilarates even as it appalls,   9
as Emily Dickinson has written. Pain is the expression of the dark underside of the body. As such, the sight of the wound, the sound of the outcry it produces, stir the imagination in a way that pleasure never can. We are drawn to the vicinity of pain by the hint of danger and death, as much as by the human desire to compare our fortunate state to that of those unluckier. Then, too, there is the undeniable relation of pain and beauty, brought to artistic flower during the Renaissance and later by the 19th-century Romantic poets. It is the writhen Christ slumping on the cross that is the emblematic vision of pain from which has come the word *excruciating*. It was Christianity that first tried to wrest meaning from pain. "Offer it up," say the Catholics, as if suffering, boredom, or even annoyance were currency to be paid on the road to sanctity. Simone Weil turned affliction into evidence of God's tenderness. Affliction is love, she wrote. To some, this represents a perversion of the senses, not unlike the masochism that welcomes pain as pleasure. To welcome pain as an approach to God is to negate mercy as proof of His love for human beings. It is an elite band of saints that can achieve ecstasy through pain. Even Christ cried out from the cross: Why hast thou forsaken me?

The artist who would prettify or soften the Crucifixion is   10
missing the point. The aim was to kill horribly and to subject the victim to the utmost humiliation. It involved a preliminary whipping with the dreaded Roman *flagrum,* a leather whip with three tails. At the tip of each tail there was tied a small dumbbell-shaped weight of iron or bone. With each

lash of the whip, the three bits dug into the flesh. The victim was tied or chained to a post and two centurions stood on either side. The wounds extended around to the chest and abdomen. Profuse bleeding ensued. Then the condemned was beaten on the face with reeds so that his face was bruised, his nose broken. To ensure maximum humiliation, the cross was set up in a public place or on an elevation of land such as the hill of Calvary. In the case of Jesus, in order to deride him further and to mock his appellation of King of the Jews, a crown of thorns was placed on his brow. Jesus, weakened by a night of fasting and prayer, as well as by the flogging and the blood loss, was not able to carry his own cross to the place of execution as the punishment required. Simon of Cyrene did it for him. Then Jesus' hands were nailed to the crosspiece, which was raised and set into a groove on the vertical piece. The height was approximately seven and a half feet. At one point, a Roman soldier hurled a spear that opened the wound in his side. To add to Christ's suffering, he was assailed by extreme thirst, as is usual in instances of severe blood loss and dehydration. Once, a disciple was able to reach up and give him a drink through a hollow straw. Death came slowly, from shock, both traumatic and hypovolemic, and from respiratory failure due to the difficulty of expelling air from the lungs in the upright and suspended position when the diaphragm does not easily rise.

I wonder whether man has not lost the ability to withstand 11 pain, what with the proliferation of pain-killing drugs and anesthetic agents. Physical pain has become a once-in-a-while experience for most of the industrialized world. Resistance to pain, like any other unused talent, atrophies, leaving one all the more vulnerable. What to a woman of the late 19th century might have been bearable is insupportable to her great-great-granddaughter. Still, for some, chronic pain is an old adversary, one whose cunning can be, if not negated, at least balanced, by hypnosis, acupuncture, biofeedback, exercise, practice of ritual, and other techniques not well understood. There is that pain which cannot be relieved by any means short of death and which must be lived *against*. Such was the pain of Montaigne who, tortured by bladder stones that occluded the outflow of urine, had to write *against* the pain. On the other hand, Aristotle was unable to philosophize because of his toothache.

Is the pain experienced in a dream any less than the pain 12 experienced while awake? I think it is not. I have a dream that has recurred many times: I am standing alone in the middle of a great empty amphitheater. It is midnight and the scene is bathed in bluish moonlight. The city is European; Milan, I think. At either end of the amphitheater, a statue stands upon a marble pedestal. One is of Caesar wearing a toga and holding up a sheaf of wheat. The other is a great marble tiger. All at once, the tiger stirs, rises to its feet, then rears as if to spring. Yes, it is about to spring! I turn to run in the opposite direction, toward Caesar, but my feet are heavy, so heavy that I cannot lift them. Already I can sense the nearness of the beast, feel its hot breath upon my neck. A moment later there is the pressure of its fangs in the supraclavicular fossa on the left—and again in the nape. And there is pain. I look down to see my shadow bearing the burden of the huge cat on its back. At that instant, I wake up. My heart is pounding; I am gasping; the bed is drenched with sweat. And in the left side of my neck there is pain as if that area had been badly bruised. The pressure of my fingers intensifies the pain that I have brought back with me from the dream, the pain that has crossed from dream to wakefulness. Slowly, my pulse returns to normal; the pain dissipates and I begin to regain a measure of equanimity. But only a measure, for I know that I shall have this dream again, that its pain and horror will be undiminished.

Lying there in the ecstasy of having survived, I wonder: 13 Had I died in the jaws of that tiger, died of a heart attack or sudden arrhythmia, died of fright, doubtless my next of kin would comfort themselves with the knowledge that I had died peacefully in my sleep. "He died the death of a righteous man," they would murmur to one another. Had I the breath for it, I would sit up in the coffin and shout: "No! No! It wasn't like that at all!"

Pain. The very word carries its own linguistic baggage, coming down to us from the Latin *poena*—punishment. It is the penalty for misdeeds; one is placed in a penitentiary and made to do penance. The pain of childbirth was inflicted upon Eve for her act of disobedience, and from her upon all those who follow. Immediately upon delivery of her young, a woman begins to distance herself from the pain which she experienced during childbirth. Such forgetfulness is nature's way of assuring the continuation of the human race. 14

It is at the very least curious that Milton in *Paradise Lost,* reinventing the birth of Eve, has the masculine effrontery to anesthetize Adam during the rib resection. In Book 8, Adam has just finished telling God of his loneliness, his sense of incompleteness. God has promised the solution. Here is Adam describing the birth of Eve: 15

> *Dazzl'd and spent, sunk down, [I] sought repair*
> *Of sleep, which instantly fell on me, call'd*
> *By Nature as in aid, and clos'd mine eyes.*
> *Mine eyes he clos'd, but op'n left the Cell*
> *Of Fancy my internal sight, by which*
> *Abstract as in a trance methought I saw,*
> *Though sleeping where I lay, and saw the shape*
> *Still glorious before whom awake I stood;*
> *Who stooping op'n'd my left side, and took*
> *From thence a Rib, with cordial spirits warm,*
> *And Life-blood streaming fresh; wide was the*
> *   wound,*
> *But suddenly with flesh fill'd up and heal'd:*
> *The Rib he form'd and fashion'd with his hands;*
> *Under his forming hands a Creature grew,*
> *Manlike, but different sex, so lovely fair. . . .*

Milton's act of anesthesia is evidence, if any further were needed, that a man cannot imagine, nor can he admit, the pain of giving birth. It is outside the precincts of his under- 16 standing. Had *Paradise Lost* been written by a woman, doubtless Adam would have felt each and every twinge.

Many is the writer who has tried to make the reader *feel* 17
pain in a fictional character. I among them, in this passage
from an essay on the subject of kidney stones:

> *Whom the stone grips is transformed in one instant* 18
> *from man to shark; and like the shark that must*
> *remain in perpetual motion, fins and tail moving*
> *lest it sink to terrible black depths of pressure, so the*
> *harborer of stone writhes and twists, bending and*
> *unbending in ceaseless turmoil. Now he straightens,*
> *stretches his limbs, only to draw them upon his trunk*
> *the next moment and fling his body from one side to*
> *the other, finding ease in neither. From between his*
> *teeth come sounds so primitive as to trigger the skin*
> *to creep. He shudders and vomits as though to cast*
> *forth the rock that grinds within. He would sell his*
> *birthright, forfeit his honor, his name, even kill to*
> *rid him of it. He toils in bed, pronged and spiked*
> *from within. Seed pearls of sweat break upon his face.*
> *In a moment his hair is heavy with it. His fingers*
> *scrabble against the bed, the wall, his own flesh to*
> *tear relief from these surfaces. But it does not pass.*
> *The impacted stone cannot push through into the*
> *lake, and from there voided. Like some terrible work*
> *of art, insatiable it screams to be extruded, let out*
> *into the air and light so as to be seen, touched, ven-*
> *erated. Never mind that the very act of deliverance*
> *will tear apart its creator.*
>
> *At last he is able to force a few drops of bloody urine* 19
> *and the pain subsides. The stone has fallen away from*
> *the point of impaction, washed loose into the bladder.*
> *He is miraculously free of the pain. It is no less than*
> *being touched by the hand of God. Still, he is afraid*
> *to move lest the lightest change of position should sink*
> *the craggy thing into some new part and the hell be*

reenacted. It has not passed. It lies within him yet, malevolent, scorpioid. It is only a matter of time before the beast will rise again.

Does this convey the pain of colic? I think it does not. No matter the metaphor and simile, all the pomp of language falls short in transmitting pain, that private corporeal experience, to the reader. It is beyond the reach of words; it is subverbal. Just as well, for to convey pain exactly would be to relive it and to suffer anew. In the matter of pain, it is better to experience it metaphorically than to know it directly. [20]

Topics for Writing
Definition

1. *Respond.* In an essay to be shared with the students in your writing class, describe the difficulty you have had in trying to describe a complex emotion in something you were writing or in a conversation that was important to you. Selzer's subject is pain, but you might want to choose another emotion, negative (anxiety, depression) or positive (relief, joy). Describe the situation and the strategies you used to communicate the emotion. Or you might reverse the situation and describe how hard it was on some occasion for you to understand and appreciate how someone else felt. (*Resources for Comparison:* George Orwell, "Shooting an Elephant," page 69; Sandra Cisneros, "One Holy Night," page 430)

2. *Analyze.* Selzer says that he has to rely on metaphor to define pain. He also describes one of our culture's most visual symbols—Christ on the cross—to define the complex associations identified with suffering. For an essay written for a course you are taking in communication or in newspaper or magazine journalism, select another such symbol to write about. You might choose a news photo of refugees or hungry children or the victims of a massacre, or you might choose a painting depicting a pleasant scene such as Renoir's *The Boating Party* or one of Mary Cassatt's pictures of a mother and child. Analyze the way the visual symbol you've chosen expresses complex emotions. (*Resources for Comparison:* Desmond Morris, "Territorial Behaviour," page 256; Kathleen Norris, "The Holy Use of Gossip," page 324)

3. *Argue.* Selzer wonders "whether man has not lost the ability to withstand pain, . . . [that what] to a woman of the late 19th century might have been bearable is insupportable to her great-great-granddaughter." Yet in some ways our society seems to encourage people to endure pain and suggests they will benefit by it. For example, the army

puts some soldiers through training programs so arduous that some participants die; some authorities believe that women should go through childbirth without anesthetic; and athletic coaches often push players to ignore their pain and continue playing. For a Guest Opinion column in your student newspaper or a column like *Newsweek*'s "My Turn," select such an example, and argue that enduring pain can be ennobling or good for the character. Or you might take the opposite view and argue that practices that cause unnecessary pain are senseless and degrading. (*Resources for Comparison:* Wakako Yamauchi, "Otoko," page 55; Rose del Castillo Guilbault, "Americanization Is Tough on 'Macho,'" page 319)

Norman Cousins (1912–1990) was born in Union Hill, New Jersey, and educated at the Teachers College of Columbia University. He started his career as a journalist, then began his long and distinguished association with *Saturday Review.* For over thirty years Cousins directed this important magazine, writing columns and hiring writers who helped shape the reading and artistic tastes of its half-million subscribers. His many books include collections of his own columns (*Writing for Love or Money,* 1949), a collection of the writing of others (*Great American Essays,* 1967), and commentaries on the central issues of our time (*Human Options,* 1981). In the mid-1960s Cousins was stricken by a collagen disease that paralyzed most of his body. When his doctors advised him that his chances for recovery were slim, he became his own physician—prescribing massive injections of vitamin C and large doses of laughter. He documented his discoveries about the causes of illness and effects of "positive emotions" in two popular books, *The Celebration of Life* (1974) and *Anatomy of an Illness* (1976). In "The Laughter Prescription" (1990), Cousins reports on some of the experiments that vindicate his assertions about the influence of laughter on good health.

The Laughter Prescription
(*Cause and Effect*)

T HE TELEPHONE CALL was from the Associated Press correspondent stationed in Chicago. 1
"How does it feel to be fully vindicated?" he was asking. 2

I drew a blank and said so.   3

"There's a report in the new issue of *JAMA* [*Journal of*   4
the American Medical Association] providing scientific evidence that you were right when you wrote that laughter is
useful in combating serious illness," he continued. "It's by
Swedish medical researchers whose experiments show that
laughter helps the body to provide its own medications. Let
me read from the report: 'A humor therapy program can
improve the quality of life for patients with chronic problems.
Laughter has an immediate symptom-relieving effect for
these patients.'

"Since you were heavily criticized by some physicians when   5

---

*Extensive experiments . . . have shown that
laughter contributes to good health.*

---

your article first appeared in the *New England Journal of
Medicine,* it must feel pretty good to have this verification."

Of course I was gratified by the report in *JAMA*. In *Anat-*   6
omy of an Illness, first published in 1976, I had reported my
discovery that ten minutes of solid belly laughter would give
me two hours of pain-free sleep. Since my illness involved
severe inflammation of the spine and joints, making it painful
even to turn over in bed, the practical value of laughter
became a significant feature of treatment.

Dr. William Hitzig, my physician, was as fascinated as I   7
was by the clear evidence that laughter could be a potent
painkiller. He tested this proposition by comparing my sedimentation rate before and after my response to amusing
situations in films or books. The sedimentation test measures
the extent of inflammation or infection in the body. Since my
sedimentation rate was in the upper range, any reduction was
to be welcomed. Dr. Hitzig reported to me that just a few
moments of robust laughter had knocked a significant number of units off the sedimentation rate. What to him was most

interesting of all was that the reduction held and was cumulative.

Even more encouraging, the retreat of pain was accompanied by a corresponding increase in mobility. At that time, little was known about the ability of the human brain to produce secretions with morphine-like molecules—endorphins and enkephalins. Looking back now, in the light of this knowledge, I realize the laughter probably played a part in activating the release of endorphins. 8

In writing of this experience, I was careful to point out that I didn't regard the use of laughter as a substitute for traditional medical care. I also emphasized that I tried to bring the full range of positive emotions into play—love, hope, faith, will to live, festivity, purpose, determination. 9

Obviously, what worked for me may not work for everyone else. Accumulating research points to a connection between laughter and immune enhancement, but it would be an error and indeed irresponsible to suggest that laughter—or the positive emotions in general—have universal or automatic validity, whatever the circumstances. People respond differently to the same things. One man's humor is another man's ho-hum. The treatment of illness has to be carefully tailored to suit the individual patient. 10

But not unnaturally, perhaps, the laughter aspects of the recovery made good newspaper copy. I was disturbed by the impression these accounts created that I thought laughter was a substitute for authentic medical care. In fact, my principal reason for writing the article about my illness in the *New England Journal of Medicine* was to correct this impression. I emphasized that my physician was fully involved in the process and that we regarded laughter as a metaphor for the full range of the positive emotions. 11

Perhaps I might have been a lot less defensive if I had known then what I know now. Medical researchers at a dozen or more medical centers have been probing the effects of laughter on the human body and have detailed a wide array of beneficial changes—all the way from enhanced respiration to increases in the number of disease-fighting immune cells. 12

Extensive experiments, working with a significant number of human beings, have shown that laughter contributes to good health. Scientific evidence is accumulating to support the biblical axiom "A merry heart doeth good like a medicine."

Of all the gifts bestowed by nature on human beings, 13 hearty laughter must be close to the top. The response to incongruities is one of the highest manifestations of the cerebral process. We smile broadly or even break out into open laughter when we come across Eugene Field's remark about a friend "who was so mean he wouldn't let his son have more than one measle at a time." Or Leo Rosten's reply to a question asking whether he trusted a certain person: "I'd rather trust a rabbit to deliver a head of lettuce." Or, as Rosten also said, "Let's go somewhere I can be alone." Or Evan Esar's definition of love: "A comedy of Eros." These examples of word play illustrate the ability of the human mind to jump across gaps in logic and find delight in the process.

Surprise is certainly a major ingredient of humor. Babies 14 will laugh at sudden movements or changes in expression, indicating that breaks in the sequences of behavior can tickle the risibilities. During the days of the silent films, Hollywood built an empire out of the surprise antics of its voiceless comedians—Harold Lloyd swinging from the hands of a giant clock, Charlie Chaplin caught up in the iron bowels of an assembly belt, or Buster Keaton chasing a zebra.

It has always seemed to me that laughter is the human 15 mind's way of dealing with the incongruous. Our train of thought will be running in one direction and then is derailed suddenly by running into absurdity. The sudden wreckage of logical flow demands release. Hence the physical reaction known as laughter.

Consider the story of the two octogenarians on a park 16 bench. One asks the other:

"Do you believe in reincarnation?" 17

"Well, Joe," replies Harry, "I've never really thought much 18 about it."

"Maybe we ought to start thinking about it," says Joe. 19 "One of us is going to go first. Let's agree that the one who is left behind will come to this park bench every Wednesday at 11:00 A.M., and the one who has departed will find a way of getting a message to him at that time about reincarnation and all those other things that are beyond our ken."

Harry agrees. 20

One month later, Joe dies peacefully in his sleep. Every week for several months, Harry takes up his station at the park bench at 11:00 A.M. 21

Then one Wednesday, at the appointed hour, he hears a voice, as though from afar. 22

"Harry, Harry, can you hear me?" the voice says. "It's Joe." 23

"Joe, for heaven's sake, what is it like?" 24

"You wouldn't believe it, Harry, about the only thing you do up here is make love. They wake you up at seven in the morning and you make love until noon. After lunch and a nap, you're at it again right through until dinner time." 25

"Good gosh, Joe, what are you and where are you?" 26

"I'm a rabbit in Montana!" 27

The brain accommodates itself to the collision of logic and absurdity by finding an outlet in the physiological response we recognize as laughter. . . . 28

Dr. Novera Herbert Spector, the neurophysiologist, sent me an account written more than a half-century ago of the physiological benefits of laughter. It was by Dr. James Walsh, then the medical director of the School of Sociology at Fordham University in New York. 29

Dr. Walsh reported on his research showing that hearty laughter stimulates internal organs, "making them work better through the increase of circulation that follows the vibrating massage that accompanies it, and heightens resistive vitality against disease." Dr. Walsh then particularized by detailing the beneficial effects of laughter on lungs, liver, heart, pancreas, spleen, stomach, intestines, and the brain. He wrote that laughter has the effect of brushing aside many of the worries and fears that set a stage for sickness. 30

Dr. William Fry, Jr., of the Department of Psychiatry at Stanford Medical School, likens laughter to a form of physical 31 exercise. It causes huffing and puffing, speeds up the heart rate, raises blood pressure, accelerates breathing, increases oxygen consumption, gives the muscles of the face and stomach a workout, and relaxes muscles not involved in laughing. Twenty seconds of laughter, he has contended, can double the heart rate for three to five minutes. That is the equivalent of three minutes of strenuous rowing.

Just in psychological terms, laughter can confer benefits.   32

In the 1950s, Dr. Gordon Allport, psychologist-teacher at   33 Harvard University, theorized that humor, like religion or climbing a mountain, provides a new perspective on one's place in society. Dr. Annette Goodheart, a psychologist in Santa Barbara, confirmed this view in her own work. She found that humor helps an individual to confront personal problems in a more relaxed and creative state. Along the same line, Dr. Alice M. Isen, of the Department of Psychology and Johnson Graduate School of Management at Cornell University, said that laughter increased creativity and flexibility of thought. One of her studies involved individuals who failed to tack a candle onto a corkboard wall in such a way as to not drip wax on the floor while it burned. Those persons who had just seen a short comedy film were better able to devise innovative approaches to the task than those who had "creative flexibility" after seeing the film. In tests of mental acuity, Isen has also found that positive feelings, induced by humorous films or the giving of a candy gift, enable persons to use language more colorfully.

Laughter has been shown to help reduce "discomfort   34 sensitivity." Drs. Rosemary and Dennis Cogan, et al., Lubbock, randomly assigned 40 undergraduates to four groups: (1) laughter, (2) relaxation, (3) informative narrative, and (4) no-treatment control. Members of groups one, two, and three each listened individually to a 20-minute audiotape appropriate to their group. The discomfort was produced by pressure from the automatic inflation of a blood pressure cuff. Subjects could withstand the highest level of discomfort after being exposed to humorous material; the next highest level after being exposed to a relaxation technique. The Cogans and their colleagues suggest that humor can be particularly useful in alleviating the pain of injections a patient must receive, as well as postoperative pain.

If laughter can improve one's perspective on life and on pain, it follows that it might be helpful in combating unusual stress. Drs. Rod A. Martin and Herbert M. Lefcourt, then of the University of Waterloo in Ontario, Canada, studied the connection between humor and adjustment to major life stresses. They gave 56 undergraduates four tests designed to measure the capacity to enjoy humor under a variety of circumstances. Three out of four tests showed that those who valued humor the most were also most capable of coping with tensions and severe personal problems. 35

Drs. Martin and Lefcourt subsequently studied 67 students and found that those who had the greatest ability to produce humor "on demand" in impromptu routines are also best able to counteract the negative emotional effects of stress. 36

Dr. James R. Averill, then of the Department of Psychology, University of California, Berkeley, measured a number of physiological reactions accompanying various emotional states. Fifty-four undergraduates were divided into three groups—a sadness group, a mirth group, and a control group. The sadness group watched a film about John F. Kennedy; the mirth group saw a Mack Sennett–type silent comedy; and the control group viewed a nonarousing documentary film. Measurements of blood pressure, heart rate, finger and face temperature, finger pulse volume, skin resistance, and respiration were taken during the showing of the films. Averill found that laughter produced respiratory changes, and that sadness yielded changes in blood pressure. The main conclusion of the study was that emotions produce measurable physiological change. 37

Dr. Paul Eckman and colleagues, of the University of California at San Francisco, School of Medicine, measured physiological differences during six emotional states—surprise, disgust, sadness, anger, fear, and happiness. They asked 16 individuals—actors and scientists—to mimic prototypical 38 emotional facial expressions and then to experience each of the six emotions by reliving a past emotional experience while measurements of heart rate, hand temperature, skin resistance, and muscle tension were taken.

The results were striking. Not only did significant physiological differences between the negative emotions and the positive emotions turn up, but different emotions produced different effects. For example, anger was characterized by a high heart rate and hand temperature increases, whereas fear was accompanied by high heart rate increases and decreases in hand temperature. Happiness was associated with low rises in heart rate and hand temperature. 39

Some of the researchers involved in these studies sent me reports of their work, saying they had been prompted by my experience as reported in *Anatomy of an Illness* to seek scientific accounts from hospitals of new facilities that featured humor and creativity as integral parts of the hospital program. 40

The first to respond was St. Joseph's Hospital in Houston, Texas. I received a telephone call from Dr. John Stehlin, oncological surgeon and medical researcher, asking if I would come to Houston to participate in the dedication ceremonies of a new feature of the hospital called the "Living Room." He said that the cancer floor had been redesigned to accommodate a large room furnished with easy chairs, hi-fi equipment, an art corner, video and audio sets, and a library. 41

"You can't imagine a setting more unlike a hospital," he said. "You would enjoy seeing how a pleasant environment can brighten the mood of the patients. Amusing films are one of our main props. You will enjoy meeting the nuns. They like the idea of making laughter a regular part of the hospital's philosophy." 42

Three weeks later, I went to Houston for the dedication ceremonies. The entire hospital was in a festive mood for the occasion. The media exhibited a strong interest in the Living Room and the idea behind it. Television crews were setting up their cameras at the entrance to the hospital and in the Living Room itself. 43

I judged Dr. Stehlin to be in his mid-50s. His appearance 44 was tall, trim, athletic, hearty. He took me into his office and told me that the hospital's experiment with laughter had been highly successful. The patients were relaxed and responsive; they appeared to be making fewer demands on the hospital staff. I met with at least a dozen patients whose arms or legs had been saved from amputation by procedures developed by Dr. Stehlin and his associates. The affected limb would be tourniqueted, protecting the rest of the body from the chemotherapy, which was then free to attack the malignancy without penalty to the rest of the body.

The Living Room was in high favor with both ambulatory   45
and wheelchair patients. They kept the videotape machine busy, viewing comedy films that Dr. Stehlin was able to get directly from the film companies with their compliments.

Dr. Stehlin said that he found himself stealing time away   46
from his desk to look at the comedies.

"You have no idea how good it makes me feel just to see   47
the patients laughing and enjoying themselves," he said. "This place is getting to be unrecognizable as a hospital—and that's all to the good. Now, before we go to the Living Room, I want you to meet the nuns, especially Mother Romano. She's almost 80 but is spry and energetic. She has fallen in with this new approach and makes a point of telling the patients funny stories. Just yesterday she was telling them about an incident at a nightclub. It seems that the headwaiter was looking around the room and saw a man slide off his chair. He rushed over to the table.

"'Madam,' he said, 'your husband has slipped off his chair   48
and fallen under the table.'

"'Sir,' she said, 'my husband has just come into the   49
room.'"

I trailed after Dr. Stehlin as he led me to the Living Room,   50
stopping along the way at the rooms of cancer patients, where he introduced me, saying that *Anatomy of an Illness* was the hospital's inspiration for the Living Room.

We met Mother Romano, a wisp of a woman but a human   51
dynamo. She pumped my arm vigorously when we were introduced and rhapsodized over the patients' response to

the Living Room. She accompanied us on visits to other cancer patients, then looked at her watch and said the dedication ceremonies were about to begin.

The Living Room was jammed with people—patients, hospital personnel, trustees, civic leaders, and press representatives. I guessed there were between 150 and 200 people. The room was brightly decorated. As Dr. Stehlin had said, it was the antithesis of everything that is popularly associated with a hospital. 52

Dr. Stehlin spoke first, then introduced Mother Romano, who described the auspicious effect of the new room not only on the patients, but on the nurses and other members of the hospital staff. Then Dr. Stehlin introduced me to the audience. 53

I said the obvious things—how grateful I was that my hospital experience played a part in the decision to create the new facility at St. Joseph's. I described the research going on at UCLA and elsewhere showing laughter could produce auspicious physiological change. 54

The meeting with Dr. Stehlin led to a close friendship. We used some of the funds placed at my disposal to support his research at the hospital in studying the salutary effects of the psychological environment surrounding the treatment of cancer patients. 55

The Living Room at St. Joseph's was only the first of two dozen or more similar programs at hospitals throughout the country. At St. John's hospital in Los Angeles, a special channel on the TV sets in each room enabled the patients to turn on comedy films day or night. As at St. Joseph's, the hospital acquired a considerable library of amusing motion pictures. I relished the opportunity given me by the nuns at St. John's to dedicate the new comedy channel. 56

I participated in six or seven similar ceremonies at hospitals in the Los Angeles area. At the L.A. County Hospital, Joseph Barbera, creator of Huckleberry Hound and Yogi Bear, presented the children's division with life-size replications of the characters made famous in his TV cartoons. 57

UCLA redecorated the hospital's children's floors, replac- 58

ing the drab whiteness with bright colors and amusing drawings. UCLA also used art throughout the entire hospital in
a program devised by Devra Breslow.

Cedars Sinai Hospital, in Los Angeles, accepted the pro-   59
posal of Marcia Weismann, a prominent art collector, to
decorate the walls of the hospital with superb reproductions
of outstanding art. Mrs. Weismann also arranged for art lec-
tures at the hospital.

Good Samaritan Hospital of Los Angeles instituted a hu-   60
mor channel for patients' TV sets, along the lines of the
program instituted at St. John's. Dr. David Cannom, head of
cardiology at Good Samaritan, arranged for piano concerts
at the hospital by Mona Golabek, an outstanding local artist.

Perhaps the most far-reaching program of all is the use of   61
not just humor but also music, art, and literature in the
treatment of the seriously ill instituted by the Duke University Comprehensive Cancer Center in Durham, North Carolina. The word "comprehensive" is to be taken literally. All
the aspects of treatment are taken into account—the emotional needs of the patient; the interests or hobbies of the
patient that can improve the climate of medical care, inside
or outside the hospital; the use of a "laugh wagon" that is
just as evident in the corridors of the hospital as the "pill
carts" of the nurses; the services of volunteers to provide
companionship or solace or to carry out errands for the
patients—all these are integral to Duke's program. Dr.
Robert Bast, the director of the center, believes that the
psychosocial factors are no less important than medical prescriptions in the structure of a hospital and medical school.

At Duke, I learned of two examples of how humor can be   62
used to lessen the problems caused by illness.

A patient at the university hospital suffered from a severe   63
case of otitis media (inflammation of the middle ear). The
nurse, recognizing that the emotional state of the patient was
important, read him stories by Woody Allen. The patient's
sense of delight blocked any nervousness, which the nurse
felt might have interfered with the efficacy of the medication.
Whether or not her strategy could be verified by physiological

measurements, her awareness that psychological factors could enhance or impair medical treatment won the commendation of the hospital authorities.

Another example concerned a man who suddenly developed what is known as a paroxysmal tachycardia—a wildly beating heart. Ordinarily, the condition is temporary, but when it is also marked by an irregular pulse, prompt medical attention is required.

The man's wife telephoned the family physician, who said he would rush over to the house. In the meantime, he instructed the wife to do everything possible to keep the patient free of panic, the effects of which could intensify and complicate the underlying problem. The woman played a videotape of "Candid Camera" reruns, one sequence of which showed Buster Keaton at a lunchroom counter struggling to keep his eyeglasses and his toupee from falling into his soup. Her husband fell to laughing over the absurdity and completely blotted out any trace of panic. By the time the doctor arrived, the pulse had settled back to normal. The doctor credited the wife with having helped to avert a potentially serious situation.

Topics for Writing
Cause and Effect

1. *Respond.* For the free weekly newspaper available at your local health-food store or restaurant, report on an experience in which you or someone you know well used laughter (or some other positive emotion) to overcome some difficulty. Like Cousins, be careful about making simplistic assertions or broad generalizations. What worked for you may not work for everybody, and there may be causes other than laughter to explain the effects you report. Nevertheless, try to support Cousins's argument that good emotions create good health. (*Resources for Comparison:* Calvin Trillin's "The Extendable Fork," page 240; William Raspberry, "The Decline of Marriage: A Bad Omen," page 380)

2. *Analyze.* For your writing group and other students in your class, consider the experiments Cousins reports in his article, especially those on students. Then conduct a simplified version of one of these tests with your writing group or friends. For example, measure some indicator of stress such as pulse rate or hand temperature before and after showing your test group (a) a funny film and then (b) a depressing film. In addition to using numbers, include interviews with subjects in your analysis. (*Resources for Comparison:* Maya Angelou, "My Name Is Margaret," page 29; Edward T. Hall, "The Arab World," page 206)

3. *Argue.* For a feature article in a special health-care supplement of your local newspaper, research the interior design and special services of one of your local hospitals or the campus health center. In what ways do they contribute to general well-being of the patients? Do any of them operate a facility such as the comprehensive "Living Room" Cousins describes? Use your research to argue for establishing such a facility in your hospital or for improving the current facility. You might write another version of such an essay

in which you suggest ways to create a positive environment in your normal living space, an environment that will enhance relaxation and reduce stress. (*Resources for Comparison:* Edward T. Hall, "The Arab World," page 206; Alice Stewart Trillin, "Of Dragons and Garden Peas," page 561)

Janice Castro was born in Oakland, California, in 1949, and was educated at the University of California at Berkeley and Columbia University. She began her professional life as a reporter for *Time,* writing articles on show business. She worked her way up to editor, writing about political and social issues, particularly as they affected the worlds of women's work. Castro currently serves as editor of *Time On Line, Time*'s daily computer magazine, and *Pathfinder, Time*'s Internet news service. In "The American Way of Health," excerpted from the introductory chapter to *The American Way of Health: How Medicine Is Changing and What It Means to You* (1994), Castro argues that changing America's health policies is ultimately a moral problem.

The American Way of Health
(Persuasion and Argument)

A SK MOST PEOPLE what they think about the state of American medicine, and they will tell you about their own doctors, or about something that happened to them during an illness. Chances are, if they see a need for health-care change, it will be very specific, based on personal experience.

On the other hand, listen to American leaders discussing health-care reform. They speak of providers. Access. Alliances. Competition. Mandates. What in Heaven's name are they talking about? The concepts seem impossibly complicated and remote from the experience of one sick person needing help. But while discussions of health-care reform may be bewildering, listen closely: they are talking about you and your needs. . . .

Medicine is too important, too personal, to be left to economists and politicians. Any broad national reform is going to affect every American. After all, the health-care debate is really about life and death. It is about those times when people need help and about whether it will be there, about one sick patient at a time and the doctor or nurse who provides care. Buried in all of the technical talk are two simple

3

Health-care reform is much more than a political issue. It is fundamentally a moral problem.

---

questions: how should that person be helped, and who will pay the bill?

Health-care reform is much more than an arcane economic policy debate, more than a political issue.

4

It is fundamentally a moral problem.

5

Viewed in that light, the challenge of health-care reform begins to come more clearly into focus. It is not really that complicated.

6

We know what we need to do.

7

We need to take care of old people when they can no longer take care of themselves. Children should see doctors and dentists. A pregnant woman should be able to check in with a doctor as the baby grows. People should not be dying in the street. Mentally ill Americans should not be wandering around, scavenging in garbage cans and sleeping in cardboard boxes. They are not someone else's problem. They are us. Families shouldn't lose their homes over the cost of coping with medical disasters. Breadwinners should not quit good jobs in order to qualify for poor people's insurance. Those with high incomes should contribute more to the cost of their

8

care. People should take responsibility for their own health and for their family's. Children should not be having children. Companies should not force people out because they might get expensive illnesses. Insurance companies should not dump you when you get sick. Medical care should make you feel better.

Most of these principles can be addressed to some extent 9 in a sound and equitable medical system that ensures access to basic care for all Americans. But meeting many of these needs also requires moral responsibility, by patients and doctors, employers and parents, and everyone else in the American family. No government program can make us better people. No financing system can guarantee quality or enforce personal responsibility for oneself, one's own family, and fellow citizens. "I don't see health care as a right," says Stuart Orsher, a Manhattan internist, "not, I mean, as something that should be available on demand. I see it as something like national defense or fire and police protection. In a civilized society, you should not expect to be shot on the street; the fire department should come when your house is burning; and doctors should not turn their backs on you when you are in need."

If we are going to ensure that every American has access 10 to decent health care, while also controlling the burgeoning costs, all of us must curb our medical greed. All of us must stop pretending that someone else is paying the bills. "What do you think most people would say if one of their parents called up and said they needed a hundred and twenty-five thousand dollars for an operation?" asks one economist. "Do you think that son or daughter would think twice and wonder whether that operation was really necessary? Of course they would. But none of us think we pay for medical care. And of course we all do."

All of us must pay our share. We must also stop the vio- 11 lence and self-destruction. When adolescents shoot children in the back, doctors can only do so much. When a friend gets drunk and plows into a family driving home, the emergency room cannot make them whole.

Something is wrong, and medicine cannot fix it. There is 12
no magic economic formula. There are no guarantees. Our
political leaders may argue for the next year or two about how
best to rearrange American health care. But no set of rules
and no system of financing can legislate compassion or moral
rectitude.

*   *   *

In a remote rural hospital in Texas, a young veterinarian is 13
sitting at a table, trying to decide what to do. She was helping
a cow through a difficult delivery when the cow slammed her
into a fence, severing most of her right middle finger. The
finger has been put on ice.

Here's her problem: because she recently left her old job 14
in the city and moved here to set up her practice, her new
insurance policy has not yet taken effect. This is a poor town,
where the doctor and the veterinarian are sometimes paid
with a gracious invitation to dinner. The doctor says that a
few months back, a poor patient showed his gratitude by
sharing a slug from a prized bottle locked away for special
occasions. The vet doesn't have much in the way of savings
or prospective revenue. The operation to reattach her finger
will cost more than $400. For less than $100, of course, they
can just sew up the stump. She's the only vet in a town full
of horses, cattle, and other animals. She is needed here.
Doing without that finger will affect her ability to make a
living, will make it harder, for example, to perform veterinary
surgery. But $400 is an awful lot of money.

She's thinking it might be better to do without the finger. 15
Her doctor is not offering to do without the fee.

A nurse in Manhattan has had it up to here with what she 16
sees every day. Sloppy doctors who seem immune to re-
proach, and other doctors and nurses, decent and hard-
pressed, who can barely keep pace with the avalanche of
problems tumbling through the doors of her hospital. Drug
addicts who have learned how to game the Medicaid system,
collecting room and board in the hospital for several days by
asserting their right to refuse a simple outpatient procedure.

Sick and frightened old people who have worked hard all of their lives, who have not had a proper pair of eyeglasses in years and can barely hear, trying to ask questions about their medications of an impatient and overworked emergency room staff. Crack babies, some of whom have been abandoned, who are now being subjected to massive medical intervention by doctors and nurses battling to save them—for what kind of life? Their best hope is often severe disability and retardation and life in an institution.

Across the street from the hospital where this nurse works 17 is a halfway house for teenage mothers. The girls sit outside talking and eating junk food. Most of them have babies and are already pregnant again. There are about a dozen trash cans on that corner, but they drop their food wrappers and soda cans on the ground. "Where is the pride?" the nurse asks. "Where are their families? What is going to happen to those children? Children shouldn't be having children. They shouldn't be allowed to have children until they are ready to love them and take care of them."

A frail old man lies on a gurney in a central California emer- 18 gency room. He was recently released from the hospital after major surgery, and now he's back. He lives alone. He is barely conscious. The doctor in charge of the emergency room impatiently asks him whether he has been taking his pills. The old man whispers that, since his operation, he has been so weak that he cannot remember which pills he is supposed to take. The doctor begins shouting at him. The same doctor approaches an extremely ill, elderly woman across the room. She is slumped in a wheelchair, waiting for help. "Did you have a nice Christmas?" he asks. "Yes," she replies. "Good, because you won't live to see another one."

A physician in Los Angeles describes the patient he has just 19 released from UCLA Medical Center after a couple of weeks of intensive treatment. "He was a Skid Row alcoholic. Of course we helped him. We did our best. But I can't get him out of my mind. In the last few weeks we spent more than a hundred thousand dollars cleaning him up, fixing him up, trying to make him better. And you know where he is right now? Back on Skid Row. We'll see him again, if he lives long enough. We can't fix his life. How come we are willing to devote all of these medical resources to saving people once they have nearly killed themselves, when we can't seem to find a way to get them off Skid Row?"

A dentist finishes up a minor repair for a long-time patient, then makes a surprising offer. The bill is $100. The patient's insurance covers 70 percent of the bill. The patient will get back $70; the visit will cost her $30.   20

"Make the check for a hundred and ten," says the dentist, "and I'll give you a bill for a hundred and thirty."   21

That way, the patient can get back $91. The visit will cost her $19. The dentist will make an extra $10.   22

Together, they commit a little fraud, adding 30 percent to the insurance bill.   23

At the Los Angeles Free Clinic, which offers free medical care to everyone regardless of income, no questions asked, a woman waits to see a doctor. Her ten-year-old son sits with her. Will he have a checkup too? "Oh no!" she says. "He has never been to the doctor! He's not old enough."   24

In Manhattan, a visiting nurse makes house calls all over town, taking care of the ailing elderly, people with AIDS, diabetics who have had their feet amputated, and others who are homebound. She checks their blood pressure, blood sugar levels, temperature, and other vital signs. She dresses their wounds, asks them how they are sleeping, how they feel in general. She administers medications, adjusting the dosage if necessary, and makes sure they know how to take them. She visits elderly women with osteoporosis, giving them injections to help build up their bone strength. She reports disturbing signs of trouble to her patients' physicians, sometimes increasing the frequency of her visits for a while when a patient suffers a setback. She visits newborn babies   25

who are in danger of abuse or neglect. She even visits middle-class mothers who are simply afraid that they do not know
how to care for their first child.

   If her patients are covered by Medicare or Medicaid, those   26
programs pay for her visits, up to a point. Other patients pay
out of pocket for her services (as much as $110 per visit), or
are covered for a few visits under their own insurance policies.
For many seriously ill patients, she is the only one who comes
to check on them. Often, though, she cannot visit them until
an escort is available to accompany her into their neighborhoods, especially at night. If she went alone, her life would
be in danger. Part of the cost of providing a visiting nurse—
and part of the reason her availability to assist the helpless is
therefore limited—is the necessary expense of protecting her
from violence.

A physical therapist in her early thirties is expecting her first   27
child. She is well insured. She is healthy. She has received
good advice on proper nutrition. She has had all of the
diagnostic tests that medicine offers. She is under the care of
an obstetrician and will deliver her baby in a major teaching
hospital. Now it is up to her and to fate. But she is not
satisfied. "If one little finger is wrong," she says, "I'm going
to sue that guy!"

A New York doctor mentions one of his patients, a famous   28
man who is a member of one of the richest families in the
country. The patient is on Medicare.

   On any given day, some of the wealthiest Americans sub-   29
mit their medical bills to Medicare. Taxpayers, many of whom
are uninsured, help to pay those bills.

                     *   *   *

In San Francisco, a billing manager for a leading teaching   30
hospital remembers the patient who called to protest an enormous bill charging him for a kidney transplant. He insisted
that he hadn't had one. The billing staff insisted he had. They
had the paperwork right there. The patient pointed out that
he was a patient in a special research program for liver trans-

plants. He said they don't give kidneys to people in that program. They said he was mistaken and sternly warned him to pay the bill.

The manager remembers the family that called to question 31 a bill for major surgery. The date of the surgery was more than a month after the patient had died. "It happens all the time. People get charged for things they never got." She tells of another patient who kept calling to say his insurance bills did not make any sense and asking for help in sorting them out. He was getting nowhere. Finally, they had to evacuate the offices one night in the summer of 1993 when he called and said he was going to blow up the place. She remembers the night her father died. The next day, the hospital began calling her mother and threatening to take action for late payment of the bills. Her mother pointed out the date of death and promised to pay. The hospital kept calling and threatening to sue. That's when the young woman decided to work in hospital administration. Somebody had to do a better job; this should not happen to people like her mother.

A doctor in Hawaii recalls the drug addict who hit the emer- 32 gency room late one night and was refusing treatment for at least one gaping bullet wound. The physician rushed in to help. "I was insisting that he needed medical care. I reached down to look at the laceration I could see, and suddenly there was a gun at my temple. We were nose to nose. He had these big starey eyes. He said he was going to kill me. I lost it. I started screaming at him, telling him he could just fucking die where he was, because he didn't have the brains to accept help when it was being offered. He stared at me, with this gun still jammed against my temple. I didn't care. I dared him to go ahead and shoot. I was fed up. He got this weird look on his face and he put the gun down. He said, 'You're crazy!' Maybe I am. What the hell are we supposed to do?"

What indeed? Guaranteeing medical coverage to all Ameri- 33 cans will not solve all of the problems that our medical system is asked to handle. It will not make us healthier. Americans must stop blaming medicine for everything that goes wrong with their health. And it is time for patients to understand that when medicine is unsuccessful, it does not always mean that a doctor has committed malpractice.

Having insurance will do nothing to curb drug abuse, 34 which cost the United States an estimated $67 billion in 1990 in medical treatment and other related expenses. Studies show that half of all people arrested for major crimes, including homicide, theft, and assault, were using illegal drugs at the time. Insurance will not make Americans more responsible about alcohol abuse, which cost the country $99 billion in 1990. It will not prevent the 11 million U.S. highway crashes every year that take some 40,000 lives; one-third of those collisions are caused by excessive speed, and many are caused by drinking. It will not take the automatic weapons out of the hands of teenagers. Every day in America, 4,900 teenagers become the victims of violent assaults.

Guaranteeing coverage will not make immoral people better parents. It will not encourage irresponsible parents to get their children the vaccinations that are readily available to them. Every day in the United States, 2,700 teenage girls become pregnant and 1,300 give birth. Families must take responsibility. Every day, 2,500 teenagers drop out of school, plunging into a lifetime of postindustrial poverty.

Nor does having insurance mean that you can get to a 36 doctor in time if you live in any one of hundreds of small towns or the broad swaths of rural America that stretch for hundreds of square miles where there are no doctors. America needs more doctors who want to take care of families, even those living in isolated or impoverished areas. Medicine is not always just, not always kind. It should be. Guaranteeing coverage will not make callous doctors compassionate or encourage selfish relatives to visit their ailing elders more often. Federal mandates do not change human behavior. Responsible people do.

Americans need to face the tough decisions about how to 37 allocate medical resources more sensibly. They need to think about how to know when to let people go. They also need to face the fact that, too often, families are ready to let someone go before the patient is ready to die. It is all too easy to blame doctors and hospitals for "wasting" money on heroic intervention at the end of life. It is easy to cite figures about all of the money spent providing care during the last six months of life. But when, exactly, do the last six months of a life start?

There are no easy answers. Every discussion about such 38 questions seems to feature a hypothetical eighty-five-year-old man who has smoked three packs of cigarettes and downed a fifth of vodka every day of his life and now wants a heart transplant. Around America's dinner tables, everyone seems ready to decide that this man must forgo the transplant so that children can have vaccinations. The equation is nonsensical. It is not that simple. The choices are seldom clear.

American medical science has now reached a level of ex- 39 pertise and skill where it can do much more than we can afford to guarantee to everyone in every case.

A health plan that seems to promise that we can have it all 40 is ducking the truth. But where do we draw the line? Who decides?

We can no longer afford to think of medicine as some sort 41 of space-age body shop. We can no longer expect the government or some other entity to pay for every physical treatment we think we need or to intervene at all costs to prevent death and decay. Nor can we continue to avoid moral responsibility for the decisions we keep shifting to medicine. We can't keep blaming the Special Interests. When it comes to health services, we are all Special Interests. It is time to have a national heart-to-heart about medical rights and responsibilities and about the social contract.

Oregon has done it, in a town-by-town, wrenching com- 42 munity discussion over which medical problems the state can promise to pay for, which needs are greatest, and, hardest of all, when some results are worth more than others. That hypothetical eighty-five-year-old is out of luck if he lives in Oregon. But the decisions faced by the people of that state were far more subtle and difficult than that. The people of

Oregon have painstakingly decided when to say no, so that they will have the ability to care for their children and for people who have a decent chance of resuming a relatively healthy life. Even at that, the state is not sure it will be able to find the money to pay for its hard-won compromises on the promise of medicine.

No other state—no other nation—has ever undertaken   43
such a process. European health leaders, facing difficult decisions themselves about how to ration medical care more severely than ever before, visit Oregon to learn how its people did it. They've never had to discuss rationing in public, though they have been doing it. Now that they must, they want to learn from the people who faced the hard choices.

No one comes from Washington, D.C.   44

Until the United States is willing to engage in such a   45
probing national dialogue, the strain on our capacity to deal with all social problems will grow.

*   *   *

"In medicine, we talk about the quandary we face when a   46
man jumps off a cliff and is floundering in the water," muses Jane Campion, an administrative nurse at the Mayo Clinic. "And a second man is standing at the edge of the cliff, trying to decide whether to jump. Whom do you save? We are always drawn to the drama of saving the man in the water. But he has already made his decision. If you can only save one of them, what about the man on the cliff, who is still trying to decide what to do?"

But how do you know when you can only save one of   47
them? How do you know the man on the cliff will jump, and whose fault is it if he does? It is not the job of medicine to make decisions about how to treat the man in the water based on how he got there. That is the job of the society. Medicine's job is to know everything it can about what happens to an injured man struggling in deep water and what it will take to restore him to the best possible health. Society's job is to decide how to pay for it.

The essential message of health reform is that for the majority   48
of Americans, who are well insured, the party's over. No more

"free" medical coverage, with an insurance company automatically paying almost any bill a patient sends to it. Many people already know this; their health coverage has come under some restrictions if, for instance, they have joined health maintenance organizations. The restrictions are going to grow tighter.

No matter which national plan for health reform prevails— 49 even if reform stalls and no broad new health law is passed— most Americans are going to pay more in the coming years to get less in health care. That does not necessarily mean that they will get less than they need. But the days of unlimited access to medical services are over. Some people will be better off than they are now; many will not. The only real issue is how we are going to organize the cutbacks.

We can preserve, even enhance, the quality of medicine 50 while curbing the price. But will we?

Topics for Writing
Argument and Persuasion

1. *Respond.* Many medical schools—for example, Harvard University Medical School and the University of Texas Medical School—put out a monthly newsletter for the general public in which a variety of health issues are discussed. For such a newsletter, narrate an incident you know of that illustrates Castro's charge that Americans are guilty of "medical greed"—that is, they believe a patient is entitled to any procedure, regardless of the cost. Use your narrative to explore what kind of limits might be put on determining who gets what kind of care and at what cost. For instance, should heart transplants be limited to certain kinds of patients? Should a very premature baby be kept alive at great cost even if the baby has a poor chance of developing normally? Who should pay? (*Resources for Comparison:* Martin Luther King, Jr., "I Have a Dream," page 455; Charles Murray, "The Coming White Underclass," page 533)

2. *Analyze.* For an essay to share and discuss with other students in your writing class, study the various examples Castro presents to make her case that "guaranteeing medical coverage to all Americans will not solve all of the problems that our medical system is asked to handle." In your essay, decide which examples have clear medical solutions. Which examples involve more complicated social and economic solutions? Analyze the way Castro arranges and presents her examples to make her point. (*Resources for Comparison:* Stephen Jay Gould, "Carrie Buck's Daughter," page 417; Wendell Berry, "The Problem of Tobacco," page 504)

3. *Argue.* In response to a newspaper story about a city council member who is proposing that bicyclists be required to wear helmets and that their bicycles be impounded for a second violation, write an editorial in which you cite and argue for Castro's assertion that "mandates

do not change human behavior." Cite an example from a recent news event that supports Castro's argument. Or you could take the position that without mandates there is no way to enforce health policies that are good for the general public. You might even be able to find a middle position to argue, one that promotes safe practices but is not overly coercive. (*Resources for Comparison:* Rosemary Bray, "So How Did I Get Here?," page 519; Arthur C. Clarke, "The Star," page 543)

CHARLES JOHNSON

Charles Johnson was born in 1948 in Evanston, Illinois, and educated at Southern Illinois University and the State University of New York at Stony Brook. He worked as a cartoonist and reporter for the Chicago *Tribune* and as a member of the art staff at *St. Louis Proud* before accepting a position as professor of English at the University of Washington in Seattle. Under the tutelage of novelist John Gardner, Johnson published his first novel, *Faith and the Good Thing* (1974), a humorous folk tale of a southern black girl's trip to Chicago. Johnson's most recent novel, *Middle Passage* (1990), won the National Book Award. Johnson has also written for two collections of drawings, *Black Humor* (1970), and *Half-Past Nation Time* (1972), written numerous scripts for PBS, most notably "Charlie's Pad" (1970) and "Booker" (1983), and published a collection of short stories, *The Sorcerer's Apprentice* (1986). The title story from that volume recounts a young boy's attempt to understand the sorcerer's lessons.

The Sorcerer's Apprentice
(Story)

THERE WAS A time, long ago, when many sorcerers 1 lived in South Carolina, men not long from slavery who remembered the white magic of the Ekpe Cults and the Cameroons, and by far the greatest of these wizards was a blacksmith named Rubin Bailey. Believing he was old, and would soon die, the Sorcerer decided to pass his learning along to an apprentice. From a family near Abbeville he selected a boy, Allan, whose father, Richard Jackson, Rubin once healed after an accident, and for this Allan loved the Sorcerer, especially the effects of his craft, which comforted the sick, held back evil, and blighted the enemies of newly freed slaves with locusts and bad health. "My house," Richard told the wizard, "has been honored." His son swore to serve his teacher faithfully, then those who looked to the Sorcerer, in all ways. With his father's blessing, the boy moved his belongings into the Sorcerer's home, a houseboat covered with strips of scrap-metal, on the river.

But Rubin Bailey's first teachings seemed to Allan to be   2
no teachings at all. "Bring in fresh water," Rubin told his apprentice. "Scrape barnacles off the boat." He never spoke of sorcery. Around the boy he tied his blacksmith's apron, and guided his hands in hammering out the horseshoes Rubin sold in town, but not once in the first month did Rubin pass along the recipes for magic. Patiently, Allan performed these duties in perfect submission to the Sorcerer, for it seemed rude to express displeasure to a man he wished to emulate, but his heart knocked for the higher knowledge, the techniques that would, he hoped, work miracles.

At last, as they finished a meal of boiled pork and collards   3
one evening, he complained bitterly: "You haven't told me anything yet!" Allan regretted this outburst immediately, and lowered his head. "Have I done wrong?"

For a moment the Sorcerer was silent. He spiced his coffee   4
with rum, dipped in his bread, chewed slowly, then looked up, steadily, at the boy. "You are the best of students. And you wish to do good, but you can't be too faithful, or too eager, or the good becomes evil."

"Now I don't understand," Allan said. "By themselves the   5
tricks aren't good *or* evil, and if you plan to do good, then the results must be good."

Rubin exhaled, finished his coffee, then shoved his plate   6
toward the boy. "Clean the dishes," he said. Then, more gently: "What I know has worked I will teach. There is no certainty these things can work for you, or even for me, a second time. White magic comes and goes. I'm teaching you

a trade, Allan. You will never starve. This is because after fifty years, I still can't foresee if an incantation will be magic or foolishness."

These were not, of course, the answers Allan longed to hear. He said, "Yes, sir," and quietly cleared away their dishes. If he had replied aloud to Rubin, as he did silently while toweling dry their silverware later that night, he would have told the Sorcerer, "You are the greatest magician in the world because you have studied magic and the long-dead masters of magic, and I believe, even if you do not, that the secret of doing good is a good heart and having a hundred spells at your disposal, so I will study everything—the words and timbre and tone of your voice as you conjure, and listen to those you have heard. Then I, too, will have magic and can do good." He washed his underwear in the moonlight, as is fitting for a fledgling magician, tossed his dishpan water into the river, and, after hanging his washpail on a hook behind Rubin's front door, undressed, and fell asleep with these thoughts: To do good is a very great thing, the *only* thing, but a magician must be able to conjure at a moment's notice. Surely it is all a question of know-how.

So it was that after a few months the Sorcerer's apprentice learned well and quickly when Rubin Bailey finally began to teach. In Allan's growth was the greatest joy. Each spell he showed proudly to his father and Richard's friends when he traveled home once a year. Unbeknownst to the Sorcerer, he held simple exhibits for their entertainment—harmless prestidigitation like throwing his voice or levitating logs stacked by the toolshed. However pleased Richard might have been, he gave no sign. Allan's father never joked or laughed too loudly. He was the sort of man who held his feelings in, and people took this for strength. Allan's mother, Beatrice, a tall, thick-waisted woman, had told him (for Richard would not) how when she was carrying Allan, they rode a haywagon to a scrub-ball in Abbeville on Freedom Day. Richard fell beneath the wagon. A wheel smashed his thumb open to the bone. "Somebody better go for Rubin Bailey," was all Richard said, and he stared like it might be a stranger's hand. And Allan remembered Richard toiling so long in the sun he couldn't eat some evenings unless he first emptied his stomach by forcing himself to vomit. His father squirreled away money in their mattresses, saving for seven years to buy the land they worked. When he had $600—half what they needed—he grew afraid of theft, so Beatrice took their money to one of the banks in town. She stood in line behind a northern-looking Negro who said his name was Grady Armstrong. "I work for the bank across the street," he told Beatrice. "You wouldn't be interested in part-time work, would you? We need a woman to clean, someone reliable, but she has to keep her savings with us." Didn't they need the money? Beatrice would ask Allan, later, when Richard left them alone at night. Wouldn't the extra work help her husband? She followed Grady Armstrong, whose easy, loose-hinged walk led them to the second bank across the street. "Have you ever deposited money before?" asked Grady. "No," she said. Taking her envelope, he said, "Then I'll do it for you." On the boardwalk, Beatrice waited. And waited. After five minutes, she opened the door, found no Grady Armstrong, and flew screaming the fifteen miles back to the fields and Richard, who listened and chewed his lip, but said nothing. He leaned, Allan remembered, in the farmhouse door, smoking his cigars and watching only Lord knew what in the darkness—exactly as he stood the following year, when Beatrice, after swallowing rat poison, passed on.

Allan supposed it was risky to feel if you had grown up, like Richard, in a world of nightriders. There was too much to lose. Any attachment ended in separation, grief. If once you let yourself care, the crying might never stop. So he assumed his father was pleased with his apprenticeship to Rubin, though hearing him say this would have meant the world to Allan. He did not mind that somehow the Sorcerer's personality seemed to permeate each spell like sweat staining fresh wood, because this, too, seemed to be the way of things. The magic was Rubin Bailey's, but when pressed, the Sorcerer confessed that the spells had been in circulation for centuries. They were a web of history and culture, like the

king-sized quilts you saw as curiosities at country fairs, sewn
by every woman in Abbeville, each having finished only a
section, a single flower perhaps, so no man, strictly speaking,
could own a mystic spell. "But when you kill a bird by
pointing," crabbed Rubin from his rocking chair, "you don't
haveta wave your left hand in the air and pinch your forefin-
ger and thumb together like I do."

"Did I do that?" asked Allan.   10

Rubin hawked and spit over the side of the houseboat.   11
"Every time."

"I just wanted to get it right." Looking at his hand, he felt   12
ashamed—he was, after all, right-handed—then shoved it
deep into his breeches. "The way you do it is so beautiful."

"I know." Rubin laughed. He reached into his coat,   13
brought out his pipe, and looked for matches. Allan stepped
inside, and the Sorcerer shouted behind him, "You shouldn't
do it because my own teacher, who wore out fifteen flying
carpets in his lifetime, told me it was wrong."

"Wrong?" The boy returned. He held a match close to the   14
bowl of Rubin's pipe, cupping the flame. "Then why do you
do it?"

"It works best for me that way, Allan. I have arthritis." He   15
slanted his eyes left at his pupil. "Do you?"

The years passed, and Allan improved, even showing a   16
certain flair, a style all his own that pleased Rubin, who
praised the boy for his native talent, which did not come from
knowledge and, it struck Allan, was wholly unreliable. When
Esther Peters, a seamstress, broke her hip, it was not Rubin
who the old woman called, but young Allan, who sat stiffly
on a fiddle-back chair by her pallet, the fingers of his left hand
spread over the bony ledge of her brow and rheumy eyes,
whispering the rune that lifted her pain after Esther stopped
asking, "Does he know what he doing, Rubin? This ain't how
you did when I caught my hand in that cotton gin." Afterwards, as they walked the dark footpath leading back to the
river, Rubin in front, the Sorcerer shared a fifth with the boy
and paid him a terrifying compliment: "That was the best I've
seen anybody do the spell for exorcism." He stroked his

pupil's head. "God took *holt* of you back there—I don't see how you can do it that good again." The smile at the corners of Allan's mouth weighed a ton. He handed back Rubin's bottle, and said, "Me neither." The Sorcerer's flattery, if this was flattery, suspiciously resembled Halloween candy with hemlock inside. Allan could not speak to Rubin the rest of that night.

In the old days of sorcery, it often happened that pupils came to mistrust most their finest creations, those frighteningly effortless works that flew mysteriously from their lips when they weren't looking, and left the apprentice feeling, despite his pride, as baffled as his audience and afraid for his future—this was most true when the compliments compared a fledgling wizard to other magicians, as if the apprentice had achieved nothing new, or on his own. This is how Allan felt. The charm that cured Esther had whipped through him like wind through a reedpipe, or—more exactly, like music struggling to break free, liberate its volume and immensity from the confines of wood and brass. It made him feel unessential, anonymous, like a tool in which the spell sang itself, briefly borrowing his throat, then tossed him, Allan, aside when the miracle ended. To be so used was thrilling, but it gave the boy many bad nights. He lay half on his bed, half off. While Rubin slept, he yanked on his breeches and slipped outside. The river trembled with moonlight. Not far away, in a rowboat, a young man unbuttoned his lover. Allan heard their laughter and fought down the loneliness of a life devoted to discipline and sorcery. So many sacrifices. So many hours spent hunched over yellow, worm-holed scrolls. He pitched small pebbles into the water, and thought, If a conjurer cannot conjure at will, he is worthless. He must have knowledge, an armory of techniques, a thousand strategies, if he is to unfailingly do good. Toward this end the apprentice applied himself, often despising the spontaneity of his first achievement. He watched Rubin Bailey closely until on his fifth year on the river he had stayed by the Sorcerer too long and there was no more to learn.

"That can't be," said Allan. He was twenty-five, a full   18 sorcerer himself by most standards, very handsome, more like his father now, at the height of his technical powers, with many honors and much brilliant thaumaturgy behind him, though none half as satisfying as his first exorcism rune for Esther Peters. He had, generally, the respect of everyone in Abbeville. And, it must be said, they waited eagerly for word of his first solo demonstration. This tortured Allan. He paced around the table, where Rubin sat repairing a fishing line. His belongings, rolled in a blanket, lay by the door. He pleaded, "There must be *one* more strategy."

"One more maybe," agreed the Sorcerer. "But what you   19 need to know, you'll learn."

"Without you?" Allan shuddered. He saw himself, in a   20 flash of probable futures, failing Rubin. Dishonoring Richard. Ridiculed by everyone. "How *can* I learn without you?"

"You just do like you did that evening when you helped   21 Esther Peters. . . ."

That wasn't me, thought Allan. I was younger. I don't   22 know how, but everything worked then. You were behind me. I've tried. I've tried the rainmaking charm over and over. *It doesn't rain!* They're only words!

The old Sorcerer stood up and embraced Allan quickly, for   23 he did not like sloppy good-byes or lingering glances or the silly things people said when they had to get across a room and out the door. "You go home and wait for your first caller. You'll do fine."

Allan followed his bare feet away from the houseboat, his   24 head lowered and a light pain in his chest, a sort of flutter like a pigeon beating its wings over his heart—an old pain that first began when he suspected that pansophical knowledge counted for nothing. The apprentice said the spell for fair weather. Fifteen minutes later a light rain fell. He traipsed through mud into Abbeville, shoved his bag under an empty table in a tavern, and sat dripping in the shadows until he dried. A fat man pounded an off-key piano. Boot heels stamped the floor beneath Allan, who ordered tequila. He sucked lemon slices and drained off shot glasses. Gradually, liquor backwashed in his throat and the ache disappeared and his body felt transparent. Yet still he wondered: Was sorcery a gift given to a few, like poetry? Did the Lord come, lift you up, then drop you forever? If so, then he was finished, bottomed out, bellied up before he even began. He had not been born among the Allmuseri Tribe in Africa, like Rubin, if this was necessary for magic. He had not come to New Orleans in a slave clipper, or been sold at the Cabildo, if this was necessary. He had only, it seemed, a vast and painfully acquired yet hollow repertoire of tricks, and this meant he could be a parlor magician, which paid well enough, but he would never do good. If he could not help, what then? He knew no other trade. He had no other dignity. He had no other means to transform the world and no other influence upon men. His seventh tequila untasted, Allan squeezed the bridge of his nose with two fingers, rummaging through his mind for Rubin's phrase for the transmogrification of liquids into vapor. The demons of drunkenness (Saphathoral) and slow-thinking (Ruax) tangled his thoughts, but finally the words floated topside. Softly, he spoke the phrase, stunned at its beauty—at the Sorcerer's beauty, really—mumbling it under his breath so no one might hear, then opened his eyes on the soaking, square face of a man who wore a blue homespun shirt and butternut trousers, but had not been there an instant before: his father. Maybe he'd said the phrase for telekinesis. "Allan, I've been looking all over. How are you?"

"Like you see." His gaze dropped from his father to the full shot glass and he despaired. 25

"Are you sure you're all right? Your eyelids are puffy." 26

"I'm okay." He lifted the shot glass and made its contents vanish naturally. "I've had my last lesson." 27

"I know—I went looking for you on the river, and Rubin said you'd come home. Since I knew better, I came to Abbeville. There's a girl at the house wants to see you—Lizzie Harris. She was there when you sawed Deacon Wills in half." Richard picked up his son's bag. "She wants you to help her to—" 28

Allan shook his head violently. "Lizzie should see Rubin." 29

"She has." He reached for Allan's hat and placed it on his 30 son's head. "He sent her to you. She's been waiting for hours."

Much rain fell upon Allan and his father, who walked as if 31 his feet hurt, as they left town, but mainly it fell on Allan. His father's confidence in him was painful, his chatter about his son's promising future like the chronicle of someone else's life. This was the night that was bound to come. And now, he thought as they neared the tiny, hip-roofed farmhouse, swimming in fog, I shall fall from humiliation to impotency, from impotency to failure, from failure to death. He leaned weakly against the porch rail. His father scrambled ahead of him, though he was a big man built for endurance and not for speed, and stepped back to open the door for Allan. The Sorcerer's apprentice, stepping inside, decided quietly, definitely, without hope that if this solo flight failed, he would work upon himself the one spell Rubin had described but dared not demonstrate. If he could not help this girl Lizzie— and he feared he could not—he would go back to the river and bring forth demons—horrors that broke a man in half, ate his soul, then dragged him below the ground, where, Allan decided, those who could not do well the work of a magician belonged.

"Allan's here," his father said to someone in the sitting 32 room. "My son is a Conjure Doctor, you know."

"I seen him," said a girl's voice. "Looks like he knows 33 everything there is to know about magic."

The house, full of heirlooms, had changed little since 34 Allan's last year with Rubin. The furniture was darkened by use. All the mirrors in his mother's bedroom were still covered by cloth. His father left week-old dishes on the hob, footswept his cigars under the bare, loose floorboards, and paint on the front porch had begun to peel in large strips. There in the sitting room, Lizzie Harris sat on Beatrice's old flat-bottomed roundabout. She was twice as big as Allan remembered her. Her loose dress and breast exposed as she fed her baby made, he supposed, the difference. Allan looked away while Lizzie drew her dress up, then reached into her bead purse for a shinplaster—Civil War currency—which she handed to him. "This is all you have?" He returned her money, pulled a milk stool beside her, and said, "Please, sit down." His hands were trembling. He needed to hold something to hide the shaking. Allan squeezed both his knees. "Now," he said, "what's wrong with the child?"

"Pearl don't eat," said Lizzie. "She hasn't touched food in two days, and the medicine Dr. Britton gave her makes her spit. It's a simple thing," the girl assured him. "Make her eat." 35

He lifted the baby off Lizzie's lap, pulling the covering from her face. That she was beautiful made his hands shake even more. She kept her fists balled at her cheeks. Her eyes were light, bread-colored, but latticed by blood vessels. Allan said to his father, without facing him, "I think I need boiled Hound's Tongue and Sage. They're in my bag. Bring me the water from the herbs in a bowl." He hoisted the baby higher on his right arm and, holding the spoon of cold cereal in his left hand, praying silently, began a litany of every spell he knew to disperse suffering and the afflictions of the spirit. From his memory, where techniques lay stacked like crates in a storage bin, Allan unleashed a salvo of incantations. His father, standing nearby with a discolored spoon and the bowl, held his breath so long Allan could hear flies gently beating against the lamp glass of the lantern. Allan, using the spoon like a horseshoe, slipped the potion between her lips. "Eat, Pearl," the apprentice whispered. "Eat and live." Pearl spit up on his shirt. Allan closed his eyes and repeated slowly every syllable of every word of every spell in his possession. And ever he pushed the spoon of cereal against the child's teeth, ever she pushed it away, gagging, swinging her head, and wailing so Allan had to shout each word above her voice. He oozed sweat now. Wind changing direction outside shifted the pressure inside the room so suddenly that Allan's stomach turned violently—it was if the farmhouse, snatched up a thousand feet, now hung in space. Pearl spit first clear fluids. Then blood. The apprentice attacked this mystery with a dazzling array of devices, analyzed it, looked at her with the critical, wrinkled brow of a philosopher, and mimed the Sor- 36 cerer so perfectly it seemed that Rubin, not Allan, worked magic in the room. But he was not Rubin Bailey. And the child suddenly stopped its struggle and relaxed in the apprentice's arms.

Lizzie yelped. "Why ain't Pearl crying?" He began repeating, futilely, his spells for the fifth time. Lizzie snatched his arm with such strength her fingers left blue spots on his skin. "That's enough!" she said. "You give her to me!"   37

"There's another way," Allan said, "another charm I've seen." But Lizzie Harris had reached the door. She threw a brusque "Good-bye" behind her to Richard and nothing to Allan. He knew they were back on the ground when Lizzie disappeared outside. Within the hour she would be at Rubin's houseboat. In two hours she would be at Esther Peters's home, broadcasting his failure.   38

"Allan," said Richard, stunned. "It didn't work."   39

"It's never worked." Allan put away the bowl, looked around the farmhouse for his bag, then a pail, and kissed his father's rough cheek. Startled, Richard pulled back sharply, as if he had stumbled sideways against the kiln. "I'm sorry," said Allan. It was not an easy thing to touch a man who so guarded, and for good reason, his emotions. "I'm not much of a Sorcerer, or blacksmith, or anything else."   40

"You're not going out this late, are you?" His father struggled, and Allan felt guilty for further confusing him with feeling. "Allan. . . ."   41

His voice trailed off.   42

"There's one last spell I have to do." Allan touched his arm lightly, once, then drew back his hand. "Don't follow me, okay?"   43

On his way to the river Allan gathered the roots and stalks and stones he required to dredge up the demon kings. The sky was clear, the air dense, and the Devil was in it if he fouled even this conjuration. For now he was sure that white magic did not reside in ratiocination, education, or will. Skill was of no service. His talent was for pastiche. He could imitate but never truly heal; impress but never conjure beauty; ape the good but never again give rise to a genuine spell. For that   44

God or Creation, or the universe—it had several names—had to seize you, *use* you, as the Sorcerer said, because it needed a womb, shake you down, speak through you until the pain pearled into a beautiful spell that snapped the world back together. It had abandoned Allan, this possession. It had taken him, in a way, like a lover, planted one pitiful seed, and said, "'Bye now." This absence, this emptiness, this sterility he felt deep at his center. Beyond all doubt, he owed the universe far more than it owed him. To give was right; to ask wrong. From birth he was indebted to so many, like his father, and for so much. But you could not repay the universe, or anyone, or build a career as a Conjure Doctor on a single, brilliant spell. Talent, Allan saw, was a curse. To have served once—was this enough? Better perhaps never to have served at all than to go on, foolishly, in the wreckage of former grace, glossing over his frigidity with cheap fireworks, window dressing, a trashy display of pyrotechnics, gimmicks designed to distract others from seeing that the magician onstage was dead.

Now the Sorcerer's apprentice placed his stones and herbs   45
into the pail, which he filled with river water; then he built a fire behind a rock. Rags of fog floated over the waste-clogged riverbank as Allan drew a horseshoe in chalk. He sat cross-legged in wet grass that smelled faintly of oil and fish, faced east, and cursed at the top of his voice. "I conjure and I invoke thee, O Magoa, strong king of the East. I order thee to obey me, to send they servants Onoskelis and Tepheus."

Two froglike shapes stitched from the fumes of Allan's   46
potion began to take form above the pail.

Next he invoked the demon king of the North, who   47
brought Ornia, a beautiful, blue-skinned lamia from the river bottom. Her touch, Allan knew, was death. She wore a black gown, a necklace of dead spiders, and entered through the opening of the enchanted horseshoe. The South sent Rabdos, a griffinlike hound, all teeth and hair, that hurtled toward the apprentice from the woods; and from the West issued Bazazath, and most terrible of all—a collage of horns, cloven feet, and goatish eyes so wild Allan wrenched away his head.

Upriver, he saw kerosene lamplight moving from the direction of town. A faraway voice called, "Allan? Allan? Allan, is
that you? Allan, are you out there?" His father. The one he
had truly harmed. Allan frowned and faced those he had
summoned.

"Apprentice," rumbled Bazazath, "*student*, you risk your   48
life by opening hell."

"I am only that, a student," said Allan, "the one who   49
studies beauty, who wishes to give it back, but who cannot
serve what he loves."

"You are wretched, indeed," said Bazazath, and he glanced   50
back at the others. "Isn't he wretched?"

They said, as one, "Worse."   51

Allan did not understand. He felt Richard's presence hard   52
by, heard him call from the mystic circle's edge, which no
man or devil could break. "How am I worse?"

"Because," said the demon of the West, "to love the good,   53
the beautiful is right, but to labor on and will the work when
you are obviously *beneath* this service is to parody them, twist
them beyond recognition, to lay hold of what was once
beautiful and make it a monstrosity. It becomes *black* magic.
Sorcery is relative, student—dialectical, if you like expensive
speech. And this, exactly, is what you have done with the
teachings of Rubin Bailey."

"No," blurted Allan.   54

The demon of the West smiled. "Yes."   55

"Then," Allan asked, "you must destroy me?" It was less   56
a question than a request.

"That is why we are here." Bazazath opened his arms.   57
"You must step closer."

He had not known before the real criminality of his deeds.   58
How dreadful that love could disfigure the thing loved. Allan's eyes bent up toward Richard. It was too late for apolo-
gies. Too late for promises to improve. He had failed
everyone, particularly his father, whose face now collapsed
into tears, then hoarse weeping like some great animal with
a broken spine. In a moment he would drop to both knees.
Don't want me, thought Allan. Don't love me as I am. Could

he do nothing right? His work caused irreparable harm—and his death, trivial as it was in his own eyes, that, too, would cause suffering. Why must his choices be so hard? If he returned home, his days would be a dreary marking time for magic, which might never come again, living to one side of what he had loved, and loved still, for fear of creating evil— this was surely the worst curse of all, waiting for grace, but in suicide he would drag his father's last treasure, dirtied as it was, into hell behind him.

"It grows late," said Bazazath. "Have you decided?" 59

The apprentice nodded, yes. 60

He scrubbed away part of the chalk circle with the ball of 61 his foot, then stepped toward his father. The demons waited—two might still be had this night for the price of one. But Allan felt within his chest the first spring of resignation, a giving way of both the hunger to heal and the anxiety to avoid evil. Was this surrender the one thing the Sorcerer could not teach? His pupil did not know. Nor did he truly know, now that he was no longer a Sorcerer's apprentice with a bright future, how to comfort his father. Awkwardly, Allan lifted Richard's wrist with his right hand, for he was right-handed, then squeezed, tightly, the old man's thick, ruined fingers. For a second his father twitched back in an old slave reflex, the safety catch still on, then fell heavily toward his son. The demons looked on indifferently, then glanced at each other. After a moment, they left, seeking better game.

Topics for Writing
Story

1. *Respond*. For a collection of personal essays that a group in your church is putting together to illustrate how different individuals have faced and dealt with illnesses, write a personal narrative in which you describe the difficulty you had overcoming an illness. Consider the various factors—emotional, intellectual, situational, and medical—that contributed to the difficulty. For example, you may want to analyze your attitudes toward illness: "I hate to admit that I am sick." or "I panic when I get a symptom that might mean cancer." You might even want to write your essay as a humorous piece, pointing out that most of the ailments you worry about never materialize. (*Resources for Comparison:* Alice Walker, "Everyday Use," page 219; Eric Liu, "A Chinaman's Chance," page 462)

2. *Analyze*. Write an essay for your literature class in which you analyze the various lessons Allan had to learn in order to complete his "medical apprenticeship." In particular, explain the significance of the final lesson Allan must learn about his ability to heal people. Analyze the evidence that indicates whether or not he has learned it. (*Resources for Comparison:* Mark Twain, "Two Views of the River," page 164; Edward Hoagland, "In the Toils of the Law," page 135)

3. *Argue*. For an article in a general-interest magazine such as *Parade, Woman's Day,* or *Vanity Fair,* write an essay in which you argue that good health is a gift, a gift that must be nurtured and appreciated, rather than a condition that can be created by tricks and spells. In other words, argue that good health is something that people control. Good luck helps. So do good doctors. But in the last analysis, people must sustain their good health through a lifetime of sensible behavior and informed routines. (*Resources for Comparison:* Anna Quindlen, "Enough Bookshelves," page 12; William Styron, "The Habit," page 497)

Ann Juralbal was born in 1974 in Haywood, California, and is enrolled at Ball State University,
where she is majoring in exercise physiology. She
works at the campus bookstore and at one of the
dormitory cafeterias. Upon graduation, Juralbal
plans to become a physical therapist. In "How to
Avoid Second-Semester Burnout," she combines
several writing strategies to advise students on how
to avoid a common health problem.

How to Avoid Second-Semester Burnout
(Student Essay)

M OST COLLEGE STUDENTS struggle through their first   1
semester only to return home to some version of the
following:

Scene #1: Your finals are over and you embrace your parents,   2
ready to regale them with your adventures. Your mother
holds you at arm's length and frets, "Honey, you look so pale!
Are you feeling well? Are you getting enough sleep?"

Your father tries to sympathize. "Sleep? During finals?   3
With all-nighters and research papers?"

Your mother is not amused. "What have you been eating?"   4

Another attempt at sympathy. "Now dear, don't you know   5
college students know only four food groups: caffeine, sugar,
fat, and starch?"

Your mother shifts into overdrive. "Well, some good   6
home-cooking will fix you up in no time."

Scene #2: You had planned to see all your friends, compare   7
notes, and find out what's happened to what's-his-name. But

seeing your old bed, you curl up for a brief nap. Six hours later, your mother calls you to dinner. You stagger down the hall, washed out, cranky, and sensing the beginning of a major headache.

Suddenly, the familiar smells of your favorite meal clear   8
your head. Your mother was right. Home-cooking sure beats potato chips, candy bars, and pizza. Famished, you ask for seconds on salad. Your mother smiles. Your father smiles. You ask for thirds on vegetables.

Scene #3: You push your chair back from the table. You're   9
stuffed. But there's no homework. No night class. Your father

---

*True burnout does not happen suddenly, in
the pressure-packed environment of finals
week, but over a long period of time.*

---

suggests you go for a walk. You open the familiar door and look at the sky. The clouds are turning scarlet and purple as the sun slips over the horizon. The night air is cool, exhilarating. You start walking. Two blocks. Four blocks. You can feel the air in your lungs. As you turn for home, you break into a jog.

You open the door, flop into a chair, and for the first time   10
feel relaxed. All the pressure is off. You want to talk. Not about reading assignments, quiz scores, or deadlines, but about why it feels so good to be home. And why, for the last two weeks, you have felt exhausted, short-tempered, and depressed. Your parents listen, their worry plain.

"We don't want you to burn out next semester."   11

You shift in the chair, sharing their concern, and make a   12
mental list of the things you will change.

*   *   *

These scenes don't illustrate burnout. True burnout does   13
not happen suddenly, in the pressure-packed environment of

finals week, but over a long period of time. It is a *chronic,* not an *acute* condition, involving more severe symptoms such as constant feelings of helplessness, hopelessness, irritability, anxiety, emotional withdrawal, and long-simmering hostility.

Burnout affects more and more people every year, and tends to affect people who are single-minded, idealistic, and highly motivated. It also affects people who have low self-esteem, don't feel in control of events, and don't have some network of support. Burnout often happens in high-stress occupations like social workers, nurses, and police officers, but it also happens in more ordinary situations when an individual's roles clash with each other. Women who work all day and then come home to families who expect them to perform all the duties of a traditional housewife are excellent candidates for burnout. So are students who struggle to keep their grades high, try to hold down part-time jobs, assume leadership positions in campus organizations, and maintain a relationship with a boy- or girlfriend. 14

People with personalities susceptible to burnout who try to balance such demands on their time and energy experience reduced creativity and enthusiasm, clinical depression, feelings of alienation, even paranoia or psychosis. Burnout can produce serious physical consequences as well, like chronic headaches, backaches, muscle pain, even heart disease and immune disorders. Such psychological and physical symptoms can lead to even more severe consequences such as alcoholism, drug abuse, school or job failure, and divorce. 15

Being stressed-out, on the other hand, is not as severe a condition. Everyone experiences stress. When you encounter unexpected situations (like missing a bus, or forgetting a deadline) your body reacts in a predictable way: your heart rate increases, your blood pressure elevates, your muscles tense up, and you start to breathe quickly. How you react to such symptoms determines whether or not you will become stressed out. If you panic, perceiving that events are overpowering you, you're on your way to being stressed-out. If you allow such feelings to escalate in everyday situations, you could be a candidate for burnout. 16

But none of this needs to happen. Before being stressed- 17

out turns into being burned-out, you can develop effective strategies to help you control your reaction to the normal stress in your life. Most of these strategies involve reversing your first-semester behavior so that you can get enough sleep, eat a balanced diet, exercise regularly, and manage your time.

Your mother is right. You need to get enough sleep. For 18 most people, about six to eight hours of sleep is sufficient. Without the proper rest, your body becomes fatigued, has greater difficulty coping with illness and is overwhelmed by stress. Sometimes when you're trying to juggle homework, research papers, and late assignments with the demands of your job and your friends—especially toward the end of the semester—you can't find enough hours in the day to sleep. If you find yourself in such a predicament, go for a walk, listen to music, or go to a movie. Any of these strategies, in moderation, can give you an effective "rest" from stress. But during the greater part of the semester, getting enough sleep is a matter of managing your time and adhering to regular routines. You don't *need* to be on-line talking to friends, lingering over pizza, or playing just one more game of Risk until 3:00 in the morning. You do need to establish a sensible time for "lights out" and stick to it, regardless.

Your mother is also right about food. Eating well gives you 19 more energy. A typical dorm cafeteria offers pop tarts, sugar frosted flakes, home fries, biscuits and sausage for breakfast. It also offers oatmeal, granola, wheat toast, grapefruit and orange juice. It's really up to you. No one is going to stop you from eating one more jelly donut or calling two cups of coffee breakfast. But when the sugar or caffeine rush is over, your energy levels will be even lower. A balanced diet from the four food groups (*not* caffeine, sugar, fat and starch, but fruits and vegetables, breads and cereals, meats and protein, and dairy products) gives you a better base for all-day alertness and energy, as well as controlling your weight and your ability to fight off colds and flu.

Your father is right. Exercise is a good idea. Playing a team 20 sport or taking an aerobics class strengthens your body and relaxes your mind. You may think there's no time for regular exercise in your busy schedule. But if you can find time to watch *Monday Night Football* or your favorite soap opera, you can find time to ride an exercise bicycle or swim a few laps. Even a brisk half-hour walk three times a week stretches your muscles, gets you out in the fresh air, and clears your mind, helping you to concentrate more effectively when you go back to studying.

The key to developing these stress management strategies is time management. Your father is right. Most students fall into the finals trap—all-nighters to cram for exams and complete term papers. But if you plan ahead you can avoid the worst of the end-of-semester crunch. The basic time management strategies are obvious. But only you can manage them. You need to pay attention to deadlines, keep up with the reading, and complete assignments on time instead of asking for extensions. Mainly, you need to set priorities among school assignments. You need to decide how much time each project is worth in relation to other projects, develop a schedule and follow it. You don't want to waste your time worrying when you can spend your time working.

When you return for your second semester you may want to take some special tools to help you follow these strategies:

1. A new alarm clock so that the more regular hours you keep, the more regular hours you sleep.
2. A pocket of coupons so that if the cafeteria or snack bar has "nothing" to eat, you can stockpile some healthy munchies in your room.
3. A new pair of walking/jogging shoes so that you can take long walks after class and take the stairs, not the elevator, to class or to your room.
4. A daily planner so that you can see at a glance what's due when and schedule the rest of your life so that you do things in an orderly way.

        *   *   *

With these strategies, a few extra tools, and the resolve to keep your promises, that phone call midway through second semester might resemble the following.

"Hi, Honey. How are you?"   28

"So far, so good, Mom. Dad . . . I'm taking a walk every   29
night after dinner."

"Good! Remember, we don't want you to burn out."   30

"Believe me, neither do I!"   31

Questions About Combining Strategies

1. What major strategy does Juralbal use to develop her purpose?
2. How does she use the pronoun *you* to identify and address her readers?
3. How does she use other strategies to attract her readers' attention and advance her purpose?

ACKNOWLEDGMENTS

DIANE ACKERMAN "The Face of Beauty," from *A Natural History of the Senses* by Diane Ackerman. Copyright © 1990 by Diane Ackerman. Reprinted by permission of Random House, Inc.

ALICE ADAMS "Truth or Consequences," from *To See You Again* by Alice Adams. Copyright © 1992 by Alice Adams. Reprinted by permission of Alfred A. Knopf, Inc.

MAYA ANGELOU "My Name is Margaret," from *I Know Why the Caged Bird Sings* by Maya Angelou. Copyright © 1969 by Maya Angelou. Reprinted by permission of Random House, Inc.

RUSSELL BAKER "The Plot Against People," Copyright © 1968 by *The New York Times Company*. Reprinted by permission.

JOHN BERENDT "The Hoax," Copyright © 1994 by John Berendt. Reprinted by permission of the author.

WENDELL BERRY "The Problem of Tobacco," from *Sex, Economy, Freedom and Community* by Wendell Berry. Copyright © 1994 by Wendell Berry. Reprinted by permission of Pantheon Books, a division of Random House, Inc.

ROSEMARY BRAY "So How Did I Get Here?" published by *New York Times Magazine,* 8 November, 1993 by Rosemary Bray. Copyright © 1993 by Rosemary Bray. Reprinted by permission.

JANE BRODY "Choosing an Exercise: What to Consider," from *Jane Brody's The New York Times Guide to Personal Health,* pp. 88–94. Copyright © 1976 by Jane Brody. Reprinted by permission of Times Books, an imprint of Random House.

BRIGID BROPHY "The Rights of Animals," from *Don't Never Forget: Collected Views and Reviews.* Holt, Rinehart & Winston, 1966. Copyright © 1966 by Brigid Brophy. Reprinted with permission from Sheil Land Associates Ltd.

MARTIN LUTHER KING, JR. "I Have a Dream." Reprinted by arrangement with The Heirs to the Estate of Martin Luther King, Jr., c/o Joan Daves Agency as agent for the proprietor. Copyright © 1963 by Martin Luther King, Jr., copyright renewed 1991 by Coretta Scott King.

ERIC LIU "A Chinaman's Chance: Reflections on the American Dream," reprinted from *Next: Young American Writers on the New Generation,* edited by Eric Liu, with the permission of W. W. Norton & Company, Inc. Copyright © 1994 by Eric Liu.

ALISON LURIE "Folktale Liberation," from *Don't Tell the Grown-Ups* by Alison Lurie. Copyright © 1990 by Alison Lurie. By permission of Little, Brown and Company.

TOM and RAY MAGLIOZZI "Inside the Engine," from *Car Talk* by Tom and Ray Magliozzi. Copyright © 1991 by Tom and Ray Magliozzi. Used by permission of Dell Books, a division of Bantam, Doubleday, Dell Publishing Group, Inc.

DAVID McCULLOUGH "FDR and Truman," from *Truman* by David McCullough. Copyright © 1992 by David McCullough. Reprinted by permission of Simon & Schuster, Inc.

BILL McKIBBEN "Nature and Televised Nature," from *The Age of Missing Information* by Bill McKibben. Copyright © 1992 by Bill McKibben. Reprinted by permission of Random House, Inc.

MARY MEBANE "Shades of Black," from *Mary* by Mary Mebane. Copyright © 1981 by Mary Elizabeth Mebane. Used by permission of Viking Penguin, a division of Penguin Books USA Inc.

DESMOND MORRIS "Territorial Behaviour." Reprinted from *Manwatching* by Desmond Morris. Published in 1977 by Harry N. Abrams, Inc., New York. All rights reserved.

CHARLES MURRAY "The Coming White Underclass." Reprinted with permission of the *Wall Street Journal,* © 1993 Dow Jones & Company, Inc. All rights reserved.

KATHLEEN NORRIS "The Holy Use of Gossip," from *Dakota.* Copyright © 1993 by Kathleen Norris. Reprinted by permission of Ticknor & Fields/Houghton Mifflin Company. All rights reserved.

FLANNERY O'CONNOR "Revelation," from *Everything That Rises Must Converge* by Flannery O'Connor. Copyright © 1964, 1965 by the Estate of Mary Flannery O'Connor. Copyright © renewed 1993 by Regina O'Connor. Reprinted by permission of Farrar, Straus & Giroux, Inc.

GEORGE ORWELL "Shooting an Elephant," from *Shooting an Elephant And Other Essays* by George Orwell. Copyright © 1950 by the Estate of Sonia Brownell Orwell and Martin Secker & Warburg Ltd. and renewed 1978 by Sonia Pitt-Rivers. Reprinted by permission of Harcourt Brace Jovanovich Inc., A. M. Heath, the Estate of Sonia Brownell Orwell and Martin Secker & Warburg Ltd.

ANNA QUINDLEN "Enough Bookshelves." Copyright © 1991 by *The New York Times Company.* Reprinted by permission.

INDEX